1976

THE LETTERS OF ALEXAN

Pushkin, 1827.   *Portrait by O. A. Kiprensky.*

The Letters of

ALEXANDER PUSHKIN

THREE VOLUMES IN ONE

Translated, with Preface,
Introduction, and Notes by

J. Thomas Shaw

The University of Wisconsin Press

MADISON, MILWAUKEE, AND LONDON

1967

Paperback edition, three volumes in one, published
by the University of Wisconsin Press
Madison, Milwaukee, and London
U.S.A.: Box 1379, Madison, Wisconsin 53701
U.K.: 26–28 Hallam Street, London W.1

Clothbound edition, in three volumes, published
by the University of Pennsylvania Press
and Indiana University Press

Printed in the United States of America
Library of Congress Catalog Card Number 67-26624

Preface

Alexander Sergeevich Pushkin is not only universally acknowledged the greatest Russian poet, but his place is also secure in world literature among the great poets of the first half of the nineteenth century. The English-reading public has long had easy access to much of his poetry and prose fiction through translations, and to knowledge of his life through a number of biographies. However, until the preparation of this edition, his letters have never been published in English translation, with the exception of excerpts in biographies.

Pushkin is as much the greatest writer of letters in Russian as the greatest poet. In their entirety, Pushkin's letters are rightly considered as constituting a prose masterpiece—some would even say his greatest work in prose. But as with most authors, the greatest service of the letters is to provide the best approach for understanding Pushkin as man and artist. The nature of his genius and particularly of his characteristic literary style, even in his prose fiction, is such as to make him difficult to accept in translation at anything like the evaluation granted him by those who know him in the original. The succinctness, the ease, simplicity, and inevitability that spring from the writer's self-imposed strictness and discipline, the absence of striking images or of any lushness or ornamentation, the continuing development toward further nakedness of utterance— these characteristics have made his poetry, dramas, and prose fiction hard to appreciate properly in translation. His style is poles apart from romantic improvisation or Elizabethan exuberance, or the realistic piling up of what Tolstoy called superfluous detail. Pushkin is always the craftsman, the builder of harmonious literary structures; every detail counts, not only in its meaning, but also in the architecture of the line, stanza, paragraph, and entire work. Pushkin's letters will provide the English-speaking reader with a gateway to his poetry and prose fiction.

The one hundred twenty-fifth anniversary of Pushkin's death in 1837 was observed throughout the world in 1962. This publication is offered as a part of this commemoration. An edition in English of Pushkin's letters was originally conceived of as part of the celebration of the one hundred fiftieth anniversary of his birth, which was celebrated in 1949. Work on this edition began in 1950. The manuscript of the first half of the letters was completed in 1955, and of the second half in 1956; the Introduction was written in 1958. The delay in publication caused by the complexities in publishing a work of this nature and scope has made it possible to include two letters which have been since discovered and published, and to utilize, during a final checking of the translation against the original texts in 1961, three of the projected four volumes of the Pushkin *Dictionary*, published by the Academy of Sciences of the U.S.S.R.

The editor of any author's letters has a difficult task in deciding what constitutes a letter. There is always the question whether to include, if they survive, receipts for laundry bills, orders to a book-seller or restaurateur, and other trivia, and in the case of Pushkin, whether to include even a surviving half-sentence of a rough draft. Furthermore, there is the question whether to include letters of neutral or unrevealing content, or letters which in all essentials duplicate each other. In this edition, an attempt has been made to include all of Pushkin's letters which have intrinsic interest as letters, and/or which reveal Pushkin the man in his character and biography, Pushkin the man of society, Pushkin the man interested and in-volved in politics and the government of his time, and Pushkin the man of letters. The Introduction gives a discussion of Pushkin under each of these various aspects, particularly as seen through his letters.

The letters reflect well the different periods of Pushkin's life; it has been thought helpful and convenient to divide them accordingly into parts. For this idea, I am indebted to the example of Professor Gordon S. Haight's edition of *The George Eliot Letters* (7 vols., New Haven: Yale University Press, 1954-1955). A Brief Note on Push-kin's Life has been provided, in which one or two paragraphs are devoted to each period of his life and literary activity.

While the first consideration in the translation has been Pushkin's thought, an effort has also been made to convey to the reader of English his rhythms, tonalities, and styles, including the official, the literary, the familiar, and all gradations among them; and also to retain Pushkin's constant word-play, including puns, allusions, parodies, and play on folk expressions. An effort has been made to discover what each word meant to Pushkin, and what may be called its specific gravity and range in his use, and to find English equivalents. In a number of cases, particularly with regard to puns, especially rhyming ones, and word-play on the literal meaning of idioms and folk expressions, it has been necessary to indicate in the notes turns of phrase which could not be adequately rendered.

For names of Russian individuals, both prenames and surnames, a popular system of transliteration, based on general English usage and the system of the Library of Congress, has been consistently applied. Only two exceptions have been allowed: (1) Alexander and Peter have been given their usual English forms, instead of Aleksandr and Petr; and (2) names of Russian rulers are given in their usual Anglicized form. Women's surnames have been retained in their Russian form (e.g., Pushkin's wife is Mme. Pushkina) but English usage has been followed in spelling out women's prenames instead of using initials for them. Pushkin's occasional use of diminutives of first names (e.g., Olya for his sister Olga) and of familiar forms of patronymics (e.g., Lev Sergeich instead of Lev Sergeevich) has been retained as a stylistic feature, with explanatory notes only when necessary. The same system of transliteration has been used not only for names of Russian origin, but also for Baltic Germans and for the Russified in general, as with the writers Fonvizin and Kyukhelbeker and for writers who made their reputations writing in Russian, such as Gogol, Bulgarin, and Senkovsky. Those considered non-Russians have their names given in Latin spelling. In the case of Russian wives of non-Russians, the Russian prenames are transliterated and non-Russian surnames are given in the original spellings (e.g., the wife of the Austrian ambassador, Count Ficquelmont, is called Darya Fedorovna Ficquelmont). Russian place names have been consistently transliterated in the same system as names of individuals. The only exceptions admitted are the Anglicized forms of Moscow and St. Petersburg; following Russian usage, the name of the latter city has been given in the "familiar" form, Petersburg, except when Pushkin himself spells it out. For items in the Brief Bibliography and for direct quotation of Russian, the international scholarly system for transliterating Cyrillic has been used.

Unless indicated otherwise, dates in the notes as well as the letters are according to the Julian calendar, which was used in Russia until 1918. In order to convert them to dates according to the Gregorian calendar, then in use in Western Europe, one should add twelve days to a given Russian date.

TEXTS

The texts of the letters have been translated from the best editions of Pushkin's works as they have been established by the extremely competent and meticulous Russian textologists. The manuscripts themselves have not been available. The basic text used has been that of Volume X of Pushkin's *Complete Works* in the "small" 1949 edition of the Academy of Sciences of the U.S.S.R. (called "small" Academy edition below), edited by the late B. Tomashevsky. The text of the "small" Academy edition has been collated against that of Volumes XIII to XVI of the "large" Academy edition of 1937-1949, the standard textual edition of Pushkin's works, and occasionally, particularly as regards punctuation, the reading of the "large" Academy edition has been followed. (For more detailed notes and bibliographical data on editions used and consulted, see the Brief Bibliography, pp. 17-19 below.) The "small" Academy edition is easily usable not only by the scholar but also by the general reader, in that abbreviations, particularly of proper names and titles of works, are spelled out, and that most variant readings and textual apparatus are omitted. In two respects the "large" rather than the "small" Academy edition has been followed: (1) in including in this edition poems which constitute integral parts of the letters; and (2) in including a small number of letters which the "small" Academy edition prints elsewhere among Pushkin's *Works*. From the Supplementary and Index volume to the "large" Academy edition, published in 1959, I have added two letters which have been discovered since the publication of the two principal editions utilized. This same volume states that the fragmentary Letter 576 of the present edition is no longer considered a letter. However, it has been retained here because of its interest and because I have not seen detailed justification for omitting it.

Headings. This edition is indebted to the Russian editions, especially the "small" Academy one, for information given in the headings to the particular letters, including the addressee, dating, and the places from and to which a letter is addressed. The Russian editions have not published justifications of dating and attribution, in the questionable cases, and hence it has not been possible to check adequately their accuracy. Quite a considerable portion of Pushkin's letters do not exist in their final versions, but only in his writer's-notebook rough drafts. In such cases, this edition follows the Russian editions in marking each of them "Rough draft." The majority of Pushkin's letters are in Russian, but a considerable portion of them are in French. All have been translated, in order to make them equally accessible to the reader of English. The French letters are marked, in the headings, "In French"; letters not so marked were all written in Russian.

The Letters Proper. The complete text of each letter is translated in full, including not only the body of the letter, but also the date and place of writing, salutation, complimentary close, and signature, when given in the original letter, even though part of this information may be duplicated in the headings. In the interests of accuracy, it has been considered desirable to translate verse quoted in the letters into English prose, rather than verse, with an indication in the notes of the nature of the work being quoted. Poems quoted in or sent along with the individual letters are included in this edition only when they are germane to the contents of the particular letters. Otherwise, there is an omission sign in square brackets, and a note indicating what materials are omitted. Pushkin's letters, as one might imagine, include a great many addressed to his editors and publishers, and many of them have rather detailed indications of textual corrections to his works. These textual corrections are included in this edition when they have importance for understanding Pushkin's attitude toward particular works or his approach to poetics; when translation of them would have little meaning in English, they have been omitted, with an omission sign in square brackets and a footnote indicating what has been left out. Omissions of such poems and textual corrections are the only instances in this edition of individual letters not being published in their entirety. In the case of fragments or rough drafts in which the beginning or end of a letter was not written or has not survived, the same indication of omission is used, with a footnote, if necessary.

One of the characteristic qualities of Pushkin's style is the occasional shifting from Russian to French or from French to Russian within particular letters, and the occasional use of expressions or even whole sentences in still other languages, including Church Slavonic, English, German, Italian, Latin, and Polish. In the body of each letter, this edition translates the basic language of the letter (Russian or French) into English and then quotes in italics in the original language any passage from a language other than the basic one of the letter; a translation of these materials is provided in the notes when the meaning might not be completely clear. In a few instances, Pushkin shifts to another language for a passage of such length that it has seemed desirable, in order to avoid masses of italics, merely to supply in square brackets the information that Pushkin has thus shifted from one language to another. This edition attempts to make it completely clear to the reader at all times what language Pushkin is using, except in such cases as the spelling of a name or address or the use of the Latin spelling for "etc."

In a number of ways I have attempted to make Pushkin's letters more easily readable, while preserving their style and effect. Standard English usage with regard to the use of quotation marks and italics has been substituted for Pushkin's inconsistencies with regard to titles of literary works and direct quotation of others' speech. Though Pushkin's paragraphing and basic sentence structure have been maintained, it has been felt desirable in separate instances to make minor modifications, such as to break up extremely long sentences consisting of series of co-ordinate clauses into separate sentences. Pushkin's punctuation has been followed where possible. One characteristic feature of Pushkin's punctuation is a much more liberal use of the dash than is normal in English. The use of dashes has been simplified when following Pushkin directly might cause ambiguity or require a rereading in English. Pushkin makes extensive use of one feature of punctuation that is not normal in English, that of *points de suspension*, to suggest that he is not expressing fully his thought. This feature has been retained in this translation, with a standardization of the number of them to three within a sentence and four at the end. Spaced dots within a letter always represent Pushkin's *points de suspension* in this translation, unless such dots are within square brackets.

A number of Pushkin's minor eccentricities of usage have been removed, except when they may have stylistic interest. Pushkin's spelling of names, occasionally careless, has been corrected and standardized. His erratic spelling in English has been retained, with note "Pushkin's English." Abbreviations have been removed, except that it has been considered desirable to leave "SPb." for St. Petersburg, when Pushkin uses it. For ease of reading and reference and to cut down the number of notes, information has occasionally been inserted in the text in square brackets, for prenames or initials, surnames, and partial titles of works. Pushkin's occasional inconsistency or (often intentional) inaccuracy in the citation of titles of works has been retained in the translation of the letters as a characteristic stylistic feature; the correct forms are given in the notes.

Two further points should perhaps be mentioned. First, with some reluctance it has been decided to follow Russian editions and to consider as unprintable in English the equivalents of words considered unprintable in Russian, and to indicate them in the conventional manner. Pushkin's attitude toward blunt speech makes unthinkable the substitution of periphrasis or softened forms. Second, any translation of an other than modern text must modernize it. Pushkin and his Russian contemporaries well knew the disease of melancholy verging upon hypochondria, which was then called in English *spleen*; Pushkin uses the English word as synonymous with Russian *xandra*. It has seemed desirable to retain the English word, even though it is now archaic in this meaning.

NOTES

For the notes, there has been the usual editor's difficult choice between giving too much and too little information. An effort has been made to make it possible for the general reader to obtain in this edition enough information to make possible a detailed understanding of the letters.

One of the functions of the notes and Index is to permit the reader to trace Pushkin's reading, his comment on literary figures, and his allusions to literary works. Since comparatively few English speakers have detailed knowledge of Russian cultural history, it has been considered desirable to give both in the notes and Index, when ascertainable, the dates indicating life-span of the Russians mentioned, including rulers. The letters and notes make it possible for the reader to obtain an understanding, not only of Pushkin's knowledge of world literature and world events, but also of Russian reception and reaction to foreign literature and culture and the history of the time. The problem of which non-Russians require identification and in how much detail is not one which will admit a satisfactory solution for all kinds of readers. The rule which has been followed is that non-Russians have been identified in the notes to the degree necessary for immediate understanding of the references in the letters. In order that the reader interested in the reception of foreign literature and culture and the reaction toward current events may easily check, if he wishes, the dates of non-Russians mentioned, they are provided in the Index. So as to avoid the constant use of the word "Russian" in identifications, the rule has been followed in the notes that all individuals mentioned are Russians, unless there is specific information indicating otherwise. Russians, except rulers, are identified and their dates given, if ascertainable, upon their first appearance. Cross-references have been omitted when it would be possible for the reader easily to check an identification by using the Index.

It has not been felt necessary to give the sources of information for the individual notes. Any edition of Pushkin's letters must rely heavily on the encyclopedic annotations of the three-volume edition of the letters from 1815 through 1833, begun by B. L. Modzalevsky (1926 and 1928), and continued by his son L. B. Modzalevsky (1935). Unfortunately, the projected fourth volume to cover the years 1834 through 1837 has never appeared, and no adequately annotated edition of Pushkin's letters has been published to cover these years. Especially for the last years, considerable reliance has been placed upon the notes in the "small" Academy edition of Pushkin's *Works*, and even more upon the notes in the "Academia" edition of Pushkin's *Works* (1936-1938), edited by M. A. Tsyavlovsky, which remains the most fully annotated complete edition. Though the "large" Academy edition has no explanatory notes, the detailed Indexes of the individual volumes and the Index volume have also been extremely useful for identifications and allusions, and for data on time of composition and of publication of Pushkin's works. (For further details on these editions, see Brief Bibliography, pp. 17-19 below.)

Russian editors of Pushkin's letters have of course not given themselves the task of providing the information needed for non-Russians. In terms of the needs of the reader of English, information in the Russian editions has been either greatly excessive, in the case of the Modzalevsky edition, or insufficient, in the others. And in all Russian editions much knowledge is assumed which few non-Russian readers possess or can easily acquire. Hence it has been by no means possible simply to translate or to abbreviate for the present edition the information available in Russian editions. With few exceptions, what was needed was supplementary information for consistency or answers to questions which for one reason or another the Russian editors had not felt it necessary to ask or answer.

In addition to the Russian editions of Pushkin's letters I have of course utilized for the annotations of this edition Russian encyclopedias, literary and general, pre-Revolutionary and post-Revolutionary; histories of Russian and other literatures; biographies of Pushkin and numerous special studies of Pushkin and of his time; journals; and old and new editions of the various authors, especially Russian ones whom Pushkin cites. Material in the annotations of Russian editions of Pushkin's letters has been checked against other sources, when possible; this checking has proved again the high level of Russian biographical scholarship on Pushkin.

Preface to the One-Volume Edition

My English-language edition of Pushkin's letters, since its appearance in 1963, in three volumes, has attracted considerable attention and has had a generally very favorable reception in the United States and abroad, including the Soviet Union. In both England and the United States there has been recognition that acquaintance with his letters makes possible a much better understanding of the man who was Russia's greatest poet, and the letters themselves have been hailed as outstanding examples of epistolary art. The present one-volume reprint of that edition will, it is hoped, make the letters accessible to a wider audience. I have taken advantage of the opportunity it gives me to correct a small number of misprints and a few minor errors or inaccuracies in the earlier edition; I am obliged to the reviewers who have called them to my attention. Except for these few changes, this edition follows the 1963 edition.

This is not the place to speak in detail about developments that have taken place in Soviet Pushkin scholarship since my edition of Pushkin's letters originally went to press. Three matters of some importance with regard to Pushkin's letters nevertheless deserve mention here. The fourth volume of the *Pushkin Dictionary* has appeared, so that I have been able to check possible errors of translation against all four volumes and to make corrections as appropriate. A new edition of Pushkin's works which has appeared in the Soviet Union should be mentioned: *Sobranie sočinenij v desjati tomax* (Moscow: State Publishing House of Artistic Literature, 1959–1962); it contains useful commentary by I. Semenko on the letters. And, in particular, all Pushkin scholars have reason to be glad of the news that the fourth and final volume of Pushkin's letters, presumably with exhaustive commentary, is slated to appear soon in the Soviet Union, to complete the edition begun by B. L. and L. B. Modzalevsky (see the Brief Bibliography, pp. 19–20 below). Until that volume appears, my edition of the letters in translation contains the most extensive commentary which has appeared anywhere for the letters of 1834–1837.

J. Thomas Shaw

The University of Wisconsin
March 22, 1967

Acknowledgments

It is a pleasure to acknowledge assistance from numerous people in the more than a decade this edition has been in preparation. The chief debt is to the generations of Russian scholars who have collected the letters, established dependable texts, and annotated them. They have provided texts which could be directly translated, and annotations which could be used as the basis for the notes to this edition.

My obligations extend to the members of several departments of Indiana University and to many colleagues in Slavic departments throughout the United States. For reading the entire manuscript and making many valuable suggestions, I am indebted to Professor Mary Elizabeth Campbell and to my wife, Betty Ray Shaw; and for the latter half of the manuscript, to Professor Mary Gaither. My translations of the Russian-language letters profited by being read for accuracy against the originals by Professor Nonna Dolodarenko Shaw, and of the French letters, by Professor Philip Duncan. I should like to express here my thanks, for reading a draft of the Introduction and for valuable suggestions, to Professors Marthe Blinoff, Deming Brown, Edward J. Brown, William B. Edgerton, Victor Erlich, Waclaw Lednicki, Thomas F. Magner, Oleg Maslenikov, Helen Muchnic, Felix J. Oinas, Edward Stankiewicz, Leon Stilman, and René Wellek. Valuable suggestions for handling certain problems were given by two Soviet Pushkinists, Academician Mikhail Pavlovich Alekseev of the Academy of Sciences, Pushkinsky Dom, Leningrad, and Mr. Ilia Lvovich Feynberg. During the years of work on the translations, I have become indebted to colleagues and Russian acquaintances, too numerous to list and who often were perhaps not aware of the assistance they were providing, for helping me to understand the nuances of Russian words and expressions and to find English equivalents. I would particularly like to acknowledge the assistance provided in this respect by Professor Serge Zenkovsky and the late Boris and Maria Mestchersky. I am grateful to Mr. Edward Czerwinski for checking the accuracy of many details. Professors Norman T. Pratt, Jr., and Edward Seeber gave helpful suggestions with regard to certain problems. Professor Otis Starkey of the Geography Department of Indiana University was kind enough to arrange for the making of the maps which appear in the end papers. I owe a debt of gratitude for encouragement, at various stages of the work, to Professors Michael Ginsburg, Renato Poggioli, Ernest J. Simmons, and Gleb Struve. A part of the Introduction, in a somewhat different form, appeared in the Summer, 1960, issue of *The Slavic and East European Journal.* For providing funds for graduate assistants and typing, I am indebted to the Graduate School of Indiana University. I am grateful to the Social Science Research Council and to the American Council of Learned Societies for a grant which covered part of the cost of publication.

I am especially indebted to the copublishers, the University of Pennsylvania Press and the Indiana University Press, for making it possible to present the Pushkin Letters in English. Mr. Bernard Perry of the Indiana University Press not only had faith in the project and the manuscript, but made the arrangements which led to this publication; I am also deeply indebted to Mr. Thomas Yoseloff of the University of Pennsylvania Press for undertaking the responsibility of the actual printing and for his co-operativeness in arranging for an adequate presentation. I am especially grateful to Miss Edith Greenburg of the Indiana University Press for many helpful suggestions while the manuscript was being prepared and to Mr. Theodore Zinn of the University of Pennsylvania Press, to whose experienced and sharp eye, in the preparation of the manuscript for the printer, this edition owes much of its consistency.

J. Thomas Shaw

The University of Wisconsin
November 10, 1961

Brief Bibliography

I. Editions Chiefly Used and Consulted.

A. Editions of Pushkin's *Works*.

1. PUSHKIN, A. S. *Polnoe sobranie sočinenij.* 10 vols. Moscow, Leningrad: Academy of Sciences of the U.S.S.R., 1949. The letters, in Volume X, were edited by B. V. Tomashevsky; they are accompanied by brief annotations by L. B. Modzalevsky and I. M. Semenko. The "small" Academy edition. The texts are based on the following item.

2. ———. *Polnoe sobranie sočinenij.* 16 vols. in 20. Moscow, Leningrad: Academy of Sciences of the U.S.S.R., 1937-1949. The letters, edited by D. D. Blagoy and N. V. Izmaylov, are in Volumes XIII-XVI. This edition establishes the basic texts and provides all textual variants and the history of publication, but no explanatory annotations. The "large" Academy edition.

Supplemented by: *Spravočnyj tom: Dopolnenija i ispravlenija; Ukazateli.* Moscow, Leningrad: Academy of Sciences of the U.S.S.R., 1959. This volume contains the letters discovered since 1949; it provides a few corrections to the complete edition and an extensive and extremely useful and detailed index, including individuals and literary works referred to as well as specifically mentioned.

3. ———. *Polnoe sobranie sočinenij.* Edited by M. A. Tsyavlovsky. 6 vols. Moscow, Leningrad: "Academia," Vols. I-V, 1936; Moscow, Leningrad: State Publishing House of Artistic Literature, Vol. VI, 1938. The letters are in Volume VI. For the letters, notes were provided by L. B. Modzalevsky, N. V. Izmaylov, and P. A. Sadikov. This edition has the best notes of any complete edition of Pushkin's *Works*, especially of the letters. The "Academia" edition.

B. Russian Editions of Pushkin's Letters.

1. MODZALEVSKY, B. L. (ed.). *Puškin: Pis'ma.* Moscow, Leningrad: State Publishing House, Vol. I (letters of 1815-1825), 1926; Vol. II (letters of 1826-1830), 1928.

MODZALEVSKY, L. B. (ed.). *Puškin: Pis'ma.* Moscow, Leningrad: "Academia," Vol. III (letters of 1831-1833), 1935.

The fourth volume, to cover the letters of 1834-1837, has not appeared.

This edition represents two whole generations of Pushkin biographical scholarship. The texts of the letters have been superseded in all respects except one, that, unlike later editions, they retain Pushkin's orthography for the letters, both in Russian and in French. The notes are by far the most detailed of any edition; they run four to five times as long as the text of the letters, and they form the basis for explanatory notes of all subsequent editions.

2. SAITOV, V. I. (ed.). *Sočinenija Puškina: Perepiska.* St. Petersburg: Academy of Sciences, Vol. I, 1906; Vol. II, 1908; Vol. III, 1911. Supplemented by TSYAVLOVSKY, M. (ed.). *Pis'ma Puškina i k Puškinu, ne sošedšie v izdannuju Rossijskoj akademiej nauk "Perepisku Puškina "*. . . . Moscow, 1925.

Textual edition, without commentary. Superseded completely by texts listed under I.A.1. and I.A.2 above.

3. Significant editions of part of the letters.

(a) *Pis'ma Puškina k Elizavete Mixajlovne Xitrovo* 1827-1832. Leningrad, 1927.

(b) *Pis'ma Puškina k N. N. Gončarovoj.* Introduction by Serge Lifar, edited by M. L. Gofman. Paris: Lifar [1936].

C. Editions of Pushkin's Letters in other languages.

1. In German.

(a) PUSCHKIN, ALEXANDER. *Briefe.* Translated by Fega Frisch. Zürich: Herrliberg [c. 1945].

(b) LUTHER, ARTHUR (ed.). *Alexander Puschkin in seinen Briefen.* Berlin, 1927.

Each offers only a small selection of the letters with little or no annotation. Luther's edition contains 166 letters.

2. In French.

MEYNIEUX, ANDRÉ (ed.). *Pouchkine: Autobiographie, Critique, Correspondance. (Oeuvres complètes,* Vol. III.) Paris: André Bonne [c. 1958]. This edition, which appeared after the present manuscript was complete, is by far the largest selection of the letters in a language other than Russian before the present edition. It contains 462 of the letters and has excellent notes. In this edition, the Russian letters are translated, and the French letters are printed in their original orthography. In the final editing for the press, the present edition is indebted to Meynieux's work in a few details.

II. Works by and on Pushkin in English.

The best biography of Pushkin in English remains the following:

SIMMONS, ERNEST J. *Pushkin.* Cambridge, Mass.: Harvard University Press, 1937.

Translations of individual works of Pushkin have been appearing in English for over a century, and there have been a number of collections of studies, particularly in connection with the centenary of his death, observed in 1937. The following brief list is confined to collections of Pushkin's works presently in print.

The most complete selection of Pushkin's works available in English is the following:

YARMOLINSKY, AVRAHM (ed.). *The Poems, Prose and Plays of Alexander Pushkin.* (Modern Library Giant G62.) New York: Modern Library, n.d. (originally published by Random House in 1936).

Two editions of selections of Pushkin's works in English translation were published in 1961:

SIMMONS, ERNEST J. (ed.). *Pushkin Reader.* (Laurel LC 129.) New York: Dell.

PUSHKIN, ALEXANDER. *The Queen of Spades and Other Tales.* Translated by Ivy and Tatiana Litvinov, and with a Foreword by George Steiner. (Signet Classics CP 70.) New York: New American Library. (The translations in this volume were originally published by the Foreign Languages Publishing House in Moscow.)

Other books in print containing works of Pushkin include *The Captain's Daughter and Other Tales,* translated by Natalie Duddington (Everyman 898, New York: Dutton), and *The Captain's Daughter and Other Great Stories* (V714, New York: Vintage).

CONTENTS OF VOLUME I

CONTENTS OF VOLUME II

ILLUSTRATIONS

MAPS
following page 880

Introduction

Pushkin's correspondence is that of a man of the world and a man of letters, reacting to life, literature, and events in a crucial period of modern Russian history. In his letters, unlike Horace Walpole, he is not deliberately the historian of his time. Nevertheless, Pushkin's place in Russian life and literature and the range of his acquaintances and interests are such that the letters have been properly called an encyclopedia of Russian life and literature of his day.

In addition, the letters provide the best source for tracing the personality and development, the internal and external biography of Russia's greatest poet. In them there is no conscious projection of a particular personality or "pose," as with some writers; one of his characteristic qualities is the lack of self-consciousness or of emphasis upon himself. Not what *I* think and feel but what I *think* and *feel* is Pushkin's subject. The self-revelation comes in snatches, between the lines, in the giving of his reactions and his judgments of men, literature, and events. The multiplicity of human experience is presented in concrete terms, rather than in generalizations. He reacts to individuals, literary works, and social and political manifestations in terms of the existing situation, rather than by the yardstick of any theory, and hence the bases of his thought remain implicit rather than directly expressed. His permanent allegiance is to values, in life as in literature, rather than to any particular theory of value, and he is capable of juxtaposing contradictions without trying to convince others—or himself—and without straining for a reconciliation. Pushkin seldom speaks of political or social theory, but speaks instead in terms of the events and the political and social situation which he himself knew; he rarely writes of critical or literary theory, but of particular authors and works. Similarly, he presents no theory of man, and rarely comments in general terms on his own character or gives judgment of his own actions.

His personality responds, in the individual letter, to what at the moment is in common between him and the person to whom he is writing. Thus each letter reflects only a part of Pushkin. His personality continued to grow and his wisdom to deepen throughout his life; the picture of him presented by the letters is a cumulative and composite one, and not infrequently contradictory in detail.

Pushkin's primary characteristic is, on the one hand, a passionate love of life, of human experience, and, on the other, an equally passionate love of creative work. The over-all characteristic of his life, as of his literary works, is of a *concordia discordium*, as strong conflicting forces are portrayed in, or moving toward, harmonious balance. In his life the strong impulse toward passionate living, in a broad sense, is combined with his equally strong inclination toward work, expressed in artistic creation, where the dross is refined away. Passion is subjected to powerful restraint and given the repose of a strict artistic conscience which saw things under the aspect of the universal. His letters show how he was able to live, grow, develop, and in the face of hardships and death itself, to remain true to himself.

His reckless acceptance of the whole of life is combined with aristocracy of birth, of intellect, of artistry, and of spirit. His love of life and experience is combined with an actively judging mind, assimilating and evaluating in human terms what he has seen and experienced, and intent on new and satisfactory artistic formulation of each stage of his observation and attained wisdom. His attitude toward life and literature is not that of the Olympian observer or the ivory-tower esthete, but that of a direct participant in the wars of the flesh and the spirit, and of one immediately involved in the literary, social, and political struggles of his day. He can change, develop, and grow, but at each moment there is harmony between thought and deed and his consciousness, and even in the whirlwind of the most violent passions, there is an essential repose.

I

Nothing is more characteristic of Pushkin than the way he lives to the full each phase of life, accepting on its own conditions the human situation he faced and the human stages of development. The letters of his youth reveal his exuberant, light-hearted acceptance of the manners and morals of the young nobles, especially the Guard officers, and they reflect the mixture in that society of the love of literature, of culture, and of social responsibility, with the impulses of "golden youth" toward, wine, women, song, gambling, riotous living, and a touchy sense of honor, ready to challenge or be challenged. Love of the theater included love of actresses. Affairs with married women, gypsy or serf mistresses, and visits to brothels were countenanced and even expected. A reckless daring was prized, not only in battle, but also at cards, in duels, and in love affairs. Loose conduct was combined with irreverence toward authority, whether religious or temporal. After sowing their wild oats, the same young men were expected to mature in conduct and attitude, and they married and settled down about the age of thirty. The letters show how Pushkin exemplified these ideals in his personal life. They reflect his youthful hot "African" blood, rapid pulse, thirst for excitement, and desire to prove his mettle as a man as well as a poet. His youth was exuberant and carefree, loose, irreverent, and rebellious. As a young man he was a Don Juan and a rake, a wit on matters of sex and religion, and the author of poems outspokenly critical of the established order. He gradually outgrew in his twenties —and before the Decembrist Uprising of 1825—his earlier attitudes toward the state, and he prepared, as he approached thirty, to settle down to domesticity. In his last years he was a loving husband and father, with a responsible attitude toward his family, society, state, and religion. The latter stages of his life were in him as natural as the earlier ones, and his epistolary skill is such that the reflection of family and business cares is as appealing as that of his volatile youth.

The seeds of his later personal development were present from the beginning. His picture of the Raevsky family in 1820 reveals his appreciation of a happy family life—so different from his own childhood experience—and which a decade later he would try to realize for himself. Interest in and latent concern with matters of religion is shown in his early irreverence, humorous use of Biblical quotations, his many witticisms on this score, and even in his impious *Gavriiliada*; his changed attitude is discernible in the letters and works of his later years. The letters give a particularly full picture of his development with regard to love. In the early ones, he is the young man panting for possession, especially in the incandescent letters to Mme. Kern, the only surviving series of his letters to a passing love. They show how hot his blood and pen could be. To the youthful Pushkin, the "whole head" disappears in legal marriage, but the letter asking for the hand of his future wife reveals a complete change in attitude.

And the correspondence with his wife shows him to be an affectionate husband and father, full of family concern. Though he never
knew affection from his parents and though in his early years he had
little love for them, after his own marriage he became a dutiful son,
even willing to undertake the financial management of his heedless
father's estate.

Though Pushkin could change and develop, to the point of
apparently changing sides on a number of issues, he manifests
constant values which remained, but deepened as he grew older.
Among these are self-respect, personal dignity, and honor. He had
an almost medieval, knightly attitude toward his personal honor.
A slap in the face was "more terrible than Atreus' cup." In his
youth, his sensitiveness to real or imaginary slights led to a score of
duels or near duels, not infrequently as a result of his making love to
other men's wives, and in a certain sense his own last, fatal duel
may be considered as retribution for his own reckless youth. It was
a point of honor with him to even scores, literary or personal.
Literary slights or attacks he repaid with epigrams; personal affronts
led to a challenge. In either case, he was quite willing to resume or
establish friendly relationships with the opponent, as soon as he had
received "satisfaction." He had a long memory for offences to be
repaid. In one instance he waited six years: after his arrest for his
political poems, in 1820, the rumor was spread that he had been
flogged; he felt so injured that he contemplated suicide or even
assassination (apparently of Alexander I himself). The first day he
was free from exile, he sent a challenge to the man who had spread
the rumor.

Pushkin early saw the moral indefensibility of duelling, and his
fatal duel occurred almost fourteen years after his last previous one.
Nevertheless, he felt that one's self-respect in good society demanded that one not endure an offense from a social equal. He was contemptuous of the "prudence of the cavalry-guard young blades" of
his last years, who would endure being publicly spat upon in the
face, for fear they might not be invited to a ball in the palace. The
society about the throne, in which Pushkin was an unwilling prisoner
in later life, found the means to prick his vanity continuously, and in
his last year there were a number of challenges and demands for
"explanations" by him. He felt compelled in the society intrigue in

which he found himself, including the tangled skein with d'Anthès-Heeckeren, to act as the "sole defender of honor" of himself and his family. He saw himself forced to defend his honor by the means then available, for the sake of his fame and calling, and for the "name" that he would leave his children.

The letters are full of his attitudes toward spiritual and financial independence. Proud of his six-hundred-year-old nobility, Pushkin was also proud of earning his own living by his pen. He was forced to earn his bread by literary efforts in a land where a writer was at the mercy of the censorship, where he was politically suspect, and where he was in competition with Philistine journalists from lower social ranks, who jeered at aristocratic pretensions and qualities. His predecessors and even elder contemporaries had governmental sinecures; in principle, he decided early that accepting "protection" was not degrading for a Russian author of the nobility, for such an author was by birth the equal of any patron. His pen was never for sale to any would-be Maecenas, whether a noble lord, a general, or the Tsar himself. Pushkin refused to flatter or to "play the clown, even for the Tsar of Heaven." After Nicholas I appointed himself Pushkin's personal censor, Pushkin was directly dependent upon the Tsar even for the right to publish and thus make his living. In the years after his marriage, he became financially more and more obligated to Nicholas, first in accepting a position in the government service to do historical research, then for financial assistance for publication, and finally even for his domestic affairs. He gradually learned that his personal financial independence was inextricably connected with personal freedom and that there was not only no political freedom, but even no privacy of family life for him under Nicholas I. But he never admitted to himself that he was in a position of real financial dependence upon Nicholas: though "assistance" from the Tsar was usually considered a gift, Pushkin insisted upon arrangements for repayment. He never demeaned himself towards Nicholas or anyone else, and he kept his spiritual independence and self-respect to the end.

Closely connected with Pushkin's attitudes toward honor and independence is his courage. In his youth, this took the form of a reckless bravado, which he proved under fire in his early duels. He showed no fear in the midst of the terrible cholera epidemic of 1830-

1831. Comparable, or perhaps even greater, bravery is exhibited in his dealing with tsars. The real measure of his fortitude can be found in the letters written during three personal crises: in 1826, when his own fate was unclear after the debacle of the Decembrist Uprising (though he was not directly involved in it); in 1834, when he attempted to resign from Nicholas' service; and in 1836-1837, in the events leading directly to the fatal duel. In the letters of 1826 and 1834 to Nicholas I, or intended for his eyes, Pushkin refused to debase himself by writing the kind of self-accusation and promises of different conduct which he knew was expected of him. The poet Zhukovsky, who acted as Pushkin's intermediary in each case, found the letters unaccountably "dry." The letters preliminary to the fatal duel with d'Anthès-Heeckeren similarly show Pushkin's calm courage, as he took all responsibility upon himself. His last letter, a business letter to a translator working for his journal, was written only a few hours before the duel; it was written with a firm hand and in a firm style, including even a gracious compliment.

Perhaps the most appealing of all Pushkin's personal qualities is his broad humanity, as manifested not only in the human impulses all through his life, but also in his respect for the personality of others. He had the knack of establishing relationships on his acquaintances' own grounds. Though his ideas and attitudes were mainly those of his social class and time, he was interested in the welfare of the enserfed peasantry, and he cared enough for the peasants to treat them as individuals, to learn their language, and to embody folklore in his artistic works. He was responsive toward human suffering—to victims of flood, of cholera, and of the Decembrist Uprising. Instead of pity, he gave sympathy; instead of bemoaning the sufferings of others, he sought ameliorative actions. In his grief at the untimely death of his dearest friend, Delvig, he thought at once of Delvig's destitute dependents: "Grief dies, but human needs go on." His humanity is also shown in his generosity, not only with his scant funds, but also with his influence on behalf of others, even when such action was indiscreet or dangerous. Particularly noteworthy in this regard are his intercessions for victims of the Decembrist Uprising.

Another of Pushkin's characteristic qualities is his capacity for friendship. His close friends came from his own social class; they included not only writers, but also men in government service, army officers, and other members of the nobility. He quickly went over to *ty*, "thou," the familiar form of address. The letters and poems show his continuing warm feelings for his Lyceum comrades. The correspondence with Delvig, Nashchokin, and Sobolevsky gives the most intimate pictures of this side of his personality. The depth of his friendship is not, however, always easily ascertainable from the tone of the letters. His letters to Vyazemsky are usually full of cold, scintillating wit, but in cases of personal crisis or grief his real affection is revealed. That he was also capable of lasting friendships with women is shown by the letters to Mme. Osipova, Mme. Khitrovo, and Princess Vyazemskaya.

The letters reflect his truthfulness, sincerity, and ingenuousness. He simply could not lie. When he felt himself to be at fault, he was ready to admit "irrationally" all he could be legitimately charged with and "trust in luck"; when he felt he was not really to blame but "explanations" were required, he could confine himself to that aspect of the truth which he was prepared to admit. Though he could hate, he was ready to forgive at the first conciliatory word. He was essentially full of good nature and trustfulness, as he himself noted ruefully. His high esteem for genuineness and sincerity was by no means based, however, upon ignorance of the ways of the world or of human nature, but upon considerations of value. He may perplex the unknowing with wit and irony, but he wished and expected to be understood, and he prized most and exemplified best what he considered the essential traits of the creative artist: to experience directly, think independently, and write with simplicity and truth.

II

From first to last, Pushkin's letters show him as an active writer. They reflect his development from his literary apprenticeship through the years of his artistic maturity, and they show him in the midst of literary activities throughout his life. The correspondence not only gives a detailed picture of Pushkin's own literary development, but also, by showing his contacts with all the leading literary men of Russia in his day, gives a broad picture of Russian literature in its Golden Age of Poetry.

Pushkin's exceptional literary gifts manifested themselves early, and he began immediately to take part in the literary interests, concerns, and struggles of the day. At eighteen he was admitted to full membership in the literary society Arzamas, to which the best writers of the immediately older generation belonged. At once he joined its members in jocose attacks on the literarily conservative Admiral Shishkov and his Conversation Society (*Beseda*) of Lovers of the Russian Word. But before Pushkin was twenty-one, he had outgrown "literary one-sidedness" and was attending meetings of the rival group. By the time of his legal majority, he showed, in his first long work, *Ruslan and Lyudmila*, that he had already become the major Russian poet. In his early twenties, Pushkin became the acknowledged master among the best Russian poets of his day.

In Pushkin's literary development there is a remarkable connection between his life and literature. He felt that the European literary tradition was part of his heritage. His early Petersburg poetry follows the tradition, already adopted in Russia, of eighteenth-century French poetry, and his poetic style was largely formed under this influence. *Ruslan and Lyudmila* reflects Italian mock-heroic poetry, which he read in eighteenth-century French versions. His southern exile gave him not only "new impressions" but also a new literary horizon. His visit to the Caucasus, the Crimea, and Bessarabia, in combination with his reading of Byron, led to his introducing into Russian literature the Byronic, or romantic, verse tale. In his first romantic verse tale he discovered that he was "no good as a romantic hero," and he soon separated himself from Byronism. But he continued to refine the romantic verse tale, giving it a new style and manner and then a new content. These verse tales gave him his first taste of financial independence, established him as *the* romantic poet in the eyes of his generation, and served as texts for Russian polemics on romanticism. The impulse for Pushkin's novel in verse, *Evgeny Onegin*, perhaps his most characteristic and original work, came from the maturer Byron's *Beppo* and especially *Don Juan*.

Pushkin's exile in Mikhaylovskoe took him away from the exotic South, from "European" and cosmopolitan Odessa, and placed him in a purely Russian geographical and historical setting, on a remote country estate, surrounded by the manors of Russian squires. He now reflected this life in *Evgeny Onegin*. Pushkin turned to Shakespeare, while writing *Boris Godunov*, for the drama of character and for psychological realism, while at the same time he drew from Karamzin's then recent *History of the Russian State* the materials for his chronicle play. Pushkin was now prepared to develop along his own path in narrative poetry and the drama, with outside influences being in stimuli rather than materials or form. He turned more and more to folk sources and manner for his masterly fairy tales in verse. In his last years he turned from poetry to prose for the greater part of his writings, and he became interested in historical research. His last major work, *The Captain's Daughter*, is firmly fixed in Russian history and the Russian countryside; it is a historical novel after— but not in—the manner of the Waverley novels of Sir Walter Scott.

Between the lines of the letters of his last decade can be sensed the gradual decline of the poet-aristocrats as an effective literary group. After the Decembrist Uprising, Ryleev and Kyukhelbeker, among other writers, were lost to Russian literature, and then Delvig died in 1831. There was an imperfect sympathy between Pushkin and a younger Moscow group, the *Ljubomudry*, or Lovers of Wisdom, a group influenced by German idealistic philosophy and esthetics. Pushkin was no lover of the abstruse, and he soon contemned their journal and ceased to contribute to it, objecting that it "sits in a pit and asks, 'What kind of thing is a rope?' " At the same time, periodicals edited by commoners and catering to mass tastes expanded and took the market away from journals and almanacs published by the gentlemen-poets. Pushkin was involved in continuous struggles, in his last years, to support and establish journals which would maintain high literary levels. He was obliged to compete, on their own terms, with uncultivated and unscrupulous journalists who managed to obtain a virtual monopoly of periodical publication. Only in his last year did Pushkin manage to establish his own quarterly, *The Contemporary*, and then it did not sell, in spite of—or because of—its high literary level.

Pushkin had trouble all his life with the censorship. During the last years of Alexander I, most literature "remained in manuscript" because of the harshness of the censors, and works that were passed might be rendered meaningless or ridiculous by omissions or changes required by the censorship. Nicholas I and Benkendorf, as Pushkin's personal censors, caused continuing difficulties. When Pushkin established his own journal, the usual censorship created endless obstacles over materials written by his contributors and by Pushkin himself, even after the Tsar had given his permission for publication. Even after his death, his works first published posthumously suffered greatly from excisions and other changes required by the censorship. Many decades passed before permission was given for the publication of various of his works, and dependable texts have been established only in our time.

The letters provide the best source for discovering Pushkin's attitude toward literature and his own writings. His numerous comments and critiques on literary works, though usually brief, are so just that no later critic has been able to overlook them in judging Pushkin, his contemporaries, and his predecessors. At the same time, Pushkin is strikingly reticent about his own works. He seldom speaks of any literary work of his while it is in progress, and only occasionally does he give detailed information about his attitude toward any of his writings. He never defends the merit nor the execution of any production of his pen, though he may indicate his intent, especially when the genre has been attacked, as with *Evgeny Onegin* and *Boris Godunov*. When he does mention a particular work of his, it is to announce its completion, to suggest or adumbrate a new idea which he later embodied, or to make a textual correction, rather than to offer a prospectus or analysis of it. There is never any presentation, as with Dostoevsky, of the creative throes of the author in search of satisfactory theme, plan, or style. Rather than give the inner growth of particular works, the letters reflect the circumstances of his life when they were written and published. Pushkin wrote only under the capricious and unpredictable prompting of inspiration, with period of literary inactivity alternating with bursts of extreme fecundity. The letters evidence his care in correcting and revising and his fury at arbitrary changes made by the censorship or a publisher. They show how he withheld writings from publication until he was satisfied with them and felt that the time for publication was ripe.

Pushkin remained honest and true to his literary self. He was aware of his own merit as a writer, and he judged himself, as he did others, by high standards. There is never any coquetry with writer-friends for favorable critiques, no evidence of his ever setting up a claque.

In a real sense he wrote for himself. He refused to have subject, style, or "aim" dictated to him: "The aim of poetry is poetry." He rejected the suggestion that he continue his early political poems after his attitude had changed; he refused to surrender his artistic independence to any "protector." Such major works as *Evgeny Onegin* and *Boris Godunov* were written in large part or in full before Pushkin had any hope that they would be passed by the censorship. When permission to publish a work in the form that satisfied him could not be obtained, he did not rewrite or basically revise, but laid it aside. Thus Pushkin refused to rewrite *Boris Godunov* as a Waverley novel at the suggestion—tantamount to a command—of Nicholas I, but kept it until, five years later, he was allowed to publish it as he had written it. Pushkin similarly refused to revise his poetic master-piece, *The Bronze Horseman*, when it did not meet the approval of his royal censor; it was published posthumously.

He manifests responsiveness to the literary movements and taste of his own day, in the forms, themes, and genres he employs, but at the same time he refuses to make any concession to public taste in style and execution. He was unwilling and "unable" to write potboilers. His artistic development followed its own inner laws, and he declined to repeat the style of work which had found favor with the public, when his own artistic development had taken him further. When he had perfected one style and literary form, he moved on to another, even when public taste much preferred the former. His own artistic conscience was ultimately his only judge.

His attitude toward the literary work of others was disinterested. There was no petty selfishness, no attempt to set off his own works or those of his literary group to advantage. He was generous in giving credit to a literary teacher, even when he had surpassed him. He was willing to recognize merit wherever it existed. He learned early to judge literary works by the laws which had guided the authors in writing them. He assumed that fellow-writers wished his honest opinion of their works and wished criticisms which might be useful in improving them. If the work had not yet been published, Pushkin might concentrate on deficiencies: "Assuming that what is good was written deliberately, I did not consider it necessary to point it out. . . ." When, in our judgment, Pushkin errs in his opinion of the work of one of his Russian contemporaries, it is usually on the side of generosity, as he judged in terms of what then existed in Russian literature and in his sense of the author's operating within the literary standards then prevalent.

III

Just as Pushkin knew every man of letters and was involved in the literary currents of Russia in his day, he was acquainted with almost every person of importance in the government and in society. His interests extended to Russia's past and present, and her place in European civilization. He was not only a keen observer of events and of political and social developments; he was directly involved in their consequences. He saw himself as more than a man of letters, even though acknowledged as the greatest of his time: he saw himself as a nobleman, a member of the responsible, old nobility, which he wished to see restored to its ancient power and influence. In his youth, he was on friendly terms with many of the participants in the Decembrist Uprising of 1825. Though his early "liberal" poems were in the hands of all the Decembrists, his volatility kept him from ever being invited to membership in any of their societies. In his later years, he utilized available opportunities to "do good" by giving frank opinions to Nicholas I and Grand Duke Michael, but his hopes of influencing policy under Nicholas I were unrealized.

The letters show throughout how difficult it was for responsible public opinion to exist under the autocracy of Alexander I or Nicholas I. Political societies were illegal, and banding together for any purpose could be interpreted as revolt. The publication of works critical of the government, the Orthodox faith, or even Russian society was impossible under the censorship. It was dangerous to express opinions on such subjects through the mail, for the postmasters acted as government spies, and all independent thinking was considered subversive. Only letters sent on an *occasion*, that is, delivered by hand, made possible the frank expression of opinion. Pushkin himself was in serious difficulty with the government in two separate instances, because letters were intercepted by the police. His letter to Chaadaev in 1836, containing his final opinions of Russia's history, mission, and society, was so dangerous that it was not sent.

Pushkin had a dual attitude toward Russia. Even the early letters evince his pride in Russia's glory and might, her history, and her powerful position in Europe after the defeat of Napoleon. Assuming that Russia was to be measured by European standards, he was at the same time painfully sensitive to her cultural and political backwardness. He was continually critical of the government and society of his day and was always concerned with the need for reforms. The central question with regard to reforms was where they were to proceed from: whether they would come in response to pressures— including possible revolution—"from below," or whether they would come from the Tsar, "from above."

The letters are full of Pushkin's patriotic interest in the glory of Russia in her past and present. There are continuing references to Russian historical figures who contributed to Russia's unification and expansion, and Pushkin often suggests to his literary friends the desirability of works on the heroes of Russia's past. He was interested in making the personal acquaintance and in publishing the memoirs of heroes of 1812. He was proud of the Russian Empire and interested in possible further expansion to the Caucasus, or even to the Balkans or to India. He wished Russia to keep territories already subjugated, and he thus took a nationalistic, anti-Polish view during the Polish Revolution of 1830-1831.

If Pushkin shows patriotism through his love of Russian glory— implicit throughout the letters but expressed only from time to time —his patriotism is no less revealed in his continually expressed attitude towards reforms. In the early works and letters, this need for reform is shown by his desire to limit the autocracy by a constitution, his hatred for "despotism," his love of freedom, and his desire for the betterment of the lot of the enserfed peasantry and the soldiers drawn from it. In all these ideas, and in his early poems on political themes, his attitudes are those of the liberal aristocracy who made up the Decembrist movement. However, during his Southern exile, and some years before the Decembrist Uprising, he had become disillusioned in the hopes of revolutionaries.

The ignominious collapse of the Decembrist Uprising in 1825, upon the accession of Nicholas I, marked the complete failure of the attempt in Pushkin's generation to impose reforms upon the Russian Tsar. Pushkin bowed to "necessity" and gave his word not to "contradict the generally accepted order of things." Freed from exile, he hoped for reforms "from above," and during the first years of the reign of Nicholas I he eagerly interpreted the Tsar's acts and gestures as harbingers of reforms. Pushkin was almost rapturous at the rumor that Nicholas would "by a counter-revolution to Peter [the Great]'s reforms," restore the ancient nobility to its former position of influence and responsibility in government and society. For a time, when Pushkin saw in Nicholas "tsar-like" qualities, especially during the terrible cholera epidemic and the Polish Revolution of 1830-1831, he obviously thought that their political views were basically the same. When in 1831 he accepted a salary from the Tsar, to do historical research, there is a strong hint that he hoped to be in the position to give disinterested and frank criticisms on affairs of state, as Karamzin had done under Alexander I.

The remaining years mark Pushkin's gradual disillusionment with Nicholas and with his reactionary and repressive reign. Instead of restoring the ancient nobility's position in society, Nicholas further degraded it in Pushkin's person, by granting him an "honor" he could not refuse, the intermediate court title of Kammerjunker, not in accordance with Pushkin's views of his birth, age, and fame, but with his nominal rank in the government service. Pushkin was inclined to blame Nicholas' advisors and the bureaucracy for the ills of government and society, but the blame went up to the Tsar himself: "When you live in a privy, you get used to the smell of s——." Pushkin never changed his opinions with regard to the human, social, and cultural values which the state should foster, but only as to how the state might be influenced to establish and safeguard these values. It was Pushkin's and Russia's tragedy that the Tsar in whom such hopes were placed was Nicholas I.

Pushkin's historical interests and researches in his last years centered on the question of two "revolutionaries." One, Peter the Great, operated in his revolutionary changes "from above," while the other, Pugachev, leader of a Cossack revolt against Catherine the Great, worked "from below." Nor was Pushkin's interest confined to Russia. He managed, through his own and friends' connections with foreign diplomats in Petersburg, to obtain forbidden foreign journals and books on the French Revolution of 1789 and on contemporary European upheavals. He was contemptuous of the "bourgeois" quality of Louis Philippe and the results of the French

Revolution of July, 1830. The sole comment on America in the letters shows him frightened by Tocqueville's picture of democracy in America.

Pushkin's birth and education gave him a position in the aristocratic society of Moscow and Petersburg. The letters give a rather detailed picture of social life in the "two capitals." Moscow is shown to be the center of the old nobility and the native Russian traditions, while in Petersburg the tone was set largely by the "new aristocracy" of descendants of eighteenth-century Russian rulers' favorites. Though he could be extremely critical of Russia, he was acutely sensitive to adverse criticism by foreigners, and he particularly disliked Russians' making clowns or fools of themselves for the amusement of visitors from abroad. He objected to the provinciality of Moscow, and to Muscovites' lack of knowledge of or interest in current events abroad, even during the European revolutions in 1830. He protested when Russians became completely preoccupied with "routs," for in them there is "no need of intelligence, nor merriment, nor general conversation, nor politics, nor literature." Court balls offered absolutely nothing to him; he dozed or stuffed himself on ices while his wife danced. The Petersburg society of his latter years evinced no interest in Alexander Pushkin, his poetry, his aspirations, or his ancient Russian nobility, but only in dancing, flirtations, intrigues, and nasty pranks, such as the fake "certificate" nominating him to the Order of Cuckolds. Pushkin summed up Russia of his time in his (unsent) letter to Chaadaev: "One must admit that the state of our society is a sad thing. The absence of public opinion, the indifferences toward all duty, justice, and truth, the cynical disdain for human thought and dignity are truly depressing."

Thus Pushkin kept his own independent mind—and demanded the same of others—with regard to Russia. He was interested in the power and influence of the autocracy and the nobility, the position of the peasant, and even such contemporary questions as the introduction of railroads into Russia. His criticisms of Russia were founded, not only on broad knowledge of Russia, but also of European history and civilization. Though sharply critical of the Russian government and society, he remained a patriot, and when his disillusionment was most complete he could nevertheless say that not for anything in the world would he wish to live anywhere else or wish Russia to have a history other than that which "God had given" her.

From all this we can say that the Pushkin of the letters is a man who lives for life and literature, but for whom literature is the product of life. He is many-faceted in his reactions to different correspondents and different situations in life. He is cosmopolitan and European, with the conviction that the same cultural and literary values are the common possession of the Western world and that Russia should be judged by the same cultural and political measure as other countries. At the same time, he is Russian, in his love of his own country and in his presentation of life there, and especially in his acceptance of the language of the people, of its life, its history, and its physical nature. The letters show him as thinking independently about matters of state and society, as well as literature. The Pushkin of the letters was perceptive, responsive, capable of growth and development, but with a core of being which is not susceptible to change or compromise; he was a disinterested critic of his own and others' literary works, a writer who would not surrender his artistic conscience, a lover of his country not unaware of her blemishes, and a lover of life who could face hardship without a whine and death without a whimper.

IV

Pushkin was conscious of letters as a literary genre and of the merits of his own. His letters were so highly esteemed in his own day that several of them were printed in whole or in part—to his indignation—without his consent. He himself proposed the publication of his correspondence with his friend Delvig, after the latter's death. Half-jokingly Pushkin expressed the hope that his wife would keep his letters, "so that nothing will be lost to [her] or posterity." The letters are in a real sense literary creations, in that, like everything he wrote, they reflect his artistic conscience and were composed, often with rough drafts and variants, like his creative works. As with his creative works, he had strong feelings as to his own right to dictate the time and conditions of their publication. He also realized that they provided the workshop where for the first time a satisfactory Russian prose language was developed.

About three-fourths of the letters are written in Russian, and the remainder are in French, the language of polite society and the court. Pushkin himself confessed that he found it easier to converse or to correspond with ladies and also to write on general subjects in French than in Russian. Thus his ideas on the dramatic theory embodied in *Boris Godunov* and on Russian history and society in the letters to Chaadaev were expressed in French. His official letters were written either in Russian or French, with no marked difference in manner or contents. He wrote to women, except his wife, almost exclusively in French; all of his letters to her while she was his fiancèe are in French, except one in Russian "because I don't know how to scold in French." After their marriage, he wrote to her only in Russian. Pushkin's French is the slightly formal conventional language of the French-speaking Russian aristocracy. He was at home in these conventions, and he uses them with charm, flexibility, and power, and with a breadth of range and effects. But the intimate, homely, familiar letters are all in Russian, and Russian was the language of his personal correspondence on matters of life and literature. His French possesses a slightly old-fashioned charm, the reflection of a society that is no more. His Russian is still fresh and immediate.

Pushkin's correspondence falls into two main categories, with an appropriate style and form for each. One group is composed of the official letters, addressed to governmental functionaries, including two tsars. The other group, the great preponderance of his correspondence, is made up of personal letters, in which the personal may be mingled, in various proportions, with matters of literary and social interest.

The major portion of the official letters were addressed to Count Benkendorf for showing, if he wished, to Nicholas I. By the nature of official correspondence, they show comparatively little variety, but each is worth careful reading, in juxtaposition with his personal letters of the same time, for what it reveals of Pushkin's life and inner self. How carefully they were composed is shown by the fact that for none of the other letters are there so many rough drafts and textual revisions. The official letters are correct, formal, and impersonal in tone, following the official amenities, but noteworthy in their brevity, severity in form, and lack of flattery, fulsomeness, or subservience. In Pushkin's personal crises, their conciseness verges upon dryness. He often takes full advantage of the conventional formal opening and complimentary close to cover up his actual feelings. He was able to maintain his self-respect in all the circumstances which required official letters of petition or self-justification; as he said of one of them, "there is nothing low in the deed [of writing the letter] or the expression."

Though the official letters "in three-cornered hat and shoes" have their importance in Pushkin's biography, his real quality is shown in the personal and personal-literary correspondence. The personal letters are like the lyrics in their saturation, their succinctness, and the immediacy of their presentation of thought and feeling. Though his letters are never lyrical—Pushkin's prose, epistolary or otherwise, is never "poetic"—they may be compared with the lyrics in their revelation of his thought, feeling, and development. And he often permits them to reflect much more of the momentary, the individual, and the private than the poetry and prose fiction.

The letters have a broad variety in style and expressiveness. They range from the burning, mad passion of the love letters to Mme. Kern, to the coldly insulting hatred of those to Heeckeren; from warm, friendly banter to scintillating brilliance; from colloquial everyday prose to gravely respectful or even severe utterance; from "spleen," or melancholy, to rapture; from blunt plain-spokenness to formal correctness; from direct statement to wit, humor, and parody. Pushkin thought that the "first task of a man of intelligence is to know whom he is dealing with": the intellectual, social, and literary level and tastes of his correspondents and also his own relationships with them are implicit, not only in the substance, but also in the tone and style of the letters.

But with all their variety, the letters have basic qualities in common. One of them is an extreme brevity and tight construction. The average length is less than four hundred words, and a great portion of them consist of only one paragraph. Pushkin comes immediately to the point, makes terse comments on each of the principal topics of the letter being answered or on matters of mutual interest at the moment, and concludes crisply. The beginning may be striking and effective—an announcement, a literary allusion, a folk expression; and the conclusion is often similarly striking and pithy. He moves from one topic to another with little or no transition; the thread of connection is provided by the successive points of the letter being answered or by a relationship between one topic and the next, suggested to him by it. He uses juxtaposition to indicate relationships, and a new paragraph to indicate a basic change in thought or tone or a break in rhythm. There are few postscripts. In a few cases, there are epigraphs, and in others folk expressions or literary allusions form a thread that binds the letter together. The unity of a letter is in the single presentation of the immediate complex of thoughts and feelings which make up the contents.

No English author has used such a naked, saturated style as that of Pushkin's formal prose or his letters. His sentence structure is stark in its simplicity: it is based on the brief simple clause, made up predominantly of noun and verb, with few adjectives and sparing use of subordinate clauses. The result is a dynamic style characterized by immediacy, swiftness, and impatient nervousness, and by abrupt sentences which, in rapid rhythm, point toward an idea, without bothering to spell it out in detail. His terseness often approaches the telegraphic, as he gives only the main heads of his judgments, leaving amplification and further discussion for later "leisure." The expression of feeling is curt and even severe; it never spills over into sentimentality or mawkishness. His vigorous phrase, in Russian and in French, often tends toward the epigrammatic: "Truly I love poetry without a plan better than a plan without poetry"; "I cannot have confidence in Mikhail or Penkovsky, seeing that I know the first and do not know the second." At the same time, the prose is flexible, moving easily, from one letter to another or within a single letter, to the expression of a wide range of tone and of ideas and emotions. Pushkin's style in the letters shows finish—not that of "literariness" or an effort at smoothness or gracefulness or elegance, but that of an artistic consciousness for which the curve of expression and the rhythm of phrase are a part of the thing expressed. And the effect is one of ease and unconstraint.

Pushkin's letters to his personal friends who are also men of letters—such as Vyazemsky—sparkle with fireworks which are not to be found elsewhere in his works. His comments, always brief and pointed, here tend toward the pithy, witty, aphoristic phrase: "anonymous (a kind of journalistic onanism)"; a ventriloquist is "a very noteworthy person (or even persons)." His letters to literary friends are full of puns and play on words: "The devil take [publishing] Onegin!" exclaimed Pushkin in exile; "I want to publish, or release, myself into the world." If a double meaning can be read into his words, one can be confident that it is intentionally there. Often young Pushkin indulged in mental gymnastics and his wit represents what can be said on a subject—especially sex and religion—rather than necessarily his own opinions at the time: "Marriage castrates the soul," he wrote in May, 1826, only five months before he himself made a proposal of marriage. The letters are saturated with literary allusions and with quotations, often from Pushkin's own works, and not infrequently used ironically. He often twists quotations or allusions to make a particular application. He seldom cites the exact or full title of a work, including his own, but substitutes a key word or the name of a character. Humor, recognition, and even criticism are often present in the form of the citation as well as in the direct comment. There are relatively few figures of speech, but when they appear they tend to be more striking and pungent than in his formal works; he found publishing a journal in Russia "all the same thing as *honey-bucketing* . . .; to clean up Russian literature means to clean out privies . . . ."

Particular effects are given in several letters by the use of parody. On occasion, Pushkin takes off the ordinary literary style, as in the following passage to Delvig: "I report to you, my master, that the present autumn has been procreative, and that if your humble vassal does not croak of the Saracen's epizootic, the cholera by name, brought back by the Crusaders, i.e., the Volga boatmen, then in your castle *The Literary Gazette* the songs of the troubadours will not become silent the whole year round." Several of the letters are humorous "Arzamasian protocols," parodying the decorousness of the old-fashioned Shishkovites. Pushkin was merely amused at the insistence that literature be solemn. His own prose style was developed, not in opposition to that of the followers of Shishkov, but to that of the Arzasmasian followers of Karamzin—and their French masters—who, in aiming for elegance and "good taste" tended toward excessive sweetness and to ornamental or euphemistic periphrasis: "And do not forget (to speak like Delille) the twisted steel which pierces the bepitched neck of the bottle—i.e., a corkscrew."

Perhaps in part as a reaction against the periphrases and the cloying sentimentality of the Karamzinists, there can be a striking bluntness and directness of speech in the style of the letters, especially the familiar ones. Pushkin felt that a "certain biblical obscenity" should remain in the language. He always used "with child" (*brjuxataja*) instead of the polite "pregnant" (*beremennaja*). There is a continuing repetition of the single most vigorous obscene expression in Russian; in one of his best-known short poems one line is left incomplete for the reader to supply this unprintable phrase. Nor does he hesitate to speak of anatomy and natural functions in the Russian equivalents of the English four-letter words, not only in letters to his men friends, but also to his wife. This non-euphemistic terminology is occasionally also applied to the creative process.

In the early letters as in the early poems, there is a sprinkling of mythological allusions, not infrequently with ironic overtones. Thus Pushkin's letter on his trip to the Caucasus and the Crimea begins "from the eggs of Leda." But, as in the poetry, mythology is replaced more and more by idiomatic folk expressions and proverbs. A whole letter is built on *sam s"eš*, "you're one yourself." The use of folk sayings is in keeping with the homely, simple tone which came to be more and more characteristics of his familiar letters. The value which Pushkin grew to find in folk wisdom is shown in his letter attempting to comfort Sobolevsky upon the death of the latter's mother: it is made up of proverbs.

The vocabulary of the Russian letters has a wide variety, from the ordinary language of his time and class, to the literary language, to the use of antiquated or high-flown words for the sake of parody, to homely folk expressions. Few of the words and expressions used by him have become archaic. Pushkin does not hesitate to employ Gallicisms, especially in his early years, for concepts or expressions for which Russian did not then provide satisfactory equivalents. There is a sprinkling of words with special literary or social connotations from still other languages, especially Latin and English; the main English words used include "vulgar," "gentleman," "spleen," "rout," "bluestocking," and "quarterly." Pushkin quoted conversations in the language in which they occurred, and thus not infrequently shifts from French to Russian, or vice versa, within a letter. Pushkin expects his reader to catch the exact feeling he gives to particular words. And occasionally his words become endowed with new, special meanings: for example, "ravings" are the result of poetic inspiration, and "talking nonsense" refers to his own friendly chatter.

There is a continuing play of irony, usually on what the over-practical or unpoetic man would think or do. At first glance it may sometimes appear to be cynicism and to have been meant to be taken at face value—and indeed not only Pushkin's acquaintances, but scholars and critics to this day, seem often to miss the point: for example, when he speaks of himself with bitter irony as "humble" or "bourgeois." In a moment of impatient anger he could apply to himself the motto *ubi bene, ibi patria*; that this motto reflected the real attitude of the despicable journalist-spy and Polish renegade, Bulgarin, was perhaps Pushkin's strongest charge against him. Occasionally the irony is elusive and may be completely missed unless one senses the smile in the tone of the passage or catches the allusion: ". . . console me; that is the sacred duty of friendship (that sacred feeling)." Pushkin sometimes covers genuine feeling with ironic hyperbole, which he may have meant to be misinterpreted: "First love is always a matter of sentiment: the sillier it is, the more delightful memories it leaves. The second, do you see, is an affair of voluptuousness. . . . Natalia . . . is my one hundred thirteenth love . . . ." He can go so far as to write a completely ironic letter to a third-rate writer whom he has "defended."

His use of irony is related to another device he used for misleading spying postal employees, if not his correspondent: "Aesopic language"—political or personal allusions hidden under apparently innocent or neutral expressions. Thus he referred to Alexander I in apparent allusions to ancient Roman rulers; in a number of letters to his wife, Pushkin alluded to Nicholas I as "he." When exiled Pushkin contemplated flight abroad, he devised for his letters code words to cover plans and contingencies. Pushkin either identified an anagram or code word for Countess Vorontsova, or else her handwriting, as is shown by Pushkin's recently discovered letter to her. Pushkin occasionally used Aesopic language in his poetry and prose fiction:

he refers to contemporary allusions concealed in *Boris Godunov*. The government under Nicholas I became extremely sensitive to hidden meanings in literary works, and Pushkin was obliged to defend his poetry—sometimes speciously—against such interpretations.

Pushkin loved anecdotes; his brief diary is made up mainly of them, and there are many in his correspondence. They range from the literary to the social to the personal. Pushkin's letters to his wife include numerous anecdotes, many of great biographical and social interest, such as the story of the forlorn rejected suitor's weeping while a wedding ceremony was being performed—the Pushkins' own. Several letters contain miniature dramatizations of events or conversations. In a few words he brings a whole scene to life. Once when Pushkin returned from a journey, "my wife was at a ball; I went to get her—and I took her away to my place, like a hussar taking off a provincial young lady from the name-day celebration of the town governor's wife."

A number of letters combine the familiar letter and the poetic epistle. Such verse epistles were particularly popular in Pushkin's youth, and a number of his separate poems are in this genre. The verse epistles included in letters are full of wit and good humor, and they are as private as the letters themselves. They are in a free, light vein.

With all the stylistic variety of the letters, their most characteristic qualities remain frankness, simplicity, and sincerity. Love is presented, not in terms of subjective perception of the emotion, but the qualities of the beloved and his experience with her; aging is seen through the eyes of the peasant woman who tells him in "plain Russian" that he has "grown old and ugly." Pushkin's view of real family happiness is presented in his unfulfilled prediction of the joy he and Pletnev will feel in seeing their sons "start playing the rake" and their daughters, "at being sentimental." But Pushkin never lays his whole heart bare. Though he revealed many and varied aspects of himself to different correspondents, behind the letters as behind the poetry and prose fiction there can be sensed the whole personality, which allows only individual facets to be revealed. Pushkin's letters are masterful in all their varied types and styles, but they are most appealing when, with the sincerity and simplicity peculiar to himself he for a moment reveals himself, in order to share a particular feeling or experience with a loved one.

A Note on Pushkin's Life

Alexander Sergeevich Pushkin was born in Moscow on May 26, 1799. The Pushkins had been nobles for more than six hundred years, and, as he liked to remember, they had taken an active and important part in Russian historical events—often on the losing side —under Alexander Nevsky, Ivan the Terrible, Boris Godunov, Peter the Great, and Catherine the Great. On his mother's side, Pushkin was descended from Gannibal, or Hannibal, an Abyssinian princeling who became the ward and favorite of Peter the Great. By Pushkin's time his family had lost its influence, but it still had a recognized, though hardly an important place in the Russian nobility. His father had literary interests and connections, and his uncle, Vasily Lvovich Pushkin, was a well-known minor poet. During Pushkin's boyhood in Moscow, many of the leading writers of the time, including Karamzin, Zhukovsky, Dmitriev, and Batyushkov, visited the Pushkin home. Young Pushkin was taught at home by a series of foreign tutors and governesses, but his chief early education was in his father's library, stocked with French classics of the seventeenth and eighteenth centuries.

In 1811 he was selected to be among the thirty students of the first class of the Lyceum of Tsarskoe Selo, which Alexander I established to educate scions of prominent families for important positions in the state. At the Lyceum, from 1811 to 1817, he received the best education available in Russia at the time. He soon not only became the unofficial laureate of the Lyceum, but found a wider audience and recognition. After one of his lyrics appeared in the journal, *The Messenger of Europe*, in 1814, more and more of his poems appeared in print. In 1815 his poem "Recollections in Tsarskoe Selo" met the approval of the venerable Derzhavin, greatest eighteenth-century Russian poet, at a public examination in the Lyceum. While still a student, Pushkin became active in the literary society Arzamas, which included the literary elite, including among others, Zhukovsky, Batyushkov, and Vyazemsky, and he was accepted to full membership in September, 1817. Upon completing the Lyceum, he was given a sinecure in the Collegium of Foreign Affairs in Petersburg. The next three years he spent mainly in carefree, light-hearted pursuit of pleasure. He was warmly received in literary circles; in circles of Guard-style lovers of wine, women, and song; and in groups where political liberals debated reforms and constitutions. In 1819 he joined the Green Lamp, a group which combined, as he did, interest in the theater and actresses with desire for political reform. Between 1817 and 1820 he reflected liberal views in "revolutionary" poems, his ode "Freedom," "The Village," and a number of poems on Alexander I and his minister Arakcheev. At the same time, he was working on his first large-scale work, *Ruslan and Lyudmila* (1817—March, 1820).

In April, 1820, his political poems led to interrogation by the Petersburg governor-general and then to exile to South Russia, under the guise of an administrative transfer in the service. Pushkin left Petersburg for Ekaterinoslav on May 6, 1820. Soon after his arrival there, he was allowed to make an extended trip to the Caucasus and the Crimea, together with the family of General Raevsky, a hero of 1812. Two months spent at spas in the Caucasus and a month in the Crimea gave him his first acquaintance with mountains and with primitive peoples. At the same time, under the Raevskys' tutelage, he fell under the spell of the poetry of Byron. On September 21, 1820, he arrived in Kishinev, Bessarabia, to which his chief in the service, General Inzov, had meanwhile been transferred. He found Bessarabia, which had been annexed from Turkey only eight years before, still "Asiatic," and the Russian society there mainly military. In Kishinev as in Petersburg, with his irritable, over-sensitive temperament, he had a number of duels, usually over trifles. Among the Russians in Kishinev he found even stronger interest in politics than in Petersburg. In Kishinev and on the estate Kamenka, Province of Kiev, he became acquainted with the more radical leaders of the secret societies. He not only had the opportunity to discuss with them desirable political reforms for Russia, but also the revolutions in 1820 in Spain and Italy. In addition, he witnessed Alexander Ypsilanti's unsuccessful attempt in 1821 to invade European Turkey from Bessarabia, as a part of the effort to free Greece from Turkish rule. During his almost three years in Kishinev, Pushkin wrote his first Byronic verse tales, *The Prisoner of the*

Caucasus (1820-1821), *The Bandit Brothers* (1821-1822), and *The Fountain of Bakhchisaray* (1821-1823). He interrupted them for his *Gavriiliada* (1821), in which the Annunication is treated with the levity which Homer accords the gods of Olympus. And two months before leaving Kishinev, he began his novel in verse, *Evgeny Onegin* (1823-1831), the chapters of which appeared as separate books from 1825 to 1832.

With the aid of influential friends, he was transferred in July, 1823, to Odessa, a busy Black Sea free port with a cosmopolitan "European" atmosphere. During his year there, he was stimulated by the Italian opera and by social life. He also had two love affairs, both with married women, one of whom was Countess Vorontsova, wife of the Russian vicegerent there. In Odessa, Pushkin's literary creativeness continued, as he completed *The Fountain of Bakhchisaray* and the first chapter of *Evgeny Onegin*, and began *The Gypsies*, the most finished of the romantic verse tales. But soon he was embroiled with Count Vorontsov, who, unimpressed with Pushkin's ancient lineage, treated him according to his low government rank and at the same time expected to be lauded by an indigent but appreciative poet. Pushkin considered himself the equal in birth of the would-be Maecenas and refused to be "protected." Vorontsov then ordered him to perform the duties of his governmental position, which had hitherto been purely nominal. Pushkin was required to make an inspection of a locust-infested region; upon returning, he angrily attempted to resign from the service. In the meantime, postal officials had intercepted a letter in which he remarked that atheism, though "not so consoling as it is usually thought" is "unfortunately" the most "plausible" belief. In tsarist Russia an offense against religion was an offense against the state: he was dismissed from the service and exiled, in open disgrace, to his mother's estate of Mikhaylovskoe in north Russia.

The next two years, from August, 1824, to August, 1826, he spent at Mikhaylovskoe, in exile and under the surveillance, not only of the police, but also of the Father Superior of the near-by Svyatye Gory Monastery. His family happened to be at Mikhaylovskoe when he arrived, and violent family dissensions arose when his father undertook to watch over him for the government. In November his family departed, and he was left alone with the servants on the estate. He found companionship in visits to the family of the widowed Mme. Osipova, on the nearby estate of Trigorskoe, and in the fairy tales of his aged serf nursemaid Arina Rodionovna. In an attempt to get away, he used aneurysm as a pretext for requesting permission from the Tsar to go abroad for treatments. But Pushkin was never allowed to leave Russia. Though his mother and his friend, the poet Zhukovsky, attempted to help, he was allowed to go only to the provincial capital of Pskov, where treatment was impossible. During his exile, Pushkin was visited twice by Lyceum comrades, in January, 1825, by Pushchin, and in April of the same year by Delvig. A visit of Mme. Anna Kern to her aunt, Mme. Osipova, in June and July, 1825, resulted in the best documented of Pushkin's love affairs. However unpleasant he may have found his virtual imprisonment in the village, he continued his literary productiveness there. During 1824 and 1825 at Mikhaylovskoe, he finished *The Gypsies*, and he wrote *Boris Godunov*, his humorous *Count Nulin*, and the second chapter of *Evgeny Onegin*.

When the Decembrist Uprising took place in Petersburg on December 14, 1825, Pushkin, still in Mikhaylovskoe, was not a participant. But he soon learned that he was implicated, for all the Decembrists had copies of his early political poems. He destroyed his papers that might be dangerous for himself or others. In late spring of 1826, he sent to the Tsar a petition that he be released from exile. In July a police agent, Boshnyak, made a secret investigation of Pushkin's activities in the Province of Pskov, and found nothing damaging. Next, on September 4, Pushkin was summoned to leave immediately for an audience with Nicholas I, then in Moscow for the coronation; he was accompanied by a special state messenger. On September 8, still grimy from the road, he was taken in to see Nicholas. At the end of the interview, Pushkin was jubilant that he was now released from exile and that Nicholas I had undertaken to be the personal censor of his works.

Pushkin thought that he would be free to travel as he wished, that he could freely participate in the publication of journals, and that he would be totally free of censorship, except in cases which he himself might consider questionable and wish to refer to his royal censor. He soon found out otherwise. Count Benkendorf, Chief of Gendarmes, gave Pushkin to know that without advance permission

he was not to make any trip, participate in any journal, or publish—
or even read in literary circles—any work. He gradually discovered
that he had to account for every word and action, like a naughty child
or a parolee. In 1827 he was questioned by the police about his poem
"André Chénier," written in early 1825, but which was being
interpreted as referring to the Decembrist Uprising. A year later he
was subjected to unpleasantness because of his authorship of *The
Gavriiliada*. Later, he had to defend his poem "Anchar" (1828)
against hidden political allusions, upon its publication in 1832, and
"On the Convalescence of Lucullus" (1835) against the charge of
contemporary applications.

The youthful Pushkin had been a light-hearted scoffer at the state
of matrimony, but freed from exile, he spent the years from 1826 to
his marriage in 1831 largely in search of a wife and in preparing to
settle down. However, there were interludes of earlier dissoluteness
and gambling fever, and several fruitless efforts to obtain permission
to travel abroad—to France, Italy, or even China. He sought no less
than the most beautiful woman in Russia for his bride. In 1829 he
met her in Natalia Goncharova, and presented a formal proposal in
April of that year. When he received an indefinite answer, he set off,
without authorization, to the military front of the Russo-Turkish
War of 1828-1829. There he obtained the Russian commander's
permission to visit the army, and with it he entered captured Erzurum, Turkey—the only time he was ever outside the boundaries of
Russia. Back in Petersburg, he was asked how he had dared to visit
the military front and the army without the express permission of the
Tsar. He renewed his suit for the hand of Natalia Goncharova, and
in April, 1830, his repeated proposal was accepted, on the condition
that his ambiguous situation with the government be clarified.
Benkendorf handsomely came through with a letter stating that his
observing and counselling Pushkin was from the Tsar's "paternal
solicitude" and "as a friend," and that Pushkin had never been under
police surveillance. As a kind of wedding present, Pushkin was given
permission to publish *Boris Godunov*—after four years of waiting for
authorization—under his "own responsibility." He was formally betrothed on May 6, 1830.

Financial arrangements in connection with his father's wedding
gift to him of half the estate of Kistenevo necessitated a visit to the

neighboring estate of Boldino, in east-central Russia. When Pushkin arrived there in September, 1830, he expected to remain only a few days; however, for three whole months he was held in quarantine by an epidemic of Asiatic cholera—the first European invasion of what was to be perhaps the most deadly disease of the nineteenth century in Europe and America. These three months in Boldino turned out to be literarily the most productive of his life. During the last months of his exile at Mikhaylovskoe, he had completed Chapters V and VI of *Evgeny Onegin*, but in the four subsequent years he had written, of major works, only *Poltava* (1828), his unfinished novel *The Blackamoor of Peter the Great* (1827), and Chapter VII of *Evgeny Onegin* (1827-1828). During the autumn at Boldino, Pushkin wrote the five short stories of *The Tales of Belkin*; the verse tale *The Little House in Kolomna*; his little tragedies, *The Avaricious Knight*, *Mozart and Salieri*, *The Stone Guest*, and *Feast in the Time of the Plague*; *The Tale of the Priest and His Workman Balda*, the first of his fairy tales in verse; the last chapter of *Evgeny Onegin*; and "The Devils," among other lyrics.

Pushkin was married to Natalia Goncharova on February 18, 1831, in Moscow. In May, after a honeymoon made disagreeable by "Moscow aunties" and in-laws, the Pushkins moved to Tsarskoe Selo, in order to live near the capital, but inexpensively and in "inspirational solitude and in the circle of sweet recollections." These expectations were defeated when the cholera epidemic in Petersburg caused the Tsar and the court to take refuge, in July, in Tsarskoe Selo. Pushkin petitioned for permission to do historical research in the government archives, and after his nationalistic poems on the Polish Revolution of 1830-1831 were written and quickly published, he was officially enrolled, as of November 14, in the government service, with a modest salary, to do historical research. In October, 1831, the Pushkins moved to Petersburg, where they lived for the remainder of his life. He and his wife became henceforth inextricably involved with favors from the Tsar and with court society. Mme. Pushkina's beauty immediately made a sensation in society, and her admirers included the Tsar himself. She became the belle of the ball in Petersburg. As Pushkin worked in the archives, his interests moved from Peter the Great to the Pugachev Revolt of 1773-1775, for a work of historical research and a historical novel. In the fall of 1833 he made a trip to the Pugachev country, in the Ural region. On the way back he stopped at Boldino, and there he had another of his short fruitful literary periods. Since 1830, he had completed only one major work, his fairy tale in verse, *Tsar Saltan* (1831); now in a month and a half he wrote *The Bronze Horseman*, "The Queen of Spades," *Angelo*, and he finished his work of historical research, *The History of Pugachev*.

On December 30, 1833, Nicholas I made Pushkin a Kammer-junker, an intermediate court rank usually granted at the time to youths of high aristocratic families. Pushkin was deeply offended, all the more because he was convinced that it was conferred, not for any quality of his own, but only to make it proper for the beautiful Mme. Pushkina to attend court balls. Dancing at one of these balls was followed, in March, 1834, by her having a miscarriage. While she was convalescing in the provinces, Pushkin spoke openly in letters to her of his indignation and humiliation. The letters were intercepted and sent to the police and to the Tsar. When Pushkin discovered this, in fury he submitted his resignation from the service, on June 25, 1834. His action was taken as the deepest "ingratitude"; in addition to other favors, the Tsar had recently lent Pushkin the money to publish *The History of Pugachev*—with the stipulation that it be renamed *The History of the Pugachev Revolt*. Pushkin was abruptly informed that the Tsar accepted his resignation, but that in that case "everything between us is over." He had reason to fear the worst from the Tsar's displeasure, and he felt obliged to retract his resignation.

Pushkin could ill afford the expense of gowns for Mme. Pushkina for court balls or the time required for performing court duties. His woes further increased when her two unmarried sisters came in autumn, 1834, to live henceforth with them. In addition, in the spring of 1834 he had taken over the management of his improvident father's estate and had undertaken to settle the debts of his heedless brother. The result was endless cares, annoyances, and even outlays from his own pocket, before he gave it up in the middle of 1835. By this time he was himself in such financial straits that he applied for a leave of absence to retire to the country for three or four years, or if that were refused, for a substantial sum as loan to cover his most pressing debts and for the permission to publish a journal. The leave of absence was brusquely refused, but a loan of thirty thousand rubles was, after some trouble, negotiated; permission to publish, beginning in 1836, a quarterly literary journal, *The Contemporary*, was finally granted as well. The journal was not a financial success, and it involved him in endless editorial and financial cares and in difficulties with the censors, for it gave importantly placed enemies among them the opportunity to pay him off. It had become meanwhile harder and harder for him to find the solitude and serenity which would make it possible for him to do creative work. Short visits to the country in 1834 and 1835 had resulted in the completion of only one major work, *The Tale of the Golden Cockerel* (1834), and during 1836 he completed only his novel on Pugachev, *The Captain's Daughter*, and a number of his finest lyrics.

Pushkin's final tragedy was played against the background of court society. Mme. Pushkina loved the attention which her beauty attracted in the highest society; she was fond of "coquetting" and of being surrounded by admirers, who included the Tsar himself. In 1834 Mme. Pushkina met a young man who was not content with coquetry, a handsome French royalist émigré in Russian service, who was adopted by the Dutch ambassador, Heeckeren. Young d'Anthès-Heeckeren pursued Mme. Pushkina for two years, and finally so openly and unabashedly that by autumn, 1836, it was becoming a scandal. On November 4, 1836, Pushkin received several copies of a "certificate" nominating him "coadjutor of the Order of Cuckolds and historiographer of the Order." Pushkin immediately challenged d'Anthès-Heeckeren; at the same time, he made desperate efforts to settle his indebtedness to the Treasury. Pushkin twice allowed postponements of the duel, and then retracted the challenge when he learned "from public rumor" that d'Anthès-Heeckeren was "really" in love with Mme. Pushkina's sister, Ekaterina Goncharova. On January 10, 1837, the marriage took place, contrary to Pushkin's expectations. Pushkin refused to attend the wedding or to receive the couple in his home, but in society d'Anthès-Heeckeren pursued Mme. Pushkina even more openly. Then d'Anthès-Heeckeren arranged a meeting with her, by persuading her friend Idalia Poletika to invite Mme. Pushkina for a visit; Mme. Poletika left the two alone, but one of her children came in, and Mme. Pushkina managed to get away. Upon hearing of this meeting, Pushkin sent an insulting letter to old Heeckeren, accusing him of being the author

of the "certificate" of November 4 and the "pander" of his "bastard."
A duel with d'Anthès-Heeckeren became inevitable. It occurred on
January 27, 1837. D'Anthès-Heeckeren fired first, and Pushkin was
mortally wounded; after he fell, he summoned the strength to fire his
shot and to wound, slightly, his adversary. Pushkin died two days
later, on January 29.

As Pushkin lay dying, and after his death, except for a few friends
court society sympathized with d'Anthès-Heeckeren, but thousands
of people of all other social levels came to Pushkin's apartment to
express sympathy and to mourn. The government obviously feared a
political demonstration. To prevent public display, the funeral was
shifted from St. Isaac's Cathedral to the small Royal Stables Church,
with admission by ticket only to members of the court and diplomatic
society. And then his body was sent away, in secret and at midnight.
His coffin was carried on a simple cart and accompanied only by an
old family friend, by Pushkin's serf "uncle," and by a captain of
gendarmes. He was buried beside his mother at dawn on February 6,
1837, at Svyatye Gory Monastery, near Mikhaylovskoe.

PART I

PRECOCIOUS POET—TSARSKOE SELO AND PETERSBURG

November, 1815–April, 1820

To Ivan Ivanovich Martynov
November 28, 1815. From Tsarskoe Selo to Petersburg.
(Rough draft)
Dear Sir, Ivan Ivanovich,[1]
Your Excellency wished me to write a piece[2] on the arrival of
the Sovereign Emperor; I am carrying out your command. If the
feelings of love and gratitude which I have depicted toward our
great monarch are not completely unworthy of my lofty subject,
how happy I would be if His Excellency, Count Alexey Kirillovich,[3]
would be so kind as to present to the Sovereign Emperor the feeble
production of an inexperienced versifier!

Relying upon your extreme indulgence, I have the honor to be,
Dear Sir,

	Your Excellency's
November 28, 1815.	Most humble servant,
Tsarskoe Selo.	Alexander Pushkin.

[2]

To Peter Andreevich Vyazemsky
March 27, 1816. From Tsarskoe Selo to Moscow.

March 27, 1816.
Prince Peter Andreevich,[1]
I confess that only the hope of obtaining from Moscow the Russian
verses of Chapelle and Boileau[2] could overcome my blessed laziness.
So be it; but don't you complain if my letter makes Your Bardic
Highness yawn; it's your own fault: why did you stir up the unfortunate Tsarskoe Selo hermit, whom the mad demon of paper-
blotching was already egging on, even as it was? For my part, I
bluntly declare to you that I do not intend to leave you in peace
until the lame Sofia[3] postman brings me some prose and verses of
yours. Think this over well and do what you please, but I have
already made up my mind, and I shall get my way.

What is there to be said to you about our solitude? Never has the

Lyceum (or Lykeum; only, for God's sake, not the *Lyceya*)[4] seemed so intolerable to me as at the present time. I assure you that solitude is indeed a very stupid thing, in spite of all the philosophers and poets who pretend that they have lived in the country and are in love with silence and quiet:

> Blessed is he who amidst the city noise dreams of solitude, who sees only from afar a deserted spot, an orchard, a country home, hills, and silent forests, a valley with a playful brook, and even . . . a herd and shepherd! Blessed is he who with good friends sits at the table until night and laughs at the Slavonic blockheads[5] in Russian verses. Blessed is he who does not abandon noisy Moscow for a hut . . . and who not in dream but in reality caresses his mistress! . . .[6]

True, the time of our graduation is approaching; one more year is left. But another whole year of plusses and minuses, of laws, of taxes, of the sublime, of the beautiful! . . . another whole year to doze in front of the teacher's desk . . . that is horrible. Really, I would gladly agree to read twelve times all twelve cantos of the notorious *Rossiada*, even with Merzlyakov's[7] most sagacious critique to boot, if only Count Razumovsky would shorten the time of my imprisonment. It is outrageous to keep a young fellow shut in and not permit him to participate even in the innocent pleasure of burying the defunct Academy[8] and the Conversation Society of Ruiners of the Russian Word.[9] But nothing can be done about it,

> All cannot have an equable fate, and one lot is quite different from another.[10]

From boredom I often write verses which are boring enough (and sometimes very boring); I often read poems no better than mine; recently I fasted and confessed—all this is completely unamusing. Dear Arzamasian![11] Console us with your poetic epistles—and I promise you, if not eternal bliss, at least the sincere gratitude of all the Lyceum.

Forgive me, Prince—you terror of all the Poet-Princes *Sh.*[12] Embrace Batyushkov[13] for the sick fellow from whom he captured *Bova Korolevich* a year ago.[14] I don't know whether I shall have time to write to Vasily Lvovich.[15] In case I don't, embrace him for his frivolous nephew. *Valeas*.[16]

Alexander Pushkin.

Lomonosov[17] greets you.

[3]

TO VASILY LVOVICH PUSHKIN
December 28(?), 1816. From Tsarskoe Selo to Moscow.

I wish you, O Nestor[1] of the Arzamas, poet reared in battles, neighbor dangerous[2] for the singers on the frightening heights of Parnassus, defender of taste, formidable *Vot!*[3] I wish you my uncle, in the new year, your merriment as of old. And here, for you is the feeble translation of my heart—an epistle in verse and prose.

In your letter you called me brother, but I have not made bold to call you by that name, which is too flattering for me.

I have not completely lost my reason as on Pegasus I jog along with Bacchic rhymes. I know my real worth, whether I like it or not; no, no, you are not my brother at all, you are my uncle and on Parnassus.

And so, most agreeable of all poet-uncles of this world, may I hope that you will forgive the nine months' pregnancy of pen of the laziest of poet nephews?

Yes, of course, I feel remorseful toward you; the hermit-rhymster is completely in the wrong; in laziness he is comparable only with the gods. He is at fault both in prose and verse, but in the new year forget what is old.

Fate seems to have destined me to only two kinds of letters—promissory and excusatory; the former at the beginning of a year's correspondence, and the latter at its last gasp. Besides, I have noted that, in all, this correspondence consists of two epistles—that seems inexcusable to me.

But you, who could laud our beautiful women with the simple songs of the reed, and with the wrathful muse of Juvenal, with ferocious satire, ridicule the bases of rude barbarity, and torment pallid Shishkov with the holy tongue of Phoebus, and brand with a single verse the sullen forehead of Shakhovskoy![4] O you who could love, dine, and write, tell me sincerely, is it possible that you can't forgive?

December 28, 1816.

P.S. Remember me to my unforgettable ones.[5] I do not have any more time for writing, but need I promise again? Farewell, all you whom my heart loves and who still love me.

Chapelle Andreevich[6] has of course forgotten me long, long ago, but I love him cordially because, in carefree manner, he loves to sing, to drink his wine, and to laugh at universal blockheads, with his sportive verses—truly, most amusingly.[7]

[4]

To Vasily Andreevich Zhukovsky
Between December 25 and 30, 1816 (?). In Petersburg.
(In French)

Sir!

We—my father and my mother—are returning to you Voltaire's *Maid of Orleans*,[1] etc.—in all   4

$$\text{total} - \frac{3}{7}$$

And in addition Mr. Kyukhelbeker[2] is sending you 4 volumes of the *Amphion*.[3] Many thanks from me. My dear Mr. Zhukovsky, I hope that I shall have the pleasure of seeing you tomorrow; *Zadig*,[4] *Tristram*,[5] etc., are very humbly requested to dine at our house today, if possible.[6]

Pushkin.

Return the sheet.

[5]

To Stepan Stepanovich Frolov
April 4, 1817. From Tsarskoe Selo to Petersburg.

April 4, 1817.
Most honored Stepan Stepanovich,[1]
Excuse it, if your ancient friend writes you only two lines and a half—in the next post he will write two pages and 1/2.

Fidget Pushkin.

[6]

To Prince Peter Andreevich Vyazemsky and Vasily Lvovich Pushkin[1]
September 1, 1817. From Petersburg to Moscow.
Dear Prince,
If you see [S. G.] Lomonosov, remind him of the letter which he was supposed to deliver into my hands and which he lost at Louis's,[2] while I was being bored in my Pskovian solitude.[3] I arrived in Petersburg quite recently, and I should like to leave it for Moscow; that is, for Vyazemsky's, as soon as possible; I do not know whether my wish will be realized. Meanwhile I am awaiting new verses of yours with impatience, and I ask you for your blessing.

September 1, 1817.   Pushkin.

Address: To The Most Reverend[4]
        Vasily Lvovich Vot
        and Peter Andreevich Asmodeus[5]
        in Moscow.

[7]

To Alexander Ivanovich Turgenev[1]
July 9, 1819. In Petersburg.
I am very sorry that I have not said good-by either to you or the two Mirabeaus.[2] Here is the epistle to Orlov[3] as a souvenir for you; put it into your fatherly pocket, print it in your own publishing house[4] and give one copy to the flaming nursling of Bellona, to the citizen faithful at the throne.[5] Apropos of Bellona: When you see white-eyed Kavelin,[6] have a talk with him, at least, for your

Christ's sake, for Sobolevsky,[7] student at the University Pension. Kavelin is persecuting him for some theological opinions, and he is forcing this young man, worthy in all respects, out of the Pension by leaving him in the lower classes, regardless of his successes and great capabilities. You have been Sobolevsky's protector; remember him, and—as the Cardinal-Nephew[8]—stop the mouth of doctor-of-theology Kavelin, who is striving to become an inquisitor. I commend myself to your prayers, and I ask Chamberlain Don Basile[9] to forget me, at least for three months.

July 9, 1819.   Pushkin.

[8]

To Nikolay Ivanovich Krivtsov
The second half of July or the beginning of August, 1819.
From Mikhaylovskoe to London.
(Rough draft)

Do you remember, inhabitant of free England, that in this world there are the province of Pskov and your lazy friend, whom you probably remember, who pines for you every day, at whom you are angry,[1] and [. . . .][2] I hate to write letters. Tongue and voice scarcely suffice for our thoughts. But the pen is so stupid, so slow—a letter cannot take the place of conversation. However that may be, I am at fault, for I knew that my letter could remind you for a moment of our Russia, of evenings at the Turgenevs and the Karamzins.[3]

[9]

To Pavel Borisovich Mansurov
October 27, 1819. From Petersburg to Novgorod.

With great difficulty I have managed to persuade Vsevolozhsky[1] to let me write a few lines to you, dear Mansurov, you marvelous Circassian![2] Are you well, my joy? Are you having fun, my charming fellow? Do you remember us, your friends (of the male sex)? We have not forgotten you, and at 1/2 past seven every day we remember you in the theater, with hand clapping and sighs—and we say: "What a fine fellow our Pavel is! Just what is he doing now in great Novgorod? He is envying us—and he is weeping because of Kr . . . .[3] (of course, with the lower duct)." Every morning a winged maiden flits to rehearsal past the windows of our Nikita [Vsevolozhsky]; as before, telescopes rise toward her, p——, too; but, alas, you do not see her, she does not see you. But let us abandon the elegiac, my friend. As your historian, I shall tell you about our fellows. Everything is going as before: the champagne, thank God, is lusty—the actresses likewise—the former gets drunk up, and the latter get f——. Amen. Amen. That's as it ought to be. Yuriev,[4] thank God, is well of the c——. I have a little dose which is clearing up; that is fine, too. N. Vsevolozhsky is gambling; the air is thick with chalk! Money is scattered all around! Sosnitskaya[5] and Prince Sha-khovskoy are growing fat and stupid—but I am not in love with them. Nevertheless, I have been loudly applauding them both—him for his bad comedy,[6] and her for her mediocre acting. Tolstoy[7] is sick—I shall not say of what—as it is, I already have too many c—— in my letter. The Green Lamp's wick needs trimming—it looks as though it may go out—and that is a pity—there is oil (i.e., our friend's champagne). Are you writing, will you write me, my pal, my nithe fewwow?[8] Tell me about yourself and about the military settlements.[9] I need all this—because I love you—and hate despo-tism. Good-by, Little Paw.

October 27, 1819.   Cricket A. Pushkin.

[10]

To Peter Andreevich Vyazemsky
About (not later than) April 21, 1820.
From Petersburg to Warsaw.

I read to my Preobrazhensky friend[1] the several lines which you wrote me in your letter to Turgenev, and I congratulated him upon a happy defecation of the Homeric feasts.[2] He answered that the s—— is yours and not his. It is to be desired that the matter stop on this—he seems to be afraid of your satirical cudgel. The first four verses with regard to him in your epistle to Dmitriev[3] are excellent. The remaining ones, necessary for the clarification of the personality, are feeble and cold—and, friendship apart, Katenin deserves some-thing a little better and more malicious. He was born too late—both in his character and mode of thinking he belongs completely to the eighteenth century. In him, as in that famed century of philosophy, is the same arrogance of the author, the same literary gossiping and intriguing. Then the quarrel of Fréron[4] and Voltaire occupied

Europe, but now you would not astonish anyone with that. No matter what you say, our age is not an age of poets—in that there would seem to be nothing to regret—but all the same it is a pity. The circle of poets is becoming tighter by the hour—soon we shall be forced, for lack of listeners, to read our verses aloud to each other. That is all right, too. Meanwhile, send us verses of yours; they are captivating and enlivening—"First Snow" is charming; "Despondency"[5] is more charming. Have you read the most recent works of Zhukovsky, who is resting in God?[6] Have you heard his "Voice from the Other World"[7] and what do you think of it? Petersburg is stifling for a poet. I thirst for foreign lands; maybe the Southern air would enliven my soul.[8] I have finished my long poem.[9] And only its last, i.e., concluding, verse brought me true pleasure. You will read fragments in journals, and you will thus receive it already printed—I am so fed up with it that I cannot bring myself to copy out scraps of it for you. My letter is boring, because since I became a personage with a history for the female gossipers of Saint Petersburg, I have been growing stupid and old, not by the week but by the hour. Farewell. Answer me, please—I am very glad that I have hit upon corresponding.

Letter 1

1. Pushkin's first surviving letter is of interest in that it concerns a poem written by him in praise of Alexander I (in contrast to his later comments and poems), and in that it shows Pushkin as the acknowledged student-poet of the Lyceum at Tsarskoe Selo. Tsar Alexander I (1777-1825), Emperor of Russia from 1801 to 1825, had established the Lyceum in 1811, for the training of selected sons of noble families for the civil and military service. Pushkin was in the first class. The Lyceum was then located in a palace in Tsarskoe Selo, the "Tsar's Village," which may be compared with the French Versailles.

Ivan Ivanovich Martynov (1771-1833), then director of the Department of Public Education, often gave assignments to students at the Lyceum.

2. Pushkin's verse epistle "To Alexander," written on the occasion of Alexander's triumphal return from Paris in 1815.

3. Count Alexey Kirillovich Razumovsky (1748-1822), then Minister of Public Education.

Letter 2

1. Prince Peter Andreevich Vyazemsky (1792-1878), Russian critic, poet, and man of letters, and one of Pushkin's closest friends and most frequent correspondents from the Lyceum days on.

2. Vyazemsky's youthful Anacreontics and satirical poems were written under the influence of the seventeenth-century French authors Chapelle and Boileau, respectively.

3. A section of Tsarskoe Selo.

4. The discussion has to do with the gender of the word in Russian; Pushkin insists that it must be masculine.

5. Members of the Conversation Society of Lovers of the Russian Word (1811-1816), headed by Vice Admiral Alexander Semenovich Shishkov (1754-1841); this group followed eighteenth-century Russian ideas of literary diction and insisted on a heavily Church Slavonic style in serious literature. They were opposed by the ideas of Nikolay Mikhaylovich Karamzin (1766-1826), Russian author and historian, and his successors, particularly by the literary society Arzamas (1815-1818), of which Pushkin, Vyazemsky, and their literary friends were members. The Arzamas group laughed to scorn the ideas of the Shishkov group.

6. This poem is typical of Pushkin's early poems in its tone and form. Whenever the verses in a letter are germane to the content of the letter, they are of course included in this edition. In the interest of precision, the translation of the verses is given in prose.

7. Alexey Fedorovich Merzlyakov (1778-1830), Professor of Literature in Moscow University, published in 1815 a long analysis of *The Rossiada* (1779), an epic in the classical style by Mikhail Matveevich Kheraskov (1733-1807). The epic had at first been popular, but it was no longer highly regarded in Pushkin's day. However, Merzlyakov considered it a great work, in spite of its defects.

8. The Russian Academy (1783-1841) had as its chief accomplishment the publication of a *Dictionary of the Russian Language* in two editions (1789-1794 and 1806-1822).

9 That is, the Conversation Society of Lovers of the Russian Word.

10. Lines from Vyazemsky's verse epistle "To a Partisan-Poet" to Denis Vasilievich Davydov (1784-1839), famous guerilla warrior in the Russo-French War of 1812 and "hussar style" poet. The poem was published in Merzlyakov's journal *Amphion* in 1815.

11. That is, member of the Arzamas. Poetic epistles were very popular in Russia at the time.

12. That is, whose names being in *Sh*; they include the literary figures Princes Alexander Alexandrovich Shakhovskoy (1777-1846), Sergey Alexandrovich Shirinsky-Shikhmatov (1783-1837), neo-classical opponents of the Arzamas, and Peter Ivanovich Shalikov (1768-1852), an extreme sentimentalist. Vyazemsky (and Pushkin) had ridiculed them in several poems.

13. The poet Konstantin Nikolaevich Batyushkov (1787-1855), poet and member of the Arzamas. He was one of the early Pushkin's poetic masters.

14. Pushkin left unfinished a planned long poem "Bova [Korolevich]" (written 1814), on the theme of the folklore romance, apparently as a result of hearing that Batyushkov intended to utilize the story.

15. Pushkin's Uncle Vasily Lvovich Pushkin (1767-1830), a wit, minor poet, and member of the Arzamas.

16. Young Pushkin not infrequently expresses "farewell" in Latin—in all the other instances, he uses the more familiar form *vale*. Pushkin similarly occasionally closes letters with the Italian *addio*.

17. Sergey Grigorievich Lomonosov (1799-1857), a Lyceum comrade, later a diplomat.

Letter 3

1. V. L. Pushkin was the oldest member of the Arzamas; hence the allusion to Nestor, the aged sage in *The Iliad* and *The Odyssey*. In the general neo-classical influence, still prevalent in Russia in Pushkin's early years, Bacchic and Anacreontic verses, a predominance of classical allusions, classical names for journals, almanacs, and so on, were generally the vogue.

2. The "battles" and "dangerous neighbor" are allusions to V. L. Pushkin's *Dangerous Neighbor* (1811), a semi-risqué, very popular, but then unpublishable poem which includes a brawl in a house of prostitution.

3. V. L. Pushkin's Arzamas nickname. The nicknames of Arzamasians were taken from ballads by the great poet and translator Vasily Andreevich Zhukovsky (1783-1852), one of the chief members of the society, and a friend and defender of Pushkin. Zhukovsky was, from the standpoint of technique, the greatest Russian poet before Pushkin, and young Pushkin's immediate master in prosody.

4. In V. L. Pushkin's *Dangerous Neighbor*, a play by Shakhovskoy is defended in a bawdy house: "Downright talent will find defenders everywhere." Shakhovskoy's play in question is *The New Sterne*, a parody on Russian works indebted to Laurence Sterne, especially to his *Sentimental Journey* (1768).

5. Vyazemsky and Batyushkov.

6. Vyazemsky; the allusion is to his poems in the style of Chapelle.

7. Pushkin was angered when his uncle published this letter without his consent.

Letter 4

1. Voltaire was always one of Pushkin's favorite authors and his *Maid of Orleans* (*La Pucelle d'Orléans*, 1755), one of Pushkin's favorite works.

2. Vilgelm Karlovich Kyukhelbeker (1797-1846), poet, later a Decembrist, and one of Pushkin's close friends from Lyceum days on, though Pushkin often laughed good-naturedly at his exaggerated enthusiasms and his violences upon the Russian language.

3. A journal published by Merzlyakov.

4. A tale (1747) by Voltaire.

5. Sterne's *Tristram Shandy* (1760-1767) was another of Pushkin's favorite books.

6. Here Pushkin is asking for the loan of more books.

Letter 5

1. Stepan Stepanovich Frolov was an inspector of the Lyceum. Pushkin's note is part of a group-letter written by eight different students of the Lyceum. "Fidget" is apparently Frolov's nickname for Pushkin. Nicknames were common in literary and social groups of the time.

Letter 6

1. The part of the sheet containing the second letter, the one to V. L. Pushkin, is torn off and lost.

2. A restaurant in Petersburg.

3. At his mother's estate of Mikhaylovskoe, in the Opochka District of the Province of Pskov, in northwestern Russia. Pushkin spent July and August there.

4. The title of an archbishop.

5. Asmodeus was Vyazemsky's Arzamas nickname. Asmodeus, in Jewish demonology, was an evil spirit, and later he was considered the king of demons; hence the joking terms of worship and reverence which Pushkin often applies to him.

Letter 7

1. Alexander Ivanovich Turgenev (1784-1845), a member of the Arzamas though not primarily a writer, and a very close friend of Pushkin and the entire Pushkin family. He was one of the most intelligent and enlightened men of his day and country.

2. A. I. Turgenev's two younger brothers, Nikolay Ivanovich (1789-1872) and Sergey Ivanovich (1790-1827). The former was like the elder Mirabeau, in that he was the author of a theoretical work on taxation; the latter was like the younger Mirabeau, in his liberal political opinions and in the fact that both were crippled. The three Turgenev brothers were from a different branch of the family from Ivan Sergeevich Turgenev (1818-1883) , whose stories and novels were later to bring Russian literature to the attention of Europe.

3. Prince Alexey Fedorovich Orlov (1786-1861), commander of the Emperor's Body Guard Cavalry Regiment, dissuaded Pushkin from the idea of joining the military service.

4. That of the Ministry of Spiritual Affairs and of Public Education. This was not done.

5. That is, to Pushkin himself; this is a quotation from Pushkin's verse epistle "To Orlov."

6. Dmitry Alexandrovich Kavelin (1778-1851), then a director of the Chief Pedagogical Institute and the Noble Pension connected with it, and of St. Petersburg University.

7. Sergey Alexandrovich Sobolevsky (1803-1870), later one of Pushkin's closest friends.

8. A. I. Turgenev was an official in the Ministry of Spiritual Affairs and as such a subordinate of Prince Alexander Nikolaevich Golitsyn (1773-1844), then Minister of Spiritual Affairs and Public Education. Hence the allusion.

9. Apparently the reference is to Prince A. N. Golitsyn. Don Basile is the singing teacher in Beaumarchais' *Barber of Seville* (1775). This is the first mention in the letters of the court ranks or distinctions, which were later to play such an important role in Pushkin's life. These ranks included, in addition to that of Chamberlain (*Kammerger*), those of Kammerjunker and Chamber-Page (*Kammerpaž*), for men and boys, and Lady in Waiting (*Frejlejn*) for women and girls.

Letter 8

1. Because Pushkin's answer was so tardy to some verses sent to him in the summer of 1818. Nikolay Ivanovich Krivtsov (1791-1843), a member of the Arzamas, was in the diplomatic service.

2. The phrase is unfinished.

3. At the homes of A. I. Turgenev and N. M. Karamzin. Pushkin always had warm friendly feelings and genuine admiration for Karamzin, who had initiated the great reforms in the Russian literary language which the Arzamas favored and Pushkin developed further. Karamzin's feelings toward Pushkin were mixed: he admired Pushkin's poetic talent, but himself favoring a strong, autocratic monarchy, he was strongly opposed to Pushkin's verses and friends of a liberal or revolutionary tendency.

Letter 9

1. Nikita Vsevolodovich Vsevolozhsky (1799-1862), a close friend of Pushkin's. The Green Lamp, a secret, illegal theatrical and literary society, met at Vsevolozhsky's house. "Green" signified hope, and "Lamp," enlightenment. The members combined their serious concerns—theatrical and literary interests and liberal political sentiments—with roisterous living and chasing after actresses.

2. Pavel Borisovich Mansurov (1795-1880's), a member of the Green Lamp. Pushkin calls him the "Circassian" probably because of the similarity of his name with that of Mansur (d. 1794), a Circassian mountaineer warrior against the Russians.

3. The dancer Maria Mikhaylovna Krylova. The name is related to the Russian word for "wing."

4. Fedor Filippovich Yuriev (1796-1860), a member of the Green Lamp.

5. Elena Yakovlevna Sosnitskaya (1800-1855), an actress.

6. *Negligent Landlords* (1819).

7. Yakov Nikolaevich Tolstoy (1791-1867), chairman of the Green Lamp.

8. *Xolosen'kij*, a lisping pronunciation.

9. Military settlements or "colonies," first set up by Alexander I in 1810, were greatly increased after 1817. Liberals considered them cruel and despotic.

Letter 10

1. Pavel Alexandrovich Katenin (1792-1853), poet, dramatist, and critic, who combined interest in experimentation in poetic form with severely classical tastes in the drama. Katenin was then an officer in the Preobrazhensky Guard Regiment.

2. Vyazemsky had mistranslated the French word *reliefs*, which in the context meant "remains, left-overs," as "bas-reliefs." Pushkin considered literary composition a natural function, and he often speaks of it in terms of physical elimination.

3. Vyazemsky denied that the lines in question referred to the poet Ivan Ivanovich Dmitriev (1760-1837), a poet of the sentimental school, a writer of fables, and one of the most prominent poets of the generation older than Pushkin.

4. Fréron was a literary opponent of the Encyclopedists and especially of Voltaire.

5. Poems by Vyazemsky.

6. That is, composing little and publishing infrequently; a frequent complaint and figure of speech of Pushkin's with regard to Zhukovsky.

7. His reworking of Schiller's "Thekla: A Ghost's Voice" (1802). Zhukovksy's translations from the German poet added much to Schiller's popularity in Russia, which was then high. Zhukovsky's poem was written in 1815 and published in 1818.

8. Pushkin was at this time being threatened with imprisonment or exile because of poems of a liberal coloring; there was considerable gossip on the subject. Later in 1820

he was indeed exiled, though under the guise of an administrative transfer as an officer in the Collegium of Foreign Affairs.

9. *Ruslan and Lyudmila*. Early in 1820 parts of it appeared in journals, *The Neva Spectator* and *The Son of the Fatherland*, and then the entire poem was published in book form in late July or early August of the same year.

PART II

SOUL-ENLIVENING SOUTHERN AIR—KISHINEV

May, 1820—July, 1823

To Lev Sergeevich Pushkin
September 24, 1820. From Kishenev to Petersburg.

Dear brother,[1] I owe you an apology; I shall try to wipe out my fault with a long letter and detailed accounts. I shall start from the eggs of Leda.[2] After arriving in Ekaterinoslav I became bored, I went boating on the Dnepr, I took a swim, and I caught a fever, as I usually do. General Raevsky,[3] who was en route to the Caucasus with a son and two daughters,[4] found me in a Jew's hovel, delirious, without a doctor, with a pitcher of iced lemonade. His son (you know our close ties and his important services, which I shall never forget)[5]—his son proposed to me a journey to the Caucasian watering places. The physician[6] who was going along with him promised not to do me in on the way; Inzov[7] gave me his blessing for a prosperous journey. I was so sick I had to lie down in the calash; I got well within a week. I lived in the Caucasus two months;[8] I needed the waters very badly, and they helped me exceedingly, especially the hot sulfur water. Incidentally, I took baths in the warm acidulous sulfur waters, the iron waters, and in the acidulous cold water. These medicinal springs are all located not very far apart in the last spurs of the Caucasian Mountains. I am sorry, my friend, that you could not see this magnificent range of mountains with me, with their icy summits, which from afar in the clear twilight look like strange, many-colored, and motionless clouds. I regret that you could not climb with me to the sharp peak of five-ridged Beshtu, of Mashuk, and of Iron, Stone, and Serpent Mountains. The Caucasian region, the torrid boundary of Asia, arouses interest in all respects. Ermolov[9] has filled it with his name and his beneficent genius. The savage Circassians have become timorous; their ancient audacity is disappearing. The roads are becoming less dangerous by the hour, and the numerous convoys are becoming superfluous. It is to be hoped that this conquered land, which until now has brought no real benefit to Russia, will soon form a bridge between us and the Persians for safe trading, that it will not be an obstacle to us in future wars— and that perhaps we shall carry out Napoleon's chimerical plan of conquering India.[10] I have seen the banks of the Kuban[11] and our guardian Cossack villages—I have looked with admiration at our Cossacks. Eternally on horseback, eternally ready to fight, eternally on guard! I traveled in sight of the hostile fields of the free mountain peoples. Sixty Cossacks were convoying us; behind us was being dragged a loaded cannon, with a lighted slow match. Although the Circassians are tame enough now, they cannot be depended upon; in hope of a large ransom they are ready to fall upon a famous Russian general. And whereas a poor officer safely gallops on post horses, His High Excellency the General may easily land on the lasso of some Circassian. You will understand how pleasing the threat of danger is to a vivid imagination. Sometime I shall read you my notes on the Black Sea and the Don Cossacks[12]—I shall not say a word about them now. The shores of the Crimea were revealed to me from the peninsula Taman, the principality of ancient Tmutarakan.[13] We came to *Kerch* by sea. Here I expected to see the ruin of Mithradates' tomb, the traces of Panticapaeum,[14] but in the cemetery on the adjacent mountain I saw a pile of stones and rough-hewn rocks and noted several steps, the work of human hands. Whether this is a tomb or whether it is the ancient foundations of a tower, I do not know. A few miles farther we stopped on the *Golden Mound*.[15] All that has remained of the city of Panticapaeum is rows of stones and a ditch now almost level with the ground. There can be no doubt that much of value is concealed under the ground, filled in by the centuries: some Frenchman[16] has been sent from Petersburg to make explorations—but he lacks both money and information, as is usual with us. We came to *Kefa*[17] from Kerch, and we stayed at the house of Bronevsky,[18] a man honored for his spotless career in the service and for his poverty. Now he is under trial—and like Vergil's Old Man,[19] he cultivates his garden on the seashore not far from the city. Grapes and almonds provide him with his income. He is not a brilliant man, but he has a great store of information about the Crimea, an important and a neglected land. From there we set off by sea, past the southern shores of Tavrida,[20] to *Gurzuf*,[21] where *Raevsky's* family was. At night aboard the ship I wrote an *elegy*, which I am sending you; send it off to *Grech*[22] without a signature. The ship sailed in front of mountains covered with poplars, grapes, laurels, and cypresses; Tatar settlements were dotted everywhere. The ship stopped in sight of Gurzuf. I spent three weeks there. My friend, I spent the happiest moments of my life in the midst of the family of honored Raevsky. I did not see in him the hero, the glory of Russian troops; I loved in him a man of lucid mind, of a simple and beautiful soul, and indulgent, solicitous friend, and a host who is always kind and affable. A witness of the Age of Catherine,[23] a memorial of '12;[24] a man without prejudices, with a strong character, and yet a sensitive person who without intending it draws to himself everyone capable of understanding and appreciating his lofty qualities. His older son is going to be more than merely well known. All his daughters are charming; the oldest is an unusual woman. Judge whether I was happy: a free and untroubled life in the circle of a pleasant family; a life which I so love and which I had never enjoyed; a happy, southern sky; a marvellous region; scenery which gratifies the imagination: mountains, orchards, the sea. My friend, my cherished hope is to see the southern shore and the Raevsky family again. Will you be with me? Shall we soon be united? Now I am alone in Moldavia, which is empty for me. At least write me. I thank you for the verses: I would have thanked you more for prose.[25] For goodness sake, honor poetry—as a good, intelligent old woman, whom one may drop in on sometimes, so as to forget for a moment the gossip, the newspapers, and the cares and bothers of life, to be diverted by her pleasant chattering and her stories; but to fall in love with her is unwise. Mikhaylo Orlov[26] with rapture is repeating [. . .][27] *unknown to the Russians*! [. . . .][27] I am, too. Good-by, my friend! I embrace you. Give me information about our folks.[28] Are they still in the country? I need money, I need it! Good-by. Embrace Kyukhelbeker and Delvig[29] for me. Do you see young Molchanov[30] occasionally? Write me about all the brotherhood.[31]

Pushkin.

[12]
TO THE ARZAMASIANS
Between September 20 and 30, 1820 (?). From Kishinev to Petersburg.
(Rough draft)
In the year 5 since the Lipetsk flood,[1] we, His Excellency Rhine and plaintive Cricket,[2] in a puddle called the *Byk*[3] in the city of Kishinev, sat and wept, remembering *you, O Arzamas*,[4] for noble geese

were majestically wallowing before our eyes in the muddy waters of the aforementioned little river. We keenly imagined Your Absent Excellencies, and with overflowing heart we resolved to give information regarding ourselves to those members of the orthodox brotherhood who are now adorning the banks of the Moyka and the Fontanka.[5]

[13]

To Nikolay Ivanovich Gnedich
December 4, 1820. From Kamenka to Petersburg.

Here I have already been leading a wanderer's life for eight months, honored Nikolay Ivanovich.[1] I have been in the Caucasus, in the Crimea, in Moldavia, and I am now in the Kiev Province, in the village of the Davydovs,[2] kind and intelligent recluses, brothers of General Raevsky. My time slips away between aristocratic dinners and democratic argumentations. Our society, now scattered, was recently a varied and gay mixture of original minds, of people well-known in our Russia, people very interesting to an unfamiliar observer. Few women, much champagne, many witty words, many books, a few verses. You will readily believe that, surrendering to the moment, I worried little about the talk of Petersburg. I have not received my poem, printed under your fatherly supervision and poetic protection—but from my heart I thank you for your kindly taking care of it. Several issues of the *Son* have reached me. I have seen the excellent translation of *Andromaque*,[3] which you read to me in your epicurean study, and the inspired stansas:

I thought that for the last time I greeted
and so on.

They revived recollections of you in me and a feeling of the beautiful, a feeling always precious to my heart. But they have not reconciled me to the critiques which I found in the same *Son of the Fatherland*. Just who is this "V."[4] who praises my chastity but reproaches me for being shameless, telling me: "Blush, unfortunate one" (which, by the way, is very impolite), who says that the *characters* of my poem are sketched with the *somber* colors of the tender, sensitive Correggio and by the *bold brush of Orlovsky*,[5] who does not take a brush in hand and who sketches only post-troikas and Kirghiz horses? I agree with the opinion of an anonymous epigrammatist—his critique for me is *so horribly weighty*.[6] The interrogator is more intelligent, but the one who took on himself the trouble of answering him[7] (gratitude and self-esteem aside) is more intelligent than any of them. In the newspapers I have been reading that *Ruslan*, published to provide a pleasant way to spend boring time, is being sold with an excellent little picture—whom am I to thank for it?[8] My friends, I hope to see you before I die! Meanwhile I have still another long poem ready or almost ready.[9] Farewell—snuff some Spanish tobacco and sneeze more loudly and yet more loudly.[10]

Pushkin.

Kamenka, December 4, 1820.

Where is Zhukovsky? Has he departed with Her Highness?[11] I embrace Delvig and Kyukhelbeker, with a brotherly kiss. I have not heard a word of them—I have not seen his[12] journal; no letters, either.

My address: In Kishinev—To His Excellency, Ivan Nikitich Inzov.

[14]

To VASILY LVOVICH DAVYDOV(?)

First half of March, 1821. From Kishinev(?) to Kamenka(?).

(Rough draft)

I am informing you of occurrences which will have consequences of importance not only for our land, but for all Europe.

Greece has revolted and proclaimed her freedom.[1] Tudor Vladimirescu, who once served in the army of the late Prince Ypsilanti,[2] in the beginning of February of the present year left Bucharest with a small number of armed Arnauts[3] and declared that the Greeks can no longer endure the oppressions and plunderings of the Turkish chiefs, that they have decided to free their native land from an illegal yoke, that they intend to pay only the taxes assessed by the government. This proclamation has alarmed all Moldavia. Prince Sutzu[4] and the Russian consul[5] have wished in vain to suppress the spreading of the revolt. Pandours and Arnauts from everywhere have hastened to the brave Vladimirescu—and in a few days he had already become the leader of 7,000 troops.

On February 21, General Prince Alexander Ypsilanti[6] with two of his brothers[7] and Prince George Kantakuzen[8] arrived in Jassy from Kishinev, where he [Ypsilanti] left his mother, sisters, and two brothers. He was met there by three hundred Arnauts, by Prince Sutzu, and by the Russian consul, and he immediately took over the command of the city. There he published proclamations which quickly spread everywhere—in them it is said that the Phoenix of Greece will arise from its own ashes, that the hour of Turkey's downfall has come, etc., and that a *great power*[9] *approves of the great-souled feat!* The Greeks have begun to throng together in crowds under his three banners, of these one is tricolored, on another streams a cross wreathed with laurels, with the text *By this conquer*,[10] on the third is depicted the Phoenix arising from its ashes. I have seen a letter by one insurgent: with ardor he describes the ceremony of consecrating Prince Ypsilanti's banners and sword, the rapture of the clergy and the laity, and beautiful moments of Hope and Freedom. . . .

In Jassy all is calm. Seven Turks were led to Ypsilanti and immediately executed—a strange novelty on the part of a European general. In Galatia, Turks—100 people in number—have been butchered; twelve Greeks have likewise been killed.

News about the rebellion has astonished Constantinople. Horrors are expected, but there have been none so far. Three fleeing Greeks have been in local quarantine since yesterday. They have scotched many false rumors. Aged Ali[11] has accepted the Christian faith and has been baptized with the name of Constantine; his two-thousand man detachment, which was on the way to unite with the Suliotes,[12] has been annihilated by the Turkish forces.

The rapture of men's minds has reached the highest pitch; all thoughts are directed to one theme, the independence of the ancient fatherland. I missed a curious scene in Odessa: in the shops, on the streets, in the inns—everywhere, crowds of Greeks had been gathering together. All had been selling their property for nothing; they had been buying sabers, rifles, pistols. Everybody was talking about Leonidas, about Themistocles.[13] All were going into the forces of the lucky Ypsilanti. The lives, the property of the Greeks are at his disposal. At first he had two million [piasters]. One *Pauli* gave 600,000 piasters, to be repaid upon the restoration of *Greece*. Ten thousand Greeks have signed up in his troops.

Ypsilanti is en route to unite with Vladimirescu. He is called Commander-in-Chief of the Northern Greek forces, and Plenipotentiary of the Secret Government. One should be aware that a secret society,[14] with the goal of the liberation of Greece, was organized as early as thirty years ago, and it has become widespread. The members of the society are divided into three degrees. The military caste has made up the lowest degree; the second, citizens. Each member of this latter degree has the right to attach comrades to himself—but not to attach soldiers, whom only the third, highest degree has been selecting. You see the simple course and chief idea of this society, the founders of which are still unknown. A separate faith, a separate language, independence of book-publishing; on the one hand enlightenment, on the other ignorance. Everything has offered favorable auspices for the freedom-loving patriots. All the merchants, all the clergy to the last monk have joined the society, which is now triumphing.

This is a detailed account for you of the most recent occurrences of our land.

A strange picture! Two great peoples,[15] who fell long ago into contemnable insignificance, are arising from their ashes at the same time, and rejuvenated, are appearing on the political arena of the world. The first step of Alexander Ypsilanti is excellent and brilliant. He has begun luckily. And, dead, or a conqueror, from now on he belongs to history—28 years old, an arm torn off, a magnanimous goal! An enviable lot. The dagger of a renegade is more dangerous for him that the saber of the Turks; Constantine-Pasha[16] after the liberation will be no more conscience-bound than Chlodwig or Vladimir,[17] for the ascendancy of the young avenger of Greece must be alarming to him. I confess I would advise Prince Ypsilanti to forestall the aged villain: the customs of the country where he is now operating approve political murder.[18]

An important question: what is Russia going to do? Shall we seize Moldavia and Wallachia under the guise of peace-loving mediators? Shall we cross beyond the Danube as allies of the Greeks and as enemies of their enemies?[19] In any case I shall let you know—

[15]

To Anton Antonovich Delvig
March 23, 1821. From Kishinev to Petersburg.

Friend Delvig, my Parnassian brother,[1] I was consoled by your prose;[2] but though it be a sin, Baron, I confess I would have been gladder of verses. . . . You yourself know that in bygone years on the shore of Castalian waters I loved to scribble long poems, odes. Jealous people saw me at the puppet theater of fashion; though I am an adherent of truth and freedom, it used to be that no matter what I would write, *for some it would not smell of Russia*. No matter what I may ask of the censorship, Timkovsky groans.[3] Now truly I can scarcely breathe; my Muse is pining away from continence, and I rarely, rarely sin with her. I am waxing cold toward chattery Fame; I still pay court to her from politeness alone, like a lazy husband, to his wife. Having bored the Muses with fruitless service, I have replaced the idol of fame with another goddess, quiet Friendship. But, my poets, I still love the magic world of fantasy, and warmed with others' flame I hearken to the sounds of your lyres. Exactly thus, forgetting for today the pranks, the games of former days, your madam looks from her couch at the gambols of young whores. . . .

I regret, Delvig, that only one of your letters has reached me, namely the one which was delivered to me by amiable Gnedich, along with virginal Lyudmila.[4] You do not talk enough about yourself and our friends; I had already heard in Kiev about Kyukhel-beker's travels. I wish him in Paris the spirit of chastity, in the chancellery of Naryshkin[5] the spirit of humility and patience; I am not worried about the spirit of love,[6] he will not be lacking in that; I say nothing of the tendency to idle words—a far-off friend cannot be too talkative. In your absence my heart reminded me of you, and the journals,[7] of your Muse. You are still the same—a man of excellent talent, but a lazy one. How long are you going to fiddle around, how long are you going to squander your genius on mere trifles? Write a fine poem, only not on the four parts of the day and not on the four seasons of the year; write your *Monk*.[8] Poetry somber, heroic, powerful, Byronic[9] is your true destiny—kill the man of old in yourself. But do not kill the inspired poet. As regards me, my joy, I shall tell you that I have finished a new poem, *The Prisoner of the Caucasus*, which I hope to send you soon. You will not be completely pleased with it, and you will be right. I shall tell you, besides, that still other poems are fermenting in my head, but that I am not writing anything now. I am digesting my memories and I hope to accumulate some new ones shortly; how are we to live, my dear fellow, as the old age of our youth approaches, if not upon memories?

I arrived in Kishinev not long ago, and I am abandoning blessed Bessarabia[10] soon—there are countries more blessed. Idle peace is not the best state of life. Even Scarmentado[11] seems wrong—there is no best state on earth, but variety is salvation for the soul.

My friend, I have a favor to ask of you. Find out and write me what is happening to my brother.[12] You love him because you love me; he is an intelligent person in the full meaning of the word, and he has a beautiful soul in him. I fear on account of his youth; I fear the education which the circumstances of his life will give him and which he will give himself—there is no other education for a creature endowed with a soul. Love him; I know they will try to erase me from his heart—they will think that beneficial. But I feel that we shall be friends and brothers, and not only in our African blood.[13]

Farewell.

A. Pushkin.

March 23, 1821.
Kishinev.

[16]

To Nikolay Ivanovich Gnedich
March 24, 1821. From Kishinev to Petersburg.

In the country where, crowned by Julia and exiled by crafty Augustus, Ovid dragged out his gloomy days and mean-spiritedly devoted his elegiac lyre to his deaf idol;[1] far from the northern capital I have forgotten your eternal fog, and the free voice of my reed disturbs the drowsy Moldavians. I am still the same as I was before; I do not go to pay respects to an ignoramus, I argue with [M. F.] Orlov, I drink little. I do not sing paeans of flattery—in blind hope—to Octavian. And I write facile epistles to Friendship, without working hard at it. You,

given by fate a bold mind and a lofty soul and doomed to
solemn songs, to comforting the solitary life, O you, who
resurrected the majestic ghost of Achilles, who manifested
Homer's Muse to us and liberated the bold singer of glory from
clanking bonds[2]—your voice has reached my isolation, where I
concealed myself from the persecution of a bigot and a proud
fool, and again it has enlivened the singer, as the sweet voice
of inspiration. Elect of Phoebus! your greeting, your praises are
precious to me; the poet is alive to the Muses and to friendship.
He disdains his enemies—he does not abase his Muse before the
people, but he lashes out with instructive rod at the carping
critic—in passing.

Your inspiring letter, honored Nikolay Ivanovich, found me in
the wilds of Moldavia; it gladdened and touched me to the bottom
of my heart. I thank you for your remembering me, for your friend-
liness, your praise, your reproaches, for the make-up of your letter—
everything shows the interest which your lively soul takes in all that
concerns me. The clothing tailored at your command for *Ruslan and
Lyudmila* is beautiful; the printed verses, the vignette, and the binding have been giving me childish pleasure for four whole days.
Feelingly I thank honored Ж ;[3] these strokes of the pen are sweet
proof to me of his amiable good will. I shall not see you soon; local
circumstances smell of a long, long separation! I pray to Phoebus and
the Holy Virgin of Kazan[4] that I may return to you with my youth,
with reminiscences, with another new long poem: the one which I
recently finished is christened *The Prisoner of the Caucasus*. You
expected much, as is evident from your letter—you will find little,
very little. From the heights of snowless Beshtu, beyond the clouds,
I saw the icy peaks of Kazbek and Elbrus only in the distance. The
setting of my poem should have been located on the banks of the
noisy Terek, on the boundaries of Georgia, in the remote ravines of
the Caucasus—I placed my hero in monotonous plains where I have
passed two months myself—where four mountains arise at a great
distance from each other, the last spur of the Caucasus. There are no
more than 700 verses in the whole poem. In a short time I shall send
it to you, for you to do with it as you will.

I greet all my acquaintances who have not yet forgotten me; I
embrace my friends. With impatience I await the ninth volume of

The Russian History.[5] What is Nikolay Mikhaylovich [Karamzin] doing? Are he, his wife, and his children well? My heart terribly misses this honored family. I am writing to Delvig in your letter.[6] *Vale.*

Pushkin.

March 24, 1821.
Kishinev.

[17]
To ALEXANDER IVANOVICH TURGENEV
May 7, 1821. From Kishinev to Petersburg.

Though I have written nothing and have received no news of you for a long time, you haven't forgotten me, have you? Honored Alexander Ivanovich, I want so badly to spend a couple of weeks in that nasty Petersburg that I don't know what to do. Without the Karamzins, without you two,[1] and also without certain other selected ones, one would be bored even in a place other than Kishinev; and far from Princess Golitsyna's hearth,[2] one would freeze even under the sky of Italy. Father, into thy hands I commend myself![3] You who are close to the inhabitants of Kamenny Ostrov,[4] can't you get me away for a few days (however, no more) from my Isle of Patmos?[5] I would bring you in reward a composition in the manner of the Apocalypse, and I would dedicate it to you, Christian pastor of our poetic flock; but first let the momentary friends of my momentary youth[6] know that they should send me some money, with which they would exceedingly oblige the *seeker of new impressions.* In our Bessarabia there is no insufficiency of impressions. Here things are really in a mess. [M. F.] Orlov has got married;[7] will you ask how it happened? I don't understand. Unless he mixed up his head and the head of his p—— and f—— his wife with the wrong one. His head is sound; his soul is beautiful; but what the devil good is that? He has got married; he will put on his dressing gown and say:

Beatus qui procul. . . .[8]

Believe that wherever I may be, my soul, such as it is, belongs to you and to those whom I have been able to love.

Kishinev.   Pushkin.

May 7, 1821.

If I should get permission to return,[9] don't say anything to anybody, and I'll come like a bolt from the blue.

[18]

To Deguilly
June 6, 1821. In Kishinev.
(In French)

Notice to M. Deguilly,[1] French ex-officer.

It is not enough to be a blackguard; one has to be one openly, too.

On the eve of a cursed duel with sabers, one does not write jeremiads and one's will under the eyes of one's wife. One does not fabricate cock-and-bull stories with the city authorities in order to escape a scratch. One does not twice compromise his second.[2]

I foresaw all that has happened; I am vexed that I did not make a bet on it.

Now it is all over, but watch out for yourself.

Accept my assurance that I feel towards you as you deserve.

June 6, 1821.   Pushkin.

Note also that henceforth in case of necessity I shall know how to exert my rights as a Russian gentleman, since you understand nothing of the laws of duelling.

[19]

To Lev Sergeevich Pushkin and to Olga Sergeevna Pushkina
July 27, 1821. From Kishinev to Petersburg.
To Brother.

Hello, Lev. I don't thank you for your letter, because you do not tell me anything sensible—I call everything sensible which has to do with you. Write me while I am still in Kishinev. I shall answer you with all possible garrulity. And write me in Russian, because, glory be to God, with my constitutional friends I shall soon forget the Russian alphabet.[1] If you resemble your relatives, you are a man of letters[2] (but please, not a poet): then write me of the news of our literature. Just what is Milonov's *Creation of the World*?[3] What is Katenin doing?

Was it he who asked questions of Voeykov in *The Son of the Father-land* last year? Who is *agin* us? You like "The Black Shawl"—you are right, but what a devil of a job they did of printing it.[4] Who printed it that way? It smells like Glinka.[5] If you see him, embrace him in a brotherly manner, tell him that he is a fine fellow—and that I love him as one should. Here is something still more important: try to see Vsevolozhsky—and get from him, at my expense, the number of copies of my works (if they are printed) which have been distributed to my friends—some thirty copies.[6] Tell him that I love him, that he has forgotten me, that I remember his evenings, his amiability, his *V.S.P.*, his *L.D.*,[7] his Ovoshnikova,[8] his Lamp,[9] and everything regarding my friend. Kiss, if you see them, Yuriev and Mansurov, wish health to the Kalmuck,[10] and write me about everything.

Send me *Tavrida*—by Bobrov.[11] *Vale.*

July 27.   Your brother A.

To Sister.
(In French)

Have you returned from your trip? Have you again visited the caverns, the castle, the cascades of Narva?[12] Did that amuse you? Do you still like your solitary promenades? Which dogs are your favorites? Have you forgotten the tragic death of Omphale and of Bizarre?[13] How do you amuse yourself? What do you read? Have you seen your neighbor Annette Vulf[14] again? Do you go riding on horseback? When are you going to return to Petersburg? How are the Korfs[15] getting along? Are you married; are you ready to be? Do you doubt my friendship? Good-by, my good friend.

[20]

To Sergey Ivanovich Turgenev
August 21, 1821. From Kishinev to Odessa.

I congratulate you, honored Sergey Ivanovich, on your safe arrival from foreign Turkey to native Turkey.[1] I would have gladly come to Odessa to chat with you a while and to breath pure European air, but I myself am in quarantine, and my warden Inzov will not let me out, as one infected with some kind of liberal plague. Will you see the Northern Stambul[2] soon? Embrace for me there our dear mufti[3] Alexander Ivanovich [Turgenev] and his brother the rebellious dragoman;[4] I have written the Right Reverend a letter to which I do not yet have an answer. It had to do with my exile—but if there is hope of war, for Christ's sake leave me in Bessarabia. I owe you an apology: every other day I reread the letter I received from you—but have not answered until now. I am relying on your magnanimous forgiveness and upon a meeting soon.

I send my respects to Hist,[5] if Hist remembers me. But Dolgoru-kov has forgotten me.

August 21.   Pushkin.

[21]

To Nikolay Ivanovich Grech
September 21, 1821. From Kishinev to Petersburg.

Forgive me, our dear Aristarchus,[1] if I disturb you again with letters and requests; do me the favor of delivering the enclosed letter to my brother.[2] The young fellow has forgotten me, and he has not even sent me his address.

Yesterday I saw in *The Son of the Fatherland* my epistle to Chaa-daev.[3] That censorship! I am sorry that it dislikes the word *freedom-loving*.[4] That word expresses so well the present-day *libéral*, it is completely Russian, and no doubt the honored A. S. Shishkov would give it the right of citizenship in his dictionary, together with *šarotyk* and *toptališče*.[5] There they have printed *the stupid philos-opher*.[6] Why *stupid*? The verses refer to Tolstoy the American,[7] who is not stupid at all; but unnecessary abuse is nothing to get worried about. And my modest letter regarding my earlier letter, apparently it won't squeeze through the censorship?[8] That's bad.

I have tried writing Delvig and Gnedich, but they don't give a hang. What might this mean? If I have simply been forgotten, then I do not reproach them: to be forgotten is the natural lot of the absent. I myself would have forgotten them, too, if I were living with epicureans, in an epicurean study, and if I could read Homer.[9] But if they are angry with me or have come to the conclusion that I have no need of their letters—then that is bad.

I would have liked to send you a fragment of my *Prisoner of the Caucasus*, but I am too lazy to do any copying; do you want to buy a whole slice of the poem from me? It is 800 verses in length; the verse is four feet in breadth; it is sliced up into two cantos. I'll let you have it cheap, so that the goods won't gather dust. *Vale*.

September 21, 1821.   Pushkin.
Kishinev.

[22]
To Peter Andreevich Vyazemsky
January 2, 1822. From Kishinev to Moscow.

Popandopulo[1] will bring you my verses; Liprandi[2] is taking it upon himself to deliver my prose to you—you saw him, I think, in Warsaw.[3] He is a good friend of mine and (a reliable guarantee of honor and intelligence) he is not loved by our government, and in his turn is no lover of it. During our long separation, nothing but stupid journals has put us in contact with each other from time to time. I thank you for your satirical, prophetic, and inspired works; they are charming—I thank you for everything in general. I have no quarrel with you except for your "Epistle to Kachenovsky."[4] How could you go down into the *arena* against that feeble fist-fighter. You knocked him off his feet, but he bespattered your poets' wreath, now inglorious, with blood, bile, and sour mash.... How could you get mixed up with him? A light horsewhip would have sufficed for him, and not your satirical cudgel. If I nicked him in my epistle to Ch[aadaev], that was not from hatred toward him, but in order to juxtapose him with Tolstoy the American, whom it is harder to contemn. Zhukovsky infuriates me—what has he come to like in this Moore, this prim imitator of deformed Oriental imagination? All of *Lalla Rookh*[5] is not worth ten lines of *Tristram Shandy*; it is time Zhukovsky had his own imagination and were master of his own fancy. But what do you think of Baratynsky![6] Acknowledge that he will surpass both Parny[7] and Batyushkov, if he will keep up the pace henceforth that he has set up till now. After all, the lucky fellow is only 23! Let us abandon all the erotic field to him, and let us hurry, each to his own forte, else we are doomed. My *Prisoner of the Caucasus* is finished. I want to publish, but I have a lot of laziness and little money—and the mercantile success of my charmer *Lyudmila* is taking away from me any desire for publishing.[8] I wish happiness to my uncle—but I am not writing him, because I am afraid of journalistic honors.[9] Will his works come out soon? *Buyanov*[10] is worth more than all of them together, but what will happen to him in future generations? I am very much afraid that my first cousin may be taken for my son—and couldn't it easily happen! Write me, send it by anybody you please and write as you please—in verse or in prose —and I swear I'll answer.

January 2, 1822.   Pushkin.

I am writing you at Rhine's. He is still the same; he has not changed, though he has got married. He began dictating a letter in his own way—but he saw fit to tear it up. He greets you and is horribly busy with the sealing wax.

Supplement.

[M. F.] Orlov has asked me to tell you that he is making sticks of sealing wax, but he has done away with sticks in his division.[11]

[23]

To Lev Sergeevich Pushkin
January 24, 1822. From Kishinev to Petersburg.

First I want to scold you a little. Aren't you ashamed, my dear fellow, to write a half-Russian, half-French letter; you are no Moscow female cousin. In the second place, your letters are too short—you are either unwilling or unable to speak to me frankly about everything. I am very sorry; the chitchat of a brother's friend-ship would be a great consolation to me. Picture to yourself that not a single friendly voice reaches my wilderness—that my friends, as if for spite, have decided to justify my elegiac misanthropy—and this state is unbearable. The letter wherein I spoke to you of *Tavrida*[1] did not reach you—that infuriates me. I gave you several errands most important in connection with me—the devil take *them*. I myself shall try to get to Petersburg for several days—then things will go differently. You say that Gnedich is angry with me; he is right. I should have turned to him with my new long poem—but my head was whirling—I had not received any news from him for a long time. I had to write Grech and on this dependable *occasion*[2] I offered him the *Prisoner*.[3] Besides, Gnedich will not haggle with me, nor I with Gnedich, with each too much considering his own profit, but I would haggle as shamelessly with Grech as with any other bearded ap-praiser of the literary mind.[4] Ask Delvig whether he is well, whether he still, thank God, drinks and eats—what he thought of my verses to him,[5] etc. Of others only vague news has reached me. I am sending some verses of mine;[6] print them in the *Son* [*of the Fatherland*] (without a signature and without any mistakes). If you want it, here is another epigram for you, which for Christ's sake do not spread; every verse in it is the truth.

One had my Aglaya,[7] because of his uniform and black moustache. Another, because of money; I understand. Another because he was a Frenchman. Cleon, because of frightening her with his intellect; Damis, because he sang tenderly. Tell me now, my Aglaya, because of what did your husband have you?

Want another? On Kachenovsky—

Talentless slanderer, he has a flair for seeking out canings, and his daily bread with monthly lying.

Please take a bite. Farewell, Foka, I embrace you.

Your friend Demian.[8]

January 24, 1822.

[24]
To Nikolay Ivanovich Gnedich
April 29, 1822. From Kishinev to Petersburg.

Parve (nec invideo) sine me, liber, ibis in urbem,
Heu mihi! quo domino non licet ire tuo.[1]

Not from hypocritical modesty I add: *Vade, sed incultus, qualem decet exulis esse!*[2] The shortcomings of this tale, long poem, or what you will, are so manifest that for a long time I could not make up my mind to publish it. I submit to you, an exalted poet, an enlightened connoisseur of poets, my *Prisoner of the Caucasus*.[3] As a reward for sending your charming Idyll (about which we shall speak at our leisure), I am willing to you the boring cares of publication. But your friendship has completely spoiled me. Call this poem a story, a tale, a long poem,[4] or do not call it anything at all; publish it in two cantos or in only one, with a preface or without. I put it completely at your disposal. *Vale.*

Pushkin.

[25]

To Pavel Alexandrovich Katenin

Between April 20 and the end of May, 1822. From Kishinev to
Petersburg.

(Fragment of rough draft)

[. . .] I do not [. . .] the honor of being a poet, but this praise would
not seem very flattering to me.

I have read of course your letter to Grech,[1] with great pleasure,
and first because you let me know about you only through the
journals [. . . .]

[26]

To Alexander Alexandrovich Bestuzhev

June 21, 1822. From Kishinev to Petersburg.

Dear Sir,

Alexander Alexandrovich,[1]

I have long been intending to call my existence to your attention.
Honoring your charming talents, and, I confess, loving your caustic
wit in spite of myself, I have been wanting to get in touch with you
by letter, not from self-love alone, but also from love for the truth.
You have anticipated me. Your letter is so kind that it is impossible
to act overly modest with you. I know that I should not give complete credence to what you say, but I believe it in spite of myself,
and I thank you, as the representative of taste and the true guardian
and protector of our literature.

I am sending you my Bessarabian ravings, and my wish is that
they may be of use to you. Give my greetings to the censorship, my
ancient girl friend; the dear creature seems to have grown still more
intelligent. I do not understand what in my elegiac fragments could
have troubled her chastity—however, we must persist, from ambition alone[2]—I put them completely at your disposal. I foresee obstacles in publishing my poem "To Ovid."[3] One may and must
deceive the old woman, for she is very stupid—apparently they have
frightened her with my name. Do not give my name, but take my
poems to her under the name of anybody you please (for example,
obliging Pletnev[4] or some tenderhearted traveller who is wandering
over Tavrida); I repeat to you, she is horribly dull-witted, but

nevertheless tractable enough. The main thing is for my name not to get to her, and then everything will get arranged.

With the keenest pleasure I noticed in your letter several lines of K. F. Ryleev; they are a pledge to me of his friendship and of his remembering me. Embrace him for me, dear Alexander Alexandrovich, as I shall embrace you when we meet.

June 21, 1822.   Pushkin.
Kishinev.

[27]
To Nikolay Ivanovich Gnedich
June 27, 1822. From Kishinev to Petersburg.

Your letter is such a substantive one that it needed nothing added to it[1] to gladden me sincerely. From my heart I thank you for your friendly solicitude. You have delivered me from great bothers by completely assuring the destiny of *The Prisoner of the Caucasus*.[2] Your notes regarding its shortcomings are perfectly just and only too indulgent. But the deed is done. Feel a little sorry for me: I live among Getae and Sarmatae;[3] nobody understands me. There is no enlightened Aristarchus with me; I write as best I can, without hearing vivifying advice, praise, or blame. But what do you think of the censorship! I confess that I by no means expected from her such great success in esthetics. Her criticism brings honor to her taste. I am forced to agree with her in everything: *Heavenly flame*[4] is too ordinary; a long kiss was said *too much at random* (*trop hasardé*). *She fully partook of his agonizing languor*—is bad, very bad—and therefore I make bold to replace this Kirghiz-Kaisak[5] verse with the following: *whatever kind* of parting kiss *you please*

Sealed the union of love.

Hand in hand, full of despondency, they went to the shore in silence—and the Russian is now swimming in the noisy deep, making the waves foam, now has attained the opposite cliffs, now is grasping them. Suddenly, etc.

With obsequiousness I submit these verses to the censorship's examination. Meanwhile, give her my congratulations. Of course some will say that esthetics is none of her business, that she must render unto Caesar what is Caesar's, and to Gnedich what is Gnedich's.[6] But who cares what they say?

I have answered Bestuzhev and sent him a thing or two. Can't he be pitted against Katenin again?[7] It would be interesting. Grech made me laugh till I cried with his comparative modesty. I have also written to Zhukovsky,[8] but he doesn't give a hang. Can't he be budged? Can't Slenin be stirred up, as well, if he has bought the remaining copies of *Ruslan*? I am impatiently awaiting *The Prisoner of Chillon*;[9] there is no comparison between that and *The Peri*; it is worthy of such a translator as the bard of Gromoboy and of the Little Old Woman. Incidentally, I think it is vexing that he translates, and translates in fragments. Tasso, Ariosto, and Homer are one thing, and the songs of Matthison and the deformed tales of Moore are another. Once he spoke to me of Southey's poem *Roderick*; give him my request that he leave it in peace,[10] notwithstanding the request of a certain charming lady. English literature is beginning to have an inflence on the Russian. I think it will be more advantageous than the influence of timid, affected French poetry. Then certain people will tumble from their pedestals, and we shall see where Iv. Iv. Dmitriev will find himself, with his *feelings and thoughts* taken from Florian and Legouvé.[11] That is how I prophesy, not in my own country,[12] but meanwhile I do not foresee the end of our separation. Here with us it is *Moldaviany* and nauseating.[13] Oh, my God, something is happening to him[14]—his fate disturbs me in the extreme. Write me about him if you answer.

June 27.   A. Pushkin.

[28]

To PAVEL ALEXANDROVICH KATENIN
July 19, 1822. From Kishinev to Petersburg.

You reproach me with forgetfulness, my dear fellow: have it your way. For a small number of chosen ones, I wish to see Petersburg again. You are of course included, but friendship is not the Italian verb *piombare;* you don't understand it very well, either.[1] I cannot make out how you could take as referring to you the verse

And dissect a sportive piece of gossip.[2]

That would be forgivable for anybody else, but not for you. Don't you know the miserable gossip I was the victim of, and am I not indebted to your friendship (at least that is the way I understood you) for the first news of it? I have not read your comedy; nobody has written me about it; I do not know whether Zelsky nicked me. Maybe, yes; more probably, no. In any case, I cannot be angry. If I were angry about anything, would I speak of you along with those I allude to? The persons and relationships are too diverse. If I had decided to do that, would I have written a line so weak and unclear, would I have chosen as the object of an epigram the excellent translation of a comedy which I had considered untranslatable? No matter from what angle one looks at it, you still offend me. I hope, my joy, that this is all a momentary cloud, and that you love me. And so let us abandon gossip and talk about something else. You have translated *The Cid*; I congratulate you and my old Corneille. *The Cid* seems to me his best tragedy. Tell me: did you have the laudable audacity to leave in, for the finicky stage of the nineteenth century, the slap in the face of the ages of chivalry?[3] I have heard that it is improper, funny, *ridicule*. *Ridicule!* A slap administered by the hand of a Spanish knight to a warrior who has grown gray under a helmet! *Ridicule!* My God, it ought to produce more horror than Atreus' cup. However that may be, I hope to see the tragedy this winter; at least I shall try. I rejoice, foreseeing that the slap must fall heavily on the cheek of Tolchenov or Bryansky.[4] Thanks for your detailed report; I know that one good turn deserves another, but *non erat his locus. . . .*[5] Farewell, Aeschylus,[6] I embrace you as poet and friend. . . .

19 July.

[29]
To LEV SERGEEVICH PUSHKIN AND OLGA SERGEEVNA PUSHKINA
July 21, 1822. From Kishinev to Petersburg.
[To. L. S. Pushkin]

You are pouting at me, dear fellow; that's not good. Write me, please, and as you like, even in six languages;[1] I shall not say a word to you. I miss you—what are you doing? Are you in the service?[2] It is time, I swear it is time. Do not take me for an example. If you let the time slip by, you will regret it afterwards—in the Russian service you absolutely must be a colonel at 26, if you ever want to amount to anything. Consequently, figure it up. You will be told: study; the service can come later. But I tell you, get in the service; studying can come later. Of course, I do not want you to be such an ignoramus as V. I. Kozlov,[3] but you yourself would not want that. Reading—that is the best study. I know that this is not what you have in mind now, but all for the best.

Tell me—have you grown up? When I left, you were a child; I shall find a young man. Tell me, with which of my friends are you best acquainted? What do you do, what are you writing? If you see Katenin, assure him, for Christ's sake, that in my epistle to Chaadaev there is not a single word about him. Imagine! He took as referring to himself the verse "And dissect a sportive piece of gossip";[4] I have received a rather tart letter from him. He complains that he has received no letters from me, but the fault is not mine. Write me the literary news. How is my *Ruslan* doing? Isn't it selling? The censorship hasn't forbidden it, has it? Let me know. . . . If Slenin has bought it, then just where is the money? I need some. How is Bestuzhev's publication going? Have you read the verses of mine which I sent him?[5] How is my *Prisoner* doing?[6] My joy, I should like to see you; I have some business in Petersburg. I do not know whether I shall get there, but I shall try. I have been written that Batyushkov has gone mad;[7] it cannot be. Put a stop to that falsehood. How is Zhukovsky, and why does he not write to me? Are you often at the Karamzins'? Answer all my questions, if you can— and hurry it up. Invite Delvig and Baratynsky to write, too. What about Vilgelm [Kyukhelbeker]? Is there news about him?

Farewell.

I am writing to Father in the village.[8]

July 21.

[To Olga Sergeevna Pushkina: in French]
My good and dear friend, I do not need your letters to reassure myself of your friendship, but I need them particularly, as something coming from you. I embrace you and I love you. Have a good time and get married.

[30]

To PETER ANDREEVICH VYAZEMSKY
September 1, 1822. From Kishinev to Moscow.

You may judge, yourself, how much your pen's scrawl[1] has glad-dened me. For almost three years I have had only unreliable and second-hand news about you—and here I do not hear a single living European word. Excuse me if I speak with you about Tolstoy;[2] your opinion is precious to me. You say that my verses are good for nothing. I know, but my intention was not to start up a witty literary war, but with a stinging insult to pay off, for his veiled insults, a person with whom I had parted friends and whom I had defended with ardor every time the opportunity arose. He thought it amusing to make an enemy of me and to give Prince Shakhovskoy's garret a laugh at my expense with his letters; I discovered everything after I had already been exiled, and, considering revenge as one of the prime Christian virtues—in the impotence of my rage from afar I plied Tolstoy with journalistic mud. My criminal accusation, you say, goes beyond the bounds of poetry; I do not agree. The scourge of satire can reach where the sword of the law cannot. Horatian satire, delicate, light, and gay, cannot hold its own against the morose indignation of a heavy lampoon. Voltaire himself felt this. You reproach me that from Kishinev, under the aegis of exile, I print abuse of a person living in Moscow. But at that time I did not doubt of my return. My intention was to go to Moscow, the only place where I can completely clear myself. Such an open attack on Count Tolstoy is not mean-spiritedness. They say that he has written some-thing horrible about me. The journalists were obligated to accept the reply of a person who has been abused in their journal. It could be thought that I am in cahoots with them, and that infuriates me. Incidentally, I have done my deed, and I do not want to have anything further to do with Tolstoy on paper. I would justify myself to you more strongly and more clearly, except that I esteem your connections with the person who resembles you so little.

"Kachenovsky is a representative of an opinion of some kind!"[3] *voilà des mots qui hurlent de se trouver ensemble.*[4] I am sorry that you do not fully esteem the charming talent of Baratynsky. He is more than an imitator of imitators; he is full of true elegiac poetry. I have not yet read *The Prisoner of Chillon.*[5] What of it I saw in *The Son of the Fatherland* is charming. . . .

On the column, like a spring flower, he hung with lowered head.

You have grieved me only too much, with the supposition that your living poetry has departed this life. If that be true, it has lived long enough for fame, but not long enough for the fatherland. Fortunately, I do not entirely believe you, but I understand you. Years incline one toward prose, and if you attach yourself to it seriously, then European Russia will have to be congratulated. Incidentally, what are you waiting for? Can it be that the monthly fame of a Pradt[6] captivates you? Undertake constant labor, write in the silence of your autocracy, fashion for us a metaphysical language,[7] which has been engendered in your letters—and let God's will be done there. People who can read and write will soon be needed in Russia; then I hope to be closer to you. Meanwhile, I embrace you with all my soul.

P.

I am sending you a poem in the mystical genre[8]—I have become a courtier.

[31]

To Lev Sergeevich Pushkin
September 4, 1822. From Kishinev to Petersburg.

By the last post (pardon me, with Dolgorukov)[1] I wrote Father, but I did not have time to write you; however, I must have a talk with you about a thing or two. In the first place, about the service. If you should go into the military, here is my plan, which I offer for your examination. There is nothing for you in the Guards; to serve four years as a Yunker[2] is no joke. Besides, you need to have them forget about you for a while. You should obtain a place in some regiment of Raevsky's[3] corps; soon you would become an officer, and then you would be transferred into the Guards—by Raevsky or Kiselev[4]—neither would refuse. Think it over, and, please, not lightly: it is a question of your whole life. Now, my joy, I shall talk a little about myself. Go to Nikita Vsevolozhsky for me and tell him for Christ's sake to wait about selling my poems until next year—if they are already sold, go with the same request to the purchaser. My flightiness and the flightiness of my comrades have made a mess of things for me. About forty subscriptions have been distributed—it goes without saying that I shall have to pay for them. In the epistle "To Ovid" make changes as follows:

> You yourself—be astonished, Naso, be astonished at most mutable fate, you who have disdained from youthful days the agitations of military life, who have become accustomed, etc.

Apropos of poetry: what I have read from *The Prisoner of Chillon* is simply charming. I am awaiting with impatience the success of *The Maidenhead of Orleans.*[5] But the actors, the actors!—unrhymed pentameter verses demand a completely new kind of declamation. From this far away I can hear the dramatically solemn roar of *Glukho-rev.*[6] The tragedy will be played with the tonality of *The Death of Rolla.*[7] What will the magnificent Semenova[8] do, surrounded the way she is? God defend and have mercy on her—but I am afraid. Don't forget to inform me on this matter, and get from Zhukovsky a ticket in my name for the first performance. I have read Kyukhelbeker's verses and prose. What a strange fellow! Only into his head could come the Jewish thought of lauding Greece—magnificent, classical, poetic Greece; Greece, where everything breathes of mythology and heroism—in Slavonic-Russian verses taken completely from Jeremiah.[9] What would Homer and Pindar have said? And what do Delvig and Baratynsky say? The "Ode to Ermolov" is better, but the verse "Thus sang Derzhavin,[10] in love with Suvorov . . ."[11] is just a little *too* Greek—the verses to Griboedov[12] are worthy of the poet who wrote once upon a time:

> Fright at the sound of bronze forces the frightened people to stream in crowds to the holy cathedral. View, O God! the number, O great One, of the despondent ones beseeching You to preserve them—the labor, belonging to many people, is complete, etc.[13]

Check about these verses with Baron Delvig.

Batyushkov is right in being angry with Pletnev; in his place I would have gone mad with indignation. "B. from Rome"[14] has no human meaning, though novelty on Olympus is very pleasing. My general opinion is that Pletnev's prose is more tolerable than his verses. He has no feeling at all, no vivacity—his style is as pale as a corpse.[15] Give my respects to Pletnev—not his style—and assure him that he is our Goethe.

A.P.

Mon père a eu une idée lumineuse—c'est celle de m'envoyer des habits— rappelez-la lui de ma part.[16]

Another word—tell Slenin to send me *The Son of a Bitch of the Fatherland* for the second half of the year. He can deduct the cost from what he owes me.

My dear fellow, where you are, someone writes that a ray of dawn used to penetrate into Khmelnitsky's prison at midday.[17] It wasn't Khvostov[18] who wrote that—that's what grieved me. What is Delvig doing? What is he thinking off?

[32]

To Yakov Nikolaevich Tolstoy

September 26, 1822. From Kishinev to Petersburg.

Dear Yakov Nikolaevich, I shall come to the point immediately. Prince Lobanov's proposal[1] is flattering to my self-esteem, but it requires several clarifications from me. At first I wanted to publish my short poems by subsciption, and about thirty subscriptions have already been sold—circumstances forced me to sell my manuscript to Nikita Vsevolozhsky and to give up publishing it myself—of course I must pay for the subscriptions which have been sold, and that is my first stipulation. In the second place, I confess to you that certain of my poems must be excluded, many must be revised, a new order for all of them must be made, and therefore I must go over my manuscript again. The third thing: in the last three years I have written much that is new: gratitude demands that I send everything to Prince Alexander, but the censorship, the censorship! . . . And so, dear friend, let us wait two or three more months. Who knows? Perhaps we shall see each other by the new year, and then everything will take a turn for the better. Meanwhile, accept my hearty thanks; you alone of all my comrades, of the momentary friends of my momentary youth,[2] have remembered me, apropos or

malapropos. For two years and six months I have not had any news
from them; no one has written a line or even a word. . . .

Are you still burning, our icon-lamp,[3] friend of vigils and
feasts? Are you effervescing, golden cup, in the hands of merry
wits? Are you still the same, friends of merriment, friends of
Cypris[4] and of poetry? Do hours of love, hours of hangover,
fly by as before at the call of freedom, laziness, and idleness?
In boring exile, I fly to you in memory every hour, burning with
ardent desire. I imagine that I see you: There it is, the hospitable refuge, the refuge of love and of the free muses, where we
confirmed our eternal union with a mutual vow, where we have
known the bliss of friendship, where sweet equality sat down in
pointed cap at our round table, where arbitrary whim was what
changed bottles, conversations, stories, the songs of the mis-
chievous, and our arguments flared up from sparks and jokes
and wine; I hear, true poets, your bewitching tongue. . . . Pour
me some wine of the comet, wish me health, Kalmuck![5]

You write me of your poems, but I am in the wilds of Bessarabia,
and I receive no journals or new books; I did not know about the
publication of your book, which would have consoled me in my
loneliness.[6] Farewell, dear fellow, until our next meeting—and until
our next letter. Embrace our fellows. How are the Vsevolozhskys?[7]
How is Mansurov? How is Barkov? How are the Sosnitskys? How is
Khmelnitsky? How is Katenin? How is Shakhovskoy? How is
Ezhova? How is Count Pushkin? How are the Semenovas? How is
Zavadovsky? How is all the Theater?

September 26, 1822.   A. Pushkin.
Kishinev.
Only yesterday I received your letter, which you wrote in July.

[33]
To NIKOLAY IVANOVICH GNEDICH
September 27, 1822. From Kishinev to Petersburg.
The Prisoners[1] have arrived, and I cordially thank you, dear Nikolay
Ivanovich. The changes demanded by the censorship served to my
advantage; I confess that I had expected to see the marks of her death-
dealing claws in other places, and I was worried. For example, if she

had changed the verse "Farewell, free Cossack villages," I would have been very sorry. But thank God! —A "bitter kiss" is simply charming.[2] But by golly, "to her of days" is no more euphonious than "of nights"; "hopeful dreams" than "ecstatic." "Onto the houses" rain and hail; "into the dales." These are the only errors I have observed. Alexander Pushkin is masterfully lithographed,[3] but I do not know whether it resembles him; the note of the publishers is very flattering[4]—I do not know whether it is just. Zhukovsky's translation is *un tour de force*. The scoundrel! In his struggles with difficulty, a man of unusual prowess![5] One would have to be Byron, to express with such terrible truth the first signs of madness, and Zhukovsky, to re-express them. Zhukovsky's style seems to me to have matured frightfully of late, although it has lost its pristine charm. He will never write another *Svetlana* or *Lyudmila* or the charming elegies of the first part of *The [Twelve] Sleeping Virgins*.[6] God grant that he begin to do creative work.

Prince Alexander Lobanov offers to print my short things for me in Paris. Save me, for Christ's sake; hold him off at least until I arrive, and I shall emerge from here and come to you. Katenin has written me; I do not know whether he has received my answer.[7] How stupid your Petersburg has become! But I would need to visit there. My being craves the theater and another thing or two. I shall write Delvig and Baratynsky. I embrace you with all my soul.

September 27. Kishinev.   A. Pushkin.

I have written my brother to coax Slenin not to print my portrait. If my consent is necessary for doing it, I do not agree to it.[8]

[34]

TO LEV SERGEEVICH PUSHKIN
Between September 4 and October 6, 1822. From Kishinev to
Petersburg.
(In French)

You are at the age when one ought to be thinking of what career he is to pursue; I have told you the reasons why the military profession appears to me preferable to all others. In any case for a long time the way you act is going to determine your reputation and perhaps your fortune.

You will have to deal with men with whom you are not yet

acquainted. Always commence by thinking of them all the evil imaginable: then you will not have to lower your opinion very much. Do not judge them by your heart, which I believe to be noble and good, and which besides is still young. Despise them as politely as you can: this is the way to be on guard against the petty prejudices and petty passions which will bruise your feelings upon your entry into society.

Be cold with everybody: familiarity always harms; but especially guard against letting yourself go with your superiors, no matter how they may lead you on. They can put you in your place very quickly, and they will take pleasure in humiliating you at the moment when you least expect it.

Avoid doing small favors; be on your guard against the kindness of which you are capable; men do not understand it, and they readily take it for servility, always being glad to judge others by themselves.

Never accept favors. A favor, most of the time, is an act of treachery. Avoid patronage completely, because it enslaves and degrades.

I should like to forewarn you against the enticements of friendship, but I haven't the courage to harden your heart at the time of its most pleasant illusions. What I have to say to you about women would be completely useless. I will point out to you only that the less one loves a woman, the surer one is of possessing her. But this pleasure is worthy of an old eighteenth-century monkey. As for the one whom you will love, I hope with all my heart that you will possess her.

Never forget an intentional offense; be a man of few or no words, and never avenge an insult with an insult.

If the state of your fortune or circumstances do not permit you to shine, do not try to conceal your hardships, but rather affect the contrary extreme; sharp cynicism makes an impression upon frivolous public opinion, whereas the petty tricks of vanity render us ludicrous and contemptible.

Never borrow; rather, suffer destitution. Believe me, it is less terrible than people imagine, and especially less so than the imminent certainty of being dishonest or of being so considered.

I am indebted to sad experience for the principles which I am proposing to you. May you adopt them without ever being forced to.

They can save you from days of anguish and fury. One day you will hear my confession. It might cost my vanity dear, but that would not stop me, when it is a matter of your life-long interest.[1]

[35]

To Lev Sergeevich Pushkin
October, 1822. From Kishinev to Petersburg.

If you were in reach, my charming one, I would pull your ears. Why did you show Pletnev my letter?[1] If in a friendly conversation I allow myself to make harsh and ill-considered judgments, they must remain between us—all my quarrel with Tolstoy proceeds from Prince Shakhovskoy's indiscretion.[2] Incidentally, Pletnev's epistle is perhaps the first piece which has been prompted by fullness of feeling. It sparkles with true beauties. He has been able to take advantage of his position, which was favorable against me; his tone is bold and noble. I shall answer him by the next post.

Tell me, my dear fellow, is my *Prisoner* making a sensation? *A-t-il produit du scandale?* [M. F.] Orlov writes me; *Voilà l'essentiel.* I hope that critics will not leave in peace the character of the Prisoner; he was created for them, my dear. I do not receive journals, so take the trouble to write me what they say—not for the sake of my correcting it, but for the sake of humbling my conceit.

I am floundering about, and perhaps I shall manage to come to you. But not earlier than next year [. . . .][3] I have written Zhukovsky, but he does not answer me; I have written to the minister[4]—he doesn't give a rap—"O friends, take my entreaties to August(us)."[5] But August looks like September. . . .[6] By the way, has my epistle "To Ovid" been received? Will it be published? How is Bestuzhev? I am awaiting his calendar. I would send you some new verses, too, but I'm too lazy. Farewell, dear fellow.

October, 1822. Kishinev.   A.P.

My friend, ask I. V. Slenin to send me and deduct it from the remainder he owes me, two copies of *Ruslan and Lyudmila*, two copies of my *Prisoner*, one of *The Prisoner of Chillon*, Grech's book,[7] and Tsertelev's ancient poems.[8] Greet Slenin for me.

[36]

To Vladimir Petrovich Gorchakov[1]

October or November, 1822. From Kishinev to Gura-Galbin, Bessarabia.

Your remarks, my joy, are very just and only too indulgent. Why did my Prisoner[2] not drown himself after the Circassian girl did? As a person he acted very sensibly, but good sense is not what is wanted in the hero of a poem. The character of the Prisoner is unsuccessful; this proves that I am no good as hero of a romantic poem. In him I wanted to depict the indifference toward life and its pleasures and the premature old age of the soul which have become the distinctive features of the youth of the nineteenth century. Of course it would have been more polite to have named the poem *The Circassian Girl*—that did not occur to me.

The Circassians, their customs and manners, occupy the larger and better part of my tale; but none of that is connected with anything else, and is a true *hors d'oeuvre*. I am very much dissatisfied with my poem on the whole, and I consider it much inferior to *Ruslan*—though the verses in it are more mature. Farewell, my joy.

P.[3]

[37]

To Peter Alexandrovich Pletnev

November or December, 1822. From Kishinev to Petersburg.

(Rough draft)

For a long time I have not answered you, my dear Pletnev; I have been intending to answer with verses worthy of yours,[1] but I have given up the idea. Your position is too favorable against me, and you know too well how to take advantage of it. If the first verse of your epistle is written as much from your heart as all the rest, then I do not repent of my momentary injustice—it gave rise to an unexpected beauty in poetry. But if you are angry with me, your verses, however charming, will never console me. Of course you would forgive my ill-considered lines, if you knew how often I am subject to so-called spleen. In these minutes I am wroth at the entire world, and no poetry stirs my heart. Do not think, however, that I do not esteem your indisputable talent. The feeling for the elegant has not

become completely dull in me—and when I am in complete possession of myself—your harmony, poetic precision, nobility of expression, beauty of structure, harmoniousness, the purity in the finish of
your verses captivate me, like the poetry of those I love most.

I do not completely confirm now what I wrote about your
Iroida,[2] but one must admit that the poem is unworthy of either you
or Batyushkov. Many have taken it for one of his poems. I know
that nothing of the kind would happen with a mediocre writer, but
Batyushkov, being displeased by your elegy, became angry with you
because of the mistake of others. And, after Batyushkov, I became
angry.

Forgive my ingenuousness, but it is a token of my esteem for you.
Sine ira, dear singer, let's strike a bargain on it, and good-by.

From my brother's letters I see that he is on friendly terms with
you. I envy you both.

[38]
To Lev Sergeevich Pushkin
Between January 1 and 10, 1823. From Kishinev to Petersburg.
My dear fellow, how do you translate *bévues*[1] into Russian? We
shall have to publish a journal *Révue des Bévues*. We would include
there excerpts from Voeykov's criticisms, Ryleev's noon-day dawn
and his coat of arms on the gates of Byzantium[2] (in the time of Oleg,
there was no Russian coat of arms, and the double-headed eagle is
the Byzantine coat of arms; it signifies the separation of the Empire
into the Western and the Eastern parts—with us it has no meaning).
Would you believe it, my dear fellow, one cannot read a single
article in our journals without finding half a score of these *bévues*;
have a talk about that with our fellows and lend a hand with regard
to our publications. You do not write me at all, and the rest of you
have fallen silent for some reason. Tell Zhukovsky for Christ's sake
to dictate to Yakov[3] a couple of lines addressed to me. Batyushkov
is in the Crimea. [M. F.] Orlov has been seeing him often. He seems
to me to be playing havoc with his mind. My greetings to Delvig;
likewise to Baratynsky. The latter is not publishing anything, and
I am forgetting how to read. Do you see [A. I.] Turgenev and
Karamzin?

What shall I regale you with? Here are verses "To F. Glinka"—

When amid the orgies of noisy life ostracism befell me, I saw
the contemptible, timid selfishness of the mindless crowd.
Without tears but with vexation I left the wreaths of feasts and
the glitter of Athens. But your voice was a solace to me, O
magnanimous Citizen! Let Fate have doomed me again to
terrible persecutions, let friendship have betrayed me, as love
has betrayed me; in my exile I shall forget the injustice of their
offenses. They are insignificant—if I shall be justified by you,
Aristides.[4]

I tried to send these verses via you, but you did not receive my
letter;[5] show them to Glinka, embrace him for me, and tell him that
all the same he is the most honored person of this world.

[39]
To Lev Sergeevich Pushkin
January 30, 1823. From Kishinev to Petersburg.

Sensible Levinka! I thank you for your letter—I regret that the
others have not arrived. I am writing you, surrounded with money,
theater programs, verses, prose, journals, letters—and all this is good,
all is well.[1] Write me about Didelot,[2] about the Circassian girl
Istomina, whom I once courted, like the Prisoner of the Caucasus.
Bestuzhev has sent me *The Star*[3]—this book is worthy of all attention. I regret that Baratynsky has grown stingy—I had counted on
him. What do you think of my poem "To Ovid"? My dear fellow,
Ruslan, The Prisoner, "Noël,"[4] and everything else are trash in comparison with it. For God's sake, love the two asterisks; they promise
a worthy rival for famous Panaev,[5] famous Ryleev, and our other
famous poets. "The Dream of a Warrior" has reduced to pensive-
ness a warrior[6] serving in the Foreign Service and now located in
the Bessarabian office. This "Dream" was published from an
erratic copy—"vocation" instead of "appeal," "*alarm-filled thoughts,*"
a phrase which has been used by famous Ryleev,[7] but which in
Russian does not mean anything. "Remembrance both of brother
and of friends" is a touching line, but in *The Star* it is simply flat. But
all that is of no consequence; if only there were money. I am glad
that my verses pleased Glinka[8]—that was my aim. As regards him,
I am no Themistocles;[9] he and I are friends, and we have not yet
quarreled over a youth. Gnedich is beating me at my own game.

Alas, in vain your sad fiancé awaited you, etc.[10]

Unforgivably charming. Would that I knew my Homer, or else there won't be room for both of us on Parnassus. Delvig, Delvig! Write me both in prose and verse; I bless and congratulate you. At last you have attained precision of language, the only thing you lacked. *En avante! marche.*

Has the Tsar arrived?[11] But I shall know that before you answer me. You are intending to go to Moscow. There you will see my friends; remind them of me. Also my relatives, who, incidentally, are little disturbed about the fate of a nephew who finds himself in disfavor. Perhaps they are right—but I am not to blame, either. . . .

Farewell, my dear fellow! If we see each other, I shall kiss, talk, and read you to death. After all, I have been writing you that I feel Kyukhelbeckery[12] in a foreign land. And where is Kyukhelbeker?

You write me about NN: *en voilà assez.*[13] *Assez* is *assez*; but I am still of my own opinion.

You order me not to complain about the weather—in the month of August(us).[14] So be it. But all the same it is unpleasant to stay shut in when one would like to be out of doors. Farewell again.

January 30.

[40]

To Peter Andreevich Vyazemsky
February 6, 1823. From Kishinev to Moscow.

You ought to be ashamed for not sending me your address; I would have written you long ago. Thank you, dear Vyazemsky! May God console you for consoling me. You cannot imagine how pleasant it is to read an intelligent person's judgment about oneself.[1] Up to now, in reading the reviews of Voeykov, Kachenovsky, etc., I have seemed to be eavesdropping at the yard gate on the literary talk of the female friends of Varyushka and Buyanov.[2] All that you say about romantic poetry is charming; you did well in being the first to raise your voice for it—the French sickness[3] would slay our adolescent literature. We have no theater; the experiments of Ozerov[4] are marked with a poetic style, but an imprecise and rusty one, though; incidentally, just where did he not follow the affected rules of the French theater? I know what makes you consider him a romantic poet: Fingal's dreamy monolog, "No! I never hearken to funeral songs." But all the tragedy is written according to all the rules of Parnassian orthodoxy. However, the romantic tragedian accepts inspiration alone for his rule. Admit it: all this is nothing but stubbornness. Thank you for the fillip to the censorship, but she is not worth even that: it is shameful that the most noble class of a nation, the class which does some thinking, of whatever kind it may be, is subject to the arbitrary, summary dealings of a cowardly fool. We laugh, but it would seem to be more sensible to take the Birukovs[5] in hand; it is time to give weight to our own opinion and to make the government esteem our voice—its disdain for Russian writers is unendurable. Think this over at your leisure, and let us unite on it. Give us a strict censorship, I agree, but not a senseless one. Have you read my epistle to Birukov?[6] If not, get it from my brother or from Gnedich. I have read your verses in *The Polar Star*; they are all simply charming—but for Christ's sake do not forget your prose. Only you and Karamzin are masters of it. "Glinka is master of the language of the feelings. . . ."[7] What a thing to say! Bestuzhev's article about our brotherhood is awfully immature,[8] but everything of ours which is published is having its effect upon Holy Russia. On the other hand, we should not slight anything, and well-intentioned notes must be printed for every article, either political or literary, if only there is a little sense in it. Who if not you is to take on himself the boring but useful duty of being overseer of our writers? My verses are seeking you over all Russia. I expected you to come to Odessa in the fall, and I would have come to you. But everything goes contrary to what I want. I do not know whether I shall see you this year. Meanwhile, write me—if by the post, then be very careful, but if by an *occasion*, say what you please. And can't I have some verses by you? I want them so badly I don't know what to do. Uncle[9] has sent me poems of his. I would have liked to write something about them, more to tweak [I. I.] Dmitriev than to gladden our bailiff; but it is impossible. He is so stupid that my tongue will not twist itself to praise him, even without comparing him with the ex-Minister–Dorat.[10] Do you see Chaadaev occasionally? He gave me a dressing down because of the *Prisoner*; he finds him insufficiently *blasé*. Chaadaev unfortunately is a connoisseur in that line; enliven his beautiful soul, Poet! You truly love him, I cannot imagine him different from formerly. Another word about *The Prisoner of the Caucasus*. You say, my dear fellow, that he is a son of a bitch for not mourning for the Circassian girl. But what should he say? "He understood everything" expresses everything. The thought of her could not help taking possession of his soul and uniting with all his thoughts—that goes without saying. It could not be otherwise. There is no need to spell it all out—this is the secret of arousing interest. Others are vexed that the *Prisoner* did not throw himself into the river to drag my Circassian girl out. Yes, shove right in; I have swum in Caucasian rivers. In them you yourself will drown, and not a devil of a thing will you find. My prisoner is an intelligent fellow, sensible, not in love with the Circassian girl. He is right in not drowning himself. Farewell, my joy.

February 6, 1823.   Pushkin.

We are having a ball day after tomorrow—come dance—the Poltoratskys[11] are inviting.

Married Happiness
Sitting at home with nothing to do, I shall tenderly say, "Ah, my dear, how you just f——; order them to fumigate."

These are the verses in fashion in Kishinev. They are not mine—but Poltoratsky's—in honor of my future marriage.

[41]
To PETER ANDREEVICH VYAZEMSKY
March, 1823. From Kishinev to Moscow.

I thank you for the letter, but not for the poem: I had no need of it—I read your "First Snow" as long ago as 1820, and I know it by heart. Haven't you written anything new? Send me something, for God's sake, or else Pletnev and Ryleev will wean me completely away from poetry. Do me the favor of writing me in detail about your suit against the censorship.[1] This concerns all the orthodox band. Your proposal for us all to gather together and complain of the Birukovs could have dire consequences. According to the military code, if more than two officers make a protest at the same time, such an action is considered mutiny. I do not know whether writers are subject to court martial, but a joint complaint on our part could

bring down on us horrible suspicions and cause great unpleasantnesses. . . . To unite secretly—but apparently to act singly—would
seem to be the more dependable way. In this situation one must look,
at poetry as, pardon the expression, a trade. Rousseau was lying
and not for the first time, when he asserted *que c'est le plus vil des
métiers.*[2] *Pas plus vil qu'un autre.*[3] Aristocratic prejudices are suitable
for you but not for me—I look at a finished poem of mine as a
cobbler looks at a pair of his boots: I sell for profit. The shop foreman judges my jack-boots as not up to the standard, he rips them up
and ruins the piece of goods; I am the loser. I go and complain to
the district policeman; all that is in the nature of things. I am thinking
of tying into Birukov soon, and I am going to break him to the
saddle in this regard. But at a distance of 1300 miles, it's a little
hard to give him a fillip on the nose. I am wallowing in Moldavian
mud, and the devil knows when I shall scramble out. As for you—
wallow in the mud of the fatherland and think:

Even the mud of the fatherland is pleasant to us.[4]

Cricket

[. . . .][5]

[42]

To PETER ANDREEVICH VYAZEMSKY
April 5, 1823. From Kishinev to Moscow.

My hopes have not been realized: this year I shall not be able to
come either to Moscow or to Petersburg.[1] If you come to Odessa
this summer, won't you make a detour to Kishinev? I would acquaint
you with heroes of Skulyany and Seku, fellow-champions of Iordaki,[2]
and with a Greek girl whom Byron kissed.[3]

Is what they say about Katenin true?[4] Nobody writes me anything. Moscow, Petersburg, and Arzamas[5] have completely forgotten me.

Has Okhotnikov[6] arrived: did he bring you the letters, etc.?

They say that Chaadaev is going abroad—he should have done it
long ago. But from selfishness I am sorry for it—my pet hope has
been to travel with him. Now God knows when we shall see each
other.

An important question, and please answer: where is Maria Ivanovna Korsakova,[7] who lives, or used to live, opposite some monastery (the Strastny, isn't it?). Is she alive, where is she? If she has died, which God forbid, where are her daughters? Are they married, and to whom, are they old maids, are they widows, etc.? I myself have no business with regard to them but I promised to find out about everything in detail.

By the way, you don't know, do you, whether the fifteen years have passed for General [M. F.] Orlov, or not yet?[8]

April 5.   A.P.

Some verses, for God's sake, some verses, and fresh ones.

[43]

To NIKOLAY IVANOVICH GNEDICH

May 13, 1823. From Kishinev to Petersburg.

I thank you, dear and honored one, for remembering the Bessarabian hermit. He keeps quiet for fear of boring those whom he loves, but he is very glad of the opportunity to have a chat with you about anything whatever.

If we may proceed to the second edition of *Ruslan and Lyudmila*,[1] it would be most expeditious for me to rely on your friendship, experience, and solicitude, but your proposals give me pause for many reasons. (1) Are you sure that the censorship, which passed *Ruslan* the first time against her will, will not collect herself and block the way for its second advent? I have not the power, nor is it my intent, to replace earlier readings with new ones to please her. (2) I agree with you that a preface is rather boring twaddle, but I absolutely cannot consent to supplementing it with any new ravings of mine;[2] I have promised them to Yakov Tolstoy and they must appear separately. True, I have a poem[3] ready, but N.B. the censorship. *Tout bien vu*, shouldn't we end the business with a foreword? Let me try; maybe I won't bore. I am somewhat in the good graces of the Russian public.

Je n'ai pas mérité
Ni cet excès d'honneur ni cette indignité.[4]

However that may be, I shall make use of my *opportunity* and shall tell the public the uncivil, but perhaps useful, truth. I know very well the extent of the understanding, taste, and enlightenment of this public. We have people who are above this public; it is too unworthy to appreciate them. There are others on its level; those it loves and honors. I remember Khmelnitsky's reading once his *Irresolute One*[5] to me; when I heard the verse "And one must give the Germans their due, that they are punctilious," I told him: "Mark my words, at this verse everybody will burst out applauding and guffawing." And what is there witty or amusing in it? I should very much like to know whether my prediction came true.

You, whose genius and labors are too lofty for this puerile public, how are you doing, how is your Homer doing? For a long time I have read nothing excellent. Kyukhelbeker writes me in tetrameters that he has been in Germany, in Paris, in the Caucasus, and that he has been falling off a horse.[6] All that is apropos of *The Prisoner of the Caucasus*. I have not received any news from my brother for a long time; none about Delvig and Baratynsky, either—but I love them, even lazy. *Vale, sed delenda est censura.*[7]

May 13. Kishinev.   Pushkin.

I have no portrait of myself—and why the devil should I have one?[8]

Do you know the Russian peasant's touching custom of setting free a little bird on Easter? Here are some verses for you on it:

> In foreign land, I piously observe a native custom of antiquity:
> I am setting free a bird on the bright holy day of spring. I have
> become accessible to consolation: Why should I murmur against
> God, when I can give freedom to even one creature?[9]

Do they publish anonymously in *The Son of the Fatherland*?

[44]
             To Alexander Alexandrovich Bestuzhev
          June 13, 1823. From Kishinev to Petersburg.
Dear Bestuzhev, permit me to be the first to overstep the bounds of the proprieties and heartily thank *thee*[1] for *The Polar Star*, for your letters, for the article on literature, for "Olga," and especially for

"An Evening at the Bivouac."[2] All of this is marked with your stamp, i.e., with your intelligence and marvelous liveliness. We might argue at our leisure about the "Glance"; I confess that there is no one that I so much like to argue with as with you and Vyazemsky—you two alone can rouse me to heated arguments. For the time being I complain to you about one thing: how could you forget Radishchev[3] in an article on Russian literature? Just whom are we going to remember? The failure to mention him is unforgivable both to you and Grech—and I did not expect it of you. Another word: Why praise the cold, monotonous Osipov,[4] but insult Maykov?[5] His *Elisey* is truly amusing. I do not know anything more amusing than the poet's saying to his underwear:

> I am thinking of you, too, underclothing, that the hope of saving you, too, was thin!

And Elisey's mistress, who burns up his trousers in the stove,

> When her stove was lighted for pies, and
> thereby became like Dido.

And Zeus's conversation with Mercury, and the hero, who fell into the sand,

> And stamped all the image of his seat in it. And
> they who go into that inn used to say
> that this same mark is visible even now in the sand.

All that is killingly funny.[6] You seem to like *The Annunciation*[7] better; however, *Elisey* is funnier, and consequently more beneficial to the health.

As regards 1824,[8] I shall try to send you my Bessarabian ravings. But can't we besiege the censorship again, and on the second assault carry off my *Anthology*? I have burned *The Bandits*[9]—and it serves them right. One fragment has survived in the hands of Nikolay Raevsky. If fatherlandish sounds—the tavern, the knout, the jail—do not frighten the tender ears of the feminine readers of *The Polar Star*, then publish it. Anyway, why be afraid of feminine readers?

There are none and will be none on Russian soil,[10] and that is nothing to regret.

I am convinced that they who attribute the new satire to Arkady Rodzyanko[11] are mistaken. He is a person of noble principles, and he is not going to resurrect the times of word and deed.[12] Denouncing an exiled person is the last degree of rabidity and baseness, and, besides, the verses in themselves are unworthy of the singer of Socratic love.

It has already been about a year since Delvig wrote me. Reproach him and embrace him for me; he will embrace you, i.e., thee, for me. Farewell, good-by.

June 13.   A.P.

[45]
To an Unidentified Woman
June or July, 1823. In Kishinev or Odessa.
(Rough draft; in French)

I am not writing to defy you, but I have had the weakness tc confess to you a ludicrous passion, and I wish to explain myselt frankly with regard to it. Do not pretend anything—that would be unworthy of you—coquetry would be a frivolous cruelty and moreover quite useless. I shall not believe in your anger, either, any more —wherein can I offend you? I love you with such tender rapture, but with such care not to be overfamiliar, that not even your pride can be wounded by it.

If I had any hopes, I would not have waited until the eve of your departure to make my declaration. You must attribute my avowal to a state of exaltation which I could no longer master, and which ended in my fainting away. I ask nothing, I do not know what I want myself—nevertheless I you [. . . .][1]

Letter 11

1. Lev Sergeevich Pushkin (1805-1852), Pushkin's only brother. This is Pushkin's first letter from his southern exile, where he was sent under the guise of an administrative transfer. The chronology of Pushkin's travels from Petersburg to Kishinev is as follows: He left Petersburg on May 6. After arriving in Ekaterinoslav and spending several days there, he became ill. About June 4, he left for the spas in the region of the Caucasus, where he arrived about June 11 and spent almost two months. He left there on August 5, and ten days later he arrived at Kerch, and on August 17 at Kefa (Feodosia). At the end of August he arrived at Gurzuf, where he spent about three weeks. He arrived in Kishinev on September 21. This letter should be compared with Letter 169, in which impressions of part of the same trip are presented for publication.

2. A Latinism. Pushkin is playing on a literal translation of the Latin *ab ovo* and an allusion to the story of Leda and the swan. In the expression there may also be an unprintable, untranslatable, and inapplicable pun in the Russian.

3. General Nikolay Nikolaevich Raevsky (1771-1829), a hero of the War of 1812 against Napoleon. Other members of the Raevsky family, which plays an extremely important part in Pushkin's life, include General Raevsky's wife, Sofia Alexeevna Raevskaya (1769-1844); two sons, Alexander Nikolaevich (1795-1868), and Nikolay Nikolaevich Raevsky the Younger (1801-1843); and four daughters, Ekaterina Nikolaevna (1797-1885), Elena Nikolaevna (1803-1852), Maria Nikolaevna (1805-1863), and Sofia Nikolaevna Raevskaya (1806-1881). Both sons are important in Pushkin's life; of the daughters, the most important are Ekaterina Nikolaevna, who in 1821 married General Mikhail Fedorovich Orlov (1788-1842), and Maria Nikolaevna, who later shared the Siberian exile of her husband Prince Sergey Grigorievich Volkonsky (1788-1865) when he was exiled for his part in the Decembrist Uprising of 1825; Pushkin may have fallen in love with either or both of these Raevsky daughters. General Raevsky was from 1815 to 1824 commander of the Fourth Infantry Corps in Kiev. Both of his sons also had military careers: A.N. became a colonel, and N.N. a major general.

4. N. N. Raevsky the Younger, and Maria Nikolaevna and Sofia Nikolaevna Raevskaya.

5. Perhaps in connection with Pushkin's being merely administratively transferred to the south of Russia, rather than being imprisoned or exiled to Siberia.

6. One Evstafy Petrovich Rudykovsky (1784-1851).

7. Lieutenant General Ivan Nikitich Inzov (1768-1845). Pushkin became administratively his subordinate upon being transferred to southern Russia. When Pushkin reached Kiev, Inzov was chief of the Board of Protection of Foreign Colonists in Southern Russia. Inzov allowed Pushkin to make this trip with the Raevskys. While Pushkin was on the trip, Inzov was made vicegerent of the Bessarabian Territory, which had been annexed by Russia from Moldavia in 1812, and hence Pushkin reported to Inzov, at the end of the trip, in Kishinev, capital of Bessarabia. Inzov treated Pushkin with friendship and indulgence.

8. Mainly in the watering spots of Zheleznovodsk, Kislovodsk, and Pyatigorsk.

9. General Alexey Petrovich Ermolov (1777-1861), then Commander-in-Chief of the Russian army engaged in the gradual conquest of the Caucasus.

10. Napoleon's Egyptian campaign (1798-1799) was to have been a prelude to the conquest of India.

THE LETTERS OF ALEXANDER PUSHKIN 117

11. The rivers Kuban and Terek formed the boundary between the Russian (Cossack) settlements and the territory of the Caucasian mountaineers.

12. Pushkin's notes regarding the Cossacks settled on the river Don have not survived.

13. Founded in 988.

14. Mithradates (or Mithridates) waged three so-called Mithradatic Wars against Rome, as King of Pontus and Bosporus; according to tradition he committed suicide at Panticapaeum, the modern Kerch, in 63 B.C.

15. Extensive archeological discoveries have been made on the Golden Mound since Pushkin's day.

16. Augustin Paul Dubrux (ca. 1774-1835) was instrumental in encouraging archaeological explorations at the Golden Mound.

17. Now called Feodosia, the Russian equivalent of its ancient Greek name Theodosia.

18. Semen Mikhaylovich Bronevsky (1764-1830), mayor of Kefa (Feodosia) from 1810 to 1816.

19. See his *Fourth Georgic*.

20. Tavrida, or Taurida, was a Russian administrative unit; it is now included in the Crimea and the southern Ukraine. Pushkin apparently means, here and elsewhere, the Crimean peninsula.

21. Called Yurzuf in Pushkin's day; the ancient Yurzuvita.

22. The "elegy" was "The Lamp of Day Has Gone Out." It was published by the journalist Nikolay Ivanovich Grech (1787-1867) in 1820 without signature in his periodical *Son of the Fatherland*.

23. That is, of Empress Catherine II (the Great, 1729-1796). General Raevsky began his army career during her reign (1762-1796).

24. The invasion of Russia in 1812 by Napoleon.

25. L. S. Pushkin had some poetic talent, but he was so overshadowed by his older brother in this respect that he soon stopped writing verse.

26. Major General M. F. Orlov, a member of the Arzamas, commander of the Sixteenth Infantry Division in Kishinev.

27. The manuscript is burned through at this point, making a hiatus.

28. His family, which included his father Sergey Lvovich Pushkin (1770-1848), his mother Nadezhda Osipovna Pushkina, nee Gannibal (1775-1836), and his sister Olga Sergeevna Pushkina (1797-1868), who in 1828 married Nikolay Ivanovich Pavlishchev (1802-1879).

29. Baron Anton Antonovich Delvig (1798-1831), poet and publisher, and perhaps Pushkin's best-loved friend, from his Lyceum days until Delvig's death.

30. Perhaps Alexander Petrovich Molchanov (1811-1828), or perhaps Pushkin's Lyceum schoolmate Nikolay Nikolaevich Molchanov (b. 1802).

31. Pushkin's reference in this and later letters to the "brotherhood" is to the brotherhood of writers.

Letter 12

1. An allusion to the playwright Shakhovskoy's comedy, *A Lesson to Coquettes, or the Lipetsk Waters* (1815). After the first performance Shakhovskoy's friends arranged an evening at which he was crowned with laurels, amid speeches of praise; the Arzamasians arranged a solemn funeral, during which a cantata composed for the occasion was presented. Shakovskoy's play satirized the Arzamasians and romantics.

2. "Rhine" was the Arzamas nickname of M. F. Orlov, and "Cricket," of Pushkin.

3. A small stream in Kishinev. There is an untranslatable play on words here: "to sit down in a puddle" means to get into a mess.

4. Pushkin is parodying Psalms 137:1, "By the rivers of Babylon, there we sat down, yea, we wept when we remembered Zion." The humorous style of this letter is typical of letters of the Arzamasians. The nickname for the Arzamasians as a group was "geese," because the Russian town of Arzamas was noted for its geese.

5. In Petersburg.

Letter 13

1. Nikolay Ivanovich Gnedich (1784-1833), poet and noted translator of *The Iliad* (1830). He and Sobolevsky together saw Pushkin's *Ruslan and Lyudmila* through the press.

2. Alexander Lvovich Davydov (1773-1833), a retired major general, and Vasily Lvovich Davydov (1792-1855), retired colonel; they were half-brothers of General Raevsky. Their village Kamenka was a gathering place for liberal-minded friends, who were later among the Decembrists.

3. Gnedich's translation of Racine's play *Andromaque*, from which the following quotation is taken.

4. Alexander Fedorovich Voeykov (1778-1839), journalist.

5. Allegri da Corregio, sixteenth-century Italian painter; Alexander Osipovich Orlovsky (1777-1832), well-known Russian artist of the time.

6. The epigram was by the greatest Russian fabulist, Ivan Andreevich Krylov (1768-1844). There is a pun on the word *tjažka*, which means both "weighty" and "hard to bear."

7. The "interrogator" was Dmitry Petrovich Zykov (d. 1827); he was answered by Alexey Alexeevich Perovsky (pseudonym: Pogorelsky, 1787-1836), well-known minor writer.

8. It was painted by Alexey Nikolaevich Olenin (1763-1843), President of the Academy of Arts.

9. *The Prisoner of the Caucasus* (written 1820-21, pub. 1822).

10. Spanish tobacco was considered particularly strong; Pushkin is alluding to the revolutionary activity going on in Spain at the time.

11. Zhukovsky was then the Russian tutor of Grand Duchess Alexandra Fedorovna (1798-1860), born Frederika Louisa Charlotta Wilhelmina, daughter of the Prussian King Friedrich Wilhelm III, wife of Tsar-to-be Nicholas I. When she went abroad in October for her health, Zhukovsky accompanied her. On several occasions Zhukovsky used his position with the Tsar's family in order to help Pushkin out of difficulties.

12. Apparently Kyukhelbeker's. He and Kondraty Fedorovich Ryleev (1795-1826), civic poet and important Decembrist, were then participating in *The Neva Spectator*.

Letter 14

1. The War of Greek Independence went on intermittently from 1821 until the independent government of Greece was set up in 1833. The Russians had been more or less encouraging such uprisings since the middle of the eighteenth century.

2. Tudor Vladimirescu (d. 1821), Rumanian leader who had led a corps of Rumanian volunteers (pandours) against the Turks in 1812, under the leadership of Prince Constantine Ypsilanti (1760-1816), who after being deposed as hospodar of Moldavia in 1805, fled to Russia and from there led an unsuccessful attempt to liberate Greece. In 1821 Vladimirescu led a Rumanian irregular force to join Prince Alexander Ypsilanti (1792-1828), oldest son of Constantine. When Vladimirescu preached a Rumanian

national crusade directed against the Phanariot Greek priests and nobles, Ypsilanti had Vladimirescu arrested and allowed him to be assassinated.

3. Albanians.

4. Prince Michael Sutzu (ca. 1784-1864), hospodar of Moldavia, later ambassador of the Greek Kingdom to Russia. Pushkin made his acquaintance in Kishinev.

5. Andrey Nikolaevich Pizani, Russian consul at Jassy, then the capital of Moravia.

6. Prince Alexander Ypsilanti had been an officer in the Russian Imperial Guard. He lost an arm in the battle of Dresden (1813). In 1821 he became the leader of the Greek insurgents in the Danubian region. A series of humiliating defeats followed, culminating in that of Dragashan on June 19, 1821. He fled to Austria, where he was imprisoned until his death.

7. Princes Georgios (1795-1829) and Nicholas (b. 1796) Ypsilanti.

8. Prince Georgy Matveevich Kantakuzen (d. 1857), a colonel in the Russian cavalry and a member of the Hetairia Society (see note 14 below).

9. I.e., Russia.

10. The motto of the Roman Emperor Constantine the Great was, according to legend, the result of a vision which caused his conversion to Christianity. The Greek's war of independence against the Mohammedan Turks was given a religious character.

11. Ali Pasha (1741-1822), Turkish pasha of Jannina, Albania. He called upon his Christian subjects to fight on his side, and he promised them concessions, but the rumor of his becoming a Christian was false. He was assassinated in 1822 by an emissary of the Sultan. Byron's impressions of him are presented in *Childe Harold*, Canto I.

12. A mixed Greek and Albanian people, now in Greece.

13. Leonidas the Spartan and Themistocles the Athenian were heroes of the battles of Thermopylae and Salamis, both in 480 B.C.

14. The Greek patriotic society Hetairia was founded by Constantine Rhigas (1760-1798).

15. The Greek, and the Italians, or perhaps the Spaniards; the secret Italian society, the Carbonari, was at this time working toward the liberation of Italy from Austria.

16. That is, Ali Pasha, of Jannina.

17. Pushkin means that continued barbarity is to be expected of barbarous converts. He gives two examples, one from western Europe, Chlodwig (Clovis I, or Chlodowech) ruler of the Franks from 481 to 511; and one from Russia, Vladimir (d. 1015), ruler of Kievan Rus from 980 to 1015, whose conversion led to Russia's Christianization (988?).

18. Prince Ypsilanti so acted in having Vladimirescu murdered.

19. When Alexander I, following the legitimist ideas of the Holy Alliance, refused to back the invasion of Danubian principalities by Alexander Ypsilanti, it collapsed entirely, leaving the Greek War of Independence to be fought in and around Greece itself.

Letter 15

1. That is, brother-poet.

2. Delvig's letter, here referred to, has not survived.

3. Ivan Osipovich Timkovsky (1776-1857), a censor; he had passed *Ruslan and Lyudmila.*

4. That is, a copy of the recently published *Ruslan and Lyudmila.*

5. For a time Kyukhelbeker served in the chancellery of Chief Chamberlain Alexander Lvovich Naryshkin (1760-1826) in Paris.

6. This passage is a paraphrase of the Lenten prayer of Ephraim the Syrian; Pushkin set the prayer to verse in 1836.

7. I.e., his publications in journals.

8. Apparently Delvig did not write such a poem.

9. Byronic poetry was becoming the rage in Russia at this time. Pushkin wrote a whole series of verse tales, beginning with *The Prisoner of the Caucasus*, based in form upon Byron's Oriental tales.

10. Pushkin spent the month of May in Odessa.

11. The hero of Voltaire's philosophical tale *The History of the Travels of Scarmentado* (1756).

12. He had been expelled from the Noble Pension a month earlier for organizing a protest against Kyukhelbeker being replaced as a teacher there.

13. Pushkin was very much interested in both sides of his ancestry. He prided himself upon the ancient noble Russian lineage of the Pushkins. He was also always conscious of his "African blood," and he attributed his passionate nature to his descent, on his mother's side, from the "blackamoor of Peter the Great," Abram (or Ibragim) Petrovich Gannibal (or Hannibal) (1697-1781). Pushkin even started a novel on the subject of his maternal great-grandfather, who was reputed an Abyssinian princeling who was abducted and sold into slavery and who eventually became the ward and favorite of Tsar Peter the Great (1672-1725, ruled 1682-1725).

Letter 16

1. Augustus Caesar exiled Ovid to Tomi, a town near the mouth of the Danube, in A.D. 8, and he exiled his own granddaughter Julia a year later. Whether there was any connection between these exilings or between Ovid and Julia is not definitely known. In exile Ovid wrote many poems to Augustus, beseeching him to allow his return to Rome. In 1821 Pushkin visited some of the spots Ovid is supposed to have visited; he writes of this in his "To Ovid" (1821). Pushkin refers to Alexander I here and elsewhere as Octavian or Augustus.

2. An allusion to Gnedich's translation of *The Iliad*, then in progress.

3. The signature "AO" of A. N. Olenin on the frontispiece to *Ruslan and Lyudmila*.

4. A famous icon.

5. Karamzin's *History of the Russian State* (11 volumes, 1816-1826), a landmark not only in Russian history, but in Russian literature, because of the artistic merit of the prose.

6. Letter 15.

Letter 17

1. A. I. and N. I. Turgenev.

2. Visitors of the literary salon of Princess Evdokia Ivanovna Golitsyna (1780-1850) would sit round her hearth almost all night.

3. A slightly changed quotation of Luke 23:46. The whole passage is full of joking allusions to Turgenev's post in the Department of Spiritual Affairs.

4. Alexander I was living in the Kamenny Ostrov Palace, and his ministers, on Kamenny Ostrov Street.

5. Where St. John is supposed to have written in banishment the Book of Revelation (the Apocalypse). Pushkin's poem here referred to is his *Gavriiliada* (Gabrieliad, 1821), a parody of the Annunciation story.

6. This expression, like the one in italics which follows, is from Pushkin's own poem "The Lamp of Day Has Gone Out."

7. To Ekaterina Nikolaevna Raevskaya.

8. "Happy the man who far away . . ." from Horace's Second *Epode*.

9. The requested leave was not granted.

Letter 18

1. Nothing more is known of M. Deguilly, except that Pushkin made a pen sketch, apparently depicting a real situation, in which a thin man, clad only in his shirt, cries out: "My wife! . . . my trousers! . . . and my duel! . . . oh, really, let her get out of it as she likes, because she wears the trousers."

2. "Nor a general who condescends to receive a scoundrel in his house."—Pushkin's note.

Letter 19

1. The members of the southern group of Decembrists, who dreamed of a constitution and a republic for Russia, apparently spoke French almost exclusively.

2. Pushkin and his uncle, V. L. Pushkin, were well known as poets. In addition, Pushkin's father was known for his witty French verses, and two other Pushkins of the time, Alexey Mikhaylovich Pushkin (d. 1825) and Andrey Nikiforovich Pushkin (d. 1831) were known as writers.

3. Unpublished poem by Mikhail Vasilievich Milonov (1792-1821).

4. Because of these misprints, Pushkin had it reprinted in the journal *The Well-Intentioned*.

5. Fedor Nikolaevich Glinka (1786-1880), a minor poet who wrote, in ornate style, almost exclusively on religious themes.

6. Pushkin had lost his poems to Vsevolozhsky at cards. There are numerous references to these poems and this event in subsequent letters.

7. Brands of wines.

8. Evdokia Mikhalovna Ovoshnikova, a ballet dancer.

9. The Green Lamp.

10. Vsevolozhsky's servant, a Kalmuck, would say, "I wish you health," when one of his master's guests made too poor or too indecent a joke.

11. The poem, by the minor poet Semen Sergeevich Bobrov (d. 1810), was published in 1798 and 1804. Pushkin was interested in the poem obviously in connection with his then recent visit to the Tavrida (Crimea).

12. On the river Narva in Estonia; Vyazemsky wrote a poem about them.

13. Apparently dogs belonging to Olga S. Pushkina.

14. Anna Nikolaevna Vulf (1799-1857), a close neighbor of the estate of Mikhaylovskoe.

15. The family of Baron Modest Alexandrovich Korf (1800-1876), a Lyceum classmate of Pushkin's. Pushkin's family was then living in the same house as the Korfs.

Letter 20

1. S. I. Turgenev was with the Russian embassy at Constantinople. The embassy went to Odessa when the Greek uprising broke out, because of the fear that the Turks would think the Russians implicated.

2. Petersburg.

3. A consulting canon-lawyer in Islam; another allusion, like "Right Reverend" (the title of a bishop) below, to A. I. Turgenev's serving in the Department of Spiritual Affairs.

4. N. I. Turgenev, called "rebellious" because of his radicalism, and called "dragoman" (a translator in the Russian embassies in Asiatic countries) because he was serving in the Asiatic Department of the Ministry of Foreign Affairs.

5. Arzamas nickname of Dmitry Vasilievich Dashkov (1788-1839); he had been in the embassy at Constantinople and had returned with Turgenev, as also had Prince Dmitry Ivanovich Dolgorukov (1796-1867), diplomat and member of the Green Lamp.

Letter 21

1. Pushkin calls Grech by the name of the noted ancient Greek grammarian and critic Aristarchus, because of Grech's Russian grammar and literary criticism.

2. It has not survived.

3. Peter Yakovlevich Chaadaev (1794-1856), famous writer and thinker, a friend of Pushkin's. The publication of his "Philosophical Letter" (written 1829) in 1836 was one of the most important events in the intellectual history of Russia in the nineteenth century (see Letter 637).

4. The censorship deleted the line containing the word *vol'noljubivyj*.

5. Shishkov hated words borrowed from other languages; *šarotyk* "sphere-poker" was his word for a billiard cue, and *toptališče* "that which gets trampled upon" for sidewalk. Shishkov was working on the second edition of the Russian Academy *Dictionary of the Russian Language*.

6. The censor deleted a line and then made the change, so that the passage would still make some kind of sense.

7. Count Fedor Ivanovich Tolstoy (1782-1846), well-known gambler, rake, and roisterer, called "the American" because he had visited the Aleutian Islands (then Russian America) and often dressed in Aleutian costume. He was an enemy, later a friend of Pushkin's.

8. Objecting to unauthorized publication of Letter 3; the letter has not survived.

9. Reference to Gnedich's study, friends, and translation (in progress) of Homer's *Iliad*.

Letter 22

1. Probably Konstantin Anastasievich Popandopulo (1787-1867), a Moscow physician.

2. Ivan Petrovich Liprandi (1790-1880), army officer and friend of Pushkin's; later a police spy.

3. Vyazemsky had been serving in Warsaw. However, he was deprived of his post and his rank of Chamberlain. He was living in Moscow.

4. Vyazemsky's verse "Epistle to M. T. Kachenovsky" was published in 1821. Mikhail Trofimovich Kachenovsky (1775-1842), editor of the journal *The Messenger of Europe*, a professor of history with conservative views, incurred Pushkin's dislike by publishing violent attacks on *Ruslan and Lyudmila*. Pushkin rejoined with several biting epigrams.

5. Zhukovsky's *Peri and the Angel* (1821) was based on *Lalla Rookh* (1817), by the Irish poet Thomas Moore.

6. Evgeny Abramovich Baratynsky (1800-1844), next to Pushkin the greatest Russian poet of his generation.

7. Batyushkov's poetry, and Pushkin's early poems, show the influence of the light erotic verse of the French poet Parny.

8. The bookseller Ivan Vasilievich Slenin (1789-1836) had bought up the edition of *Ruslan*, but he paid Pushkin only in driblets.

9. Another reference to his uncle's publishing Letter 3 without Pushkin's consent.

10. V. L. Pushkin's *The Dangerous Neighbor*, of which Buyanov was the principal character. Pushkin, who smiled at his uncle's poetic talent, did not want the poem attributed to himself. He feared that Buyanov, as his uncle's literary "son" and hence Pushkin's literary "first cousin," might be considered his own literary "son."

11. General Orlov had started a sealing-wax plant near Kishinev. In the division under his command, he had abolished corporal punishment, which was widespread at the time.

Letter 23

1. See Letter 19.

2. The Russian word *okazija* (a transliteration of the French *occasion*), "occasion, opportunity," is used frequently by Pushkin, as here, to mean an opportunity to have a letter delivered by a friend, acquaintance, or a servant, instead of by the post, where letters were often opened and read by the police. Here a trip to Moscow by Liprandi furnished the *occasion*.

3. Pushkin nevertheless sent *The Prisoner of the Caucasus* to Gnedich, who had published *Ruslan and Lyudmila*.

4. I.e., merchant.

5. In Letter 15.

6. Liprandi delivered the verses, as well as this letter.

7. Aglaya Antonovna Davydova (1787-1847), wife of A. L. Davydov.

8. Foka and Demian were characters in Krylov's fable "Demian's Fish Chowder" (1813).

Letter 24

1. "Little book (and I do not grudge it), you will go to the city without me. Alas for me, your master, who is not permitted to go." This passage, like the quotation italicized immediately after it, is from the opening verses of the first elegy of the first book of Ovid's *Tristia*. Pushkin is again alluding to his exile near the place of Ovid's exile over eighteen hundred years earlier.

2. "Go, but unadorned, as becomes the book of an exile."

3. Gnedich purchased the poem, but he paid Pushkin only five hundred paper rubles for it, to Pushkin's great dissatisfaction. Gnedich's idyll here referred to is probably "The Fishermen" (published in *The Son of the Fatherland*, 1822).

4. *Skazka, povest', poèma.*

Letter 25

1. Katenin's open letter with regard to Grech's "Attempt at a Short History of Russian Literature" (in *The Son of the Fatherland*, 1822).

Letter 26

1. A. A. Bestuzhev (1797-1837), pen name Marlinsky, a man of letters and a Decembrist. He became extremely popular for his tales of adventure.

2. Untranslatable pun on *čestoljubie* (love of honors; ambition) and Pushkin's implied coinage *čistoljubie* (love of purity); the sound would be almost identical in Pushkin's pronunciation.

3. The censorship passed the poem "To Ovid," which Pushkin included in his "Bessarabian ravings." It was published without signature in Bestuzhev's *Polar Star for* 1823.

4. Peter Alexandrovich Pletnev (1792-1865), man of letters, and Pushkin's friend and long his literary agent.

Letter 27

1. Pushkin is punning etymologically on the Russian expressions for "substantive, noun" and "adjective." What was "added" was no doubt the five hundred rubles in payment for Pushkin's *Prisoner of the Caucasus*. Pushkin was actually angered at what he considered the niggardliness of Gnedich in paying no more. The poem immediately became extremely popular and Gnedich made large profits on it.

2. That is, by publishing it.

3. Savage peoples who in antiquity lived about the Black Sea; here Pushkin means barbaric, uncivilized people.

4. This and further expressions and the quotation have to do with the text of *The Prisoner of the Caucasus*.

5. Central Asian peoples; here barbaric, cacophonic.

6. Paraphrase of "Render unto Caesar the things that are Caesar's and unto God the things that are God's," Mark 12:17; cf. Matthew 22:21, Luke 20:25.

7. In polemics with Grech and Katenin, Bestuzhev had been advocating a literary language based on the Russian vernacular, rather than the heavily Church Slavonic literary language accepted in the eighteenth century as appropriate for the "higher genres" of literature.

8. It has not survived.

9. That is, Zhukovsky's translation (1822) of Byron's poem (1816). *The Peri* is Zhukovsky's *The Peri and the Angel*, based on Moore's *Lalla Rookh*; Gromoboy and the Little Old Woman are characters in ballads by Zhukovsky.

10. Pushkin means that if Zhukovsky wishes to translate, rather than do creative work, he should translate, *in toto*, such works as Tasso's *Jerusalem Delivered*, Ariosto's *Orlando Furioso*, and Homer's *Iliad* and *Odyssey*, rather than poems by his English contemporaries, Thomas Moore and Robert Southey, or the German, Friedrich von Matthisson. Zhukovsky did translations from the last three authors. Late in life he translated Homer's *Odyssey*.

11. The reference is to the sentimentality and moralizing in Dmitriev's works, which Pushkin here charges with being derived from the minor eighteenth-century French authors, Jean-Pierre Claris de Florian, author of fables and moralizing novels, and Gabriel-Marie Legouvé (or Le Gouvé), author of didactic long poems and high-flown tragedies. Dmitriev had been one of the first poets of the older generation to sense Pushkin's poetic promise; Pushkin's negative reaction to him as expressed here is perhaps occasioned in part by Dmitriev's lack of enthusiasm for Pushkin's first work of large scope, *Ruslan and Lyudmila*.

12. "A prophet is not without honor save in his own country," Matthew 13:57; Mark 6:4; cf. John 4:44.

13. Pushkin is here playing on the concluding phrase of an epigram (1818), attributed to Pushkin, and on Kyukhelbeker: "Kyuhelbekery and nauseating." The epigram is said to have been called forth by Zhukovsky's commenting that "I was a little nauseated somehow last night; besides Kyukhelbeker came." In this passage Pushkin replaces the specific reference to Kyukhelbeker with one to Moldavia, which only in 1812 had ceded to Russia the territory of Bessarabia, where Pushkin was living in exile. Pushkin often alludes to the epigram.

14. Kyukhelbeker. He had been serving with the army in the Caucasus, but he had to retire in consequence of a quarrel with a nephew of General A. P. Ermolov.

Letter 28

1. Apparently the reference to *piombare*, "to fall, hang vertically, coat with lead," is a private one.

2. A line in Pushkin's "To Chaadaev"; the allusion was to Tolstoy the American. Katenin may have considered the line an allusion to his comedy *Gossip* (1820), in which the hero Zelsky was considered by some to be a take-off on Pushkin. Katenin's play was based on, or freely translated from, *The Naughty One* (1747), by the French dramatist Jean-Baptiste Gresset.

3. Katenin left in the scene in which Count Gomès slaps old Don Diègue. It will be

observed here and elsewhere that Pushkin's own ideas of honor have much in common with those of the Middle Ages.

4. Pushkin had no high opinion of the abilities of either of these actors, Pavel Ivanovich Tolchenov (d. 1840's) and Yakov Grigorievich Bryansky (1760-1853).

5. "For such things, this was not the place"—Horace's *Art of Poetry*, line 19.

6. That is, writer (or translator) of tragedies. Katenin had already translated Racine's *Esther* and Corneille's *Cid*, and he later translated Racine's *Andromaque*.

Letter 29

1. Pushkin obviously thought he might have offended his brother by his complaint in Letter 23 of his brother's "half-Russian, half-French" letter.

2. L. S. Pushkin did not go into the service until 1824.

3. Vasily Ivanovich Kozlov (1792-1825), a minor writer.

4. See Letter 28.

5. For Bestuzhev's "publication" and Pushkin's verses sent to him, see Letter 26, note 3.

6. It was then, as a matter of fact, through the censorship and in the press; it appeared in August.

7. The first signs of Batyushkov's madness, which lasted the rest of his life, had begun to appear.

8. The letter has not survived.

Letter 30

1. Vyazemsky's handwriting was eccentric.

2. The following passage has to do with Pushkin's attack on Tolstoy the American in his poem "To Chaadaev." Prince Shakhovskoy had shown Tolstoy some uncomplimentary remark of Pushkin's about him, and Tolstoy responded with an epigram on "Chushkin." Shakhovskoy's "garret" was his literary salon. Pushkin felt that he could be "completely cleared" only by a duel with Tolstoy. Pushkin was further angered when Grech, publisher of *The Son of the Fatherland*, in which "To Chaadaev" appeared, refused to publish Tolstoy's epigram, because this could give rise to the idea that Pushkin was involved in journalistic cliques and intrigues.

3. Quotations from Vyazemsky's letter.

4. "Here are the words that scream at finding themselves together." The earlier mention of Voltaire in the letter leads to a quotation from him.

5. Zhukovsky's translation.

6. Dominique de Pradt, whose essays had great contemporary appeal not only in France, but also in Russia.

7. That is, such as would be suitable for writing on serious subjects like philosophy and criticism. In Pushkin's day such writing in Russia was customarily done in French.

8. A facetious reference to his *Gavriiliada* and an allusion to the mysticism and religiosity then characterizing Alexander I and his court.

Letter 31

1. Prince Pavel Ivanovich Dolgorukov (1787-1845), then an official in Kishinev. The letter sent on this *occasion* has not survived.

2. Term then used for non-commissioned officer from the nobility.

3. General N. N. Raevsky.

4. General Pavel Dmitrievich Kiselev (1788-1872).

5. It may be noted that Pushkin gives a similarly profane and irreverent treatment to another title in the postcript of this letter. The reference here is to Zhukovsky's translation (1820-1821) of Schiller's play, *Die Jungfrau von Orleans* (1801).

6. "Dull roar"; pun on the name of the actor Glukharev.

7. Play by Kotzebue; it had been translated into Russian in 1802, but it was presented in Russian only in 1822.

8. Ekaterina Semenovna Semenova (1786-1849), tragic actress.

9. Kyukhelbeker's poem "God's Voice Was to Me. . . ."

10. Gavriil Romanovich Derzhavin (1743-1816), greatest Russian poet of the eighteenth century; noted particularly for his odes.

11. Field Marshal Count Alexander Vasilievich Suvorov (1729-1800), considered the greatest of all Russian military leaders.

12. Alexander Sergeevich Griboedov (1795-1829), Russian playwright and diplomat, famous for his play *Woe from Wit* (written 1823-24, pub. 1833).

13. The verses here quoted by memory appeared in the manuscript Lyceum journal *The Messenger*, brought out by Delvig, in 1811.

14. Pletnev's "B[atyushkov] from Rome," which speaks in the first person of the poet's losing his inspiration abroad, had been attributed to Batyushkov himself.

15. L. S. Pushkin showed this letter to Pletnev, and thus incurred Pletnev's anger against Pushkin, and thereby Pushkin's against his brother. See Letter 35.

16. "My father has had a brilliant idea—to send me some clothes—say that I asked you to remind him." Pushkin's correspondence with his father is in French, and hence when he thought of his father's "brilliant idea," he thought in French.

17. Ryleev changed the passage in his "Bogdan Khmelnitsky" (1822), so as to remove this error.

18. Count Dmitry Ivanovich Khvostov (1757-1835), poetaster often ridiculed by Pushkin and other Arzamasians.

Letter 32

1. Prince Alexander Yakovlevich Lobanov-Rostovsky (1788-1866), a Russian statesman, bibliophile, and bibliographer. The proposal was to publish a collection of Pushkin's poems; Pushkin had lost them at cards in 1820 to Vsevolozhsky.

2. Self-quotation. See Letter 17, note 6.

3. That is, the Green Lamp.

4. Aphrodite, Venus.

5. For the Kalmuck, see Letter 19. The "wine of the comet" is of the vintage of 1811, noted for its excellence, the year the largest comet of the nineteenth century appeared.

6. Tolstoy's *My Idle Time* (1821).

7. The people listed here are members of the Green Lamp or are connected with the theater. The ones who appear in the Letters here for the first time include the following: Alexander Vsevolodovich Vsevolozhsky; Dmitry Nikolaevich Barkov (1796-1855), writer and member of the Green Lamp; Nikolay Ivanovich Khmelnitsky (1789-1845), playwright; Ekaterina Ivanovna Ezhova (1787-1837), actress. The Sosnitskys include not only the actress Elena Yakovlevna Sosnitskaya, but also her husband, the actor Ivan Ivanovich Sosnitsky (1794-1871). Pushkin is Count Vasily Valentinovich Musin-Pushkin-Bryus (1773-1836), army officer and, later, Decembrist. The Semenovas are the actress Ekaterina Semenovna Semenova and her sister, the opera singer Nimfodora Semenovna Semenova (1789-1876). Zavadovsky is probably Count Vasily Petrovich Zavadovsky (1798-1855), an officer.

Letter 33

1. Printed copies of Pushkin's *Prisoner of the Caucasus* and of Zhukovsky's translation of Byron's *Prisoner of Chillon*.

2. The changes here listed were made at the demand of the censorship, except for the "bitter kiss" of parting, a suggestion of Gnedich's.

3. The portrait was lithographed, not engraved.

4. Regarding Pushkin's "unusual gift."

5. Quotation from Vyazemsky's epistle "To V. A. Zhukovsky" (1821).

6. Ballads written by Zhukovsky in 1812, 1808, and 1809-1817, respectively.

7. Letter 28.

8. It was not printed.

Letter 34

1. This letter gives the extreme statement of Pushkin's youthful cynicism and disenchantment. Much bitter personal experience, particularly with regard to the service and his exile, is no doubt here reflected. It may be remarked that Pushkin never himself followed the advice he gives here. He rejects this attitude in *Evgeny Onegin*, Chap. IV, stanza 7.

Letter 35

1. Letter 31.

2. See Letter 30.

3. Hiatus in manuscript.

4. Pushkin's letters to Zhukovsky and to Karl Vasilievich Nesselrode (1780-1862), Minister of Foreign Affairs and, as such, head of the department in which Pushkin was nominally serving, have not survived.

5. A line, placed in Ovid's lips in Pushkin's "To Ovid"; in Russian *avgust* for the man and the month. Here it is an allusion to Alexander I. Pushkin's "To Ovid" appeared in Bestuzhev's "calendar," or almanac, *Polar Star for* 1823.

6. Pushkin is quoting from a poem by Nikolay Mikhaylovich Yazykov (1803-1846), "We Love Noisy Feasts." After Pushkin and Baratynsky, Yazykov is regarded as the greatest Russian poet of his generation.

7. Grech's "Attempt at a Short History of Russian Literature" (1822).

8. Prince Nikolay Andreevich Tsertelev (1790-1869) published in 1820 two booklets: *Of the Works of Ancient Russian Poetry* and *A Glance at Russian Fairy Tales and at Songs and the Tale in the Spirit of Ancient Russian Poems.*

Letter 36

1. Vladimir Petrovich Gorchakov (1800-1867), a friend of Pushkin's in Kishinev.

2. The hero of Pushkin's *Prisoner of the Caucasus*; the Circassian girl is the heroine.

3. On a separate sheet Pushkin gives corrected readings for misprints in his poem.

Letter 37

1. Pletnev had written a poetic epistle to Pushkin in response to Pushkin's remark about Pletnev's writing (see Letters 31, 35). Pletnev's first verse was "I am not angry at your caustic reproach."

2. I.e., Herodiada, monstrosity; Herod's name is used in Russian colloquial address in the meaning of "monster." The reference is to "B[atyushkov] from Rome."

Letter 38

1. "Howlers."

2. In his "Oleg the Seer" (1822). Oleg, the second ruler of Kievan Rus in the Rurik dynasty, made his expedition against Constantinople in 907, and "nailed his shield" to the gates of the city. Pushkin utilized the incident in his "Oleg's Shield" (1829). Ivan

III, the Great (1440?-1505, ruled 1462-1505), adopted the Byzantine coat of arms, the double-headed eagle, in 1472.

3. Zhukovsky's valet.

4. Under the guise of a poem about ancient Athens, Pushkin transparently refers to his own "ostracism" from Petersburg; his Aristides "the Just" was Glinka. In this little poem Pushkin is good-naturedly following to a considerable degree Glinka's florid style. The poem was written in response to a poetic epistle by Glinka to Pushkin in 1820.

5. The letter is unknown.

Letter 39

1. Quotation from Derzhavin's poem "Morning" (1800).

2. Charles Louis Didelot (1767-1837), French choreographer in Petersburg. He composed a ballet on the subject of Pushkin's *Prisoner of the Caucasus*; it was presented in 1823 with the dancer Evdokia Ilinichna Istomina (1799-1848) playing the part of the heroine, the Circassian girl.

3. *The Polar Star for* 1823. Poems by the Russian poets (except Glinka) mentioned in this paragraph appeared in this publication. Pushkin's contributions included "To Ovid" and "War" (which he here calls "The Dream of a Warrior"). They appeared with two asterisks instead of the poet's name.

4. "Fairy Tales: A *Noël*" (1818), a bitter poem by Pushkin in the form of a Christmas carol by the Virgin Mary to the Christ child, ridiculing as "fairy tales" the idea that the Tsar (i.e., Alexander) would give the people their rights (i.e., a constitution).

5. Vladimir Ivanovich Panaev (1792-1859), poetaster.

6. I.e., Pushkin.

7. In Ryleev's poem, "Boris Godunov."

8. See Letter 38.

9. Themistocles was a rival of Aristides, by which name Pushkin called Glinka, in his poetic epistle to him, quoted in Letter 38.

10. Quoted from Gnedich's "Tarentine Maid" (1823) from André Chénier. Pushkin had recently been borrowing from Chénier, whose complete works had appeared only in 1819, twenty-five years after his death. Pushkin jokingly suggests that he would compete with Gnedich, who was then translating *The Iliad*, in that, too, if he could.

11. In Petersburg from the Congress of Verona. He had arrived on January 21, 1823.

12. See Letter 27 and note 13. Kyukhelbeker was then living on his sister's estate in the Province of Smolensk.

13. "Enough of that." "NN" in Russian refers to an unnamed person, with an "N" standing for each prename. The allusion of this paragraph is unclear.

14. Another allusion to Alexander I. See Letter 35 and note 6.

Letter 40

1. Vyazemsky's article about Pushkin's *Prisoner of the Caucasus*, in *The Son of the Fatherland* (1822).

2. I.e., prostitutes. Varyushka was a prostitute and Buyanov one of her clientèle in V. L. Pushkin's *Dangerous Neighbor*.

3. Here, French influence; the "French sickness" is syphilis.

4. Vladislav Alexandrovich Ozerov (1769-1816), tragic dramatist defended by Vyazemsky, but of whom Pushkin had no high opinion. Pushkin's allusion is to his *Fingal* (1805), based on Macpherson's *Fingal* (1762).

5. I.e., censors; Alexander Stepanovich Birukov (1772-1844) was one of them.

6. "Epistle to the Censor" (1822).

7. A quotation from Bestuzhev's "Glance at Old and New Literature in Russia," in *The Polar Star for* 1823.

8. Literally, young; an allusion to the Russian saying "young, green," i.e., immature, not thought out.

9. V. L. Pushkin, the Arzamas "bailiff" because the oldest member.

10. Claude Joseph Dorat, French poet and dramatist.

11. Alexey Pavlovich Poltoratsky (1802-1863) and Mikhail Alexandrovich Poltoratsky, officers, friends of Pushkin in Kishinev. It is doubtful that either of them wrote the quoted verses.

Letter 41

1. When the censor Alexander Ivanovich Krasovsky (1780-1857) delayed, and then largely rewrote, an article by Vyazemsky against Kachenovsky in 1822, Vyazemsky made a formal complaint, which is here called a "suit."

2. "That it is the lowest of trades."

3. "It is no lower than any other." Pushkin's rejoinder, as usual with him, is in the language of the original remark.

4. Pushkin is parodying a line from Derzhavin's "Harp" (1798): "Even the smoke of the fatherland is sweet and pleasant to us."

5. Pushkin concludes by quoting five of his verse epigrams.

Letter 42

1. Pushkin's requests for a leave were turned down.

2. That is, fighters for Greek liberation. Pushkin speaks of Yorghakis Olympios (1772-1821) also in his *Kirdzhali* (1834). In 1821 battles were fought between fighters for the Greeks and the Turks at Skulyany and Seku.

3. Calypso Polvchroni; she fled from Constantinople to her mother in Kishinev upon the outbreak of the Greek uprising. The only evidence of any relationship between her and Byron is her own assertion. Pushkin had an affair with her.

4. Katenin had been exiled to his country estate in November, 1822, for hissing the actress Semenova in the theater.

5. In listing the three cities thus, Pushkin is referring to his friends in Moscow and Petersburg, and the members of the Arzamas Society, which had taken its name from the city of Arzamas.

6. Konstantin Alexeevich Okhotnikov, an officer in M. F. Orlov's division; the reference is probably to Letter 40.

7. Maria Ivanovna Rimskaya-Korsakova (d. 1832). Pushkin was apparently once in love with one of her daughters, Alexandra Alexandrovna (1803-1860), who is mentioned in the seventh chapter of Pushkin's *Evgeny Onegin*.

8. Probably the question has to do with his length of service as an officer. In point of fact, he had been in the service since 1805.

Letter 43

1. It appeared in 1828.

2. By "ravings" Pushkin means hitherto unpublished poems of his. He is refusing to attempt to augment the sale of the second edition of *Ruslan and Lyudmila* by adding other poems.

3. *The Fountain of Bakhchisaray.*

4. "I have deserved neither this excess of honor nor this indignity."—Racine, *Britannicus*, Act II, Scene iii.

5. N. I. Khmelnitsky's comedy, *The Irresolute One, or Seven Fridays in a Week*, was first presented on the stage in 1820.

6. In a verse epistle, "To Pushkin" (pub. 1871).

7. "Farewell, but the censorship must be destroyed."—Pushkin substitutes, as chief enemy, the censorship, for Carthage, in his adaptation of the familiar quotation from Cato the Censor.

8. Gnedich probably wanted it for the proposed second edition of Pushkin's *Ruslan and Lyudmila*.

9. The poem, "A Little Bird," was first published in 1823 in *Literary Leaves*, whose publisher was Faddey Venediktovich Bulgarin (1789-1859). This was the first connection between Pushkin and Bulgarin, a Pole who had fought on the side of Napoleon against Russia in 1812, but who settled down in Petersburg, became the most faithful servant and even spy of the Russian Tsar, especially after 1825, and became an extremely successful journalist, with a government-granted monopoly of news of a political nature. His publications enjoyed special government protection, which he used to smear and denounce all who might compete with him in popularity with the public. Pushkin's relationships with Bulgarin began correctly enough, but they gradually deteriorated, reaching the point of bitter warfare in the late 1820's and early 1830's, as the numerous references to Bulgarin in the Letters show. The Polish form of Bulgarin's name was Tadeusz Bułharyn.

Letter 44

1. Pushkin italicizes the word to emphasize his use of the familiar form of "you," *ty*, instead of the formal *vy*. Pushkin was quick at making personal and literary friends and in shifting to the familiar form of "you." It has been impossible to maintain this distinction in modern colloquial English; *ty* has been translated as "thou, thee' when Pushkin emphasizes the use of the familiar form.

2. In *The Polar Star for* 1823 Bestuzhev published his "Glance at Old and New Literature in Russia" and two tales, "Roman and Olga" and "An Evening at the Bivouac."

3. Alexander Nikolaevich Radishchev (1749-1802), famous for his *Journey from Petersburg to Moscow* (1790), with its attack upon serfdom. Bestuzhev's and Grech's omission of mention of him may have been because of the censorship; Pushkin himself never obtained permission to publish an article on Radishchev, though he went to considerable lengths in the attempt in 1836.

4. Nikolay Petrovich Osipov (1751-1799), author of humorous works including a parody (1791) of Vergil's *Aeneid*.

5. Vasily Ivanovich Maykov (1728-1778), poet; author of the mock epic, the humorous *Elisey, or Angry Bacchus* (1771).

6. Pushkin was fond of the word *umoritel'no*, "killingly funny." The word is double-edged, from "humor" and also from the root "to kill, to die."

7. Pushkin's *Gavriiliada*.

8. *The Polar Star for* 1824.

9. Pushkin called the part which survived in the hands of N. N. Raevsky the Younger, *The Bandit Brothers* (written 1821-1822, pub. 1825).

10. In Ryleev's "Ivan Susanin" (1823), which Pushkin is here quoting, the reference is to traitors.

11. Pushkin was mistaken. The poem in point, a satire on liberals which has not survived, really was by Arkady Gavrilovich Rodzyanko (1793-1846). Rodzyanko was author of coarse poems on subjects such as "Socratic love." In spite of what he says here,

Pushkin resumed friendly relationships with Rodzyanko (see Letter 94, which is addressed to him).

12. That is, of denunciation to the authorities, and of execution by them. The reference may be to the time of Ivan the Terrible (1530-1584, ruled 1533-1584) in the sixteenth century, or of Empress Anne (1693-1740, ruled 1730-1740), in the eighteenth.

Letter 45

1. There have been various conjectures with regard to the addressee of this letter but none has been established. The letter breaks off with an unfinished sentence.

PART III

UNPROTECTED POET—ODESSA

July, 1823—July, 1824

To Peter Andreevich Vyazemsky
August 19, 1823. From Odessa to Moscow.

I am bored, dear Asmodeus, I am ill, I feel like writing, but I am not myself. I have a piece of business for you: Gnedich wants to buy the second edition of *Ruslan* and of *The Prisoner of the Caucasus* from me—but *timeo danaos*,¹ i.e., I am afraid he might behave with me as before. I promised him a foreword—but prose nauseates me. Correspond with him—take upon yourself this second edition and hallow it with your prose, the only prose in our prosaic fatherland. Do not praise me in it, but scold Russia and the Russian public— stand up for the Germans and the English—destroy these marquises of classical poetry. . . .² One more request: If you undertake the editing, do not be sly with me, but take from me what it is worth. Do not donate to me—for this reason alone I have not been inclined to do business with you, my dear aristocrat. Answer me by *extra*-post!³

I owe my brother a letter. What kind of person is he? They say **he** is a fine fellow and a Moscow dandy—is it true?

Farewell, my charming one. I shall write you more intelligibly in the future. And [M. F.] Orlov?

August 19.

[47]

To Lev Sergeevich Pushkin
August 25, 1823. From Odessa to Petersburg.

I should like, my dear fellow, to write you a whole novel—the last three months of my life. Here is what has happened: I had been needing sea baths for my health for a long time; with difficulty I talked Inzov into letting me go to Odessa—I left my Moldavia and put in my appearance in Europe. The restaurant and the Italian opera reminded me of old times, and by golly they refreshed my soul. Meanwhile Vorontsov arrives, receives me very affably,¹ declares to me that I am transferring to his command, that I am to remain in Odessa—and it seems fine. But then a new sadness wrung my bosom—I began to regret my abandoned chains.[2] I came to Kishinev for several days; I spent them in an unutterably elegiac manner, and after leaving there forever, I sighed for Kishinev. Now I am again in Odessa and still cannot become accustomed to the European mode of life—I do not go anywhere, however, except to the theater. Tumansky[3] is here. He is a fine fellow, but sometimes he lies. For an example, he writes to Petersburg a letter wherein he speaks in passing about me: "Pushkin immediately opened his heart and his *portefeuille*[4] to me—love, etc."—a phrase worthy of V. Kozlov. What happened is that I read to him fragments from *The Fountain of Bakhchisaray* (my new poem), saying that I would not like to publish it, because many passages relate to a certain woman with whom I was for a very long time, and very stupidly, in love, and because the role of Petrarch is not to my taste.[5] Tumansky took this for a heartfelt confidence, and he is conferring Shalikov-hood upon me. Help! —Raich[6] is here, too. Do you know him? Rodzyanko the traitor[7] will be here—I await him with impatience. Write me to Odessa—but let's have a talk about business.

Make it clear to Father that I cannot live without some money from him. It is impossible for me to live by the pen under the present censorship; I have not learned the cabinet-makers' trade; I cannot become a teacher, although I know the essentials of the faith and the four arithmetic functions—but I am in the service and not of my own will—and it is impossible to retire.[8] Everything and everybody deceive me—on just whom can one rely, I wonder, if not on the near and dear? I am not going to sponge on Vorontsov—I do not want to, and that's that. One extremity could lead to another—it hurts me to see my father's indifference toward my situation, though his letters are very pleasant. This reminds me of Petersburg: when, sick, in the autumn mud or hard frosts I used to take a cab from the Anichkov Bridge, he would always scold about the eighty kopeks (which surely neither you nor I would have begrudged a servant). Farewell, my dear fellow. I feel melancholy—and this letter has not cheered me up.

Odessa. August 25.

So be it; I shall send *The Fountain* to Vyazemsky—omitting the love delirium—but it's a pity!

[48]

To Peter Andreevich Vyazemsky
October 14, 1823. From Odessa to Moscow.

As you advised, dear Asmodeus, I let Gnedich know that I am
entrusting to you the publication of *Ruslan* and *The Prisoner*;[1] consequently, the deed is done. I do not remember whether I asked you
for an introduction, a foreword, etc., but I thank you heartily for
your promise. Your prose will assure the fate of my verses. What
changes did Raich speak to you about? I never could correct what I
have once written. In *Ruslan* there is need only to add an epilogue
and several verses, for the sixth canto, which I delivered to Zhukovsky too late. *Ruslan* is printed accurately; there are no mistakes,
except "fresh sleep" at the very end. I do not remember how it was
in the manuscript, but fresh sleep has no meaning here. *The Prisoner
of the Caucasus* is a different matter.

[. . . .][2]

Fate sent down for her lot not many glad *to her of days.*

The censorship has cut my throat! I cannot say, I must not say,
I dare not say,[3] "to her of days" at the end of the verse.[4] Nights,
nights—for Christ's sake

Fate had sent for her lot few nights.

What a difference! *Nights*, for she did not see him in the daytime—
—look at the poem. And just wherein is the night more unseemly
than the day? Just which of the twenty-four hours are repugnant to
the spirit of our censorship? Birukov is a fine fellow; persuade him,
or I shall take to my bed.

[Textual corrections]

And here are two more notes, in the way of answers to criticism.[5]
(1) "Under the wet burka":[6] A *burka* does not get wet through, and
it is moist only on top; consequently one may sleep under it when
there is nothing else to cover oneself with, and there is no need to

dry it. (2) "On the bank of the forbidden waters." The Kuban is the boundary. There is a quarantine on it, and the Cossacks are strictly forbidden to cross over *ob" on" pol"*.[7] Explain this as clearly as you can to the wags of *The Messenger of Europe*. Now a typographical note: "He understood everything. . . ." several periods in the manner of Shalikov—and "with a farewell gaze" should be *à la ligne*.[8] I now agree that this passage is too skimpy, but I am not up to correcting it or adding to it. *Sur ce*[9] I embrace you with hope and gratitude.

I received your letter via Fournier,[10] and I answered by the post. Your friendship with Shakhovskoy gladdens my peace-loving soul.[11] He is truly a fine fellow, a middling author, and an excellent pander. Here is some news of the same kind. Monarchial Sturdza[12] is here; I am not only a friend of his, but we think identically about a thing or two, and we are not sly with each other. Have you read his last *brochure* about Greece? Count Langeron[13] assures me *qu'il y a trop de bon Dieu*.[14] Severin[15] is here, but I have quarreled with him, and we are not on speaking terms. Vigel[16] was here, but he has gone to Sodom-Kishinev, where I think he will be the vice governor. It is boring and cold here. I am freezing under the Southern sun.

October 14. Odessa.   A.P.

Your observations regarding my *Bandits*[17] are unjust; that as a story *c'est un tour de force* is not praise—but the contrary. But, as for the style, I have written nothing better. *The Fountain of Bakhchisaray*, between us, is trash, but its epigraph[18] is simply charming. Apropos of epigraphs—do you know the epigraph of *The Prisoner of the Caucasus?*

Under the storms of fate, a firm stone; in the agitations of passion, a light leaf.[19]

You understand why I did not leave it. But I would give three-fourths of my poem for your four verses. *Addio*.

[49]
To ALEXANDER NIKOLAEVICH RAEVSKY
Between October 15 and 22, 1823. In Odessa.
(Rough draft; in French)
I answer your P.S., it being what interests your vanity most. Madame Sobanskaya[1] has not yet returned to Odessa; consequently

I have not yet been able to make use of your letter; in the second place, since my passion has cooled considerably and since in the meantime I have fallen in love with somebody else, I have thought it over. And seated on my sofa like Lara Hansky,[2] I have decided not to mix in that affair any more. That is, I shall not show your letter to Mme. Sobanskaya, while concealing only what would cast on you any intriguing quality of the Melmoth[3] type, as I intended at first. And this is what I propose to do: your letter will be quoted only with suitable omissions; on the other hand, I have prepared a lengthy, fine answer in which I give myself just as much the better of it over you as you have over me in your letter. I begin by telling you: "I am not your dupe, dear Job Lovelace:[4] I see your vanity and weakness through your affectation of cynicism," etc. The rest is in the same vein. You may be sure that this would produce an effect. But since I always think of you as my mentor as regards ethics, for all this I ask your permission and especially your advice—but hurry it up, because they will arrive shortly. I have had news of you; I have been told that Atala Hanskaya has made you foppish and boring. Your last letter is not boring. I hope mine may be able to divert you for a moment in your sorrows. Your uncle,[5] who as you know is a swine, has been here. He has set everybody at variance with each other and has quarreled with everybody. I am preparing for him a fine letter in basso profundo, and this time he is going to be told what a great blackguard he is, so that, like everybody else, he may be in on the secret.

[50]
To Filipp Filippovich Vigel
Between October 22 and November 4, 1823. From Odessa to Kishinev.
(Rough draft)

Accursed city Kishinev! the tongue would tire of berating you. Sometime heavenly thunder will roar onto the old roofs of your soiled houses, and I won't find any traces of you. The dirty shops of the Jews and the many-colored house of Varfolomey[1] will fall, will perish in flames. Thus it was, if Moses be believed, that unlucky Sodom[2] perished. But I do not dare compare Kishinev with this town—I am too well acquainted with the Bible (and not at all accustomed to flattering!). Sodom, you know, was distinguished not only by the polite sin, but by enlightenment, feasts, hospitable houses, and the beauty of unaustere maids. I am sorry that Jehovah's wrath, with thunders, leveled it. In bliss, in the amusements of society, I, a man chosen by God, would have quietly spent my day there. But in Kishinev, as you yourself see, you won't find attractive ladies, nor a madam, nor a bookseller. I, lamenting your fate, do not know whether toward evening three handsome fellows will come to you. In case they don't, my sad friend, as soon as I have leisure, I shall say farewell to Odessa; I shall come to you. I shall be glad to serve you with my random conversation, with verses, prose, with all my soul, but, Vigel, spare my rear!

These are verses, and consequently a joke—do not be angry, but smile, dear Filipp Filippovich. You are bored in the den of iniquity where I was bored for three years. I wish to distract you for at least a minute. And I enclose the information which you asked of me in your letter to Shvarts.[3] Of your three acquaintances, good use could be made of the smallest; N.B. he sleeps in the same room with his brother Mikhail, and they tumble about unmercifully—you can deduce valuable conclusions from this; I leave them to your experience and good sense. The older brother, as you have already observed, is as stupid as a bishop's staff. Vanka j—— off. Consequently, the devil take them. Embrace them for me in friendly manner—the sister likewise. And tell them that Pushkin kisses Maiguine's[4] hands and wishes her happiness on earth—not to speak of the heavens, about which I have not yet received sufficient information. Disclose to Pulkheria Varfolomey[5] as a secret that I am head over heels in love with her and that I shall be in a few days a constable and a kammerjunker in imitation of my friend Zavalievsky.[6] My greetings and my old friendship to the Poltoratskys![7] To Alexeev[8] likewise, and something more. Where and how is Liprandi? My being craves seeing him. Here it is cold and muddy. We dine gloriously. I drink, like Lot of Sodom, and regret that I have not a single daughter with me. Not long ago we had a fine day here. I was president of the drinking-bout; everybody got drunk, and we made the rounds of the whorehouses.

[51]

To Peter Andreevich Vyazemsky
November 4, 1823. From Odessa to Moscow.

November 4. Odessa.

Here, dear and honored Asmodeus, is my recent poem for you.[1] I have thrown out what the censorship would have thrown out if I hadn't, and what I did not want to exhibit before the public. If these disconnected fragments seem to you worthy of printing, then publish them, and do me the favor not to make any concession to that bitch, the censorship; snarl back for every verse, and gnaw her to shreds if you can, in remembrance of me. I have no protectors *there* except you. Another request: add to *Bakhchisaray* a foreword or addendum, if not for my sake, then for the sake of your lascivious Minerva, Sofia Kiseleva.[2] I am enclosing a police epistle[3] as material; draw information from it (being silent of course about the source). Also take a look at the article on Bakhchisaray in Apostol-Muraviev's *Travels*.[4] Excerpt from it the most endurable part—and cast a spell on all this with your prose, the wealthy heir of your charming poetry for which I am wearing mourning. Enough of this; won't it rise from the dead, like the one who pulled that stunt? What has come into your head, to write an opera[5] and subordinate the poet to the musician? Observe precedence properly. I wouldn't budge even for Rossini.[6] As for what I am doing, I am writing, not a novel but a novel in verse[7]—a devil of a difference. It's in the genre of *Don Juan*. There's no use even to think of publishing; I am writing the way I feel like writing. Our censorship is so arbitrary that it is impossible to determine the sphere of one's activity with it. It is better not even to think of it—and if you're going to take something, take it, else why dirty your claws?[8]

A.P.

The new edition is very nice—God speed it—dear angel or *aggel*[9] Asmodeus. Can you imagine, I still have not read your article which vanquished the censorship.[10] That's what it is like to live in the Asiatic manner and read no journals. Odessa is a European city— that is why Russian books are not to be found here.

A.P.

My greeting to my Uncle Vasily Lvovich, and I shall write in a few days.

[52]

To PETER ANDREEVICH VYAZEMSKY
November 11, 1823. From Odessa to Moscow.

Here are my *Bandits*[1] for you. A true occurrence gave rise to my writing this fragment. In 1820 during my stay in Ekaterinoslav, two bandits, chained together, swam across the Dnepr and escaped. Their resting on the little island and the drowning of one of the guards were not my invention. Certain verses remind one of the translation of *The Prisoner of Chillon*. That is my misfortune. I coincided with Zhukovsky accidentally; my fragment was written at the end of 1821.

November 11.

[53]

To ANTON ANTONOVICH DELVIG
November 16, 1823. From Odessa to Petersburg.

My Delvig, I have received all your letters, and I have answered almost all of them.[1] Yesterday I smelled the aroma of Lyceum life; glory and my gratitude for it to you and my Pushchin![2] You are bored; we are bored; shall I tell you the story of a white bull?[3] My dear fellow, you write too little; at least you publish too little. Incidentally, I am living in the Asiatic manner, and I do not read your journals. A few days ago your charming sonnets came my way— I read them avidly, with rapture, and with gratitude for the inspired remembrance of our friendship. I share your hopes regarding [N. M.] Yazykov and your ancient love for Baratynsky's impeccable muse. I can hardly wait for your verses to appear in print; as soon as I receive them I shall slaughter a lamb, glorify the Lord, and decorate our hut with flowers—even though Birukov thinks that too voluptuous. I do not care for the satire "To Gnedich,"[4] even though the verses are excellent; there is too little pepper in them; "ununiformed Somov" is unforgivable. Is it becoming for a person who is enlightened, a satirist who is a Russian, to laugh at a writer's independence? That is a joke worthy of the College Counsellor Izmaylov.[5] I am also awaiting *The Polar Star*. I regret that my elegies are written against religion and the government: I am half a Khvostov: I love to write (but not to copy) verses; I do not like to give them to the press (though I like to see them in print).[6] You request *The Fountain of Bakhchisaray*. It was sent to Vyazemsky a few days ago. It is made up of disconnected fragments, for which you will chide me, but all the same you will praise me. I am now writing a new poem,[7] in which I chatter to the limit. Birukov will not see it because he is a capricious child that cannot say anything but "fie." God knows when we shall read it together. It is boring, my joy—that is the refrain of my life! If only brother Lev would gallop to me to Odessa! Where is he; how is he? I know nothing. Friends, friends, it is time for me to exchange the honors of exile for the joy of meeting again. Is it true what Rossini and the Italian opera are coming where you are? My God! They are representatives of heavenly paradise. I shall die of yearning and envy.

November 16. A.P.

Order the German *Prisoner*[8] to be sent to me.

[54]

To ALEXANDER ARDALIONOVICH SHISHKOV

Between early August and the end of November, 1823. From Odessa to Tiflis.

You have gone out of your mind, dear Shishkov;[1] you wrote me several months ago using expressions like "dear sir, your flattering acquaintance, I have the honor, your very obedient servant . . . ," so that I did not even recognize my Tsarskoe Selo comrade. If you should see fit to write me, I beg you henceforth to be on the old footing with me. Otherwise I shall be grieved. I still regret, dear fellow, that you and I did not run into each other in the Caucasus; we could have acted as in the old days, and played the rake and chattered a bit. Incidentally, our fates seem to be identical, and we were apparently born under the same constellation. Does our mutual friend Kyukhelbeker write to you? He has been pouting at me, God knows why. Reconcile us. What about your verses? Where have you buried your golden talent? Under the snows of Elbrus, under the Tiflis vineyards? If you have something, send it to me—my heart is truly longing for it.

I embrace you—my letter is incoherent, but I don't have the time to be more intelligible.

A.P.

Not long ago I discovered that you are an acquaintance and a relative of our honored Alexander Ivanovich.[2] He is providing me with the opportunity to get in touch with you, but he himself is snowed under with papers and affairs. For loving you he has enough time, but for writing you—hardly.

[55]

To Nikolay Ivanovich Krivtsov
October or November, 1823 (?). From Odessa(?) to Tula.

My dear Krivtsov, do you remember Pushkin? Do not think that this is the first time he has written you since we parted. But God knows why my letters have not been reaching you. Only vague rumors of you reach me. And you have not gladdened the exile with a single line. Is it true that you have become an aristocrat?[1] That's the stuff. But don't forget your democratic friends of 1818. We have become a scattered lot. We have all changed. But friendship, friendship—

[56]

To Madame Maiguine and an Unknown Woman
November (after the 4th), 1823. From Odessa to Kishinev.
(Rough draft; in French)

Yes, unquestionably I have guessed rightly who the two charming women are who have been so kind as to remember the Odessa hermit, formerly the Kishinev hermit. I have kissed a hundred times these lines, which reminded me of so much madness, torment, wit, and grace, of parties, the mazurka, etc. Lord, how cruel you are, Madame, to think that I can be amused where I can neither meet you nor forget you. Alas, dear Maiguine, separated from you I am quite unwell, quite despondent, my faculties are dwindling away. I have lost even my talent for caricatures, though the family of Prince Mourouzi[1] is so very worthy of inspiring some. I have only one thought—of returning again to your feet and devoting to you, as a fine poet used to say, the little remnant of life which remains for me. . . . Do you recall the little correction which you made in the page of A[retino]?[2] Lord, if you would only repeat it here! But is it true that you are intending to come to Odessa? Come, in heaven's name; to lure you we shall have balls, Italian operas, parties, con-

certs, *cicisbei*, admirers, everything that will please you; I shall imitate
a monkey,[3] I shall slander, and I shall draw for you Mme. de [. . .][4]
in the thirty-six poses of Aretino.[5]

Apropos of Aretino, I shall tell you that I have become chaste
and virtuous; that is to say, in words, because my conduct has always
been such. It is a real pleasure to see me and hear me talk—won't this
impel you to hasten your arrival? Once more, come, in heaven's
name, and pardon me the liberties I take in writing to women who
have too much sense to be prudes, but whom I love and whom I
respect with all my heart.

As for you, charming, sulky one, whose handwriting (which by
great luck was not disguised a bit) has made me tremble, do not say
that you know my character; you would not have pained me by
pretending to doubt my devotion and my regrets.

Guess who, in your turn.

S.,[6] who was reputed to have unnatural tastes, has moistened the
end of a thread and put it through the eye of a needle. A. says of
him that he has always excelled where patience and saliva were
needed—

[57]

To ALEXANDER IVANOVICH TURGENEV
December 1, 1823. From Odessa to Petersburg.

You remember Kiprensky,[1] who in *The Son of the Fatherland*
published his greeting and respects to you from poetic Rome. I
embrace you from prosaic Odessa, not thanking you for anything,
but appreciating in full measure both your remembering me and
your friendly solicitude, to which I am obligated for the change in
my fate.[2] One must, like me, spend three years in stifling Asiatic
imprisonment, in order to feel the value even of the unfree European
air. Now everything would be completely all right for me, if it were
not for the absence of a certain person or two. When we see each
other again, you will not recognize me; I have become as boring as
Gribko,[3] and as sensible as Chebotarev,[4]

> My first liveliness has disappeared; will you forgive me my
> occasional reticence, my despondence? . . . Endure it, O friends,
> endure it, if only because I am attached to you.[5]

Apropos of verses: you wished to see the ode on the death of Napoleon. It is not very good; here are the most endurable stanzas for you: [. . . .][6]

Here is the last one: [. . . .][7]

This last stanza now has no meaning, but it was written in the beginning of 1821. Incidentally, this is my last liberalistic delirium; I have sworn off that,[8] and a few days ago I wrote an imitation of a fable by the moderate democrat Jesus Christ (*Izyde sejatel' sejati semena svoja*): [. . . .][9]

My greeting to your brothers[10] and to the brotherhood. I thank you for reassuring me with regard to Nikolay Mikhaylovich and Katerina Andreevna Karamzina[11]—but what is the poetic, unforgettable, constitutional, anti-Polish, heavenly Princess Golitsyna doing? Is it possible that I still miss your Petersburg?

It is a sin on Zhukovsky's part; wherein am I worse than Princess Charlotta,[12] that he won't write me a single line for three years? Is it true that he is translating *The Giaour*?[13] But at my leisure I am writing a new poem, *Evgeny Onegin*, wherein I am choking on my bile. Two cantos are already finished.

[58]
To Peter Andreevich Vyazemsky
Between December 1 and 8, 1823. From Odessa to Moscow.

Of course you are right,[1] and here are some changes for you—

Do wounding kisses remind you of your doses of the c——?[2] Put *piercing*. That will be something new. The point is that my Georgian girl bites, and this absolutely must be made known to the public. I do away with the expression the *cold castrate* out of esteem for Anna Lvovna's[3] virginity of such long standing.

[. . . .][4]

Bobrov led me into temptation: he says in his *Tavrida*: "Under the guard of the castrates of the harem." I wanted to steal something from him, and besides I should like for a certain biblical obscenity to remain in the Russian language. I hate to see in our primitive language traces of European affectation and French refinement. Rudeness and simplicity are more becoming to it. I preach from internal conviction, but as is my custom I write otherwise. [. . .][5]

Apostol has written up his travels about the Crimea; they are being published—but there is no need to wait for it.

What about Griboedov! I have been told that he has written a comedy on Chaadaev; under present circumstances that is extremely noble of him.[6]

I am sending *The Bandits*.

Now, how do I have it? "He fixed his motionless gaze"? Put *curious*, and all the same the verse is Kalmuckish.

[59]

To PETER ANDREEVICH VYAZEMSKY
December 20, 1823. From Odessa to Moscow.

[. . . .][1]

I should like to know whether we cannot somehow avoid the post in our correspondence. I would send you a couple of things too weighty for it.[2] It is more suitable for us here in Asia to write on an *occasion*. How is Krivtsov? His Excellency could halloo at me. I am awaiting *The Polar Star* [*for* 1824] in hope of seeing you extensively in print. How is Anacharsis Cloots–Kyukhelbeker's[3] journal? Let's leave the sketch of the fountain[4] until the next edition. Hurry and print; I ask, not for the sake of glory but of Mammon.

December 20.

I congratulate you upon the birth of our Savior, the Lord Jesus Christ.[5]

You appear to have the intention of making a description of Bakhchisaray without seeing it. Don't. Verses in praise of Sofia Pototskaya[6] are a different matter. Incidentally, the description of the palace in its present condition, in my epologue, is detailed and accurate, and Zontag[7] would not observe any more than I did. What if you were to drop in on us in the South this spring? We would spend the summer in the Crimea, where a world of sensible people, women and men, are planning to be. Do come: it is gayer here, I swear, than where you are in the North.

[60]

To ALEXANDER ALEXANDROVICH BESTUZHEV
January 12, 1824. From Odessa to Petersburg.

Of course I am angry with you and I am ready, with your permission, to scold you even till tomorrow. You have published[1] exactly the verses which I asked you not to: you do not know to what degree that annoys me. You write that the elegy would make no sense without the last three verses.[2] What an important matter! And just what kind of meaning have [. . .]?[3]

I long since ceased getting angry about misprints, but in the old days I would often chatter in verses, and it is painful for me to see that I am being treated as though I were dead, with no respect for my wishes or my poor possessions. That is forgivable for Voeykov, but *et tu autem, Brute!*

Gnedich is making jokes with me of a different kind. He has spread the word that all the new verses which I promised Yakov Tolstoy had already been sold to him, Gnedich. Tolstoy has written me an extremely dry letter in which he justly complains at my light-mindedness; he has given up publishing my poems, has left for Paris, and I don't hear even a whisper about him. He is in correspondence with you in *The Son of the Fatherland;* write him a word or two about me, justify me in his eyes, and send his address.[4]

I repeat to you for the last time my complaints and requests, and I embrace you *sans rancune* and with gratitude for everything— prose and poetry. You are always you, i.e., kind, lively, intelligent. Baratynsky is a charm and a marvel; his "Declaration" is perfection. After him I am never going to print my elegies, even though the typesetter should swear to me on the Gospels to act more graciously with me than he has done before. Ryleev's *Voynarovsky* is incomparably better than any of his *Dumy;*[5] his style has grown more mature and is becoming a truly narrative one—which we still almost completely lack. Delvig is a fine fellow. I shall write to him. I am ready to give you the three Easter kisses in verse, but please . . . spare me. Farewell, my dear *Walter.*[6] I have not seen Tumansky yesterday or today, and I have not given him your letter. He is a fine fellow, but I do not care for him as a poet. God grant him great wisdom.

January 12, 1824.   Odessa.   A.P.

[61]
To FADDEY VENEDIKTOVICH BULGARIN
February 1, 1824. From Odessa to Petersburg.

I received the first issue of *The Northern Archive*[1] with sincere gratitude, supposing that I am indebted to its most honored publisher for it; with the same feeling I saw your indulgent comment about my Tatar poem.[2] You belong to the small number of those men of letters whose strictures or praises can be and must be respected. You will oblige me very much if you will insert in your pages the two pieces[3] here enclosed. They were printed in *The Polar Star* with such mistakes that they make no sense. That is no great misfortune with people, but verses are not people. I assure you of my sincere respect.

Odessa. February 1, 1824.   Pushkin.

[62]
To LEV SERGEEVICH PUSHKIN
Between January 12 and early February, 1824. From Odessa to
Petersburg.

Since I have waited until there is an *occasion*, I shall write you as I wish. N. Raevsky[1] is here. He did not bring me enough news of you; why did you stand on ceremony with him and not come to see me? Didn't you have the money? We would have squared accounts afterward—but, as it is, God knows when we shall come together. You know that I have twice asked Ivan Ivanovich[2] through his ministers for a leave—and twice has followed his most gracious refusal. One thing remains—to write to him directly—to such-and-such, in the Winter Palace, opposite the Fortress of Peter and Paul,[3] or else, on the quiet, to take my cane and cap and go have a look at Constantinople. Holy Russia is becoming unbearable to me. *Ubi bene ibi patria.*[4] And it's *bene* for me, buddies, where grows a certain insignificant plant.[5] If only there were money—but where am I to get it? As for fame, it is hard to be satisfied with that alone in Russia. Russian fame may be flattering to some V. Kozlov, to whom Petersburg acquaintances are also flattering, but a person with any decency disdains all of that. *Mais pourquoi chantais-tu?*[6] To this question of Lamartine's I answer: I have sung as a baker bakes, as a tailor sews, as Kozlov writes, as a physician kills—for money, for money, for money. This is what I am like in the nakedness of my cynicism. Pletnev writes me that my *Fountain of Bakhchisaray* is already in everybody's hands.[7] I thank you, my friends, for your gracious solicitude for my fame! I especially thank [A. I.] Turgenev, my benefactor; I thank Voeykov, my high protector and illustrious friend! It remains to be seen whether even one printed copy will be bought by those who already have complete manuscripts. However, this is a trifle. A poet must not think about his livelihood, but he must, like Kornilovich,[8] write with the hope of stealing a smile from the fair sex. My dear fellow, I am so vexed I am nauseated. Whatever I look at, everything is such muck, such baseness, such stupidity— can this continue long? Apropos of muck, I have been reading Lobanov's *Phèdre*.[9] I have been wanting to write a critique on it, not for Lobanov's sake, but for the sake of the Marquis Racine—my pen tumbled out of my hand. Where you are they are making a noise about it, and our journalists are calling it a most beautiful translation of Mr. Racine's famous tragedy! *Voulez-vous découvrir la trace de ses pas*[10]—do you hope to find

Theseus' warm trace or dark paths—

the m——-f—— s.o.b.! That's how it's all translated. And what is Ivan Ivanovich[11] Racine characterized by if not verses full of meaning precision, harmony! The plan and the characters of *Phèdre* are the acme of stupidity and insignificance in their invention. Thésée is nothing but Molière's first cuckold. Hippolyte *le superbe, le fier Hippolyte—et même un peu farouche*,[12] *Hippolyte* the stern Scythian[13] bastard—is nothing but a well-bred child, polite and respectful—

D'un mensonge si noir . . . , etc.[14]

Read all that belauded tirade, and you will be convinced that Racine had no understanding of how to create a tragic character. Compare it with the speech of the young lover in Byron's *Parisina*,[15] and you will see the difference between minds. And Thérèmene the abbot and pimp—*Vous-même où seriez vous*,[16] etc. . . .—here is the acme of stupidity! I am becoming reconciled with Ryleev. His *Voynarovsky* is full of life. How is Kyukhlya?[17] I shall write Delvig,[18] but if I don't get around to it tell him that he should get my "Oleg the Seer" from Turgenev and publish it.[19] Perhaps I shall send him fragments from *Onegin*; it is my best work. Do not believe N. Raevsky, who is inveighing against it. He expected romanticism from me, and thought he found satire and cynicism. But he did not get a really good whiff.

[63]

To Alexander Alexandrovich Bestuzhev
February 8, 1824. From Odessa to Petersburg.

You obviously have not received my letter.[1] I am not going to repeat what one time was enough to say. Of your tale[2] in *The Polar Star*, I shall say that it is incomparably better (i.e., more interesting) than those which were published last year, *et c'est beaucoup dire*.[3] Kornilovich is a fine fellow and gives much promise—but why does he write "for the indulgent attention of the gracious lady NN" and await "the encouraging smile of the fair sex" before continuing his interesting works? All that is old and unnecessary, and smells too much of Shalikovian innocence. Bulgarin said that N. Bestuzhev[4] is distinguished by "the novelty of his thoughts." The word *thoughts* ought to be treated with greater respect. The Arabian fairy tale[5] is simply charming; I advise you to hold fast to this Senkovsky. I do not see Gnedich among the poets, and that is annoying; Yazykov is not there, either—and I am sorry for that; the (obscene) madrigal by A. Rodzyanko[6] could have been left for the late Nakhimov;[7] "yesterday . . . I am loving and thinking" will eventually be put into a grammar as an example of nonsense. Pletnev's "Native Land" is good. The Baratynsky is marvelous. My pieces are poor. There for you is all I have to say about the *Polar*.

I am glad that my *Fountain* is stirring up a rumpus. The insufficiency of plan is not my fault. I superstitiously set to verse the story of a young woman.

> *Aux douces loix des vers je pliais les accents*
> *De sa bouche amiable et naïve.*[8]

Incidentally, I wrote it solely for myself, but I am publishing it because I need money.

My third and most essential point, and with the epigraph "without ceremony," is: you ask for half a score of pieces from me, as if I had hundreds of them. I can scarcely gather even five together, and even so don't forget my relations with the censorship. I am not going to take money from you for nothing; besides, I have promised Kyukhelbeker, who probably needs my verses more than you do. There is no point in even thinking about my long poem[9]—if it is ever published, it will probably not be in either Moscow or Petersburg. Farewell. Give my greetings to Ryleev, embrace Delvig, your brother, and the brotherhood.

February 8, 1824.

[64]

To Peter Andreevich Vyazemsky
March 8, 1824. From Odessa to Moscow.

I thank you with all my heart, dear European, for the unexpected epistle, or rather, parcel. I am beginning to respect our booksellers and to think that our trade is truly no worse than another. One thing troubles me; you have sold the whole edition[1] for 3,000 rubles, but how much did it cost you to print it? All the same you are donating to me, you shameless fellow! For Christ's sake deduct what is due you from the remaining money, and send the rest here. It can't be expected to grow. But with me it won't gather any dust, though I am certainly no spendthrift. I shall pay old debts and sit down to my new poem.[2] Considering that I do not belong to our writers of the eighteenth century, I write for myself, but I publish for money, and not in the slightest for the smiles of the fair sex.[3]

I am impatiently awaiting my *Fountain*, i.e., your foreword. Not long ago I read your recent notes on Bulgarin;[4] this is the best of your polemical articles. I have not yet seen "The Life of Dmitriev."[5] But, dear fellow, it's a sin for you to belittle our Krylov. Your opinion must be law in our literature, but with unforgivable partiality you judge against your conscience and act as protector to the devil knows whom. And just what is Dmitriev? All his fables together are not worth one good fable by Krylov; all his satires together are not worth one of your epistles, and all the rest is not worth any poem of Zhukovsky's. You once called him [Dmitriev] *le poète de notre civilisation*. If so, we have a fine *civilisation!*

The errand you gave me of finding a house for you delighted me inexpressibly. There's no hurry; however, please explain to me a little more intelligibly what you mean by "at the beginning of the summer" and "not expensive." Lev Naryshkin,[6] with whom I have already discussed this matter, is going abroad "at the beginning of the summer." He is renting a house here for five hundred rubles per month, and a summer house for I don't remember exactly how much. I would advise you, for the children, to rent the summer house, because the dust in the city is unendurable. I shall look into it further. Incidentally, I don't understand your "too expensive"; you will spend all your money anyway, if not for that, then for something else. I am awaiting your answer. S. Volkonsky[7] is no longer here.

March 8, 1824.

[65]
To Ivan Nikitich Inzov(?)
About March 8, 1824. From Odessa to Kishinev (?)
(Rough draft; in French)

I am sending you, General, the 360 rubles which I have owed you so long. Please accept my sincere thanks; as for excuses, I am not so audacious as to make any to you. I am embarrassed and humiliated at not having been able to repay you this debt until now—the fact is that I have been perishing of poverty.[1]

Accept, General, the assurance of my profound respect.

[66]
To Lev Sergeevich Pushkin
April 1, 1824. From Odessa to Petersburg.

Here is what Vyazemsky writes me: "In *The Well-Intentioned*[1] I have read that your *Fountain* was read in some learned society, still before its publication. Who ever heard of the like? And in Petersburg a thousand manuscript copies are circulating—after that, who will buy it? I do not have the sin on my conscience, etc."

Nor do I. But I shall be told: "What's it to you? After all, you have taken your 3,000 rubles, and what happens there is no skin off your back." All that may be so, but it would be a pity if our booksellers, having acted for the first time in a European manner, should play the wrong card and lose on it—and in the future I won't be able, either, to sell anything at a profit. Thus I am indebted for absolutely everything to the friends *of my fame*—the devil take them and it, too; I have to look to it that I don't croak from hunger, and they shout *fame!* You see, my dear fellow, I am peeved at all of you; I ask one thing of you: write me how the *Fountain* is selling—or I shall join the Count Khvostovs[2] and buy up half the edition myself. What are the journalists doing to me! Bulgarin[3] is worse than Voeykov. How could one publish private letters—of no matter what comes into my mind in friendly correspondence? But they would publish it all. That's banditry. I've decided: I am breaking off correspondence with them all—I do not want to have anything to do with them. And as for them, let them stupidly berate or stupidly praise me. It's all the same to me—I shan't give a hoot. And I consider the public as on the same level as the booksellers—let them buy and then say whatever nonsense they please.

April 1, 1824.

This letter will be delivered to you by Senyavin,[4] Count Vorontsov's adjutant, a very fine fellow and my friend; he will furnish you all the information you may wish about me. I have been told that you are intending to come to see me. As if you could! Unless at government expense and in the company of a gendarme. Write me. Neither you nor Father writes me a word in answer to my elegiac fragments[5]—neither of you sends me any money—but you undermine my book trade. How very fine!

[67]

To Peter Andreevich Vyazemsky
Early April, 1824. From Odessa to Moscow.

I have just returned from Kishinev,[1] and I find letters, parcels, and *Bakhchisaray*. I don't know how to thank you.[2] The "Conversation" is simply charming, both in the ideas and in the brilliant form of their expression. Your judgments are indisputable. Your style has progressed marvellously. Not long ago I read your life of Dmitriev, too; all the reasoning in it is excellent. But this article is a *tour de force et affaire de parti*. While reading your critical compositions and letters, I have been collecting my own thoughts, and I am thinking of writing a thing or two about our poor literature in a few days,[3] about the influence of Lomonosov,[4] Karamzin, Dmitriev, and

Zhukovsky. Maybe I shall even print it; then *du choc des opinions jaillira de l'argent.*[5] Do you know what? Your "Conversation" is written more for Europe than for Russia. You are right with regard to romantic poetry. But does the old classical whore you attack fully exist with us? That is still the question. I swear to you again by the Gospels and the Holy Sacrament that Dmitriev, notwithstanding his influence of old, does not have and must not have any more weight than Kheraskov or Uncle Vasily Lvovich. Does he alone really represent our classical literature, and does Mordvinov[6] comprise in himself all the opposition? And wherein is he a classicist? Where are his tragedies, his didactic or epic poems? Is he a classicist in his epistles to Severina or in the epigraphs translated from Guichard?[7] One cannot take seriously the opinions of *The Messenger of Europe,* and it is impossible to be angry with *The Well-Intentioned.* Just where are the enemies of romantic poetry? Where are the pillars of classicism? Let's talk about all this at leisure. Now let's talk about business, i.e., about money. Slenin offers me as much as I want for *Onegin.* Who would have thought it of Russia! What, she really is in Europe—and I had thought that was a geographer's error! Now it's the censorship that's holding things up, and it's no joking matter to me because what is involved is my future fate, the independence which I must have. In order to get *Onegin* published, I'm ready to — — —, i.e., either to eat a fish or sit down on my p——.[8] The ladies take this saying backwards. However that may be, I am ready even for the noose. To Kyukhelbeker, to Matyushkin,[9] to Verstovsky, my cordial greetings; I shall answer them without delay. I have reproached my brother for *Bakhchisaray*'s becoming known in manuscript. What do you think of Bulgarin and all the brotherhood! They are not bandit-nightingales, but bandit-rooks.[10] Farewell, dear fellow—and send me some money.

A.P.

You did not understand me when I spoke to you about sending mail on an *occasion*[11]—the postmaster will trust me with credit, but I don't trust him.

[68]

To Vilgelm Karlovich Kyukhelbeker (?)
April or the first half of May(?), 1824. From Odessa to (?).
(Fragment)[1]

[. . .] reading Shakespeare[2] and the Bible, the Holy Spirit is sometimes to my liking, but I prefer Goethe and Shakespeare. You want
to know what I am doing. I am writing the motley stanzas of a
romantic poem[3]—and I am taking lessons in pure atheism. An
Englishman is here, a deaf philosopher,[4] the only intelligent atheist
I have yet met. He has covered some thousand pages with writing
to prove *qu'il ne peut exister d'être intelligent Créateur et régulateur*,[5]
destroying in passing the flimsy evidence of the immortality of the
soul. His philosophic system is not so consoling as it is usually
thought to be, but unfortunately it is the most plausible.

[69]

To Alexander Ivanovich Kaznacheev
May 22, 1824. In Odessa.
(Second rough draft)

Honored Alexander Ivanovich! Being completely unfamiliar with
procedures regarding official documents, I do not know whether I
have the right to make a reply to His Excellency's orders.[1] However
that may be, I rely on your indulgence, and I am making bold to
explain myself frankly with regard to my position.

For the past seven years I have not devoted any attention to the
service; I have not written a single document; I have not had any
dealings with a single department chief. These seven years, as you
know, are completely lost for me. Complaints on my part would be
out of place. I myself blocked up my own way, and I chose another
goal. For God's sake do not think that I have looked upon the
writing of poetry with the childish vanity of a rhymester or as being
merely recreation for a man of feeling: it is simply my trade, a branch
of an honorable industry which furnishes me with a livelihood and
with domestic independence. I do not think Count Vorontsov
would wish to deprive me of either of these.

I may be told that, since I am receiving seven hundred rubles, I am
obligated to serve. You know that the book trade can be conducted

only in Moscow or Petersburg, for only there are the journalists, censors, and booksellers to be found. I am constantly forced to refuse most profitable offers solely for the reason that I am 1300 miles from the capitals. The government sees fit to recompense my losses to a certain degree; I accept these seven hundred rubles, not as the salary of an official, but as the ration allowance of an exiled prisoner. I am ready to give them up, if I cannot be master of my own time and occupations. I enter into these details because I value the opinion of Count Vorontsov, as well as yours, just as I value the opinion of every honorable person.

I repeat here what Count Mikhail Semenovich[2] knows already: if I wished to serve, never would I choose for myself a superior other than His Excellency; but, feeling my complete lack of capability, I have already given up all the advantages of the service and every hope of future success in it.

I know this letter is enough to annihilate me, as the saying goes. If the Count orders me to retire, I am ready; but I feel that if my dependence on him were to cease, I would lose much, and I have no hope of gaining anything.

One more word: perhaps you do not know that I have aneurysm.[3] For eight years now I have been carrying death within me. I can present the certificate of any doctor you please. Can I not be left in peace for the remainder of my life, which probably will not last long?

I assure you of my deep respect and heartfelt devotion.

[70]
To Alexander Ivanovich Kaznacheev
The beginning (after the 2nd) of June, 1824. In Odessa.
(Rough draft; in French)

I am very sorry that my resignation has caused you so much trouble, and the distress which you show at it touches me sincerely. As for the fear you have regarding the consequences this resignation[1] could have, I do not believe it well founded. What would I regret? My ruined career? I have already had time to resign myself to that idea.—My salary? Since my literary endeavors can procure me more money, it is completely natural for me to sacrifice to them my duties in the service. You speak of protection and of friendship.

The two things are incompatible. I neither can nor will pretend to the friendship of Count Vorontsov, still less to his protection: nothing I know of degrades more than patronage, and I esteem this man too much to wish to bemean myself before him. On this matter I have democratic prejudices which are quite as valid as the pride of the Aristocracy.

I am tired of depending on the good or bad digestion of such-and-such a superior; I am tired of being treated in my native land with less respect than the first English scamp[2] who comes to parade his dullness and his gibberish among us.

I aspire only to independence—pardon me the word in considera-tion of the thing. By dint of courage and perseverance I shall end by enjoying it. I have already overcome my repugnance to writing and selling my verses for a living—the greatest step has been taken. Though I still write only under the capricious prompting of inspira-tion, I regard my verses, once written, as nothing but merchandise at so much per piece. I cannot understand my friends' *consternation*[3] (I do not know very well who "my friends" are).

There is no doubt that Count Vorontsov, who is an intelligent man, will be able to put me in the wrong in public opinion—a very flattering triumph which I shall let him enjoy to his heart's desire, since I am as little concerned about public opinion as about the dis-approbation or the admiration of our journals.

[71]

To Peter Andreevich Vyazemsky
June 7, 1824. From Odessa to Moscow.

Your wife[1] arrived today; she brought me your letters and Vasily Lvovich's madrigal,[2] in which he tells me: "you will live with a charming princess." Don't believe him, my dear fellow, and don't be jealous. Your letters gladdened me in many respects: you seem to have calmed down since your epigram.[3] Would that it had happened long ago! There is no such thing as criticism among us Chuvashes.[4] Cudgels are, somehow, unseemly; it would be ridiculous and stupid even to think of a duel. Your chick-chick, or shush-shush[5] is more like it. Send me Griboedov's epigram.[6] In yours there is an in-accuracy: "and such a *squeal*"; it should be "and such a *squeak*." Nevertheless, your epigram is charming. What you say about a journal[7] has already been fermenting in my head for a long time. The situation is that as regards Vorontsov nothing is to be hoped for. He is cold to everything other than himself, and playing the Maecenas has gone out of style. None of us would wish for the "magnanimous protection of an enlightened noble lord"; that fell into decay along with Lomonosov. Our contemporary literature is and must be nobly independent. We alone must undertake this task and we must unite. But just here there is a misfortune! We are all lazybones, one on top of another—we have the materials, we have the materialists, but *où est le cul de plomb qui poussera ça*?[8] Where will we find our compiler, our Kachenovsky, so to speak (in Milonov's sense—that a publisher, at least of *The Messenger of Europe*, need have only an a——)? Another misfortune. You are a *Sectaire*, and in this matter a lot, an awful lot of tolerance would be needed. I would consent to see Dmitriev on our band's title page, but would you let me have my Katenin? I renounce Vasily Lvovich; will you renounce Voeykov? Another misfortune: we are all accursed and scattered over the face of the earth—intercourse between us is difficult; there is no unanimity; every moment a golden *apropos*[9] slips away from us. The first thing: we must take all the periodicals in hand and make them respected— nothing would be easier if we were together and if we could publish on the morrow what we decided on at supper the day before. But now you send from Moscow to Odessa an observation on some stupidity of Bulgarin's, I send it to Birukov in Petersburg, and then after two months publish it in the *Révue des Bévues*.[10] No, my dear Asmodeus, let us give up the notion; we don't have a chance.[11]

I am glad that I was able to be of service to you with my half-kopek; please don't be in a hurry. I shall send you the first canto of *Onegin* by your wife. Maybe with the change of the ministry,[12] it can be published—meanwhile I am being offered two thousand rubles for the second edition of *The Prisoner of the Caucasus*. What do you think? Should I consent? After all, a third one is not out of the question.

Farewell, dear fellow; I am writing you half-drunk and in bed. Do answer.

[72]

To Lev Sergeevich Pushkin
June 13, 1824. From Odessa to Petersburg.

You ask my opinion with regard to Bulgarin's rubbish[1]—the devil take it. Why should you want to have anything to do with journalists in speech, or why should Vyazemsky in writing? One should have respect for himself. You, Delvig, and I can all three spit at the rabble of our literature—this is all my advice to you. Instead, write me something about *The Northern Flowers*.[2] Will it come out, and when will it come out? With the change of the ministry[3] I expect also a change of the censorship. And it is a pity . . . *le coupe était pleine*.[4] Birukov and Krasovsky were unbearably stupid, arbitrary, and oppressive. That couldn't last long. On what footing did Grandfather Shishkov begin his activities? He hasn't forbidden *The Fountain of Bakhchisaray* out of esteem for the sacred *Academic Dictionary* and his sinlessly formed word *vodomet*,[5] has he? All jokes aside, I expect good for literature on the whole, and I send him a kiss, not as a Judas-Arzamasian, but as a Bandit-Romantic.[6] I shall try to shove through to the gates of the censorship with the first chapter or canto of *Onegin*. Maybe we shall squeeze through. You demand of me details about *Onegin*—that is boring, my dear fellow. Some other time. Now I am not writing anything; I have bothers of a different kind. There are unpleasantnesses of every kind; it's boring and dusty. Princess Vera Vyazemskaya has arrived here, a good and a nice female—but I would have been gladder to see her husband. I have received the Zhukovsky.[7] The late departed was a capital fellow; may God grant him the heavenly kingdom! Listen, my dear fellow: I need money. Sell rights for a year to *The Prisoner of the Caucasus* for two thousand rubles. But, then, to whom? [. . . .][8] Farewell.

[73]

To Peter Andreevich Vyazemsky
June 24 or 25, 1824. From Odessa to Moscow.

I have been waiting for Trubetskoy's[1] departure, so that I can write you what I have a mind to. I shall begin with what concerns me most nearly. I quarreled with Vorontsov and engaged in a polemical correspondence[2] with him, which ended with my submitting my resignation. What the powers that be will end by doing is still un-known. Tiberius will be glad to take advantage, and European talk about the European mode of thinking of Sejanus[3] will make me responsible for everything. Meanwhile do not speak of this to any-one. And my head is whirling. By your letters to Princess Vera[4] I see that you too are Kyukhelbekery and nauseated;[5] you are sad about Byron, but I am very glad of his death,[6] as a sublime theme for poetry. Byron's genius paled with his youth. In his tragedies, not excluding even *Cain*, he is no longer that flaming demon who created *The Giaour* and *Childe Harold*. The first two cantos of *Don Juan* are superior to the following ones. His poetry noticeably changed. He was created completely topsy-turvy; there was no gradualness in him, he suddenly matured and attained manhood, sang his song, and fell silent; and his first sounds did not return to him again—after the fourth canto of *Childe Harold* we did not hear Byron, but rather some other poet wrote with a high, human talent. Your idea of glorifying his death in a fifth canto of his Hero[7] is charming. But it is not in my power—Greece defiled this idea for me. About the fate of the Greeks one is permitted to reason, just as of the fate of my brothers the Negroes[8]—one may wish both groups freedom from unendurable slavery. But it is unforgivable puerility that all enlightened European peoples should be raving about Greece. The Jesuits have talked our heads off about Themistocles and Pericles, and we have come to imagine that a nasty people, made up of bandits and shopkeepers, are their legiti-mate descendants and heirs of their school-fame. You will say that I have changed my opinion. If you would come to us in Odessa to look at the fellow countrymen of Miltiades, you would agree with me. And take a look at what Byron himself wrote several years ago in the notes to *Childe Harold*—where he alludes to the opinion of Fauvel, the French consul in Smyrna, if I remember correctly.[9] I promise you, however, some rhymes on His Excellency's death.[10]

I should like to chat with you about the change of the ministry.[11] What do you think about it? I am both glad and not glad. The motto of every Russian has long been "the worse, the better." The Russian opposition, made up, thanks to the Russian God, of our writers of all kinds whatever, was already approaching a certain im-patience, which on the sly I have been egging on, expecting some-thing to happen. But now Fita Glinka[12] is allowed to tell his mistress that she is divine, that she has heavenly eyes, and that love is a sacred feeling; the result will be that all the riff-raff will again calm down, that journals will begin to spout nonsense in their turn, the higher orders in their turn, and Russia in her turn. That is how Shishkov will turn the entire Mass into s——. On the other hand, money, *Onegin*, the holy scriptures of the Koran[13]—in general my selfishness.[14] Another word: I have given my brother permission to sell the second edition of *The Prisoner of the Caucasus*. I needed the money, and (as I have been saying) a third edition is always a possibility. And you are playing dirty tricks on me: You are being charitable to me and getting mixed up with the devil knows whom. You are a contention-provoking publisher—and although Gnedich[15] may not be a profitable friend, on the other hand he won't be charitable to the extent of a single kopek, and he peacefully stays at home, not quarreling with either Kachenovsky or Dmitriev.[16]

A.P.

You ought to send me some verses, too.

[74]

To ALEXANDER ALEXANDROVICH BESTUZHEV
June 29, 1824. From Odessa to Moscow.

Dear Bestuzhev, you were mistaken in thinking that I am angry with you—laziness alone has prevented me from answering your last letter (I have not received the other one). Bulgarin is a different matter. It is dangerous to correspond with that man.[1] It is much more fun to read him. You yourself judge: I happened once to be madly in love. I usually write elegies in such a case, just as another soils his bed. But is it a friendly deed to hang out my wet sheets to public view? God forgive you, but you disgraced me in the current [*Polar*] *Star*—by printing the three last verses of my elegy.[2] What the devil possessed me to write apropos of *The Fountain of Bakhchisaray* some additional, sentimental lines and to mention my elegiac beauty at this point! Imagine my despair when I saw them in print. The journal may fall into her hands. Just what will she think, seeing with what willingness I talk about her "with one of my Petersburg friends"? How could she know that I did not mention her name, that Bulgarin unsealed and published the letter, that the devil knows who delivered the Elegy to you, and that no one is to blame. I confess that I value one of this woman's thoughts more than the opinions of all the journals in the world and of all our public. My head has begun to whirl. I wanted simply to publish in *The Messenger of Europe* (the only journal I have no right to complain of), that Bulgarin had no right to make use of the correspondence of two private persons, still living, without their consent. But, crossing myself, I consigned all that to oblivion. I dashed it off and got it over with. I am sad, my dear fellow, that you are not writing anything. Just who will write? M. Dmitriev and A. Pisarev? They are fine ones! If the deceased Byron had got into a quarrel with the half-deceased Goethe,[3] even then Europe would not have budged to egg them on, or to dash cold water on them. The century of polemics has passed. Who cares about Dmitriev's opinion of Vyazemsky's opinion or about Pisarev's opinion of himself? I was forced to get mixed up with it, for I was summoned by M. Dmitriev for testimony.[4] But I shall not do it any more. My *Onegin* is growing. But there's not a devil of a chance to get it published. I thought our censorship would become more intelligent under Shishkov, but I see that with the old, things still go as of old. If you need my consent for the publication of *The Bandits*, seriously I absolutely shall not give it if they don't allow *žid* [Jew, or Yid, the deprecatory term] and *xarčevni* [dives] (the beasts! the beasts! the beasts!), and as for the *pop* [parish priest], to the devil with him. I shall end with a friendly commission—try to see Nikita Vsevolozhsky, the best of the momentary friends of my momentary youth.[5] Remind that dear, forgetful egotist that a certain A. Pushkin exists, just such another egotist, and an agreeable verse-writer. The same Pushkin sold him once upon a time a collection of his poems for a thousand rubles in paper money. Now he wants to buy them back from him at the same price. Will Aristippus[6] Vsevolodovich agree? I would offer him my friendship to boot, *mais il l'a depuis longtemps, d'ailleurs ça ne fait que* 1000 *roubles.*[7] Show him my letter. Take heart, and give me a quick answer, as the God of Job or Lomonosov says.[8]

[75]
To Peter Andreevich Vyazemsky
July 5, 1824. From Odessa to Moscow.
(Jottings)

The French are not a whit below the English in the field of history. If primacy is worth anything, remember that Voltaire was the first to take the new road—and to bring the lamp of philosophy into the dark archives of history. Robertson[1] said that if Voltaire had taken the trouble to indicate the sources of what he said, then he, Robertson, would never have written his *History*. Secondly, Lémontey[2] is a genius in the 19th century. Read through his *Survey of the Reign of Louis XIV*, and you will place him above Hume[3] and Robertson. Rabaut de Saint-Etienne[4] is trash.

July 5, 1824. Odessa.

The age of romanticism has not yet come for France. Delavigne[5] is floundering in the old nets of Aristotle[6]—he is a student of the tragedian Voltaire, and not of nature.

Tous les recueils de poésies nouvelles dites Romantiques sont la honte de la littérature française.[7]

Lamartine is good in his "Napoleon," in "The Dying Poet"[8]— generally speaking, he is good, with a certain new harmony.

No one loves charming André Chénier better than I do—but he is a classicist's classicist—he is simply redolent of ancient Greek poetry.[9]

Mark my words: the first genius in the fatherland of Racine and Boileau will break forth into such unrestrained liberty, into such literary Carbonarism,[10] that your Germans won't amount to a thing. But for the time being there is less poetry in France than here with us.

[76]
To Alexander Ivanovich Turgenev
July 14, 1824. From Odessa to Petersburg.

You have already learned, I suppose, that I have submitted my resignation; I am awaiting with impatience the determination of my fate, and I am looking toward your North with hope.[1] Isn't it strange that I reached an understanding with Inzov, but I could not manage to get along with Vorontsov; what happened was that he suddenly began to treat me with indecent disrespect. I could expect great unpleasantnesses, and with my request I anticipated his wishes. Vorontsov is a Vandal,[2] a courtier boor,[3] and a petty egotist. He saw in me a collegiate secretary, but I confess that I think somewhat differently of myself. Old Inzov would put me under arrest every time I would give a Moldavian boyar a beating.[4] True. But on the other hand the good mystic[5] at the same time would come to visit me and chat with me about the Spanish revolution. I do not know whether Vorontsov would put me under arrest, but he certainly would not come to me to discuss the constitution of the Cortes.[6] I shall eschew evil and do good:[7] I shall quit the service and take up rhyme. Knowing your old bent for the pranks of the accursed Muse, I meant to send you several stanzas of my *Onegin*, but I'm too lazy. I do not know whether they will allow this poor *Onegin* into the heavenly kingdom of print; in case they might, I shall try. The most recent change of ministry would have gladdened me completely if you had remained in your former post. This is a genuine loss for us writers; the dismissal of Golitsyn can scarcely compensate for it.[8] Farewell, dear and honored one! This letter will be delivered to you by Princess Volkonskaya,[9] whom you so love and who is so amiable. If you have not seen her daughter for a long time, then you will be astonished at the rightness and justness of her charming head. I embrace everybody; that is, very few indeed. I kiss the hands of Katerina Andreevna Karamzina and the Princess Golitsyna, *constitu-tionelle ou anti-constitutionelle, mais toujours adorable comme la liberté.*[10]

July 14.   A.P.

[77]
To Peter Andreevich Vyazemsky
July 15, 1824. From Odessa to Moscow.

Why are you chiding me in your letters to your wife? For my retirement, i.e., for my independence? Why don't you write to me? Will you come to see us in the southern dust? God grant it! But whether you would be able to get along with the local authorities— that is a question which I don't care to answer, although I could. Kyukhelbeker[1] is coming here. I am awaiting him with impatience. But he does not write me anything, either; why does he not answer my letter?[2] Have you given him *The Bandits*[3] for his *Mnemosyne*? I would send you something from *Onegin* but I can't: everything is branded with the stamp of rejection. I was about to get *The Prisoner* off my hands; but Oldekop's swindle[4] kept me from it. He has pirated *The Prisoner*, and I shall have to petition for redress under the laws. Farewell, my joy. Give me your blessing, Most Reverend Asmodeus.

July 15.

[78]

To VASILY LVOVICH DAVYDOV(?)
Between early June, 1823, and the end of July, 1824. From Kishinev or Odessa to Kamenka (?).
(Rough draft)

With astonishment I hear that you consider me an enemy of the liberation of Greece and an advocate of Turkish slavery. Apparently my words have been strangely misinterpreted to you. But whatever you may have been told, you ought not to have believed that my heart would ever feel ill-will for the noble efforts of a people in the process of being reborn. Regretting that I am compelled to justify myself to you, I shall repeat here, too, what I have said on occasion about the Greeks.

People, for the main part, are self-centered, uncomprehending, light-minded, ignorant, stubborn; an old truth which all the same bears repeating. They will rarely endure contradiction, and they never forgive disrespect; they are easily carried away by fine phrases, and they are glad to repeat anything new; and, having become accustomed to the new, they can no longer do without it.

When anything is generally held, then the general stupidity harms it to the same degree that unanimity helps it. Among the Europeans the Greeks have many more harmful advocates than reasonable friends. Nothing has yet been so much *of a people* as the Greek affair, although many things have been more important for Europe in a political sense.

[79]

To VASILY LVOVICH DAVYDOV (?)
Between early June, 1823, and the end of July, 1824. From Kishinev
or Odessa to Kamenka(?).
(Rough draft; in French)

[. . .]¹ from Constantinople—a crowd of cowardly beggars, thieves, and vagabonds² who were not even able to sustain the first fire of the worthless Turkish musketry, would form a strange troop, even in Count Vitgensteyn's³ army. As for the officers, they are worse than the soldiers. We have seen these new Leonidases in the streets of Odessa and Kishinev—we are personally acquainted with a number of them, we attest of their complete worthlessness—they have found the art of being dull even at the monent when conversation with them ought to interest every European—not the slightest idea of the art of war, no concept of honor, no enthusiasm—the French and the Russians who are here show them disdain of which they are only too worthy; they will endure anything, even blows of a cane, with composure worthy of Themistocles. I am neither a barbarian nor an apostle of the Koran,⁴ the cause of Greece interests me acutely; this is just why I become indignant when I see these poor wretches invested with the sacred office of defenders of liberty—

Letter 46

1. "I fear the Greeks [bearing gifts]."—Vergil, *Aeneid*, II, 49. Pushkin is again expressing his dissatisfaction at the mere five hundred rubles Gnedich had paid him for the first edition of *The Prisoner of the Caucasus*. Gnedich was a "Greek" because of his translation, then in progress, of Homer's *Iliad*.

2. Pushkin in various places expresses a negative reaction toward contemporary French literature, especially in the 1820's. Pushkin greatly preferred the English literature of his time to the German, but he preferred German literature to that of France, where Romanticism, with its rejection of classicism, came late.

3. That is, on an *occasion*, so that he could talk frankly.

Letter 47

1. Pushkin obtained a transfer to the chancellery of Count Mikhail Semenovich Vorontsov (1782-1856), later prince and field marshal, then newly appointed Governor General and Vicegerent of the Odessa and Bessarabia Territory. Vorontsov was noted for his Anglomania and his aristocratic ideas.

2. Pushkin is quoting Zhukovsky's translation of Byron's *Prisoner of Chillon*. New applications of sighing for "abandoned chains"—such as this passage—soon came to be almost commonplace in Russian.

3. Vasily Ivanovich Tumansky (1800-1860), minor poet then serving in Vorontsov's chancellery.

4. As elsewhere, Pushkin uses the word here with a double meaning, both "wallet" and "portfolio."

5. When Pushkin published the poem, he omitted ten lines at the end containing the autobiographical comments (probably relating to Maria Nikolaevna Raevskaya), for he had no wish to sing of unrequited love.

6. Semen Egorovich Raich (1792-1855), minor poet and translator, and journalist.

7. See Letter 44.

8. Pushkin received the small salary of seven hundred rubles in paper money for his post in the service. The stinginess of Pushkin's father was well known.

Letter 48

1. That is, the second editions (1828). The corrections noted by Pushkin were included in the second edition.

2. Pushkin gives textual corrections.

3. A paraphrase of a line from Zhukovsky's "Smaylho'me Castle" (1822), a translation of Sir Walter Scott's "Eve of Saint John" (1800).

4. Pushkin's objection is to sound as well as sense; as "corrected" by the censor the verse ends with an internal rhyme: *ej dnej*.

5. To an anonymous review in *The Messenger of Europe*.

6. A *burka* is a garment worn by mountaineers in the Caucasus. It is a kind of cloak or cape of felt and goat fur. The factuality of Pushkin's approach to the materials of poetry may be noted in Pushkin's self-defense here.

7. "To yon side." The expression is in Church Slavonic.

8. "On the next line." The two expressions here quoted make up a tetrameter line, but Pushkin wants the second expression printed, indented, on a second line.

9. "Upon this." In several letters Pushkin uses this tag.

10. Victor André Fournier, a Frenchman living with the Raevskys.

11. Pushkin, as an Arzamasian, had been on bad terms with Shakhovskoy in his Lyceum days.

12. Alexander Skarlatovich Sturdza (1791-1854), government official, and writer who defended the monarchy and Orthodoxy. His *brochure* was *La Grèce en* 1821-22.

13. Count Andrault de (Russ.: Alexander Fedorovich) Langeron (1763-1831), French general in Russian service, Governor General of New Russia, 1815-1823.

14. "That there is too much of the religiose in it."

15. Dmitry Petrovich Severin (1791-1865), Arzamasian and friend of Vyazemsky's; Pushkin had written an epigram on him in 1822.

16. Filipp Filippovich Vigel (1786-1856), Arzamasian, friend of Pushkin's, a pederast —hence the comment about Sodom-Kishinev; he was made Vice Governor of Bessarabia on December 1, 1824.

17. *The Bandit Brothers*.

18. Taken from the thirteenth-century Persian poet Saadi: "Many, like me, have visited this fountain, but some of them are no more; others have journeyed farther." Pushkin found the quotation in Moore's *Lalla Rookh*.

19. From Vyazemsky's verse epistle to Tolstoy the American, "To Tolstoy" (1818). Pushkin did not "leave" the epigram, because he did not wish to give the idea that Tolstoy the American was the original of the hero of the poem, and, besides, Pushkin was on very bad terms with him at this time.

Letter 49

1. A famous beauty, Karolina Adamovna Sobanskaya (1794-1885), one of Pushkin's loves in Odessa.

2. The Hanskys mentioned in this letter were a brother and sister or perhaps man and wife; Vatslav Hansky (Russian: Gansky, d. 1841) was then married to Evva (Evalina) Adamovna Hanskaya (1803-1882), who later married the French novelist Balzac, and they were living in Odessa. Pushkin gives Hansky as nickname the name of the hero of Byron's *Lara* (1814), and Mme. Hanskaya that of the heroine of Chateaubriand's *Atala* (1801). Mme. Hanskaya was Mme. Sobanskaya's sister.

3. The hero of the then popular Gothic novel *Melmoth the Wanderer* (1820), by Charles Robert Maturin.

4. Job, no doubt because of his patience, like the biblical patriarch's; Lovelace, as an unprincipled lady-killer, like the hero of Richardson's *Clarissa* (1747-1748).

5. Probably A. L. or V. L. Davydov.

Letter 50

1. Egor Kirillovich Varfolomey, rich and hospitable Kishinev noble.

2. See Genesis, Chaps. 13—19. Pushkin's poem is full of allusions to Vigel's being a sodomite. The allusion to Lot and his daughters, later in the letter, is to the same biblical story.

3. Dmitry Maximovich Shvarts (1797-1839), an official serving under Count Vorontsov; the "three acquaintances" are unknown.

4. A Kishinev lady: Pushkin's Letter 56 is addressed to her.

5. Pulkheria Egorovna Varfolomey (ca. 1800-1863), daughter of E. K. Varfolomey.

6. Nikita Stepanovich Zavalievsky (d. 1864), a government official under Count Vorontsov.

7. A. P. and M. A. Poltoratsky.

8. Nikolay Stepanovich Alexeev (1789-1850's-1860's), one of Pushkin's closest friends in Kishinev.

Letter 51

1. *The Fountain of Bakhchisaray.*

2. Sofia Stanislavovna Kiseleva, wife of General P. D. Kiselev. She was a famous beauty of the time, and Vyazemsky, who called her the "lascivious Minerva," was very much attracted to her.

3. Unknown.

4. *Journey over the Tavrida* (1823), by Ivan Matveevich Muraviev-Apostol (1768-1851).

5. Vyazemsky and Griboedov had written a comic opera with music by Alexey Nikolaevich Verstovsky (1799-1862), *Who Is the Brother; Who Is the Sister? Or, Deceit After Deceit.*

6. In Odessa Pushkin came to know and love Rossini's operas, including, among others, *The Barber of Seville* (1816).

7. Here we have the first mention in Pushkin's letters of his *Evgeny Onegin*, his most extensive work, both in size and in time of composition. It is also Pushkin's most famous, best loved, and most influential single work. He worked on it from 1823 to 1831, and later thought of returning to it (see Letter 576 and note). It is noteworthy that in his first reference to *Evgeny Onegin* Pushkin admits that the point of departure was Byron's epic satire, *Don Juan* (1819-1824). But see his disclaimer in Letter 111.

8. The quotation is from Krylov's "Little Raven" (1811).

9. "Angel of darkness, devil"—a pun in connection with Vyazemsky's "diabolical" nickname.

10. See Letter 41.

Letter 52

1. This note accompanied the manuscript of Pushkin's *Bandit Brothers*, which was subsequently published in Bestuzhev's and Ryleev's *Polar Star for* 1825. This "fragment" is the third of Pushkin's Byronic verse tales. Zhukovsky's translation of Byron's *Prisoner of Chillon* was in progress at the same time that Pushkin, not knowing of it, was writing his poem, and the Byronic genres and materials led to similarities. It was Pushkin's "misfortune" that Zhukovsky's translation appeared first (1822).

Letter 53

1. This correspondence has not survived.

2. Ivan Ivanovich Pushchin (1798-1859), one of Pushkin's two or three dearest friends from his Lyceum days.

3. The allusion is probably to Voltaire's tale, *Le Taureau blanc.*

4. Baratynsky's poetic epistle "To Gnedich, Who Advised the Poet to Write Satires"; it was published in 1827, without the allusion to Orest Mikhaylovich Somov (1793-1833), who worked for the Russian-American Company as a private citizen rather than a government official (hence "un-uniformed").

5. Alexander Efimovich Izmaylov (1779-1831), man of letters and publisher of the journal *The Well-Intentioned*, was also a government official with the rank of College Counsellor.

6. Khvostov, in his verse epistle "To Ivan Ivanovich Dmitriev," says "I love to write verses and give them to the press."

7. *Evgeny Onegin.*

8. Translation, into German, by Alexander Evstafievich Vulfert, of Pushkin's *Prisoner of the Caucasus*, as *Der Berggefangene*, and published in Petersburg in 1823.

Letter 54

1. Alexander Ardalionovich Shishkov (1799-1832), friend of Pushkin's from the Lyceum days.

2. Alexander Ivanovich Kaznacheev (1788-1881), official in Vorontsov's chancellery in Odessa.

Letter 55

1. While in the diplomatic service in England, Krivtsov had fallen in love with the mode of life of the British aristocracy and with castles. In 1823 he was the Governor of Tula.

Letter 56

1. Probably the family of Prince Mourouzi, former Hospodar of Jassy.

2. The manuscript here is very unclear. Instead of the reading *feuille de A[retino]*, the "small" Academy edition prefers the reading *temple de l'a[mour]*, "temple of love."

3. Pushkin had an exaggerated opinion of his own ugliness. He often compared his appearance to that of a monkey.

4. The manuscript is illegible here. The reading accepted in early editions, Mme. de Vorontsova (Countess Elizaveta Ksaverievna Vorontsova [1792-1880], wife of Count M. S. Vorontsov), is now rejected.

5. The reference is to *The Wandering Harlot*, usually attributed to Aretino. It contains descriptions of not thirty-six but thirty-eight erotic poses.

6. "S.," like "A.," below, has not been identified.

Letter 57

1. Orest Adamovich Kiprensky (1783-1836), artist-portraitist. His "Letter from Rome" was written and published in 1817.

2. A. I. Turgenev had helped get Pushkin transferred from Kishinev to Odessa.

3. Probably Otton Nikolaevich Gribko, an official close to Turgenev.

4. Probably Andrey Kharitonovich Chebotarev (1784-1833). a teacher and eccentric; the comment is apparently ironic.

5. Quotation from I. I. Dmitriev's "To My Friends" (1800).

6. Pushkin quotes stanzas four through six of the fifteen stanzas of his ode "Napoleon," which was written in July, 1821, not in the beginning of the year as he states. Napoleon died on May 5, 1821.

7. Pushkin quotes the last (fifteenth) stanza of the poem.

8. In 1820 Pushkin promised Karamzin that he would write nothing further against the state for two years.

9. Pushkin uses the Church Slavonic biblical quotation, "A sower went forth to sow his seed" (Luke 8:5), as epigraph of his "The Sower of Freedom in the Wilderness," which he quotes in the letter.

10. N. I. and S. I. Turgenev. The brotherhood may be their mutual acquaintances or perhaps the Arzamas society.

11. Ekaterina Andreevna Karamzina (1780-1851), wife of N. M. Karamzin, and half-sister of Prince Vyazemsky.

12. Zhukovsky had written verses in 1823 to Princess Charlotta (1807-1873), daughter of the Duke of Würtemburg, the affianced of Grand Duke Michael (1798-1840). Upon accepting the Orthodox faith, she changed her name to Elena Pavlovna.

13. From Byron, Zhukovsky translated only *The Prisoner of Chillon*. The gentle Zhukovsky translated only that with which he was in spiritual sympathy, and this did not include the darker or rebellious side of Byron.

Letter 58

1. In objections to details in *The Fountain of Bakhchisaray*.

2. The word *jazvitel'nyj* "biting, caustic, mordant" has the same root as *jazva* "ulcer."

Pushkin's use of the word to mean "wounding" is uncommon in modern literary Russian.

3. Anna Lvovna Pushkina (d. 1824), Pushkin's maiden aunt.

4. Pushkin supplies a new reading, omitting the offending expression.

5. Pushkin gives further textual corrections.

6. Griboedov's comedy was his *Woe from Wit*, one of the two or three best comedies in the Russian language. The rumor was that the "hero," Chatsky, was modeled on Chaadaev. Pushkins' wry comment about "present circumstances" is called forth by the following situation: When the "revolt" of enlisted men took place in the Semenovsky Regiment, in 1820, Chaadaev, who had appeared to be slated for a brilliant career, was ordered to report on the "revolt" to Alexander I, who was then abroad. When the "revolt" was sternly dealt with, Chaadaev was put in an ambiguous position with regard to all liberals. The upshot was that Chaadaev retired from the military service in 1822.

Letter 59

1. Pushkin gives textual corrections for *The Fountain of Bakhchisaray.*

2. Pushkin of course meant letters that he did not want the police to see, but Vyazemsky took Pushkin's "too weighty" literally (see Letter 68).

3. Kyukhelbeker's journal was *Mnemosyne*, which he published together with Prince Vladimir Fedorovich Odoevsky (1803-1869), Russian man of letters and later close associate of Pushkin. Pushkin calls Kyukhelbeker by the name of Anacharsis Cloots (1755-1794), a revolutionary fanatic of Prussian extraction, because of Kyuhelbeker's revolutionism and also his unrestraint and enthusiasm.

4. It was not published in either of the first two editions.

5. That is, "Merry Christmas."

6. The reference is to Vyazemsky's "Madrigal (To Two Beauties—Mother and Daughter)" (1823), to Sofia Stanislavovna Kiseleva and her mother, Sofia Konstantinovna Pototskaya, called "the beautiful Phanariot."

7. Anna Petrovna Zontag (1785-1864), a niece and friend of Zhukovsky's and a writer.

Letter 60

1. Pushkin's complaints here and his comments and titles cited below have to do with *The Polar Star for* 1824.

2. The reference is to Pushkin's lyric "The Flying Bank of Clouds Is Thinning Out." The concluding lines refer to Ekaterina Nikolaevna Raevskaya. When Pushkin himself printed the poem two years later, he left out the last three lines.

3. Pushkin quotes misprints.

4. Bestuzhev, in a letter of March 3, 1824, offered to Yakov Tolstoy to buy the rights to publish Pushkin's poems, if Tolstoy no longer wished to do so.

5. Ryleev used the word *duma*, a Ukrainian folk song, for the genre word for his lyrical-epical narrative poems on historical subjects. Pushkin did not think highly of Ryleev's works in this genre. Ryleev's *Voynarovsky* (1825) was a romantic verse tale following Pushkin and Byron.

6. Bestuzhev's story, "Castle Neuhausen," was written in the spirit of and in imitation of the historical novels of Sir Walter Scott, then very much in vogue.

Letter 61

1. The first of several journals published by Bulgarin. He began publication of *Literary Leaves* in 1823, and, with Grech, *The Northern Bee* in 1825.

2. An announcement, in *Literary Leaves*, of the imminent appearance of *The Fountain of Bakhchisaray*.

3. "The Flying Bank of Clouds Is Thinning Out" and "Nereid." See Letter 60 above. Bulgarin published the poem at Pushkin's request.

Letter 62
 1. N. N. Raevsky the Younger.
 2. Here, Alexander I.
 3. A joking reference to the usual manner of addressing letters at the time. For examples, see Letters 92, 144, 202.
 4. "Where it is well, there is the fatherland." Pushkin later applied the expression in bitter polemics to the Polish-Russian journalist Bulgarin.
 5. A quotation from a satirical song by Ryleev and Bestuzhev: "Ah, Where Are the Islands Where the *Tryn-Trava* Grows, Buddies!" Apparently freedom is meant by *tryn-trava* here; it grows in never-never land.
 6. "But why did you sing?" The question is from Lamartine's "Dying Poet."
 7. That is, in manuscript form. A. I. Turgenev and Pushkin's father quoted from the poem to acquaintances. The allusion to Voeykov has to do with unceremonious dealing with others' property, including pirating.
 8. Alexander Osipovich Kornilovich (ca. 1795-1834), journalist and historian, used this expression in dedicating an article in *The Polar Star for* 1824 to a baroness.
 9. The translation (1823) of Racine's *Phèdre* by Mikhail Evstafievich Lobanov (1787-1846), an untalented poet and dramatist.
 10. "Do you wish to discover his footprints. . . ." This quotation, like the remainder of the quotations in French in this letter, is from Racine's *Phèdre*. Pushkin begins with objecting to the inaccuracy of Lobanov's translation, and proceeds to a critique of Racine's play.
 11. Russianized form of Racine's given name.
 12. "Haughty, proud, and even a little savage, Hippolyte."
 13. The Scythians were an Asiatic people who in ancient times occupied the territory north of the Black Sea. Pushkin (and Russians in general) use the word to mean barbaric, savage; here the use is ironical.
 14. "Of a lie so black. . . ."
 15. Hugo's speech to his step-mother, to whom he had been affianced before his father married her, in Byron's *Parisina* (1815).
 16. "Where would you yourself have been. . . ?"
 17. Nickname for Kyukhelbeker.
 18. Letter unknown.
 19. Perhaps enclosed in Letter 57. Pushkin's "Lay of Oleg the Seer" was written in 1822 and published in Delvig's almanac *Northern Flowers for* 1825.

Letter 63
 1. See Letter 60.
 2. "Castle Neuhausen."
 3. "And that is saying a lot."
 4. Nikolay Alexandrovich Bestuzhev (1791-1855), older brother of A. A. Bestuzhev and, like him, a man of letters.
 5. *The Warrior of the Dun Steed,* by Osip Ivanovich Senkovsky (Polish: Jósef Sękowski, 1800-1858), Russian man of letters of Polish birth, professor of Arabian at the University of Petersburg. Later he edited the journal *A Library for Reading* and became an extremely popular writer under the pseudonym Baron Brambeus.

6. The poem "To My Dear One."

7. Akim Nikolaevich Nakhimov (1783-1815), poetaster.

8. "I bent the accents of her lovable and naive lips to the sweet laws of verse."— André Chénier, "Ode XI: The Young Captive Girl."

9. Pushkin's novel in verse, *Evgeny Onegin*. In the rough draft of this letter, Pushkin added, "It is written in stanzas perhaps even freer than the stanzas of *Don Juan*."

Letter 64

1. Of *The Fountain of Bakhchisaray*; apparently Vyazemsky's "parcel" contained part of the sale money.

2. Either *Evgeny Onegin* or *The Gypsies* (written 1823-24).

3. A phrase of Kornilovich; see Letters 62 and 63.

4. In *Literary News* (1823).

5. Vyazemsky's article on I. I. Dmitriev's life, included in the sixth edition of the latter's *Poems* (1823); Vyazemsky here compares Dmitriev and Krylov to the advantage of Dmitriev, an opinion in which posterity had not concurred. Pushkin's opinion of their relative merits is today universally held.

6. Lev Alexandrovich Naryshkin (1785-1846), a cousin of M. S. Vorontsov.

7. Prince S. G. Volkonsky.

Letter 65

1. This letter shows Pushkin's financial straits during his Kishinev and Odessa period.

Letter 66

1. A journal (1818-1826), published by A. E. Izmaylov.

2. Count Khvostov bought up his own works and donated them to friends and acquaintances; nobody would buy them.

3. Bulgarin published in his *Literary Leaves* in 1824, without permission, fragments from Letters 63 above and 74 below.

4. Ivan Grigorievich Senyavin (1801-1851).

5. Pushkin's letters to his father, here referred to, have not survived.

Letter 67

1. A two-weeks visit.

2. For seeing *The Fountain of Bakhchisaray* through the press and for his article "Instead of an Introduction: A Conversation Between the Publisher and a Classicist from the Vyborg Side or from the Vasilievsky Island," published together with it.

3. A fragment survives, dated 1823 or 1824, usually called "Of the Causes Delaying the Advance of Our Literature."

4. Mikhail Vasilievich Lomonosov (1711-1765), great Russian scientist and man of letters, a universal genius.

5. "From the clash of opinions, money will spring forth." Pushkin humorously substitutes the word "money" for "truth" in the saying.

6. Admiral Nikolay Semenovich Mordvinov (1754-1845), member of the State Council; he favored the liberation of the serfs.

7. Jean François Guichard (1731-1811), minor French poet.

8. That is, he would do anything to get *Onegin* published. Pushkin humorously paraphrases the Russian expression "to eat a fish (i.e., succeed in catching and eating a fish), or else go aground"—i.e., to succeed at whatever cost, or crash.

9. Fedor Fedorovich Matyushkin (1799-1872), a Lyceum comrade of Pushkin's; later a naval explorer and admiral.

10. Pushkin here compounds an allusion to an "Arsamasian" epigram with a pun.

Nightingale the Bandit is a hero of Russian folklore. In the epigram in point, which is probably directed at Count Khvostov, the poet is called, not a nightingale, but a "nightingale-bandit." Pushkin plays on the name of Bulgarin's fellow journalist and later associate Grech, as similar to *grač*, "rook."

11. In Letter 59.

Letter 68

1. This letter exists only in this fragmentary form, as excerpted in the document, *Of the Exile from Odessa to the Pskov Province, of the Collegiate Assessor Pushkin*. The letter was intercepted and read by the police; it resulted in Pushkin's being discharged from the civil service and exiled to his mother's estate of Mikhaylovskoe. Pushkin's "exile" to Kishinev and Odessa had been under the guise of an administrative transfer. After the judgment passed on him because of this letter, he was in actual exile and open disgrace. Some Russian editors think the letter was addressed to Vyazemsky.

2. About this time Pushkin began to be interested in and influenced by Shakespeare. The chief traces of this influence are in Pushkin's *Boris Godunov*, *Angelo* (a reworking of *Measure for Measure* into a narrative poem), and *Count Nulin* (a sort of parody of *The Rape of Lucrece*).

3. *Evgeny Onegin*.

4. One Dr. William Hutchinson, who came to Russia as personal physician to the Vorontsovs. He is reputed to have become, some five years later, a zealous priest of the Church of England.

5. "That no intelligent being, Creator and governor, can exist."

Letter 69

1. This letter was called forth by Pushkin's having been ordered to make an inspection trip to investigate a plague of locusts. Pushkin considered this assignment humiliating; however, he went.

2. Vorontsov.

3. This is the first mention in the Letters of Pushkin's real or imaginary aneurysm which he again tried to use later as a pretext for requesting release from exile.

Letter 70

1. Pushkin was not allowed to retire from the government service. See Letter 68 and notes.

2. An allusion to Vorontsov's well-known Anglophilism.

3. That is, at Pushkin's submitting his resignation from the service. Pushkin's attitude was that if he was required to perform the duties of his hitherto nominal position in the government service, then he had the right to resign.

Letter 71

1. Princess Vera Fedorovna Vyazemskaya (1790-1886), an intelligent woman who became one of Pushkin's best friends.

2. Unknown.

3. On Mikhail Alexandrovich Dmitriev (1796-1866), minor author who wrote a criticism of Vyazemsky's Introduction to Pushkin's *Fountain of Bakhchisaray*.

4. A tribe in east central Russia; Pushkin means barbarians, uncivilized people.

5. An allusion to Vyazemsky's epigram "To Journal Twins"; the two terms are to call and to quiet down chickens. Pushkins' emendation below is for the same epigram.

6. On M. A. Dmitriev and Alexander Ivanovich Pisarev (1803-1828), minor author of vaudevilles and translator.

7. For many years Pushkin wished to publish a journal or gazette; only in 1836 was this wish realized, with his *Contemporary*.

8. "Where is the lead bottom who will push this forward?"

9. *Kstati*. The emphasis is Pushkin's.

10. *Review of Howlers*. See Letter 38.

11. Pushkin juxtaposes and slightly paraphrases two colorful folk sayings: Pushkin's passage reads, literally, "for a snipe it's a long time to St. Peter's day [June 29] and still farther for an old peasant woman to St. Yury's day [November 26]."

12. I.e., a new head of the censorship. Admiral A. S. Shishkov was made Minister of Public Education on May 15, 1824. Pushkin had high hopes from this appointment, in spite of the earlier differences between the Arzamasians and members of Shishkov's literary group.

Letter 72

1. A carping note about the "high price" paid to Pushkin for his *Fountain of Bakhchisaray*.

2. Delvig's almanac *Northern Flowers for 1825*.

3. Shishkov was the new Minister of Public Education; see Letter 71.

4. "The cup was full," an ironical allusion to Psalm 23:5. Pushkins' point here is "the worse, the better," as in Letter 73.

5. Shishkov insisted that, rather than naturalizing foreign words into Russian, new words should be constructed on Russian roots. Thus he objected to *fontan*, which Pushkin uses, as borrowed from the French *fontaine*, preferring *vodomet* "water-thrower" for the word *fountain*. See also Letter 21.

6. That is, not as a traitor to the Arzamasians, a literary group which had been inimical to Shishkov's circle, but as the author of romantic verse tales, including among others *The Bandit Brothers*. Pushkin's point is that he is to be considered a literary "criminal" because he is a romanticist rather than a classicist, not because of his new ideas of diction and style.

7. Exactly what is not known.

8. Pushkin gives textual changes for *The Prisoner of the Caucasus*. One of them was that "for God's sake" it be "nights" instead of "days," as he had insisted in Letters 33 and 48.

Letter 73

1. Prince Peter Petrovich Trubetskoy (1793-1840), then in the civil service in Odessa.

2. It has not survived.

3. By Tiberius and his favorite, Sejanus, Pushkin means Alexander I and Count Vorontsov, respectively.

4. Princess Vera Fedorovna Vyazemskaya, his wife.

5. See Letter 27, note 13.

6. Vyazemsky, in his letters to his wife, then in Odessa, chiming in the general European lament over Byron's death at Missolonghi on April 19, 1824, kept on expressing the hope that Pushkin would write on Byron's death.

7. That is, a fifth canto of *Childe Harold*.

8. Another allusion to Pushkin's Abyssinian blood.

9. In the notes to *Childe Harold*, Canto II, Byron alludes to the opinion of Fauvel, the French consul in Athens. Byron quotes Fauvel's unfavorable opinions of the Greeks, but he blames the undesirable qualities of the Greeks of the time on their "slavery" under Turkish rule.

10. Several lines about Byron are included in Pushkin's "To the Sea" (1824).

11. Shishkov's appointment.

12. The Russian word *fita* (the name of the Russian letter beginning Glinka's first name, Fedor) means a scribbler.

13. A self-quotation of a line from *The Fountain of Bakhchisaray*; the verse rhyming with this one speaks of the "will of the khan"—i.e., the allusion is to Alexander I and Pushkin's exile.

14. In this elliptic passage, Pushkin expresses the opinion that a relaxation of the censorship was occurring under Shishkov; this he objects to, in that it might reduce the oppositional spirit of Russian writers and might also result in bad writing. Then he thinks of the advantages for himself in such a change from the severe censorship—the possibility of publishing *Evgeny Onegin* profitably, and even, he dares suggest, of his obtaining freedom from exile.

15. An allusion to Pushkin's dissatisfaction at Gnedich's payment for *The Prisoner of the Caucasus*.

16. Vyazemsky was then engaged in polemics with M. A. Dmitriev and Kachenovsky over Pushkin's *Fountain of Bakhchisaray*.

Letter 74

1. See Letter 66 and notes.

2. See Letter 60 and notes.

3. Byron had died in April, 1824; Goethe died eight years later, in 1832, at the age of 83.

4. M. Dmitriev expressed the opinion that Pushkin regretted the publication of Vyazemsky's foreword to *The Fountain of Bakhchisaray*.

5. See Letter 17.

6. Pushkin calls his friend Vsevolozhsky by the name of Aristippus, ancient Greek philosopher who taught that pleasure is the chief end of life.

7. "But he has had it for a long time already; besides, that makes only 1000 rubles."

8. Pushkin slightly changes a line from Lomonosov's "Ode IX: Taken from Job."

Letter 75

1. William Robertson, eighteenth-century Scotch historian. The source of Pushkin's quotation has not been discovered.

2. Pierre Edouard Lémontey. His *Essai sur l'établissement monarchique de Louis XIV* ... was published in 1818.

3. The reference is to David Hume's *History of England* (5 vols., 1754-1761).

4. Jean Paul Rabaut de Saint Etienne, French revolutionary and historian.

5. Casimir Delavigne, French poet and dramatist.

6. That is, he was concerned with the so-called "Aristotelian" unities of action, time, and place.

7. "All the miscellanies of the new poetry called Romantic are the shame of French literature."

8. Two of the "meditations" in Lamartine's *Nouvelles méditations poétiques* (1824).

9. Pushkin took this comment about Chénier from the rough draft of Letter 51.

10. I.e., revolutionism, like the political revolutionaries called Carbonari in Italy and France in the early nineteenth century.

Letter 76

1. Pushkin did not know that it had been decided on July 8, 1824, that he was to be exiled to Mikhaylovskoe.

2. That is, a barbarian.

3. *Xam*, here translated "boor," is the proper name Ham, after Noah's son in the Bible, who laughed when he saw his father drunk. The word had been given general usage in Russian in a "technical" sense by N. I. Turgenev.

4. Todoraki Balsh, a Moldavian nobleman whom Pushkin slapped when the former's wife insulted him; Pushkin has a rough draft of a poem on this event (1822).

5. Inzov was a Freemason.

6. The Spanish national legislature.

7. I Peter 3:11.

8. Another allusion to Shishkov's replacing A. N. Golitsyn as Minister of Public Education; Turgenev was Golitsyn's subordinate and this "change of ministry" resulted in his removal from this position.

9. Princess Sofia Grigorievna Volkonskaya (1786-1868); her daughter was Princess Alexandra Petrovna Volkonskaya (1804-1859).

10. "Pro-constitution, or anti-constitution, but always as adorable as liberty."

Letter 77

1. Pushkin's friends were trying to obtain a position for him in South Russia at the time; nothing came of it. Kyukhelbeker and Prince V. F. Odoevsky were then engaged, in Moscow, in publishing the almanac *Mnemosyne*.

2. It has not survived.

3. Pushkin's *Bandit Brothers* was published in *The Polar Star for* 1825.

4. In 1824 Evstafy Ivanovich Oldekop (d. 1845), without Pushkin's permission, published in Petersburg the Russian text of Pushkin's *Prisoner of the Caucasus*, together with Vulfert's translation of the poem into German (see Letter 53 and note).

Letter 79

1. The beginning of the letter is torn off and lost.

2. The reference is to the Greek revolutionaries.

3. General Peter Khristianovich Vitgensteyn (1768-1843).

4. That is, neither a Turk nor an adherent of the Turks.

PART IV

EXILE UNDER DOUBLE SURVEILLANCE—
MIKHAYLOVSKOE

August, 1824—December, 1825

80

To Alexey Nikolaevich Vulf
September 20, 1824. From Mikhaylovskoe to Dorpat.

Greetings, Vulf,[1] my friend! Come here in winter and drag
along Yazykov the poet to my place with you, to do some
horseback riding, to do some pistol-shooting. Lion,[2] my
curly-haired brother (not the Mikhaylovskoe steward), will
bring us, really, a treasure. . . . What? A box full of bottles.
Silence! We shall feast. Marvellous is the life of an anchorite!
In Trigorskoe until night and in Mikhaylovskoe until dawn;
the days are devoted to love, glasses reign at night; as for us,
now we are head-over-heels drunk, now dead-in-love.

Really, my dear fellow, I am awaiting you with open arms and
with uncorked bottles. Persuade Yazykov, and give him my letter.
Since I am under strict surveillance,[3] if you both see fit to answer me,
send your letters in a double envelope addressed to your sister Anna
Nikolaevna.

Good-by, my dear one.

A.P.

81

To Peter Andreevich Vyazemsky
October 8 or 10, 1824. From Mikhaylovskoe to Moscow.

My dear one, finally you have spoken up—I received your business
note[1] all right. Here is your answer. Oldekop stole and lied; my
father did not make any kind of bargain with him. I would send you
a power of attorney, but you'll have to wait. The official stamped
paper is in the city, a certain kind of witnessing must be performed in
the city—and I am in a remote village. If you can get along without
it, begin actions, my sole, active friend! By my uncle's letter I see
that Princess Vera Fedorovna has gotten there; you are in no way
worthy of your wife (unless in your verses, and you no longer write
them). I shall write her without delay; I have been wanting to know
for sure where she now is. *En attendant mettez moi à ses pieds et dites*

lui qu'elle est une âme charmante.[2] I shall not tell you anything about
my way of living—it is boring, and that is all.

What is Count Vorontsov like?

Half-hero, half-ignoramus, and, to boot, half-scoundrel! . . .
But in the last instance there is however the hope that at last
he will be a complete one.[3]

Apropos of verses: today I have finished my poem *The Gypsies.* I
do not know what to say about it. For the time being I am sick of
it; I have just finished it and have not had time to wash off my
besweated balls. I am sending you a small memento for the repose of
the soul of God's servant Byron[4]—I would have undertaken a whole
requiem, but it is boring to write for myself alone or multiplying in
my head by Birukov's stupidity and dividing by Krasovsky's.
Brother Lion sends you greetings. Send me some verses; I am dying
of boredom.

[82]
To Vasily Andreevich Zhukovsky
The end of October, 1824. From Mikhaylovskoe to Petersburg.

I do not know whether you have received my very essential
letter;[1] in case you have not, I shall repeat briefly a matter which
touches me to the quick. Eight-year-old Rodoes Sophianos, the
daughter of a Greek who fell a hero in the battle of Skulyany, is
being brought up in Kishinev at Katerina Khristoforovna Krupen-
skaya's, the wife of the former vice governor of Bessarabia.[2] Can't
the orphan be given refuge? She is the niece of a Russian colonel,[3]
and consequently can be considered of noble rank. Move Maria's[4]
heart, O poet! and we shall justify the ways of providence. I have no
intention of talking about myself. I cannot calmly think all this
through; perhaps I would anger you, if I poured out what I have on
my heart. My brother will take you verses of mine. I am awaiting
yours as a consolation. I embrace you warmly, though sadly.
Remember me to the family of Karamzin, and tell them that for
them I am the same as before. Embrace for me the ones of them you
can; to the others—all my soul.

[83]

To PETER ALEXANDROVICH PLETNEV
The end of October, 1824. From Mikhaylovskoe to Petersburg.
(Rough draft)

You published my uncle:[1] The creator of *The Dangerous Neighbor* was very deserving of that, even though the defunct Conversation Society did not spare his personage. . . . Now publish, friend, the fruits of my vain labors;[2] but for Phoebus' sake, my Pletnev, when will you publish yourself?

I am nonchalantly and joyfully relying on you with regard to my *Onegin*! Call my Areopagus together: you, Zhukovsky, Gnedich, and Delvig—I am awaiting for this court to hold trial over it, and I shall humbly accept its decision.

I am sorry that Baratynsky is not among you; he is writing, they say.[3]

[84]

To VERA FEDOROVNA VYAZEMSKAYA
The end of October, 1824. From Mikhaylovskoe to Odessa.
(Rough draft; in French)

Beautiful, good Princess Vera, charming and generous soul! I shall not thank you for your letter, for words would be too cold and too feeble to express to you my emotion and my gratitude. . . . Your sweet friendship would suffice any soul less selfish than mine; it alone has consoled me, such as I am, for many sorrows, and it alone has been able to calm the attack of ennui which is consuming my stupid existence. You wish to know of this stupid existence. What I foresaw has come true. My presence in the midst of my family has only redoubled my afflictions, already real enough. I have been reproached with my exile. They believe that they are involved in my misfortune. They claim that I am preaching atheism to my sister, who is a heavenly creature, and to my brother, who is very amusing and very young, who has been admiring my verses, and whom I very assuredly bore. God only knows whether I am thinking of him. My father has had the weakness to accept an employment which in any case places him in a false position with regard to me;[1] as a result, I spend on horseback and in the field all the time I am not in bed. All that reminds me of the sea saddens me—the noise of a fountain makes me literally ill. I believe that a beautiful sky would make me weep with frenzy; *no slava bogu nebo u nas sivoe, a luna točnaja repka.* . . .[2] As regards my neighbors, I simply made a point of rebuffing them in the beginning; now they do not bother me. I enjoy among them the reputation *of an Onegin*—and so I am a prophet in my own country.[3] So be it. As my sole expedient, I often see a good old neighbor-woman[4]—I listen to her patriarchal conversations. Her daughters, unappealing enough in all respects, play for me some Rossini which I sent for. I am in the best possible position to complete my novel in verse, but boredom is a frigid Muse, and my poem is progressing but little. Here, however, is a stanza[5] which I owe you—show it to *Prince Peter.*[6] Tell him not to judge it all from this sample.

Farewell, my esteemed Princess, I am very sadly at your feet; show this letter only to those whom I love and who take interest in me from friendship and not from curiosity. In the name of heaven, a word about Odessa—about your children! Have you consulted Mily's[7] doctor? what is he doing, *i čto Mili?*[8]

The prince has [. . . .]

[85]
To Nikita Vsevolodovich Vsevolozhsky
The end of October, 1824. From Mikhaylovskoe to Petersburg.
(Rough draft)

I cannot bring myself to believe that you have forgotten me, dear Vsevolozhsky—you do remember Pushkin who has spent so many merry hours with you—Pushkin whom you have often seen both drunk and in love, not always faithful to your Saturdays,[1] but your invariable comrade in the theater, the confidant of your pranks, Pushkin who sobered you up on Good Friday and led you by the hand into the church of the theatrical management, so that you might pray to the Lord God and look your fill at Mme. Ovoshnikova.[2] This same Pushkin has the honor to remind you now of his existence, and he is proceeding to a certain matter which touches him closely. . . . Do you remember that I half sold, half lost at cards to you the manuscript of my poems? For, you know, bad luck at gambling

gives rise to recklessness. I repented, but too late. Now I have
decided to atone for my sins, beginning with my poems; a large part
of them are below mediocrity and deserve only complete destruction,
but I should like to save certain ones. Dear Vsevolozhsky, the Tsar is
not giving me freedom! Sell me back my manuscript, for the same
price of 1,000[3] (I know you are not going to quarrel with me; I
would not wish to take them for nothing). I shall deliver you the
money with gratitude as soon as I net it—I hope my verses will not
gather dust at Slenin's. Think it over, and give me an answer. I
embrace you, my joy; I also embrace your tiny Vsevolod. Some day
we shall see each other . . . some day. . . .

[86]
To BORIS ANTONOVICH ADERKAS
The end of October (31 ?), 1824. From Mikhaylovskoe to Pskov.
(Fragment)
Dear Sir, Boris Antonovich,
    The Sovereign Emperor, of His Highest Will, has deigned to
send me to my parents' estate, thinking thus to ease their grief and
their son's fate. The government's insignificant charges against me
have had a powerful effect on my father's heart and have exacerbated
his mistrustfulness, forgivable to old age and to his tender love for
his other children. I have decided, for his peace of mind and for my
own, to ask His Imperial Majesty to be so kind as to transfer me to
one of his fortresses. I am awaiting this last favour from Your
Excellency's intercession.[1]

[87]
To VASILY ANDREEVICH ZHUKOVSKY
October 31, 1824. From Mikhaylovskoe and Trigorskoe to
Petersburg.
    Dear fellow, I resort to you. Judge of my position. When I came
here I was met by all as well as could be, but soon everything
changed. My father, frightened by my exile, has been constantly
reiterating that the same fate awaits him. Peshchurov,[1] appointed to
have surveillance over me, had the shamelessness to offer my father
the duty of unsealing my correspondence, in short, of being my spy.
My father's hot temper and irritable touchiness would not permit

me to have an explanation with him; I decided to be silent. My father began to reproach my brother to the effect that I was teaching him godlessness. I still kept silent. They received a document regarding me. Finally, desiring to remove myself from this painful position, I went to my father, I asked his permission to explain my position frankly. . . . My father flared up. I bowed, mounted a horse, and left. My father called my brother and ordered him to have nothing to do *avec ce monstre, ce fils dénaturé.* . . .[2] (Zhukovsky, think of my position, and judge.) My head began to seethe. I went to my father, I found him with my mother, and I blurted out everything that had been bothering me for three whole months. I ended by saying that I was talking to him for the last time. My father, taking advantage of the absence of witnesses, dashed out and declared to the whole household that "I had beat him, wanted to beat him, raised my hand threateningly, could have given him a thrashing. . . ." I am not justifying myself to you. But just what does he want for me, in accusing me of a felony? The mines of Siberia and the deprivation of honor? Save me, either with a fortress or with the Solovetsky Monastery.[3] I say nothing to you of what my brother and sister are enduring on account of me. Once more, save me.

October 31.   A.P.

Hurry: my father's accusation is known to the whole household. Nobody believes it, but everybody repeats it. The neighbors know. I do not wish to make explanations to them. If it should reach the government, judge what would happen. To try to prove in court my father's slander would be horrible for me, but there is no court for me. I am *hors la loi.*[4]

P.S. You need to know that I have already written a paper to the governor, in which I make the request to him regarding the fortress, without saying anything about the reasons.[5] Praskovia Alexandrovna Osipova, at whose house I am writing you these lines, has persuaded me to make this confidence to you. I confess, I am a little vexed at myself, and, my dear fellow, my head is going round and round.

Anna Petrovna Kern, 1820's.   *Silhouette.*

Pushkin's Sketch for Chapter 1 of *Evgeny Onegin*.

[88]

TO LEV SERGEEVICH PUSHKIN

Between November 1 and 10, 1824. From Trigorskoe to
Petersburg.

My affairs are still in the same condition. I am rarely in Mikhaylovskoe. Annette[1] is very amusing; our sister will recount my new
stunts to you.[2] Everyone there is sorry for you, but I am jealous of
you and I berate you. Deadly boredom is everywhere.

Tell Zhukovsky from me to keep mum about the occurrences he
knows about.[3] I have absolutely no desire to wash our dirty Mikhaylovskoe linen in public—and you, dear fellow, keep your tongue in
check.

Have you seen all the saints? Is Peter[4] full of hubbub? How was
your arrival, and how about *Onegin*?[5]

N.B. Send me (1) *Oeuvres de Le Brun*,[6] odes, *élégies*, etc.—you'll find
them at St. Florent's.[7] (2) Sulphur matches. (3) Cards, i.e., playing
cards (tell Mikhaylo[8] about this; let him keep and sell them). (3) *The
Life of Emelka Pugachev*.[9] (4) Muraviev's *Journey over the Tavrida*. (5)
Some mustard and cheese, but you will bring this to me yourself.
How are our literary aristocrats and how are the riff-raff?

I am toiling for the glory of the Koran,[10] and I have written a
thing or two besides—I'm too lazy to send it.

Farewell. You'll have to give up Nashchokin,[11] Saburov,[12] wine,
and Voeykova[13] by and by—or else you will be a *freluquet*[14]—which
is much worse than a *Mirtil*[15] and a *godelureau dissolu*.[16]

Yazykov will be in Dorpat no earlier than January.

My greeting to everybody—write and be lively about it.

[88a]

TO LEV SERGEEVICH PUSHKIN

Between November 1 and 10, 1824. From Mikhailovskoe to
Petersburg.

Brother, here is a little picture for *Onegin*—find an artist with a
skilful and rapid pencil.[1]

If the picture is a different one, have everything in the same
position. The same scene, do you hear? I absolutely must have that.

And send me galoshes by Mikhail.[2]

[89]

To Lev Sergeevich Pushkin

The first half of November, 1824. From Mikhaylovskoe to
Petersburg.

Brother, will you send me the German critique of *The Prisoner of
the Caucasus*[1] (ask Grech for it), and some books, for God's sake,
some books. If the publishers do not wish to honor me by sending
me their almanacs, then tell Slenin to forward them to me, including
Bulgarin's *Thalia*.[2] Apropos of *Thalia*,[3] a few days ago Evpraxia[4] and
I compared measurement with a belt and our waists turned out to be
identical. One of two things follows: either I have the waist of a
fifteen-year-old girl, or she has the waist of a twenty-five-year-old
man. Evpraxia pouts and is very sweet. I quarrel with Anetka; I am
fed up with her! Some more errands: send me my manuscript book
and the portrait of Chaadaev,[5] and the *ring*[6]—I am sad without it;
risk it with Mikhaylo.[7] I hope the bandits have not plundered you.
N.B.: How can you travel without a weapon! That is not done even
in Asia.

How is *Onegin* doing? [. . . .][8]

Don't forget to write, not *Fon-Vizin* but *Fonvizin*.[9] What kind of
an infidel is he? He is a Russian of the most Russian. Rumor here has
it that the governor[10] is inviting me to Pskov. If I do not receive a
special *command*, I probably shall not budge from the place—unless
Father and Mother drive me away. But I am ready for everything.
However, have a chat, my intercessor, with Zhukovsky and with
Karamzin. I am not asking half-mercies of the government; that
would be a half-measure, and a most pitiful one. Let them leave me
as I am, until the Tsar decides my fate. Knowing his firmness and,
if you like, his stubbornness, I would have no hope for a change of
my lot, except that toward me he has acted not only sternly, but even
unjustly. I rely not on his indulgence, but on his justice. However
that may be, I do not wish to be in Petersburg, and I shall probably
not set foot at home again.[11] I send sister many kisses.[12] My friends
likewise, you especially. Some poems, poems, poems! *Conversations
de Byron*! Walter Scott![13] That is food for the soul. Do you know
how I spend my time? I write memoirs[14] until dinner; I dine late.
After dinner I ride on horseback. In the evening I listen to fairy tales,

and thereby I am compensating for the insufficiencies of my accursed upbringing. How charming these fairy tales are! Each is a poem! Oh, my God, I almost forgot! Here is a task for you: the historical, dry information about Senka Razin,[15] the only poetic figure in Russian history.

Farewell, my joy. How about Baratynsky's Finnish girl?[16] I am waiting.

[90]
To Lev Sergeevich Pushkin
The early 20's of November, 1824. From Mikhaylovskoe to Petersburg.

Tell my guardian genie, my Zhukovsky, that, thank God, all has ended. My letter to Aderkas is in my possession.[1] Our folks have reached their destination, I should think; and I am alive and well. What are you having? a flood?[2] It serves accursed Petersburg right! *voilà une belle occasion à vos dames de faire bidet.*[3] I am sorry about Delvig's *Flowers;*[4] and will he be delayed long in the Petersburg mire? What about the wine cellars? I confess that my heart aches for them, too. Will no Noah be found among you, to plant a vineyard? It is no joke to go about stark naked in Holy Russia; the Hams would laugh.[5] That's all nonsense, though. And here is something important: Aunty has died![6] I am going to Svyatye Gory tomorrow, and I shall order prayers or a requiem to be sung, whichever is cheaper. I think our folks will set out for Moscow; pleasant journey! Publish, publish *Onegin* and the "Conversation"[7] with it. Embrace Pletnev and Gnedich; I shall write both by the next post. Here is something for you: Anna Nikolaevna [Vulf] is angry with you. Rokotov[8] told Praskovia Alexandrovna [Osipova] what was in your letters to *Lubny*[9] and to Mother. Again gossip! and you're a fine fellow! All the same, she ordered me to kiss you soundly, you *trifler.* Evpraxia [Vulf] is killingly funny; I am suggesting to her that she start up a philosophical correspondence with you. She keeps on envying her sister for writing and receiving letters. Send by Mikhaylo [Kalashnikov] everything that has escaped destruction in the Alexandrian conflagration,[10] and the books I mention in my letter to Sister. Send me a Bible, a Bible! and without fail one in French. The way I am living is still the same: I am not writing any poems, I am continuing my Memoirs, and I am reading *Clarissa*.[11] What an insufferably boring fool she is! I am waiting for letters from you: How is Vsevolozhsky? How about my manuscript? What about my letter to Princess Vera Fedorovna? Will the little picture be in *Onegin*?[12] What are the *Polar* gentlemen doing?[13] How is Kyukhlya? Farewell, my dear fellow. Stay well, and don't drink yourself drunk, as the aforementioned did after his flood.[14] N.B. I am very glad of this flood, because I am peeved: You will have a famine, do you hear? Hurry Delvig along, and send me Baratynsky's Finnish girl,[15] or else I shall curse you. Tell Sister that I received a letter to her from dear cousin Countess Ivelich[16] and I unsealed it, supposing that it was as much an answer to me as to her: in it is a notification about the flood, about Kolosova;[17] it shows intelligence, amiability, and everything. Kiss her for me, i.e., Sister Olga, and my friendly handclasp to Countess Ekaterina [Ivelich]. Tell Saburov not to play the fool; shame him out of it. Write me.

Ah, dear one, a rich thought! I unsealed my letter on purpose. *Barrels* no doubt *per fas et nefas*[18] are being sold in Petersburg—buy what you can, the cheapest and the best. This flood is an occasion.

[91]
To Vasily Andreevich Zhukovsky
November 29, 1824. From Mikhaylovskoe to Petersburg.

I regret, dear, honored friend, that I have caused all this alarm;[1] but what was I to do? I was exiled for a line of a stupid letter;[2] what would have happened if the government should find out about my father's accusation? That smells of the hangman and the prison camp. My father said afterward: "What a fool, what he is justifying himself in! and he would even have dared to beat me, too! and I would have had him bound!" Just why did he accuse his son of such unheard-of evil-doing? "And how did he dare, while talking with his father, to gesticulate improperly?" This is inconsequential. "And he has killed his father with his words!" A play on words, and nothing else. No matter what you say, even poetry won't help in this.

What about it, dear fellow? Will there be something for my little Greek girl?[3] She is in a pitiful plight, and her future is even more pitiful. The daughter of a hero, Zhukovsky! Heroes are akin to poets through poetry. But half-Milord Vorontsov[4] is not even a half-hero.

I regret that he is immortal in your verses, but nothing can be done about that now. Yesterday I received a letter from Vyazemsky, a killingly funny one. How has he been able to preserve his merry disposition in Russia? You will see the Karamzins—I love you and them with passion. Tell them, from me, whatever you like.

November 29.

[92]
TO PETER ANDREEVICH VYAZEMSKY
November 29, 1824. From Mikhaylovskoe to Moscow.

I am fed up with Oldekop, the m—— f—— s.o.b.! Let's spit on him and call it quits. Your proposal regarding my elegies is unrealizable, and here is why: In 1820 I copied out my rubbish, and I intended to publish it by subscription; I printed tickets and disposed of about forty. Then I lost my manuscript at cards to Nikita Vsevolozhsky (of course, with a certain proviso). Meanwhile I have been compelled to flee from Mecca to Medina,[1] my Koran started going from hand to hand, and the true believers are still awaiting it. Now I have given my brother the task of seeking out and buying back my manuscript, and then we shall proceed to the publication of the elegies, poetic epistles, and the miscellaneous things. It must be announced in the newspapers that, since the tickets may have been lost on account of the lengthy delay in publication, the name and address will suffice for the receipt of copies, for (let us tell the lie, to be on the safe side) the names of all the ladies and gentlemen subscribers are in the Publisher's hands. If I incur losses and do lose several copies, there will be nobody to complain of; I myself am to blame (this must remain *between us*). My brother took *Onegin* to Petersburg and will print it there. Don't be angry, dear fellow; I feel that I am losing in you the one who would best look out for my interests, but in my present circumstances any other publisher of mine would willy-nilly attract attention and displeasure upon himself. I am astonished at how Tanya's letter[2] has turned up at your house. N.B.: Explain this to me. I answer your criticism: A *neljudim* is not a misanthrope, i.e., one who hates people, but one who flees from people. Onegin is a *neljudim* for his country neighbors; Tanya supposes that the reason for this is "in the wilds, in the village, everything is boring to him," and that only glitter can attract him. . . . Anyway, if the sense is not completely exact, then by the same token there is more truth in the letter; it is the letter of a woman, what's more of one of seventeen, and what's still more of one in love! My dear fellow, what about your prose about Byron? I can hardly wait. Hasn't the death of my aunt *frétillon*[3] inspired Vasily Lvovich to make any translation? Isn't there at least an epitaph?

Write me: In care of Her Excellency Paraskovia Alexandrovna Osipova, Opochka, the village Trigorskoe, for delivery to A.S., and that is all, but for the envelope find a hand a little more legible than yours. Farewell, kind listener; answer me to what I say between the lines. I have written Princess Vera; has she received my letter?[4] I send her not my respects but my adoration.

November 29.

[. . . .][5]

[93]
To Lev Sergeevich Pushkin and Olga Sergeevna Pushkina
    December 4, 1824. From Mikhaylovskoe to Petersburg.
Kyukhlya ought to be ashamed for printing, incorrectly, "my demon."[1] "My demon!" After this he will print even the Creed with mistakes. Just for that, don't give him "The Sea" or a drop of poetry from me.
    N.B.: Publisher of *Onegin*,

Verses are only an amusement for you, it costs you *little* to sit down to them.[2]

Do you understand? And, in addition, couldn't the date 1823 be placed under the "Conversation"? The verse "Whether all life alone, whether two nights," must be removed, and that's a pity—it is a good one. It is a pity too, that the poet did not rail at posterity in the presence of his bookseller. *Mes arrière-neveux me devraient cet ombrage.*[3] Do what you please with the journalists. I give you my trifles for pocket money; sell or give away what you can remember, but I am not up to copying them. Mikhaylo[4] brought me everything all right, except that there is no Bible. The Bible is for a Christian what a history is for a nation. Karamzin's *History* at first began with this phrase, turned around.[5] I was present when he changed it. Closing the theater and forbidding balls is a sensible measure.[6] Decency demanded it. Of course, the populace does not participate in the amusements of the upper class, but in time of public misfortune it must not be exasperated with offensive luxury. Shopkeepers, seeing a brightly illuminated main floor, might break out the plate-glass windows, and there would be losses. You see that I am being impartial. I should like to praise other measures of the government, too, but the newspapers speak only of the million which has been distributed. A million is a great amount—but what about salt, bread, oats, and wine? It would do no harm to think about this in the winter, either by oneself or in a committee. I cannot get the flood out of my mind. It is by no means so funny as it might seem at first glance. If you should take the notion to help any unfortunate one, help him with *Onegin* money. But, I ask you, without any ado, either oral or written. It is by no means funny to stand in *The Invalide*[7] alongside the idyllic collegiate assessor Panaev. Send me Baratynsky's *Eda*. Oh! What a Finn he is! But if she is nicer than my Circassian girl,[8] I shall hang myself from the two pines,[9] and I shall never have anything to do with him again.

December 4.

Dear Olya, I thank you for your letter. You are very sweet, and I love you very much, even though you do not believe it. *Si ce que vous dites concernant le testament d'Anna Lvovna est vrai, c'est très joli de sa part. Au vrai j'ai toujours aimé ma pauvre tante, et je suis fâché que Chalikof ait pissé sur son tombeau.*[10] Our nursemaid[11] has fulfilled your commission; she went to the Svyatye Gory and had them do a requiem or whatever was necessary. She kisses you; I do, too. Your Troegorskoe[12] girl friends are unendurable fools, except their mother. I am seldom at their house. I am staying at home and waiting for winter.

Lev! Burn up my letter.

Give my greetings to Vasily Vasilievich Engelgardt[13] and to Gnedich, and to Pletnev, and to *Onegin*, and to Slenin. Send me *Antiquity*:[14] that is a pleasant novelty. Hurry Delvig up;[15] I hope he has not incurred any losses. How is blind Kozlov?[16] Have you read *Onegin* to him?

[94]

TO ARKADY GAVRILOVICH RODZYANKO
December 8, 1824. From Mikhaylovskoe to Lubny.

Dear Rodzyanko, your greetings delighted me; since you have remembered me, won't you bring yourself to write me a few lines? They would solace my loneliness.

Explain to me, dear one, just what Anna Petrovna Kern is like, who has written a lot of kind things about me to her cousin?[1] They say she is an extremely sweet thing—but *the grass is greener across the fence at Lubny.*[2] In any case, knowing your amorousness and your *unusual talents* in all lines, I suppose your business is done or half done. I congratulate you, my dear fellow: write me an elegy or at least an epigram on all that.

Enough rubbish. Let us talk about poetry, i.e., about yours. What about your romantic poem *Ukrainian*?[3] You rascal! Don't crowd me at my own trade—write satires, even on me, but don't undercut me in my romantic shop. Incidentally, Baratynsky has written a poem (do not get angry—about a Finnish girl), and they say this Finnish girl is marvelously sweet.[4] And I, about a Gypsy Girl;[5] what do you think of me? Hurry up and pass along your *Ukrainian Girl*—'at a boy, Parnassus! 'at a boy, heroines! 'at a boy, honorable company! I can imagine how Apollo, looking at them, will cry out: "Why are you bringing me the wrong one?" But just what kind do you want, accursed Phoebus? A Greek girl? An Italian girl? Wherein are they worse than a Finnish girl or a Gypsy girl? C—— is all the same — f——! That is, enliven us with a ray of inspiration and glory.

If Anna Petrovna is as sweet as they say, then no doubt she is of my opinion. Check with her and see. My greetings to Porfiry[6] and to all my old friends.

Farewell, Ukrainian sage, vicegerent of Phoebus and Priapus! Your straw hat is more comfortable than any other crown; your Rome is the village; you are my Pope; bless me, singer.

December 8.

[95]

To Dmitry Maximovich Shvarts
About December 9, 1824. From Mikhaylovskoe to Odessa.
(Rough draft)

The tempest seems to have died down, and I dare peek out of my nest and chirp at you, dear Dmitry Maximovich. Here I have already been in this remote village four months. It is boring, but nothing can be done about it; there is no sea here, no southern sky, no Italian opera.[1] But on the other hand there are no locusts[2] or milords Uorontsov.[3] My isolation is complete—idleness is triumphal. There are few neighbors near me; I am acquainted with only one family[4] and I see it rather seldom. I am on horseback the whole day, and in the evening I listen to fairy tales being told by my nursemaid, the original of Tatiana's nursemaid;[5] I think you saw her once. She is my only girl friend—and only when with her am I not bored. About Odessa, not a whisper. My heart begs for news. For a long time I have not dared to engage in correspondence with the comrades I left behind—for a long time I have held back, but I couldn't restrain myself. For God's sake, a living word about Odessa—tell me what is going on with you. Tell me, first, whether little Countess Gurieva[6] has recovered; I cordially wish you every happiness, honor, and blessing.

[96]

To Lev Sergeevich Pushkin
About (not later than) December 20, 1824.
From Mikhaylovskoe to Petersburg.

[Alexey Nikolaevich] Vulf is here; I have not said anything to him yet,[1] but I am waiting for you—come either with Praskovia Alexandrovna [Osipova] or with Delvig; we must have a conference without fail.

I wrote you a letter and sent it with Rokotov—get this letter without fail. From the stupidity of my years, I sent you a little Christmas carol.[2] Thoughtless young Rokotov might lose the letter —and it would not amuse me in the slightest to land in the fortress *pour des chansons*.[3]

In the name of Christ and God I beg you to hurry and drag *Onegin* out from under the censorship.⁴ As for fame, f—— it; I need money. Do not bargain long over the verses—cut, tear, shred, even all 54 stanzas, but some money, for God's sake, some money!

A most amusing affair has arisen with me and the Trigorskoe people—I don't have time to tell it to you, but it is killingly funny. I thank you for the books, and send me all possible calendars, except the Court and the Academic.⁵ By the way, the beginning of old man Shishkov's speech touched me, but the end made a mess of everything.⁶ How about the censorship now? Write me something concerning

Karamzin, -a, -s
Zhukovsky
A. Turgenev
Severin
Ryleev and Bestuzhev

And concerning what the public is talking about in general: Have they begun badgering Vorontsov? They say the Tsar is furious—one would ask what for, but people are like that!⁷

Send me some letter paper and some plain paper, some wine, and also some cheese, and do not forget (to speak like Delille)⁸ the twisted steel which pierces the bepitched neck of the bottle—i.e., a corkscrew.

I am devilishly displeased at the Petersburg gossip about my flight. Why should I flee? It is so good here! When you are with me, we are going to discuss a *banker, our correspondence, the place where Chaadaev is*. These are the points which you can already inquire about.

Who is thinking of dropping in on me? Deliver me

From the stupid sleep-invoker, from the impudent awakener.⁹

All are welcome, though. By messenger send whatever you think of—*addio*.

Have you received my letter of the Flood, wherein I tell you *voilà une belle occasion pour nos dames de faire bidet*?¹⁰ N.B. N.B.

I wanted to send you some verses, but I am too lazy.

[97]

To Lev Sergeevich Pushkin

Between December 20 and 23, 1824. From Mikhaylovskoe to
Petersburg.

Brother! Greetings. I wrote you a few days ago; that is enough for
you. I congratulate you upon the birth of our Lord, and I beg you to
hurry Delvig along. Send me *The Flowers* [*for* 1825] and *Eda*, and go
to Engelgardt's dinner. Give my greetings to Mr. Zhukovsky. Drop
in on Pushchin and Malinovsky.[1] Kiss Matyushkin, love and honor
Alexander Pushkin.

And send me the ring,[2] my Lion.

[98]

To Kondraty Fedorovich Ryleev

January 25, 1825. From Mikhaylovskoe to Petersburg.

I thank you for the *thou* and the letter.[1] Pushchin[2] will bring you a
fragment from my *Gypsies*. I hope you will like it. I am awaiting *The
Polar Star* impatiently, do you know why? For *Voynarovsky*. Our
literature has been needing this poem. Bestuzhev writes me a lot
about *Onegin*—tell him he is wrong: Does he really want to banish
everything light and merry from the province of poetry? What would
then become of satires and comedies? That would mean that it
would be necessary to destroy *Orlando Furioso*,[3] and *Hudibras*, and
Pucelle, and *Vert-Vert*, and *Reineke-Fuchs*, and the best part of
Dushenka, and the tales of La Fontaine, and Krylov's fables, etc., etc.,
etc., etc., etc. That is a little severe. Pictures of society life enter into
the realm of poetry, too. But enough of *Onegin*.

I agree with Bestuzhev in his opinion of Pletnev's critical article,[4]
but I do not completely agree with his stern verdict on Zhukovsky.
Why should we bite our wet nurse's breasts? Because we have cut
our teeth? Whatever you may say, Zhukovsky has had a decisive
influence on the spirit of our literature; besides, his translational style
will forever remain the model. Ugh! that's what the republic of
literature is like. Why does it condemn, why does it bestow laurels?
As regards Batyushkov, let us esteem in him the misfortunes and the
unrealized hopes.[5] Farewell, poet.

January 25.

[99]

To Peter Andreevich Vyazemsky

January 25, 1825. From Mikhaylovskoe to Moscow.

Why have you become silent? Did you receive the letter from me wherein I spoke to you of Oldekop, of the collection of my elegies, of Tatiana, etc.?[1] I ran across you in *The Flowers*, and I almost choked with laughter reading your "Feature of the Locality." It is a charming little thing. "A Simple-Hearted Answer"[2] is long-winded; the rhyme "tears," "roses" [*slëzy, rozy*] led you astray. Brevity is one of the virtues of epigrammatical speech. "Through coughing and through tears" is very amusing, but all the husband's speech down to "jealousy torments beyond the grave" is long-winded and far-fetched. "Still twice more tormenting" can hardly be other than pleonasm. Here is a critique for you longer than your piece. But you alone can introduce and perfect this kind of poem. Rousseau[3] is the model in it, and his obscene epigrams are a hundred times better than his odes and hymns. I have read in *The Invalide*[4] an announcement about *The Telegraph*.[5] What of mine is in it? "The Sea" or "The Cart"? How is my Kyukhlya, who makes me suffer, but whom I keep on loving? They say his circumstances are not good—wherein are they not good? I am expecting my brother and Delvig to see me soon[6]—meanwhile, I am completely alone; I live like a *nedorosl*![7] I lounge around on the stove-shelf and listen to old fairy tales and songs. Verses just won't come. I think I wrote you that my *Gypsies* is not worth anything: Don't believe it—I lied—you will be very much pleased with it. *Onegin* is being printed; my brother and Pletnev are looking after its publication. I did not expect that it would scrape through the censorship—all honor and glory to Shishkov! Do you know my "Second Epistle to the Censor"? [. . . .][8]

That's the way an Arzamasian now speaks about Grandpa Shishkov, *tempora altri*![9] That is why I have decided, as you advised, not to have recourse to him in my action against Oldekop. In base actions a certain nobility is needed.[10] But I have acted meanly in a well-intentioned manner, having in view the welfare of our literature and the pacification of arrogant Krasovsky. Farewell, greet your Princess for me—and kiss the children. My letter is reminiscent of

Vasily Lvovich's *le faire*,[11] isn't it? Here are some rhymes for you in his spirit. [. . . .][12]

Print them somewhere.

January 25.

What do you think of the article which our Pletnev wrote?[13] What a jumble! You're asleep, Brutus! And tell me, who of you from Moscow so warmly took the part of the Germans against Bestuzhev (whom I have not read).[14] Do you want another epigram? [. . . .][15]

Don't give me away, dear one; don't show this to anybody; for *Fita*[16] is a friend of my heart, a fine man, good-natured; I eschew all evil.[17]

[100]

TO PETER ANDREEVICH VYAZEMSKY

January 28, 1825. From Trigorskoe to Moscow.

Pushchin will bring you six hundred rubles. Give them to Princess Vera Fedorovna and with my gratitude.[1] Savelov is a great scoundrel. I am sending him enclosed a friendly letter. Forward it (in an envelope) to Odessa *on an occasion*, or else he will say, by the post, that he did not receive it. I readily excuse and understand him,

But an intelligent person cannot help being a swindler![2]

Apropos: I have read Chatsky—there is much of the witty and the amusing in the verses, but in the whole comedy there is no plan, no main idea, no truth. Chatsky is by no means an intelligent man, but Griboedov is very intelligent. Send me your *Telegraph*.[3] Has Khvostov been published in it? How charming his epistle is![4] It is as good as the best of his times. As it was, he was on the point of becoming mediocre, like Vasily Lvovich, Ivanchin-Pisarev,[5] etc. What do you think of Filimonov[6] in his *Invalide* announcement? Dear fellow, only stupidities can entertain and make me laugh now. All glory to Filimonov!

I am writing to you while I'm on a visit and with a banged-up hand—I fell on the ice, not from my horse but with my horse: a great difference to my equestrian pride.

[101]

TO ALEXANDER ALEXANDROVICH BESTUZHEV

The end of January, 1825. From Mikhaylovskoe to Petersburg.

Ryleev will deliver my *Gypsies*[1] to you. Chide my brother for not keeping his word[2]—I did not want the poem to become known ahead of time. Now nothing can be done about it—I am forced to publish it, before they pilfer it a piece at a time.

I have heard Chatsky,[3] but only once, and not with the attention which he deserves. Here is what I managed to note in passing:

One must judge a dramatic writer by the laws which he acknowledges for himself. Consequently I do not condemn the plan, the exciting force, or the proprieties in Griboedov's comedy. His goal is in the characters and a sharp picture of manners. In this regard Famusov and Skalozub are superb. Sofia is not sketched clearly: she is not exactly a whore, not exactly a Moscow female cousin. Molchalin is not glaringly base enough; shouldn't he have been made a coward, too? That is an old mainspring of action, but a civilian coward in high society between Chatsky and Skalozub could be very amusing. *Les propos de bal*, gossip, Repetilov's tale about the club, Zagoretsky, who is known by all as an inveterate scoundrel and is received everywhere—here are traits of a truly comic genius. Now, a question. In the comedy *Woe from Wit* who is the intelligent personage? The answer: Griboedov. And do you know what Chatsky is? A fiery, noble, and fine fellow who has spent some time with a very intelligent man (namely Griboedov) and who has become steeped in his ideas, witticisms, satirical observations. Everything he says is very intelligent. But to whom does he say all this? To Famusov? To Skalozub? To Moscow grandmothers at a ball? To Molchalin? That is unpardonable. The first mark of an intelligent man is to know at first glance whom he is dealing with, and not to cast pearls before Repetilovs and such like.[4] By the way, what is Repetilov? In him there are two, three, ten characters. Why make him loathsome? It is enough that he is thoughtless and stupid with such simple-heartedness; it is enough that he should momentarily confess his stupidities, without going into loathsome things. This meekness is extremely new in the theater, although to whom of us has it not happened *to be put to the blush*, hearing similar penitents? Among the masterful traits of this charming comedy, Chatsky's distrustfulness in Sofia's love for Molchalin is charming!—and how naturally handled! This is what the whole comedy should have turned on, but Griboedov apparently didn't want it thus—but let him have it as he pleases. I say nothing of the verses: half of them should become proverbs.

Show this to Griboedov. Perhaps I have erred in something. While I was listening to his comedy, I was not criticizing, but enjoying. These observations came into my mind afterwards, when I was no longer able to check. At least I am speaking directly, without any beating around the bush, as to a truly talented man.

You do not seem to like my "Oleg";[5] you are mistaken. The comradely love of the old prince for his horse and his solicitude about its fate is a trait of touching simple-heartedness, and the occurrence has in itself much of the poetic in its simplicity. Turn the sheet round;[6] for this time, enough.

I have not received Bulgarin's *Literary Leaves*, the issue with your criticism on Bowring.[7] Order it sent.

[102]
To Peter Andreevich Vyazemsky
The end (after the 28th) of January, 1825. From Mikhaylovskoe to Moscow.

I do not have the time to write the Princess. Thank her for her solicitude, for her reproaches, even for her advice, for all that bears the stamp of her friendship, which is precious to me. You are of course right; I must esteem myself more than ever—to humble myself before the government would be a stupidity. Grabbe by himself is enough of that.[1]

I wrote you a few days ago, and I sent some verse. You write me: send me *all your verses*. That's easy to say! Pushchin will bring you fragments from *The Gypsies*—for the time being there is nothing of the forbidden variety.[2]

[103]
To Lev Sergeevich Pushkin
The end of January or the first half of February, 1825.
From Mikhaylovskoe to Petersburg.

I am not scolding you (though I feel like it), for 18 reasons: (1)

because it would do no good. . . .[1] Nothing can be done about it, I'll copy and send *The Gypsies* to you, and you print it.[2] Your apprehensions about coming to see me are completely unjust.[3] I am not in the Shlisselburg,[4] and to deprive two brothers of seeing each other when there is a physical possibility of it would be cruelty without purpose, and consequently not at all in the spirit of our times, not. . . .

I am awaiting the uproar over *Onegin*;[5] for the time being I am rather bored. You do not send me the *Conversations de Byron*, fine! But, my dear one, if it is at all possible, seek out, buy, beg, steal Fouché's *Memoirs*,[6] and let me have them here. I would give all Shakespeare for them; you can't imagine what Fouché is like! In my opinion, he is more fascinating than Byron. These memoirs ought to be a hundred times more instructive, more interesting, more striking than Napoleon's memoirs,[7] i.e., as politics, because I don't understand a damned thing about war. On his cliff (God forgive my transgression!) Napoleon grew stupid. In the first place he tells lies like a child;[8] (2) he judges of a thing not like a Napoleon, but like a Parisian pamphleteer, some Pradt or Guizot.[9] Somehow it very, very much seems to me that Bertrand[10] and Montholon were bribed! All the more so that precisely the most important pieces of information are absent. Have you read Napoleon's memoirs? If not, read them: by the way this book, is among other things, an excellent novel, *mais tout ce qui est politique n'est fait que pour la canaille.*[11]

Enough about trash; let us talk about something important. *My* Konshin[12] has written a piece, "A Maid to a Poet in Love," that's a very nice thing, by golly, except for *by authórs.*[13] But what a Konshin he is! What do you think of his elegy in *The Flowers*? Your judgment about Griboedov's comedy is too harsh. I have written to Bestuzhev about it in detail; he will show you my letter. By the journals I see there is an unusual fermentation of ideas; that augurs a change in ministry on Parnassus. I am the minister of foreign affairs, and I should think this matter does not touch me. If *Paley* continues as it began, Ryleev[14] will become a minister. Pletnev harmed Baratynsky with his indiscreet zeal;[15] but *Eda* will set everything right. How is Baratynsky? . . . And will it be soon, will it be long? . . . How can one learn? Where is the messenger of redemption?[16] Poor Baratynsky, when I think of him, I am ashamed, in spite of myself, for being despondent. Farewell, there are no new verses—I am writing Memoirs, but I am fed up even with despised prose.

Has Count Vorontsov come? Find out and write me how he has spoken of me in society—and I don't need to know about anything else.

Advise Ryleev to put our grandfather in Peter I's suite, in his new poem.[17] His ugly blackamoor phiz would produce a strange effect on the whole picture of the Battle of Poltava.

[104]
To PETER ANDREEVICH VYAZEMSKY
February 19, 1825. From Mikhaylovskoe to Moscow.

Tell Mukhanov[1] from me that it is a sin for him to play journalistic pranks on me. Without a by your leave, he took the beginning of my *Gypsies* and spread it over the world. The barbarian! Why, that's my blood; why, that's money! Now I must break out *The Gypsies*, and it is not at all timely.

Onegin has been printed; I think it has already been released. You will see a compliment to Prince Shalikov in the "Conversation of a Poet and a Bookseller." He is a nice poet, a person worthy of respect, and I hope that sincere and full praise from me will not be unpleasant to him. He is the very poet of the fair sex. *Il a bien mérité du sexe, et je suis bien aise de m'en être expliqué publiquement.*[2]

What about the promised[3] *Telegraph*? Have you published my "Cart," you prankster? I receive all the other journals—and more than ever I feel the need of some kind of *Edimboorg review*.[4] But Christ is my witness that I am fed up with literature—my guts crave some of your prose. What about the publication of your Fonvizin?[5]

February 19.

I bow to the Princess and kiss her hands, though that has gone out of style.

[105]
To NIKOLAY IVANOVICH GNEDICH
February 23, 1825. From Mikhaylovskoe to Petersburg.

Onegin seems to be indebted to you for Shishkov's protection and for its happy deliverance from Birukov. I see that your friendship has not changed, and that consoles me.

My present circumstances do not permit me even to wish for letters from you. But I await your verses, either printed or in manuscript. Your Greek songs are charming and are a *tour de force*.[1] May I talk a little about your witty preface? The similarity in the poetic songs of the two people₂ is obvious—but the reasons? . . . My brother has told me of the early completion of your Homer. That will be the first classical, European feat in our fatherland (may the devil take this fatherland). But when you have rested after your *Iliad*, what will you take up in the full flower of your genius, after you have matured in the temple of Homer, like Achilles in the Centaur's den? I am expecting an epic poem from you. "The shade of Svyatoslav is wandering, unsung," you once wrote me. And Vladimir? and Mstislav? and Donskoy? and Ermak? and Pozharsky?[2] The history of a people belongs to the poet.

When your ship, laden down with the treasures of Greece, is entering the haven while the crowd awaits expectantly, I am ashamed to speak to you of my small-wares shop No. 1. I have much that is begun; nothing is finished. I am sitting by the seashore and awaiting a change in the weather. I am not writing anything, and I am reading little, because you publish little.

February 23, the day of Alexander Ypsilanti's announcement of the Greek uprising.

[106]
To Lev Sergeevich Pushkin
The end of February, 1825. From Mikhaylovskoe to Petersburg.

I have received, my dear one, your kind letter. I am awaiting Delvig with impatience. I am sorry about the severe measures which have been taken with regard to you.[1] I have read the announcement about *Onegin* in *The Bee*: I am expecting a sensation. If the edition is bought up, then proceed at once to another or come to an agreement with some bookseller. Write me of the impression it makes. A change has taken place here in my ministry: I have been forced to give Roza Grigorievna[2] the sack for her indecent behavior and for words which I did not have to put up with. Otherwise she would have worried to death my nursemaid, who had begun to get thin on account of her. I ordered Roza to surrender her accounts to me. She testified to me

that for the two years (1823 and 1824) she had been paid nothing(?).
And she calculates, at the rate of 200 rubles per year, the sum of
400 rubles. According to my calculation, she is due 100 rubles. She has
300 rubles of money on hand. Of this I shall give her 100, and send
200 to Petersburg. Find out and write me back in detail precisely
how much has been set for her gratuity and whether anything has
been paid her during these two years. I appointed a committee made
up of Vasily, Arkhip,[3] and the overseer. I ordered the grain to be
remeasured, and I discovered certain malpractices, i.e., several
concealed shares. Anyway, she is a scoundrel and a thief. For the
time being I have taken over the reins of management.

You ask why I write Bulgarin.[4] Because he is a friend of mine. I
have still other friends: Yashka Saburov, Mukhanov, Davydov, etc.
These friends are incomparably worse than Bulgarin. One of these
days they will cut my throat—meanwhile I have sent honored Faddey
Venediktovich [Bulgarin] two fragments from *Onegin*, which neither
Delvig nor Bestuzhev has, has had, or will have. . . . And who is to
blame? Nobody but my friends, nobody but my thrice-damned
friends.[5]

Greet my friend Voeykov.[6] The words "An Idyll of Moschus"
should have been placed over or under "Sea and Land." That
wouldn't throttle me, and old Bion would keep what belongs to
him. The same also with regard to Ivan Ivanovich Parny[7]—but here
I myself am to blame.

If a packet comes to you addressed to Delvig, open it—I permit it.
I kiss Pletnev, and I shall write him.

And send me *Antiquity* and *Thalia*; God have mercy, one can't ask
and get anything from you. Here is a letter to the Publisher or
Flublisher[8] of *The Neva Almanac*.[9] Read and deliver it. The rascal, he
lies about me in announcements and sends me his lying—fine! The
beginning of Izmaylov's *Tomcat*[10] is very nice.

P.S. A blind priest[11] has translated *Sirach* (look at such-and-such an
issue of *The* [*Russian*] *Invalide*), is publishing it by subscription—
subscribe for several copies.

[107]

To Lev Sergeevich Pushkin

Between the beginning of February and the beginning of March,
1825. From Mikhaylovskoe to Petersburg.

I would send this to *The Son of the Fatherland*, but this journal seems
to be about to rebel against me, judging by the dry announcement
in *The Bee*.[1] In such case it would not do for me to appear there as a
tributary of the Ataman Grech and the Esaul Bulgarin.[2] I give the
fragments[3] to you: print them where you wish.

[108]

To Lev Sergeevich Pushkin

March 14, 1825. From Trigorskoe to Petersburg.

Brother, I embrace you and fall at your feet. I embrace also the
Algerian Vsevolozhsky.[1] You send me my damned manuscript—
and let me blot out, copy, and publish.[2] How sorry I am that you
won't be with me! The task would go more quickly and better. I am
awaiting Delvig,[3] even though he would not help. He has your taste,
but not your handwriting. My elegies are to be copied, then come
the epistles, then the miscellaneous things, and then I shall cross
myself, and off to the censorship with them.

My dear fellow, send me some mustard, some rum, something in
vinegar, and some books: *Conversations de Byron, Mémoires de Fouché,
Thalia, Antiquity*, and Sismondi (*littérature*),[4] and Schlegel (*drama-
turgie*),[5] if St. Florent has them. I should also like to have the *New
Edition of the Collection of Russian Poems*,[6] but it is expensive—75
rubles. I'm not giving that much even for all Russia. However, take
a look at it.

Kachenovsky has rebelled against me. Write me whether the tone
of his criticisms[7] is seemly—if not, I shall send an epigram.

There is heresy where you are. They are saying that in verses the
verses are not the main thing.[8] Then what is the main thing? Prose?
That heresy must be stamped out before it gets out of hand, with
persecution, the knout, stakes, songs to the air "Alone I Sit in the
Company,"[9] etc.

Anna Nikolaevna [Vulf] greets you and regrets very much that
you are not here, because I have fallen in love and am playing the

Myrtilus.[10] Do you know her cousin Anna Ivanovna Vulf?[11] *Ecce femina!*

I want to see Delvig so badly I don't know what to do. Have I written to you about galoshes? I don't need them. I have received Gnedich's songs.[12] In a few days I shall write him of my grievances. Meanwhile, thank him—I suppose you have presented him a copy of *Onegin* from me. As regards the above-mentioned ladies, I hope it's a joke. But I wouldn't be surprised! However, that would be in any case very unpleasant for me.

Trigorskoe.

March 14.

Obtain my short poems from Ryleev or Bestuzhev, and hurry and send them to me.

"Just why did you promise to send *me* Parny?"[13]

[109]

To LEV SERGEEVICH PUSHKIN
March 14, 1824. From Mikhaylovskoe to Petersburg.

Upon receiving the manuscript. March 14.

You are wrong in imagining that I am angry with you—I had not even thought of such a thing. I have written you several times, but apparently nothing has reached you yet. Vsevolozhsky is having his little joke with me. I owe him 1000 and not 500; talk it over with him, and thank him very much for the manuscript. He's a fine fellow, even though he is getting married. I shall get busy on the new collection at once, and send it to you.

For God's sake, wait a little with respect to your retirement. Perhaps you are being persecuted without the Tsar's knowledge.[1] Your petition might be considered the result of a suggestion by me, etc., etc., etc. Wait at least for Delvig.

Inform me about Baratynsky—I'll light a candle for Zakrevsky,[2] if he will rescue him.

[110]
To Lev Sergeevich Pushkin and Peter Alexandrovich Pletnev
March 15, 1825. From Mikhaylovskoe to Petersburg.

Brother Lev
and brother Pletnev!

Day before yesterday I received my manuscript.[1] Today I am sending off all my new and old verses. I have hurriedly washed out my dirty linen, and I have basted up the new. But I hope with your help that the lady-public will not smack me on my cheeks as having been a slapdash laundress.

I beg you to correct the mistakes of spelling, the punctuation, the misprints, the instances of nonsense yourselves—my eyes won't be up to it. Also abide by your best judgment as to the order of the pieces. Only do not imitate the edition of Batyushkov[2]—eliminate, blot out without hesitation. I permit, I even beg you to do it. But for this labor take for your helpers Zhukovsky, without arousing the wrath of Bulgarin; and Gnedich, without arousing the wrath of Griboedov.[3] Either no epigraph or one from A. Chénier. A vignette[4] would not be bad; why, you even may—you even must—even, for Christ's sake, have one made, namely, "Psyche pensive over a flower." (By the way: what is more charming than Zhukovsky's stanza "He thought that you and he are of the same kind"[5] and the following one? I don't like the end.) What if the magic brush of F. Tolstoy would. . . .[6]

No! It's too expensive! But how terribly nice![7]

Besides, except for Utkin's,[8] nobody's chisel is a match for his pencil. That's all surface, though. It is captivating with another charm. . . .

Counting over the poems which I am sending you, I find 60 or thereabouts (for the part to be consigned to the gods of the underworld cannot be foreseen). Birukov is an enlightened man; I don't want to deal with anybody but him. Even in the *terrible time*[9] he was gracious and compassionate. Now I submit myself unconditionally to his verdicts.

What should I say to you about the edition? Print each piece on a separate page, without errors, neatly, like the last edition of Zhu- kovsky—and please without ⌒⌒⌒⌒⌒⌒⌒⌒⌒⌒ ——————— + ——————— and without ══════════.[10] All this fancy stuff is hideous and reminds one of Asia. The title in capital letters—and *à la ligne*. But print each thing separately—even if it consists of only four lines (if only two, then you may do the next one also *à la ligne*).[11]

Sixty pieces. Will that be enough for a volume? Shouldn't I send you, to piece it out, "Tsar Nikita and His Forty Daughters"?[12]

Brother Lev! Don't anger journalists! It's bad politics!

Brother Pletnev! Don't write *kind* critiques! Be sharp-tongued and fear the cloying![13]

Farewell, children! I'm drunk.

March 15.

[111]
To ALEXANDER ALEXANDROVICH BESTUZHEV
March 24, 1825. From Mikhaylovskoe to Petersburg.

In the first place, send me your address, so that I won't bother Bulgarin. I am not writing to Ryleev. I am waiting for his *Voy- narovsky* before I do. Tell him that as regards Byron's opinion he is right.[1] I would have liked to speak against my conscience, but I did not succeed. Both Bowles and Byron talked nonsense in their con- troversy; I have a very apt rebuttal to it. Want me to send it? It's boring to copy. Where did you get the notion that I am flattering Ryleev?[2] I stated my opinion about his *Dumy* loudly and clearly; about his long poems, too. I know very well that I am his master in poetic diction, but he is going along his own road. He is a poet in soul. I am afraid of him in earnest, and I regret very much that I did not shoot him down when I had the chance—the devil knows why I didn't.[3] I am awaiting *Voynarovsky* impatiently, and I shall send him all my observations on it. For Christ's sake! If he would only write, and more, more!

Your letter is very intelligent, but all the same you are mistaken, all the same you are looking at *Onegin* from the wrong point of view, all the same it is my best work. You compare the first chapter with *Don Juan*. Nobody esteems *Don Juan* more than I do (the first five cantos; I have not read the others), but there is nothing in common with *Onegin* in it. You talk of the Englishman Byron's satire and compare it with mine, and demand of me the very same thing! No, my dear fellow, you want too much. Where do I have *satire*? There is not even a hint of it in *Evgeny Onegin*. My embankment would crumble[4] if I were to touch satire. The very word *satirical* ought not to appear in the preface. Wait for the other cantos. . . . Oh! If I could only lure you to Mikhaylovskoe! . . . You would see that if *Onegin* is to be compared at all with *Don Juan*, then perhaps in one respect: which is the nicer and more charming (*gracieuse*), Tatiana or Julia?[5] The first canto is simply a rapid introduction, and I am satisfied with it (which very seldom happens with me). Whereupon I conclude our polemics. . . . I am awaiting *The Polar Star*. Give it here. I foresee that I shall agree with you in your literary opinions. I hope that you will finally give Katenin his just due.[6] That would be, incidentally, noble, worthy of you. To make errors and to perfect one's judgments is natural to a thinking creature. A *disinterested* admission of the same demands spiritual strength. Incidentally, I would be glad for Katenin if this happened, but for myself I am awaiting tales of yours; and get busy on a novel—who's holding you? Just imagine: you would be the first among us in all senses of the word; in Europe you would also receive your evaluation—in the first place, as a man of true talent; in the second, for the novelty of subjects, colors, etc. . . . Think this over, brother, at your leisure. . . . But you want to become a captain of cavalry.[7]

March 24. Mikhaylovskoe.

[112]

To VERA FEDOROVNA VYAZEMSKAYA
March 24, 1825. From Mikhaylovskoe to Moscow.
(In French)

Dear and esteemed Princess, your letter has cut me to the heart. I had no idea of the misfortune which has befallen you;[1] I shall not try to console you, but from the bottom of my soul I share your sorrows and your anguish. I hope that by this time the Prince and the children are recovering. Since *Onegin* may distract him, this moment I am going to set about copying it, and I shall send it to him. I shall also write my brother, to send whatever verses of mine he may have. I ask only of the Prince that he keep it all for himself alone, and that he not read any of it to anybody in the world.

Pushchin was in the wrong to speak to you of my anxieties and my conjectures, which turned out to be false.² I have no contact with Odessa; I know absolutely nothing of what is going on there.

Dear Princess, be calm, if that is possible. Give me news of your family, and count me always among those most devoted to you.

March 24.

[113]

To Lev Sergeevich Pushkin
March 27, 1825. From Mikhaylovskoe to Petersburg.

My dear fellow, how charming Grandmother's Tomcat is!¹ I re-read the whole tale twice and in one breath, and now I do nothing but rave of Trifon Faleleich Murlykin. I step forth lightly, screwing up my eyes, turning my head, and arching my back. Pogorelsky is Perovsky, isn't he?

I have received the news of Vyazemsky. Send him, my dear fellow, everything you have on paper and in your memory from my new compositions. By so doing you will oblige me very much, and you will wipe out your dirty tricks of your mad passion for giving readings.²

Have you received my poems?³ Here is what the preface must consist of: Many of these poems are trash and unworthy of the attention of the Russian public, but since they have often been published by God knows whom, with the devil knows what titles, with the corrections of the typesetter and with the errors of the publisher—here they are; be so good, sir, as to have a bite, sir, although this, sir, is s———, sir (say this a little more mildly). (2) We (that is, the publishers) had to throw out of the complete edition many things which might have seemed obscure because of having been written in circumstances which are unknown or of little interest to the most honored (Russian) public, or which could be of interest only to certain private personages; or which are too immature, for Mr. Pshk. saw fit to publish his rhymes in 1814 (i.e., when he was fourteen); or as you please.

(3) Please, without the slightest praise to me. That is an unfitting thing, and in *The Fountain of Bakhchisaray* I forgot to remark of this

to Vyazemsky. (4) All this must be expressed romantically, without buffoonery. On the contrary. I am relying on Pletnev in all this. If I should say that his prose is better than mine, he would not believe it—but it is at least as good. Is he satisfied?[4] But, to be on the safe side, send this preface to Mikhaylovskoe, and I shall send you my observations.

When you send my verses to Vyazemsky, write him to give them to nobody, because if he does, I shall be robbed again—I have no ancestral village, with nightingales and bears.[5] Farewell. Kiss sister. Good Friday.

I am very much pleased with *The Telegraph*[6]—I am thinking of giving it my support. Tell Zhukovsky this, too. Still no Delvig!

Since Voeykov is behaving well, I am thinking of sending even him some verses. It's much better not to steal, not to berate obscenely, not to pirate,[7] not to intercept letters, etc.—people won't censure, and I shall say thanks.

Print also the verses to Princess Golitsyna-Suvorova;[8] get them from her. I think that the epistle "To Ovid," "Yesterday Was a Day of Noisy Parting," and "To the Sea" can, for the sake of variety, be placed among the Elegies—and in general you may change the entire order. R.S.V.P.

Oughtn't "Recollections in Tsarskoe Selo" be printed at the end with the *Note* that it was written by me at 14, and with an excerpt from my Memoirs (about Derzhavin),[9] eh?

No.[10]

And also print my "Little Bird" and the quatrain *about friendship*: "What Is Friendship? The Light Flame of a Hangover."[11]

[114]
To PETER ANDREEVICH VYAZEMSKY
The end of March or the beginning of April, 1825.
From Mikhaylovskoe to Moscow.

I hope you have recovered—I am awaiting official news to this effect with impatience. My brother will send you verses of mine, and I am copying *Onegin* for you—my desire is that it will help you smile. For the first time, a reader's smile *me sourit*.[1] (Excuse this banality: it's in the blood! . . .)[2] And meanwhile be grateful to me—I have never copied anything for anybody in my life, not even for Golitsyna.[3]

From which it follows that I am in love with you, like Kyukhel-beker's Derzhavin with Suvorov.[4]

Does Russian literature still interest you? I was about to bristle up considerably at Polevoy on account of *The Neva Almanac* and the parody of Zhukovsky.[5] But now I have made my peace with him. I am even of the opinion that we absolutely must support his journal. Want to? I agree to.

My poems have been sent off to Petersburg in care of Birukov.[6] Almost everything is already known. But everything needed to be joined together. Of all that had to be consigned to oblivion, I lament most of all for my epigrams—there are about fifty in all, and all are original—but unfortunately I can say, like Chamfort, *Tout ceux contre lesquels j'en ai fait sont encore en vie.*[7] But enough—I don't want to quarrel with the living.

From my epistle "To Chaadaev," I blotted out the verses which you did not like[8]—I did it solely for you, out of respect for you, and not because they go against others' grain.

Greet Davydov, who has forgotten me. My sister Olga is in love with him, and it serves him right. Apropos or not: he has criticized Zarema's eyes in *The Fountain of Bakhchisaray* for her. I would agree with him, if the East weren't involved. The Eastern style was a model for me, insofar as it is possible for us, rational, cold Europeans. Apropos again, do you know why I dislike Moore? Because he is excessively Eastern. He imitates childishly and in an ugly manner the childishness and ugliness of Saadi, Hafiz, and Mohammed.[9] A European, even in the rapture of Oriental splendor, must preserve the taste and eye of a European. That is why Byron is so charming in *The Giaour*, in *The Bride of Abydos*, etc.

[115]

To PETER ANDREEVICH VYAZEMSKY
April 7, 1825. From Mikhyalovskoe to Moscow.

April 7.

Today is the anniversary of Byron's death—I have ordered a mass this evening for the repose of his soul. My priest[1] was astonished at my piety, and gave me part of the host from the mass for the repose of God's servant the Boyar Georgy.[2] I am sending it to you.

I am copying *Onegin*.[3] It will get to you without delay.

I have just received *Voynarovsky* and the *Dumy*,[4] together with Pushchin's letters—it looks as though I shall have to decline Selivanovsky's offer of 12,000 rubles for the three long poems,[5] because of a new typographical swindle. *The Fountain of Bakhchisaray* has been pirated.[6]

Farewell, dear one. I have the spleen, and there is not a single thought in my head. Greet your wife for me. I am devoted in soul to you both.

[116]
To Lev Sergeevich Pushkin
April 7, 1825. From Trigorskoe to Petersburg.

I just now received a letter from you, and a little tale, probably from Pletnev. Without reading the letter, I let Anna Nikolaevna [Vulf] have it, and then burned it up at once (out of apprehension or out of jealousy, as you wish). She is offended by your endearments, and that in writing them you forgot yourself. I have not yet received *The Polar*.[1] For God's sake, check about my *Fountain*. Selivanovsky is offering me 12,000 rubles, and I must refuse it.[2] This way I'll die of hunger—what with Father and with Oldekop. Farewell. I am furious.

Thank you very much for the *Fragment* from *Baratynsky's* letter. Delvig is not here yet.

On vous permet d'écrire des lettres—**mais sous l'adresse de notre soeur** (get it!). *C'est ainsi, voyez-vous, que j'écris à Anna Ivanovna Vulf, sous le nom d'Euphrosine*. Lord Jesus Christ! *Quelles misères!* . . .[3] Kiss Olga.

Here is my yesterday's *im-promptu*

From family love and tender friendship, I praise you, Sister! Not in front, but behind.

Burn that after you have shown it to her.

Variantes en l'honneur de Mlle. NN[4]
From honor, love, and tender friendship, I praise you, my dear, both in front and behind.

Mlle. NN finds the first text is suitable for you. *Honny* [sic] *soit*,[5] etc. . . .

I have ordered a mass for the repose of Byron's soul (today is the anniversary of his death). Anna Nikolaevna [Vulf] has, too, and special services have taken place in both the churches of Trigorskoe and Voronich. This is a little reminiscent of *la messe de Frédéric II pour le repos de l'âme de M-r de Voltaire.*[6] I am sending Vyazemsky part of the host from Father Prank's mass for the repose of the poet.

[117]

To ALEXANDER SEMENOVICH SHISHKOV

About April 7, 1825. From Mikhaylovskoe to Petersburg.

(Rough draft; unsent)

Mr. Oldekop last year, in 1824, reprinted my composition *The Fountain of Bakhchisaray*[1] without my authorization, by doing which he has deprived me of 3,000. Although my father, State Councillor S. L. Pushkin, complained to Your High Excellency for this disregard of my property, not only has he not received any satisfaction, but I have even become convinced from your letter that Mr. Oldekop enjoys Your High Excellency's protection. Excluded from the service and consequently not receiving salary, and not having any other income except from my compositions, I have decided to have recourse to Your High Excellency yourself with my complaint, hoping that you will not wish to deprive me of my bread and butter —this I do not out of personal dissatisfaction against Mr. Oldekop, who is completely unknown to me, but solely in order to protect myself from theft.

[118]

To LEV SERGEEVICH PUSHKIN

April 22 and 23, 1825. From Mikhaylovskoe to Petersburg.

Fouché, Œuvres dramatiques de Schiller, Schlegel, Don Juan (the last cantos, 6th and following), the new Walter Scott, *all of The Siberian Messenger*[1]—and all that through St. Florent, and not through Slenin. Wine, wine, rum (12 bottles), some mustard, *Fleur d'orange,*[2] a trunk for the road. Some *limburger cheese*, a book about horseback riding (I want to break in some stallions—a free imitation of Alfieri and Byron).

How glad I was of the Baron's coming![3] He is very nice! Our young ladies have all fallen in love with him. But he is as indifferent as a block of wood; he loves to lie in bed, enraptured by the Chigi-rinsk bailiff.[4] He orders me to greet you, kissing you mentally 100 times, and he wishes 1000 good things for you (for example, oysters).

23.

I have just now received a letter from you. Thank you for the promise of a preface.[5] I think I may cross myself and begin. Of the epistle "To Chaadaev" I shall say to you that there is no need to repeat slaps in the face.[6] Tolstoy will appear in all his glory in the fourth canto of my *Onegin*, if his lampoon is good enough for that, and for this reason ask Vyazemsky to let you have the epigram on him, etc., back (without fail). My lad, you don't find any sense in my moon.[7] What's to be done? Just go ahead and print it as it is. If Saburov has not left yet for Odessa, tell him not to tell any lies there about me. I am sorry that I cannot be assured of your reticence, either. Tell Sister that I have stirred up a quarrel between her and Anna Nikolaevna [Vulf], by accidentally showing her and not reading the letter in which she says: *Elle me boude mais je m'en fous*[8] or some-thing to that effect. I have assured Aneta [Anna N. Vulf] that Sister is very angry with her, and all through your gossip.

Des bretelles
Des bottes[9] (or you needn't)

A greeting and a couple of words to Pletnev. I shall write him in a few days.

[118a]

To Lev Sergeevich Pushkin
April (not later than 24), 1825. From Mikhaylovskoe to
Petersburg.

Deliver this to Vyazemsky, repeating my request that he not show it to anybody, and don't you do me dirty.[1]

[119]

To Peter Andreevich Vyazemsky
Between April 20 and 24, 1825.
From Mikhaylovskoe to Moscow.

Delvig is here with me. Via him I am sending you the second chapter of *Onegin* (solely to you and copied out only for you). For the conversation[1] with her [Tatiana's] nursemaid, not including her letter, my brother has received 600 rubles. You see that this is money; consequently it must be kept under lock and key. I haven't received a whisper from you. I hope you are well; I do not dare to hope for anything else, but one would think that fate might be satisfied.

Smile, my dear one; here is "The Elegy on the Death of Anna Lvovna"[2] for you:

Oh, Aunty! Oh, Anna Lvovna, sister of Vasily Lvovich! You were loving toward mama; you were kind to papa; you were loved more than silver by Lizaveta Lvovna; Matvey Mikhaylovich met you amidst the court like a blood-relation. Has it been long since with Olga Sergevna, has it been long since with Lev Sergeich, you shared bread and salt, as though laughing at wrathful fate? Alas! Why did Vasily Lvovich bepiss your grave with verses, and why did Krasovsky, the scoundrel, the priest's son, let him do it.[3]

(I and Delvig.)

By the way, why haven't you wished to answer Delvig's letters? He is a person worthy of esteem in all respects, and nothing like your Saint Petersburg literary riff-raff. Please, for my sake, support his *Flowers*[4] for next year. We shall all do our best for them. What do you think of *The Polar*? . . . Have you any news about Odessa? Send me something on that subject.

[120]
To Alexander I
Between April 20 and 24, 1825.
From Mikhaylovskoe to Petersburg.
(Rough draft;[1] in French)

I would have considered it my duty to bear my disgrace in respectful silence, if necessity did not constrain me to break it.

My health was severely impaired in my early youth; up until the present I have not had the means of treating it. My aneurysm, which I have had for ten years, may also necessitate a prompt operation. It is easy to verify what I am stating.

I have been reproached, Sire, with having relied once upon a time upon the generosity of your character; I admit that today I have recourse only to it. I beseech Your Majesty to permit me to withdraw to some place *in Europe*, where I will not be deprived of all succor.

[121]

To Vasily Andreevich Zhukovsky
Between April 20 and 24, 1825.
From Mikhaylovskoe to Petersburg.

Here is a human answer for you.[1] I have borne my aneurysm for 10 years, and with God's help I can bear it for three more years or so. Consequently, there is no hurry, but Mikhaylovskoe is stifling to me. If the Tsar would let me go abroad for treatments, that would be a benefaction for which I would be eternally grateful to him and to my friends. Vyazemsky writes me that my friends have lost faith in me as regards the powers that be: wrongly. I promised Nikolay Mikhaylovich [Karamzin] not to write anything against the government for two years, and I kept my word. "The Dagger"[2] was not written against the government; though the verses are not completely pure as regards their style, the intention in them is above reproach. But now I am fed up with all that; and if they will leave me in peace, then probably I shall think of only unrhymed pentameters. Boldly relying on your decision, I am sending you the rough draft for the most White;[3] there is no meanness, I think, either in the action or in the expression. I wrote him in French, because that language is the one of affairs, and it comes more easily to my pen. Incidentally, thy will be done.[4] If this seems unfitting, then it can be translated, and my brother will copy and sign it for me.[5]

All that doesn't matter two straws. I have not said anything to you about your *Poems*.[6] Why do you listen to the Marquis Bludov?[7] It is time you were convinced of the one-sidedness of his taste. Besides I don't see in him even disinterested love for your fame. Though he tossed out and blotted out arbitrarily, he did not exclude from the collection the *epistle to him*—a work which of course is weak. No. Zhukovsky,

> I wish Bludov a merry trip to the ancient Danube, the m——
> f—— s.o.b.[8]

"The Inscription to Goethe," "Ah, if Only My Dear One," "To

a Genie"[9]—all that is charming; but where is it? Do you know what will happen? After your death all that will be published with mistakes and supplemented by the verses of Kyukhelbeker. It is terrible to think of. Delvig will tell you of my literary activities. I regret that I do not have your advice or at least your presence—it is an inspiration. Finish, for God's sake, "The Diver."[10] You ask what is the aim of *The Gypsies*? Here, take it! The aim of poetry is poetry, as Delvig says (if he didn't steal it). Ryleev's *Dumy* aim, all right, but continually miss the mark.[11]

[122]
To Lev Sergeevich Pushkin
The first half of May, 1825. From Mikhaylovskoe to Petersburg.
[. . . .][1]

Here is the requested epigram on Kachenovsky; send it to Vyazemsky. And in the meantime send me the issue of *The Messenger of Europe* in which the second conversation of the false Dmitriev[2] is published; I need it for the preface to *The Fountain of Bakhchisaray*. It wouldn't be bad if you sent me the entire trial proceedings (both *The Messenger* and *The Ladies' Journal*).

The signature of the blind poet[3] touched me inexpressibly. His tale is charming. Whether this will anger him or not, "I wanted to forgive—I could not forgive" is worthy of Byron. The vision, the end are excellent. The epistle[4] is perhaps better than the poem itself—at least the terrible place where the poet describes his becoming blind will remain forever the epitome of poignant poetry. I should like to answer him in verses; if I have time to do it, I shall send them along with this letter.

Didn't Gnedich receive my letter?[5] Too bad; as far as I remember, it was very amusing. In the same packet were two very important ones—to you and to Pletnev. Why has Pletnev become silent? Of course the poor fellow is sick, or dissatisfied with *Voynarovsky*[6]—by the way, what do you think of my obervations on it? I hope you won't say that I am flattering him—but excuse me: I like *Voynarovsky* very much. I am even bored because it is not here with me.

If you can, send me the last *Genlis*[7]—and *Childe Harold*—Lamartine[8] (that must be rubbish!), and generally speaking something new, and also *The Antiquity*.[9] I have received *Thalia*[10] and the letter from the publisher. I have not had time to skim through it yet; *The Sorceress* seemed to me *du bon comique*. And Khmelnitsky, an old love of mine. I have such weakness for him that I am ready to insert in his honor a whole passage in the first canto of *Onegin* (but what the devil! they say he gets angry if he is referred to as a dramatic writer). Vyazemsky is right—but all the same I am angry with him. I hope that Delvig and Baratynsky will also bring for me Anacharsis Cloots,[11] who probably is angry with me because I don't care for "the playfully skipping blood of Griboedov."

My embraces are open for Delvig. I am waiting for some letters from him on account of my selfishness, aneurysm, etc.

I have at last deciphered Zhukovsky's letter. How charming his devilish, heavenly soul is! He is a saint, though he was born a romantic and not a Greek, and a man, and what a man!

Print "Tsarskoe Selo" and the Note along with it.[12] The announcement about *The Bandit Brothers*[13] was incorrect. It, too, might be printed among the *Various Poems*. The idea of publishing "Napoleon" is rich, but the censorship. . . . The best stanzas would be swallowed up.

[123]
To Kondraty Fedorovich Ryleev
The second half of May, 1825. From Mikhaylovskoe to Petersburg.

I think you have already received my observations[1] on your *Voynarovsky*. I shall add one thing: every place that I said nothing, you must understand praise, exclamation points, "excellent," etc. Assuming that what is good was written deliberately, I did not consider it necessary to point it out for you.

What shall I say to you about the *Dumy*? Lively verses are to be met in all of them; the concluding stanzas of "Peter in Ostrogozhsk"[2] are extremely original. But generally speaking they are weak in invention and exposition. They are all cut to the same pattern. They are made up of *points in common* (*loci topici*): the description of the site of the action, the hero's speech, and the moral. There is nothing national, nothing Russian in them, except the names (I exclude "Ivan Susanin," the first *Duma* which made me begin to suspect you of having true talent). You were wrong in not correcting in "Oleg" *the coat of arms of Russia*. The ancient coat of arms, Saint George, could not have been on the shield of the pagan Oleg; the most recent, the two-headed eagle, is the Byzantine coat of arms and was accepted in our country in the time of Ivan III,[3] no earlier. The chronicler simply says: "He also hung up his shield on the gates to show the victory."[4]

Of "The Confession of Nalivayko" I shall say that it is hard in our country to publish anything truly good in that genre. I find this fragment long drawn out, but even here you of course affixed your own imprint.[5]

You are bored in Petersburg, and I am bored in the village. Boredom is one of the appurtenances of a thinking creature. What can be done about it. Farewell, poet—shall we see each other some fine day?

[124]

To ANNA NIKOLAEVNA VULF
Between early March and the end of May, 1825(?).
From Mihkaylovskoe to Trigorskoe.
(In French)

Here, Mademoiselle, is another letter for my brother. I beseech you to take it under your protection. For mercy's sake, send the quill pens which you had the magnanimity to sharpen for me and which I had the insolence to forget! Please don't be vexed with me over this.

[125]

To ALEXANDER ALEXANDROVICH BESTUZHEV
The end of May or the beginning of June, 1825.
From Mikhaylovskoe to Petersburg.

I am answering the first paragraph of your "Glance."[1] With the Romans the age of mediocrity preceded the age of the *geniuses*—it is a sin to take this term away from such men as Vergil, Horace, Tibullus, Ovid, and Lucretius, although, with the exception of the last two, they[2] went along the well-marked road of imitation. We do not have any Greek criticism. In Italy Dante and Petrarch preceded Tasso and Ariosto, the latter ones preceded Alfieri and Foscolo. With the English, Milton and Shakespeare wrote before Addison and Pope, after whom appeared Southey, Walter Scott, Moore, and

Byron. It is hard to draw any conclusion or rule from this. Your words are fully applicable to French literature alone.

"We have criticism, but we do not have a literature."[3] Just where did you get that idea? Criticism is just what we lack. Hence the reputations of Lomonosov[4] and Kheraskov, and if the latter has fallen in general opinion, then surely not from Merzlyakov's criticism. Derzhavin's idol, 1/4 gold and 3/4 lead, has not yet been assayed. His "Ode to Felitsa" stands alongside "The Noble Lord," and the ode "God" alongside the ode "On the Death of Meshchersky"; the "Ode to Zubov" was discovered not long ago.[5] Knyazhnin[6] is serenely enjoying his fame: Bogdanovich is numbered in the choir of great poets; Dmitriev, too. We have not a single commentary, not a single book of criticism. We do not know just what Krylov is, Krylov who is as much above La Fontaine as Derzhavin is above J. B. Rousseau. Just what are you calling criticism? *The Messenger of Europe* and *The Well-Intentioned?* Grech's and Bulgarin's bibliographical news? Your own articles? But admit it: this still cannot establish any kind of real opinion among our public; it cannot be considered a code of taste. Kachenovsky is dull-witted and boring; Grech and you are sharp-witted and amusing—that is all that can be said about the lot of you. But just where is the criticism? No. Let us turn your phrase around and say it: We have literature of a sort, but we have no criticism. Incidentally, you agree with this yourself, a little further along.

With only one nation did criticism precede literature—with the Germans.

"Why have we no geniuses and so few men of talent?" In the first place, we have Derzhavin and Krylov; in the second, just where are there *a lot* of men of talent?

"We have no literary encouragement—and thank God!" What do you mean we haven't? Derzhavin and Dmitriev were made ministers *as encouragement.*[7] The age of Catherine is the age of encouragement; it is no worse than another on that account. Karamzin seems to have been encouraged. Zhukovsky cannot complain; Krylov cannot, either. Gnedich is completing his great achievement in the quiet of his study; we shall see when our Homer will appear. I see only myself and Baratynsky in the ranks of the unencouraged—and I do not say "thank God!" "Encouragement can fledge only mediocre talents." I do not speak of the Augustan Age,[8] but Tasso and Ariosto left evidence in their poems of a prince's encouragement; Shakespeare wrote his best comedies *at the command* of Elizabeth; Molière was one of Louis's valets[9]—his immortal *Tartuffe*, the fruit of the most powerful exertion of his comic genius, was indebted for its existence to the monarch's intercession; Voltaire wrote his *best* long poem under the protection of Frederick. . . .[10] Three rulers of Russia encouraged Derzhavin.[11] You did not say what you meant; I shall say it for you.

So! We can be justly proud: our literature, though it yields to others in the profusion of men of talent, has the distinguishing trait in comparison with them that it does not bear the stamp of servile abasement. Our men of talent are noble, independent. The voice of flattery became silent with Derzhavin—and just what was his flattery like?

> O recall how, in that rapture, prophesying, I praised you: mark,
> I said, that triumph lives but for a moment, but virtue for ages.[12]

Read the epistle to Alexander (by Zhukovsky, in 1815).[13] That is how a Russian poet speaks to a Russian Tsar. Take another look at our journals, everything current in literature. . . . Of only our lyre may one say what Mirabeau[14] said about Sieyès,[15] *Son silence est un calamité publique.* Foreigners are amazed at us—they give us our just due in full, but they do not understand how it has been accomplished. The reason is clear. Our writers come from the upper class of society. In them aristocratic pride is combined with authors' self-esteem. We do not want to be protected by our equals. This is what the scoundrel Vorontsov does not understand. He imagines that a Russian poet will come to his antechamber with a dedication or an ode, but instead the poet comes with a demand for esteem, as a noble of six-hundred-years standing—a devil of a difference!

All you say about our education, about foreign and intestine (simply charming!) imitators is excellent, expressed powerfully and with heartfelt eloquence. Generally speaking, ideas seethe in you. You did not come out and say what you had on your heart with regard to *Onegin*; I sense why and thank you, but why not disclose your opinion clearly? So long as we are guided by our personal relationships we shall not have any real criticism—whereas you are worthy of creating it.

Your *Tournament*[16] is reminiscent of *W. Scott's* tournaments. Away with those furriners, and turn to us Orthodox; and enough of your writing *rapid* tales with romantic transitions—that is all right for a Byronic poem. But a novel requires *chatter*: say everything out plainly. Your Vladimir[17] speaks the language of the German drama, he looks at the sun at midnight,[18] etc. But the description of the Lithuanian camp and the carpenter's conversation with the sentry are charming; the end, likewise. Incidentally, extraordinary vivacity is everywhere.

Ryleev will of course show you my observations on his *Voynarovsky*, and you send me your objections. Meanwhile, I embrace you with all my heart.

Another word: in 1822[19] you saw fit to complain about the fogs of our literature—and this year you did not even say thanks to old Shishkov.[20] To just whom, if not to him, are we obligated for our revival?

[126]

To Anton Antonovich Delvig
Between June 1 and 8, 1825.
From Mikhaylovskoe to Petersburg.

I keep on waiting for letters from you—and none come. Haven't you taken the deceased Nikita[1] into your service again. Or are you waiting for an *occasion*?—accursed *occasion*. For God's sake write me something: you know that I have had the misfortune to lose my grandmother Chicherina and Uncle Peter Lvovich[2]—I received these pieces of news without any preparation, and I am in a terrible state. Solace me; that is the sacred duty of friendship (that sacred feeling).[3]

How are my *Various Poems* doing? Has Birukov the Terrible seen them?[4] I am not receiving a single line from Pletnev; what about my *Onegin*? Is it selling? By the way: tell Pletnev that he may give Lev money of mine for pocket money, but not for commissions for me, because that is to no purpose: such another shameless agent as Lev does not exist and never will. After your departure I reread all Derzhavin, and here is my final opinion. That strange man knew neither the Russian ABC's nor the spirit of the Russian language

(and that is why he is below Lomonosov). He had no understanding
of either style or harmony—or even of the rules of versification.
That is why he must infuriate every fastidious ear. He not only does
not sustain an *ode*, but he cannot sustain even a stanza (with the
exception of you know which ones). Here is what is in him: *thoughts,
pictures, and movements which are truly poetic*; in reading him you seem
to be reading a bad, free translation of some marvelous original. By
golly, his genius thought in Tatar—and he did not know the Russian
ABC's from lack of leisure.[5] Derzhavin, when he has in due course
been translated, will amaze Europe, and because of national pride
we shall not say what we know about him (to say nothing of his
ministry). Some eight odes and several fragments of Derzhavin's
must be preserved, but burn up the rest. His genius can be compared
with Suvorov's genius—it's too bad that our poet too often crowed
like a rooster. Enough of Derzhavin—what is Zhukovsky doing?
Send me his opinion of the second chapter of *Onegin*, and of what I
now have on my embroidery frame.[6] What kind of operation has
Krylov undergone?[7] God grant him many years! His "Miller" is
good, like his "Demian and Foka."[8] Have you seen Nikolay
Mikhaylovich [Karamzin]? Is his *History* moving forward?[9] Where
will it stop? Not at the election of the Romanovs? The ingrates!
Six Pushkins signed the election charter, and two made an "X,"
not being able to write![10] And I, their literate descendant, how am I?
Where am I? . . .

[127]
To Peter Andreevich Vyazemsky and Lev Sergeevich Pushkin
          May 25, and near the middle of June, 1825.
          From Mikhaylovskoe to Moscow.
     You ask whether I am pleased with what you said about me in *The
Telegraph*.[1] What kind of a question is this? European articles are so
rare in our journals! But both taste and the partiality of friendship
guide your pen. But you are too protective of me with regard to
Zhukovsky. Rather than a successor, I am precisely a disciple of his,
and I succeed only in that I do not presume to push onto his highway, but wander on a byway. Nobody has had or will have a style
equal to his in power and variety. In his struggles with difficulty,
he is a man of unusual prowess.[2] Translations have spoiled him,

made him lazy; he himself does not want to create, but like Voss[3] he is a genius at translation. In addition, it is ridiculous to speak of him as one who has blossomed and withered, when as a matter of fact his style is still maturing. The past will recur,[4] and I still look for the resurrection of the dead.[5] I have read your thing about *The Black Monk*;[6] you fulfilled your heart's duty. This poem is of course full of feeling and is *more intelligent* than *Voynarovsky*, but in Ryleev there is more abandon or dash in the style. He has in the poem a hangman, with rolled-up sleeves,[7] for whom I would give a great deal. On the other hand, the *Dumy* are trash and the name comes from the German *dumm*, and not from the Polish,[8] as it would seem at first glance. The verses of Neelov[9] are charming; not without reason I once called him *le chantre de la merde!*[10] (Be that spoken between us and posterity.) I have not read Shalikov's articles and verses.[11] Can it be that he is offended by my verses? Why, herein I am innocent as a lamb! Ask brother Leon: he will tell you that seeing the name of Prince Shalikov in my stuff he advised me to replace it with Batyushkov—I was about to heed him, but I felt it would be a pity, *et j'ai remis bravement Shalikov!*[12] I can prove it with the rough draft. Your puns are very nice—the local maids find them extremely amusing, but all the same I am awaiting your thing about Byron. Thank you for Casimir. (How could a *calembour* be cut out of him? Figure it out.)[13] You seem to love Casimir, but I, no such thing. Of course he is a poet, but all the same no Voltaire, no Goethe. . . . It's a long way from a snipe to an eagle! The first genius *there* will be a romantic, and God knows where he will carry French heads away to. By the way, I have noticed that everybody (including you, too) has a most hazy understanding of romanticism. We shall have to have a discussion on this matter when we have the leisure, but not now; I am so tired I don't know what to do. I have written everybody— even Bulgarin.[14]

May 25.

You volunteer to pander Polevoy to me. The point is that I would be glad to help him, but I probably would not carry out any commitments—and hence I don't want his money. But you look out for him —for God's sake! He sometimes talks nonsense, too. For example, "*Don Quixote* eradicated knights errant in Europe"!!! "In Italy, except for Dante, there has been no romanticism." But it was in Italy that it arose. Just what is Ariosto? And his predecessors, beginning with *Buovo d'Antona*[15] up to *Orlando Inamorato*?[16] How can one write so at random? And don't you disdain short journal articles: Napoleon engaged in them and was the best journalist of Paris (as Fouché, I think it was, noted).

[Postscript to L. S. Pushkin][17]

To Vyazemsky, who will be where you are in a few days. Otherwise, send to A. I. Turgenev for delivery to Moscow.

I am not writing anything to you, Monsieur *Lion*, because it is already your turn for several answers.

[128]

TO PETER ANDREEVICH VYAZEMSKY

The beginning of July, 1825. From Mikhaylovskoe to Tsarskoe Selo.

I should think you have already received my answer to *The Telegraph*'s proposal.[1] If it needs my verses, then send it whatever falls your way (except *Onegin*), but if it wants my name as a collaorator, I shall not agree on account of noble pride, i.e., self-esteem: the Telegraph is a decent fellow and an honorable one—but a twaddler and an ignoramus; and the twaddle and ignorance of the journal are shared by its editors; I have no intention of entering into that part. Notwithstanding the change of ministry and the improvement of the censorship, all the same I cannot answer for Krasovsky and his brotherhood; perhaps I shall contract to write at the rate of so many pieces, but the journal can be the loser if God and Birukov will it that way. I have always been inclined to play the aristocrat, and since the plague has descended upon the Pushkins,[2] I have begun to put on airs even more: I trade in verses *en gros*, and I am locking up my small wares shop No. 1. Besides, between us, my brother Lev is on my hands—he'll not get any money from our father for wenches and champagne; so let the Telegraph make a deal with him, and God grant them both to get rich trading on my lucky hand. *A demain les affaires sérieuses.* . . .[3] What song from Béranger did Uncle Vasily Lvovich translate? It wasn't *Le Bon Dieu*,[4] was it? Declare to him as a secret that in Petersburg he is being suspected of it, and that an investigative commission is already being prepared, made up of Count Khvostov, Magnitsky,[5] and Mme. Khvostova (the author of "The Hearth" and consequently a rival of

Vasily Lvovich).[6] It wouldn't be a bad idea to inform him that he would have been exiled long ago if it were not for the *extrême popularité* of his *Dangerous Neighbor*. They are afraid of a sensation! What a pity that Alexey Mikhaylovich [Pushkin] has died! And that I did not see uncle being baited! But Dmitriev is alive, not everything is lost yet.[7] I sent my *misprint*[8] to *The Bee* and not to *The Telegraph*, because the post takes an insufferably long time to reach Moscow; Polevoy unjustly felt hurt, you not unjustly added the word *journalistic*, and I not unjustly made my response, *et le diable n'y perd rien*.[9] Here is another epigram on *The Well-Intentioned*, which is said to have criticized my "Friends":

[. . . .][10]

It has been sent off to Polevoy. I'll bet you are already barefoot and are splashing in the sea-puddle, but I am reveling in the pungent odor of resinous beech buds under the sprinkler of the Pskov sky, and I am waiting until Someone on high turns off the sprinkler and the shower of gold ceases. Fita[11] aside, it is cold and muddy here—I am waiting for my fate to be settled.

[129]
To Vasily Andreevich Zhukovsky
The beginning of July, 1825. From Mikhaylovskoe to Petersburg.

His Majesty's unexpected favor[1] has touched me indescribably, all the more that the local governor[2] had already proposed that I have my abode in Pskov, but I was adhering strictly to the commands of the highest authorities. I have checked about the Pskov surgeons; a certain Vsevolodov[3] was pointed out to me, very skilful in veterinary work, and well known in the learned world for his book on the healing of horses.

Notwithstanding all that, I decided to remain in Mikhaylovskoe, though being sensible of His Majesty's paternal condescension.

I am afraid they may consider my slowness in taking advantage of the Monarch's favor as being disdain or recalcitrant obstinacy. But could one suppose such hellish ingratitude in the human heart?

The point is that after my having taken no thought of my aneurysm for ten years, I see no reason suddenly to raise a lot of fuss about it. I am still expecting that from his humane heart, the Em-

peror maybe somehow will permit me to seek a land according
to my heart and a physician according to the credulity of my
own reason, and not according to the command of the highest
authorities.

I embrace you warmly.

1825.   A. Pushkin.

Mikhyalovskoe.

[130]

To PETER ANDREEVICH VYAZEMSKY

July 13, 1825. From Mikhaylovskoe to Tsarskoe Selo.

My brother wrote me that you were in Tsarskoe Selo, that he has
copied my verses for you, and I keep on waiting, waiting for a letter,
and I don't get any. How are you? Are you in Reval yet or not?[1]
And what about your Byron or Beyron (*Toi dont le monde encore
ignore le vrai nom!*).[2] I have just read your observations on Denis'
observations on Napoleon's observations[3]—they are marvellously
good! Your style, lively and original, is here even more lively and
more original. You did well in openly coming out in defense of
Gallicisms. Sometime is must be said aloud that the Russian metaphysical language[4] is still in a savage condition with us. God grant
that some day it be formed similar to the French (the clear, precise
language of prose, i.e., the language of ideas). I have some three
stanzas on that in *Onegin*.[5] My article about Mme. de Staël[6] follows
yours. But don't noise it about: in this there is nothing but *magnanimity*, put there, in the first place, for the sake of the censorship, and,
in the second, for the greater glory of *anonymous* (a kind of journalistic onanism). Probably you already know of the Tsar's favor toward me and his permission for me to go to Pskov. I checked on the
surgeons there; Vsevolodov was recommended to me, a very skillful
horse-doctor;[7] we shall see. Meanwhile, my dear fellow, I have
undertaken a literary feat for which you will cover me with kisses:
a romantic tragedy![8] Look, don't you say a word: very few indeed
know about it. Have you read my "A. Chénier in Prison?"[9] Judge
it as a Jesuit would—according to its intention.

My dear fellow! My intention is to embrace you, but the flesh is
weak. Good-by, farewell. Is your Swan-Princess with you? Greet
her from an Arzamasian goose.[10]

July 13.

My tragedy is before me. I cannot restrain myself from copying out the title: *A Comedy About the Real Misfortune to the Moscow State, About the Tsar Boris, and About Grishka Otrepiev, Written by God's Servant Alexander the Son of Sergey Pushkin in the Year 7333, on the Site of the Ancient Fort of Voronich.*[11] What do you think of it?

[131]

To Peter Alexandrovich Pletnev
About (not later than) July 19, 1825.
From Trigorskoe(?) to Petersburg.

[. . . .]¹

Why don't I hear anything from you! We are having autumn; the rain is making a noise, the wind is making a noise, the forest is making a noise—it is noisy, but boring. Is Delvig getting married?² Describe all the ceremony for me. How handsome he should be under the crown! A pity that I shall not be his best man.

Tell Kozlov³ from me that not long ago our region was visited by a charming person⁴ who sings in heavenly manner his "Venetian Night," to the air of a gondolier's recitative—I promised to inform the dear, inspired blind man about it. A pity that he will not see her, but let him imagine beauty and deep sincerity—God grant him at least to hear her!

Questo è scritto in presenza della donna, come ognun puo veder. Addio caro poeta. Scrivete me, vi prego.

*Tutto il vostro.*⁵

[132]

To Anna Nikolaevna Vulf
July 21, 1825. From Mikhaylovskoe to Riga.
(In French)

I am writing to you after being gloomily drunk; you see that I am keeping my word.

Well! Are you in Riga? Have you made some conquests? Will you get married soon? Have you found some uhlans? Inform me of all this in the greatest detail, because you know that in spite of my bad jokes I am truly interested in all that concerns you. I was wanting to scold you, but I do not have the heart at such a respectable distance. As for moralizing and advice, you shall have them. Listen well: (1) In the name of heaven, be scatter-brained only with your men friends; they will profit by it only for themselves, whereas your *girl friends* will do you harm; for get it into you head that they are as vain and as garrulous as you yourself. (2) Wear short dresses, because you have pretty feet, and do not fluff up your hair at your temples even when that may be the style, since you have the misfortune to have a round face. (3) You have become very erudite of late but do not act like it, and if an uhlan tells you *čto s vami nezdorovo val' sirovat'*![1] do not laugh, do not smirk, do not appear proud of it: blow your nose, turn your head, and talk of something else. (4) Do not forget the latest edition of Byron.[2]

Do you know why I was wanting to scold you? No? A perverse girl, without feeling, and without, etc. . . . and what about your promises, have you kept them? There now, I shall not say any more to you about them, and I forgive you, especially since I remembered it myself only after your departure. It is strange—just what was I thinking of? And now let us talk of other things.

All Trigorskoe is singing *Ne mila ej prelest' noči*,[3] and it wrings my heart; yesterday, Mr. Alexey [Vulf] and I talked for four hours on end. Never have we had such a long conversation. Guess what suddenly brought us together. Boredom? *Conformity of feeling?* I do not know. I take a walk every night in my garden; I say: she[4] was there. The stone against which she stumbled is on my table in front of a faded heliotrope. I am writing a lot of verse. All that, if you like, is very much like love, but I swear to you that it is nothing of the kind. If I were in love, on *Sunday* I would have had convulsions of madness and of jealousy, but I was only nettled. . . .[5] However the thought that I mean nothing to her, that after having aroused and taken possession of her imagination I have only diverted her curiosity, that the memory of me will not make her more absent-minded in the midst of her triumphs or more gloomy in the days of sadness, that her beautiful eyes will cling to some Riga fop with the same heart-rending and voluptuous expression . . . no, this thought is unendurable to me; tell her that I shall die of it. No, do not tell her that; she would make fun of me for it, this delightful creature. But tell her that if her heart does not hold a secret tenderness, a melancholy and mysterious inclination toward me, I despise her, do you understand? Yes, I despise her, in spite of all the astonishment which a feeling so new must cause her.

Farewell, Baroness. Please accept the respects of your prosaic adorer.

July 21.

P.S. Send me the recipe which you promised me; I have pulled so many stunts that more I cannot do—*accursed visit, accursed departure*!

[133]

To Anton Antonovich Delvig

July 23, 1825. From Mikhaylovskoe to Petersburg.

Just now I discover that you have written to me, but your letter has not reached me; God grant that the new Nikita[1] enjoy it! I am extremely disturbed for you. You didn't say anything superfluous or ill-considered, did you? The sympathy of friendship can be interpreted in another manner—and I fear that I may be the cause of unpleasantnesses for the best of my friends.

Peter Alexandrovich [Pletnev] writes me that they intend to make another petition on my behalf.[2] There's no use; my mother's letter is clear; the answer is final. In Pskov of course there are doctors—what more could I want?

I have no intention of entering into any kind of dealings with my brother. He knew my circumstances, and of his own free will he has been making them more difficult. As for money, I do not have a single kopek for a rainy day; I do not know when and how I shall get any money. The nonchalance and thoughtlessness of self-centeredness are excusable only to a certain degree. If he would get the notion of copying my verses, instead of reading them at suppers and embellishing Voeykova's album with them, then I would be grateful to him; if not, then let him give my manuscript to you, and then you and Pletnev have the copying done.

I have heard that you are getting married in August; I congratulate you, my dear one—be happy, though that's devilishly hard to do. I kiss your fiancée's hand, and sight unseen I love her as the daughter of Saltykov and the wife of Delvig.[3]

July 23.

Praskovia Alexandrovna [Osipova] has left, and I am alone.

Why was my sensible and reasonable letter[4] replaced by my

mother's letter? Weren't they relying on the susceptibility. . . .?
. . . .[5] An important error! In the former case I would have been
acting straightforwardly; in the second, they could only suspect me
of slyness and unyieldingness.

A certain Vibius Serenus, upon being denounced by his own son,
was sentenced by the Roman Senate to being confined on a certain
waterless island. Tiberius opposed this decision, saying that a man
to whom life has been granted must not be deprived of the means for
sustaining life. Words worthy of a lucid and humane mind! The more
I read Tacitus,[6] the more reconciled I am to Tiberius. He was one
of the greatest intellects among the rulers of antiquity.

[134]

To Anna Petrovna Kern
July 25, 1825. From Mikhaylovskoe to Riga.
(In French)

I had the weakness to ask you for permission to write you, and
you the thoughtlessness or the coquetry to permit me to do it. A
correspondence leads to nothing, I know; but I do not have the
strength to resist the desire to have a word from your pretty hand.

Your visit to Trigorskoe has left me with a stronger and more
painful impression than our meeting at the Olenins[1] produced once
upon a time. The best I can do in the depths of my sad village is to
try not to think of you any more. You would also wish me not to,
if only you had any pity in your soul—but frivolity is always cruel,
and you women, while you are turning heads right and left, are
delighted to know of a soul suffering to your honor and glory.

Farewell, divine one. I am frantic, and I am at your feet. A
thousand amiabilities to Ermolay Fedorovich [Kern][2] and my
compliments to Mr. [Alexey N.] Vulf.

July 25.

I take up my pen again, because I am dying of boredom, and I
can't get you off my mind. I hope you will read this letter in secret—
will you hide it again in your bosom? Will you answer me at considerable length? Write me all that comes into your head, I entreat
you. If you fear my indiscretion, if you do not wish to compromise
yourself, disguise your handwriting, sign with a fictitious name—
my heart will be able to recognize you. If your words should be as

sweet as your glances, alas! I shall try to believe them or to be deceived; it's all the same. Do you know in rereading these lines, I am ashamed of their sentimental tone—what will Anna Nikolaevna say? *Ax vy čudotvorka ili čudotvorica!*[3]

Do you know what? Write me this way and that;[4] it is so nice.

[135]

To Praskovia Alexandrovna Osipova
July 25, 1825. From Mikhaylovskoe to Riga.
(In French)

Here, Madame, are two letters addressed to you and which have just come. One is from Pletnev and was enclosed in one to me.

I hope that you will have arrived in Riga gaily and happily before you receive these letters. My Petersburg friends were convinced that I would accompany you. Pletnev writes me a rather strange piece of news: His Majesty's decision has seemed to them a misunderstanding, and they have decided to speak to him of it again.[1] My friends are going to go to such lengths that it will end with me being locked in the Shlisselburg, where most certainly I would not have the proximity of Trigorskoe, which, all deserted as it is now, is still a consolation for me.

I am awaiting very impatiently some news of you—give me some, I implore you. I do not speak to you of my respectful friendship or my eternal gratitude. I greet you from the bottom of my soul.

July 25.

[136]

To Lev Sergeevich Pushkin
July 28, 1825. From Mikhaylovskoe to Petersburg.

If Pletnev had shown you my letters, you would have understood my position. Now I am writing you from necessity. You knew that I would need money; I was relying on you as a brother—meanwhile a year has passed, and I don't have a cent. If I had dealt with nobody but booksellers I would have had some 15 thousands.[1]

You took 2000 rubles from Pletnev to buy up my manuscript,[2] and you paid out 500; have you paid up the remaining 500? And isn't anything left from the remaining thousand?

Have the 600 rubles been paid to Vyazemsky?[3]

I sent my manuscripts to you in March—they are still not arranged, still not through the censorship. You read them to your friends until they spread them by heart to the Moscow public. I thank you.

Delvig's letters do not reach me. The publication of my long poems will never go forward. Meanwhile I have refused Zaikin's offer.[4] Now I ask you, if possible, to renew the negotiations. . . .

In a word, I must have money or hang myself.[5] You knew that; you promised me capital in less than a year—and I relied on you.

I am not going to reproach you, but by golly there is nothing to thank you for.

July 28.

Zaikin's letter is enclosed. I am not burdening you down with new things to do for me. I ask you solely to explain in full to Pletnev my circumstances—I am relying on his friendship. And if you should take a notion to dictate *The Gypsies* so that it can be given to the censorship[6] before I send my copy, I shall consider myself very much obliged.

[137]
To Ivan Filippovich Moyer
July 29, 1825. From Mikhaylovskoe to Dorpat.

The news has just now been received by me that V. A. Zhukovsky has written you[1] of my aneurysm and has requested that you come to Pskov to perform an operation; you will no doubt consent to do it. But I beseech you, for God's sake do not come and do not disturb yourself about me. The operation which my aneurysm requires is of too little importance to take a famous man away from his occupations and his place of abode. Your benefaction would be agonizing for my conscience. I must not and cannot consent to accept it; I boldly call to witness your own way of thinking and the nobility of your heart.

Permit me to testify of my deepest esteem for you, as a famous man and Zhukovsky's friend.

The Village Mikhaylovskoe.   Alexander Pushkin.

July 29, 1825.

[138]
To Praskovia Alexandrovna Osipova
July 29, 1825. From Mikhaylovskoe to Riga.
(In French)

A pointless letter came for you from Pskov; I have destroyed it. I am sending you another from Batovo and still another from my mother. You will see what a beautiful soul Zhukovsky is.[1] However, since I absolutely cannot have the operation performed by Moyer, I have just written him to implore him not to come to Pskov. I do not know where my mother's hopes are coming from, but I have not believed in hopes for a long time.

[I. M.] Rokotov came to see me the day after your departure; he would have been kinder to have let me be bored by myself. Yesterday I paid a visit to the Trigorskoe manor house, to its garden, to its library. Its solitude is truly poetic, because it is full of you and the memory of you. The kind people who live there really should hurry up and return, but this hope smacks too much of my family selfishness. If Riga amuses you, have a good time and remember sometimes the exile of Trigorskoe (i.e., of Mikhaylovskoe). You see that I continually mix up our dwelling places from force of habit.

July 29.

In the name of heaven, Madame, do not write anything to my mother concerning my refusal to Moyer. That would only cause a useless uproar, for my mind is made up.

[139]
To Nikolay Nikolaevich Raevsky the Younger
July (after the 19th), 1825.
From Mikhaylovskoe to Belogorodka or to Belaya Tserkov.
(Rough draft; apparently not sent; in French)

Where are you? I have seen in the newspapers that you have changed regiments.[1] I hope that amuses you. What is your brother[2] doing? You say nothing of him to me in your letter of May 13; is he undergoing treatments?

Here is what concerns me: My friends have exerted themselves considerably, in order to obtain permission for me to go to take treatments; my mother wrote His Majesty, and thereupon I was granted permission to go to Pskov and even to live there, but I shall do nothing of the kind. I shall only go there for several days. In the meantime I am very isolated: the only neighbor woman whom I have been going to see has left for Riga,[3] and I have literally no company except my old nursemaid and my tragedy;[4] the latter is making headway, and I am satisfied with it. While writing it, I have reflected on tragedy in general. It is perhaps the most misunderstood genre. The classicists and the romanticists have all based their laws on *verisimilitude*, and that is precisely what the nature of drama excludes. Not to speak of time, etc., what the devil verisimilitude is there in a hall cut in two halves, of which one is occupied by two thousand people who are supposed to be unseen by those who are on the boards? (2) *The language*. For example, La Harpe's Philoctète says in good French after hearing a tirade by Pyrrhus: "Alas! I hear the sweet sounds of the Greek language, etc."[5] Consider the ancients: their tragic masks, their double roles—isn't all that a conventional un-verisimilitude? (3) Time, place, etc., etc. The true geniuses of tragedy have never troubled themselves about verisimilitude. Look how Corneille boldly managed *The Cid*. Oh, you wish the rule of 24 hours? So be it, and thereupon he piles up enough events for four months. There is nothing more vain in my opinion than small changes of the accepted rules. Alfieri is profoundly struck by the absurdity of the *aside*; he does away with it and thereupon lengthens the monologue and thinks he has made a revolution in the system of tragedy. What puerility!

Verisimilitude of situations and truth of dialogue—here is the real rule of tragedy.[6] (I have not read Calderon or Vega) but what a man this Shakespeare is! I can't get over it. How paltry is Byron as tragedian in comparison with him! This Byron who never conceived but one sole character (women do not have any character; they have passions in their youth; and this is why it is so easy to paint them), this Byron, then, has parceled out among his characters such-and-such a trait of his own character; his pride to one, his hate to another, his melancholy to a third, etc., and thus out of one complete, gloomy, and energetic character he has made several insignificant characters—there is no tragedy in that.

There is still another mania: when a character is conceived, all that he is made to say, even what is most foreign to him, bears his essential stamp (like the pedants and sailors of Fielding's old novels). One conspirator says "Give me something to drink" conspiratorially —that is only ludicrous. Look at Byron's hater (*ha pagato*),[7] at this monotony, this affectation of the laconic, of continual fury—is it nature? Thence comes this constraint and this timidity of dialogue. Look at Shakespeare. Read Shakespeare; he is never afraid of compromising a character of his, he makes him speak with all the unconstraint of life, because he is sure to find the language of his character for him at the right time and place.

You will ask me: "Is your tragedy a tragedy of character or a historical tragedy?"[8] I have chosen the easier genre, but I have tried to unite both of them. I am writing and thinking. Most of the scenes require only the reason; when I arrive at a scene which demands inspiration, I wait for it or I skip over the scene—this manner of working is completely new for me. I feel that my soul has become fully developed; I can create.

I [. . . .]

[140]

To NIKOLAY ALEXEEVICH POLEVOY
August 2, 1825. From Mikhaylovskoe to Moscow.

Dear Sir,

I am at fault toward you; I have been long in answering your letter; bothers of every kind have given me no peace, not even for a minute. Neither have I thanked you yet for sending *The Telegraph* and for the pleasure which you afforded me in my isolation—all this is unforgivable.

I rejoice that my verses can be of use for your journal[1] (the best, of course, of our journals). I have written Prince Vyazemsky to take the trouble to deliver them to you—he has a lot of my ravings.

I rely on your indulgence, and I hope that they will please our public.

I assure you of my sincere esteem.

August 2.   Alexander Pushkin.
Mikhaylovskoe.

[141]

To PRASKOVIA ALEXANDROVNA OSIPOVA
August 8, 1825. From Mikhaylovskoe to Riga.
(In French)

Yesterday I received, Madame, your letter of the 31st [of June], the day after your arrival in Riga. You could not imagine how deeply I felt that mark of affection and memory. It went straight to my soul, and from the bottom of my soul I thank you for it.

I received your letter at Trigorskoe. Anna Bogdanovna[1] told me that you are being expected toward mid-August. I dare not hope it. Just what has Mr. Kern[2] been saying to you concerning Mr. Aderkas' paternal supervision with regard to me? Are there any actual commands? Has Mr. Kern anything to do with them? Or are these only public rumors?

I suppose, Madame, that at Riga you are better informed about European news than I am at Mikhaylovskoe. As for news from Petersburg, I know nothing of what is going on there. We are expecting autumn, but we still have several beautiful days to come, and thanks to you I still have flowers in my window.

Farewell, Madame. Please accept the assurance of my tender and respectful devotion. Believe me, there is nothing true or good on earth except friendship and liberty. You have made me appreciate the charm of the former.

August 8.

[142]

To PETER ANDREEVICH VYAZEMSKY
August 10, 1825. From Mikhaylovskoe to Reval.

Have you had your fill of bathing in the sea, and where are you thinking of leaving Reval for? Please write. But I shall not budge from Mikhaylovskoe.[1] What about your Byron?[2] Send it to me before the press; and are there no verses by the deceased poet Vyazemsky, at least some epigrams? Do you know his best epigram? "What's the use? the prudent one says," etc. Excuse me! I despotically made some changes in it, transposing the verses in the following manner:[3] 1, 2, 3-7, 8-4, 5, 6. Shouldn't it be printed, so as to read: "No, I shall go into the antechamber, the profitable way." If the censorship will not pass the eighth line, then we'll get along without it. The main charming thing is: "I am not a poet, but a nobleman!" And it is still more charming after the dedication of *Voynarovsky*, concerning which Delvig's anger is killingly funny.

How are the Karamzins? I would write them but I am afraid of the proprieties—but I still love them with all my heart. Zhukovsky is playing such pranks with me that it is impossible not to adore him and not to be angry with him.[4] What do you think of our current literature? A real case of the c——! I'm sorry that the inclination for journals has been knocked out of Kyukhelbeker; he is a clever man with a pen in his hands—even though he is a madcap. I am waiting for his analysis of Shikhmatov.[5] What rot it will be, I'll bet! I have just read Polevoy's counter-criticism.[6] No, my dear fellow, that's not it and that's not the way! The analysis "Of the New Poetics of Fables"—that's criticism.[7] Some fine day we'll start a journal! I want to so badly that I don't know what to do, but meanwhile at least look after Polevoy. What shall I regale you with? Here are my bon mots for you (for the sake of the salt, imagine that this was said to a sentimental maiden,[8] of some 26 years): *Qu'est ce que le sentiment?—Un supplément du tempérament.*

What do you like better, the smell of rose or of mignonette?— The smell of herring.[9]

August 10.

[143]
To Praskovia Alexandrovna Osipova
August 11, 1825. From Mikhaylovskoe to Riga.
(In French)

Shall I speak to you of my gratitude? It is indeed kind of you, Madame, not to forget your hermit. Your letters enchant me, just as your generous concern touches me. I do not know what my future may hold, but I know that the feelings which I have avowed to you will be eternally the same. I have been to Trigorskoe again today. The little one[1] is in the best of health, and she is very pretty. Like you, Madame, I believe that the rumors which have reached Mr. Kern are false, but you are right: they must not be disregarded. A few days ago I was at Peshchurov's, the glib lawyer[2]—as you call him—he believed me to be in Pskov (N.B.).[3] I am counting on seeing my old negro of a Great-Uncle,[4] who is, I suppose, going to die one of these fine days, and I must have some memoirs from him concerning my great-grandfather.

I present my respects to all your kind family, and I am, Madame, yours sincerely.

August 11.

[144]
To Vasily Ivanovich Tumansky
August 13, 1825. From Mikhaylovskoe to Odessa.

The storm seems to have calmed down; I dare to peep out of my nest. My dear Tumansky, I have a request to make of you, and I hope that you will not refuse to do me a real favor. Here is what it is: several days before my departure from Odessa, Savelov and I were playing at Luchich's:[1] Luchich lost 900 rubles to me, of which he paid me 300 the very next day, and he transferred the remaining debt of 600 to Savelov, who also consented. Upon my sudden departure I borrowed these 600 rubles from Princess Vyazemskaya (with the consent of Savelov). Afterward I discovered that he [Savelov] is repudiating his debt. The money is gone; so be it. But I am afraid this may be misinterpreted by my friends, of whom I have a lot, and all lovers of gossip. Tell all this simply, *par manière de conversation*, to Luchich. He is an honorable man, and I do not suppose that he would lie in a matter touching his honor. I repeat that I do not need this money, and that I have no intention of even bothering with Savelov. Write me Luchich's response, and that is all.

Of Odessa I know nothing, except the newspaper news; write me something. Of myself I shall tell you that I am completely alone; the Tsar has given me permission to go to Pskov for an operation for my aneurysm, and Moyer wanted to come to me—but I asked him not to trouble himself—and I do not think I shall budge from my village. My friends have petitioned on my behalf against my will, and they seem only to have spoiled my lot. How are you? How is your poetry? Only now and then and too seldom do your verses find their way to me. Please do not forget your talent. I am afraid the prose of your life may overcome the poetry of your soul. Your "Maid to the Poet in Love" is charming! "Sitting with authórs" is the only thing about it that isn't good.[2]

Shouldn't it be this way:

> If you carry on conversations with me, what you note most is
> mistakes in my style. Your looks without expression, etc.

Give my greeting to all my former comrades; I testify to my
respect for Varvara Dmitrievna and Alexander Ivanovich.[3] Farewell, my dear fellow.

August 13.
My address: to Opochka, to the village Trigorskoe, in care of Her
Honor, Praskovia Alexandrovna Osipova.

[145]
To Anna Petrovna Kern
August 13 and 14, 1825. From Mikhaylovskoe to Riga.
(In French)
I am rereading your letter up and down and crosswise, and I am
saying: "*milaja! prelest'!* divine! . . . and then: *ax, merzkaja! . . .*"[1]
Forgive me, beautiful and sweet one, but that is the way it is. There is
no doubt that you are divine, but sometimes you don't have common
sense; forgive me again and be comforted, for you are only the more
charming this way. For example, what do you mean by this seal
which is *to suit you and please you* (happy seal!) and for which you ask
a subject of me? If there is no hidden meaning there, I do not understand what you wish. Are you asking me for a motto? That would
be just like Netty.[2] Enough, keep the *Ne skoro, a zdorovo,*[3] providing
that this is not the motto of your trip to Trigorskoe—and let's talk of
something else. You tell me that I do not know your character.
What do I care about your character? I don't care a straw—should
pretty women have character? The essential things are their eyes,
their teeth, their hands, and their feet (I would have added a heart,
but your girl cousin has discredited that word too much). You say
that it is easy to come to know you; did you wish to say to love you?
I am sufficiently of that opinion and I am even the proof of it. I have
behaved with you like a boy of 14—it is shameful. But since I no
longer see you, I am little by little regaining the ascendant which I
had lost, and I employ it to scold you. If we ever see each other
again, promise me. . . . No, I do not want your promises, and,

besides, a letter is so cold; there is no force nor emotion in an entreaty by mail, and a refusal has neither charm nor voluptousness. Hence good-by—and let us talk of something else. How is your husband's gout coming along? I hope he had a good attack of it on the second day after your arrival. *Podelom emu!*[4] If you knew what aversion mixed with respect I feel for that man! Divine one, in heaven's name see to it that he gambles and has the gout, the gout! That is my only hope.

In rereading your letter, I find a terrible *if* which I did not notice at first. "If my girl cousin[5] remains, I shall come this autumn," etc. In the name of heaven then, may she remain! Try to amuse her, nothing is easier; order some officer of your garrison to fall in love with her, and when the time comes for her to leave, annoy her by taking her admirer away from her; again, nothing is easier. At least do not show her this: from stubbornness she is capable of doing the complete opposite of what she ought. What are you doing with your cousin [Alexey Vulf]? Inform me of it, and frankly. Hurry up and send him to his university; I don't know why, but I don't care for students any more than Mr. Kern does. Mr. Kern is a very worthy man, a wise, prudent man, etc. He has only one shortcoming—that of being your husband. How can anyone be your husband? I cannot imagine it, any more than paradise.

All this was written yesterday. Today, the post day, I do not know why I had gotten it in my head that I would receive a letter from you. That has not happened, and I am in a bitch of a humor, the most unjustly so in the world; I know I ought to be grateful for the last time; but what would you have? I beesech you, divine one—be compassionate to my weakness, write me, love me, and then I shall try to be lovable. Farewell, *dajte ručku.*[6]

[146]

To Olga Sergeevna Pushkina

Between August 10 and 15, 1825. From Mikhaylovskoe to Petersburg.
(In French)

My good friend, I suppose you have arrived. Let me know when you expect to leave for Moscow, and give me your address. I am very sad on account of what has happened to me, but I had predicted it, which is very consoling, as you know. I do not complain of my mother;[1] on the contrary I am grateful to her. She believed she was doing something good for me, she set about it warmly; it is not her fault that she was mistaken. But my friends have done exactly what I had implored them not to do. What madness is this, to take me for a fool and to thrust me into a misfortune which I had foreseen, and which I had pointed out to them? They are embittering His Majesty, they prolong my exile, they make fun of my mode of living, and when they are astonished at all these blunders, they pay me compliments on my excellent verses, and then they go out to dine. What can you expect? I am sad and discouraged. The idea of going to Pskov appears extremely ridiculous to me, but since they will be very glad to know that I am outside Mikhaylovskoe, I am waiting to be notified of the order. All that comes of light-mindedness, of inconceivable cruelty. One more thing: my health requires another climate; not a word was said to His Majesty about that. Is it his fault if he knows nothing of it? They tell me that the public is indignant; so am I, but it is because of the thoughtlessness and the frivolity of those who interfere in my affairs. Oh, my God, deliver me from my friends!

Njanja zaočno u vas, Ol'ga Sergeevna, ručki celuet golubuške moej.[2]

[147]
TO PETER ANDREEVICH VYAZEMSKY
August 14 and 15, 1825. From Mikhaylovskoe to Reval.
August 14.

My dear fellow, poetry is your native language,[1] as is audible from your pronunciation, but just who is to blame that you speak it as rarely as the ladies of 1807 spoke Slavonic-Russian?[2] And over you there is no Shishkov nor Sergey Glinka nor nursemaid Vasilisa, to shout at you, "Be so good as to scold in rhymes, be so good as to complain in verses." I thank you very much for "The Waterfall."[3] Let us muddy it up at once.

. . . *with wrath* the *angry* ruler of the moisture—

Vla Vla[4] are musical sounds, but can one, for example, call lightning "the ruler of heavenly fire"? A waterfall itself consists of moisture, just as lightning itself is fire. Come on and change it some way or other, "from some kind of *rapids, heights,*" etc.

The second stanza is charming!—The rain is spattering *from*

> (some kind of) clashing
> Of your *mutual* waves.

Mežduusobnyj [mutual] means *mutuel*, but it does not include the idea of warfare, quarrel[5]—you absolutely must fill out the meaning here.

The 5th and 6th stanzas are charming.

> But you, the nursling of secret storm.

Not a nursling, rather a parent—and that is not good—shouldn't it be rival? *Secret*, speaking of a thundering waterfall is not good— nor about a physical storm. "The plaything of deaf war" is not completely precise. "You are not a mirror," etc. Wouldn't it be clearer and more lively: "You do not *accept* their azure," etc.[6] Precision would require "you do not reflect." But your repetition of *you* is necessary here.

"Under the terrible banner," etc. "You preserve," etc., but all the stanza is confused. "The embryo of bad weather" in a waterfall; it's hazy. "Eternally beating *fire*" is a triple metaphor. Oughtn't you strike out the whole stanza?

"Having torn into" is marvelously good. "As amid the desert," etc. You ought not to distract the attention here with a double comparison, and the comparison is not precise, at that. Come on and destroy "the whirlwind" and "the desert"—look what will come of it:

> Like you, it will suddenly flame up.

Here, do you see? You spoke of the *fiery* waterfall metaphorically, i.e., "sparkling, like fire," but here you transfer to the heat of passion this same waterfall-flame (I couldn't express myself worse, but you understand me). And so, isn't it better:

> Like you, it will *as in a desert* burst forth

etc. Eh? Or something else. But "it will flame up" is too far fetched.

Write me wherein you agree with me. I need your letters for my mind much more than an operation for my aneurysm. They enliven me exactly like an intelligent conversation, like Rossini's music, like the lusty coquetry of an Italian girl. Write me; in Pskov that would be a benefaction for me. "I called *unexpected* guests together" is charming[7]—wouldn't "uninvited" be still better? No, *cela serait de l'esprit.*[8]

Enclosed is a business document; for God's sake make business use of it.

[On a separate sheet:]

In 1811 my uncle Vasily Lvovich, in accordance with his favorable inclination toward me and all my family, during a trip from Moscow to Saint Petersburg, borrowed from me 100 rubles in paper money which had been given to me for pocket money by my late grandmother[9] Varvara Vasilievna Chicherina and my late aunt Anna Lvovna. The witness of this loan was a certain Ignaty; but Vasily Lvovich himself, in the nobility of his heart, will not deny the same. Since more than ten years have already passed without any exaction or presentation for the same, and since I have already lost my legal right to exact the repayment of the above-mentioned 100 rubles (with interest for 14 years, which makes more than 200 rubles), I humbly beg His High Nobility, Dear Sir, my uncle, to pay me these 200 rubles according to Christian duty—I name as my plenipotentiary to receive this same money Prince Peter Andreevich Vyazemsky, a well-known man of letters.

Collegiate Secretary
Alexander son of Sergey Pushkin.

August 15, 1825.
The Village Mikhaylovskoe.

[148]

To Vasily Andreevich Zhukovsky
August 17, 1825. From Mikhaylovskoe to Petersburg.

Father, into thy hands I commend my spirit. I am truly ashamed that my veins are disturbing all of you so much. An operation for aneurysm is of no significance, and by golly the first Pskov horse-doctor[1] could manage it. I shall go to Pskov no sooner than deep autumn; I shall write you from there, bright soul. A few days ago

I saw an amateur doctor at Peshchurov's; he gave me more re-assurance—only it's Kyukhelbekery[2] for me here. I agree that my life has sometimes strayed toward an epigram, but in general it has been an elegy, something like Konshin's. Apropos of elegies, my tragedy is coming along, and I shall finish it, I think, by winter;[3] conse-quently I am reading only Karamzin and chronicles. What a marvel these two last volumes of Karamzin[4] are! What life! *C'est palpitant comme la gazette d'hier,*[5] as I have written to Raevsky.[6] One request, my charming one: Can't you obtain for me either the life of the *Iron Pointed Cap* or the life of some holy fool?[7] In vain I have sought for Vasily the Blessed in *The Menologion*[8]—I need it very badly.

I embrace you from my soul. I see by the newspapers that Perov-sky[9] is where you are. Fortunate man! He has seen Rome and Vesuvius.

August 17.   P.

[149]

To Anna Petrovna Kern
August 21(?), 1825. From Mikhaylovskoe to Riga.
(In French)

You are disheartening.[1] I was in the mood to write you foolish things which would have made you die laughing, and then your letter came to sadden me, right in the middle of my verve. Try to rid yourself of the twitches which make you so interesting, but which, I warn you, are not worth the devil of a thing. Just why do I have to scold you? If you had your arm in a sling, there was no need to write me. What an unruly thing you are!

But tell me, what has your poor husband done for you? Is he not by chance jealous? Oh, well, I swear to you that he would not be wrong; you do not know how (or what is even worse) you do not wish to deal tactfully with people. A pretty woman is indeed mistress . . . of being the mistress. My God, I am not going to preach morals. But yet respect is due a husband, else nobody would want to be one. Do not oppress the vocation too much; it is necessary in the world. Consider! I am speaking to you with an open heart. At 250 miles distance you have found the means of making me jealous; what then would happen at four steps? (N.B.: I should very much like to know why your cousin [A. N. Vulf] left Riga only on the

15th of this month, and why his name turns up on the point of your pen three times in your letter to me? Would it be rude to inquire?) Forgive me, divine one, if I tell you frankly my manner of thinking. It is a proof of the true interest I take in you; I love you more than you believe. Try, then, at least a little, to get along with the accursed Mr. Kern. I well understand that he may not be a great genius, but, after all, no more is he a complete imbecile. Some gentleness, some coquetry (and above all, in the name of Heaven, refusals, refusals, and refusals) will put him at your feet, a place which I envy him from the bottom of my soul; but what can one do? I am in despair at Annette's² departure; whatever happens, you absolutely must come here or else to Pskov this autumn. An illness of Annette's could be the pretext. What do you think? Answer me, I beseech you; and do not say anything about it to Alexey Vulf. You will come, won't you? Until then, do not decide anything with regard to your husband. You are young, your whole lifetime is before you—but he. . . . Well, you may be sure that I am not among those who would never counsel a violent course—sometimes it is unavoidable. But first you must try to be reasonable and try not to create a needless scandal.

Farewell; night is falling, and your image appears before me, all sad and all voluptuous—I fancy I see your glance, your parted lips.

Farewell. I fancy I am at your feet, I press them, I feel your knees —I would give my life's blood for one minute of reality. Farewell, and believe in my delirium; it is absurd but true.

[150]
To Anna Petrovna Kern
August 28, 1825. From Mikhaylovskoe to Riga.
(In French)

Here is a letter for your aunt; you may keep it for her if she by chance is no longer in Riga. Tell me, is it possible to be as flighty as you are? How could a letter addressed to you have fallen into hands other than yours? But, since what is done is done, let us talk of what we shall have to do.

If your husband wearies you too much, leave him—but do you know how? Leave all the family there, take post horses for Ostrov, and come . . . where? To Trigorskoe? Not at all. To Mikhaylovskoe!

Here is the fine project which has been plaguing my imagination for the past quarter of an hour. But can you conceive of how happy I would be? You will tell me: "And the hullabaloo, and the scandal?" The devil with it! When a woman leaves her husband, the scandal is already complete; the rest is nothing or very little.[1] But won't you admit that my project is romantic? Conformity of character, hatred of barriers, a very pronounced organ of flight, etc., etc. Can you conceive of your aunt's[2] astonishment? A rupture would ensue. You would see your cousin [Anna N. Vulf] in secret; that is the way to make friendship less dull. And once Kern is dead, you are as free as the air. . . . Now then, what do you say about it? Didn't I tell you that I was in the mood to give you a bold and striking piece of advice!

Let us speak seriously; that is, coldly: shall I see you again? The idea that I shall not makes me shudder. You will tell me: "Console yourself." Very well, but how? Fall in love? Impossible. First I would have to forget your twitches. Go abroad? Strangle myself? Get married? All these things present great difficulties; I am loath to do any of them. . . . Oh! by the way, how am I going to get your letters? Your aunt is opposed to this correspondence, so chaste, so innocent (and how else . . . at 250 miles?). Our letters will probably be intercepted, read, commented upon, and then burned with ceremony. Try to disguise your handwriting, and I shall see to the rest. But write me, and a lot, lengthwise and crosswise and diagonally (a geometrical term). This is what *diagonal* means.[3] But above all give me the hope of seeing you again. If not, really, I shall try to fall in love with somebody else. I was about to forget: I have just written Netty a very tender, very humble letter.[4] I am extremely fond of Netty. She is naive—and you are not. Why aren't you naive? I am much more amiable by the post than face to face, am I not? Well, if you come, I promise to be extremely amiable—I shall be gay on Monday, exalted on Tuesday, tender on Wednesday, light-hearted on Thursday, and on Friday, Saturday, and Sunday I shall be whatever will please you, and all the week at your feet. *Farewell.*

August 28.

Do not unseal the enclosed letter.[5] That is not nice. Your aunt would get angry.

But marvel at how the good Lord mixes things up: Mme. Osipova unseals a letter to you, you unseal a letter to her, I unseal a letter from Netty—and we all find something there to edify us. Truly we are under a spell!

[151]

To Praskovia Alexandrovna Osipova
August 28, 1825. From Mikhaylovskoe to Riga.
(In French)

Yes, Madame, evil be to him who evil thinks. Oh, these evil-minded people who believe that a correspondence could lead to anything![1] Could it be that they know from experience? But I forgive them; you do the same, and let us proceed.

Your last letter (of midnight) is charming; I laughed heartily. But you are too severe toward your amiable niece. It is true that she is feather-brained, but have patience: another score of years and she will correct herself, I promise you. As for her coquetry, you are completely right; it is disheartening. Why isn't she satisfied at pleasing Sire Kern, since she has that good fortune? No, she must also turn the head of your son, her cousin.[2] When she came to Trigorskoe she took the notion to captivate Mr. Rokotov[3] and me. That is not all: when she arrived at Riga, she saw a confounded prisoner in the confounded fortress, she became the coquette Providence of the damned *katoržnik!*[4] Nor is that all. You inform me that there are more uniforms in the affair, too! Oh, it is indeed too much: Mr. Rokotov will find out, and we shall see what he will have to say. But, Madame, do you seriously believe that she would play the coquette *indifferently*? She says not, I should like to believe that, and what reassures me still more is that everybody does not have the same manner of paying court, and if only the others are respectful, timid, and fastidious, that is all I need. I thank you, Madame, for not delivering my letter;[5] it was too tender, and in the present circumstances it would be ludicrous of me. I am going to write her another, with my characteristic impertinence, and I am going to break with her decisively. Let it not be said that I have tried to bring trouble into the bosom of a family, that Ermolay Fedorovich[6] could accuse me of not having any Principles and that his wife could be making fun of me. You are very nice, aren't you, to have found that the portrait resembles her: "Bold in," etc.[7] She still tells me that it does not, but that's all over; I shall not believe her any more.

Farewell, Madame. I await your arrival with great impatience. We shall speak ill of Netty of the North,[8] whom I shall always regret having seen, and still more not having possessed. Pardon this avowal, a little too sincere, made by one who loves you very tenderly, although very differently.

Mikhaylovskoe.

[152]
To KONDRATY FEDOROVICH RYLEEV
Between the second half of June and the end of August, 1825.
From Mikhaylovskoe to Petersburg.
(Rough draft)

I am vexed that Ryleev does not understand me.—What is the matter? That "with us literature is not protected"[1] and that "thank God"? But why talk about it? *Pour réveiller le chat que dort?*[2] That's wrong. We are obliged, for the spirit of our present-day literature, to the indifference of the government and the oppression of the censorship. What more do you want? Take a glance at the journals, look how many times in the course of six years I have been mentioned, how many times I have been praised rightly and wrongly— and not even a murmur about our friend,[3] as though he did not exist. Why is this? Certainly not because of the pride or the radicalism of such-and-such a journalist. No. And everybody knows that even if he himself should start playing the scoundrel, nobody would say thanks or give him five rubles—so it is better to be an honorable man for nothing. You are angry at my bragging of my 600-year-old nobility (N.B.: My nobility is more ancient). How is it you do not see that the spirit of our literature depends in part on the status of writers? We cannot offer up our compositions in tribute to noble lords, for we consider ourselves their equals in birth. Hence the pride, etc. Russian writers must not be judged like foreigners. There writing is done for money, but here with us (except for me) from vanity. There they live on their poems; here with us Count Khvostov went broke on them. There if one has nothing to eat, he writes a book; but here with us if one has nothing to eat, let him go into the government service, but not write books. My dear fellow, you are a poet, and I am a poet. But I judge more prosaically than you do, and I am scarcely wrong in doing so. Farewell, my dear fellow. What are you writing?

[153]

To Alexey Nikolaevich Vulf
The end of August, 1825. From Mikhaylovskoe to Dorpat.

Dear Alexey Nikolaevich,

I haven't got around to thanking you for your friendly efforts with regard to my accursed compositions; the devil take them and the Censor, and the typesetter,[1] and *tutti quanti*.[2] That is not the point now. My friends and parents are eternally playing pranks on me. Now they have sent my calash to Moyer so that he can come in it to see me, and then leave, and send the poor calash back again.[3] Make him understand. Give him from me my word of honor that I do not want this operation, although I should be very glad to become acquainted with him. And do me the favor of writing a couple of words about the calash. How is it? Where is it? etc.

Vale, mi fili in spirito.[4] Give my greetings to Yazykov. A few days ago I wrote an imitation of his Elegy "Go Away."[5]

[154]

To Pavel Alexandrovich Katenin
Between September 1 and 14, 1825.
From Mikhaylovskoe to Kologriv.

You cannot imagine, dear and honored Pavel Alexandrovich, how I was gladdened by your letter, a sign of your unchanged friendship. . . . Our connection is not based on an identical mode of thinking, but on love for identical pursuits. You pain me with your protestation that you have abandoned poetry—our common mistress. If that is true, then what will console you, and who will console her? . . . I had been thinking that you were doing creative work in your wilds; but no—you are fussing about and litigating. And in the meantime the years are hastening by.

Heu fugant, Posthume, Posthume, labuntur anni.[1]

And what is worst of all, together with them the passions and inspiration are flying away. Heed me, dear one, lock yourself in and get started on a romantic tragedy in eighteen acts[2] (like Sofia Alexeevna's tragedies).[3] You would accomplish a revolution in our literature, and nobody is more worthy of that than you. I have read in Bulgarin[4] your third act, which is charming in its majestic simplicity. It keenly reminded me of one of the best evenings of my life. Do you remember? . . . In Prince Shakhovskoy's garret.[5]

What do you think of the first Act of *Venceslas*?[6] In my opinion it is marvelously good. I confess I have not read old Rotrou; I do not know the Spanish language, but I am in rapture over Zhandr; is the whole tragedy finished?

What shall I tell you of myself, of my pursuits? For the time being I have deserted verses, and I am writing my *mémoires*; that is, I am making a smooth copy of my boring, confused, rough-draft notebook. I have four cantos of *Onegin* ready, and also a multitude of fragments. But I don't feel like fooling with them. I am glad that the first canto is to your liking—I like it myself; though I look at all my verses rather indifferently, as on my old pranks with K. . . . ,[7] with the theatrical major,[8] etc.: I won't do it any more! *Addio, Poëta, a rivederla, ma quando?* . . .[9]

[155]

To PETER ANDREEVICH VYAZEMSKY

September 13 and 15, 1825. From Mikhaylovskoe to Moscow.

"You're one yourself!" Have you noticed that in our journals all answers to criticism[1] are based on "you're one yourself"? Bulgarin says to Fedorov:[2] "You're lying"; Fedorov says to Bulgarin, "You're lying yourself." Pinsky[3] tells Polevoy, "You're an ignoramus"; Polevoy retorts to Pinsky, "You're an ignoramus, yourself." One screams: "You are plagiarizing!"; the other, "You are plagiarizing, yourself!" And all are right. And similarly, you're one yourself, my dear fellow; you are looking for noon at 2 p.m., yourself.[4] It was very natural that I was grieved by the Tsar's favor, for I dare not hope for any new favor—and Pskov is worse for me than the village, where at least I am not under the surveillance of the police. It is easy for you to reproach me with ingratitude, at your leisure, but if you were in my place (which God preserve you from), then perhaps you would have become even more enraged than I have. My friends make efforts in my behalf, and the result is that it becomes worse and worse for me. Flaring up, I curse them. Then I think better of it, I thank them for their intention, as a Jesuit would, but just the same it is no easier for me. For five years I cherished my aneurysm as the last pretext for my deliverance, the *ultima ratio libertatis*—and suddenly my last hope is shattered by the accursed permission for me to go take treatments in exile! My dear fellow, in spite of myself my head is going round and round. They are solicitous about my life; I thank them. But what the devil good is such a life? Why, it would be much better to die in Mikhaylovskoe from lack of treatments. At least then my tomb would be a living reproach, and on it you could write an agreeable and useful epitaph. No. Friendship is entering into a conspiracy with tyranny and is undertaking to justify it, in order to avert my indignation. For me they summon Moyer, who could of course perform the operation even in a Siberian mine. They deprive me of the right to complain (not in poetry but in prose, a devil of a difference!), and then they forbid me to be enraged.[5] Nothing doing! I know that the right to complain, like everything else, amounts to little, but it exists in the nature of things. Just you wait. Do not play the demon, Asmodeus: your ideas about public opinion, about the vanity of persecution and martyrdom are (let us suppose) just. But good gracious! . . . That is my religion; I am no longer a fanatic, but I am still devout. Do not take away the hope of heaven and the fear of hell from the *sximnik*.[6]

Why am I unwilling to consent to Moyer's coming to me here? I am not wealthy enough to summon famous doctors and pay them for treating me. Moyer is Zhukovsky's friend, but he is not Zhukovsky. I want no charity from him. And that's all there is to it.

You admit that in your "Waterfall" you were writing of a passionate person, rather than of water. Hence the imprecision of certain expressions. From my soul I thank Karamzin for the Iron Pointed Cap which he is sending me; in exchange I shall send him my colored[7] one, which I have lugged about enough. Really, why shouldn't I become a holy fool; perhaps I would be more blessed![8] Today I finished the second part of my tragedy[9]—I think there will be four in all. My Marina is a fine female: a real Katerina Orlova! Do you know her? But don't tell this to anybody. I also thank you for Karamzin's observation[10] on Boris' character. It has been very useful to me. I had been looking at Boris from the political point of view, without observing his poetic side. I shall set him down to the Gospels, make him read the story of Herod,[11] etc. You want a *plan*? Take the end of the tenth and all the eleventh volume,[12] and there is a *plan* for you.

Oh, my dear fellow, here is a pun for you on my aneurysm; my friends are fussing around about *my vein, but I about my vein of life.*[13] What do you think of it?

September 15.

Résumé: You consider the permission for me to go to Pskov a step forward, but I think it is a step backwards. However, enough about aneurysm—I am fed up with it, just as with our journals.

I am sorry Mukhanov[14] (if it was Raevsky's adjutant) wrote about Staël. He is my friend, and I would not touch him. But all the same he is at fault: Mme. Staël is ours—don't touch her. Anyway, I have spared him. How sorry I am that Polevoy in your absence has plunged into writing answers to criticism. He is long-winded and boring, a pedant and an ignoramus. For heaven's sake put a curb bit in his mouth and break him—at your leisure. I shall have some verses, but wait a little.

Gorchakov[15] vividly reminded me of the Lyceum. He seems not to have changed much—though he has matured and consequently has dried up a little. You have hammered it into his head that I am getting fed up with persecution. Oh, my dear fellow—it makes me sick at my stomach. . . . But one has to eat what one is offered.

[156]

To Alexander I
Between the beginning of July and the end of September, 1825.
From Mikhaylovskoe to Petersburg.
(Rough draft; not sent; in French)

Some unconsidered remarks, some satirical verses attracted public attention to me; the rumor spread that I had been taken to the secret chancellery and whipped.

I was the last to learn of this rumor, which had become universal. I saw myself as sullied in public opinion. I became despondent. I duelled—I was 20 in 1820. I pondered whether I would not do well to commit suicide or to assassinate—V [. . . .][1]

In the former case I would have only confirmed a rumor which dishonored me. In the latter, I would not have avenged myself, since no outrage had been committed; I would have committed a crime; I would have sacrificed to the opinion of a public which I disdain a man on whom everything depended and whose talent I had involuntarily admired.

Such were my reflections. I imparted them to a friend[2] who was completely of my opinion. He counselled me to take steps justifying myself to the authorities—I felt the uselessness of it.

I resolved to put so much impropriety and insolence in my speech and writings that finally the authorities would be obliged to treat me as a criminal—I hoped for Siberia or the fortress as rehabilitation.

The magnanimous, generous conduct of the authorities,[3] in uprooting entirely a ridiculous calumny, touched me profoundly. From that time up to my disgrace, if sometimes complaints escaped me against the established order of things, if sometimes I abandoned myself to juvenile declamations, I am nevertheless very sure that I have always treated with respect the Person of Your Majesty both in my writings and in my speech.

Sire, I have been accused of having counted on the generosity of your character—I have told you the truth with a frankness which one could not be capable of toward any other sovereign in the world.

Today I appeal to that generosity. My health was greatly impaired in my youth—aneurysm of the heart necessitates a prompt operation or prolonged treatment. Residence in Pskov, the town which has been assigned me, could not provide me any relief, and I beseech Your Majesty to permit me to reside in one of our capitals or else to designate a locality in Europe where I could take care of my life.

[157]

To Anna Petrovna Kern
September 22, 1825. From Mikhaylovskoe to Riga.
(In French)

In heaven's name do not send Mme. Osipova the letter which you found in your packet.[1] Don't you see that it was written solely for your own personal edification? Keep it to yourself, or you're going to cause a misunderstanding between us. I had undertaken to make peace between you, but I despair of it after your last thoughtless acts. . . . Incidentally—you swear to me by all that is holy that you are not playing the coquette with anyone, and you "thou" your cousin;[2] you say to him, "I disdain thy mother." That's dreadful; you should say "your mother," and, indeed, it is not necessary to say anything at all, because that sentence has had a devilish effect. Jealousy aside, as a friend who is truly devoted to you, without mincing matters and without affecting airs, I advise you to break off that correspondence. I don't understand what your object is in playing the coquette with a young student (who is not a poet) at such a respectable distance. When he was near you, you know that I found all that natural—for one must be reasonable. That's settled, isn't it? No correspondence at all—I guarantee you that he will not be less in love on account of that. Are you speaking seriously in appearing to approve my scheme? Annette had goose flesh from it, and my head whirled with joy; but I don't believe in happiness, and it is completely pardonable that I don't. Would you like, angel of love, to convince an unbelieving and withered soul? But come at least to Pskov; that will be easy for you. My heart pounds, I can't see clearly, and I languish at only the idea alone. Could this be only a vain hope, like so many others? . . . Let's come to the point: first a pretext is necessary: a sickness of Annette's—what do you say of that? Or else, won't you make a trip to Petersburg? . . . You will let me know, won't you? Don't deceive me, beautiful angel! May I be indebted to you for knowing happiness before leaving this life! Don't speak to me of admiration; that feeling is not the one. Speak to me of love; I thirst for it. But above all, don't speak to me of verse. . . . Your advice to write to His Majesty[3] has touched me, as a proof that you have thought of me—I thank you for it on my knees, but I cannot follow it. Fate must determine my life; I don't wish to interfere with it. . . . The hope of seeing you again, still beautiful and young, is the only thing that is dear to me. Once more, don't deceive me.

September 22. Mikhaylovskoe.

Tomorrow is your aunt's birthday; so I shall be at Trigorskoe. Your idea of marrying off Annette, in order to have a refuge, is delightful, but I have not communicated it to her. Answer, I beg you, the principal points of this letter, and I shall believe that the world is still worth the trouble of living in it.

[158]

TO PETER ANDREEVICH VYAZEMSKY
Between September 15 and 24, 1825.
From Mikhaylovskoe to Moscow.

[A. M.] Gorchakov will deliver my letter to you. We met and parted rather coldly—at least on my part. He has dried up horribly— but that's the way it must be. We have no ripeness in the North, we either dry up or we rot; the first, all the same, is the better. From having nothing to do, I read him several scenes from my comedy.[1] Ask him not to talk about them or else they will start talking about it, and it will become repulsive to me, just as my *Gypsies* did, which I couldn't finish for that reason. I rejoice, however, at the fortune of my song "Cut Me."[2] It is a very close translation; I am sending you the wild melody of the original. Show it to Vielgorsky[3]—the air seems an extremely happy one. Give it to Polevoy together with the song. My sister writes me from Moscow—do you ever see her? For God's sake prove to Vasily Lvovich that the Elegy on the death of Anna Lvovna[4] is not a production of mine but of some other lawbreaker. He exclaims, "But she left his sister 15,000!". . . That is reminiscent of the tea he gave Milonov to drink.[5] The point is that of course Delvig is more at fault than I am. Intercede for me, my dear fellow, as for a brother—

> Satirist and poet of love, our Aristippus and Asmodeus, you are not the nephew of Anna Lvovna, my deceased aunt. You are a tender, keen, witty writer; my uncle is not your uncle. But my dear one—our Muses are sisters, and so all the same you are my brother.

Variante: "Vasily Lvovich is delicate, witty."

Give my regards to your Princess and my sister—I don't have time to write any more.

[Pushkin enclosed a sheet with the musical score; on the back of it he wrote:]

Do not lose this score; if it does not get printed, show it to Verstovsky.

[159]

To Vasily Andreevich Zhukovsky

October 6, 1825. From Trigorskoe to Petersburg.

A few days ago I saw autumn through my window, and I got in my carriage and galloped to Pskov. The governor[1] received me very nicely. I chatted with him about my blood vessels, consulted with a very kind doctor, and then I came back to my Mikhaylovskoe. Now that I have detailed information about my aneurysm, I shall talk about it sensibly. Praskovia Alexandrovna Osipova, when she was in Riga, spoke of me with all the solicitude of friendship to the surgeon Ruehland.[2] The operation is no trick, he said, but the aftereffects could be grave: the patient must lie motionless several weeks, etc. No matter what you say, my dear fellow, I shall not consent to have it done either in Pskov or Mikhaylovskoe; it's all the same to die, whether of boredom or of aneurysm, but the former death is surer than the latter. I shall not endure being bedridden, come what may. Secondly, the Pskov doctor says that I can get along even without the operation, but strict precautions are necessary. I must not go about much on foot, not ride on horseback, not make any violent movements, etc., etc. I call everybody to witness: what will there be for me to do in the village or in Pskov, if every physical movement is forbidden me? The governor promised to report that it is impossible for me to receive treatments in Pskov—and so let's wait and see, maybe the Tsar will decide on something in my favor.

Now for the third § (and most important one), I positively don't want Moyer. You write, "Accept him, as if it were I." That's hard to do. I am not wealthy enough to order famous surgeons for myself. And I have no intention of receiving treatments gratis—he is not you. Of course I would gladly and with gratitude let you cut off not only my spinal cord, but even my head. A benefaction from you would not be burdensome for me, but from another I don't want it, no matter how good a friend of yours he may be, even Karamzin's son.

My dear fellow, let us await by the seaside for a change in the weather. I shall not die; that is impossible. God wouldn't want *Godunov* to be destroyed with me. Let's wait it out: I greedily accept your prophecy; let my tragedy redeem me. . . . But is our callous age up to tragedies? At least leave me hope. I feel that an operation would take it away from me. It would enslave me to ten years of life in exile. I would no longer have either hope or pretext. It is terrible to think of it, Father! Do not scold me and do not be angry when I am enraged; think of my position; it is not at all enviable, whatever they may be saying. It is enough to drive anyone mad.

Trigorskoe.
October 6.

[160]
To ALEXEY NIKOLAEVICH VULF
October 10, 1825. From Mikhaylovskoe to Dorpat.

Dear Alexey Nikolaevich, I give you my deeply felt thanks for your friendly carrying out of my errands, etc. I thank honored Moyer from my heart. I fully feel and value his good will and his intention to help me—but I repeat positively: I have no intention of taking treatments either in Pskov or in my wilds. I make bold to bring you a most humble request regarding my calash.[1] If (as it may happen) you have the money, hire horses and order it to be sent off to Opochka; if (which also happens) you don't have any money, then write me how much will be needed.—At all events, let's hurry, before the roads become impassable. . . . What news shall I tell you of? You of course already know everything relating to the arrival of Anna Petrovna [Kern]. Her husband is a very nice person;[2] we became acquainted and made friends with each other. I should very much like to fulfill your desire regarding my imitation of Yazykov,[3] but I don't find it at hand. Here is the beginning:

How wide, how deep! No, for God's sake, let me from behind—
etc.

Hasn't Yazykov written something else of the same kind? Or of another? Send it to us—we shall be very grateful.

October 10.

[161]

To Peter Andreevich Vyazemsky

About November 7, 1825. From Mikhaylovskoe to Moscow.

In the wilds, worn out by a life of fasting, with a broken-down stomach, I do not soar like an eagle—I sit and am ill of diarrheic idleness.

I am saving a supply of paper; I am foreign to the effort of inspiration; I rarely go onto Parnassus, and only for great need.

But your ingenious manure tickles my nose pleasantly: It reminds me of Khvostov, the father of toothy pigeons,[1] and it invites my soul again to the defecation of former days.

Thank you, my dear fellow, and I kiss you on your poetic little a——. Since I have been in Mikhaylovskoe I have guffawed only twice: at your critique of the "New Poetics of Fables"[2] and at the dedication of your s—— to s——. How can I help loving you? How can I help groveling before you? However, I am ready to grovel, but no matter what you say I shall not copy—it would be the death of me, and nothing else.

Congratulate me, my dear fellow, upon my romantic tragedy. In it the principal personage is Boris—Godunov! My tragedy is finished; I reread it aloud, alone, and I clapped my hands and shouted, 'at a boy, Pushkin, 'at a boy, you son of a bitch! My holy fool is a very funny young fellow. Marina will make you get a hard on—because she is a Pole and very good looking (of the type of Katerina Orlova, have I told you?). The others are very appealing, too, except for Captain Margeret,[3] who swears obscenely all the time—the censorship won't pass him. Zhukovsky says that the Tsar will forgive me, as a result of my tragedy—hardly, my dear one. Although it is written in a good spirit, there's no way I could hide my ears completely under the pointed cap of the holy fool. They stick out! Your criticism of Krylov is killingly funny: be quiet, I know that myself, but that rat is an old crony of mine.[4] I have called him a representative of the *spirit* of the Russian people[5]—I don't vouch that it does not stink in some respects. In antiquity our common people were called *smerd*[6] (cf. Mr. Karamzin). The point is that Krylov is a most original carcass, Count Orlov is a fool, but we are bumpkins, etc., etc.

I wrote you from Pskov a killingly funny letter, but I burned it up. The bishop there, Father Evgeny,[7] received me as the father of Evgeny.[8] The governor[9] was also extremely gracious. He gave me his own verses, sir, to correct. What do you think of that! Farewell, my dear one.

[162]

To Anton Antonovich Delvig
October or the first half of November, 1825.
From Mikhaylovskoe to Petersburg.

The Tsar, knitting his brows, said: "Yesterday a storm toppled Peter's monument." The other became frightened. "I didn't know it! . . . Really?"—The Tsar guffawed. "April fool, brother."

*

He said with woe to the Ladies in Waiting of the Court: "Beyond the sea men are hanged by[1] their two b——. That is, I mean," he suddenly added, "they are hanged by the neck, but the law is cruel."

Here, my dear fellow, is for you an offshoot of the rhymes of Eristov.[2] Kiss him on the forehead for me. I remember him as the boy who got away from the Polotsk Jesuits. I bless him in the name of Phoebus and noseless Saint Boboly.[3]

I have written my brother about my "André Chénier." Incidentally, have it your holy way. I am afraid that the volume of *Various Poems* may be too thin. Take all the portrait of Tatiana up to "Mad about Richardson" and also the end from "Returned to his Penates"[4] on. What do you think? Write, while you are still not married.

Give my regards to the honored, most intelligent Arzamasian, your future father-in-law,[5] and make an Arzamasian out of your wife without fail.

I am expecting some letters.

[163]
To Peter Andreevich Vyazemsky
The second half of November, 1825. From Mikhaylovskoe to
Moscow.

I had been thinking that you received long ago from Lev Sergeich
the 600 rubles which were stolen by Savelov. I discover that Lev has
squandered them; excuse him and wait for the quitrent which I shall
collect in a few days from my village Saint Petersburg.[1]

Dear one, I am fed up with writing to you, because I cannot appear
to you in my dressing gown, unbuttoned, and with drooping
sleeves.[2] Our conversation is like Mr. Lémontey's introduction.[3]
You and I don't discuss anything but Polevoy and Bulgarin—and
they are unbearable even in a paper binding. You are intelligent,
no matter what you talk about—and compared to you I am a complete fool. Let's come to an agreement: write me and don't wait for
answers.

Is the article about Byron's Abbey yours?[4] What a marvellous
thing *Don Juan* is! I know only the first five cantos; when I read the
first two, I told Raevsky[5] at once that this is Byron's *chef-d'oeuvre*, and
I was made very glad when I saw later that Walter Scott is of my
opinion. I need the English language[6]—and this is one of the disadvantages of my exile: I haven't the means to study, while I have
the time. It's a sin on the part of my persecutors! And I, like A.
Chénier, can tap myself on the head and say: *Il y avait quelque chose
là.* . . .[7] Excuse this poetic bragging and prosaic spleen. I'm so angry
I don't know what to do: I haven't had a good nap or a good
crap.

Why do you regret the loss of Byron's notes? The devil with them!
Thank God they are lost. He made his confession in his verses, in
spite of himself, carried away with the rapture of poetry. In cool
prose he would have lied and acted crafty, now trying to sparkle
with sincerity, now bedaubing his enemies. He would have been
caught in the act, just as Rousseau was caught in the act[8]—and spite
and slander would have triumphed again. Leave curiosity to the
crowd and be at one with Genius. Moore's deed is better than his
Lalla Rookh (as regards poetry). We know Byron well enough. We
have seen him on the throne of glory; we have seen him in the tor-

ments of his great soul; we have seen him in his coffin in the midst of
Greece's rising from the dead. Why should you want to see him on a
chamber pot? The crowd greedily reads confessions, memoirs, etc.,
because in its baseness it rejoices at the abasement of the high, at the
weaknesses of the strong. It is in rapture at the disclosure of anything
loathsome. "He is small like us; he is loathsome like us!" You are
lying, you scoundrels: he's small and he's loathsome, but not the
way you are—differently. To write ones *mémoires* is tempting and
pleasant.[9] There is no one you love, no one you know, so well as
your own self. It's an inexhaustible subject. But it's difficult. Not to
lie is possible, but to be sincere is a physical impossibility. The pen
will sometimes stop, as from a running start before a chasm—on
what an outsider would read with indifference. To contemn—
braver—other people's judgment is not difficult; to contemn one's
own judgment is impossible.

[164]
To Alexander Alexandrovich Bestuzhev
November 30, 1825. From Mikhaylovskoe to Petersburg.
I was made very glad by your letter, my dear fellow; I was already
beginning to think that you were pouting at me—and I am glad of
the things you are doing. The study of modern languages must in our
day replace Latin and Greek—such is the spirit of the age, and its
demands. You—and, I think, Vyazemsky—are the only ones of our
men of letters who are learning; all the others are unlearning. Too
bad! The high example of Karamzin ought to have brought them to
reason. You are going to Moscow; have a chat there with Vyazemsky
about a journal;[1] he himself feels the necessity of it, and it would be a
marvellously good thing. You complain to me for not publishing—
I am fed up with publishing—with misprints, critiques, defenses,
etc. . . . However, my long poems will soon come out.[2] I am fed up
even with them; *Ruslan* is a milksop; the *Prisoner* is a greenhorn, and
in comparison with the poetry of nature in the Caucasus, my poetry
is Golikov-like[3] prose. Incidentally: who was it that wrote about the
mountaineers in *The Bee*? Wasn't it Yakubovich,[4] the hero of my
imagination? When I tell lies to women, I assure them that I played
the bandit with him in the Caucasus, shot Griboedov, buried
Sheremetev, etc.—there is indeed a great deal of romanticism in him.

Too bad I didn't meet him in Kabarda[5]—my poem would have been better. An important thing! I have written a tragedy,[6] and I am very much pleased with it; but it's terrifying to publish it—our timid taste will not endure true romanticism. Among us, romanticism means Lamartine. However much I have read about romanticism, what's said is all wrong; even Kyukhelbeker talks nonsense. What is his *Spirits* like?[7] I haven't read it yet. I'm waiting for a new tale of yours, but just take on a whole novel—and write it with all the freedom of conversation or of a letter, else the style will keep on slipping into Kotzebuese.[8] I give my regards to the "planster" Ryleev, as the late Platov[9] used to say—but truly I love poetry without a plan better than a plan without poetry. My friends, I wish you health and inspiration.

November 30.

[165]

To PAVEL ALEXANDROVICH KATENIN
December 4, 1825. From Mikhaylovskoe to Petersburg.

Your letter gladdened me for several reasons: (1) that it was written from Petersburg,[1] (2) that finally your *Andromache*[2] has been given to the theater, (3) that you are planning to publish your poems, (4) (and which ought to stand first) that you love me as of old. Perhaps the present change of regime will bring me together with my friends. As a faithful subject, I must of course be sad at the death of the ruler;[3] but, as a poet, I rejoice at the accession of Constantine I. There is much romanticism in him; his stormy youth, his campaigns together with Suvorov, his enmity with the German Barklay, all call to mind Henry V.[4] Besides, he is intelligent, and with intelligent people somehow everything is better; in a word, I hope for much good from him. How good it would be if I were a witness and a participant in your triumph this winter! a participant, for your success cannot be alien to me; but will the thought of me occur to them? God knows. I am truly ashamed that they have talked to you so much about my *Gypsies*. That's good enough for the public, but I hope to present to you something more worthy of your attention. I'm fed up with *Onegin*, and it is dormant; I haven't abandoned it, though. I rejoice at the success of Karatygin[5] and I congratulate him upon your approval. I confess I want to come to see you so badly I don't know what to do. Farewell, dear and honored one. Remember me during the first performance of *Andromache*.

December 4.

[166]
TO VILGELM KARLOVICH KYUKHELBEKER
Between December 1 and 6, 1825. From Mikhaylovskoe to Moscow.

Before I thank you, I want to scold you a little. When I received your comedy, I hoped to find a letter in it, too. I shook and shook it, and waited to see whether at least a sheet of writing paper folded into four would not fall out; in vain: no come came, and with spitefulness of spirit I read your *Spirits*,[1] at first to myself, and then aloud as well. Do you want my criticism? You don't, do you? All the same I shall criticize. You admit that the character of the poet is not plausible. The confession is praiseworthy, but this implausibility should be justified, excused, in the comedy itself, not in the preface. The poet himself might have been ashamed of his own superstitition: from this there could be new, comic traits. On the other hand, Caliban is charming. I don't understand why you should want to parody Zhukovsky. That is forgivable in Tsertelev, but not in you. You will say that the laugh will be on his imitators, rather than on him. Dear fellow, remember that though you may write for us, you publish for the mob; it takes things literally. It sees your disrespect for Zhukovsky and is glad of it.

Your word *sir* [orphaned] is an old one. Some will read *syr* [cheese], etc. Your word is very nice and sensible. We must be weaned away from affectation. "I have herded the flocks of my head." (Lice?) But everywhere the poet raves like Shakespeare, his *light ethereal creation*, the speech of Ariel, and the last long speech—it is excellent. Of your versification I shall say that it is negligent, not always natural, the expressions not always precisely Russian—for example, to listen *into both ears*, [. . .],[2] etc. I forgive you all this because of your Caliban, who is marvellously appealing. You see, my dear fellow, that I am frank with you as before, and I am convinced that I shall not anger you thereby. But this I shall anger you with: Prince Shikhmatov, notwithstanding—and withstanding—your long critique, is a soulless, cold, inflated, boring

windbag.... Ouch, ouch, I won't do it any more! Don't beat
me.

[167]
To Peter Alexandrovich Pletnev
Between December 4 and 6, 1825.
From Mikhaylovskoe to Petersburg.

Dear fellow, the point here is not poems—listen *into both ears:*[1] If
I haven't done too thorough a job of weaning my friends away from
interceding for me, probably they will remember me now. . . .[2] If
you're going to take something, then take it—else, why dirty your
conscience.[3] For God's sake don't ask the Tsar for the permission
for me to live in Opochka or Riga; what the devil do I care about
them?—*but request permission to enter the capitals or to go to foreign
lands.* I should like to come to the capital on account of you, my
friends—I should like to talk nonsense with you a while before I die,
but of course it would be more sensible to go overseas. What is there
for me to do in Russia? Show this letter to Zhukovsky, who may be
angry at me. He will manage it somehow. And can't the ladies be
aroused to help? . . . Dear fellow! I am a prophet, by golly a prophet!
I shall order my "André Chénier" published in Church Slavonic
letters in the name of the Father and of the Son, etc. Get me away
from here, my handsome ones, or else I won't be the one who will
read you my tragedy.[4] Incidentally: Borka[5] has also portrayed a holy
fool in his novel. And he is playing the Byron, describing himself![6]
My holy fool is much nicer than Borka's, though—you will see.
Here are letters for you to two more holy fools.[7] Voeykov can't be
up to some mischief, can he? I have not read his September issue.
He is playing the coward with me for some reason. Kyukhelbeker's
Spirits is trash; there are very few good verses; there's no imagination at all. The only thing that is fairly good is the preface. Don't tell
him this—he would be pained.

Ilia Muromets is by Zagorsky, now isn't it?[8] If not, then whom
does the pseudonym belong to? If so, what a pity that he has died!

[168]

To Anna Petrovna Kern
December 8, 1825. From Trigorskoe to Riga.
(In French)

I little expected, enchantress, that you would remember me;[1] from the bottom of my soul I thank you for doing so. Byron has just acquired a new charm for me—all his heroines will assume unforgettable features in my imagination. I shall see you in Gulnare and in Leila—the ideal one of Byron himself could not be more divine. So it is you, always you, that fate sends to enchant my solitude! You are the angel of consolation—but I am only an ingrate, for I still complain. . . . You are going to Petersburg; my exile weighs on me more than ever. Perhaps the change which has just taken place[2] will bring me closer to you; I do not dare to hope so. Let us not believe in hope; she is only a pretty woman who treats us like old husbands. What is yours doing, my sweet genie? Do you know, I imagine the enemies of Byron, including his wife, as having his features.

December 8.

I take my pen again to tell you that I am at your knees, that I still love you, that I detest you sometimes, that the day before yesterday I said horrible things about you, that I kiss your beautiful hands, that I kiss them again pending something better, that I am at the end of my tether, that you are divine, etc.

[169]

To Anton Antonovich Delvig
Between December 15, 1824, and December 15, 1825.
From Mikhaylovskoe to Petersburg.

I read[1] the *Journey over Tavrida* with extreme pleasure. I was on the peninsula the same year and almost at the same time as Ivan Muraviev-Apostol. I am very sorry that we did not meet. I omit comment on his witty researches; to check them one would need the wide knowledge of the author himself. But do you know what struck me most of all in that book? The difference between our impressions. Judge yourself.

We crossed from Asia to Europe on our ship. I immediately set off for the so-called *Tomb of Mithradates* (the ruins of some tower), there I plucked a flower as a souvenir, and I lost it the next day with no regret whatever. The ruins of Panticapaeum had no stronger effect upon my imagination. I saw traces of streets, a half-grown-up gully, old bricks—and nothing else. I traveled from Feodosia all the way to Gurzuf by sea. I stayed awake all night. There was no moon; the stars were twinkling; before me, in the fog, extended the southern mountains. . . . "There is Chatyrdag," the captain said to me. I could not discern it, and I was not even curious. I fell asleep before dawn. Meanwhile, the ship halted in sight of Gurzuf. I awoke and saw a captivating picture: the many-colored mountains were shining; the flat roofs of the Tatar huts from afar seemed to be beehives pasted to the mountains; poplars, like green columns, gracefully rose among them; to the right, enormous Ayu-Dag. . . and all around, this clear blue sky and bright sea, and the radiance and the southern air. . . .

I lived in Gurzuf, going nowhere, I bathed in the sea and stuffed myself on grapes; I became accustomed to southern nature at once, and I enjoyed it with all the indifference and nonchalance of a Neopolitan *lazzarone*.[2] I loved, when I would wake up at night, to hear the roar of the sea—and I spent whole hours listening to it. Two steps from the house grew a young cypress; every morning I visited it, and I became attached to it with a feeling similar to friendship. That is all that my stay in Gurzuf has left in my memory.

I traveled around the southern shore, and the journey of Muraviev-Apostol has revived in me many memories; but his fearful crossing along the cliffs of Kikeneis has not left the slightest trace in my memory. We clambered up the mountain steeps on foot, holding our Tatar horses by the tail. This amused me extremely, and it seemed like some mysterious, Oriental ritual. We crossed the mountains, and the first object, which astonished me, was a birch, a northern birch! My heart was wrung. I even then began to feel nostalgia for the pleasant south—though I was still in the Tavrida, and was still seeing poplars and grape vines. The St. George Monastery and its steep steps to the sea left a strong impression on me. At the same place I saw also the fabulous ruins of the temple of Diana. Apparently mythological legends are luckier for me than historical memories; at least here rhymes paid me a visit, I thought in verses. Here they are:
[. . . .][3]

I arrived in Bakhchisaray ill. I had heard earlier of the strange monument of the khan in love. K———[4] described it to me poetically, calling it *la fontaine des larmes*. When I entered the castle, I saw a ruined fountain; water was falling drop by drop from a rusty iron pipe. I went around the castle with great vexation at the negligence which is reducing it to dust, and at the semi-European alteration of certain rooms. N.N.[5] almost by force took me up the rickety stairs into the ruins of the harem and to the khan's cemetery

but at that time it was not that my heart was full of—

a fever was tormenting me.

As regards the monument to the khan's mistress, which Muraviev-Apostol speaks of, I did not remember it when I was writing my poem—otherwise I would have made use of it without fail.

Explain to me now why the southern shore and Bakhchisaray have an inexpressible charm for me? Why is the wish in me so strong to visit again the places which I left with such indifference? Or is memory the strongest quality of our soul, and is everything charmed by it, subject to it? etc.[6]

Please do not show this letter to anybody, even to my friends (unless when already copied), and indeed the beginning is unnecessary.

Letter 80

1. Alexey Nikolaevich Vulf (1805-1881), friend of Pushkin's and son of Praskovia Alexandrovna Osipova (1781-1859), Vulf by first marriage. She owned Trigorskoe, an estate near Pushkin's mother's estate of Mikhaylovskoe. At this time Vulf and the poet Yazykov were students at the University of Dorpat. The entire Osipova-Vulf family plays a large role in the remainder of Pushkin's life and correspondence. The other members of the family are identified in Letter 84, note 4.

2. That is, Lev (Leo).

3. Pushkin was under the "strict surveillance" not only of the civil authorities but also of the spiritual. Pushkin's father, at the request of Boris Antonovich Aderkas (d. 1831), Governor of Pskov, undertook this surveillance. Pushkin was exasperated, as subsequent letters indicate, at his father's accepting such a task.

Letter 81

1. An official notification informing Pushkin that Oldekop's edition of Pushkin's *Prisoner of the Caucasus* was on sale in Moscow and that Oldekop claimed to have made arrangements for his edition with Pushkin's father, S. L. Pushkin; Vyazemsky requested that Pushkin send him or his uncle, V. L. Pushkin, a power of attorney, to make it possible to stop the sale, if it was without authorization.

2. "Meanwhile tell her that I am at her feet and that she is a charming soul."

3. Another version exists: "Half-milord, half-merchant, half-sage, half-blockhead, half-scoundrel, but there is hope that finally he will become a complete one." Milord is a reference to Vorontsov's Anglomania.

4. Pushkin's "To the Sea," containing lines about Byron.

Letter 82

1. It has not survived.

2. Matvey Egorovich Krupensky.

3. Her father's brother was a lieutenant colonel in General M. F. Orlov's division. Attainment of sufficient rank in the Russian military or civil service made a person and his descendants Russian nobles.

4. The Dowager Empress Maria Fedorovna (1759-1828) ,wife of Paul I, mother of Alexander I and Nicholas I, was protectress of women's educational and other institutions. Zhukovsky, as tutor to the royal family, had the opportunity to present this case to her.

Letter 83

1. That is, V. L. Pushkin's *Poems*, in 1822. As an Arzamasian, V. L. Pushkin had been an enemy of Shishkov's Conversation Society of Lovers of the Russian Word, which in 1816 had ceased to exist.

2. Chapter I of *Evgeny Onegin*.

3. He was engaged in writing the verse tale *Eda* (pub. 1826).

Letter 84

1. This "employment" was to keep Pushkin under strict surveillance for the government (see Letter 80, and note 3).

2. "But thank God our sky is gray, and the moon is just like a turnip."

3. In *Evgeny Onegin*, Chap. II, stanza 5, written while Pushkin was still in Odessa, Pushkin describes how Onegin rebuffs his country visitors.

4. Praskovia Alexandrovna Osipova (identified, together with her son Alexey Nikolaevich Vulf, in Letter 80, note 1). Her family enters much into Pushkin's correspondence henceforth, and includes her children Alexey Nikolaevich Vulf, Mikhail Nikolaevich Vulf (1808-1832), Valerian Nikolaevich Vulf (1812-1845), Anna Nikolaevna Vulf, Evpraxia Nikolaevna Vulf (1810-1883), Maria Ivanovna Osipova (1820-1895), Ekaterina Ivanovna Osipova (1823-1908), and also a step-daughter Alexandra Ivanovna Osipova (d. 1864). Pushkin became an intimate friend of all the family, and these close ties lasted until his death.

5. Which stanza of *Evgeny Onegin* is unknown.

6. I.e., Prince Peter Andreevich Vyazemsky, her husband.

7. Perhaps a young Countess Gurieva, daughter of the Governor of Odessa.

8. "And how is Mily?"

Letter 85

1. Usual day for meetings of the Green Lamp in Vsevolozhsky's home.

2. A ballet dancer.

3. Vsevolozhsky returned the manuscript to Pushkin, asking only 500 rubles for it.

Letter 86

1. This letter was not delivered. For Pushkin's reasons for writing it, see Letter 87.

Letter 87

1. Alexey Nikolaevich Peshchurov (1779-1849), the Opochka District Marshal of the Nobility.

2. "With this monster, this unnatural son."

3. The Shlisselburg Fortress, then used as a prison, the Solovetsky Monastery, and exile to Siberia were the three punishments which threatened Pushkin in 1820, before his friends managed to get his exile commuted to an administrative transfer. By "fortress" Pushkin could also have meant the Fortress of Peter and Paul in Petersburg.

4. "An outlaw."

5. Letter 86. On November 22, Mme. Osipova wrote Zhukovsky that the person by whom Pushkin sent the letter to Aderkas brought it back undelivered, and that Pushkin had destroyed it.

Letter 88

1. Anna Nikolaevna Vulf.

2. Pushkin's sister Olga took this letter to Petersburg with her.

3. See Letter 87.

4. Russian familiar nickname for Petersburg.

5. L. S. Pushkin took the first chapter of *Onegin* for submission to the censorship.

6. Ponce Denis Le Brun was a French lyric poet.

7. Petersburg bookseller.

8. Mikhail Ivanovich Kalashnikov (ca. 1768-1858), then serf manager of the estate of Mikhaylovskoe; after 1825, of Boldino.

9. Published in Moscow in 1809. The repetition of the "(3)" is Pushkin's.

10. Pushkin was then working on his "Imitations of the Koran."

11. Probably Pavel Voinovich Nashchokin (1800-1854), later one of Pushkin's closest friends.

12. Yakov Ivanovich Saburov.

13. Alexandra Andreevna Voeykova (1795-1829), wife of A. F. Voeykov.

14. "Whipper-snapper."

15. A traditional name for a shepherd in love, in eighteenth-century pastorals; from the mythological Myrtilus.

16. "Profligate, countrified gallant."

Letter 88*a*

1. An illustration based on Pushkin's sketch was first printed, not with the first separate edition of the first chapter of *Evgeny ,Onegin* as Pushkin wished, but only in 1829.

2. Mikhail I. Kalashnikov.

Letter 89

1. Probably Karl Friedrich von der Borg's *Poetic Production of the Russians* . . . (in German), Riga and Dorpat, 1823.

2. *The Russian Thalia for* 1825, an almanac published by Bulgarin.

3. The play on words here is untranslatable; the spelling of Thalia, the Greek Muse of Comedy, and the word for "waist" (French: *taille*), are the same in Russian, *talija*.

4. Evpraxia Nikolaevna Vulf. Anetka is Anna Nikolaevna Vulf.

5. What portrait and why Pushkin wanted it are not known.

6. Probably a talisman ring with a Hebrew inscription which had been given to him by Countess Elizaveta Ksaverievna Vorontsova.

7. M. I. Kalashnikov.

8. Pushkin next gives textual corrections.

9. In *Evgeny Onegin*, Chap. I, stanza 17. Denis Ivanovich Fonvizin (1745-1792) was the most important eighteenth-century Russian writer of comedies.

10. B. A. Aderkas.

11. Pushkin hoped to be allowed to go abroad.

12. Pushkin is perhaps indirectly thanking his sister Olga for her sympathy in his exile and also in his recent difficulties with his father.

13. In Pushkin's library were the French edition (Paris, 1824) of Thomas Medwin's *Conversations of Lord Byron*, and also various of Scott's novels in English and in French translation.

14. Pushkin burned them after the Decembrist Uprising in 1825.

15. Senka or Stenka (Stepan Timofeevich) Razin (d. 1671), Cossack hetman and rebel, who led the uprising called by his name, in the seventeenth century.

16. Baratynsky's *Eda*; the title character and heroine was a Finnish girl.

Letter 90

1. The final version of Letter 86. See also Letter 87 and note 5.

2. The terrible flood of November 7, 1824; it later provided the locale and setting for Pushkin's *Bronze Horseman*.

3. "Here is a fine opportunity for your ladies to make their *bidet*."

4. The almanac *Northern Flowers for* 1825.

5. See Genesis 10:20 for the story of Ham and Noah. See also Letter 76 and note 3.

6. Pushkin's maiden aunt Anna Lvovna Pushkina. His references to her are usually ironical. Pushkin and Delvig wrote a joking epitaph on her in 1825. Svyatye Gory (Holy Mounts) was a monastery near Mikhaylovskoe.

7. "Conversation of a Bookseller and a Poet."

8. Ivan Matveevich Rokotov (1782-1840's), a rich landowner who lived near Mikhaylovskoe.

9. Letters to Anna Petrovna Kern (1800-1879), niece of Praskovia A. Osipova. Pushkin later fell in love with her. Anna Petrovna Kern was then living in Lubny, a town in the Ukraine.

10. The burning of Alexandria in 48 B.C. Pushkin's reference is to the Petersburg flood. Alexandria was suggested by the name of Tsar Alexander I.

11. In Pushkin's library, there were three novels by Richardson, not only *Clarissa*, but also *Pamela* and *Sir Charles Grandison* in the London, 1824, edition.

12. Pushkin had sent a sketch on the basis of which he wished a picture to be drawn for *Evgeny Onegin*; it came out without the picture. See Letter 88a, accompanying sketch, and notes.

13. A. A. Bestuzhev and Ryleev.

14. That is, Noah.

15. *Eda*.

16. Countess Ekaterina Markovna Ivelich (1795-1838), an acquaintance, not a cousin.

17. Alexandra Mikhaylovna Kolosova (1802-1880), an actress.

18. "By fair means or foul."

Letter 91

1. Referring to his alleged threat of physical violence to his father. See Letters 86, 87, and 88.

2. See Letter 68.

3. Rodoes Sophianos.

4. See Letter 81.

Letter 92

1. That is, from Odessa to Mikhaylovskoe. Pushkin, who was at this time working on his "Imitations of the Koran," jokingly compares himself with Mohammed; here Pushkin's "Koran" is made up of his early poems.

2. Tanya is the diminutive of Tatiana. The reference is to Tatiana's letter from Chapter III of *Evgeny Onegin*.

3. Pushkin, with his tongue in cheek, applies to his recently deceased maiden aunt, Anna Lvovna Pushkina, the term *frétillon* "fidget," the title of a poem by the French poet Béranger, of whom V. L. Pushkin was very fond. The heroine of Béranger's poem is a woman of light character. V. L. Pushkin published a poem on his sister's death, "To Her," in 1825.

4. Letter 84.

5. Pushkin concludes by quoting his poem "The Cart of Life."

Letter 93

1. Pushkin's poem "Demon," inspired by A. N. Raevsky, was published by Kyukhelbeker incorrectly in *Mnemosyne* as "My Demon." Pushkin objects to the incorrect interpretation which would arise from this error, that A. N. Raevsky was his "demon." Delvig published it with the correct title in *The Northern Flowers for* 1825. In spite of what Pushkin says here, his "To the Sea" was published in *Mnemosyne*, and with mistakes.

2. A correction for Pushkin's "Conversation of a Bookseller and a Poet," published together with *Onegin*, Chapter I.

3. "My descendants would be indebted to me for this shade," quotation from "The Old Man and the Three Young Men" (1678-1679), by La Fontaine. Even though the

old man will not live to enjoy the tree he is setting out, it will provide shade for his descendants.

4. M. I. Kalashnikov.

5. Karamzin's *History* begins with the words, "History in a certain sense is the holy book of nations. . . ."

6. The allusion is to the Petersburg flood of November 7, 1824.

7. Contributions were being listed in the newspaper *Russian Invalide*.

8. The heroine of Pushkin's *Prisoner of the Caucasus*. The heroine of Baratynsky's *Eda* was a Finnish girl.

9. Two pines on the Mikhaylovskoe estate.

10. "If what you say concerning Anna Lvovna's will is true, it is very kind of her. Truly, I have always loved my poor aunt, and I am vexed that Shalikov would have urinated on her tomb." Shalikov had written a lachrymose poem, "To Vasily Lvovich Pushkin: On the Passing Away of His Sister, Anna Lvovna Pushkina." Anna Lvovna Pushkina had bequeathed her estate to several nieces, including Olga Pushkina.

11. Arina Rodionovna (1754-1828).

12. I.e., Trigorskoe; Pushkin puns on the name, so as to make it mean a "threesome" (of hills). The reference is to Anna and Evpraxia Nikolaevna Vulf and their mother Praskovia Alexandrovna Osipova.

13. Vasily Vasilievich Engelgardt (1785-1837), retired colonel and member of the Green Lamp.

14. *Russian Antiquity*, an almanac published by A. O. Kornilovich.

15. Delvig planned to visit Pushkin after finishing work on *The Northern Flowers for 1825*; Pushkin's hope was that Delvig had not suffered losses because of the flood.

16. Ivan Ivanovich Kozlov (1779-1840), blind poet and translator, best known for his translation of Byron's *Bride of Abydos* and for his *Monk*, a verse tale greatly indebted to Byron's *Giaour*.

Letter 94

1. Rodzyanko's greeting and the "kind things" about Pushkin were included in Anna Petrovna Kern's letter to her cousin, Anna Nikolaevna Vulf.

2. Literally, "*Lubny* is glorious beyond the mountains," a paraphrase of the folk expression "the tambourines [*bubny*] are glorious beyond the mountains."

3. Rodzyanko answered Pushkin that his narrative poem *The Ukrainian Girl* had come to an end with the fragments which he had read to Pushkin.

4. *Eda*.

5. Pushkin's *Gypsies*.

6. Porfiry Gavrilovich Rodzyanko, brother of A. G. Rodzyanko.

Letter 95

1. Pushkin had very much liked the Italian opera at Odessa.

2. See Letter 69, note 1.

3. I.e., Worontsov; Pushkin spells Vorontsov's name in such a manner as to get an English pronunciation, to go along with "milord" and to point up further Vorontsov's Anglomania.

4. Praskovia Alexandrovna Osipova and her family.

5. Pushkin's childhood nursemaid Arina Rodionovna; Tatiana is the heroine of *Evgeny Onegin*.

6. See above, Letter 84, note 7.

Letter 96

1. About Pushkin's scheme to flee abroad. There is direct reference below to this plan, and also in the expression "where Chaadaev is staying" (i.e., Switzerland). Among the plans was one suggested by A. N. Vulf, for Pushkin to go abroad with Vulf, disguised as his serf servant.

2. That is, a political poem in the form of a Christmas carol, like Pushkin's earlier "Fairy Tales: A *Noël*."

3. "On account of songs."

4. The censorship passed *Evgeny Onegin*, Chapter I, on December 29, 1824.

5. The words "calendar" and "almanac" were used interchangeably for annuals. The *Court Calendar* included court ranks and possessors of the various orders; the *Academic Calendar* contained lists of all officials. Pushkin wanted almanacs such as *The Polar Star*, *The Russian Thalia*, etc.

6. Shishkov's speech to the Chief Directorate of Educational Institutions, on September 11, 1824, concluded with a declaration against teaching literacy to the whole people or "too large a part of it." Shishkov had a new Censorship Code drawn up, which was adopted by Nicholas I (1796-1855, ruled 1825-1855) in 1826; it was extremely harsh.

7. Apparently Pushkin is thinking of Vorontsov's and Alexander I's anger at him.

8. Jacques Delille, French abbé, poet, and translator of Vergil and Milton. Pushkin contemned the periphrastic style he typified.

9. A quotation from his own "Blessed Is He Who in a Far-Off Spot" (1822), a translation of "Solitude," by the French author Antoine Vincent Arnault.

10. See Letter 90.

Letter 97

1. Ivan Vasilievich Malinovsky (1795-1873), one of Pushkin's friends and Lyceum classmates.

2. See Letter 89, note 6.

Letter 98

1. Ryleev's letter which Pushkin is answering started formally with *vy* and then shifted to the familiar *ty*.

2. Pushkin's close friend Pushchin visited him at Mikhaylovskoe on January 11, 1825, and Pushkin dictated the first part of *The Gypsies* to him for publication in *The Polar Star for* 1825. Ryleev's *Voynarovsky* did not appear in this almanac, but separately.

3. Pushkin's list of humorous poetic works includes Ariosto's *Orlando Furioso* (pub. 1516-1532); Samuel Butler's *Hudibras* (pub. 1663-1678); Voltaire's *Pucelle*; Gresset's *Vert-Vert* (1734); the medieval Flemish satirical poem *Reineke-Fuchs* (*Reynard the Fox*)— which Goethe reworked in 1794; and *Dushenka* (1783) by Ippolit Fedorovich Bogdanovich (1743-1803).

4. Pletnev's article, a defense of Russian writers as against the French, was published in *The Northern Flowers for* 1825. Bestuzhev's opinion was expressed in a letter to Pushkin.

5. The reference is to Batyushkov's madness.

Letter 99

1. Letter 92.

2. Vyazemsky's two poems discussed here were printed in *The Northern Flowers for* 1825.

3. Jean Baptiste Rousseau, French poet and dramatist.

4. *The Russian Invalide.*

5. *The Moscow Telegraph,* a journal published by Nikolay Alexeevich Polevoy (1796-1846), began to appear in 1825. At first Pushkin supported it; his "Cart of Life" appeared in the first issue and also the first lines of his "To the Sea."

6. They did not come at this time.

7. The hero of Fonvizin's play of the same name (1782), usually translated "the adolescent"; it means an adolescent, half-shaped, unformed, ill-educated.

8. Pushkin gives a passage from the poem.

9. "Other times," i.e., how times have changed.

10. A self-quotation from "Once a Tsar Was Told...," written about this time, but published only in 1863.

11. "Manner."

12. Pushkin gives his poem "To Friends."

13. See Letter 98, and note 4.

14. Bestuzhev indicates a low opinion of German poetry in a review of Sir John Bowring's *Specimens of the Russian Poets* (published in English, 1821-1823); Bestuzhev's review was published in *Literary Leaves,* 1824.

15. Pushkin quotes his epigram on F. N. Glinka.

16. F. N. Glinka.

17. I Peter 3:11, or Job 1:1 or 2:3.

Letter 100

1. Princess Vyazemskaya had lent Pushkin six hundred rubles before he left Odessa for Mikhaylovskoe on exile. She was supposed to receive the sum from the gambler Avtonom Petrovich Savelov, to whom a card debt in this amount, owed to Pushkin, had been transferred (see Letter 144). Savelov had not paid as he agreed.

2. A line from Griboedov's *Woe from Wit*; Chatsky is the central character of this play.

3. "Your" *Moscow Telegraph* because Vyazemsky was then taking active part in the journal.

4. Khvostov's "Epistle to N.N. on the Inundation of Petropolis ...." (1825); Pushkin's praise is sarcastic.

5. Nikolay Dmitrievich Ivanchin-Pisarev (1790-1849), an untalented writer.

6. Vladimir Sergeevich Filimonov (1787-1858), minor author: Pushkin's amusement was aroused by his announcement of the forthcoming appearance of *The Art of Living* (1825).

Letter 101

1. Pushchin had delivered to Ryleev a fragment from Pushkin's *Gypsies.*

2. Pushkin's brother Lev knew *The Gypsies* by heart; Pushkin had exacted a promise that Lev would not make a copy of the poem for anybody. Bestuzhev himself knew of the poem from Lev Pushkin's reading it from memory, and he wrote of it in an article in *The Polar Star for* 1825.

3. That is, Griboedov's *Woe from Wit.* Chatsky, Famusov, Skalozub, Molchalin, Sofia, Zagoretsky, and Repetilov are characters from this play. Pushkin's friend Pushchin had brought along a manuscript copy of Griboedov's play. Pushkin's judgment is on the basis of reading it aloud once.

4. "Gresset's Cléon does not parade his wit before Géronte or Chloé"—Pushkin's note. Cléon, Géronté, and Chloé are characters from Gresset's *Naughty One.*

5. Pushkin's "Lay of Oleg the Seer" recounts in verse the story from the *Primary*

Chronicle of how Oleg (d. ca. 912), Prince of Kiev (882-ca. 912), laughs at soothsayers who told him his favorite horse would kill him; as he looks at the horse's skeleton, a snake crawls out of the horse's skull and its bite is fatal to him.

6. Pushkin had filled up the sheet of letter paper; the remainder of the letter is written in the margin.

7. See Letter 99 and note 14.

Letter 102

1. Pavel Khristoforovich Grabbe (1789-1875), army officer, had been deprived of his command and exiled at home in 1822; he was allowed to return to the service in 1823.

2. That is, none unsuitable for publication.

Letter 103

1. Pushkin gives only one of his "18 reasons."

2. Pushkin is referring to Lev Pushkin's reading *The Gypsies* aloud and of his letting it be known in manuscript copies, necessitating its publication.

3. Probably in connection with Pushkin's projected flight abroad.

4. The Shlisselburg Fortress was then used for political prisoners.

5. *Evgeny Onegin*, Chapter I, appeared on February 15, 1825.

6. The *Memoirs* of Joseph Fouché, Duc d'Otrante, French statesman and minister of police under Napoleon, appeared in 1824, four years after his death. His family declared them faked.

7. *Memoirs to Serve as a History of France Under Napoleon, Written by the Generals Who Shared His Captivity and Published with the Manuscripts Corrected Completely by the Hand of Napoleon* (8 vols., 1822-1823), published by Generals Comte Charles Tristan de Montholon and Baron Gaspard Gourgaud.

8. "Manifestly"—Pushkin's note.

9. François Pierre Guizot, French historian and statesman.

10. Comte Henri Gratien Bertrand, French general who accompanied Napoleon on all his campaigns and to St. Elba and St. Helena.

11. "But all that has to do with politics is done only for the rabble."

12. Pushkin is laughing at Pletnev's liking for the minor poet Nikolay Mikhaylovich Konshin (1793-1859); Pushkin's "Konshin" was V. I. Tumansky. Tumansky's "Elegy" was published in *The Northern Flowers for* 1825.

13. That is, Pushkin objects to the misplaced accent. In Letter 144 Pushkin suggests to Tumansky a substitution for the line containing the mispronunciation.

14. A fragment of Ryleev's unfinished long poem *Paley* appeared in 1825.

15. In an article in *The Northern Flowers for* 1825. Baratynsky was serving in Finland as an enlisted soldier as punishment for a prank he had committed when he was only fourteen.

16. Quotation from Zhukovsky's "Gromoboy."

17. That is, in *Voynarovsky*; Ryleev did not include Pushkin's maternal great-grandfather Gannibal, nor did Pushkin in his own *Poltava* (written 1828), which also presented the Battle of Poltava (1709) in which Peter the Great's forces crushed those of Charles XII of Sweden.

Letter 104

1. Peter Alexandrovich Mukhanov (1799-1854), whom Pushkin had known in Odessa, and who must have come into possession of these verses from letters of Pushkin's, which have not survived, which he had for delivery to Pushkin's literary friends.

2. "He has deserved well of the sex, and I am very glad that I have expressed myself publicly to this effect."

3. Pushkin uses the biblical word *obetovannyj*, which is used to refer to the Promised Land. His "Cart of Life" appeared in the first issue of *The Moscow Telegraph*.

4. Pushkin cites the title in English, and in his own eccentric spelling, here as elsewhere. Pushkin long wanted to have his own journal, before he was finally given permission to found *The Contemporary* in 1836. Pushkin's prime models were the great English quarterly reviews.

5. Vyazemsky's biography of Fonvizin, begun in 1819, but not published until 1848.

Letter 105

1. Gnedich's translation of twelve *Folk Songs of the Modern Greeks* (1825), printed together with the originals and with explanatory comments. Gnedich thought the Greek folk songs very similar to Russian folk songs.

2. Pushkin lists a number of heroes of Russian history as suitable subjects for epic poems. Svyatoslav (d. 972 or 973, ruled ca. 945-972) and Vladimir (see Letter 14 and notes) were princes of Kiev; Mstislav (d. 1036) founded the ancient principality of Tmutarakan; Dimitry Donskoy (1350-1389, ruled in Moscow, 1359-1389) defeated the Tatars at Kulikovo in 1380; Ermak Timofeevich (d. 1584) conquered Western Siberia for Russia; Prince Dmitry Mikhaylovich Pozharsky (1578-ca. 1642) was Commander-in-Chief of the Russian Army against the Poles at the end (1610-1613) of the Time of Troubles.

Letter 106

1. Apparently their parents' strict measures with regard to L. S. Pushkin's visiting the poet.

2. Roza Grigorievna was the housekeeper at Mikhaylovskoe; she had been hired by Pushkin's mother.

3. Vasily and Arkhip were serfs on the Pushkin estate.

4. This correspondence has not survived; Bulgarin did not print the fragments from *Onegin.*

5. The reference is to Pushkin's "friends" who allowed his poems to be disseminated from the manuscript before appearing in print.

6. Pushkin's use of the word "friend" is sarcastic. Under the title of "Land and Sea" the poem appeared in Voeykov's *Literary News* in 1825 without Pushkin's attribution of it to Moschus. Here by Bion, Moschus' friend and teacher, Pushkin jokingly means his "friend" Voeykov.

7. Pushkin jokingly calls the French poet Parny "Ivan Ivanovich"; Pushkin's poem "Proserpine," a free paraphrase of the twenty-seventh picture in Parny's *Les Déguisements de Vénus*, was published in *The Northern Flowers for* 1825.

8. *Izdatel'* . . . *P——atel'*.

9. Egor Vasilievich Aladiin (1796-1860); Pushkin's letter to him has not survived. Aladiin lied, in saying that works by Pushkin would appear in his almanac; none did.

10. Izmaylov's "Black Tomcat" appeared in *The Neva Almanac for* 1825 and in *The Well-Intentioned* in 1825.

11. Gavriil Abramovich Pakatsky (d. 1830); his verse translation of The Book of Wisdom of Jesus, Son of Sirach, or Ecclesiasticus, appeared in 1825.

Letter 107

1. A short and ambiguous announcement about the appearance of the first chapter of *Onegin* appeared in Bulgarin's *Northern Bee* in 1825. Bulgarin and Grech (publisher of

The Son of the Fatherland) were then in substantial agreement on all major questions; hence Pushkin's further comment.

2. An ataman and an esaul were Cossack officers. Pushkin is referring to the likelihood of their rising against him, as the proverbially rebellious Cossacks did against the Russian Tsar.

3. Exactly what fragments are meant is unknown.

Letter 108

1. N. V. Vsevolozhsky. Why Pushkin calls him the "Algerian," the editor has been unable to discover.

2. Pushkin's brother finally recovered for him the manuscript of his early poems (see Letter 92). Pushkin revised them, and they appeared as *Poems of Alexander Pushkin* on December 30, 1825, with the date of 1826.

3. Delvig came to see Pushkin at the end of April.

4. Pushkin wished Simonde de Sismondi's *Of the Literature of the South of Europe* (second French edition, 1819).

5. Pushkin wanted *Of Dramatic Art and Literature* (1809-1811), by August Wilhelm von Schlegel.

6. *Collection of New Russian Poems, Appearing from 1821 to 1823* (Part I) and . . . *from 1823 to 1825* (Part II), 1824-1826. They were published by Voeykov.

7. Kachenovsky had published in his *Messenger of Europe* an article, not by him, considering *Onegin* a "bad" poem and hence Pushkin a "negative magnitude" in poetry.

8. A discussion was conducted in *The Moscow Telegraph* during 1824-1825 over the nature or essence of poetry. The position was taken that the essence of poetry is not in the form (Pushkin interprets this as *verses*) but in the poetic rapture, or afflatus.

9. Apparently a popular song.

10. See Letter 88, note 15.

11. Anna Ivanovna Vulf (d. 1835), nicknamed Netty, cousin of Anna Nikolaevna Vulf and niece (by first marriage) of Praskovia Alexandrovna Osipova.

12. *Folk Songs of the Modern Greeks.*

13. Why Pushkin put this question in quotation marks, and what he had in mind are not clear. Perhaps he meant that he knew Parny by heart and had no need of his works.

Letter 109

1. For some reason at this time there was a police check into L. S. Pushkin's behavior and service.

2. General Arseny Andreevich Zakrevsky (1783-1865), at this time Governor General in Finland, where Baratynsky was serving in the army as an enlisted man. Baratynsky was indeed commissioned an officer in 1825 and allowed to retire from the army in 1826. At this time Baratynsky was in love with General Zakrevsky's wife, Agrafena Fedorovna Zakrevskaya (1799-1879), to whom Pushkin was later attracted himself (see Letter 234).

Letter 110

1. See Letter 108 and note 2.

2. Batyushkov's *Attempts in Verse and Prose* (1817), published by Gnedich.

3. Apparently neither Zhukovsky nor Gnedich participated in the edition. The juxtaposition of Gnedich's and Griboedov's names here is an allusion to a literary quarrel they had in 1816 over a translation by Katenin; apparently the juxtaposition of the names of Zhukovsky and Bulgarin is a joke.

4. None was published.

5. From Zhukovsky's "Butterfly and the Flowers" (1824); the butterfly had taken the flower as being another butterfly.

6. Count Fedor Petrovich Tolstoy (1783-1873), well-known dilettante painter and illustrator.

7. Quotation from I. I. Dmitriev's poem "The Fashionable Wife" (1791).

8. Nikolay Ivanovich Utkin (1780-1863), most famous of nineteenth-century Russian engravers.

9. That is, before Shishkov became Minister of Public Education.

10. Pushkin means that he wishes the poems to be published without decorative typographical frills.

11. Pushkin means that he wishes the titles printed on a separate line, with paragraph indentation, and that two couplet-poems may be printed on the same page, with proper spacing and paragraph indentation for the second poem.

12. The idea of sending Pushkin's risqué, humorous "Tsar Nikita and His Forty Daughters," which Pushkin had written in 1822, was a joke. The poem could not possibly be passed by the censorship of the time, as Pushkin was well aware.

13. Pushkin has in mind Pletnev's extreme good nature and the way he avoided polemics.

Letter 111

1. Byron had taken the position in his quarrel (1819-1821) with William Bowles, that a poet describing a deck of cards well is better than one who describes a tree badly. The quarrel was over which is more important in poetry, the subject or the artistry, natural subjects or artificial ones. Pushkin agrees with Ryleev (and Bowles) that "the poet describing a deck of cards better than another does trees, is not always above his competitor," that is, the subject, as well as execution, matters.

2. The comments have not been preserved.

3. Pushkin is apparently joking. There is no evidence of ill-feeling, to say nothing of a duel, between them.

4. The allusion is to Petersburg's site on the Neva River and also, no doubt, to the then recent flood. Pushkin's drawing for Onegin showed him and his hero on the embankment (see Letter 88a).

5. Tatiana is the heroine of *Evgeny Onegin*; Julia is a character of the first canto of *Don Juan*. Pushkin would have been fairer if he had asked for comparison of Tatiana and Haidée.

6. Bestuzhev did not mention Katenin in his "Glance at Russian Literature" in *The Polar Star for* 1825.

7. Bestuzhev was then a Staff-Captain in a hussar regiment.

Letter 112

1. The death of the Vyazemskys' son Nikolay Petrovich (1818-1825).

2. The reference is to Pushkin's idea of fleeing from Russia. Rumor had it that the Countess Vorontsova herself, in Odessa, was willing to help Pushkin flee abroad.

Letter 113

1. The hero of Perovsky's (pseudonym Pogorelsky) "Lafertovsky Poppy-Cakes Woman"; the hero's name is Aristarchus (not Trifon) Faleleich Murlykin (the surname means "meow"). Pushkin immediately quotes from the story.

2. Pushkin alludes again to his brother's giving public readings from memory of Pushkin's as-yet unpublished works, and hence cutting down sales.

3. The manuscript for *Poems of Alexander Pushkin*.

4. Pushkin is apparently thinking of his earlier unfavorable comment about Pletnev's writing (in Letter 31), which his brother had shown Pletnev.

5. A mark of opulence. That is, Pushkin was poor, and could not afford to be "robbed."

6. The first issue of *The Moscow Telegraph* included an article giving a high evaluation of Pushkin as a poet, and especially of *The Fountain of Bakhchisaray*.

7. One of Pushkin's poems had appeared in the preceding issue of Voeykov's *Literary News*. The expression "to Voeykovize" came to be used to mean to pirate, to publish without permission.

8. "Long Ago Recollection of Her . . ." (1823), addressed to Princess Maria Arka-dievna Golitsyna, nee Princess Suvorova-Rymnitskaya (1802-1870). The remainder of the titles cited are of lyrics by Pushkin.

9. The excerpt from his notes about Derzhavin was not printed, and it was destroyed with Pushkin's other notes, after the Decembrist Uprising. Pushkin wrote another auto-biographical note (1833), portraying his rapture when Derzhavin, then an old man, the greatest Russian poet of his time, expressed his approbation when Pushkin, still a Lyceum student, recited this poem.

10. Pushkin struck out the preceding paragraph, and instead of it wrote the single word "No."

11. The quatrain was first published by Mikhail Petrovich Pogodin (1800-1875) in his almanac *Urania for* 1826.

Letter 114

1. "Pleases me" (lit., "smiles on me").

2. Pushkin's father and his uncle V. L. Pushkin were also punsters and wits.

3. Princess Evdokia Ivanovna Golitsyna.

4. In Kyukhelbeker's epistle to Ermolov. See Letter 31.

5. In *The Neva Almanac for* 1825 appeared Polevoy's "Elegy," a parody of Zhukov-sky's famous first translation (1802) of Gray's "Elegy in a Country Churchyard" (1751).

6. That is, to the censorship.

7. "All those against whom I have written are still alive." Sébastien Chamfort was an eighteenth-century French writer and wit.

8. The four lines against Tolstoy the American. See Letter 30.

9. Saadi and Hafiz were Persian poets: in speaking of Mohammed, Pushkin is think-ing of *The Koran*.

Letter 115

1. Illarion Evdokimovich Raevsky, nicknamed Prank (Škoda), the priest of a neighboring village, Voronich.

2. That is, for Lord Byron. Pushkin Russianizes the title and also the given name, George.

3. Pushkin was copying the second chapter of *Onegin*, not yet published at that time, to console Vyazemsky in his bereavement (see Letters 112, 113).

4. By Ryleev.

5. Pushchin's letter gave Pushkin the information about the bookseller Semen Ioannikievich Selivanovsky's desire to obtain the right to publish these poems.

6. Pushkin was misinformed. His *Fountain of Bakhchisaray* had not been pirated. A French translation appeared in Paris in 1826.

Letter 116

1. *The Polar Star for* 1825.

2. See Letter 115 and note 5. Pushkin was afraid *The Fountain of Bakhchisaray* was being pirated, and hence that he would not be able to sell a second edition.

3. "You are permitted to write letters, but *under the address of our sister.* . . . That's the way, you see, that I write Anna Ivanovna Vulf, under the name of Euphrosine. . . . What bothers!" Euphrosine was Evpraxia Nikolaevna Vulf.

4. Anna Nikolaevna Vulf.

5. "May he be ashamed [who evil thinks]."

6. "Frederick II's mass for the repose of the soul of M. de Voltaire." Frederick II of Prussia was Voltaire's patron and host from 1751 to 1753. Though these relationships ended with mutual recriminations, unpleasantnesses, and open enmity, Frederick is said to have had a mass said for Voltaire, upon the latter's death, twenty-five years later. The point of Pushkin's comment seems to be that for him, in exile for "atheism," to have a mass said for Byron is as odd as for Frederick II to have a mass said for Voltaire, in that, as men of the Enlightenment, both were free-thinkers. For "Father Prank" see Letter 115, note 1.

Letter 117

1. A slip of the pen; Oldekop pirated *The Prisoner of the Caucasus.*

Letter 118

1. A journal published by Grigory Ivanovich Spassky (1784-1864) from 1818 to 1824; renamed *The Asiatic Messenger*, it was published from 1825 to 1827.

2. Orange-flower toilet water.

3. Delvig. He spent several days with Pushkin, and left on April 26.

4. "The Death of the Chigirinsk Bailiff," a fragment from Ryleev's unfinished long poem *Nalivayko*, had just appeared in *The Polar Star for* 1825.

5. For Pushkin's *Poems*; it was signed by the "publishers."

6. The lines on Tolstoy the American in the poem.

7. Apparently L. S. Pushkin had objected to four mentions of the moon in two stanzas of *Onegin* (Chap. III, stanzas 20-21).

8. "She is sulking at me, but I don't give a damn."

9. "Some suspenders, some boots."

Letter 118*a*

1. Enclosed with this note was the second chapter of *Onegin*, which Pushkin had copied out especially for Vyazemsky. Pushkin also again asks his brother not to do readings from his poems or allow copies to be made. In the publication situation of that day, such readings and manuscript copies could greatly cut down the sale of literary works.

Letter 119

1. Tatiana's conversation, in *Onegin*, Chapter III. The passage was sold to Bestuzhev and Ryleev, for inclusion in *The Little Star*, an almanac which was to replace *The Polar Star*. The printing ceased with page eighty, when both editors were implicated in the Decembrist Uprising of December, 1825; in 1827 Pushkin returned the 600 rubles to the widow of the executed Ryleev and the mother of the exiled Bestuzhev.

2. This poem was called forth by the tenderly sentimental attitude of Pushkin's uncle, shown in his poem "To Her," upon the death of his sister Anna Lvovna Push-

kina. Much family ill-feeling was quite naturally aroused by the poem, and Delvig finally claimed sole authorship, in order to remove the onus from Pushkin. Lizaveta Lvovna Solntseva (1776-1848) was the sister of Pushkin's father, his Uncle Vasily, and his Aunt Anna Lvovna; Matvey Mikhaylovich Solntsev (1779-1847) was Solntseva's husband.

3. That is, why did the censorship pass his uncle's poem.

4. "And don't you have some prose, too?"—Pushkin's note.

Letter 120

1. This rough draft was forwarded to Zhukovsky, together with Letter 121. It was not given to Alexander I, because, instead, Pushkin's mother addressed a petition to the Tsar to allow Pushkin to go to Riga or elsewhere for treatments. Her request was denied, Pushkin being allowed permission to go only to the neighboring town of Pskov. Pushkin's aneurysm appears to have been merely a pretext; he had already advanced this pretext in Letter 69.

Letter 121

1. Zhukovsky had asked Pushkin to give a "human" and not a "madcap" answer to the question whether Pushkin really was suffering from aneurysm.

2. (1821).

3. Pushkin at this time was writing *Boris Godunov* (written 1824-1825, pub. 1831), which, under the influence of Shakespeare, is in blank verse. Blank verse in Russian is called "white verse"; the "most White" here is Alexander I. The "rough draft" is Letter 120. The subject of Pushkin's play is the career of Boris Godunov (1551?-1605), who served as elective tsar (1598-1605), after the end of the Rurik Dynasty.

4. Pushkin applies to Zhukovsky the "thy" of the Lord's Prayer. At various critical junctures, Zhukovsky acted as Pushkin's spiritual father.

5. L. S. Pushkin's handwriting was very similar to his brother's.

6. The third, corrected and augmented edition of Zhukovsky's *Poems* appeared in 1824.

7. Dmitry Nikolaevich Bludov (1785-1864), member of the Arzamas. Pushkin's calling him "Marquis" is a reference to his love and knowledge of French.

8. This is a parody of the opening of Zhukovsky's "To Bludov, Upon His Departure to the Turkish Army" (1810).

9. "To a Portrait of Goethe" (1819), "The Dream" (1818), "To a Genie-Acquaintance . . ." (1819), all poems by Zhukovsky.

10. Zhukovsky's translation of Schiller's "Diver" (1797) was completed in 1831, with the title "The Goblet."

11. Once more Pushkin expresses his low esteem for Ryleev's twenty-five little poems on historical themes (1821-1823), which, together, Ryleev called *Dumy*.

Letter 122

1. Pushkin quotes his epigram on Kachenovsky, "Richard Is Himself Again."

2. M. A. Dmitriev, in contradistinction to I. I. Dmitriev, the poet; Pushkin is asking for Vyazemsky's polemics with M. A. Dmitriev. The historical False Dimitry claimed to be the Tsarevich Dimitry Ivanovich (1581-1591); he held power in Russia 1605-1606 and was murdered. He is one of the chief characters of Pushkin's *Boris Godunov*.

3. I. I. Kozlov. He had sent Pushkin an autographed copy of his Byronic verse tale *The Monk* (1824).

4. Kozlov's poetic epistle "To My Friend V. A. Zhukovsky" was printed together with *The Monk*; it describes Kozlov's becoming blind.

5. Probably Letter 105. The letter to L. S. Pushkin is number 106; what letter to Pletnev Pushkin has in mind is unknown.

6. A paraphrase of lines in I. I. Dmitriev's fable "The Sparrow and the Finch" (1794): "The Nightingale has become silent! Of course the poor fellow is sick or displeased with his girl friend." Ryleev's *Voynarovsky* had just appeared.

7. The ten-volume *Memoirs* of the Countess de Genlis were published in Paris in 1825.

8. Lamartine's *Dernier chant du pèlerinage d'Harold* (1825).

9. The almanac *Russian Antiquity*.

10. In the almanac *Russian Thalia for* 1825 Pushkin found Prince Shakhovskoy's *Sorceress* and several fragments of plays by Khmelnitsky. Pushkin does not mention Khmelnitsky in *Onegin*.

11. Kyukhelbeker. The expression is in his verse epistle to Griboedov.

12. See Letter 113.

13. *The Bandit Brothers* appeared separately in 1827. "Napoleon " was published in Pushkin's *Poems*, but with four whole stanzas omitted.

Letter 123

1. They have not survived.

2. "Peter the Great in Ostrogozhsk" (1823), "Ivan Susanin" (1823), and "Oleg the Seer" are poems among Ryleev's *Dumy*.

3. See Letter 38, note 2.

4. See *The Primary Chronicle* under the year 907.

5. Ryleev had specifically asked Pushkin's opinion of *Nalivayko*, regarding which Pushkin had been silent in his previous comments. Three sections of the thirteen of *Nalivayko* were published in *The Polar Star for* 1825. Pushkin speaks of only one of them.

Letter 125

1. Bestuzhev's "Glance at Russian Literature in the Course of 1824 and at the Beginning of 1825," published in *The Polar Star for* 1825, begins with the contention that the first age of each literature has always been that of the geniuses. Pushkin disputes the point, in terms of several literatures: the Latin, Italian, English, and, in detail, the Russian. Pushkin gives three grouping of the Italian and of the English writers. With the Italian, he ends with the late neo-classical authors Alfieri and Foscolo, both of whom wrote on patriotic themes; with the English, he comes up to his own day. The names which Pushkin chooses from each of these literatures are interesting, especially those from then contemporary or almost-contemporary literature, as indications of the reception of foreign literatures in Russia.

2. "My error: Horace is not an imitator"—Pushkin's note.

3. In this letter, Pushkin quotes from Bestuzhev's article, and then proceeds to give a refutation.

4. "I esteem him as a great man, but of course not as a great poet. He understood the true source of the Russian language and its beauty; this is his chief contribution."—Pushkin's note.

5. Pushkin mentions the odes of Derzhavin's which are in his opinion the best: "Felitsa" (1782), "Noble Lord" (1794), "God" (1784), "On the Death of Prince Meshchersky" (1797), and "On the Return of Count Zubov from Persia" (written 1797, pub. 1805).

6. Yakov Borisovich Knyazhnin (1742-1791), neo-classical dramatist.

7. Derzhavin was Minister of Justice from 1802 to 1803, and Dmitriev from 1810 to 1814. From 1803 on, Karamzin received an annual pension of 2,000 rubles as historiographer. From 1816 on, Zhukovsky received an annual pension of 4,000 rubles. In 1812

Krylov was given an annual pension of 1,500 rubles; later the amount was increased. From March, 1825, on, Gnedich received an annual pension of 1,500 rubles, plus his full salary in the government service (he was engaged in the translation of Homer's *Iliad*).

8. Practically all the great writers of the Augustan Age, including Vergil, Horace, Propertius, and others, had as patrons Emperor Augustus himself, or men in high positions, such as Maecenas and Messalla.

9. Molière had the reversion of his father's office of the king's valet—tapestry-maker. His *Tartuffe* (1664) was allowed on the stage (1669) only after considerable intercession of Louis XIV with the church dignitaries.

10. Perhaps Pushkin has in mind Voltaire's *Poem on the Natural Law* (1752-1756), or perhaps his *Pucelle*.

11. Catherine II, Paul I (1754-1801, ruled 1796-1801), and Alexander I.

12. From Derzhavin's "On the Return of Count Zubov from Persia."

13. Zhukovsky's "Song to the Russian Tsar from His Warriors" (1815).

14. The younger Mirabeau.

15. Emmanuel Joseph Sieyès, leader in the French Revolution.

16. Bestuzhev's "Tournament of Reval," published in *The Polar Star for* 1825, was written under the inspiration of Scott's historical novels.

17. Hero of another tale by Bestuzhev, "The Traitor," published in the same almanac.

18. "Page 330"—Pushkin's note.

19. In his "Glance at Old and New Literature in Russia," in *The Polar Star for* 1823.

20. As new Minister of Public Education and thus head of the censorship.

Letter 126

1. Delvig's valet, well know among Delvig's friends for his laziness.

2. Varvara Vasilievna Chicherina (ca. 1742-1825), Pushkin's great-aunt by marriage; Peter Lvovich Pushkin (d. 1825), an uncle of Pushkin's.

3. This passage is a good example of the personal, or even private nature of Pushkin's epistolary prose. His comment here is an ironical allusion to his short article, "Of Prose," which he did not allow to be published during his lifetime. In objecting to Russian prose writers of the time, he said: "These people will never say *friendship* without adding 'this sacred feeling, whose noble flame, etc.' One ought to say that it is early in the morning, but they say, 'Hardly had the first rays of the rising sun illuminated the eastern edges of the pale blue sky.' Oh, how new and fresh all that is—as though it were better only because it is longer!"

4. L. S. Pushkin had not yet delivered them to the censor, whom Pushkin jokingly calls by the appellative commonly applied to Ivan IV.

5. The expression "did not know the ABC's from lack of leisure" is quoted from I. I. Dmitriev's epitaph "Passer-By, Halt!" (1805), where the reference is to a warrior.

6. L. S. Pushkin could quote to Zhukovsky from memory passages from the as yet unpublished second chapter of *Onegin*; Pushkin was then working on *Boris Godunov*.

7. Krylov underwent no operation at this time.

8. Krylov's "Miller" appeared in *The Polar Star for* 1825 and his "Demian's Fish Chowder," about Demian and Foka, appeared in 1813.

9. Karamzin's *History*, which he did not live to finish, was to have taken the history of Russia up to the founding of the Romanov dynasty (1613). In 1825 he was working on the twelfth volume, which remained unfinished.

10. Recent investigations have indicated that five Pushkins signed the document and two "affixed their hand." Pushkin is also playing, untranslatably, on two meanings of *gramota*—"charter" and "ABC's, literacy."

Letter 127

1. In Vyazemsky's article, "Zhukovsky: Pushkin: Of the New Poetics of Fables," in *The Moscow Telegraph* (1825), he had called Pushkin a "successor" of Zhukovsky.

2. The entire sentence is a quotation of Vyazemsky's own judgment about Zhukovsky, in his verse epistle "To V. A. Zhukovsky."

3. Johann Heinrich Voss, the German poet, translator, and critic.

4. Quotation from Zhukovsky's poem "I Used to Meet the Young Muse . . ." (1823).

5. Paraphrase from the Nicene Creed.

6. Vyazemsky's article about I. I. Kozlov's *Monk* was published in another issue of *The Moscow Telegraph* in 1825.

7. Pushkin is indebted to the scene of the hangman in Ryleev's *Voynarovsky* for a scene in *Poltava*; Ryleev had adapted it from Byron's *Parisina*.

8. The German word *dumm* means "stupid"; the Polish word *duma* means a kind of song. Ryleev took the word and genre from Ukrainian, in which it means a kind of lyrical-narrative poem.

9. Sergey Alexeevich Neelov (1778-1852), author of witty and satirical verses, many of them unprintable.

10. "The singer of s——."

11. "To A. S. Pushkin (On His Swearing Off Singing of Women)" (1825). The allusion is to the mention of Shalikov in Pushkin's "Conversation of a Bookseller and a Poet."

12. "And I boldly replaced Shalikov."

13. Casimir Delavigne. His first name means Kerseymere, or Casimir-satinette, a kind of cloth; hence the pun could be "cut out."

14. The letter has not survived.

15. Medieval Italian tale.

16. Boiardo's mock-heroic epic was written in 1482 and published in 1487.

17. The postscript was written on the back of the letter, which Pushkin sent to his brother for delivery to Vyazemsky.

Letter 128

1. The proposal of N. A. Polevoy, editor of *The Moscow Telegraph*, that Pushkin collaborate in that journal. See Letter 127.

2. Pushkin is speaking of the recent deaths of several of his relatives, including an aunt, an uncle, and a great-aunt. A distant relative, Alexey Mikhaylovich Pushkin, had also died recently.

3. "Till tomorrow for serious matters."

4. V. L. Pushkin had indeed translated this poem, in which God is made to deny what is done on Earth in His name; the work was considered sacrilegious. Pushkin is joking at his uncle's timorousness toward the authorities and at the mysticism then in vogue in high government circles. The "investigative commission" Pushkin jokingly suggests is stacked.

5. Mikhail Leontievich Magnitsky (1778-1855), high government official and obscurant.

6. Alexandra Petrovna Khvostova (1765-1853), author of several works with a mystical coloring, was author of "The Hearth and the Brooklet" (1796). V. L. Pushkin had written a verse epistle "To the Hearth."

7. A. M. Pushkin and many other friends of V. L. Pushkin, including Dmitriev, liked to tease V. L. Pushkin.

8. Pushkin's epigram "To Friends" was printed in *The Moscow Telegraph* as "To Journalistic Friends"; Pushkin asked *The Northern Bee* to print the title correctly there. Vyazemsky himself took all the responsibility for the change of title.

9. "All of us caught hell there."

10. Pushkin quotes his epigram, *Ex ungue leonem*.

11. F. N. Glinka; Pushkin is parodying Glinka's style.

Letter 129

1. Instead of being given permission to go to Riga or abroad for treatments for aneurysm, Pushkin was given permission to go to Pskov for treatments.

2. B. A. Aderkas.

3. Vsevolod Ivanovich Vsevolodov (1790-1863). He had published several books on veterinary problems.

Letter 130

1. Vyazemsky stopped off several days for visiting in Tsarskoe Selo, while en route to Reval, on the Estonian coast, for sea baths.

2. "You whose true name the world does not yet know!"—a pun and joke on the various spellings and pronunciations of Byron's name then current in Russia, and on what Lamartine had in mind in "L'Homme" (1819), his poetic epistle to Byron.

3. Vyazemsky's article on Denis Davydov's objections to Napoleon's minimizing partisan warfare in the Russian-French War of 1812; Vyazemsky praised Davydov's literary style as well as his military exploits. Vyazemsky's article appeared in *The Moscow Telegraph* (1825).

4. That is, the language of exposition, of ideas, abstract language.

5. *Onegin*, Chap. III, stanzas 26-29.

6. Pushkin's article "Of Mme. Staël and Mr. A. M——v" was signed O. Ar. (i.e., Old Arzamasian). In his article Pushkin defends Mme. de Staël.

7. See Letter 129. Curiously enough, Vyazemsky missed Pushkin's sarcasm here.

8. *Boris Godunov.*

9. Published as "André Chénier," with considerable changes and great omissions. Pushkin later had considerable difficulty because of the poem.

10. The Arzamasians called themselves "geese."

11. The play is *Boris Godunov*. Grigory (Grishka) Otrepiev became the False Dimitry. Calculation of dates from "the beginning of the world" (5508 B.C.) was common in Russia up to the eighteenth century (7333 — 5508 = 1825).

Letter 131

1. Pushkin gives textual corrections to "André Chénier."

2. Delvig was married on October 30, 1825. In the Russian Orthodox marriage ceremony, crowns are held over the bride's and bridegroom's heads.

3. I. I. Kozlov.

4. Anna Petrovna Kern.

5. "This was written in the presence of that lady, as anyone may see. Farewell, dear poet. Write me, I pray you. All yours."

Letter 132

1. "It's unhealthy to waltz with you."

2. Anna Petrovna Kern shortly afterwards sent Pushkin the latest edition of Byron as a present.

3. "The charm of night does not appeal to her," a quotation from Kozlov's "Venetian Night."

4. Anna Petrovna Kern.

5. After visiting Mme. Osipova, Mme. Kern had left on Sunday, July 19. Pushkin was "nettled" because Alexey N. Vulf, who also was in love with Anna Petrovna Kern, left in a carriage with her and his sister Anna N. Vulf.

Letter 133

1. Delvig's servant.

2. Another application for Pushkin to be allowed to go elsewhere than to Pskov for treatment for his alleged aneurysm.

3. Delvig's fiancée was Sofia Mikhaylovna Saltykova (1806-1888), daughter of Mikhail Alexandrovich Saltykov (1767-1851), a member of the Arzamas.

4. Letter 120.

5. That is, on the Tsar's susceptibility to a mother's appeal.

6. The incident is given in *The Annals* (IV, 30).

Letter 134

1. Pushkin first made the acquaintance of Anna Petrovna Kern in 1819 at the home of A. N. Olenin, in Petersburg.

2. General Ermolay Fedorovich Kern (ca. 1770-1841), Anna Petrovna's husband.

3. "Oh, you sorceress or necromancer."

4. This clause was written across the paper in different directions.

Letter 135

1. The reference is to the Tsar's permission for Pushkin to go to Pskov for treatments for aneurysm.

Letter 136

1. After this letter Pushkin ceased to utilize the services of his brother as his agent, a function the latter had performed since 1821; Pushkin's correspondence with his brother also came to almost a complete halt.

2. The manuscript of Pushkin's early poems, which he had lost at cards to Vsevolozhsky.

3. The 600 rubles which Pushkin had borrowed in Odessa from Princess Vyazemskaya. Pletnev paid the money on March 26, 1826, from money received for the sale of Pushkin's *Poems*.

4. From Alexey Ivanovich Zaikin (1793-1831), bookseller and publisher, or his brother Ivan Ivanovich Zaikin (d. 1834).

5. This comment led to new rumors in Petersburg that Pushkin was about to flee abroad and needed money for this purpose.

6. Apparently L. S. Pushkin did not do so, for *The Gypsies* was not passed by the censorship until December, 1826, and published in 1827.

Letter 137

1. Ivan Filippovich Moyer (1786-1858), professor of surgery at the University of Dorpat and a friend of Zhukovsky's, consented to go to Pskov to perform the operation; Pushkin's friends had hoped that Pushkin would obtain permission to go to Dorpat to see Moyer and that the latter would certify to the authorities that he needed treatments abroad.

Letter 138

1. The reference is to Zhukovsky's persuading Moyer to go to Pskov and operate on Pushkin.

Letter 139

1. N. N. Raevsky had transferred on January 1, 1824, from the Kurland Hussar Regiment to the Kharkov Hussar Regiment.
2. A. N. Raevsky.
3. Praskovia Alexandrovna Osipova.
4. *Boris Godunov.*
5. In La Harpe's neo-classical play, *Philoctète* (1781).
6. "Shakespeare has seized upon the passions; Goethe, manners,"—Pushkin's rough draft variant.
7. "He has paid." The reference is to the closing words of Byron's *Two Foscari* (1821); upon the death of the older Foscari, Loredano says "he has paid me . . . nature's debt and *mine.*" Byron's dramas, with the exceptions of *Cain* and *Manfred,* were determinedly neo-classical in form.
8. That is, a historical drama. Pushkin's text reads as follows: *Votre tragédie est-elle une tragédie de charactère ou de costume?* Costume, in this sense, was borrowed from Italian, and means the truth to customs (*moeurs*) which is reproduced by poets, writers, or artists.

Letter 140

1. Several poems by Pushkin appeared in *The Moscow Telegraph,* of which Polevoy was the editor, during 1825.

Letter 141

1. A servant at Mme. Osipova's house.
2. Apparently Pushkin thought that General Kern had given some commands with regard to the surveillance over him, which was under the supervision of the Pskov governor, B. A. Aderkas.

Letter 142

1. That is, Pushkin did not intend to go to Pskov for treatments.
2. A promised article on Byron.
3. The discussion has to do with Vyazemsky's epigram on a sycophantic poem written by the poetaster Pavel Petrovich Sviniin (1788-1839), in which the latter expressed preference for the estate Gruzino, belonging to Alexey Andreevich Arakcheev (1769-1834), powerful reactionary political advisor to Alexander I, to "the fruitless ruins of Palmyra, Troy, and Athens." Pushkin changes the line "No, I shall go to Gruzino, the profitable way," to "No, I shall go into the antechamber, the profitable way." The main effect of Pushkin's changes is to conclude the poem with the line he admires, "I am not a poet, but a nobleman"; this line suggests to Pushkin Ryleev's dedication to *Voynarovsky,* which concludes, "I am not a poet, but a citizen." Pushkin rejoined to Ryleev's line that if one wants to be only a citizen, one can be that in prose.
4. Zhukovsky's persuasion of Moyer to to to Pskov to operate on Pushkin.
5. Kyukhelbeker, an admirer of the works of the poetaster Shirinsky-Shikhmatov, was engaged in writing a detailed critique of the latter's *Peter the Great* (1810).
6. Polevoy had attacked *The Northern Bee,* in response to an article in that publication attacking *The Moscow Telegraph.*
7. Vyazemsky's article; see Letter 127, and note 1.

8. It was said to Anna N. Vulf.

9. This "bon mot" was probably also said to Anna N. Vulf, who was hopelessly and unrequitedly in love with Pushkin. Pushkin addressed verses to her which were even more plainspoken, and in no better taste.

Letter 143

1. The two-year-old Ekaterina Ivanovna Osipova.

2. Alexey Nikitich Peshchurov (1779-1849), Opochka Marshal of the Nobility. The appellative is an allusion to the then still-popular French comedy *Glib Lawyer* (1704) by David Augustin de Brueys and Jean Palaprat, Sieur de Bigot.

3. For medical treatments.

4. Peter Abramovich Gannibal (1742-ca. 1825), a retired artillery general, the second son of Abram Petrovich Gannibal, Pushkin's Abyssinian great-grandfather.

Letter 144

1. Filipp Lukianovich Luchich, Odessa merchant and banker.

2. See Letter 103. Pushkin is still objecting to the misplaced accent on the word "authors."

3. Alexander Ivanovich Kaznacheev and his wife Varvara Dmitrievna Kaznacheeva (1793-1859).

Letter 145

1. "Dear one! You charming one! . . . Oh, loathsome one!"

2. Anna Ivanovna Vulf.

3. "Not hurriedly, but soundly."

4. "Serves him right."

5. Anna Nikolaevna Vulf. Anna Petrovna Kern, together with her husband, visited Trigorskoe in October, 1825.

6. "Give me your little hand."

Letter 146

1. This is another reference to Pushkin's mother's petition to the Tsar with regard to his aneurysm.

2. "Nurse kisses your hand, Olga Sergeevna, my little dove." The nurse is Arina Rodionovna. Pushkin is obviously quoting her exact words.

Letter 147

1. In Vyazemsky's letter which Pushkin is here answering, Vyazemsky had complained that poetry was to him a sort of foreign language.

2. After the Treaty of Tilsit (1807), Alexander I and Napoleon were allied, and Gallomania reached its height in Russia. Among those objecting were Admiral Shishkov and Sergey Nikolaevich Glinka (1775-1847), the latter of whom founded the patriotic journal *The Russian Messenger* to fight against Gallicisms and Gallomania.

3. Vyazemsky's "Narva Waterfall" was published in 1826; Vyazemsky accepted practically none of Pushkin's suggestions.

4. That is, alliteration. Vyazemsky had, in the same line, the words *vlagi vlastelin*.

5. The word *mežduusobnyj* now means "internecine."

6. "That's captiousness, though."—Pushkin's note.

7. Pushkin is quoting a correction to a verse in his "Black Shawl" (written 1820, pub. 1821) which had been sent him by Vyazemsky as from a girl in Reval.

8. "That would be forced wit."

9. Really his great-aunt. The document is a parody of the usual style of documents of the time.

Letter 148

1. The allusion is to V. I. Vsevolodov.
2. I.e., Kyukhelbekery and nauseating; see Letter 27.
3. He finished it on November 7, 1825.
4. Volumes X and XI of Karamzin's *History*.
5. "It is as thrilling as yesterday's newspaper."
6. N. N. Raevsky the Younger.
7. For the *jurodivyj* or holy fool or simpleton in *Boris Godunov*. The *jurodivyj* called the "Large Pointed Cap" died in 1589, nine years before Boris Godunov became Tsar; Pushkin's holy fool's dire maledictions to Boris are based on Large Pointed Cap's statements. Pushkin did not hesitate to utilize this anachronism in his play for one of its most striking scenes.
8. A Saint's Calender (*Čet'i Minei*) compiled by Makary (1482-1563), Metropolitan of Moscow (1542-1563). Vasily the Blessed was another sixteenth-century *jurodivyj*.
9. Vasily Alexeevich Perovsky (1795-1857), brother of A. A. Perovsky, had recently described Vesuvius, Herculaneum, and Pompeii in a letter from Italy published in *The Moscow Telegraph* (1824).

Letter 149

1. This letter was sent via Mme. Osipova; she did not deliver it.
2. Anna Nikolaevna Vulf.

Letter 150

1. Quotations from Pushkin's scabrous "Tsar Nikita," where "nothing or very little" has to do with female anatomy.
2. Mme. Osipova.
3. This phrase was written diagonally from one corner of the letter to the other.
4. The letter here referred to, to Anna I. Vulf, has not survived.
5. Pushkin wished so to arouse Anna Petrovna Kern's curiosity that she would open and read the enclosed letter (Letter 151), addressed to Mme. Osipova, but really intended for the eyes of Mme. Kern.

Letter 151

1. This letter did not find Mme. Osipova in Riga, for she had quarreled with Anna Petrovna Kern over corresponding with Pushkin and had left. In Letter 157 Pushkin "beseeches" Anna Petrovna Kern not to send this letter on to Mme. Osipova.
2. Alexey N. Vulf.
3. I. M. Rokotov.
4. "Convict."
5. Letter 149.
6. Ermolay Fedorovich Kern, Anna Petrovna's husband.
7. Pushkin's "portrait" of Anna Petrovna Kern, is quoted by her in her *Memoirs*, as follows [in French]:

"Do you want to know what Mme. Kern is like? She is pliant, she understands everything; she is easily grieved and easily consoled; she is timid in her manner, but bold in her actions; but she is quite attractive." This fragment is dated between the end of July and the first half of August, 1825, and it was sent from Mikhaylovskoe to Riga.

8. Anna Ivanovna Vulf.

Letter 152
1. In this letter Pushkin continues the arguments presented in Letter 125. Pushkin's letter is in answer to Ryleev's objections that Pushkin is confusing literary "encouragement" (*odobrenie*) with "patronage" (*pokrovitel'stvo*).
2. "To awaken the sleeping cat [i.e., dog]?"
3. Alexander I.

Letter 153
1. This letter is connected with Pushkin's schemes of fleeing abroad. Pushkin had hoped that permission could be obtained for him to go to Riga to see Dr. Moyer, on the pretext of aneurysm, and that Moyer could be persuaded to prescribe treatments abroad. Here the words "composition," "censor," and "typesetter," and, below, "calash" are code words in connection with these plans. The most important of these words was "calash," which stood for Pushkin himself. Alexey Vulf had taken Pushkin's calash to Dorpat with him, and he was to report that he was keeping it there, or sending it back, in accordance with whether Moyer would agree or not to help in these plans of escape.
2. "All such things."
3. These words indicate to Vulf that Pushkin had given up all hopes of escaping abroad and had abandoned the attempt (for the code meaning, see note 1). Pushkin had already consented to go to Pskov for a physical examination. He still wanted Vulf to explain to Moyer that, as we have already seen in Letter 137, Pushkin did not want to be operated on for aneurysm—and certainly not in Pskov.
4. "Farewell, my son in spirit."
5. Pushkin quotes the beginning of his "imitation" of Yazykov's risqué poem, in Letter 160.

Letter 154
1. "Alas, Posthumus, Posthumus, the years glide swiftly by."—Horace, *Odes*, II, xiv, 1-2, quoted a little inaccurately.
2. Katenin had reminded Pushkin of his joking promise to write a poem of twenty-five cantos; Katenin himself was on the whole a literary conservative.
3. Tsarevna Sophia (Sofia Alexeevna, 1657-1704), Regent of Russia from 1682 to 1689; a lover of the drama, who, according to tradition, herself composed plays. Pushkin errs in attributing to her *A Comedy About St. Catherine*; it was composed by her sister, Grand Duchess Natalia.
4. In Bulgarin's theatrical almanac *Russian Thalia*; the reference is to Katenin's translation of Racine's *Andromaque*.
5. That is, of Prince Shakhovskoy's literary circle; though as a member of the Arzamas Pushkin was a literary opponent of Shakhovskoy's group, his personal relationships with it were excellent.
6. Fragments from the French tragedy *Venceslas* (1647), by Rotrou, in the translation of Andrey Andreevich Zhandr (1789-1873), author and civil servant, were published in *The Russian Thalia for* 1825. The plot of Rotrou's play was borrowed from a play by the seventeenth-century Spanish playwright Francisco de Rojas Zorilla.
7. Probably Peter Pavlovich Kaverin (1794-1855), an officer and friend of young Pushkin, and a member of the Green Lamp.
8. A Ukrainian named Denisevich, whom Pushkin offended by hissing a play which Denisevich liked; this almost led to a duel.
9. "Farewell, Poet, until we meet again, but when?"

Letter 155

1. Criticism, criticism of criticism, and criticism of criticism of criticism were extremely common in the journals of the time.

2. Boris Mikhaylovich Fedorov (1794-1875), untalented man of letters and journalist.

3. Matvey Mikhaylovich Karniolin-Pinsky (1796-1866), teacher and civil servant.

4. A Gallicism for "missing the obvious, looking for difficulties where none are"; Pushkin translates into Russian the expression which Vyazemsky had applied to him (*chercher midi à quatorze heures*). Vyazemsky missed the point of Pushkin's efforts to get out of his immediate locality for treatments for aneurysm—the hope of being allowed to go abroad for "treatments"; police interception of letters made it impossible for Pushkin to speak more plainly. The "Tsar's favor" was permission to go for treatments only to Pskov.

5. Vyazemsky argued in his letter that there was no use for Pushkin to complain of his persecution or suffering, because the public was not interested in that, however much the public might like his poetry.

6. A monk who has taken the strictest vows.

7. That Pushkin had in mind the color red, as a symbol of revolutionary sympathies, is clear from his poetic epistle to V. S. Filimonov (1828). There is also a pun involved: in Russian the "colored metals" are the non-ferrous ones. Pushkin had promised Karamzin in 1820 that he would not write anything further against the state for two years.

8. The *jurodivyj*, or wandering holy fool, was considered blessed and often given this appellative.

9. *Boris Godunov*. Marina is the Polish voevoda's daughter with whom the False Dimitry falls in love: Katerina Orlova was Ekaterina Nikolaevna Orlova, nee Raevskaya.

10. Vyazemsky reported to Pushkin that Karamzin said: "You must have in mind in depicting the character of Boris a savage mixture: piety and criminal passions. He constantly reread the Bible and sought in it justifications for himself. That is a dramatic contradiction."

11. That is, the slaughter of the innocents (see Matthew 2), because of Boris' responsibility for the murder of young Dimitry, the heir to the throne.

12. Of Karamzin's *History*.

13. Pushkin puns on *žile*, *žil'e*. There is also play on the Russian word *xlopotat'*, which means both "to fuss about" and "to intercede."

14. The article was by Alexander Alexandrovich Mukhanov (1800-1834), not Pushkin's friend P. A. Mukhanov. Pushkin had countered with a sharp attack on the article and a defense of Mme. de Staël. See Letter 130.

15. Pushkin saw his Lyceum comrade Prince Alexander Mikhaylovich Gorchakov (1798-1883) at the home of A. N. Peshchurov in September, 1825.

Letter 156

1. Perhaps *Vous*, "You," or *Votre Majesté*, "Your Majesty." Pushkin left the word and sentence unfinished.

2. Perhaps Chaadaev.

3. In giving Pushkin an administrative transfer at that time, instead of exiling or imprisoning him.

Letter 157

1. Letter 151.

2. Alexey N. Vulf.

3. See Letter 156.

Letter 158
1. *Boris Godunov.*
2. "Cut Me" is the song of the Gypsy heroine of Pushkin's *Gypsies.* The song, together with the music, was published in *The Moscow Telegraph* later in 1825.
3. Count Mikhail Yurievich Vielgorsky (1788-1856), talented dilettante composer.
4. See Letter 119, and notes.
5. When V. L. Pushkin was pricked by the satires of M. V. Milonov, he interjected, "Why, how many times he has been at my house and drunk tea!"

Letter 159
1. B. A. Aderkas.
2. Heinrich Christian Matthew Ruehland (1784-1837), surgeon of German birth.

Letter 160
1. Code word relating to Pushkin's plans to flee Russia; see Letter 153.
2. The Kerns at this time were visiting Mme. Osipova.
3. Vulf had obviously asked Pushkin to send him Pushkin's "imitation"of Yazykov's risqué "Go Away" (see Letter 153).

Letter 161
1. Khvostov, in his "Two Pigeons," a poetic fable, speaks of a pigeon which, having falled into a snare, bites through the knots with its "teeth." Pushkin's doggerel is in response to a poem of Vyazemsky's in similar vein, in a letter of October, 1825.
2. See Letters 127 and 142.
3. The French spelling is conjectural; the Russian, transliterated, is *Maržeret.*
4. Pushkin was amused at the way Vyazemsky in his letter had objected that to present the "lackey" Krylov as typical of the Russian people would be like painting a person's backside as the differentiating human characteristic. Pushkin manages to agree and at the same time remain of the same opinion, by quoting the concluding lines from Krylov's "Council of Mice" (1811). In this poem, the mice had decided that mice with the longest tails had the most intelligence, and they called a council of the most intelligent mice, according to this standard. A tailless rat appeared. When one of the young mice objected, a gray old mouse made the rejoinder Pushkin quotes here.
5. In Pushkin's article—to which Vyazemsky had objected—"Of Mr. Lémontey's Preface to the Translation of the Fables of Krylov," published in *The Moscow Telegraph* in 1825. Count Grigory Vladimirovich Orlov (1777-1826) had published a French and Italian edition of Krylov's *Fables* earlier in the same year.
6. "Stench." The reference is to Karamzin's *History.*
7. Evgeny Kazantsev (1778-1871), then Bishop of Pskov.
8. That is, Evgeny Onegin.
9. B. A. Aderkas.

Letter 162
1. The Russian word *za* here is ambigious, meaning both "by" and "on account of."
2. Dmitry Alexeevich Eristov (1797-1858), minor poet and lexicographer; he had been a member of the second class of the Lyceum. Before that, he had attended the Jesuit college at Polotsk.
3. Andrey Boboly, a Jesuit monk who was tortured to death by Cossacks in the seventeenth century.
4. I.e., for Delvig's *Northern Flowers for* 1826; the fragments from *Evgeny Onegin,*

Chap. II, stanzas 24-29 and 37-40, here referred to, were published in it, along with other things.

5. M. A. Saltykov; his daughter was Sofia M. Saltykova.

Letter 163
1. That is, from the publication of his *Poems*.
2. Another allusion to police interception of letters.
3. To G. V. Orlov's edition in French and Italian of Krylov's fables.
4. The reference is to the article "Newstead Abbey: From the Works of Lord Byron," preceded by a short introduction signed "V," and published in *The Moscow Telegraph* in 1825. In this introduction Vyazemsky mentioned the destruction of Byron's notes of 1818 to 1820 by Thomas Moore after Byron's death.
5. N. N. Raevsky the Younger.
6. Apparently Pushkin was first introduced to the study of English in 1820, when he was with the Raevsky family. In 1828 he learned to read English fluently.
7. "There was something here," the (apochryphal) comment of Chénier just before his execution.
8. The reference is to Jean Jacques Rousseau's *Confessions* (1782).
9. Pushkin's perceptive remarks about the writing of memoirs are the fruit of his own then recent experience in writing his own memoirs. Unfortunately, the memoirs he wrote at this time had to be burned, as a precautionary measure, after the Decembrist Uprising in 1825, because of the comments there about his many Decembrist friends and acquaintances. He himself later very much regretted that they had had to be destroyed. The main surviving material of a comparable character is in Pushkin's diary, which he kept with more or less regularity from 1833 to 1835.

Letter 164
1. Pushkin himself was dreaming of being permitted to publish his own journal.
2. Pletnev was trying to persuade Pushkin to publish his long poems in a companion volume to that of his short poems, then in the press.
3. Ivan Ivanovich Golikov's (1735-1801) *Acts of Peter the Great* (12 vols., 1788-1789, with 18 volumes of Supplements, 1790-1797) was written in a heavy, ornate style.
4. Alexander Ivanovich Yakubovich (1792-1845) was noted for his bravery in fighting in the Caucasus; he dueled with Griboedov, and he was a second in a duel in which Vasily Vasilievich Sheremetev (d. 1817) was killed in a quarrel over the actress Istomina. Yakubovich's article about the Caucasus was published in *The Northern Bee* in 1825 with the signature "A. Ya."
5. That is, when Pushkin was in the Caucasus; the poem referred to is *The Prisoner of the Caucasus*.
6. *Boris Godunov*.
7. Kyukhelbeker's *Shakespeare's Spirits* (1825) was based on Shakespeare's *Tempest*.
8. The facile, shallow style of Kotzebue.
9. Count Matvey Ivanovich Platov (1756-1818), ataman of Don Cossacks; apparently the expression has to do with "scientific" preparations for battle or war.

Letter 165
1. Katenin's exile from Petersburg had been brought to an end.
2. Katenin's translation of Racine's *Andromaque* was staged in 1827. His poems were published in 1832.
3. Alexander I had died on November 7, 1825, at Taganrog on the Black Sea; the news reached Petersburg only on November 27. At this time it was not generally

known that Constantine (1779-1831) had renounced the succession to the throne in favor of his brother Nicholas. Each of the brothers declared fealty to the other before Constantine made a final renunciation of the succession. December 14, 1825, was the day that the oath of fealty to Nicholas was to be sworn. On this day, a group of Russian nobles, mainly army officers, who hoped to liberalize the autocratic regime of Russia, staged the so-called Decembrist Uprising, which was, however, speedily put down.

During Constantine's "stormy youth," Catherine II had for a time the idea of taking Constantinople and installing Constantine there as ruler, but Turkish might and European power politics made if preferable for her to turn Russian ambitions in other directions. He took part in Suvorov's Italian campaign of 1799 and in the campaign of 1812-1813, when he had sharp disagreements with Prince Mikhail Bogdanovich Barklay de Tolly (1761-1818), Russian field marshal of Scottish descent. Constantine was Governor General of Poland from 1815 until his death.

4. The allusion is to Henry's personality as Shakespeare conceived it both in *Henry V* and in the two parts of *Henry IV*.

5. Vasily Andreevich Karatygin (1802-1853), tragic actor.

Letter 166

1. *Calembourg* [sic]! *Reconnais-tu le sang?* ["Pun! Do you recognize the strain?"]—Pushkin's note. The allusion is to the reputation for wit of Pushkin's whole family, especially his father and his Uncle Vasily. The work in question is Kyukhelbeker's *Shakespeare's Spirits*, a play based on Shakespeare's *Tempest*, and keeping the characters Ariel and Caliban. The poet in Kyukhelbeker's play parodies Zhukovsky's poems.

2. Pushkin gives other examples.

Letter 167

1. Quotation from Kyukhelbeker's *Shakespeare's Spirits*. See Letter 166.

2. That is, Pushkin is hoping that his friends will intercede in his behalf with the new Tsar.

3. A slight paraphrase of Krylov's expression, "If you are going to take something, then take it—else why dirty your claws?" in his "Little Raven" (quoted in Letter 51).

4. *Boris Godunov.*

5. Boris M. Fedorov has a *jurodivyj* in his novel *Prince Kurbsky*; his poem "Byron" was published in 1826.

6. For Pushkin's more extensive comments on this point, see Letter 139.

7. To Kyukhelbeker (Letter 166), and, it is supposed, to Voeykov; the latter letter has not survived. Pushkin is referring to the September issue of Voeykov's *Literary News.*

8. *Ilia Muromets*, by Mikhail Pavlovich Zagorsky (1804-1824), appeared posthumously in fragments in *Literary News* (1825).

Letter 168

1. Anna Petrovna Kern had sent Pushkin the *Works* of Byron. Gulnare is one of the heroines of Byron's *Corsair*, and Leila is the heroine of *The Giaour*.

2. The death of Alexander I and the accession to the throne of his successor, Nicholas I.

Letter 169

1. This letter was written for publication, with indicated omissions, in connection with Pushkin's *Fountain of Bakhchisaray*, which had appeared in 1824. Its subject is Pushkin's visit to the Crimea in 1820, which he had described in detail to his brother

Lev in a letter of September 20, 1820 (Letter 11). Pushkin's two presentations of these experiences should be compared: one, in an intimate personal letter, while the visit was fresh in his memory, and the other, four or five years later and for publication. This letter, with the omission of the first paragraph and the last two, was published in *The Northern Flowers for* 1826. Since 1830 it has been printed as an appendix to Pushkin's *Fountain of Bakhchisaray*, together with an excerpt from Muraviev-Apostol's *Journey Over the Tavrida*, with regard to the monument to the khan's mistress.

2. "Mendicant."

3. Pushkin quotes his poem "To Chaadaev." It was published in 1825, before the publication of this letter.

4. Pushkin uses the letter "K" here to mislead readers, who might think (rightly) that one of the Raevsky daughters is meant.

5. N. N. Raevsky the Older.

6. This entire paragraph was struck through in the manuscript.

PART V

DECEMBER AND AFTER—MIKHAYLOVSKOE

December, 1825—August, 1826

Mikhaylovskoe, 1837.   *Lithograph.*

To Peter Alexandrovich Pletnev
Between January 15 and 25, 1826.
From Mikhaylovskoe to Petersburg.

Dear fellow, thank you for *Poems of Alexander Pushkin.*[1] The edition is very pretty; there are mistakes here and there, but nothing to speak of. Again I give you my hearty thanks and a friendly embrace.

What's going on where you are, in Petersburg? I don't know a thing, and everybody has ceased writing to me. You probably suppose I am in Nerchinsk.[2] Wrongly; I have no intention of going there—but lack of information about the people with whom I have been closely connected torments me. I have been hoping the Tsar will be gracious toward them. By the way: can't Zhukovsky find out whether I can hope for the Sovereign's condescension; I have been in disgrace for six years, and whatever you may say—I am only 26 in all. The late emperor in 1824 exiled me to my village for two irreligious lines[3]—I don't know of any other evil deeds on my part. Won't our young Tsar[4] permit me to remove myself to some place where it would be a little warmer—if indeed I can't somehow be allowed to appear in Petersburg—eh?

Farewell, dear fellow; I am so bored I don't know what to do.

[171]

To Anton Antonovich Delvig
Between January 20 and 29, 1826.
From Mikhaylovskoe to Petersburg.

Dear Baron! You are disturbed about me, and to no purpose. I am a peaceful man. But I am disturbed—and God grant that it be to no purpose. I have been told that A. Raevsky[1] is under arrest. I have no doubt of his political guiltlessness. But he has trouble with his legs, and the dampness of the casemates[2] would kill him. Find out where he is, and reassure me. Farewell, my dear friend.

P.

[172]

To Vasily Andreevich Zhukovsky
Between January 20 and 29, 1826.
From Mikhaylovskoe to Petersburg.

I have not written to you, firstly because I have not felt like talking of myself;[1] secondly, from lack of a dependable opportunity. Here is the point: it is hard for me to ask for your intercession with the Sovereign; I do not want to involve you in my mess. Probably the government has ascertained that I do not belong to the conspiracy, and had no political ties with the rebels of December 14—but in the journals it has announced disgrace for those, as well, who had any information of the conspiracy and did not announce it to the police. But just who, except the police and the government, did not know about it? There was shouting about the conspiracy in every alley, and that is one of the reasons I am guiltless. All the same I still have not got away from the gendarmes; they can perhaps easily convict me of political conversations with somebody or other of the accused. And among them there are enough of my friends (N.B.: Have both the Raevskys[2] been taken, and are they really in the fortress? Do me the favor to write and tell me). Now let us suppose that the government should even want to put an end to my disgrace; I am ready to come to terms with it (if conditions are necessary), but I tell you positively not to answer or vouch for me. My future behavior depends on the circumstances, on the way the government treats me, etc.

And so it remains for you to rely on my good sense. You can ask evidence from me of this new quality. Here it is.

In Kishinev I was on friendly terms with Major Raevsky, with General Pushchin, and with Orlov.[3]

I was a Mason in the Kishinev Lodge; i.e., in the one on account of which all the lodges in Russia were done away with.[4]

Lastly, I had connections with the greater part of the present conspirators.

The late Emperor, when he exiled me, could reproach me only with unbelief.[5]

This letter is of course unwise, but one must sometimes put his trust in luck. Farewell, be happy, that is for the time being my prime wish.

Before you burn this letter, show it to Karamzin and ask his advice. I should think that it might be said to the Tsar: "Your Majesty, if Pushkin is not implicated, then can he not at long last be permitted to return?"

They say you have written verses on the death of Alexander[6]—a rich subject! But your lyre was silent during the last ten years of his reign. That is the best reproach against him. Nobody has more right than you to say that the voice of the lyre is the voice of the people. Consequently I was not completely wrong in hissing him to the very grave.[7]

[173]

To ANTON ANTONOVICH DELVIG
The beginning of February, 1826.
From Mikhaylovskoe to Petersburg.

You finally wrote me, and then without making sense, dear fellow. Get it into your head that here in the wilds I know exactly nothing, my correspondence from everywhere has been broken off, and you write me as though we were together all day yesterday and had our fill of talking with each other. Of course I am not implicated in anything, and if the government has leisure to think about me a little, it will easily be assured of that. But I am somehow ashamed to petition, especially now; my way of thinking is known. Persecuted six years in a row, stained by expulsion from the service, exiled to an out-of-the-way village for two lines of an intercepted letter,[1] I of course could not bear good will toward the late Tsar, although I gave full justice to his true merits. But I never preached rebellion or revolution—on the contrary. Writers as a class, as Alfieri noted, are more inclined to speculation than to action,[2] and if December 14 proved it different with us, then there is special cause for it. However that may be, I should like to be reconciled *fully* and *sincerely* with the government, and of course that depends on nobody but it. In this wish there is more good sense than pride on my part.

I am impatiently waiting for the determination of the fate of the unfortunate ones and the divulging of the conspiracy. I firmly rely on the magnanimity of our young Tsar. Let us not be either superstitious or one-sided—like French tragedians. But let us look

at the tragedy with the eyes of Shakespeare. Farewell, my dear
fellow.

Pushkin.

You borrowed 2000 rubles of mine,[3] and you did well, but arrange
it so that Pletnev will have it back again before Lent.

[174]

To PETER ALEXANDROVICH KATENIN
The first half of February, 1826.
From Mikhaylovskoe to Petersburg.

I shall answer you point by point. The verses about Kolosova[1]
were written in a letter which has not reached you. I did not give your
full name, because it would seem a little strange for me to talk with
Katenin in verses about nothing but my quarrel with an actress.
The future almanac[2] gladdens me indescribably, if it will awaken
you to poetry. My soul begs for some verses of yours; but do you
know what? Instead of an almanac, shouldn't we start up a journal
of the type of the *Edimburgh* [sic] *Review*? We need a voice of true
criticism; just who, if not you, can take public opinion in hand and
give a new, true direction to our literature? Meanwhile, except for
you, we do not have a critic. Many people (including also me) are
greatly obligated to you; you weaned me away from one-sidedness in
literary opinions, and one-sidedness is the bane of thought. If you
would consent to set down your conversations on paper, you would
bring a great benefit to Russian literature. What do you think?
And how are your *Andromache* and the collection of your verses
doing?

[175]

To ANTON ANTONOVICH DELVIG
February 20, 1826. From Mikhaylovskoe to Petersburg.

Baron, my friend, I have not been pouting at you, and I have
magnanimously excused your long silence with your hymeneal

Io hymen Hymenaee io,
Io hymen Hymenaee![1]

i.e., may the devil take your wedding, may your wedding the devil take. When my friends get married, it's fun for them, but misery for me. But so be it. The Apostle Paul says in one of his epistles that it is better to take oneself a wife than to go to hell and eternal fire.[2] I embrace and congratulate you—commend me to the good graces of Baroness Delvig.

I am very grateful for your news; I rejoice that the Teuton Kyukhlya was not a Slav[3]—but is suffering for others' faults. The conduct of the Grand Duke Mikhail with regard to him is very noble. But what about Ivan Pushchin? I have been told that on the 20th, i.e., today, their fate is to be decided. My heart is in my throat. But I firmly hope for the Tsar's graciousness. The government's measures have proved its decisiveness and its might. Greater confirmation would seem unnecessary. The government can disdain the embitteredness of certain ones who have been unmasked. . . .

I have written Zhukovsky—and I am awaiting his answer. Meanwhile I am entirely alone. Praskovia Alexandrovna [Osipova] has left for Tver; I am writing her now and sending her *Eda*[4]—how charming this *Eda* is! Our critics will not grasp the originality of the story. But what variety! The Hussar, Eda, and the poet himself all speak their own way. And the descriptions of nature in Liflyandia! and the morning after the first night! and the scene with her father! It is marvellous! I have also seen the Slepushkin;[5] didn't somebody correct for him his "Christmas Holidays," "Carnival," "Wooden House"? He has genuine talent, *his own*. Please send him from me a copy of *Ruslan* and of my *Poems*—and tell him that he is not to imitate me, but to continue to go his own road. I am waiting for *The [Northern] Flowers* [*for* 1826].

[176]

To Praskovia Alexandrovna Osipova
February 20, 1826. From Mikhaylovskoe to Tver.
(In French)

Madame,

Here is a new poem by Baratynsky,[1] which Delvig has just sent me; it is a masterpiece of grace, elegance, and feeling. You will be enchanted with it.

I assume, Madame, that you are now in Tver; I hope that you have been spending your time agreeably there, but not enough to allow you to forget completely Trigorskoe, where we have been missing you and where we are already beginning to expect you.

Accept, Madame, the assurance of my high esteem and of my complete devotion.

February 20.

Madame, please present my regards to your daughter, as well as to Mlle. Netty.[2]

[177]
To Peter Alexandrovich Pletnev
March 3, 1826. From Mikhaylovskoe to Petersburg.

Karamzin is ill! My dear one, that is worse than a lot of things together—for God's sake reassure me, or else I'll be twice as afraid[1] to unseal the newspapers. Gnedich will not die before he completes his *Iliad*—or I shall say in my heart, there is no Phoebus.[2] You know that I am a prophet. There will be no *Boris* for you until you summon me to Petersburg—indeed, what is this? It's a shameful business. To Sle-Pushkin they give a caftan and a watch, and a half-medal,[3] but to the complete Pushkin—a fig. So be it: I renounce my frock coat, trousers, and even the Academy quarter-ruble[4] (which is due me); at least let them permit me to abandon damned Mikhaylovskoe. The question is: Am I innocent or not? But in either case I should have been in Petersburg long ago. This is what it is like to be a loyal subject! They forget you, and are quits with you. Have my friends received my sensible, i.e., business letters?[5] Then why don't they answer? And you're a fine fellow! You write me: "Copy and hire Opochka copyists, and publish *Onegin*." I don't feel like fooling with *Onegin*. The devil take *Onegin*! It's myself I want to publish, or release into the world. Holy Fathers, help me.

March 3.

[178]
To Vasily Andreevich Zhukovsky
March 7, 1826. From Mikhaylovskoe to Petersburg.

Entrusting myself to the intercession of your friendship, I am setting forth in brief the history of my disgrace. In 1824 the manifest ill will of Count Vorontsov forced me to submit my resignation. My health, which has long been upset, and a kind of aneurysm which has needed treatment without delay, served me as a sufficient pretext. It did not please the late Sovereign Emperor to take this into consideration. His Majesty expelled me from the service and ordered me exiled to my village on account of a letter written three years or so ago,[1] in which there was a judgment about atheism, an ill-considered judgment, deserving of course of any kind of reproach.

The accession to the throne of the Sovereign Nikolay Pavlovich gives me joyful hope. Perhaps His Majesty will see fit to change my lot. Whatever may have been my political and religious way of thinking, I am keeping it to myself, and I have no intention of insanely opposing the generally accepted order of things, and necessity.[2]

March 7, 1826.   Alexander Pushkin.
The Village Mikhaylovskoe.

[179]

To Peter Alexandrovich Pletnev
March 7(?), 1826. From Mikhaylovskoe to Petersburg.

My dear fellow, I am very grateful to you for all the news.— Together with your letter I received another one from Zaikin, notifying me of the sale of the *Poems of Alexander Pushkin*,[1] and making me offers. You tell me, my dear one, that the censor will no longer pass certain pieces; just which ones? "A. Chénier"? And so let's wait a bit with a new edition. There will still be time, everything will come out all right—then we shall publish the second, augmented, corrected edition. (But tell me: was there really any displeasure on the occasion of my *Poems*? Or was this nothing but your presuppositions?) Do you know what? If something really ought to be published, then let's latch on to *The Gypsies*. I hope my brother will at least copy it. Then send me the manuscript—I shall supply a preface and perhaps notes, and off my hands, away with it! Otherwise every time I think about it or read a word in the journals, my blood will boil. In the collection of my poems, for a novelty, let's place another tale, of the type of *Beppo*,[2] which I have in stock. I await your answer.

Enclosed is a letter to Zhukovsky in a three-cornered hat and shoes.[3] I dare not hope, but it would be sweet to receive my freedom from Zhukovsky, rather than from another. Incidentally, I abide by the Stoic proverb: rejoice not at finding, weep not at losing.

What *Boris* do you want, and for what lectures? In my *Boris* there is profanity in all languages. This tragedy is not for the fair sex.[4]

Farewell, my dear fellow. Hold fast to my money; don't give any of it to anybody. I need it. And make Delvig pay up, too.

[180]
To Ivan Ermolaevich Velikopolsky
About (not later than) March 11, 1826. From Mikhaylovskoe to Pskov.

Dear Sir, Ivan Ermolaevich,[1]

I heartily thank you for your letter, a pleasing sign of your good will toward me. I have received the poems of Slepushkin, and I am rereading them with more and more astonishment. Your excellent idea of improving the condition of the poet-peasant will, I hope, not go for naught. I do not know whether I shall make up my mind to go to you again at Pskov; you do not completely take away from me the hope of seeing you in my out-of-the-way place; and I thank you meanwhile even for that.

I send my greetings to Prince Tsitsianov;[2] I regret that I did not take back my portrait from him. What is new in your regions?

I remain with sincere esteem your most humble servant.

Alexander Pushkin.

[181]
To Peter Andreevich Vyazemsky
The end of April or the beginning of May, 1826.
From Mikhaylovskoe to Moscow.

My dear Vyazemsky, you are silent and I am silent; and we do well—sometime we shall have a chat at leisure. But for now that is not the point. This letter will be handed to you by a very sweet and kind girl[1] whom one of your friends has indiscreetly knocked up. I rely on your humaneness and friendship. Give her refuge in Moscow and give her as much money as she needs—and then send her to Boldino (my father's estate, where there are chickens, roosters, and bears). You see that here is something that a whole epistle in the style of Zhukovsky's "Of the Priest"[2] might be written about; but posterity does not need to know about our humane feats.

In addition, with paternal tenderness I ask you to look after the little one to be, if it is a boy. I don't feel like sending him to the Foundling Home. But can't he be sent to some village for the meantime—say to Ostafievo?[3] My dear fellow, I swear I am ashamed . . . but it's a little late for that now. Farewell, my angel, whether you are sick or not; we are all sick—each of something. Answer me, and in detail.

[182]
To ALEXEY NIKOLAEVICH VULF
May 7, 1826. From Pskov or Ostrov to Dorpat.

You promised to write me from Dorpat, but you don't write. Fine. However I am waiting for you, dear Philister,[1] and I hope to embrace you at the beginning of next month. You will bring us the inspired one,[2] too, won't you? Tell him that I ask this of him in the name of the glory and honor of Russia. Meanwhile, tell me—won't Zhukovsky pass through Dorpat en route to Karlsbad? Yazykov ought to know that. Are you receiving any letters from Anna Nikolaevna [Vulf] (we N.B. completely made it up before her departure), and what is the Whore of Babylon,[3] Anna Petrovna [Kern], doing? They say that Boltin[4] has been dealing cards very luckily against honored Ermolay Fedorovich [Kern]. That is none of my business, but what would you say? I have written her: *Vous avez placé vos enfants, c'est très bien. Mais avez-vous placé votre mari? Celui-ci est bien plus embarrassant.*[5] Farewell, dear Alexey Nikolaevich; bring Yazykov, and with some verses of his.

May 7.

I saw certain immodest hexameters in Sinsk,[6] and I heartily envied them.

[183]
To PETER ANDREEVICH VYAZEMSKY
Between May 15 and 24, 1826.
From Mikhaylovskoe to Moscow.

Fate doesn't stop playing bad tricks on you. Don't be angry with her, for she knoweth not what she doth. Imagine her as a huge monkey which is given its way completely. Who will put her on a chain? Not you, not I, nobody. Nothing can be done about it, and so there is nothing to be said.

Have you seen my Eda?[1] Has she handed you my letter? She is very sweet, isn't she?

I have not thanked you for your stanzas to Olga.[2] How can you be astonished at my stubbornness and attachment to my present situation? I am more fortunate than André Chénier—I, being still alive, hear the voice of inspiration.

Your verses to the Imaginary Beautiful Woman (ah, excuse me, Happy Woman) are too intelligent. But poetry, Lord forgive me, must be rather stupid. This characterization is harsh. What an *unpacifiable* thing you are, as my nursemaid says. *Seven Fridays* is your best vaudeville.

Write me something, my joy. Without letters from you I grow stupid: that is unhealthy, even though I am a poet.

Is it true that Baratynsky is getting married?[3] I fear for his mind. Lawful c—— is like a warm cap with ears. One's whole head disappears into it. You are perhaps an exception. But even in your case I am convinced that you would be more intelligent if you had remained a bachelor ten more years. Marriage castrates the soul. Farewell, and write.

Mikhaylovskoe.
May.

[184]

To Peter Andreevich Vyazemsky
May 27, 1826. From Pskov to Petersburg.

You are right, favorite of the Muses.[1] I shall take advantage of the rights of the prodigal son-in-law and future master, and I shall settle the whole affair with a letter.[2] Do I owe you anything or not? Answer. Didn't my servant get something from you, the one I discharged for his bad tone and bad conduct? It's about time for us also to discharge Bulgarin, and *The Well-Intentioned*, and our friend Polevoy. I don't feel like it now, but I swear that sometime I'll take up a journal.[3] I'm sorry that you just don't get along with Katenin at all. But for a journal—he's a find. I've read in the newspaper that Ancelot[4] is in Petersburg; who the devil is he? I have also read that

30 men of letters gave him a dinner. Who are these immortals? I am counting on my fingers, and I can't count that far. When you arrive in Petersburg, take control of this Ancelot (I don't remember a single rhyme of his), and don't let him get loose among the pigsties of the literature of our fatherland. In our dealings with foreigners we have neither pride nor shame—in the presence of Englishmen we make a fool of Vasily Lvovich [Pushkin]; before Mme. de Staël we make Miloradovich distinguish himself in the mazurka.[5] A Russian squire shouts: "Boy! amuse Little Hector" (a great Dane). We guffaw and translate these squirish words for the curious traveler. All this pops into his diary and gets published in Europe. It's loathsome. I of course despise my fatherland from head to foot—but it vexes me if a foreigner shares that feeling with me. You, who are not on a leash, how can you remain in Russia? If the Tsar gives me *liberty*, I won't remain a month. We live in a sad age, but when I imagine London, railroads, steamships, English journals, or Paris theaters and brothels, then my out-of-the-way Mikhaylovskoe fills me with boredom and rage. In the fourth canto of *Onegin* I have depicted my own life.[6] Sometime you will read it and ask with your pleasant smile: "But where is my poet? Talent is perceptible in him." You will hear, dear one, in answer: "He bolted off to Paris and will never return to accursed Russia[7]—'at a boy, clever fellow."

May 27.

Farewell.

I suspect you are still in Petersburg, and this letter will head for there. It grieves me that I shall not be able to say farewell to the Karamzins[8]—God knows whether we shall ever see each other. I am now in Pskov, and a young doctor, three sheets in the wind, told me that without an operation I shall not last to thirty years of age. It's not funny to die in the district of Opochka.

[185]

TO IVAN ERMOLAEVICH VELIKOPOLSKY
June 3, 1826. From Preobrazhenskoe to Pskov.

The occasion has arisen for me to square accounts with you again, singer of love, now playful, now despondent; you play very prettily on the lyre; you play rather badly at shtoss.[1] The 500 rubles which you lost are cash witnesses of that. My fate is like yours; immediately, my friend, you will see why.

Do me the favor to pay the five hundred rubles which you owe me, not to me but to Gavriil Petrovich Nazimov,[2] by doing which you will very much oblige me, one devoted to you in soul.

June 3, 1826.   Alexander Pushkin.
Preobrazhenskoe.

[186]
To Nicholas I
Between May 11 and the middle of June, 1826.
From Mikhaylovskoe to Petersburg.

Most gracious Sovereign!

In 1824 I had the misfortune to incur the wrath of the late Emperor by an ill-considered judgment regarding atheism set down in a letter,[1] and I was expelled from the service, and exiled to the village where I still am under the surveillance of the provincial authorities.

Now, with reliance upon Your Imperial Majesty's magnanimity, with sincere remorse, and with the firm intention for my opinions not to be at variance with the generally accepted order (in which matter I am ready to obligate myself by my signature and by my word of honor), I have decided to have recourse to Your Imperial Majesty with my most humble request.

My health, which was shattered in my early youth, and a kind of aneurysm, have now for a long time been needing constant treatment, in support of which I present the testimony of physicians:[2] I make bold to request most humbly the permission to go for this purpose to Moscow, to Petersburg, or to foreign lands.

Most gracious Sovereign,
Your Imperial Majesty's
Loyal subject,
Alexander Pushkin.

[On a separate sheet]

I, the undersigned, obligate myself henceforth not to belong to any secret societies, under whatever name they may exist; I hereby certify that I have not belonged and do not belong to any secret society, and that I never had knowledge of them.

Civil servant of the Tenth Class Alexander Pushkin.[3]

11 May
1826.

[187]

To Peter Andreevich Vyazemsky
July 10, 1826. From Mikhaylovskoe to Petersburg.

Your short letter grieved me for many reasons. In the first place, what do you mean by my epigrams against Karamzin? It's enough that there is one,[1] which I wrote at a time when Karamzin had quit having anything to do with me, and thus deeply wounded my self-esteem and also my heartfelt attachment toward him. Even now I cannot remember it with equanimity. My epigram is pointed, and not offensive in the slightest. But the others, as far as I know, are stupid and rabid: you don't attribute them to me, do you? In the second place, whom are you calling madcaps and rascals? Ah, my dear fellow, you hear the accusation without hearing the justification, and make your decision: that's an unjust trial. If that's the way even Vyazemsky does, then what about the others? I'm grieved, brother, so grieved that now I'm even ready for the noose.

As I read the articles in the journals on the death of Karamzin, I am in a fury. How cold, stupid, and base they are. Can it be that not a single Russian soul will bring a worthy tribute to his memory? The fatherland has the right to demand that of you. Write his life for us; that will be the thirteenth volume of his *Russian History*; Karamzin belongs to history. But tell *everything*; for that you will have to use sometimes the eloquence which Galiani[2] defines in his letter on the censorship. I wrote to you in Petersburg, while I still did not know of the death of Karamzin. Have you received the letter? Write and tell me. Your advice seems good to me—I have already written the Tsar, immediately upon the termination of the investigation, and I concluded my petition in your exact words.[3] I am awaiting the answer, but my hopes are poor. I have never liked revolt and revolution, that is true; but I had ties with almost all and was in correspondence with many of the conspirators. All the subversive manuscripts went under my name, just as all obscene ones go under the name of Barkov.[4] If I had been called up by the commission, I would of course have cleared myself, but I have been left in peace, and I suspect that bodes no good. Only the devil knows, though. Farewell; write.

July 10.

How is Katerina Andreevna [Karamzina]?

[188]

To PETER ANDREEVICH VYAZEMSKY
August 14, 1826. From Mikhaylovskoe to Petersburg.

So the sea, the ancient killer of men, is inflaming your genius?
With golden lyre you glorify the trident of awesome Neptune.
Do not glorify him. In our vile age Gray Neptune is the ally of
Land. In all the elements man is tyrant, traitor, or prisoner.

I give you my hearty thanks for the verses.[1] Now every impulse from the material world is precious for the soul. Let us postpone criticism until another time. Is it true that Nikolay Turgenev[2] has been taken by ship to Petersburg? Here is what your vaunted sea is like! I still am in hopes for the coronation: the hanged are hanged;[3] but penal servitude for 120 friends, brothers, comrades, is horrible. From my memoirs I have preserved only several pages, and I shall send them to you, for you alone. Farewell, dear one.

August 14.

You find my letter[4] cold and dry. It could not be otherwise. It is well that it is written. My pen wouldn't budge now.

[189]

To PRASKOVIA ALEXANDROVNA OSIPOVA
September 4, 1826. From Pskov to Trigorskoe.
(In French)

I suppose, Madame, that my sudden departure with a *Fel'd-Eger'*[1] surprised you as much as it did me. Here is the thing: with *us* nothing can be done without a *Fel'd-Eger'*. I have been given one, for greater safety. According to a very pleasant letter from Baron Dibich,[2] I should be proud of it. I am going straight to Moscow, where I expect to be on the eighth of the present month. As soon as I am free, I shall return in all haste to Trigorskoe, where from now on my heart is fixed forever.

Pskov. September 4.

Letter 170

   1. Dated 1826, they appeared on December 30, 1825.
   2. That is, exiled to Siberia, in connection with the Decembrist Uprising.
   3. See Letter 68.
   4. Nicholas I.

Letter 171

   1. A. N. Raevsky. The rumors proved false; Nicholas I had a talk with Raevsky and became convinced of his innocence of participation in the Decembrist Uprising of 1825.
   2. Of the Fortress of Peter and Paul, then a dungeon.

Letter 172

   1. Pushkin learned of the interregnum about December 10, 1825, and of the Decembrist Uprising in Petersburg, of December 14, about December 20. After hearing of the interregnum, Pushkin was about to set off for Petersburg, breaking his exile, but he was held back by superstitiousness when hares crossed his path and he met a priest. If he had gone, he would have gone directly to the house of Ryleev and he would have arrived just when the uprising was starting. In that case, no doubt he would have participated. Pushkin was right in thinking that there was no evidence implicating him directly in the conspiracy; however, copies of early revolutionary poems by Pushkin were found in the possession of all the Decembrists. Pushkin burned his autobiographical notes, in anticipation of search and seizure.
   2. A. N. Raevsky and N. N. Raevsky the Younger; both were cleared of the charges of being Decembrists.
   3. Major Vladimir Fedoseevich Raevsky (1795-1872), General Pavel Sergeevich Pushchin (1785-1865), and General Mikhail Fedorovich Orlov. Pushkin was very close in friendship and political views to all three of these people, during his stay in Kishinev, 1820-1823. General Pushchin was founder of the Masonic lodge in Kishinev, and he was a member of the Union of Welfare, before it was abolished in 1821. He was freed from complicity in the Decembrist Uprising. General Orlov had also been a member of the Union of Welfare before 1821, and like Pushchin he had ceased activity in secret societies after that time. But he and Major Raevsky were implicated in another matter which was considered as having revolutionary implications, an "uprising" of soldiers under their command in 1822, when an attempt was made to abolish the more liberal treatment of soldiers which these two officers had instituted. Orlov was allowed to resign and to go to his village under surveillance; in 1831 he was allowed to settle in Moscow. Raevsky was found guiltless by one investigatory commission after another; however, in 1828, he was sentenced to exile in Siberia, where he spent the rest of his life.
   4. Masons were regarded as "free thinkers" in a political sense, and all lodges in Russia were abolished in 1822. The government had long known through its secret agents that Pushkin was a member of the Kishinev lodge.
   5. See Letter 68.
   6. Zhukovsky only mentions Alexander I in his poem "The Choir of Maids of Catherine's Institute . . ." (1826).
   7. Pushkin is known definitely to have written two poems "Fairy Tales: A *Noël*" and the epigram beginning "Reared to the Beat of a Drum . . ." on Alexander I; several others have been attributed to him with dubious accuracy.

Letter 173

1. Letter 68.

2. In his work *Of the Prince and of Literature* (1785-1786). Russian writers implicated in the Decembrist Uprising included, among others, Ryleev, A. A. Bestuzhev, Kyukhelbeker, Zhandr, and Kornilovich.

3. Money from the sale of Pushkin's *Poems*. Delvig borrowed the money from Pushkin's agent Pletnev.

Letter 174

1. Pushkin's poem "Who Will Send Me Her Portrait," written in 1821 and published in his *Poems*. Pushkin had written an epigram about Kolosova in 1819; he later repented and wrote this poem in her praise. The letter to Katenin containing these verses has not survived; it was written in 1821.

2. The almanac, planned by Katenin's friend Nikolay Ivanovich Bakhtin (1796-1869), did not materialize.

Letter 175

1. The burden from Catullus' Epithalamium (Poem LXI). Delvig's marriage took place the preceding October.

2. I Corinthians 7:8-9. St. Paul's line of thought is somewhat different from Pushkin's here; he says that "it is better to marry than to burn [i.e., with desire]."

3. Contrary to Pushkin's supposition, the "Teuton" Kyukhelbeker was a "Slav"— that is, a member of the Secret Society of the United Slavs. Both Kyukhelbeker and Ivan Pushchin were condemned to life imprisonment for participating in the Decembrist Uprising.

4. Eda and the Hussar are the two principal characters in Baratynsky's *Eda*, the setting of which was Finland, and not Liflyandia, the earlier name of a territory comprising modern Latvia and parts of modern Estonia and Lithuania.

5. Fedor Nikiforovich Slepushkin (1783-1848), peasant poet. Pushkin is referring to his poems "Christmas Fortune-Telling," "Carnival in the Country," and "Wooden House."

Letter 176

1. *Eda*.

2. Her daughter here referred to was Anna Nikolaevna Vulf. "Netty" was Anna Ivanovna Vulf. Mme. Osipova's second estate, Malinniki, was located near Tver, as was also the estate of Anna Ivanovna Vulf's father.

Letter 177

1. That is, an additional fear to that for the fate of the Decembrists.

2. Humorous paraphrase of Psalms 14:1, "The fool hath said in his heart, there is no God."

3. The peasant poet Slepushkin was given various prizes by Nicholas I and the Empress; the Russian Academy gave him a gold medal.

4. Pushkin is referring to the medal given each member of the Russian Academy after each meeting attended.

5. That is, letters regarding his being freed from his exile.

Letter 178

1. Letter 68.

2. This letter was written as an official letter which could be shown to the Tsar.

Letter 179

1. The edition of 1200 copies was sold out in two months.
2. Byron's *Beppo* (1818); Pushkin is referring to his own *Count Nulin* (written 1825, pub. 1827).
3. That is, an official letter; Letter 178.
4. Zhukovsky had requested Pushkin's *Boris Godunov*, probably for his "lectures" in Russian literature to Grand Duchess Elena Pavlovna.

Letter 180

1. Ivan Ermolaevich Velikopolsky (1797-1868), a military man, poet, and friend of Pushkin's.
2. Prince Fedor Ivanovich Tsitsianov (1801-1832), army officer; nothing is known of the portrait given him by Pushkin.

Letter 181

1. Olga Mikhaylovna Kalashnikova, one of the serfs at Mikhaylovskoe. Little is known of her further fate, except that she was married unhappily to one Pavel Stepanovich Klyucharev, and that during Pushkin's last years she lived at Boldino, in her father's care. Two letters of hers to Pushkin in 1833, requesting help, survive. Nothing is known of Pushkin's child by her.
2. The poem is unknown.
3. Vyazemsky's estate.

Letter 182

1. Pushkin erroneously uses as meaning "student" the word used among German students to mean a "non-student"; A. N. Vulf and N. M. Yazykov were then students at the University of Dorpat.
2. Yazykov, the poet.
3. See Revelation 17.
4. Unknown.
5. "You have disposed of your children—that is very good. But have you disposed of your husband? That is much more bothersome to manage." Pushkin's letter to her containing these words is unknown.
6. A post station on the road from Mikhaylovskoe to Novgorod.

Letter 183

1. Olga M. Kalashnikova (see Letter 181); Pushkin calls her by the name of the heroine of Baratynsky's *Eda*, who was seduced by a Russian hussar.
2. Verses by Vyazemsky dedicated to Olga Sergeevna Pushkina and published in *The Northern Flowers for* 1826. His poems "To an Imaginary Happy Woman" and "Seven Fridays in a Week" were also published there.
3. Baratynsky was married to Anastasia Lvovna Engelgardt (1804-1860) on May 10, 1826

Letter 184

1. Quotation of the opening words of Batyushkov's "Epistle to I. M. Muraviev-Apostol" (1815).
2. Pushkin is replying to Vyzemsky's suggestion that he write Olga Kalashnikova's father a frank "half-affable, half-landownerish letter" pointing out that Pushkin will be Kalashnikov's master and will hold the father responsible if anything happens to the daughter.

3. I.e., Pushkin hoped to publish a journal which would put out of business Grech's and Bulgarin's *Son of the Fatherland*, Izmaylov's *Well-Intentioned*, and Polevoy's *Moscow Telegraph*.

4. Jacques Arsène François Ancelot, French poet and dramatist. In a book published the following year he justified Pushkin's premonitions.

5. The story must have been traditional; the event is not included in Mme. de Staël's book *Ten Years of Exile* (1821). General Count Mikhail Andreevich Miloradovich (1771-1825), Governor of Petersburg (1819-1825), was killed while attempting to put down the Decembrist Uprising.

6. *Onegin*, Chap. IV, stanzas 37-39, 43-51.

7. Pushkin is parodying the final words of I.I. Dmitriev's poem "To Masha" (1803-1805), where, with a "pleasant smile," the girl will ask, "Where is my poet?" and will receive the answer, "The unfortunate one did not live long; he is no more."

8. Karamzin planned to go abroad for his health, but he did not go.

Letter 185

1. A card game.

2. Gavriil Petrovich Nazimov (1794-1850), Pushkin's host on his estate of Preobrazhenskoe.

Letter 186

1. Letter 68.

2. The attached certificate was signed by the Pskov Inspector of the Medical Council, V. Vsevolodov, testifying that Pushkin actually had *varicositus totius cruris dextris*.

3. That is, Collegiate Secretary, the same rank in which Pushkin entered the government service in 1817.

Letter 187

1. Several epigrams on Karamzin have been attributed to Pushkin, but it is not definitely known which one he admits having written. Vyazemsky, in accusing Pushkin of having written the epigrams on Karamzin, who had died on May 26, 1826, said that he was doing it to amuse "madcaps and rascals."

2. Abbé Ferdinand Galiani (1728-1787); his *Correspondence* was published in 1818. His definition is as follows: "It is the art of saying everything, without being clapped in the Bastille, in a country where it is forbidden to say anything."

3. Letter 186.

4. Ivan Semenovich Barkov (1732-1763) is famous for his pornographic poems.

Letter 188

1. Vyazemsky's poem "The Sea."

2. N. I. Turgenev was convicted *in absentia* of conspiracy in the Decembrist Uprising; he spent the rest of his life abroad.

3. Five were hanged, including Ryleev. Many of Pushkin's friends were among the exiled. Pushkin's hopes for a coronation amnesty were not realized.

4. The reference is to Letter 186.

Letter 189

1. "State messenger." The Russian expression is a simple transliteration of the German *feldjäger*.

2. Count Ivan Ivanovich Dibich-Zabalkansky (1785-1831), German-born soldier in Russian service, then Head of the Chief Staff. Dibich's letter conveyed the information

that Pushkin was to be summoned, in company of a *fel'd-eger'*, but not as one under arrest, to see Tsar Nicholas I.

The *fel'd-eger'* arrived in Mikhaylovskoe on the night of September 3, and Pushkin left with him within a half hour. Nobody knew what to expect, and naturally their expectations were of the worst. When Pushkin arrived at Pskov, he discovered that there it was thought that he was to be forgiven by Nicholas I. Pushkin wrote this letter from Pskov, to ease the anxiety of his friends.

CONTENTS OF VOLUME II

ILLUSTRATIONS

PART VI

FORGIVEN POET—MOSCOW AND PETERSBURG

September, 1826—March, 1830

Pushkin, 1827. *Portrait by V. A. Tropinin.*

190

To Praskovia Alexandrovna Osipova
September 16, 1826. From Moscow to Trigorskoe.
(In French)

Here I have been in Moscow eight days, without having had the time yet to write you, which proves to you, Madame, how busy I have been. The Emperor received me in the most amiable manner.[1] Moscow is noisy and in the midst of festivities, to such a degree that I have already become tired of them, and I am beginning to sigh for Mikhaylovskoe, that is, for Trigorskoe. I expect to leave, at the latest, in two weeks. Today, September 15, we are having the grand public festival.[2] Over a mile of tables will be set up in Devichie Field; meat pies have been provided by the *sažen'*,[3] like lumber. It has been several weeks since the meat pies were baked, so that it will be difficult to swallow and digest them, but the respected public will have fountains of wine to wash them down with. This is the news of the day. Tomorrow there is a ball at the Countess Orlova's;[4] an immense riding school has been turned into a hall; she has borrowed 40,000 rubles worth of bronze,[5] and a thousand people have been invited. Much is being said about new, very severe, regulations concerning duels, and concerning a new code of the censorship;[6] I have not seen it, so I can say nothing about it. Excuse the disconnectedness of my letter. It portrays perfectly for you the disconnectedness of my present life. I suppose the Mlles. Annette[7] are already at Trigorskoe. I greet them from afar, and with all my heart, just as I do all your charming family. Please accept, Madame, the assurance of my profound esteem and the unalterable attachment which I have pledged to you for life.

Moscow. September 15.[8]   Pushkin.

191

To Vasily Petrovich Zubkov (?)
November 1 or 2, 1826 (?). In Moscow.
(In French)

I was hoping to see you and to speak with you again before my departure, but my evil fate pursues me in all I desire. So farewell, dear friend. I am going to bury myself in the country until the first of January—I am departing with death in my heart.[1]

[192]
To Vera Fedorovna Vyazemskaya
November 3, 1826. From Torzhok to Moscow.
(In French)

I hasten, Princess, to send you the belts.[1] You see that I have an excellent opportunity to compose you a madrigal apropos of the girdle of Venus, etc.—but the madrigal and the sentiment have become equally ridiculous. What shall I tell you of my trip? It is continuing under the happiest auspices—except for a detestable road and for some unendurable *jamŝčik*.[2] The jolts, elbow pokes, etc., are greatly inconveniencing my two travelling companions—I ask their pardon for my taking such great liberty, but when people decide to travel together, they have to endure a few things. S. P.[3] is my good angel; but *the other*[4] is my demon; the latter troubles me in my poetic and amorous meditations at the worst possible times.

Farewell, Princess. I am going to bury myself among my neighbors.[5] Pray God that my soul rest in peace. If you will be so kind as to send to Opochka a little letter of four pages, that will be an extremely kind act of coquetry on your part. Won't you, who know how to turn a note better than my deceased aunt,[6] have this extreme goodness? (N.B.: *a note* is from now on a synonym of *music*.) So farewell. I am at your feet, and I shake your hand, like the English, since you absolutely forbid me to kiss it.

Torzhok. November 3.

Are there enough hints?[7] In the name of God, do not give your husband the key to them. I am categorically opposed to it.

[193]
To Sergey Alexandrovich Sobolevsky
November 9, 1826. From Mikhaylovskoe to Moscow.

My dear Sobolevsky—I am in my own wooden house again. I was on the road eight days; two wheels broke down, and I arrived by post chaise. On the road I berated you unmercifully;[1] but in proof of my friendship (this sacred feeling) I am sending you my *Itinéraire* from

Moscow to Novgorod. This will be a Guide for you. In the first place, lay in a supply of wine, for you won't find any decent wine anywhere. Then

To the Air: "Once There Was a Turkey Cock"[2]	At Galiani's or Cologne's[3] in Tver order for yourself macaroni and parmesan, and have an omelet prepared.
	Dine at Pozharsky's in Torzhok at your leisure. Try fried cutlets (be sure it is cutlets), and set off, not weighted down.
	When the peasant drags his heavy coach to Yazhelbitsy, then my friend will goggle his epicurean eye!
	They will bring you trout! Order them to be boiled at once: when you see that they have turned blue, pour a glass of Chablis in the broth.
	In order that the broth may be to your taste, you may put a little pepper and a piece of onion in the boiling liquid.

Yazhelbitsy is the first station after Valday. In Valday, ask whether there is any fresh herring. If not

> From the compliant peasant girls (which Valday is famous for) buy some barankas for your tea, and you will leave the sooner.

I advise you to throw an empty bottle out of the calash at every station; thus you will have an occupation to keep you from boredom. Farewell; write.

[194]
To Peter Andreevich Vyazemsky
November 9, 1826. From Mikhaylovskoe to Moscow.
Here I am in the village. I arrived all right, without any incidents worthy of note. The most unpleasant occurrence was that my wheels broke down; they had been jolted to pieces in Moscow by my

friend and well-wisher Mr. Sobolevsky. The village somehow rejoiced my heart. There is a kind of poetic delight in returning, free, to one's abandoned prison. You know that I do not wax sentimental, but meeting my domestics, my boors, and my nursemaid—I swear it tickles the cockles of my heart more delightfully than fame, the enjoyments of my egotism, the social whirl, etc. My nursemaid[1] is killingly funny. Just imagine, at seventy she has learned by heart a new prayer "for the softening of the heart of the Sovereign and for the taming of his soul's ferocity," a prayer which was probably composed under Tsar Ivan.[2] Priests are bawling out a prayer service in her room now, and are preventing me from getting anything done. Has the Princess received the belts and my letter from Torzhok? I shall not stay here long, but I shall not go to Petersburg. I shall be in Moscow by the first . . . she[3] commanded it! My dear one, Moscow left an unpleasant impression on me, but even so it is better to see you than to correspond with you. Besides, there is the journal. . . .[4] I have not said anything to you about your definite intention to unite with Polevoy, but by golly it's sad. So, decent men of letters in our country will never produce anything together! Everything gets done in isolation. Polevoy, Pogodin, Sushkov,[5] Zavalievsky, whoever may publish a journal—it's all the same. The point is that we must possess our own journal and rule it autocratically and absolutely. We are too lazy to translate, make extracts, make announcements, etc., etc. This is the dirty work of a journal; that is why the editor exists; but he must (1) know Russian grammar, (2) write and make sense, i.e., make the substantive agree with the adjective and join them to a verb. But Polevoy can't do even that. Read, for Christ's sake, the first paragraph of his account of the deaths of Rumyantsev and Rostopchin.[6] And grant me that it is impossible to entrust to him the editing of a journal sanctified with our names. There's nothing that can't still be done, though. Perhaps not Pogodin but I shall be the proprietor of a new journal. Then you'll have to send Polevoy up his mother's a——. Farewell, Prince Weathercock, give my greetings to the Princess of the Winds,[7] who, I hope, has completely convalesced. How are our friends? How is Forbidden Rose?[8] How is Timasheva?[9] What a pity that I didn't succeed in starting up a noble intrigue with her! But that can still be done, too.

November 9.

I have just reread my pages about Karamzin[10]—there is nothing publishable. Pluck up your spirit and write. What you did for Dmitriev[11] (N.B.: you are still the only one who is standing up for him), we ask of you for the shade of Karamzin—who must not be compared with Dmitriev. Here I found some verses by Yazykov.[12] You will be amazed at how he has developed, and at what will come from him. If indeed I ought to be jealous, here is the one I ought to be jealous of. Amen, amen, I say unto you. He'll eclipse all us old men. Ah! a pun! Tell the Princess that she will eclipse all Moscow charms when she puts on my belts.[13]

[195]
To Nikolay Mikhaylovich Yazykov
November 9, 1826. From Mikhaylovskoe to Dorpat.

Dear Nikolay Mikhaylovich—I have just arrived from Moscow, I have just seen *your* Trigorskoe[1]—I hasten to embrace and congratulate you. You have written nothing better, but you will write much that is better. God grant you health, discretion, and a prosperous and peaceful life! The Tsar has freed me from the censorship. He himself is my censor. The advantage is, of course, enormous. Thus we shall print *Godunov*. Regarding the censorship regulations—to be continued. Write me. I embrace you and [Alexey] Vulf.

Have you received my verses?[2] I have no copy of them. Send them to me, and, incidentally, also my first epistle.[3]

I shall write you a lot about Moscow.

[196]
To Mikhail Petrovich Pogodin
November 29, 1826. From Pskov to Moscow.

Dear and honored one, for God's sake, stop as soon as possible everything bearing my name and now in the Moscow censorship[1]— *such is the will of the Highest Authorities.*[2] Meanwhile I cannot even participate in your journal[3]—but everything will be ground out fine, there will be flour, and bread and salt for us. I do not have time to go into explanation; until we meet again soon. I am sorry that our contract did not go through.

November 29.   Alexander Pushkin.
Pskov.

[197]

To Alexander Khristoforovich Benkendorf
November 29, 1826. From Pskov to Petersburg.

Dear Sir,

Alexander Khristoforovich,

Being completely unfamiliar with the procedures regarding official documents, I did not know whether I ought to answer the letter[1] which I was honored with receiving from Your Excellency, and by which I was touched to the depths of my heart. Of course no one feels more keenly than I the graciousness and magnanimity of the Sovereign Emperor, and also Your Excellency's indulgent good will.

Since I actually did read my tragedy to certain persons in Moscow (of course not from disobedience, but only because I badly understood the Sovereign's most high Will), I consider it my duty to forward it to Your Excellency in the same form as it was when I read it, so that you yourself may see the spirit in which it was composed; I have not made bold before now to present it to the eyes of the Emperor, for I intended first to expunge certain indelicate expressions. Since I do not have another copy, I make bold to request Your Excellency to return this one to me.

I felt ashamed to disturb, with my insignificant literary endeavors, a man of state, amid his enormous cares. I have given several of my short poems to various journals and almanacs, at the requests of the editors; I ask Your Excellency's forgiveness for this unintentional fault, if I do not succeed in stopping them in the censorship.

With the profoundest feeling of esteem, gratitude, and devotion, I have the honor to be,

Dear Sir,
Your Excellency's
Most humble servant,
Alexander Pushkin.

Pskov.
1826. November 29.

[198]

To Nikolay Stepanovich Alexeev
December 1, 1826. From Pskov to Kishinev.

Come, O friend, give former inspirations, breathe life of the past on me! . . .[1]

I cannot express to you my feeling when I received your letter—your neat and stiff handwriting, the sounds of Kishinev, the shore of the Byk, Jewess, Solovkina, Calypso.[2] My dear one, you took me back to Bessarabia! I was again in my ruins[3]—in my dark room, before the trellised window, or at your place, my dear fellow, in the bright, clean little wooden house, bedaubed with Moldavian s——. Again Rhine wine, again champagne, and Pushchin, and Varfolomey,[4] and everything. . . . How intelligent it was of you to write me first! That happy thought might never have come into my head, even though I often remember you, and I regret that I can neither throw you into a rage nor observe your maneuvers around the jail. I was in Moscow, and I thought: God is merciful, maybe I shall see my dark-complexioned friend sitting decorously somewhere in the theater loge or in a restaurant with a bottle. No. So I left for Pskov—so I now again am going to white-stoned Moscow.[5] There's no hope or very little.[6] At least write me as often as you can, and I will regale you with the Moscow news in exchange for the Kishinev news. I'll play the pander of your old mistresses for you—I'll bet they have aged devilishly. Write which ones. To this day I have been ready to follow in your footsteps, consoling myself with the thought that I shall put horns on a friend.

I send Liprandi a friendly embrace; I regret that we have made round trips at government expense[7] at various times but have not bumped into each other anywhere.

Farewell, Bessarabian hermit, sly friend of my soul—gladden me, not with an Arabian fantasy, but with your Russian truth.

December 1.   A.P.

[199]

To Peter Andreevich Vyazemsky
December 1, 1826. From Pskov to Moscow.

My Vyazma angel or my Vyazma spice cake,[1] I have received your wife's letter and your postscript. I thank you both. I am on the way to Moscow, and I can hardly wait. What do you think! They're wearing me down! . . .[2] I'll explain later. In the village I wrote despised prose,[3] but inspiration is not stirring. In Pskov, instead of writing the seventh chapter of Onegin, I am losing the fourth at shtoss; it's not funny! I have received letters from all directions, and I am answering them in all directions. *Adieu, couple si étourdi en apparence, adieu,*[4] Prince and Princess Weathercock.[5] You see that I lack even my own simplicity for corresponding.

December 1. Pskov.

Enclosed is a letter to Alexeev[6] (a type like my Sushkov); give it, for delivery to him, to Kiselev, Kiseleva, the Kiselevs, as you please.

[200]

To Vasily Petrovich Zubkov
December 1, 1826. From Pskov to Moscow.
(In French)

Dear Zubkov, you have not received any letter from me, and here is the reason: I wanted to drop in on you like a bomb on December 1, i.e., today, and so I left my accursed village five or six days ago by *perekladnaja*[1]—on account of the detestable roads. The Pskov *jamščik*[2] have had nothing more important to do than to overturn me; I have a wrenched side, a sore chest, I cannot breathe; in my rage, I am gambling and losing. Enough of that: I am waiting until I am even a tiny bit better, to take post horses again.

Your two letters are charming; my arrival would have been the best answer to the reflections, objections, etc. But since I am here in the inn in Pskov instead of at Sofia's[3] feet, let us chatter, i.e., let us reason.

I am twenty-seven years old, dear friend. It is time for one to begin to live, i.e., to know happiness. You tell me that happiness cannot be eternal: a fine piece of news! It is not my own happiness which disturbs me—could I be other than the happiest of men beside her? I tremble at the mere thought of the fate which perhaps awaits her—I tremble that I may not be able to make her as happy as I should like. My life up to the present, so wandering, so stormy; my character, crotchety, jealous, touchy, violent, and weak, all at the same time—this is what gives me moments of painful reflection. Ought I unite to a fate so sad, to a character so unfortunate, the fate of a being so sweet, so beautiful? . . . My God, how pretty she is! and how stupid my behavior toward her has been. Dear friend, try to blot out the bad impressions which it may have given her—tell her that I am more rational than I have appeared to be, and as evidence say—*čto tebe v golovu pridet. Merzkij ètot Panin, dva goda vljublen, a svatat'sja sobiraetsja na Fominoj nedele—a ja vižu raz ee v lože, v drugoj na bale, a v tretij svatajus'*![4] If she thinks that Panin is in the right, she must believe that I am mad, mustn't she? So explain to her that I am the one in the right, that when one has seen her, there can be no hesitating, that I do not for a moment suppose that I could fascinate her, that I have acted very well in coming absolutely straight to the conclusion, that once one falls in love with her, it is impossible to love her more, just as it is impossible to find her still more beautiful with the passing of time, because it is impossible to be more beautiful. *Angel moj, ugovori ee, uprosi ee, nastrašťaj ee Paninym skvernym i ženi menja.*[5]

A.P.

In Moscow, I shall tell you something. I prize my turquoise,[6] completely vile as it is. I congratulate Count Samoylov.[7]

[201]
To Sergey Alexandrovich Sobolevsky
December 1, 1826. From Pskov to Moscow.

Here is the point: though freed from the censorship, I must nevertheless, before I publish anything, present it Higher,[1] even though it is only a trifle. I have already been given a dressing down (very nicely, very politely).[2] Of course I shall fulfill the Sovereign's will to the letter, and to that end I have written Pogodin[3] to let it be known to the censorship that nothing of mine is to be passed anywhere. I see for myself a great benefit from this: liberation from the *almanacsters, journalsters*, and other *writersters* dealing in small wares. Pogodin and I shall come to another agreement.

Send the letter on to Zubkov, without the slightest delay.[4] Your guesses are loathsome; my prospects are smooth as silk.[5] In a few days I shall be at your house; meanwhile I am sitting, or lying, in Pskov. They write me that you are sick: what did you overeat on?[6] I shall stop at your house.[7]

[202]
To Nikolay Mikhaylovich Yazykov
December 21, 1826. From Moscow to Dorpat.

I received you letter in Pskov, and I wanted to answer you from Novgorod, worthy singer of both places.[1] I am writing, however, from Moscow—to which I brought your "Trigorskoe" yesterday. You know by the newspapers that I am participating in *The Moscow Messenger*, consequently you should, too. Address your verses to Moscow, Molchanovka to the house of Renkevicheva, and from there I shall give them to the temple of immortality. Be ours without fail. Pogodin earnestly sends his greetings.

I am tired and ill—therefore I shall not write you any more. I send greetings to [Alexey] Vulf, promising my high protection.

November[2] 21.

Your "Trigorskoe," with your permission, will be published in the second issue of *The Moscow Messenger*.

Are you glad of the journal? It is time to throttle the almanacs. Delvig is ours.[3] Only Vyazemsky has remained firm and faithful to *The Telegraph*—it's a pity, but what's to be done?

[203]
To Alexander Khristoforovich Benkendorf
January 3, 1827. From Moscow to Petersburg.

Dear Sir, Alexander Khristoforovich,

I have received, with the feeling of the most profound gratitude, Your Excellency's letter informing me of His Majesty's most gracious comment with regard to my dramatic poem.[1] I agree that it resembles a historical novel more than a tragedy, as the Sovereign Emperor deigned to observe. I regret that I have not the power to re-do what I have once written.

I shall shortly have the honor, in accordance with Your Excellency's command, to send you my short poems.

With the feeling of most profound respect, gratitude, and devotion, I have the honor to be

Your Excellency's
Most obedient servant,
Alexander Pushkin.

January 3, 1827.
Moscow.

[204]

To PETER PAVLOVICH KAVERIN
February 18, 1827. From Moscow to Borovsk.

Here is an amber for you,[1] my dear Kaverin. Just how are you getting along in your swinish little city?[2] Here it is dull as before. Zubkov is going to his boors[3] in a few days. Our police sector is in good condition. The sector police chief Sobolevsky swears and scuffles as before. Spies, dragoons, whores, and drunks loaf around at our place from morning till evening.

Farewell until we meet again.

February 18.

[205]

To VASILY IVANOVICH TUMANSKY
February (not later than 25), 1827. In Moscow.

My dear Tumansky, you surely have written to me, because you surely love me as of old, but I have not received a single line from you. The post is to blame, isn't it? Check on it, and take your own measures. So that I'll be sure to get it, write me in care of Pogodin, to the bookseller Shiryaev in Moscow. By the way: I am relying on you, as on a stone wall. Pogodin is nothing but a *name, an empty sound*—the spirit is I, i.e., all of us, the orthodox.[1] Buttress us with your prose, and solace us with your verses. Farewell; send my fragment "Odessa."[2]

[206]

To ANTON ANTONOVICH DELVIG
March 2, 1827. From Moscow to Petersburg.

My dear one, a few days ago I became angry at you and your silence, and I wrote Venevitinov a stern letter.[1] Excuse me: we were having spring, a thaw, and I had not received a single word from you for about two months. One can't help getting furious. Now we are having freezing weather again, we have sent fool spring packing,[2] I have received a letter from you—everything, thank God, is all right. I am awaiting *The Gypsies*, and I shall publish at once. You complain to me about *The Moscow Messenger*, and about German metaphysics. God sees how I hate and despise it. But what is to be done? Enthusiastic, stubborn lads have gathered together; to the parish priest his own, and to the devil his own. I say, Gentlemen, why should you want to mill the wind—all that is fine for the Germans, already saturated with positive knowledge, but we. . . . *The Moscow Messenger* sits in a pit and asks, "What kind of thing is a rope?"[3] (incidentally, this metaphysical question could be answered, but enough said).[4] But my time is a thing such that I am not going to waste it on any *Messenger*. So much the worse for them, if they do not listen to me.

Lev [Pushkin] was here—he's a nimble young fellow, but it's a pity that he drinks. He went four hundred rubles in debt at your Andrieux's, and he had debauched the wife of a garrison major. He imagines that his estate is in disorder and that he had drained all the cup of life. He is en route to [Caucasian] Georgia, to restore his withered soul. Killingly funny.

Pletnev, our misanthrope, writes me a touching letter; he complains of me, of you, of your *grand patience*, and he says, "It is terrible to think, that's what people are like!"[5] Pletnev, my dear fellow! What's terrible about that? People—that is to say, trash, s——. Spit on them and call it quits.

March 2.

Hurry up with *The Gypsies*. And what are your *Flowers* like—tiny blossoms?[6]

[207]

To ALEXANDER KHRISTOFOROVICH BENKENDORF
March 22, 1827. From Moscow to Petersburg.

Dear Sir, Alexander Khristoforovich,

I have not for a long time had in my possession the poems which Baron Delvig delivered to Your Excellency.[1] I gave them to him for his almanac *Northern Flowers*, and they were to have been published in the beginning of the present year. Following the Highest's Will, I stopped their publication and I directed Baron Delvig to submit them to Your Excellency before doing anything else.

I give you my deeply felt thanks for your benevolent observation regarding the piece "October 19." Without fail I shall write Baron Delvig to expunge from it the capital letters of the names—and generally speaking everything that could give occasion for conclusions and interpretations unfavorable for me.[2]

The tardiness of my answer proceeds from the fact that the last letter which I was honored to receive from Your Excellency was addressed by mistake to Pskov.

With the feeling of most profound respect and heartfelt devotion, I have the honor to be,

Dear Sir,
Your Excellency's
Most humble servant,
Alexander Pushkin.

March 22
1827
Moscow.

[208]

To Lev Sergeevich Pushkin
May 18, 1827. From Moscow to Tiflis.

Why don't you write me, and why doesn't your commander[1] write me? Tomorrow I am going to Petersburg to see our dearest parents, *comme on dit*,[2] and to put my financial affairs in order. From Petersburg I shall go either to foreign lands, i.e., to Europe, or to my own, i.e., to Pskov. But more probably I shall go to Georgia, not on account of your beautiful eyes, but on account of Raevsky. My letter will be delivered to you by Maria Ivanovna Rimskaya-Korsakova, an extremely charming representative of Moscow. Come to the Caucasus and make her acquaintance —but I ask you not to fall in love with her daughter.[3]

Has the war ended where you are? Have you seen Ermolov,[4] and how are things for all of you after his departure? Write me in care of our sister, and she will forward your letter to me sometime.

May 18.   A.P.[5]

[209]

To Praskovia Alexandrovna Osipova
About (not later than) June 10, 1827.
From Petersburg to Trigorskoe.
(In French)

I am very much to blame toward you, but not so much as you may think. When I arrived in Moscow, I immediately wrote you, addressing my letters *na Vaše imja v Počt-amt.*[1] It turns out that you have not received them. That discouraged me, and I have not taken up my pen again. Since you are so kind as to be still interested in me, what shall I tell you, Madame, of my stay in Moscow, and of my arrival in Petersburg?[2] The insipidness and stupidity of our two capitals are equal though different, and since I have pretensions to impartiality, I shall say that if I had been given the choice between the two, I would have chosen Trigorskoe—more or less like Harlequin, who upon the question which would he prefer, to be broken on the wheel or hanged, answered: "I prefer some bread and milk." I am here on the point of my departure, and I am definitely counting on coming to spend several days at Mikhaylovskoe. Meanwhile with all my heart I greet you and all of yours.

[210]

To Mikhail Petrovich Pogodin
June 10, 1827. From Petersburg to Moscow.

I am very grateful to you, and I hasten to send off the proof sheets.[1] 'At a boy, Sobolevsky, 'at a boy, Sluggard! What nonsense he has piled up here![2]

I have received a letter from him, and I shall answer in a few days —meanwhile I am thinking lustfully of Sillery[3] at eleven rubles in bills.

[211]

To Sergey Alexandrovich Sobolevsky
July 15, 1827. From Petersburg to Moscow.
July 15.

Last night I learned of your grief,[1] and I received your two letters. Don't cry over spilled milk; rejoice not upon finding, weep not upon losing. I am sending you the cash I have on hand; the remaining 2,500 will follow. My *Gypsies* is not selling at all; this money is hard-earned, won at cards in the sweat of my face from our friend Poltoratsky.[2] Come to Petersburg if you can. I should like to see you and talk over the future. Bear in manly fashion the change in your fate, i.e., cut your coat according to your cloth—everything will be ground out fine, there'll be flour. You see that, except for proverbs,[3] I shall not be able to say anything sensible to you. Farewell, my friend.

[212]

To ELIZAVETA MIKHAYLOVNA KHITROVO
July 18, 1827(?). In Petersburg.
(In French)

Madame,[1]

I do not know how to express to you all my gratitude for the interest which you are so kind as to take in my health; I am almost ashamed to be so well. An extremely irksome circumstance deprives me of the happiness of being at your house today. Please accept my regrets and my excuses, as well as the assurance of my high esteem.

July 18.   Pushkin.

[213]

To ALEXANDER KHRISTOFOROVICH BENKENDORF
July 20, 1827. In Petersburg.

Dear Sir, Alexander Khristoforovich,

In 1824 State Counsellor Oldekop, without my consent or knowledge, reprinted my poem *The Prisoner of the Caucasus*, and thereby deprived me irrevocably of the profits of a second edition, for which booksellers at the time were offering me three thousand rubles. As a consequence of this, my father, State Counsellor Sergey Lvovich Pushkin, addressed a petition to the authorities, but he received no satisfaction. Instead he was answered that Mr. Oldekop had said he had reprinted *The Prisoner of the Caucasus* so that the original could be checked with the German translation; that, besides, no law exists in Russia against reprinting books; and that he, State Counsellor Pushkin, could prosecute Oldekop, if at all, only as a swindler, which

I did not dare to agree to, from esteem for his profession and fear of having to pay for slander.

Not having any other means for providing for my financial status except the profits from my labors as I find strength to do them, and now personally encouraged by Your Excellency, I make bold at last to have recourse to the Highest's protection, in order to guard myself against such an encroachment on my property in the future.[1]

I have the honor to be, with the feeling of most profound respect, gratitude, and devotion,

Your Excellency's,
Dear Sir,
Most humble servant,

St. Petersburg.   Alexander Pushkin.
July 20, 1827.

[214]

To ANTON ANTONOVICH DELVIG

July 31, 1827. From Mikhaylovskoe to Reval.

[. . . .][1]

Here is the promised elegy for you, my dear fellow. Now you have a fragment from *Onegin*,[2] a fragment from *Boris*, and this piece. I shall try to send you something else. Remember that I have *The Moscow Messenger* on my hands and that I cannot leave it to the mercy of fate and Pogodin. If I finish the epistle to you about your grandfather's skull,[3] let's print it, too. I am in the village, and I hope to do a lot of writing; at the end of autumn I shall be with you. Inspiration hasn't come so far; meanwhile I have taken up prose.[4] Write me about what you are doing. How about prose of yours, and how about poetry of yours? Has knightly Reval awakened your sleepy-headed Muse?[5] Is Bulgarin there? By the way, Somov has spoken to me about Bulgarin's "Evening at Karamzin's."[6] Don't publish it in your *Flowers*. By gosh, it's unseemly. Of course a dog is free to bark even at a lord, but let it bark outdoors and not in your own rooms. Our silence with regard to Karamzin, even so, is unseemly, but Bulgarin is not the one to break it. That would be still more unseemly. How is your wife?[7] Has the sea helped her? My nursemaid kisses her, and I send her my greetings. Write.

July 31. Mikhaylovskoe.

[215]

To MIKHAIL PETROVICH POGODIN
August 31, 1827. From Mikhaylovskoe to Moscow.

Victory, victory! The Tsar has passed my *Faust*, except for the two lines: "And the fashionable disease, it /Was presented to you not long ago." Tell this as from me to the gentleman who asked us *how we dared* put such verses before *His* Honor's eyes.[1] Show him this letter, and ask His Honor, from me, to be more civil and indulgent henceforth. Pletnev will deliver the "Scene" to you, together with a copy of Benkendorf's memorandum. If the Moscow censorship should all the same be obstinate, then write me, and I shall disturb the Sovereign Emperor again with a most humble petition and with complaints at disrespect toward His Highest Will.

Now let us turn to another subject. You want to publish *Urania*! ! ![2] *Et tu, Brute*! ! . .[3] But consider: Is that the thing to do? You, the editor of a European journal in Asiatic Moscow, you, an honorable man of letters among the shopkeepers of literature, you! . . . No, you wouldn't want to muss your hands with almanac mud. You have "many articles which have piled up, and which aren't getting into the journal"; but just what kind? *Quod licet Uraniae, licet* all the more to *The Moscow Messenger*; not only *licet*, but *decet*.[4] "And there are also other reasons." What kind? Money? There'll be money, there'll be money. Don't abandon *The Messenger*, for God's sake; I promise you *unconditionally* that I shall participate actively in publishing it next year: to this end I am breaking off absolutely all ties with the almanac-men of both capitals. Our chief mistake has been that we have wanted to be too intelligent. Our poetry section is fine, our prose is perhaps still better; but here is the rub: there is too little nonsense in it.[5] You no doubt have a tale for *Urania*, don't you? Give it to *The Messenger*. Apropos of tales: they absolutely must be an essential part of the journal, like fashions in *The Telegraph*.[6] With us it's not the way it is in Europe—here tales are a rarity. They constituted the initial fame of Karamzin; his tales are still being talked about here with us.

Your Indian fairy tale "The Crossing"[7] would, in a European journal, attract general attention, as a curious disclosure of erudition, but here with us they see only a tale, and they solemnly find it to be stupid. Do you feel the difference? *The Moscow Messenger*, in my un-biassed, honest opinion, is the best of Russian journals. Only the zealous industry is praiseworthy in *The Telegraph*—and only Vyazem-sky's articles are good. But on the other hand for one of Vyazemsky's articles in *The Telegraph* I would give three intelligent articles of *The Moscow Messenger*. His criticism is superficial or unjust, but the mode of his incidental ideas and the expression of them are sharply original. He thinks, angers one, and he makes one think and laugh: an impor-tant merit, especially in a journalist! If you see him, tell him that I owe him an apology, but that I still intend to make amends for my fault. I do not know whether I shall see you now; at least I should like this winter to visit white-stoned [Moscow]. Good-by, dear and amiable one. I am all yours, without ceremony.

August 31. Mikhaylovskoe.

P.S. Another word: publishing *Urania*, by golly, could harm you, albeit unjustly, in the general opinion of decent people. Read what Vyazemsky said about the almanac of the publisher of *The Well-Intentioned*;[8] he is perfectly right. Our public is stupid, but one must not bamboozle it. It's just exactly as with the journalistic detective Serezha;[9] he is stupid, but one must not win his money by cheating at cards. The editor of a journal must use all his might to make his journal as perfect as possible, and must not dash off after profits. It would even be better to cease publication than that; but that would be shameful. I am speaking to you simply and directly, because I sincerely esteem you. Farewell.

Publication of the "Stanzas" to the Tsar is permitted by him; the "Songs About Stenka [Razin]" were not passed.

[216]

To Anna Petrovna Kern

September 1, 1827. From Trigorskoe to Petersburg.

Anna Petrovna, I complain to you of Anna Nikolaevna—she has not kissed me in the eyes, as you commanded. *Adieu, belle dame.*

All yours,

Apple Pie.[1]

[217]

To ALEXANDER KHRISTOFOROVICH BENKENDORF
September 10, 1827. From Opochka to Petersburg.

Dear Sir, Alexander Khristoforovich,

With reverence and gratitude I have received via Your Excellency the Sovereign Emperor's comment. I count it happiness to submit in everything to His Highest Will.

As regards my affair with Mr. Oldekop, I shall not make bold to disturb Your Excellency about it again. You have deigned to observe justly that whereas there are positive laws regarding the pirating of books, it is not forbidden to publish translations together with the originals. But this relates only to the compositions of ancient or dead writers; if it should be permitted among us that a translation gives the right to reprint the original, then it would be impossible to guard literary property against the encroachments of the pirate.

In venturing this my opinion for Your Excellency's consideration, I submit that in drawing up fixed rules for guaranteeing literary property, the question of the right of reprinting a book along with a translation, notes, and a preface, is extremely important.[1]

With the most profound respect and with complete devotion, I have the honor to be,

Dear Sir,
Your Excellency's
Most humble servant,

Opochka.   Alexander Pushkin.
1827
September 10.

[218]

To FADDEY VENEDIKTOVICH BULGARIN
November 21, 1827. In Petersburg.

You were wrong in thinking, most amiable Faddey Venediktovich,[1] that I could forget my promise—Delvig and I will appear at your place without fail with a guilty but repentant stomach today at 3½ o'clock. My head and heart have long been yours. A. Pushkin.

[219]

To SERGEY ALEXANDROVICH SOBOLEVSKY

November (after the 10th), 1827. From Petersburg to Moscow.

Scatterbrain! Stop writing stupidities to Anna Petrovna [Kern], and write me a sensible word. Where is the second part of *Onegin*? Here it is being asked for, and on account of it the sale of the other chapters has stopped.¹ And who is to blame? You, Belly, Caliban,² etc. Another word: you transferred my debt to Trubetskoy,³ and he stood it a whole month. And when he couldn't stand it any longer, he suddenly began to importune me, "Give me some money!" Some money—but where am I to get it? How are your fellows, i.e., ours?⁴ Pogodin has written me, but, excuse me, I have got completely lazy. I have not answered him yet, and I have not sent any verses—but those fellows themselves have discouraged me. Here in Petersburg they give me (*à la lettre*) ten rubles per line. But with you in Moscow they want me to work for nothing and to work exclusively for the journal. And, besides, they say: he is rich, what the devil is money to him? Let us suppose it is so, but then I am rich from my trading in verses, and not from ancestral estates, which are in the hands of Sergey Lvovich [Pushkin].

A.P.

The Baroness [Delvig] sends her greetings and kisses you tenderly.

[220]

To MIKHAIL PETROVICH POGODIN

About (not later than) December 17, 1827.

From Petersburg to Moscow.

Now I must apologize to you very much for my long silence. Incomprehensible, irresistible, inexplicable laziness overcame me; that is my best justification. I am sending you the Tumansky (except for "Blue Eyes,"¹ which has been taken for Delvig), a fragment from *Onegin*,² and the "Stanzas"³ which have been passed by the censorship. In a few days I shall send "Moscow"⁴ and others. Make my excuses to Kalaydovich;⁵ absolutely nothing of mine is left from the local almanac harvest, and as yet there has been no time to write.

All yours, A.P.

I have not been deprived of the rights of citizenship, and I can be censored by your censorship, if I want to. And I shall not pester the Highest Censor[6] with every moralizing quatrain—tell them that.

[221]
To SERGEY ALEXANDROVICH SOBOLEVSKY
December, 1827 (?). From Petersburg to Moscow.

If you had simply written me when you arrived in Moscow that you couldn't send me the second chapter,[1] I would have reprinted it without making any fuss about it. But you kept on promising—and thanks to you, the sale of the first and third chapters has stopped in all the bookshops. I humbly thank you.

What follows from this?

That you are scatterbrained.

That you are playing the Oldekop and Voeykov,[2] in pirating us exemplary Great People—Merzlyakov, two Pushkins,[3] Veliko-polsky, Podolinsky,[4] Polevoy, etc.

A fine fellow you are!

[222]
To PRASKOVIA ALEXANDROVNA OSIPOVA
January 24, 1828. From Petersburg to Trigorskoe.
(In French)

I am so ashamed, Madame, of having gone so long without writing you, that I scarcely dare to take up my pen; it is only the memory of your friendship, a memory which will be eternally delightful to me, and the assurance that I have the indulgence of your kindness, which embolden me again today. Delvig, who is abandoning his *Flowers* for diplomatic thorns,[1] will tell you of our life in Petersburg. I confess to you that this life is rather foolish, and that I am burning to change it somehow or other. I do not know whether I shall come to Mikhaylovskoe again. However, that would be my desire. I confess to you, Madame, that the noise and the tumult of Petersburg have become completely alien to me—I endure them with impatience. I prefer your beautiful garden and the pretty bank of the Sorot.[2] You see, Madame, that my tastes are still poetic, in spite of the nasty prose of my present life. But truly it is difficult to write you and not be a poet.

Accept, Madame, the assurance of my esteem and of my complete

devotion. I greet with all my heart your entire charming family.
How is Mlle. Euphrosine [Evpraxia Nikolaevna Vulf] finding her
stay at Torzhok?[3] And is she making a lot of conquests there?
    January 24.   Pushkin.

[223]
To Elizaveta Mikhaylovna Khitrovo
February 6, 1828. In Petersburg.
(In French)
    How kind you are, to have thought of solacing the boredom of
my reclusion by remembering me. All kinds of difficulties, vexations,
unpleasantnesses, etc., have kept me more remote from the world
than ever, and only when I was ill myself[1] did I learn of the Countess's accident. Arendt[3] has had the kindness to give me the news of it
and to tell me that she is getting along much better. As soon as my
condition permits me, Madame, I hope to have the pleasure of
coming at once to present to you my respectful compliments; meanwhile I am bored, without having even the distraction of physical
suffering.
                                                          Pushkin.
    Monday.
    I take the liberty, Madame, of sending you the fourth and fifth
parts of *Onegin*, which have just appeared; I hope with all my heart
that they may make you smile.

[224]
To Elizaveta Mikhaylovna Khitrovo
February 10, 1828. In Petersburg.
(In French)
    Such a sad sick person as I little deserves having such an amiable
nurse as you, Madame. But I am very grateful for this completely
Christian and completely charming charity. I am delighted that you
are protecting my friend Onegin;[1] your critical observation is as just
as it is discriminating, like all that you say; I would hasten to come
and collect others, if I did not still limp a little, and if I were not
afraid of staircases. Up to the present I permit myself only the ground
floor.

Be so kind as to accept, Madame, the expression of my gratitude and of my complete esteem.

Friday. Pushkin.

[225]

To Mikhail Petrovich Pogodin
February 19, 1828. From Petersburg to Moscow.

You are absolutely right, and you guessed correctly that I had absolutely nothing to do with Bulgarin's note—not in deed nor in word nor in consent nor in knowledge.[1] If I had seen the proof sheets of it, then certainly I would not have let pass the scurvy trick which is disturbing you. Print your objection, if you think *The Northern Bee* is worth it, but I shall not get mixed up in the business, for it is my rule not to touch you-know-what. Nobody here observed the observation, though.

O hero Shevyrev! O great-hearted knight! Continue your heroic exploits![2] And you, dear Mikhaylo Petrovich, be consoled, and, as Trediakovsky says,[3] spit on the bitch *Northern Bee*.

February 19.

In a few days I shall send you some prose[4]—and for Christ's sake don't insult my little orphan verses with misprints, etc.

I am writing to Shevyrev separately.[5] It's a sin for him not to feel Baratynsky's poetry—but God is his judge.

[226]

To Sergey Alexandrovich Sobolevsky
The second half of February, 1828. From Petersburg to Moscow.

Scatterbrain!

You don't write me anything about the 2100 rubles I owe you, but you write me about Mme. Kern, whom, with God's help, a few days ago I f——. Here's what I want to know: if you want to receive that sum from *The Moscow Messenger*, find out whether they are in a position to pay me 2100 for the present year,[1] and give me the answer —if not, you will get it from Smirdin[2] in installments. Well, my dear Caliban?[3] How does this please you? Write me about your business affairs and your plans. Who is producing there, and who is consuming? Who is this *Athenaeum* sage who analyzed so well the fourth and fifth chapters? Zubarev? or Ivan Saveliich?[4] I have been intending to come to see you, my dear ones, but I don't know whether I shall get there; in any case I'm not remaining in Petersburg.

[227]
TO PRASKOVIA ALEXANDROVNA OSIPOVA
About (not later than) March 10 (?), 1828.
From Petersburg to Trigorskoe.
(In French)

I am taking the liberty of sending you the last three cantos of *Onegin*;[1] I hope that they may merit your approbation. I am enclosing also a copy for Mlle. Euphrosine,[2] thanking her very much for the laconic answer which she has been so kind as to make to my question. I do not know, Madame, whether I shall have the pleasure of seeing you this year; they say that you have been wanting to come to Petersburg. Is it true? Nevertheless, I am still counting on the proximity of Trigorskoe and of Zuevo.[3] In spite of fate, we absolutely must eventually meet again under the ash trees of the Sorot. Accept, Madame, you and all your family, the assurance of my respect, of my friendship, of my missing you, and of my complete devotion.

[228]
TO IVAN ERMOLAEVICH VELIKOPOLSKY
The end of March, 1828. From Petersburg to Moscow.

Dear Ivan Ermolaevich,

Bulgarin has shown me your very pretty stanzas in answer to my joke. He told me that the censorship won't pass them without my consent, as being an allusion to a particular person. Unfortunately, I cannot consent. Your verse,

The second chapter of *Onegin* modestly rode on the ace,

and your note are of course both an allusion to a particular person and an impoliteness.[1] And the whole stanza is unworthy of your pen. The others are very pretty. You seem to me to be a little displeased with me. Are you? At least your most recent poem leaves a rather bitter aftertaste. You would not want to quarrel with me in earnest and make me, your peace-loving friend, include hostile stanzas in the eighth chapter of *Onegin*, would you?[2] N.B.: I didn't gamble away the second chapter, but I paid my debt with copies of it, just exactly as you paid me yours with your parents' diamonds and with the thirty-five volumes of the Encyclopedia. What if I were to print this well-intentioned retort? But I hope that I have not lost your friendship and that upon our first meeting we shall peaceably get down to cards and verses.

Farewell.

All yours, A.P.

[229]
To Alexander Khristoforovich Benkendorf
April 21, 1828. In Petersburg.

Dear Sir, Alexander Khristoforovich,

Although sincerely regretting that my wishes could not be ful-filled,[1] I accept with veneration the decision of the Sovereign Emperor, and I express my heartfelt gratitude to Your Excellency for your indulgent intercession in my behalf.

Since I shall probably remain in inactivity for the next six or seven months, I should like to spend this time in Paris,[2] something which I would perhaps not succeed in doing subsequent to that time. If Your Excellency would deign to obtain for me from the Sovereign this precious permission, then you would do me a new, true bene-faction.

I make use of this latest opportunity, in order to solicit from Your Excellency confirmation of the permission which you gave me orally, to issue again the long poems of mine which have already been printed.[3]

Again entrusting my fate to your magnanimous intercession, I have the honor, with the most profound respect and heartfelt gratitude, to be,

Dear Sir,
Your Excellency's
Most humble servant,
SPb. 1828.   Alexander Pushkin.
April 21.

[230]

To Vera Fedorovna Vyazemskaya
April 26, 1828. From Petersburg to Moscow.

Your Highness! His Highness, notwithstanding his jealousy, has permitted My Nobility[1] to write you several stanzas (i.e., lines). In the first place, permit me to prostrate myself at Your Highness' little feet and express my most humble gratitude for the little dog (the symbol of my faithfulness toward you), embroidered on canvas with your own little hands and sent to me in my Finnish isolation.[2] What are you doing, peerless Princess, in your Saratov steppe, and what is His Highness Pavel[3] doing, whose letters constitute our only consolation? [In French:] In the second place, I thank you for the charming letter which you honored me with. At the moment I do not have it on my heart (that is, in my pocket), and that is why I am reserving for another time the pleasure of chattering and of making you the full and complete confession which you ask of me. Greetings.

A.P.

[231]

To Mikhail Petrovich Pogodin
July 1, 1828. From Petersburg to Moscow.

Forgive me for my long silence, Mikhaylo Petrovich; every day, truly, I have been reproaching myself for inexcusable laziness, every day I have been intending to write you, but I still haven't gotten it done. By the same token I haven't sent you anything for *The Moscow Messenger*, either. True, there hasn't been anything to send; but give me time—autumn is at the gates; I shall sneak off to the village, and I shall send you my quitrent in full. Our journal must be published next year, too. It of course is, be it said between us, the best, the only journal in Holy Russia. We must with patience, conscientiousness, nobility, and especially with perseverance justify the expectations of the true friends of literature and the approbation of great Goethe.[1] Honor and glory to our dear Shevyrev! You did excellently in publishing the letter of our German Patriarch. I hope it will give Shevyrev more weight in public opinion. And that's just what we need. It is time for Intelligence and Knowledge to supplant Bulgarin and Fedorov; here at my leisure I am poking fun at the variance between their opinions and Goethe's. For their long critique of "A Thought,"[2] one of the most noteworthy poems of current literature, our Northern bumblebees[3] have already got what for from Krylov, who has censured them and Shevyrev, each according to his deserts. Forward! And long live *The Moscow Messenger*! Have you made the Telegraph[4] understand that he is a fool? Ksenofont Telegraph, while he was in Petersburg, came close to agreeing with me on this matter (but keep this between us: The Telegraph is a good and honest man, and I do not want to quarrel with him). Give my greetings to Caliban.[5] I shall write to him in a few days. I shall send him some money, and you some verses. Whereupon I embrace you with all my heart.

July 1.

By the way: praise *The Slav*;[6] we need it as plowland needs manure, as the kitchen needs pork, and as the Russian Academy needs Shishkov.[7] [. . .][8]

[232]
To Sergey Alexandrovich Sobolevsky
July 3, 1828. From Petersburg to Moscow.

I am sending you what I have been able to get together so far: 1750 rubles. Send 250 of it to Zubkov, for Christ's sake. For now I don't have time to write. Farewell; glut yourself for your health.

July 3.

My address: in care of Pletnev, Peter Alexandrovich—to the Catherine Institute.

[233]
To Alexander Khristoforovich Benkendorf
The second half (not earlier than the 17th) of August, 1828.
In Petersburg.
(Rough draft)[1]

In pursuance of the Highest's Command, the Chief of Police has asked from me a signed statement that henceforth I, without the usual preliminary censorship [. . . .][2] I am complying with your will which is sacred for me; nevertheless this step is painful for me. The Sovereign Emperor at a moment I could never forget deigned to free me from the censorship; I gave the Sovereign my word of honor, which I cannot betray, on account of my profound, sincere attachment to the Tsar and the man, not even to speak of the honor of a nobleman. The demand for a signed police statement humiliates me in my own eyes, and I firmly feel that I do not deserve it, and I would give my word of honor to this effect, if I still dared to hope that it has its value. As regards the censorship, if the Sovereign Emperor sees fit to do away with the favor he has shown me, then, accepting with grief the sign of the Tsar's wrath, I ask Your Excellency to resolve for me the question, what is the proper manner for me to deal henceforth with my compositions, which, as you are aware, make up my only property.

I hope that Your Excellency will understand and not take amiss the boldness with which I bring myself to make my explanations. It is a sign of the sincere esteem of a man who feels himself[. . . .]

[234]

To Peter Andreevich Vyazemsky
September 1, 1828. From Petersburg to Penza.

I am grateful to you for your letter—it caught me amid all kinds of bothers and unpleasantnesses.[1] I shall answer all your inquiries hastily.

> Perhaps some day she will weep over me

is a verse of Gnedich's (who is now here), in his translation of Voltaire's *Tancrède*:

> *Un jour elle pleurera l'amant qu'elle a trahi;*
> *Ce coeur qu'elle a perdu, ce coeur qu'elle déchire.*[2]

Have you calmed down? While Kiselev and the Poltoratskys[3] were here, I continued the mode of life which I have sung of in this manner:

> But on gloomy days they often gathered, together. They doubled the stakes, the m——-f—— s.o.b.'s, from 50 to 100. And they would win and note it down with chalk. Thus on gloomy days they occupied themselves with business.[4]

But now we have all scattered. Kiselev, they say, is already in the army; *Junior* is in the village: Golitsyn is messing around with Glinka and is establishing celebrations for his aristocratic relatives. I have begun to mix in society, because I am havenless. If it were not for your bronze Venus,[5] I would have died of ennui. But she is consolingly amusing and sweet. I am writing verses to her. And she has made me one of her panders (to the doing of which I was drawn by my usual inclination and the present condition of my own well-intentioned, about which one may say the same as was said of its printed namesake: "The intention is good, but, by golly, the fulfillment is bad").[6]

You invite me to Penza, but if you don't watch out, I shall go farther

Straight, straight to the east.[7]

An extremely stupid joke has draped itself around my neck. *Gavriiliada* has finally reached the government; it is being attributed to me, denunciations against me have been made, and I shall probably answer for another's pranks, if Prince Dmitry Gorchakov[8] does not appear from the other world to defend his rights to his own property. Let this be between us. None of this is very amusing, but Prince Pavel's criticism amuses me as a charming blossom, which with time promises fruit. Ask him to send me his observations; I shall answer them without fail. I thank you with my mind and heart, i.e., with my taste and my self-esteem—for the portrait of Pelagea Nikolaevna.[9] I am not sending her any verses, for even the Turks don't shoot at such a distance. I do not care to raise my eyes before Princess Vera [Vyazemskaya]; however, I inquire what she thinks of the occurrences in Odessa ([A. N.] Raevsky and the Countess Vorontsova).[10]

Addio, idol mio—write me everything, to Petersburg—so long—
September 1.

[235]
To Elizaveta Mikhaylovna Khitrovo
Between early August and the middle of October, 1828 (?).
In Petersburg.
(In French)

Good Lord, Madame, in speaking at random, I never dreamed of making any improper allusions. But that is what you are all like, and that is why genteel women and grand sentiments are what I fear most in the world. Long live the grisettes. With them it is much more direct and much easier. If I do not come to your house, it is because I am very busy, because I can leave home only when it is late, because I have a thousand people whom I ought to see and whom I do not see.

Do you wish me to speak to you quite frankly? Perhaps I am elegant and genteel in my writings; but my heart is completely vulgar and my inclinations are all of the third estate. I am surfeited with intrigues, feelings, correspondence, etc., etc. I have the misfortune to have a liaison with an intelligent, sickly, and passionate woman who drives me wild, although I love her with all my heart.[1] So much for my cares, and especially, for my temperament.

My frankness will not anger you, will it? Then pardon me some expressions which had no common sense and which, besides, did not relate to you in any way.

[236]
To Elizaveta Mikhaylovna Khitrovo
Between early August and the middle of October, 1828 (?).
In Petersburg.
(In French)

Where the devil do you get the idea that I am angry? But I am over my head in difficulties. Pardon my brevity and my Jacobin style.
Wednesday.

[237]
To Nikolay Vasilievich Putyata[1]
Between January and the middle of October, 1828 (?). In Petersburg.
(In French)

Yesterday when I was approaching a lady who was speaking to

M. de Lagrené,[2] the latter said to her loudly enough for me to over-hear: "Send him away." Finding myself obliged to demand the reason for this remark, I pray you, Sir, to be so good as to call on M. de Lagrené and to speak with him accordingly.

Pushkin.

R.S.V.P.

[238]
To ALEXEY NIKOLAEVICH VULF
October 27, 1828. From Malinniki to Petersburg.

The Tver Lovelace[1] wishes the St. Petersburg Valmont[2] health and successes.

———

I have the honor to report that in this province, which is filled with your memory, all goes well. I was received with all due respect and affability. They allege that you are *much worse than I* (as regards morals), and therefore I dare not hope for successes equal to yours. I have given the elucidations demanded of me with regard to your conduct in Petersburg, with frankness and simple-heartedness, as a result of which certain tears began flowing and certain unbenevolent exclamations burst forth, such as, for example, "what a scoundrel, what a vile fellow!"[3] But I pretended that I did not hear. I take this reliable opportunity to report that Maria Vasilievna Borisova[4] is a flower in the desert, a nightingale among the wild birds of the forest, a pearl in the sea, and that I intend to fall in love with her one of these days.

Greetings. My regards to Anna Petrovna [Kern], a friendly hand-clasp to the Baroness [Delvig], etc.

October 27.

[239]
To PRASKOVIA ALEXANDROVNA OSIPOVA
November 3, 1828. From Malinniki to Trigorskoe.
(In French)

A thousand thanks, Madame, for the interest which you are so kind as to take in your devoted servant. I would have come to you without fail, but night surprised me, I hardly know how, right in the middle of my reveries. My health is as good as possible.

Until tomorrow, then, Madame, and please accept once more my tender thanks.

November 3.

[240]

To Anton Antonovich Delvig

The middle of November, 1828. From Malinniki to Petersburg.

[. . . .][1]

Here for you is an "Answer to Katenin," for the *Flowers*, instead of an answer to Gotovtsova,[2] which is not ready. I have completely unlearned how to act amiable: it is as hard for me to get through a madrigal as through a maidenhead. And Sofia Ostafievna[3] is all to blame. I do not know whether I shall stay long in these parts. I am waiting for an answer from Baratynsky. I shall probably put in my appearance there in Finland[4] by the new year. I am having fun here. I love Praskovia Alexandrovna [Osipova] with all my soul; it's a pity that she is ailing and is always disturbed. The neighbors come to look at me, as at the dog Munito;[5] tell this to Count Khvostov. Peter Markovich[6] has become very merry and is nice in a killingly funny way. A few days ago there was a gathering at one of the neighbors'; I had to go to it. His kinswoman's children, spoiled brats, wanted to go there without fail. Their mother brought them some raisins and some black plums and thought to sneak away from them on the sly. But Peter Markovich got them all stirred up; he ran in to them: "Children! children! Your mother is deceiving you— don't eat the black plums. Go with her. Pushkin will be there. He's all made of sugar, and his rear is of apple; they'll cut him up and each of you will get a piece." The children began to howl, "We don't want black plums, we want Pushkin." Nothing could be done about it. They were taken, and they ran up to me, licking their chops— but seeing that I am not made of sugar but of skin, they were completely taken aback. Here there are very many pretty wenches (or maids, as Boris Mikhaylovich commands that they be called),[7] but my relationships with them are Platonic, and as a result I am getting fat and improving in health—farewell, kiss yourself in the navel, if you can. My sister is asking for my *Raven* for her *Pigeon*;[8] do as you think best. Let my brother-in-law engrave, and you print. *Vale et mihi favere*, like Evgeny Onegin.⁹ I say nothing to the Baroness—however, I kiss her little hand, but in an extremely prim manner.

[241]
To Anton Antonovich Delvig
November 26, 1828. From Malinniki to Petersburg.
[. . . .]¹

Here for you is an answer to Gotovtsova (the devil take her); what do you think of *ces petits vers froids et coulants*?² Just what did my Vyazemsky write for her? But there is little gain for her from me. And what does she bluntly reproach me for? Impoliteness against the fair sex, or of obscenities, or of improper conduct?³ The Lord knows. Is it true that you are going to bury yourself in the Smolensk grits?⁴ You see what a mess you have cooked up. You send me after Baratynsky, and you, yourself, have hightailed it away. What am I to do with you? I am having a lot of fun here, because I love village life very much. Here they think that I have come to garner stanzas for *Onegin*, and they frighten their children with me, as a bogeyman. But here I go riding on the new-fallen snow, I play whist at eighty kopecks per rubber—and in this way I am sticking to the charms of virtue and shunning the toils of vice—tell this to our ladies. I shall come to them rejuvenated in body and soul— — — but enough. What nonsense I've been spouting with you today!
November 26.
How about *The Iliad* and how about Gnedich?⁵

[242]
To Peter Andreevich Vyazemsky
January 5 or 7, 1829. In Moscow.

Baratynsky is here with me—and I am leaving in three hours or so. I shall not wait for dinner, but we shall have breakfast, a kind of *en petit couragé*.¹ We shall try to get drunk, not *en grand cordonnier*, like cobblers, but so as to be *en petit couragé*, unconstrained. Come, my angel.

[243]

To Peter Andreevich Vyazemsky
About January 25, 1829. From Petersburg to Penza.

Have you left Moscow? I suspect not—in case you have, I am writing you to Penza, where you will read my epistle sometime. I have been at Zhukovsky's. He takes a lively, warm, Arzamasian—not a courtier's[1]—interest in you. When he received the first news about you, he was about to write an official letter to the Sovereign, but he changed his mind, and he seems to be right. The opinions, the words of Zhukovsky must have great weight, but explanations and proofs are needed to eradicate the preconceptions hostile to you—and so much the better, for Prince Dmitry[2] can present both. Zhukovsky told me of his advice for you to write officially to Benkendorf. But I know that would be unpleasant and painful for you. He is of course not in the right with regard to you; in his position one ought not to pay any attention to police gossip, and still less ought he let knowledge of it reach *aux personnes qui en sont l'objet. Mais comme au fond c'est un brave et digne homme, trop distrait pour vous garder rancune et trop distingué pour chercher à vous nuire, ne vous laissez pas aller a l'inimitié et tâchez de lui parler tout franchement.*[3] Be kind enough to forget the expression, "his profligate conduct"; it simply does not mean anything. Zhukovsky said, with a laugh, that they say you were drunk at the wenches', and he maintains that what gave the basis for the charge was our visit to *Butterfly* Filimonov,[4] in indecent Kolomna, Filimonov is of course of the brothel, and his *Butterfly* is of course a one-ruble Parnassian Varyushka,[5] into whom it would be pitiable and repulsive to slip anything of ours. But even if you had gone into an unmetaphorical brothel, there still would be no great harm done.

I drop into your pleasant house, as a freethinker drops into a cathedral.[6]

The government is no lady, no *Princess Moustache*:[7] it is not becoming for it to play the prude. Amen. Let's talk about something else. I've been in Petersburg about a week, no more. I found all society here in astonishing agitation. They're making merry here till they fall down and till they get up, i.e., at routs,[8] which are coming into great fashion here. We should have guessed it long ago: we were created for routs, for in them there is no need of intelligence, nor merriment, nor general conversation, nor politics, nor literature. You walk on others' feet as on a rug, you ask pardon—and here already is a substitute for conversation. As for me, I am in raptures over routs, and I am resting up from Zinaida's damned dinners. (God grant her neither bottom nor lid, i.e., neither Italy nor Count Ricci!)[9] I have not read the journals yet. They say that Bulgarin is praising you.[10] For what reason? Have you read *The Flowers*? What do you think of Zhukovsky's "Sea," and of his Homer,[11] at which Gnedich is angry, like a tax-farmer at bootlegging?[12] Farewell, there is neither the time nor the space.

[244]

To Ivan Mikhaylovich Snegirev
April 9, 1829. In Moscow.

Dear Sir, Ivan Mikhaylovich,

Do me the favor of explaining on what basis you do not pass the observation which I provided for *The Moscow Telegraph*.[1] It is essential to me for it to be published, and I shall be obliged in case of refusal to make an official complaint to the Highest Authorities of your partiality toward I do not know whom.

I entrust myself to your benevolence, and I beg you to accept the assurances of my sincere esteem and devotion.

A. Pushkin.

[245]

To Ivan Alexeevich Yakovlev
The second half of March or April, 1829 (?). In Moscow.

Dear Ivan Alexeevich,

It is painful for me to be at fault toward you; it is painful also to make excuses, all the more that I know your *delicacy of gentlemen*.[1] You are leaving in a few days, and I am still in debt to you. My debtors do not pay me, and God grant that they not be completely bankrupt, but I (between ourselves) have already gambled away about 20 thousand rubles. In any case you will be the first to receive your money. I still hope to pay it before you leave. Otherwise, permit me to hand it to Alexey Ivanovich, your father, and do me the favor to tell him in advance that you have lent me these 6 thousands.[2] At the end of May or the beginning of June I shall have a wad of money, but meanwhile I am floundering about in the shallows.

All yours, A.P.

[246]

To Natalia Ivanova Goncharova
May 1, 1829. In Moscow.
(In French)

On my knees, pouring forth tears of gratitude—that is how I should write you, now that Count [F. I.] Tolstoy has brought back your answer to me: this answer is not a refusal;[1] you allow me hope. However, if I still murmur, if some sadness and bitterness are mixed with my feelings of happiness, do not accuse me of ingratitude; I understand a mother's prudence and tenderness! But pardon the impatience of a heart which is sick and devoid[2] of happiness. I am departing at once, and I am taking with me in the depths of my soul the image of the celestial one who owes her being to you. If you have any commands to give me, please direct them to Count Tolstoy, who will see that they reach me.

Be so kind, Madame, as to accept the expression of my profound esteem.

May 1, 1829.   Pushkin.

[247]

To Fedor Ivanovich Tolstoy
Between May 27 and June 10, 1829. From Tiflis to Moscow.
(Rough draft)

I have just now discovered that a letter to me has been here; I suspect, dear Count, that it is from you. I very much regret that it has already been sent off to the active detachment, which I am not likely to get to so easily or so quickly—nothing can be done about it. My journey was boring enough.[1] To begin with, I set off for Orel and not directly for Voronezh, I made about 130 extra miles, but on the other hand I saw Ermolov. Although you do not look on him with much favor, I am obliged to tell you that I found in him a striking resemblance to you not only in his turn of mind and in his opinions, but even in his facial features and their expression. He was gracious to an extreme. The road through the Caucasus is vile and dangerous—by day I dragged along on foot with a convoy of infantry, and I slept all night at each halt; on the other hand, I saw Kazbek and the Terek, which are worthy of Ermolov. Now I am sweating it out in Tiflis, awaiting Count Paskevich's permission.[2]

[248]
To Nikolay Nikolaevich Raevsky the Younger
January 30 or June 30, 1829.
From Petersburg to the Caucasus or in Erzurum.
(Rough draft; in French)

Here is my tragedy,[1] since you absolutely must have it, but before you read it I insist that you skim through the last volume of Karamzin.[2] My play is full of good jokes and delicate allusions to the history of the time, like our innuendos of Kiev and Kamenka.[3] It is a *sine qua non* that they be understood.

Following the example of Shakespeare, I have restricted myself to developing an epoch and historical personages, without seeking after theatrical effects, the romantically moving, etc. . . . . The style of it is a mixture. It is coarse and low where I have been obliged to bring in vulgar and gross personages—as for the gross indecencies, pay no attention to them: that was written with a hasty pen, and will disappear in the first copy. A tragedy without love appealed to my imagination. But apart from the fact that love entered greatly into the romantic and passionate character of my adventurer, I have rendered Dimitry enamored of Marina[4] in order the better to throw into relief the strange character of the latter. It is still no more than sketched out in Karamzin. But most certainly she was a strange, beautiful woman. She had only one passion and that was ambition, but to such a degree of energy, of frenzy that one can scarcely imagine it. After having tasted of royalty, watch her, drunk of a chimera, prostitute herself with one adventurer after another—share now the disgusting bed of a Jew, now the tent of a Cossack, always ready to give herself to anyone who could present her the feeble hope of a throne which no longer existed. Watch her boldly face war, destitution, shame, and at the same time negotiate with the king of Poland as one crowned head with another—and end miserably a most stormy and most extraordinary life. I have only one scene for her, but I shall return to her, if God grants me life. She troubles me like a passion. She is horribly Polish, as the cousin of Mme. Lubomirska[5] used to say.

Gavrila Pushkin[6] is one of my ancestors; I have painted him as I found him in history and in my family papers. He had great talents; he was a man of war, a man of the court, a man of conspiracy above all. He and Pleshcheev, with unheard-of audacity, assured the success of the Pretender. Afterwards I found him again in Moscow, one of the seven leaders who defended it in 1612, then in 1616 with a seat in the Duma beside Kuzma Minin, then *voevoda* in Nizhny, then among the delegates who crowned Romanov, then ambassador. He was everything, even an incendiary, as a *gramota*[7] proves which I found at Pogoreloe Gorodishche—a city which he burned down (to punish it for I don't know what), in the manner of the proconsuls of the National Convention. . . .[8]

I expect also to return to Shuysky.[9] He shows in history a singular mixture of audacity, pliability, and force of character. A flunky of Godunov's, he is one of the first boyars to go over to the side of Dimitry. He is the first who conspires, and it is he himself, note that, who undertakes to pull the chestnuts back out of the fire, it is he himself who shouts, who accuses, who from a leader becomes a lost child. He is at the point of losing his head; Dimitry grants him a pardon on the scaffold himself; he exiles him, and with that hare-brained generosity which characterized this appealing adventurer he recalls him to his court, he showers him with possessions and honors. What does Shuysky do, who had had such a close scrape with the axe and the block? He has nothing better to do than to conspire anew; he succeeds in it, is elected Tsar, falls, and preserves in his downfall more dignity and fortitude than he had during his whole life.

There is much of Henry IV[10] in Dimitry. Like him he is brave, generous, and a swashbuckler, like him indifferent to religion—both abjure their faith for political cause, both love pleasures and war, both give themselves up to chimerical projects—both are the object of conspiracies. . . . But Henry IV does not have Ksenia[11] to reproach himself with—it is true that this horrible accusation is not proved, and as for me I make it a point of conscience not to believe it.

Griboedov has criticized my character Iov—the patriarch, it is true, was a man of much intelligence. I inadvertently made a fool of him.

While writing my *Godunov* I reflected on tragedy, and if I should get involved in making a preface, I would arouse an uproar—it is perhaps the most misunderstood genre. They have tried to base its laws on verisimilitude, and that is precisely what the nature of drama excludes. Not to speak of time, place, etc.—what the devil verisimilitude is there in a hall cut in two parts, of which one is occupied by 2000 people, supposedly unseen by those on the boards?

(2) *The language*. For example, the Philoctète of La Harpe says in good French after having heard a tirade by Pyrrhus: "Alas, I hear the sweet sounds of the Greek language." Isn't all that only a conventional unverisimilitude? The true geniuses of tragedy never troubled themselves over any verisimilitude other than that of characters and situations. Look how Corneille boldly managed *The Cid*: "Oh, you want the rule of twenty-four hours? So be it." And thereupon he piles up for you events for four months. Nothing is more ludicrous than small changes of the accepted rules. Alfieri was profoundly struck by the ridiculousness of the *aside*; he suppresses it and thereupon lengthens the monologue. What puerility!

My letter is much longer than I had wished to make it. Keep it, I request you, because I shall have need of it if the devil tempts me to do a preface.

A.P.

1829
30 J[indecipherable]

[249]
To MIKHAIL PETROVICH POGODIN
Between late September and October 12, 1829 (?). In Moscow.
Excuse me, for God's sake. There is an obligation, so to speak, a sacred one. . . .[1] Good-by. Excuse me again.

A.P.

[250]

To ALEXEY NIKOLAEVICH VULF
October 16, 1829. From Malinniki to Petersburg.

En route from Erzurum[1] to Petersburg, I swung to the right and arrived at the Staritsa District to collect certain arrears.[2] What a pity, dear Lovelace Nikolaevich,[3] that we did not meet here! how we would have infuriated the Barons and simple noblemen! At least I have the honor to present to you a detailed account of our and others' affairs.

(I) *In Malinniki* I found Anna Nikolaevna [Vulf] alone with a gumboil and with [Thomas] Moore. She received me with her usual amiability and announced to me the following:

(a) Evpraksia Nikolaevna [Vulf] and Alexandra Ivanovna [Osipova] have left for Staritsa to see the new uhlans.[4]

(b) Alexandra Ivanovna has busied her imagination partly with Kusovnikov's waist and back part, partly with Yurgenev's[5] sideburns and lisping pronunciation.

(c) Gretchen[6] is becoming prettier, and *by the hour is becoming more innocent.* (Anna Nikolaevna has just now declared that she does not find it so.)

(II) *In Pavlovskoe* Frederika Ivanovna[7] is suffering from a gumboil; Pavel Ivanovich is versifying with excellent success. A few days ago he corrected the verses you and I wrote, as follows:

> Coming up to Izhory, *I glanced up at the heavens and remembered* your glances, your dark blue eyes.

This is very pretty, isn't it?

(III) *In Bernovo*[8] I missed fat-a——d Minerva.[9] She had set off with her jealous one for Saratov. On the other hand, *Netty*[10]—tender, languorous, hysterical, *plumpened Netty*—is here. Do you know that Miller[11] in despair threw himself at her feet, but she was not touched by that. This is already the third day that I have been in love with her.

(IV) *Various News.* The priest's daughter (your Clarissa)[12] is in Tver. Somebody gave Pisarev a beating, and he has been ordered to resign. Prince Maksyutov[13] is more in love than ever. *Ivan Ivanovich*[14] is on a strict diet (he screws his odalisques once a week). Not long ago we learned that *Netty*, when she goes to bed, has the habit of making the sign of the cross over all the objects surrounding her bed. I shall try to obtain (as a souvenir of my chaste love) a vessel which has been made holy by her. . . . Upon this, permit me to conclude my instructive letter.

October 16.

[251]

To Alexander Khristoforovich Benkendorf
November 10, 1829. In Petersburg.
(In French)

General,

With most profound sorrow I have just learned that His Majesty was displeased with my trip to Erzurum.[1] Your Excellency's indulgent and bountiful goodness and the interest which you have always deigned to show toward me inspire me with the confidence to have recourse to you again and to explain myself frankly.

When I arrived in the Caucasus, I could not resist the desire to see my brother, who is serving in the Nizhny Novgorod Dragoon Regiment, and from whom I had been separated for five years. I believed that I had the right to go to Tiflis. When I arrived there, I found that the army was no longer there. I wrote Nikolay Raevsky [the Younger], a friend of my childhood, to obtain permission for me to come to the camp. I arrived on the day of the crossing of the Sagan-lu.[2] Once there, it seemed awkward for me to avoid taking part in the engagements which were about to take place, and thus it happened that I was present in the campaign, half a soldier, half a traveler.

I feel how false my position was and how heedless my conduct, but at least there has been only heedlessness in it. The idea that any other motive might be attributed to it would be unendurable. I would prefer to suffer the most severe disfavor rather than to be accounted an ingrate in the eyes of him to whom I owe everything, for whom I am ready to sacrifice my life, and this is no mere phrase.

I beseech Your Excellency to be my providence on this occasion, and I am, with the highest esteem,

My General,

Your Excellency's

Most humble and most obedient servant,

November 10   Alexander Pushkin.

1829

St. P.

[252]

TO SERGEY DMITRIEVICH KISELEV

November 15, 1829. From Petersburg to Moscow.

Dear Sergey Dmitrievich,[1]

I arrived in Petersburg a few days ago; I am letting you know of this, for your agent-friend has perhaps already been here in my absence. My address is *at Demut's*.[2] How are you? How are our fellows? In Petersburg there's anguish, anguish. . . .

If you see Vyazemsky again, hurry him here. We are all awaiting him with impatience. Give our regards to our inalienable Ushakovas.[3] Will it be soon, my God, that I shall come from Petersburg to the *Hôtel d'Angleterre* close by the Kars![4] At least I want to so badly I don't know what to do.

November 15.   All yours,

SPb.   Pushkin.

[253]

TO EKATERINA FEDOROVNA TIZENGAUZEN

January 1, 1830. In Petersburg.

(Verses in Russian; letter in French)

Losing tongue and mind simultaneously, I look at you with a single eye: the sole eye in my head. If the Fates had willed that I have a hundred eyes, all hundred would be looking at you.

It goes without saying, Countess, that you will be a true Cyclops.[1] Accept this commonplace remark as a proof of my complete submission to your commands: if I had a hundred heads and a hundred hearts, they would all be at your service.

Please accept the assurance of my high esteem.

January 1.   Pushkin.

[254]

To Nikolay Ivanovich Gnedich
January 6, 1830. In Petersburg.

I am glad, I am happy, that the several lines which I timidly jotted down in *The Gazette*[1] could touch you to such a degree. Ignorance of the Greek language prevents me from proceeding to a full-scale critique of your *Iliad*. This analysis is not necessary for your fame, but it may be necessary for Russia. I embrace you with all my heart. If you will be at Andrieux's, I shall look in there. I shall see you before that.

All yours,
Pushkin.

[255]

To Alexander Khristoforovich Benkendorf
January 7, 1830. In Petersburg.
(In French)

Having called upon Your Excellency and not having had the good fortune to find you in, I take the liberty of addressing to you a request which you have permitted me to make to you.

While I am still neither married nor attached to the service, I should like to make a trip either to France or to Italy. However, if this is not granted to me, I would request the favor of visting China with the mission which is about to set out for there.[1]

May I dare to trouble you further? Mr. Zhukovsky had wished to publish my tragedy[2] during my absence, but he has not received formal authorization to do so. It would inconvenience me, in view of my lack of fortune, to be deprived of some fifteen thousand rubles which my tragedy can bring me, and it would sadden me to renounce the publication of a work which I long meditated over, and with which I am most satisfied.[3]

Relying entirely on your good will, I am, General,
Your Excellency's
Most humble and most obedient servant,
January 7, 1830.   Alexander Pushkin.

[256]
To Mikhail Nikolaevich Zagoskin
January 11, 1830. From Petersburg to Moscow.
Dear Sir, Mikhaylo Nikolaevich,[1]

I interrupt the captivating reading of your novel to thank you heartily for sending me *Yury Miloslavsky*, a flattering mark of your good will toward me. I congratulate you upon your complete and deserved success, and the public upon one of the best novels of the present epoch. Everybody is reading it. Zhukovsky spent a whole night at it. The ladies are in rapture over it. There will be an article about it by Pogorelsky in *The Literary Gazette*. If everything is not said in it, I shall try to say the remainder. Farewell. God grant you many years, i.e., God grant us many novels.

With sincere esteem and devotion, I have the honor to be
Your most humble servant,
A. Pushkin.

January 11, 1830.
SPb.

[257]
To Elizaveta Mikhaylovna Khitrovo
The first half of January, 1830. In Petersburg.
(In French)

You must consider me very ungrateful, a very bad lot. But I entreat you not to judge by appearances. It is impossible for me to come at your command today. Although, not to speak of the happiness of being at your house, curiosity alone would suffice to lure me there. Some verses of a Christian, of a Russian bishop, in answer to some skeptical stanzas:[1] That is really a piece of good luck!
A.P.

[258]

To ALEXANDER KHRISTOFOROVICH BENKENDORF
January 18, 1830. In Petersburg.
(In French)

General,

I have just received the letter which Your Excellency has deigned to write me.[1] God forbid that I should make the least objection to the will of the one who has showered me with so many benefactions. I would even submit myself to it with joy, if I could only be sure of not having incurred his displeasure.

I am choosing my time very badly, General, to have recourse to your good will, but a sacred duty obliges me to do so. Bonds of friendship and of gratitude attach me to a family which is very unfortunate today: the widow of General Raevsky[2] has just written me, to urge me to take steps in her behalf with those who can see to it that her voice reaches the throne of His Majesty. The choice which she had made, of me, proves how devoid indeed she is of friends, of hopes, and of resources. Half her family has been exiled,[3] the other half is on the verge of complete ruin. Their income scarcely suffices to pay the interest on an immense debt. Madame Raevskaya solicits a pension of the full salary of her late husband, revertible to her daughters[4] in case of her death. This will suffice to preserve her from beggary. As I apply to you, General, it is rather the warrior than the minister, the good and sensitive man rather than the statesman, that I hope to interest in the fate of the widow of a hero of 1812, of a great man whose life was so brilliant and whose death was so sad.

Deign to accept, General, the expression of my high esteem.

I am, with respect,
Your most humble and most obedient servant,
January 18, 1830.   Alexander Pushkin.
St. P.

[259]

To Mikhail Osipovich Sudienko
January 22, 1830. From Petersburg to Ochkino.
(In French)

My dear Sudienko,[1] if up to now you have not been paid, it is the fault of my agent, who has mislaid the address of yours. As for me, I had completely forgotten his name, and your four thousand have been all sealed up awaiting you for more than six months.

When I arrived in Petersburg, I wrote you at Chernigov, to find out your exact address, in order to congratulate you upon your marriage, and in order to propose that you take fifty rubles. You inform me that you have lost your appetite and that you no longer breakfast as in days of old. That's a pity; take some exercise, travel by post to Petersburg, and it will come back. [In Russian:] Here, with us, it is impossibly boring: there is no card-playing, but I am losing, all the same. I have sad news about [I. A.] Yakolev. He is in Paris. He is not playing, he is not visiting the wenches, but he is learning English. Dolgorukov[2] arrived a few days ago. This fellow shows promise. For the time being, I am dying of boredom. Come, my dear fellow, or out of woe, I'll come to you. Farewell, my dear fellow, be happy and forgive my involuntarily not keeping my word.

January 22, 1830.   A. Pushkin.
St. Petersburg.

[260]

To Peter Andreevich Vyazemsky
The end of January, 1830. From Petersburg to Moscow.

Hurry up and send Delvig off to me, if you are not coming yourself. It is boring to publish The [Literary] Gazette alone, with the aid of Orest,[1] my intolerable friend and comrade. All Orestes and Pylades[2] are just alike. I thank you very much for your prose—give me more of it. You berate Miloslavsky;[3] I praised it. Every cloud has a silver lining. Of course, in it much is lacking, but much is present: liveliness, gaiety which Bulgarin couldn't dream of even in his sleep.[4] How do you find the Polevoy?[5] Reading Polevoy's History has replaced for Zhukovsky the reading of Muraviev the state secretary.[6] But nobody ever heard of the like of Pogodin's criticism.[7]

How would it be to infuriate Kachenovsky?[8] Let's pit him and Polevoy against each other.

Is it true that my Goncharova[9] is marrying Archive Meshchersky?[10] And what's Ushakova—the one that's mine—doing?[11] I am planning to go to Moscow[12]—may we not miss each other on the road. I published your "To Them" against Zhukovsky's will. Of course I would not let anything too bitter, too full of animosity, be printed. But when a noble person cannot stand it any longer, he is permitted to express an elegiac m——-f—— s.o.b.[13] I send greetings to all of you and to my formidable critic Pavlusha.[14] I wrote a very abusive answer to his criticism, in the style of *Galatea*[15]—taking for the epigraph "Pavlusha brazen fellow—a polite term!"[16] I was intending to send it to him, but I don't know where I put it.

[261]

To KAROLINA ADAMOVNA SOBANSKAYA
February 2, 1830. In Petersburg.
(Rough draft; in French)

Today is the ninth anniversary of the day I saw you for the first time. That day decided my life.

The more I think about it, the more I see that my life is inseparable from yours; I was born to love you and follow you—any other care on my part is error or folly; far from you, I have felt only remorse for the happiness which I have not been able to sate myself upon. Sooner or later I shall have to abandon everything and come and fall at your feet. The idea of being able to have some day a bit of land in the Crimea is the only one which appeals to me and cheers me up in the midst of my sad regrets. There I shall be able to come on pilgrimage, to wander about your house, to meet you, to catch a glimpse of you. . . .[1]

[262]

To KAROLINA ADAMOVNA SOBANSKAYA
February 2, 1830. In Petersburg.
(Rough draft; in French)

You make light of my impatience; you seem to take pleasure in disappointing me. I shall see you, then, only tomorrow—so be it. Meanwhile I cannot think of anything but you.

Although to see you and to hear you is happiness for me, I prefer writing to you to speaking with you. There is in you an irony, a maliciousness, which embitter and discourage one. Feelings become painful, and words from the heart turn into mere jests in your presence. You are the demon, that is, "the one who doubts and denies," as the Scripture says.[1]

Not long ago you spoke cruelly of the past. You told me what I have been trying not to believe—for seven whole years. Why did you do that?

Happiness is so little made for me that I did not recognize it when it was before me. Do not speak of it any more, for Christ's sake. Remorse, if indeed I had known it at all, remorse would have had its own voluptuous pleasure—such a regret leaves in my mind only frenzied, blasphemous thoughts.

Dear Ellénore, permit me to call you by this name, which recalls for me the ardent reading of my youthful years[2] and the sweet phantom which then fascinated me, and your own life, so violent, so stormy, so different from what it ought to have been. Dear Ellénore, as you know, I have come under your full sway. I am obligated to you for having come to know everything that is most convulsive and painful in the intoxication of love, just as everything that is most stupid. Of all that, only a convalescent's feebleness remains for me, a very sweet, very sincere liking, and only a little timorousness which it is impossible for me to overcome.

If you ever read this, I well know what you will think: What clumsiness—he is ashamed of the past, that's all. He well deserves for me to make light of him some more. He has all the self-conceit of Satan, his master. Isn't this correct?

However, in taking up my pen, I wished to ask you for something—I no longer know what. Oh! yes—it is for friendship. This request is very banal, very. . . . It is as though a beggar were asking for bread—the fact is that I need your close friendship.

And nevertheless you are still as beautiful as the day of the crossing or even that of the baptism, when your fingers touched my forehead. This impression still remains with me—cool, moist. This is what has made me a Catholic. But you are going to fade; this beauty is soon going to fall like an avalanche. Your soul will remain standing for a while longer, amid so many fallen charms—and then it will depart from them, and perhaps never will it meet mine, its timid slave, in the infinity of eternity.

Well, what is a soul? It has neither glance nor melody—melody perhaps. . . .

[263]

To Konstantin Matveevich Borozdin[1]
About (after) February 4, 1830. In Petersburg.
(Rough draft)

Recently Professor Shcheglov[2] has been assigned to the publishers of *The Literary Gazette* as censor instead of K. S. Serbinovich;[3] with his observations he momentarily calls to mind the best times of Birukov and Krasovsky. In proof allow me to adduce for you one of a thousand examples: [Denis] Davydov in a certain epistle to Zaytsevsky and Kazarsky says:

O be you both the shield of the fatherland, the Perun of the everlasting state![4]

The censor doubted whether one may be permitted to call thus two Lieutenant-Captains, and blotted out the greeting as not in accordance with their rank.

The publishers have decided to have recourse to your protection and to ask, if only it is possible, to be given another, less arbitrary censor, if it is no longer possible to restore Mr. Serbinovich.

[264]

To Mikhail Osipovich Sudienko
February 12, 1830. From Petersburg to Starodub.
(In French)

You wrote me, my dear Sudienko, such a horribly ceremonious letter than I am completely stunned. The four thousand rubles in question had been awaiting you, all sealed up, since the month of July; but I lost your agent's address, and I did not have yours. A month ago Mr. Lerch[1] came to claim the sum, and he was paid it immediately. I wanted to send you the receipt which he left me, but I do not know what I have done with it. Pardon me, once more, and thank you for having been so obliging as to wait so long.

I am leaving Petersburg in a few days; I shall probably spend the summer in the country. Perhaps I shall come into your section of the country. You will permit me, I hope, to come and knock on your door. If you wish to write in the meantime, address your letters to His High Nobility Peter Alexandrovich Pletnev, the Catherine Institute. *Addio, a rivederla.*

February 12, 1830.   A. Pushkin.

[265]

To Peter Andreevich Vyazemsky
March 14, 1830. From Moscow to Petersburg.

Day before yesterday I arrived in Moscow, and straight from my carriage I landed in a concert where all Moscow was present. The first people whom I chanced to meet were N[atalia Nikolaevna] Goncharova and Princess Vera, and after them the brothers Polevoy. The arrival of the Sovereign has made a great impression.[1] Those under arrest were summoned to Benkendorf, who in the name of the Tsar and in the presence of Volkov and Shulgin announced that everything occurred because of misunderstanding, that the Tsar regrets it all very much, that Shulgin is at fault, etc. Volkov added that he rejoices at his own justification before the Moscow nobility, that he has only to solicit the forgiveness of, or rather reconciliation with, Countess Potemkina—and thus everything is at an end and everybody is satisfied.

Princess Vera spoke very prettily and very intelligently about you to Benkendorf. He was apologizing to Potemkina: *Quant a Mme. Kartsova tout ce qu'elle dit c'est comme si elle chantait.* . . . And your wife: *Vous eussiez pu remarquer, Général, qu'elle chantait faux.* Then followed explanations. *Puisque nous sommes sur le pied de la franchise vous me permettrez, Général, de vous répéter la demande de la C-sse Potemkine: la réhabilitation de mon mari.*[2] He told her that he was dissatisfied with your memorandum. I have not read it: what is it like? You regret that you were not in Moscow, but I, not in the least. Do you know the difference between a cannon and a mortar? A cannon is one thing, and a mortar is another.[3] Potemkin and Sibelev are one thing, and you are another. One must not confuse these two things. Here you would of course have been included in the general amnesty, but you deserve and must insist on an individual rehabilitation—and not on this reliable opportunity. But all that is a trifle, and here is what's important: Kiselev is marrying Lizaveta Ushakova, and Katerina [Ushakova] says that they are so happy it's repulsive. Yesterday I dined at [I. I.] Dmitriev's with Zhikharev.[4] Dmitriev is angry with Polevoy[5] and with the censor [S. N.] Glinka: I have not lost my hope of dragging him into polemics. Give me time. Farewell; mention me at an evening at Katerina Andreevna's [Karamzina], and write me at Kopp's.[6]

March 14.

Seal and send off the note to Theatrical Gagarin.[7]

And here is another letter for you.

[266]

To Peter Andreevich Vyazemsky
March 16, 1830. From Moscow to Petersburg.

On my table I have a letter which I wrote you a long time ago[1]— I was afraid to send it to you by the post. Your wife has probably told you more fully and sensibly what is going on. When the Sovereign departed, he left in Moscow a plan of a new organization, a counter-revolution to Peter's revolution.[2] Here is an opportunity for you to write a political pamphlet, and even publish it, for the government is acting or intends to act in the spirit of the European enlightenment. The limiting of the nobility, the suppressing of the bureaucracy, new rights for the petty bourgeoisie and the serfs—these are great subjects. What do you think? I am thinking of launching into some political prose. How is your health? What kind of footing are you on with the ministers, and will you be in a new branch of the service?[3] Do you know who in Moscow has raised his oppositional voice above everybody's?[4] [M. M.] Solntsev. What do you think of that! He declared himself insulted on Sibelev's behalf, and in a coach-and-six he went to the guard house to see him, notwithstanding the tears of Lizaveta Lvovna and the tender requests of Olga Matveevna. Moscow has quieted and calmed down. I am awaiting the concerts and the uproar *over the project*. I shall give you my observations about the spirit of the Moscow Club. Farewell; my greetings to your folks. I still cannot get accustomed to not spending my evenings with them. It seems to me that I am becoming profligate.

March 16.

[267]

To ALEXANDER KHRISTOFOROVICH BENKENDORF
March 21, 1830. From Moscow to Petersburg.

Dear Sir, Alexander Khristoforovich,

In 1826 I received from the Sovereign Emperor the permission *to live in Moscow*, and from Your High Excellency the permission to go to Petersburg for the following year. Since then I have spent *every winter* in Moscow and the fall in the village, without ever asking for preliminary permission and without receiving any reproof. This was partly the reason for my involuntary offense, my trip to Erzurum, for which I have had the misfortune to earn the displeasure of the Authorities.

As early as the beginning of the winter I had the intention of coming to Moscow, and when I met you once out strolling, to Your High Excellency's question of what I intended to do, I had the happiness to inform you of it. You even deigned to observe to me, *Vous êtes toujours sur les grands chemins.*[1]

I hope that my conduct has not given the government grounds for being displeased with me.[2]

With sincere and profound respect and with complete devotion, I have the honor to be, Dear Sir,

Your High Excellency's
Most obedient servant,

March 21, 1830.   Alexander Pushkin.
Moscow.

[268]

To ALEXANDER KHRISTOFOROVICH BENKENDORF
March 24, 1830. From Moscow to Petersburg.
(In French)

General,

The letter which you have honored me with has caused me genuine distress; I beseech you to grant me a moment of indulgence and attention. Notwithstanding four years of good conduct, I have not been able to obtain the confidence of the authorities. I am grieved to see that the least of my acts arouses suspicion and ill will. Pardon me, General, for the liberty of my complaints, but, in the name of heaven, deign for an instant to enter into my position and see how embarrassing it is. It is so precarious that every moment I see myself on the verge of a misfortune which I can neither foresee nor avoid. If up to the present I have not fallen into some disgrace, I owe it not to cognizance of my rights, of what is due me, but solely to your personal good will. But if tomorrow you were no longer minister, the day after tomorrow I would be in prison. Mr. Bulgarin, who says he has some influence with you, has become one of my most rabid enemies, apropos of a critique which he has attributed to me.[1] After the infamous article which he has published about me, I believe him capable of anything. I cannot but inform you about my relationships with this man, because he could do me infinite harm.

I was intending to go from Moscow to my Pskov estate; however, if Nikolay Raevsky [the Younger] comes to Poltava, I beseech Your Excellency to permit me to go there to see him.[2]

Accept, General, the expression of my high esteem and my complete devotion.

Your Excellency's

Most humble and most obedient servant,

March 24, 1830.   Alexander Pushkin.
Moscow.

[269]
To Nikolay Alexeevich Polevoy
March 27, 1830. In Moscow.

Do me the favor, my dear sir, Nikolay Alexeevich, to let me know what I am to do with Pisarev,[1] with his society, and with my certificate of membership. All this is troubling me exceedingly.

All yours,
A. Pushkin.

[270]

TO PETER ANDREEVICH VYAZEMSKY
The second half (after the 17th) of March, 1830.
From Moscow to Petersburg.

I am sending you something precious, Sumarokov's[1] denunciation of [M. V.] Lomonosov. I have seen the original with a signature
in his own hand, at Ivan Ivanovich Dmitriev's. It was discovered in
the papers of Miller, *torn* probably in the governmental office, and
it probably was preserved by Miller as a document of Lomonosov's
debauchery; they were enemies. Cook up an article from this and
print it in *The Literary Gazette*. This letter will be delivered to you
by Goncharov,[2] a brother of the beauty: now you will guess what is
disturbing me in Moscow. If you can make Eliza [Khitrovo] fall in
love with you, then do me this divine favor. I have preserved my
chastity, leaving in her hands not my cloak but my shirt (check with
Princess Meshcherskaya),[3] but she is pursuing me even here with
letters and packets. Save me from Potiphar's wife. Bulgarin astonished me with what he perpetrated;[4] one mustn't be angry, but he
could be given a beating, and I think he must. But the slush, laziness,
and [Natalia N.] Goncharova don't let me out of Moscow, and there
is no oak cudgel 500 miles long in Russia, except Count Panin's.[5]
I see your wife often, i.e., every day. Our mode of living is endurable. My uncle is alive, [I. I.] Dmitriev is very nice, Zubkov is a
member of the [English] Club. Ushakov[6] is one-eyed. Here is a
request for you. Pogodin has made preparations to go abroad; he
can manage without financial aid, but all the same it would be
better. Talk it over with Bludov, and with warmth. Stroev[7] has
written an essential book, *tables des matières* for Karamzin's *History*.
It must be published; talk to Bludov about this, too. Farewell. My
cordial greetings to all your family.

In the denunciation the word "insulting" has been left out.
Batyushkov is dying.[8]

Letter 190

1. Pushkin arrived in Moscow on September 8. He was taken directly to the Emperor, without being allowed to wash, change his clothes, or get any rest. Nicholas I managed to charm Pushkin completely. The Tsar granted Pushkin "free" residence in Moscow and Petersburg and declared that he himself would henceforth be the poet's censor.

2. The celebration in Moscow was in honor of Tsar Nicholas I's coronation; the celebration was on September 16 and 17 (hence it is clear that Pushkin made a slip of the pen in dating this letter).

3. A Russian measure, approximately seven feet.

4. Countess Anna Alexeevna Orlova-Chesmenskaya (1785-1848), a wealthy Muscovite and a protectress of monasteries.

5. The hall was said to have been illuminated by seven thousand candles.

6. The new, extremely severe censorship code was drawn up by Admiral Shishkov and Prince Shirinsky-Shikhmatov; it was affirmed by Nicholas I on June 10, 1826.

7. Anna Nikolaevna Vulf and Anna Ivanovna Vulf.

8. Pushkin erred in the date: the letter was written on September 16.

Letter 191

1. In the fall of 1826 Pushkin was courting Vasily Petrovich Zubkov's (1799-1862) sister-in-law Sofia Fedorovna Pushkina (1806-1862), a distant relative. Apparently this letter has to do with his unsuccessful courtship.

Letter 192

1. Pushkin was en route to Moscow; Torzhok, a town on the route, was noted for its morocco embroidered with gold and silver.

2. "Coachman."

3. "It is not Sergey Pushkin, of course."—Pushkin's note. Pushkin means that his "good angel" was Sofia F. Pushkina, and not his father, Sergey L. Pushkin. Pushkin's relationships with his father were strained at the time, as the police were aware from intercepted letters in which Sergey Pushkin made blunt statements about his son.

4. Anna N. Vulf, then in love with Pushkin and showering him with letters.

5. The family of Praskovia A. Osipova.

6. Anna Lvovna Pushkina.

7. Pushkin was of course coquetting with Princess Vyazemskaya. She answered on November 19: ". . . you so often changed the *object* that I don't know who *the other* is. My husband assures me that I *hope* that it is *I*. But Heaven preserve us both from that— to begin with, I do not at all wish to travel with you. I am too weak for that and too old to roam about the highways. . . ."

Letter 193

1. See Letter 194.

2. A poem, "Herons" (1825), by Sobolevsky and Baratynsky.

3. Galiani was an Italian restaurateur in Tver; *Cologne* is Italian for dolt, fool. Pozharsky was an innkeeper at Torzhok. Yazhelbitsy and Valday were post stations, the former noted for its trout, and the latter, for its girls of light morals (already celebrated in Radishchev's *Journey from Petersburg to Moscow*), and its *barankas* (ring-shaped rolls).

Letter 194

1. Arina Rodionovna.
2. That is, Ivan the Terrible; the prayer had been preserved in oral tradition some 250 years.
3. Sofia Fedorovna Pushkina.
4. *The Moscow Messenger*, which began in 1827, and was edited by Mikhail Petrovich Pogodin. The journal was the organ of a group of Moscow disciples of the German philosopher Schelling. Several of Pushkin's friends, Delvig, Yazykov, and others, contributed to *The Moscow Messenger*, but Vyazemsky continued his ties with Polevoy's *Moscow Telegraph*.
5. Nikolay Vasilievich Sushkov (1796-1871), minor writer and civil servant.
6. Count Nikolay Petrovich Rumyantsev (1754-1826), Grand Chancellor of Russia; Count Fedor Vasilievich Rostopchin (1763-1826), Russian soldier, politician, and writer —governor of Moscow in 1812. The article appeared in 1826 in *The Moscow Telegraph*.
7. That is, Princess Vyazemskaya.
8. Princess Elizaveta Petrovna Lobanova-Rostovskaya (d. 1854); Vyazemsky published a poem to her with this title in 1826.
9. Ekaterina Alexandrovna Timasheva (1798-1881), a Moscow high-society beauty.
10. See Letter 188; a fragment which Pushkin preserved from his notes when he burned them.
11. Vyazemsky's article on the life and works of Dmitriev.
12. "Trigorskoe" (1826).
13. Pushkin has an untranslatable play on words. The Russian expression "to eclipse" is literally "to put behind the belt."

Letter 195

1. Pushkin is speaking of the Osipova-Vulf estate and of Yazykov's poem "Trigorskoe"; Yazykov spent six weeks visiting at Trigorskoe during the summer of 1826.
2. "To Yazykov" ("Yazykov, Who Inspired You"; written 1826, pub. 1827).
3. "To Yazykov" ("From Ancient Times the Sweet Union"; 1824).

Letter 196

1. When Pushkin was "forgiven" by Nicholas I and the Tsar declared himself Pushkin's personal censor, Pushkin supposed that this meant that he could continue to have his works passed by the usual censorship, like other writers, and only in case of difficulties there, he would apply to the Tsar. Under this misapprehension, he made agreements for publication of several of his works and sent them to the usual censorship. Then he found out the actual situation. Pushkin discovered that he could publish nothing, not even the most innocuous trifle, without permission from the Tsar, through the head of the secret police, Count Alexander Khristoforovich Benkendorf (1783-1844), who remained Pushkin's intermediary with the Tsar for the remainder of his life. Thus Pushkin was forced to write the present letter and recall all the things he then had in the censorship. In addition, Pushkin received a polite but pointed dressing down from Benkendorf for having given readings from *Boris Godunov* in Moscow literary circles, without preliminary examination of the manuscript by the Tsar. Thus Pushkin learned that his words and actions were under the watchful ears and eyes of the secret police. Pushkin struggled for the rest of his life against the double censorship of the Tsar and Benkendorf, on the one hand, and the usual censorship, on the other.

2. The "Highest Authorities" means the Tsar himself, or Benkendorf speaking for him.

3. *The Moscow Messenger.*

Letter 197

1. The reference is to Benkendorf's letter to Pushkin of November 22, 1826, in which Benkendorf made it clear that Pushkin should not have read *Boris Godunov* in public before it had been seen by the Emperor. Pushkin's and Benkendorf's correspondence is conducted in the tone of extreme politeness, but Pushkin's letters to him, after Pushkin began to suspect the true state of affairs, should be read between the lines.

Letter 198

1. From Zhukovsky's dedication to "The Twelve Sleeping Virgins."

2. The Kishinev women acquaintances whom Pushkin mentions are the "Jewess," Maria Egorovna Eikhfeldt, the wife of an official, and mistress of Alexeev; Elena Fedorovna Solovkina, the wife of an officer; and Calypso Polychroni, whom in Letter 42 Pushkin called "the Greek girl whom Byron kissed."

3. An allusion to an earthquake in Kishinev in 1822.

4. General Pavel Sergeevich Pushchin; Egor Kirillovich Varfolomey.

5. Pushkin often uses this common epithet for Moscow; it appears in *Onegin*, Chap. VII, stanza 36.

6. Paraphrase from Pushkin's scabrous "Tsar Nikita and His Forty Daughters." What the daughters lacked was "a nothing or very little."

7. Like Pushkin, Liprandi made a trip to the capital under the surveillance of a *fel'd-eger'* in connection with the Decembrist Uprising.

Letter 199

1. Pushkin has here a multiple play on words. The Princes Vyazemsky had ruled over Vyazma. "Angel" is a jocose allusion to Vyazemsky's "demon" Arzamas nickname, Asmodeus; the town of Vyazma was famous for its spice cakes.

2. An allusion to his relationships with Benkendorf and Nicholas I.

3. A note "Of Popular Education," written at the command of Nicholas I.

4. "Farewell, couple ostensibly so flighty, farewell."

5. Pushkin had called Vyazemsky by this nickname in Letter 194.

6. Letter 198.

Letter 200

1. "Post horses."

2. "Coachman."

3. Sofia Fedorovna Pushkina, whom, with Zubkov's help, Pushkin hoped to marry.

4. ". . . Whatever comes into your head. That vile Panin, in love for two years, and he is planning to send the matchmakers during St. Thomas' Week—I see her once in the loge, a second time at a ball, and the third, I send the matchmakers!" Valerian Alexandrovich Panin (1803-1880) and Sofia F. Pushkina were married on December 8, 1826.

5. "My angel, persuade her, prevail upon her, scare her away from nasty Panin, and marry me off."

6. Pushkin was superstitious and believed in omens and talismans. He had several talisman rings, one of which was set with a small turquoise. Apparently here he is predicting success in his suit for the hand of Sofia F. Pushkina.

7. The reference has to do with rumors regarding the marital difficulties of Count Nikolay Alexandrovich Samoylov (d. 1841), apparently as reported to Pushkin in a letter from Zubkov.

Letter 201

1. To Nicholas I, via Benkendorf.
2. Benkendorf's letter of November 22, 1826; Pushkin's answer is Letter 197.
3. Letter 196.
4. Letter 200.
5. The reference is to Pushkin's courtship of Sofia F. Pushkina.
6. Pushkin often teased Sobolevsky about his weakness for overeating, and he had several unflattering nicknames for him alluding to this propensity.
7. Pushkin stayed in Sobolevsky's house in Moscow from December 18, 1826, until May 20, 1827.

Letter 202

1. Yazykov's "Trigorskoe" contained references to Pskov.
2. Slip of the pen for December.
3. That is, he will contribute to *The Moscow Messenger*.

Letter 203

1. Nicholas I's comments about *Boris Godunov* were as follows: "I consider that Mr. Pushkin's goal would be fulfilled if, along with *necessary expurgation*, he would change his comedy into a historical tale or novel, similar to Walter Scott's" (letter of Benkendorf to Pushkin, of December 14, 1826).

Letter 204

1. Probably a mouthpiece for a pipe.
2. The name of the town Borovsk is related to the word *borov*, "boar, hog, pig."
3. That is, to his own estate.

Letter 205

1. This letter was apparently sent along with another, perhaps by Pogodin, asking Tumansky to contribute to *The Moscow Messenger*, of which Pogodin was the editor. Alexander Sergeevich Shiryaev (d. 1841) was a Moscow bookseller. The "orthodox" are Pushkin and his literary friends.
2. A fragment from the seventh chapter of *Onegin*; it afterwards was incorporated into "Fragments from Onegin's Journey." The fragment was published in the March, 1827, issue of *The Moscow Messenger*.

Letter 206

1. It has not survived. Dmitry Vladimirovich Venevitinov (1805-1827) was a poet and member of the Lovers of Wisdom (Lyubomudry) group, under the influence of German idealistic thought, who were backing the publication of *The Moscow Messenger*. This letter clearly indicates that Pushkin was no lover of abstract thought in literature or of German idealistic metaphysics.
2. Pushkin similarly expresses dislike for spring, with its thaws and its rains, in *Evgeny Onegin* and in "Autumn" (1833).
3. Pushkin paraphrases Ivan Ivanovich Khemnitser's (1745-1784) fable "The Metaphysician."

4. Pushkin is undoubtedly alluding to the hanging of five Decembrists, including Ryleev, in 1826.

5. The gentle Pletnev had written Pushkin a despondent letter, lamenting the meager prospects for literature in Petersburg, because Pushkin was not there, Baratynsky had left, and Delvig was about to give up literary work for playing cards. The card game of *grand patience*, popular in France and then the rest of Europe from the time of the American Revolution, had not lost its popularity in Russia.

6. Delvig's *Northern Flowers for* 1827 appeared late in March, 1827. Pushkin is alluding to the Russian expression, "those are the tiny blossoms, but the berries are yet to come," that is, the worst is yet to come.

Pushkin wrote Delvig's address on the outside of the letter in Cyrillic, Gothic, and in Russian cursive.

Letter 207

1. Five poems, including *The Gypsies* and "October 19." Pushkin is answering Benkendorf's letter which gave permission to publish the poems but which expressed astonishment that Pushkin had used an intermediary, Delvig, in dealing with him. Why Benkendorf addressed Puskin in Pskov when he had Pushkin under surveillance in Moscow is unclear.

2. "October 19," one of the great poems on friendship, was the first of a number of poems by Pushkin commemorating the graduation of his class, the first one, from the Lyceum of Tsarskoe Selo. Benkendorf objected to Pushkins's giving even the first letters of the surnames of his Lyceum classmates who were then in exile, as participants in the Decembrist Uprising. This poem, written in 1825, was published in *The Northern Flowers for* 1827, with asterisks substituted for individuals' names, and with one stanza omitted.

Letter 208

1. N. N. Raevsky the Younger, then commander of a regiment in the Caucasus, where the Persian Campaign of 1826-1828 was in progress.

2. Pushkin had not seen his parents for two and a half years. The "as they say" shows how warm their relationship really was.

3. This may be a hint that Pushkin was not indifferent at this time to one of her two daughters. There is evidence that he was in love with Alexandra Alexandrovna Rimskaya-Korsakova.

4. Ermolov had been relieved by Nicholas I of command of the Russian army in the Caucasus.

5. The letter was addressed "To Lev Sergeevich Pushkin in Asia."

Letter 209

1. "To the post office, under your name."

2. Pushkin was seeing Petersburg again for the first time in seven years.

Letter 210

1. Proof sheets of the second chapter of *Onegin*, then being seen through the press by S. A. Sobolevsky, whom Pushkin calls here by one of his nicknames, "Sluggard."

2. Sobolevsky's letter to which Pushkin refers has not survived.

3. A variety of champagne.

Letter 211

1. The death of Sobolevsky's mother. Sobolevsky was an illegitimate son. As his mother lay dying, he refused to let her be bothered about arranging an inheritance for him; he was left penniless upon her death.

2. Sergey Dmitrievich Poltoratsky (1803-1884), a friend of Pushkin's, bibliophile, one of the founders of *The Moscow Messenger*, and an ardent gambler.

3. In 1830, Pushkin similarly presents the use of proverbs to offer consolation for grief, in "The Snowstorm," one of *The Tales of Belkin*, with the difference that in the story there is an admixture of good-natured irony.

Letter 212

1. Elizaveta Mikhaylovna Khitrovo (1783-1839) was the daughter of the great Russian Field Marshal Prince Mikhail Ilarionovich Golenishchev-Kutuzov (1745-1813), hero of the war against Napoleon in 1812. Mme. Khitrovo was a good and true friend of Pushkin's, and she was passionately but unrequitedly in love with him. She provided Pushkin's best connection with the highest Petersburg society, to which Pushkin did not belong. She had a famous salon in Petersburg.

Letter 213

1. Benkendorf answered that it was permissible for a translation to be published together with the original without infringing upon the author's rights.

Letter 214

1. Pushkin quotes "Under the Blue Sky of Her Native Land" (1826), on the death of Amalia Riznich (d. 1825).

2. *Onegin*, Chap. IV, stanzas 1-9; the passage was nevertheless published in *The Moscow Messenger* instead of Delvig's *Northern Flowers*.

3. A few months later when Pushkin and A. N. Vulf visited Delvig, they brought along the skull of one of Delvig's ancestors, which had been dug up by Yazykov, and Pushkin's poem "Epistle to Delvig" (1827) about the skull. They followed the Romantic tradition and drank healths from the skull.

4. His unfinished novel, *The Blackamoor of Peter the Great* (written 1827).

5. An allusion to Delvig's proverbial laziness.

6. Bulgarin's article, under the title "A Meeting with Karamzin (1819)," published in the almanac *Album of Northern Muses* (1828).

7. Delvig's wife was ill and had gone to Reval to take sea baths.

Letter 215

1. The reference is to Pushkin's "Scene from Faust," which was passed also by the usual censorship and published in 1828. The "gentleman" was the censor Ivan Mikhaylovich Snegirev (1793-1868).

2. Pogodin did not publish *Urania for* 1828.

3. See Letter 60 and note.

4. "What is permitted to *Urania* is permitted . . . *is permitted* . . . *is becoming*." This is a paraphrase of the Latin expression *Quod licet Jovi, non licet bovi*, "What is permitted to Jove is not permitted to an ox."

5. That is, it is too solemn, or perhaps Pushkin means there is too little "chatter," plenitude, in it.

6. Pictures of current European fashions in clothing, furniture, etc., were published in *The Moscow Telegraph*.

7. Translated from the French by Prince V. F. Odoevsky and published in *The Moscow Messenger* in 1827.

8. A. E. Izmaylov's *Calendar for the Muses for* 1826 and *for* 1827; Vyazemsky said the contents were a mere continuation of *The Well-Intentioned*.

9. Perhaps S. D. Poltoratsky.

Letter 216

1. Pushkin's letter is a part of a collective letter written by Alexey N. Vulf, Anna N. Vulf, and Pushkin. Pushkin's closing here was called forth by Alexey Vulf's comment that he was as fond of nuts as Anna Petrovna Kern was of apple pie.

Letter 217

1. Benkendorf neither answered this letter nor took any action as a result of it.

Letter 218

1. Pushkin's polite letter to Bulgarin is particularly interesting in view of the opinions of Bulgarin which he expresses in many letters. Nevertheless, his literary relationships with Bulgarin continued good until 1829, after which they changed sharply for the worse and continued so for the rest of Pushkin's life.

Letter 219

1. That is, the sale of Chapters I and of III-VI was being held up by Chapter II being out of print.

2. More of Pushkin's nicknames for Sobolevsky.

3. Unknown.

4. Members of the editorial staff of *The Moscow Messenger*.

Letter 220

1. Published as "To Beautiful Eyes" (1828); Pushkin probably sent Tumansky's "Little Song" (1828) to Pogodin.

2. *Onegin*, Chap. IV, stanzas 27-30, "Albums."

3. "Stanzas" ("In Hope of Glory and of Good"); published in 1828.

4. *Onegin*, Chap. VII, stanzas 36 ff.

5. Konstantin Fedorovich Kalaydovich (1792-1832) began the journal *The Russian Spectator* in 1828.

6. Nicholas I (and Benkendorf).

Letter 221

1. Of *Onegin*; see Letter 219.

2. That is, pirating; Sobolevsky did not carry out his plan.

3. A. S. and V. L. Pushkin. Pushkin's putting himself in this company is, of course, a joke.

4. Andrey Ivanovich Podolinsky (1806-1886), minor poet.

Letter 222

1. Delvig served in the Ministry of Internal Affairs; he planned to visit Mme. Osipova while en route on official business.

2. That is, Trigorskoe, which lay on the bank of this small river.

3. Mme. Osipova's other estate Malinniki, in Novotorzhok, some 250 miles from Trigorskoe, and 150 miles northwest of Moscow. Pushkin visited her there in 1829.

Letter 223

1. It is not known what was Pushkin's illness. Perhaps it was rheumatism, or, perhaps, aneurysm. Cf. Letter 224.

2. Probably Mme. Khitrovo's younger daughter, Countess Ekaterina Fedorovna Tizengauzen (1803-1888).

3. Nikolay Fedorovich Arendt (1785-1859), a well-known physician and surgeon of the time. He later became the Pushkins' family physician.

Letter 224

1. The then recently published fourth and fifth chapters of *Evgeny Onegin*. Pushkin personifies the work in terms of its hero.

Letter 225

1. Pushkin was so angry because of misprints in stanzas from *Onegin* published in *The Moscow Messenger* that he sent them to Bulgarin, asking that they be published in *The Northern Bee* accurately. Bulgarin gladly complied, using the opportunity for a gratuitous slap at *The Moscow Messenger*, the "note" from which Pushkin is seeking to exonerate himself with Pogodin.

2. Stepan Petrovich Shevyrev (1806-1864), poet, critic, historian of literature, later professor in Moscow University and Slavophile, had included in his "Survey of Russian Literature for 1827," published in *The Moscow Messenger*, a devastating negative evaluation of Bulgarin.

3. In "Little Song," by the eighteenth-century poet Vasily Kirillovich Trediakovsky (1703-1769).

4. Unknown.

5. The letter has not survived.

Letter 226

1. According to the agreement, Pushkin was to receive 10,000 rubles from 1200 copies sold of *The Moscow Messenger*.

2. Alexander Filippovich Smirdin (1795-1857), Petersburg bookseller and publisher.

3. A nickname for Sobolevsky.

4. An anonymous, completely negative critique of the fourth and fifth chapters of *Onegin* appeared in the journal *Athenaeum* in 1828. Zubarev is Dmitry Eliseevich Zubarev (1802-1850), minor literary figure; Pushkin's other guess is a joke: Ivan Savelievich Salnikov was a well-known and extremely popular professional jester, kept by a nobleman.

Letter 227

1. That is, the most recent ones, four, five, and six.

2. Evpraxia N. (Zizi) Vulf. The copy had the inscription "Yours from yours." Pushkin makes allusion to her in *Onegin*, Chap. V, stanza 32. Nothing is known of Pushkin's question to her or her answer.

3. Another name by which Mikhaylovskoe was known locally.

Letter 228

1. Pushkin plays on the similar words *ličnost'* and *nepriličnost'*. In 1828 Velikopolsky

published a poem, "To Erast (A Satire on Gamblers)," to which Pushkin responded with his "Epistle to V., Composer of a Satire on Gamblers," published without signature in *The Northern Bee*. Velikopolsky recognized the authorship of the verses, and immediately wrote and sent to the editor of *The Northern Bee*, Bulgarin, "I Recognized You at Once by Your Manner," a little poem including the lines Pushkin quotes here, having to do with Pushkin's wagering his poetry at cards. As an obvious reference to a person, these lines, according to the censorship code of the day, required that person's consent before they could be published. In this letter Pushkin refuses to grant that permission.

2. Pushkin had made a similar threat with regard to Tolstoy the American (Letter 118); neither was carried out.

Letter 229
1. To be allowed to go to the Caucasus and fight, in the army, against the Persians.
2. This request was not transmitted to the Tsar.
3. *The Prisoner of the Caucasus* and *Ruslan and Lyudmila*; the permission was granted.

Letter 230
1. This letter is Pushkin's postscript to a letter written by Vyazemsky to his wife.
2. That is, Petersburg; Pushkin is teasing about the isolation of Princess Vyazemskaya on the Saratov steppe, where she was visiting her step-father.
3. The Vyazemsky's son Prince Pavel Petrovich Vyazemsky (1820-1888).

Letter 231
1. Goethe answered a certain N. Borchard with a letter including flattering comments about Russian literature in general and especially about a critique of *Faust* by Shevyrev; the letter was published in *The Moscow Messenger* in 1828.
2. A poem (1828) by Shevyrev, attacked by Bulgarin.
3. That is, the editors of *The Northern Bee*, Bulgarin and Grech.
4. N. A. Polevoy, publisher of *The Moscow Telegraph*; "Ksenofont Telegraph" was his brother and co-worker, Ksenofont Alexeevich Polevoy (1802-1867).
5. Sobolevsky.
6. A "military-literary" weekly journal, published 1827-1830 by Voeykov.
7. Admiral Shishkov was President of the Russian Academy from 1813 to 1841; the Academy came to an end within six months after his death.
8. Pushkin concludes his letter by quoting a passage from Yazykov's "To A. N. Vulf" ("Don't Call Me Poet," pub. 1830), in which *The Athenaeum* is characterized as the "Moscow *Well-Intentioned*." Izmaylov's *Well-Intentioned* had ceased to exist in 1827.

Letter 233
1. This letter was probably not sent.
2. The phrase is unfinished. Pushkin was asked to sign a statement to the effect that he would not write blasphemous works in the future. The secret police had begun its investigations in the case of Pushkin's *Gavriiliada*, which Pushkin denied, in depositions, having written or having copies of. Pushkin then wrote a letter which apparently only the Tsar saw, and which does not survive, in which he obviously must have admitted the authorship, for the investigation of the authorship was suddenly dropped. Pushkin was extremely repentant for having written the poem, and he was angered and hurt at mentions of it during the rest of his life.

Letter 234

1. Over *Gavriiliada*. See Letter 233.

2. "Some day she will beweep the lover she has betrayed, the heart she has lost, the heart she is rending". Pushkin's quotation from Gnedich's translation (1816) of Voltaire's *Tancrède* is not completely accurate.

3. The friends mentioned in this letter include: Nikolay Dmitrievich Kiselev (1802-1869), who shortly before left to be secretary of the embassy in Paris; A. P. and M. A. Poltoratsky; Alexey Alexeevich Olenin (*Junior*, 1798-1855), son of Alexey Nikolaevich Olenin, President of the Academy of Arts; Sergey Grigorievich Golitsyn (1806-1868); and Mikhail Ivanovich Glinka (1804-1857), the composer.

4. Pushkin used these verses as the epigraph to the first chapter of his "Queen of Spades" (written 1833, pub. 1834) with the substitution of another phrase for the unprintable words.

5. Agrafena Fedorovna Zakrevskaya. She is the subject of several of Pushkin's poems.

6. The quotation is the poet M. V. Milonov's witticism on the journal *The Well-Intentioned*. The tone of Pushkin's comment is that of Vyazemsky's letter he is answering.

7. Quotation of a line from Zhukovsky's "Traveler" (written 1809, pub. 1810).

8. Prince Dmitry Petrovich Gorchakov (1758-1824), minor poet known for his unprintable poems, was dead and hence uninjurable in person or in fame. Pushkin no doubt wrote these lines, thinking his letter might be read by the police, and hoping to get Vyazemsky to tell the same story.

9. Pelagea Nikolaevna Vsevolozhskaya; Pushkin is speaking of a poetic portrait of her written by Vyazemsky and enclosed in Vyazemsky's letter which Pushkin is answering.

10. A. N. Raevsky had long been in love with the Countess Vorontsova. The jealous Count Vorontsov denounced Raevsky to the government as having made remarks against the government and the then current military operations; as a result, Raevsky was transferred to Poltava.

Letter 235

1. Some think this a reference to Agrafena Fedorovna Zakrevskaya; others, to his Muse.

Letter 237

1. Nikolay Vasilievich Putyata (1802-1877), an officer, man of letters, and friend of Pushkin's.

2. Théodore Joseph de Lagrené was then secretary of the French embassy in Petersburg. Pushkin's note was written in such a form that Putyata could show it to Lagrené; it is a demand for satisfactory explanations or a preliminary to a challenge to a duel. Lagrené told Putyata that Pushkin must have misheard him, that his opinion of Pushkin was nothing like what Pushkin had thought he heard him express; Putyata so informed Pushkin, putting an end to the matter.

Letter 238

1. The "Tver" Lovelace because Vulf's mother's estate Malinniki, where Pushkin was visiting, was in the Province of Tver. The allusion is to the unprincipled seducer Lovelace in Richardson's *Clarissa*. Vulf had not wished Pushkin to visit Malinniki, because he feared for the reputations of his mother and his sister, neither of whom was indifferent to Pushkin.

2. The Vicomte de Valmont, the amoral chief character of Pierre Ambrois Choderlos de Laclos' novel *Les Liaisons dangereuses* (1782).

3. The one who asked for the "elucidations" and who did the exclaiming was Elizaveta Petrovna Poltoratskaya, a sister of Anna Petrovna Kern. Some idea of the mores of the time and the character of Vulf can be gathered from the fact that not only Mlle. Poltoratskaya, but also the other two ladies mentioned in the closing lines of this letter, Mme. Kern and Baroness Delvig, were on terms of intimate relationships with Vulf at one and the same time.

4. A young orphan living in the home of Vulf's uncle, Peter Ivanovich Vulf (1768-1832).

Letter 240

1. Pushkin quotes his poem "Answer to Katenin" (written 1828, pub. in *The Northern Flowers for* 1829).

2. Anna Ivanovna Gotovtsova; Vyazemsky had sent Pushkin some verses by her and requested some verses from Pushkin to her in answer. Pushkin is punning on her name, which is related to the Russian word meaning "ready."

3. The madam of a "high society" house of prostitution in Petersburg.

4. That is, Petersburg.

5. A performing dog then being shown in Moscow.

6. Peter Markovich Poltoratsky (ca. 1775-after 1851), father of Anna Petrovna Kern.

7. In his critique of the fourth and fifth chapters of *Onegin*, B. M. Fedorov was disturbed that Pushkin calls "noble maids" wenches, and a simple village "wench" a maid.

8. In 1828 Pushkin's sister Olga married Nikolay Ivanovich Pavlishchev (1802-1897); she wanted Pushkin's "One Raven Flies to Another," a redoing of "The Twa Corbies," one of the poems included by Walter Scott in *Minstrelsy of the Scottish Border* (1802-1803), for her husband's almanac *Lyrical Album for* 1829. Pushkin complied with her request. The word "pigeon" is used in Russian affectionately of a person.

9. "Farewell and be favorably disposed to me." Evgeny Onegin knew enough Latin to write *vale* at the end of his letters (*Onegin*, Chap. I, stanza 6). Pushkin is smiling at the practice, which he himself had not infrequently followed, of ending letters with a Latin tag.

Letter 241

1. Pushkin quotes "Both Mistrustfully and Greedily" (written 1828, pub. 1829), his poetic epistle to Mme. Gotovtsova, as requested by Vyazemsky (see Letter 240, and note).

2. "These cold and flowing little verses." The quotation is from Voltaire's "Epistle to Mme. de Saint-Julien" (1782).

3. Two verses in Mme. Gotovtsova's epistle to Pushkin were omitted, with the omission indicated by rows of periods; Pushkin assumes that the omitted lines were a reproach.

4. Pushkin is playing on the expression "to bury oneself like a mouse in the grits." The word can also mean "hominy snow." Delvig was making the trip on business.

5. Gnedich had been ill and convalescing in Odessa from August, 1827, to August, 1828; his translation of *The Iliad* appeared in 1829.

Letter 242

1. This letter contains some interesting "Petersburg French," where *encouragé*

"encouraged" gets separated by *petit* "little" and gets special applications. The expression *en petit couragé* received currency after a member of the theatrical directorate expressed himself as wanting not one of the important "orders" or decorations across his shoulder, but a *petit encouragé* in his buttonhole. Pushkin became fond of the expression in the sense of a poor substitute for the genuine article, and he used the expression with regard to love affairs, as well as drinking bouts and eating.

Letter 243

1. Pushkin's expression *ne pridvornyj* in this context is a pun on *ne pritvornyj* "not hypocritical." The first part of this letter has to do with plans for the rehabilitation of Vyazemsky, who had been accused by the Tsar of "loose conduct" and harmful influence upon younger people, including Pushkin. Apparently the Tsar's displeasure at Vyazemsky was called forth by a denunciation made by Bulgarin, on the suspicion that Vyazemsky might start a newspaper which would compete with his publications.

2. Prince Dmitry Vladimirovich Golitsyn (1771-1844), the Moscow Military Governor General at the time.

3. ". . . people who are the subject of it. But since basically he is an honorable and worthy man, too much occupied with other things to store up rancor against you, and too noble to seek to harm you, do not give way to enmity, but try to speak of the matter with complete frankness."

4. Filimonov, publisher of a bi-weekly journal *Butterfly* (1829-1831), lived in Kolomna, a remote part of Petersburg. One night Zhukovsky, Vyazemsky, and Pushkin were invited by him to a party; they returned home late, and this gave rise to the police report that they had spent the night at a house of prostitution.

5. Varyushka was a prostitute in V. L. Pushkin's *Dangerous Neighbor*.

6. From Baratynsky's verse epistle "To * *" (1824).

7. Princess Natalia Petrovna Golitsyna (1741-1837). In her old age she received great attention and courtesy from everybody, even including the imperial family; she was extremely strict with the young, and she considered almost everybody young. In her old age she was extremely ugly, with a beard and large moustaches. Pushkin apparently used her as his model for the old countess in his "Queen of Spades."

8. The Russians had borrowed the English word "rout," now archaic in this meaning, for an evening party without dancing.

9. Princess Zinaida Alexandrovna Volkonskaya (1792-1862) had a salon in Moscow. Count Ricci was an Italian singer who had taken part as hero in privately performed operas at Princess Volkonskaya's. Pushkin is playing here upon a colorful Russian curse which usually means something like "to hell with," "may all one's wishes come to naught."

10. At the same time Bulgarin was giving a secret denunciation against Vyazemsky to the Tsar, he was praising him in his *Northern Bee*.

11. Zhukovsky's "Sea" (written 1822) and translation of fragments of *The Iliad* appeared in *The Northern Flowers for* 1829. Gnedich's translation of *The Iliad* was then in the press, and he was angry at the publication of this competitive translation.

12. The government's practice of farming out taxes was common at the time, especially in the liquor business.

Letter 244

1. Possibly Pushkin's epigram "There Where Ancient Kochegovsky" on Kachenovsky, which Snegirev passed later in the month; possibly a note which has not survived.

Letter 245
  1. Pushkin's English.
  2. Ivan Alexeevich Yakovlev (1804-1882), a wealthy landowner, friend of Pushkin's, and a gambler. Pushkin had probably lost the six thousands to him at cards.

Letter 246
  1. Natalia Ivanovna Goncharova, nee Zagryazhskaya (d. 1848) became Pushkin's mother-in-law when Pushkin married her daughter Natalia Nikolaevna Goncharova (1812-1863) in 1831. Pushkin saw Natalia Nikolaevna in Moscow early in 1829 and fell passionately in love with her. Count F. I. Tolstoy the American acted as Pushkin's intermediary in Pushkin's proposal, which, according to form, was delivered to Natalia Ivanovna (since Natalia Nikolaevna's father, Nikolay Afanasievich Goncharov [1788-1861], was *non compos mentis*). Natalia Ivanovna's answer was unclear and not a flat rejection of Pushkin's suit.
  Other members of the Goncharov family who enter considerably into Pushkin's life (and correspondence) include Natalia Nikolaevna's grandfather, Afanasy Nikolaevich Goncharov (ca. 1760-1832), then the head of the family; two sisters, Ekaterina Nikolaevna (1809-1843) and Alexandra Nikolaevna Goncharova (1811-end of the 1870's), and three brothers, Dmitry Nikolaevich (1808-1859), Ivan Nikolaevich (1810-1881); and Sergey Nikolaevich Goncharov (1815-1865).
  2. Pushkin's word was not clearly written: perhaps "drunk with."

Letter 247
  1. From Moscow to Tiflis; Pushkin's trip to the Caucasus was made without preliminary permission from Benkendorf. Pushkin left Moscow for the Caucasus on May 1, 1829. Tolstoy the American had acted as Pushkin's intermediary in his proposal to Natalia Nikolaevna Goncharova; Pushkin obviously thought the letter alluded to might concern this matter.
  2. Adjutant General Count Ivan Fedorovich Paskevich-Erivansky (1782-1856) had succeeded Ermolov as Command-in-Chief of Russian forces in the Caucasus. The permission Pushkin sought was that of visiting his brother Lev and his old friend N. N. Raevsky the Younger, who were serving in the Russian army active against the Turks. Pushkin was granted the desired permission, and he was present at the entry of Russian troops into Erzurum. Pushkin spent, in all, four and a half months in the Caucasus on this trip. He describes his experiences in his *Journey to Erzurum* (1836), including his impressions of Ermolov. It is known that Pushkin wrote several other letters while he was on this trip, but none have survived, except Letter 248.

Letter 248
  1. This letter should be compared with Letter 139, also about *Boris Godunov*.
  2. Karamzin's *History*, Vol. XI.
  3. Apparently the allusion is to some words or expressions given special meaning by the members of the Secret Society in Kiev and on the Davydov estate Kamenka, which Pushkin visited in 1820-1821.
  4. The False Dimitry, the Pretender in *Boris Godunov*, fell in love with Marina Mniszek (d. 1614), daughter of a Polish *voevoda*, or governor of a province. Both are historical figures.
  5. An unidentified member of a very high-ranking Polish family.
  6. Gavrila Grigorievich Pushkin (d. after 1634), one of Pushkin's ancestors, was presented in *Boris Godunov*, as well as another Pushkin, Afanasy Mikhaylovich, whom Pushkin

invented for the drama. Other figures from Russian history whom Pushkin mentions in this context are the following: Alexey Romanovich Pleshcheev (d. 1607), an adherent of the False Dimitry; Kuzma Minin (or, correctly, as Pushkin elsewhere notes, Kuzma Minich Zakhariev-Sukhoruky, d. 1616), a Novgorod merchant who was a hero in the Russian struggle against the Poles during the Time of Troubles; and "Romanov" here is Michael I (1596-1645) the first tsar of the Romanov line in Russia, who was elected tsar in 1613 and ruled to 1645.

7. "Document, charter."

8. Pushkin has in mind the French revolutionaries (1792-1795), who, for example, had Lyons largely destroyed (1793).

9. Vasily Ivanovich Shuysky (1552-1612; Tsar of Russia, 1606-1610), another important character in *Boris*.

10. Henry IV, King of France (1589-1610), first of the Bourbon line, and perhaps the most popular French king. Brought up as a Protestant, he accepted Catholicism in order to strengthen his hold on his kingdom. He was famed also as warrior and lover.

11. Tsarevna Ksenia Borisovna Godunova (d. 1622), daughter of Boris Godunov, upon her father's death and the accession of the False Dimitry became the latter's concubine for several months and then was sent to a convent, where she spent the rest of her life.

Letter 249

1. That of appearing immediately upon his arrival from the Caucasus at the home of Natalia Nikolaevna Goncharova, whom he eagerly wished to marry.

Letter 250

1. Pushkin was present at the engagement of Russian troops and the Turks at Erzurum in 1829; he describes it in his *Journey to Erzurum*.

2. Malinniki, Mme. Osipova's estate, was located in the Staritsa District of the Tver Province. The "arrears" were personal relationships with Osipova-Vulf family.

3. Pushkin called himself Lovelace in Letter 238; he calls Vulf the Tver Lovelace in Letter 608.

4. Officers of the Orenburg Uhlan Regiment were then stationed in the town Staritsa.

5. Alexey Mikhaylovich Kusovnikov (d. 1853), a colonel in the Orenburg Uhlan Regiment and an acquaintance of Pushkin's from his Lyceum days; Alexander Tikhonovich Yugenev (ca. 1785-1867), a landowner of the Staritsa District.

6. Ekaterina Vasilievna Veliasheva (1813-after 1860), a cousin of Vulf's. Vulf's sisters called Pushkin "Mephistopheles," Alexey N. Vulf "Faust," and Veliasheva "Gretchen"; but "Gretchen" remained unmoved by their efforts. The passage of poetry quoted below was composed by Pushkin to her (and published in 1830).

7. Frederika Ivanovna Vulf (d. 1848), the wife of A. N. Vulf's uncle Pavel Ivanovich Vulf (1775-1858), the proprietor of the estate Pavlovskoe.

8. Bernovo was the estate of Ivan Ivanovich Vulf (1776-1860), father of both the ladies mentioned in this paragraph.

9. Ekaterina Ivanovna Gladkova, nee Vulf (b. 1805), a distant cousin of A. N. Vulf. Pushkin may be quoting what Vulf himself called her; at any rate, he is alluding to her coldness and virtuousness when Vulf attempted to seduce her. Vulf piquantly records in his diary the details of his attempts to make love to her, and how her jealous husband's presence interfered.

10. Pushkin had known and been attracted by Netty Vulf (Anna Ivanovna Vulf) at intervals since 1825, but never really seriously (see Letter 108). Pushkin's love affairs with her usually lasted, like this one, about three days.

11. Unidentified.

12. Ekaterina Evgrafovna Smirnova (1812-after 1888), daughter of the priest at Bernovo. A. N. Vulf, thinking she was in love with him, attempted seduction, but without success; hence the reference to the heroine of *Clarissa*, who was violated by an unprincipled seducer.

13. Dmitry Ivanovich Pisarev (1805-after 1865) and Prince Maksyutov were army officers then stationed at Staritsa.

14. Ivan Ivanovich Vulf; he had a harem of serf girls on his estate. A. N. Vulf later did the same thing at Malinniki.

Letter 251

1. Pushkin's letter is in response to a letter from Benkendorf asking in the Tsar's name who gave him permission to make the trip to Erzurum and asking in his own why Pushkin "broke his word" and went to the trans-Caucasus region. When Nicholas I asked Pushkin how he dared to go to the army, and Pushkin answered that it was because the Commander-in-Chief permitted, Nicholas I rejoined: "You should have asked me. Don't you know the army is mine?"

2. A mountain ridge.

Letter 252

1. Sergey Dmitrievich Kiselev (d. 1851) was a military man and a friend of Pushkin's.

2. A hotel in Petersburg.

3. Elizaveta Nikolaevna Ushakova (1810-1872), whom Kiselev married in 1830, and Ekaterina Nikolaevna Ushakova (1809-1872).

4. The Moscow English Club was near the Moscow house of Natalia Nikolaevna Goncharova, as impregnable, it then seemed to Pushkin, as the Turkish fortress of Kars. There is nevertheless hope in Pushkin's use of the term "Kars." The Russians had recently captured the fortress of Kars, and Pushkin had visited it during the summer of 1829 and seen it under Russian occupation.

Letter 253

1. Countess Tizengauzen, dressed as a Cyclops, attended a costumed ball on January 4, 1830, at which she pronounced to the royal couple these verses which Pushkin had written for her for the occasion. Pushkin did not attend the ball.

Letter 254

1. A short, unsigned note in *The Literary Gazette*, praising Gnedich's translation of *The Iliad*, which had just appeared; Gnedich guessed the author, and invited Pushkin to meet him at Andrieux's, a Petersburg restaurateur and hotel keeper.

Letter 255

1. Pushkin had long been dreaming, since at least 1823, of going abroad, but in his status he could not go without the Tsar's explicit permission. Pushkin was in this instance refused permission to go to France or Italy; he was informed also that the officials to go to China had already been appointed and could not be changed without the approval of the court at Peking. He was further reminded that a trip to Europe would upset his financial affairs and take him away from his work.

The only time Pushkin was ever able to leave the political boundaries of Russia was the short time in the summer of 1829 when he accompanied the victorious Russian army for some distance into Turkish territory.

2. *Boris Godunov.*

3. In the rough draft of this letter, Pushkin stated that *Boris Godunov* was the work which he had "thought over *most* and the *only* one with which [he was] satisfied" (italics mine). Pushkin also removed from the final version of the letter his assurance that the "political ideas" of the play are "completely monarchistic."

Letter 256

1. Mikhail Nikolaevich Zagoskin (1789-1852), dramatist and historical novelist; he became famous in Russia for his historical novel *Yury Miloslavsky* (1829). As a matter of fact, Pushkin himself (not Pogorelsky, pen name of Perovsky) wrote the article about Zagoskin's novel which appeared in *The Literary Gazette* in 1830.

Letter 257

1. The Metropolitan of Moscow, Filaret (Vasily Mikhaylovich Drozdov; 1783-1867) had rewritten Pushkin's despondent, "skeptical" stanzas "Vain Gift, Chance Gift" (written 1828, pub. in *The Northern Flowers for* 1830). The Metropolitan revised Pushkin's verses to an acceptance of God and self-accusation. Pushkin answered Filaret's verses with the ironical poem "In Hours of Amusement or Idle Boredom" (1830), which concludes that as a result of Filaret's poem, "the poet hears the harp of the seraphim in holy horror."

Letter 258

1. Refusing permission for Pushkin to go abroad.

2. Sofia Alexeevna Raevskaya; her husband, General Nikolay Nikolaevich Raevsky the Older, had died in 1829. She eventually received a pension of twelve thousand rubles.

3. Those exiled included two sons-in-law, M. F. Orlov and Prince S. G. Volkonsky; a brother-in-law, V. L. Davydov; and a son, A. N. Raevsky.

4. That is, to her then still unmarried daughters Elena Nikolaevna and Sofia Nikolaevna Raevskaya.

Letter 259.

1. Mikhail Osipovich Sudienko (1802-1874), a rich landowner and friend of Pushkin's. He was living on his estate Ochkino, in the Novgorod-Seversky District, in the Ukraine.

2. Probably Prince Vasily Andreevich Dolgorukov (1804-1868), cavalry officer, later Minister of War and Chief of the Third Section.

Letter 260

1. Vyazemsky shortly afterwards moved to Petersburg; Delvig was then in Moscow. In Delvig's absence, Pushkin and Orest Mikhaylovich Somov published Delvig's *Literary Gazette*, which appeared every five days. Pushkin thanks Vyazemsky for prose for this publication.

2. Pushkin probably has in mind Racine's *Andromaque*, in which the inseparable friends Oreste and Pylade are characters.

3. Zagoskin's *Yury Miloslavsky*.

4. Pushkin is referring to Bulgarin's novels, *Dimitry the Pretender* (1830) or *Ivan Vyzhigin* (1829).

5. Polevoy's *History of the Russian People* (6 vols., 1829-1833); the advertisements for subscriptions had promised that there would be twelve volumes and that it would go up to 1829; it stopped with Ivan the Terrible. Polevoy's *History* was designed to replace Karamzin's. However, it was ridiculed by most critics, including Pushkin.

6. Zhukovsky liked very much Nikolay Nazarievich Muraviev's (1775-1845) *Certain of the Amusements of Relaxation, Since* 1805, three parts of which appeared in 1828; fourteen parts appeared in all, the last in 1851. Vyazemsky considered many passages in the work ludicrous.

7. Pogodin's extremely sharp and unfavorable criticism of Polevoy's *History* (*The Moscow Messenger*, 1830).

8. A critique favorable to Polevoy's *History* (by Nadezhdin) appeared in Kachenovsky's *Messenger of Europe* in 1830.

9. Natalia Nikolaevna Goncharova.

10. Prince Platon Alexeevich (1805-1889), or his brother Prince Alexander Alexeevich (b. 1807), Meshchersky, then working in the Moscow Archives of the Collegium of Foreign Affairs.

11. Ekaterina Nikolaevna Ushakova.

12. He went early in March.

13. Vyazemsky's poem was provoked by the denunciations against him and his being out of favor as a result of them.

14. Vyazemsky's ten-year-old son Pavel Petrovich.

15. S. E. Raich's journal *Galatea* was then engaged in harsh polemics with *The Moscow Telegraph*.

16. The first verse of A. E. Izmaylov's fable "The Liar" (1824), on the journalist Pavel Petrovich Sviniin. The second verse continues ". . . had a great gift for lying."

Letter 261
1. Pushkin had been very much attracted to Mme. Sobanskaya during the years 1821-1823. See Letter 49.

Letter 262
1. This letter, written on the same day as Letter 261, continues the same train of thought. It is not known whether either was sent. It is in response to a note from Mme. Sobanskaya, postponing for a day a meeting they were to have had.

The quotation goes back, not to the "Scriptures," but to Goethe's *Faust*. Pushkin is quoting almost verbatim from his own unfinished note (1825) on his own "Demon" (written 1823, pub. 1824). In this note Pushkin first rejects the interpretation of any certain person as being the "demon" of the poem. Then, citing *Faust*, where "the eternal enemy of mankind" is called "the spirit who denies," Pushkin's note, which is written in the third person, continues with the rhetorical question whether Pushkin "did not wish, in his demon, to personify *this spirit of denial or doubt*" (the italics are mine).

2. The heroine of Constant's novel *Adolphe* (1816).

Letter 263
1. Konstantin Matveevich Borozdin (1781-1848), as Chairman of the Petersburg Censorship Committee, had the responsibility of assigning works for censoring to the individual censors.

2. Nikolay Prokofievich Shcheglov (1794-1831), Professor of Physics at the Petersburg University; he was assigned as censor for *The Literary Gazette* from January 26, 1830, on.

3. Konstantin Stepanovich Serbinovich (1796-1874), a Petersburg censor from 1826 until 1830; censor of *The Literary Gazette* until January 20, 1830.

4. In "To Zaytsevsky, Poet and Sailor" (1830). Efim Petrovich Zaytsevsky (d. ca. 1860) was a sailor and a minor poet; Alexander Ivanovich Kazarsky (1797-1833) was a

naval officer and hero in the Turkish War. Perun was the ancient Russian pagan god of the thunder.

Letter 264

1. Apparently Sudienko's agent.

Letter 265

1. Nicholas I's unexpected appearance in Moscow on the night of May 5 was called forth partly by the event alluded to further in Pushkin's letter. In the private Moscow French Theater, managed by Sofia Vasilievna Kartsova, her secretary slapped the actress Alfred, a favorite of the Moscow public. Then Alfred was discharged, not being allowed even to appear in her benefit performance. Her admirers raised such a hubbub at the theater, demanding that Alfred be allowed to present her benefit, that Nicholas I himself felt that he had to take steps. Dmitry Ivanovich Shulgin, the Moscow Chief of Police, the General of Gendarmes Alexander Alexandrovich Volkov, and even Prince D. V. Golitsyn, Governor General of Moscow, were involved in the steps taken. Nicholas I had Shulgin reprimanded for not taking immediate steps which would have prevented the hubbub, and he had the "chief instigators," Count Sergey Pavlovich Potemkin (1787-1858) and a Sibelev (probably Evgraf Ivanovich, ca. 1759-1839) arrested. All Moscow visited those imprisoned, and the imprisonment turned into a farce. Countess Potemkina (below in the letter) was Elizaveta Petrovna Potemkina, the wife of Count Sergey Pavlovich Potemkin.

2. "As for Mme. Kartsova, all her talking was as though she was singing."
—"You might have noted, General, that she was singing off key."
"Since we are speaking frankly, you will permit me, General, to repeat to you Countess Potemkina's request, that of the rehabilitation of my husband."
Vyazemsky was still in disgrace, on the charge of "profligate conduct" (see Letter 243). He had sent a self-justification to Benkendorf via Zhukovsky a month earlier.

3. *Puška sama po sebe, a edinorog sam po sebe.*

4. Stepan Petrovich Zhikharev (1788-1860), a lover of the theater.

5. Over articles in *The Moscow Telegraph* in which Polevoy defended romanticism, whereas Dmitriev was an adherent of the ideas of classicism; in these articles Polevoy attacked Karamzin's *History*, and various other literary figures including Dmitriev. Dmitriev's anger at S. N..Glinka is at his being the censor who passed the articles which Dmitriev found offensive. Pushkin wished to draw Polevoy into polemics over Polevoy's *History*.

6. Kopp operated a hotel and restaurant in Moscow at the time.

7. Prince Sergey Sergeevich Gagarin (1795-1852), at this time Director of the Imperial Theaters.

Letter 266

1. Probably Letter 265.

2. According to rumor, the government was about to promulgate great reforms, including the liberation of the serfs, with land, and the abolition of the system set up by Peter the Great, whereby a person could become a member of the hereditary nobility by achieving a certain status in the civil or military service. Almost nothing came of the hopes for such reforms.

3. Vyazemsky at his own request was taken back into the civil service in 1830, in the Ministry of Finance. He had been out of the civil service since 1821.

4. The reference is to the theatrical incident cited in Letter 265. Matvey Mikhaylovich Solntsev was Pushkin's uncle by marriage; his wife was Elizaveta (Lizaveta) Lvovna

Solntseva, nee Pushkina (1776-1848); Olga Matveevna Solntseva (d. 1880) was their daughter.

Letter 267
1. "You are always on the road."
2. Pushkin is answering a letter from Benkendorf, in which the latter demanded Pushkin's reasons for going to Moscow without his permission and threatening "unpleasantnesses" if the excuse is not a good one.

Letter 268
1. Bulgarin, thinking Pushkin the author of an unfavorable critique by Baron Delvig on Bulgarin's novel *Dimitry the Pretender*, published a lampoon on Pushkin in the form of an "anecdote," supposedly borrowed from an English journal, jeering at Pushkin and praising himself.
2. Benkendorf answered with assurances that Pushkin's position was by no means as shaky and undependable as it seemed to him, but refused permission for him to visit N. N. Raevsky the Younger in Poltava.

Letter 269
1. Alexander Alexandrovich Pisarev (1780-1848) was then Chairman of the Moscow University Society of Lovers of Russian Literature, which elected Pushkin to membership in December, 1829, along with Baratynsky, the composer Verstovsky, and Bulgarin. Polevoy answered that no action was necessary but that the fee for the parchment certificate of membership was twenty-five rubles. Pushkin's personal and literary relations with Polevoy were at this time at a low level; why he wrote to Polevoy about this matter at this time is not clear.

Letter 270
1. Alexander Petrovich Sumarokov (1718-1777), eighteenth-century dramatist and theatrical director. Gerard Friedrich Miller (1705-1783), of German birth, became a historiographer and academician in Russia.
2. Ivan Nikolaevich Goncharov.
3. Ekaterina Nikolaevna Meshcherskaya, nee Karamzina (1806-1867), daughter of the historian. Pushkin jokingly likens his situation with Khitrovo with that of Joseph and Potiphar's wife (Genesis 39).
4. Publication of a lampoon on Pushkin; see Letter 268, note 1.
5. Count Alexander Nikitich Panin (1791-1850), educational official in Moscow, noted for his severity.
6. The writer Vasily Appollonovich Ushakov (1795-1838), a friend of Bulgarin and Polevoy and a co-worker on *The Moscow Telegraph*. He was cross-eyed. Pushkin's comment may have been suggested by the rhyme *živ* "alive" and *kriv* "one-eyed."
7. Pavel Mikhaylovich Stroev (1796-1876), historian; the Index was published in 1836.
8. Batyushkov had gone mad, but the rumor that he was dying was false; he died in 1855.

PART VII

ENGAGED—MOSCOW, BOLDINO

April, 1830—February, 1831

Pushkin, 1827 or 1828. *Lithograph by G. Gippius.*

To Natalia Ivanovna Goncharova
April 5, 1830. In Moscow.
(In French)

Now, Madame, that you have granted me the permission to write to you, I am as agitated, upon taking up my pen, as I was in your presence. I have so many things to say, and the more I think of them, the more melancholy and discouraging thoughts occur to me. I am going to reveal them to you in all their sincerity and all their diffuseness, imploring your patience and, above all, your indulgence.

When I saw her for the first time, her beauty was just beginning to be noticed in society. I fell in love with her; my head whirled; I asked for her hand. Your answer, all vague as it was, gave me a moment of delirium. I departed the same night for the army. You ask me what I was going to do there? I swear to you that I do not know at all, but an involuntary anguish was driving me from Moscow. There I would not have been able to bear either your presence or hers. I wrote you. I hoped, I waited for an answer—it did not come. The errors of my first youth presented themselves to my imagination. They were only too violent, and calumny has added to them further; talk about them has become, unfortunately, widespread. You might have believed it; I dared not complain, but I was in despair.

What torments awaited me on my return! Your silence, your cold air, Mlle. Natalia's reception of me, so nonchalant, so inattentive. . . . I did not have the courage to explain myself, I went to Petersburg with death in my soul. I felt that I had played a rather ludicrous role; I had been timid for the first time in my life, and timidity in a man of my age could hardly please a young person of your daughter's age. One of my friends went to Moscow and brought me back a kind word which restored me to life,[1] and now when those gracious words which you have been so kind as to address to me should have overwhelmed me with joy—I am more unhappy than ever. I shall try to explain.

Only habit and a long intimacy could win for me your daughter's affection. I can hope to make her become attached to me in the course of time, but I have nothing to please her with. If she consents to give me her hand, I shall see only the proof of the calm indifference of her heart. But surrounded as she will be with admiration, with homage, with enticements, will this calmness last? She will be told that only unfortunate fate has prevented her from forming other ties, more fitting, more brilliant, more worthy of her—perhaps such remarks may be sincere, but she will assuredly believe them to be so. Will she not have regrets? Will she not regard me as an obstacle, as a fraudulent ravisher? Will she not take an aversion to me? God is my witness that I am ready to die for her, but that I should die to leave a dazzling widow, free to choose a new husband tomorrow— this idea is hell.

Let us speak of finances; I set little store on that. Mine have sufficed me up to the present. Will they suffice me, married? Not for anything in the world would I bear that my wife should come to know privations, that she should not go where she is invited to shine, to amuse herself. She has the right to insist upon it. In order to satisfy her, I am ready to sacrifice to her all my tastes, all the passions of my life, a mode of life quite free and quite reckless. Still, will she not murmur if her position in society is not as brilliant as that which she deserves and which I would wish for her?

Such are, in part, my anxieties. I tremble that you may find them only too just. There is still another one which I cannot resolve to commit to paper. . . .

Deign to accept, Madame, the expression of my complete devotion and of my high esteem.

Saturday.   A. Pushkin.

[272]
To Sergey Lvovich Pushkin and to
Nadezhda Osipovna Pushkina
Between April 6 and 11, 1830. From Moscow to Petersburg.
(Rough draft; in French)

My most beloved parents, I am turning to you at a moment which will determine my lot for the rest of my life.

I wish to marry a young woman whom I have been in love with for a year—Mlle. Natalia Goncharova. I have her consent and that of her mother. I ask you for your blessing, not as an empty formality, but in the deep conviction that this blessing is necessary for my well-being—and may the last half of my life be more consoling for you than my sad youth was.

The finances of Mme. Goncharova being very disarranged and depending in part on those of her father-in-law, this point is the only obstacle which stands in the way of my happiness. I do not have the strength even to consider renouncing it. It is indeed easier for me to hope that you will come to my aid. I beseech you, write me what you can do for [. . . .][1]

[273]

To ALEXANDER KHRISTOFOROVICH BENKENDORF
April 16, 1830. From Moscow to Petersburg.
(In French)

I am very much embarrassed to have to apply to the Authority in a purely personal matter, but my position and the interest which you have been so kind as to evince toward me up to the present oblige me to do so.

I am to marry Mlle. Goncharova, whom you must have seen in Moscow.[1] I have her consent and that of her mother. Two objections have been made to me: my finances and my situation with respect to the government. As regards finances, I was able to answer that they have been sufficient, thanks to His Majesty, who has given me the possibility of living honorably from my labors. As for my situation, I was not able to conceal that it has been false and equivocal. I was excluded from the service in 1824; this stigma remains on me. After leaving the Lyceum in 1817 with the rank of civil servant of the tenth class, I never received the two ranks which should have fallen to me by right, my superiors neglecting to present me for them, and I not caring to call their attention to it. It would be painful for me to re-enter the service now, in spite of my willingness. A completely subordinate position, such as my rank permits me to occupy, could not suit me. It would take me away from my literary pursuits, which provide my livelihood, and would do nothing but give me vexations without end and without any useful purpose. So I ought not even to think of it any more. Mme. Goncharova is afraid that she might be giving her daughter to a man who has the misfortune of being in the Emperor's disfavor. . . . My happiness depends on a word of good will from him toward whom my devotion and my gratitude are already pure and unbounded.[2]

Another favor: In 1826 I brought to Moscow my tragedy of *Godunov*, written during my exile. It was sent to you in the form that you saw it, only in order to exculpate me. The Emperor deigned to read it, and he made me several criticisms on passages which are too free, and I must confess that His Majesty is only too right. Two or three passages also attracted his attention, in that they seemed to present allusions to circumstances which were then recent;[3] in re-reading them at present, I doubt that one could find such a meaning in them. All public disturbances resemble each other. The dramatic author cannot be answerable for the words which he places in the mouth of historical personages. He must make them speak according to their known character. One must therefore pay attention only to the *spirit in which the entire work is conceived,* to the impression which it must produce. My tragedy is a work of good faith, and I cannot in good conscience suppress what appears to me to be essential. I beseech His Majesty to pardon me the liberty which I am taking to contradict him; I well know that this opposition by a poet can evoke laughter, but up to now I have always steadfastly refused all proposals of the booksellers; I have been happy to be able to make in silence this sacrifice to His Majesty's will. Present circumstances are pressing me, and I now beseech His Majesty to unbind my hands and to permit me to publish my tragedy as I think proper.

Once more, I am very much ashamed of having talked to you so long of myself. But your indulgence has spoiled me, and although I have done nothing to merit the Emperor's benefactions, I nevertheless hope and believe in him.

I am, with the highest esteem,

Your Excellency's

Most humble and most obedient servant,

April 16, 1830.   Alexander Pushkin.

Moscow.

I beseech you, General, to keep my secret for me.[4]

[274]

To Daria Fedorovna Ficquelmont
April 25, 1830. From Moscow to Petersburg.
(In French)

Countess,

It is very cruel of you to be so amiable and to make me feel so keenly the sorrow of being banished from your salon. In the name of heaven, Countess, do not believe, however, that the unhoped-for happiness of receiving a letter from you would have been needed to make me miss an abode which you embellish. I hope that your mother's[1] indisposition has not had any bad consequences and that it no longer gives you anxiety. I would have wished to be already at your feet and to thank you for your graciously remembering me, but my return is still very uncertain.

Permit me to tell you, Countess, that your reproaches are as unjust as your letter is enticing. Believe that I shall always remain the most sincere admirer of your so natural graces, of your so affable and so lively conversation, even though you have the misfortune to be the most brilliant of our ladies of the nobility.

Deign, Countess, to accept once more the expression of my gratitude and of my high esteem.

April 25, 1830.   A. Pushkin.
Moscow.

[275]

To Vera Fedorovna Vyazesmskaya
The end (not later than the 28th) of April, 1830.
From Moscow to Ostafievo.
(In French)

You are right in finding *The Ass*[1] delightful. It is one of the most remarkable works of the moment. It is being attributed to V. Hugo— I see more talent in it than in *The Last Day*,[2] where there is a great deal of it. As for the phrase which embarrassed you—I shall tell you first not to take seriously all an author advances. Everybody has exalted first love, but he has found it more piquant to speak of the second. Perhaps he is right. First love is always a matter of sentiment: the sillier it is, the more delightful memories it leaves. The second, do you see, is a matter of voluptuousness. One could push the parallel much further. But I hardly have the time to do it. My marriage to Natalia (who, parenthetically, is my one hundred thirteenth love)[3] has been decided. My father is giving me two hundred peasants whom I am pledging in the loan office,[4] and I want to pledge you, dear Princess, to be my *posaženaja mat'*.[5]

At your feet, A.P.

Erratum, variant: after 200 *peasants*:
I am pledging them at the loan office and you, divine Princess, to be my *posaženaja mat'*.

[276]

To Stepan Petrovich Shevyrev
April 29, 1830. From Moscow to Rome.

Accept my cordial greetings, too, dear Stepan Petrovich. We dwellers of prosaic Moscow make bold to write to you in poetic Rome,[1] relying on your friendship. Return enriched with memories, with new knowledge, with inspirations; return and enliven our somnolent northern literature.

A.P.

[277]

To Peter Andreevich Vyazemsky
May 2, 1830. From Moscow to Petersburg.

I thank you, my dear one, for your congratulations and madrigals[1] —I shall transmit them to my fiancée to the letter. Is it true that you are planning to come to Moscow? I am afraid of the Countess Ficquelmont.[2] She will keep you in Petersburg. They say that your position is that of special commissions for Kankrin, but that your actual service is for her. Come, my dear fellow, and fall in love with my wife, and we shall talk over *The [Literary] Gazette* or an almanac. Delvig really is lazy; however, his *Gazette* is good; you have enlivened it greatly. Support it while we have no other. It would be shameful to yield the field to Bulgarin.[3] The fact is that a purely literary gazette cannot exist among us; one must take as ally either Fashion or Politics. To compete with Raich and Shalikov is somehow shameful.[4] But Bulgarin hasn't been given a monopoly on political news, has he? It isn't possible, is it, that except for *The*

Northern Bee not a single journal of ours dares to announce that there has been an earthquake in Mexico and that the House of Deputies had adjourned until September? It isn't impossible to obtain this permission, is it? You check with the young ministers and also with Benkendorf. The point here isn't political opinions, but a dry account of occurrences. And besides it's not decent for the government to enter into an alliance with the likes of Bulgarin and Grech. Please have a talk about this, but on the quiet; if Bulgarin should suspect it, then he, in his usual way, would let go with denunciations and slander—and you wouldn't get the better of him in that.

Why was my dedication to you not published in the third edition of *The Fountain*?[5] Didn't my censor[6] pass it? That's very vexing to me. Find out, please, how and why.

Today I am taking [M. M.] Solntsev to my fiancée's. It's a pity I shall not be presenting him in his former appearance, which obtained for him the rank of Chamberlain. She would have more veneration for his, a relative's, paunch. Uncle Vasily Lvovich wept, too, when he learned of my engagement. He is planning to present us some verses on the wedding. A few days ago he came within a hair's breadth of dying and then within a hair's breath of coming back to life. God knows what he is living on or for. Have you told Katerina Andreevna [Karamzina] about my engagement? I am convinced of her sympathetic interest. But give me her words— they are needful for my heart, which is not completely happy even now. Farewell, my dear one; I embrace you and Zhukovsky.

May 2.

[278]
To Sergey Lvovich Pushkin, Nadezhda Osipovna Pushkina,
AND Olga Sergeevna Pavlishcheva
May 3, 1830. From Moscow to Petersburg.
(In French)

My dear Parents, I have received two more letters from you. I can tell you in answer only what you already know: that everything has been arranged, that I am the happiest of men, and that I love you with all my heart.

His Majesty has done me the favor of showing me his kindly disposed satisfaction at the marriage which I am going to contract.

He has permitted me to publish my tragedy as I felt proper.[1] Tell my brother to repeat this to Pletnev—who, parenthetically, is forgetting me, just as Delvig is.

I have delivered your letter to Mme. Goncharova; I suppose she will answer you today. My uncle Matvey Mikhaylovich [Solntsev] paid a call on her the day before yesterday. He and my aunt [Solntseva] have taken the greatest pleasure *in my happiness* (I am completely dumbfounded at using this expression). It has been several days since I have seen my uncle Vasily Lvovich. I know he is better.

Thank you, my dear Olga, for your friendship and for your compliments. I have read your letter to Natalia [N. Goncharova], who laughed over it, and who embraces you.

I embrace you, too, my dear Parents. Perhaps one of these days I shall make a trip to Kaluga to Natalia's grandfather's.[2] I should very much like for the nuptials to take place before the fast[3] which is approaching. Farewell once more.

May 3.

[279]
To Afanasy Nikolaevich Goncharov
May 3, 1830. From Moscow to Polotnyany Zavod.
Dear Sir, Afanasy Nikolaevich!

With the feeling of heartfelt veneration I address you as the head of the family to which I shall belong from now on. When you gave Natalia Nikolaevna your blessing, you gave your blessing to me, too. I am obligated to you for more than life. The happiness of your granddaughter will be my sacred, my sole goal, and all I can requite you with for your benefaction.

With the deepest esteem, devotion, and gratitude, I have the honor to be,

                    Dear Sir,
                         Your most humble servant,
May 3, 1830.   Alexander Pushkin.
Moscow.

[280]
To Peter Alexandrovich Pletnev
About (not later than) May 5, 1830. From Moscow to Petersburg.

Dear fellow! Victory! The Tsar is permitting me to publish *Godunov* in its pristine beauty. Here is what Benkendorf writes to me:

Pour ce qui regarde votre tragédie de Godounof, Sa Majesté vous permet de la faire imprimer sous votre propre responsibilité.[1]

Just listen, my provider: I shall send you my tragedy with my corrections—and you, my benefactor, go to Fon-Fok[2] and get a written authorization from him (is it necessary?).

I am thinking of writing a preface.[3] My hands are itching to crush Bulgarin. But is it fitting for me, Alexander Pushkin, appearing before Russia with *Boris Godunov*, to start talking of Faddey Bulgarin? It seems unfitting. What do you think? Decide.

Tell me, did *The Northern Bee's* review[4] have any influence on the sale of *Onegin*? I am curious to know. Do you know what? I have some extremely amusing materials for a novel, *Faddey Vyzhigin*.[5] Now there's no time, but in due course I shall be able to write it. What effect did the article about Vidocq[6] produce, in general and in particular? Please write and tell me.

Ah, my dear fellow, what a little wife I have caught for myself!

I have just now received your letter—I thank you, my dear fellow. Contract terms as you wish—only can't it be three years instead of four years—haggle even six months off it.[7] Shouldn't we sell Smirdin the tragedy, too? Your commission regarding my fiancée has been fulfilled.[8] Sight unseen, she commends herself to you and your wife.[9] As regards my future abode, I do not know myself—it seems that I shall not be able to get away from Petersburg. The Tsar is very nice to me.

[281]
To Alexander Khristoforovich Benkendorf
May 7, 1830. From Moscow to Petersburg.
(In French)

General,

I owe the new favor with which the Emperor has just overwhelmed me to Your Excellency's solicitude; please accept the expression of my profound gratitude. Never in my heart have I been unmindful of the benevolence, I dare to call it completely paternal, which His Majesty has borne me; never have I wrongly interpreted the interest which you have always been kind enough to show toward me; my request was made only in order to reassure a mother[1] who was apprehensive and whom calumny had given further affright.

Please accept, General, the expression of my high esteem.

Your most humble and most obedient servant,

May 7, 1830.   Alexander Pushkin.
Moscow.

[282]

To Elizaveta Mikhaylovna Khitrovo
May 18, 1830. From Moscow to Petersburg.
(In French)

I do not yet know whether I shall come to Petersburg—the chaperones[1] whom you have the kindness to promise me are very brilliant for my poor Natalia. I am at their feet and at yours, Madame.

May 18.

[283]

To Mikhail Petrovich Pogodin
Between May 15 and 20, 1830. In Moscow.

Do me the favor of telling me whether I can hope to have 5000 rubles by May 30, either at 10 percent for a year, or at 5 percent for six months.[1] How is the fourth act?[2]

A.P.

[284]

To Elizaveta Mikhaylovna Khitrovo
Between May 19 and 24, 1830. From Moscow to Petersburg.
(In French)

First permit me, Madame, to thank you for *Hernani*. It is one of the works of our day which I have read with the most pleasure. Hugo and Sainte-Beuve are unquestionably the only French poets of the epoch, particularly Sainte-Beuve—and apropos of him, if it is possible to get his *Consolations*[1] in Petersburg, do a deed of charity, and for heaven's sake send it to me.

As for my marriage, your thoughts on that subject would be perfectly just, if you had judged me less poetically. The fact is that I am a decent sort of fellow and that I ask nothing better than to grow fat and be happy—the former is easier than the latter. (Pardon me, Madame: I see that I have commenced my letter on a torn sheet—I do not feel like starting again.)

It is very kind of you, Madame, to interest yourself in my situation in relation to the boss.[2] But what position would you have me occupy in his service? I do not see any which would suit me. I have an aversion for business affairs and *boumagui*,[3] as Count Langeron says. I am no longer of the right age to be a Kammerjunker,[4] and then what would I do at court? Neither my means nor my pursuits permit it. My wife's parents trouble themselves very little about her and me. I repay them with the same, with all my heart. These relationships are very agreeable, and I shall never change them.

[285]

To Mikhail Petrovich Pogodin

Between May 19 and 24, 1830. In Moscow.

Do me the divine favor of helping me. By Sunday I must have the money without fail, and all my hope is in you.[1]

A.P.

[286]

To Ivan Fomich Antipin and Faddey Ivanovich Abakumov

May 27, 1830. At Polotnyany Zavod.[1]

Alexander Pushkin, with feeling of keenest gratitude, accepts the token of the flattering attention of his honored fellow-countrymen Ivan Fomich Antipin and Faddey Ivanovich Abakumov.[2]

May 27, 1830.

Polotnyany Zavod.

[287]

To Alexander Khristoforovich Benkendorf
May 29, 1830. From Moscow to Petersburg.
(In French)

My General,

I beseech Your Excellency to pardon my importunity once more.

My intended's great-grandfather once had permission to erect a monument to the Empress Catherine II[1] on his estate of Polotnyany Zavod. The collossal statue of her which he had cast in bronze in Berlin was a complete failure and could never be erected. It has been buried for more than 35 years in the cellar of the house. Dealers in copper have offered 40,000 rubles for it, but the present owner, Mr. Goncharov, has never been willing to consent to that. He has prized this statue, all misshapen as it is, as a memento of the benefactions of the Grand Sovereigness. He was afraid that if he destroyed it he might consequently lose the right of erecting a monument. His granddaughter's marriage, which has been unexpectedly decided upon, has found him completely without funds, and except for the Emperor there is scarcely anyone except the Emperor's late august Grandmother who could remove us from the difficulty. Mr. Goncharov consents, although against his inclinations, to part with the statue, but he fears to lose a right which he holds dear. I therefore beseech Your Excellency to be so kind as to see to it that I obtain, first, the permission to have the statue in question melted down; secondly, the favor of retaining for Mr. Goncharov the right of erecting, as soon as he can, a monument to the benefactress of his family.

Accept, General, the expression of my complete devotion and of my high esteem.

Your Excellency's
Most humble and most obedient servant,
Alexander Pushkin.

May 29, 1830.
Moscow.

[288]
To Mikhail Petrovich Pogodin
May 29, 1830. In Moscow.

Rescue me, if possible, and I, my wife, and my little children will pray to God for you.[1] Shall I see you tomorrow, and isn't something ready (in the tragedy, I mean)?[2]

May 29.   A.P.

[289]
To Natalia Nikolaevna Goncharova
The beginning of June, 1830.
From Moscow to Polotnyany Zavod.
(Rough draft; in French)

Here I am in Moscow, which is so sad, so boring, when you are not here. I have not felt up to going along the Nikitskaya,[1] still less to go and ask Agrafena[2] for the news. You cannot imagine the anguish which your absence gives me. I am sorry I left the Zavod— all my fears keep returning, more vivid and more gloomy. I should like to be able to hope that his letter may find you no longer at the Zavod—I am counting the quarter-hours which separate me from you.[3]

[290]
To Mikhail Petrovich Pogodin
Between May 20 and June 6, 1830. In Moscow.

What do you think, is there hope in Nadezhdin, or is Nadoumko perplexed?[1]

A.P.

[291]
To Mikhail Petrovich Pogodin
Between May 30 and June 6, 1830. In Moscow.

Can I drop in on you, and when? And will there be some money?[1] God, of course, has a lot of everything, but instead of lending He gives to whom He takes the notion; so I am depending on you rather than on Him (the Lord forgive my transgression).

A.P.

Post-scriptum et Nota bene: Rumyantsev *did away with chevaux-de-frise* and introduced the Kaluga *carrés*.[2]

[292]

To MIKHAIL PETROVICH POGODIN
Between May 30 and June 6, 1830. In Moscow.

If just a part, then the greater, for God's sake.[1]

A.P.

[293]

To MIKHAIL PETROVICH POGODIN
Between May 30 and June 6, 1830. In Moscow.

Although Nadezhdin does a thorough job of *rough-hewing* us sometimes, or he *scratches* us, etc., it would be better if he could *give us comfort* now.[1] Two thousand is better than one, Saturday is better than Monday, etc.

All yours, etc.

[294]

To AFANASY NIKOLAEVICH GONCHAROV
June 7, 1830. From Moscow to Polotnyany Zavod.

Dear Sir, Afanasy Nikolaevich,

Every day I have been expecting the promised money and necessary documents from Petersburg,[1] but so far I have not received them. That is the reason for my involuntary silence. I think that I shall be forced at the end of this month to set off for Petersburg for several days, in order to bring my affairs into order.

As regards the monument,[2] I wrote to Benkendorf about it immediately upon my arrival in Moscow. I do not know whether he has departed with the Sovereign or where he is now. His answer will probably not be long delayed.

Permit me, Dear Sir, Afanasy Nikolaevich, to give you once more my heartfelt thanks for the paternal favors which you have rendered to Natalia Nikolaevna and to me.[3] I make bold to hope that in the course of time I shall earn your good will. At the least my life will be henceforth dedicated to the happiness of her who has honored me with her choice and who is so close to your heart.

With the deepest respect and with boundless devotion, I have the happiness to be,

Dear Sir,

Your most humble servant,

June 7, 1830.   Alexander Pushkin.
Moscow.

[295]

To MIKHAIL PETROVICH POGODIN
June 8 or 9, 1830. In Moscow.

Glory to God in the highest, and on earth to you, dear and honored one![1] I have received with gratitude your 1800 rubles in bills, and the sooner you obtain the rest, the more you will oblige me.[2] I have not obligated myself to a definite date, though.

All yours,
A.P.

[296]

To MIKHAIL PETROVICH POGODIN
June 12, 1830. In Moscow.

I feel that you are becoming fed up with me, but nothing can be done about it. Do me the favor of telling me precisely when I can hope to receive the remaining sum.

Thursday.   A.P.

[297]

To AFANASY NIKOLAEVICH GONCHAROV
June 28, 1830. From Moscow to Polotnyany Zavod.

Dear Sir, Afanasy Nikolaevich,

I have only just now received your agent's paper, and I have not succeeded yet in skimming through it. I make bold to repeat to you what I have already told Zolotov:[1] the most important thing is not to stir up Kankrin[2] against yourself, for I absolutely do not see how you can manage without him. The Sovereign, upon receiving your petition, is sure to refer it to the consideration of the Minister of Finance, and the Minister, if he should once refuse, would want to persist in his refusal. Temporary assistance (of two or three hundred thousands), although a very difficult thing, is nevertheless easier, for it depends solely on the Sovereign's fancy. I am going to Petersburg in a few days, and if your paper does not have the desired success, I am ready (if you command) to petition both Benkendorf and Kankrin for this assistance. As regards mortgaging the Zavod, though I am convinced of the consent of the young male members of your family,[3] and of their obedience to your will, I do not make bold to take action by-passing them in their absence. I hope that my candor will not harm me in your good inclination toward me, which is so precious to me; I thought it better to explain myself straightforwardly and frankly than to promise and not fulfill.

Awaiting your future commands, I commend myself to your good inclination, and I have the honor to be with the most profound respect and heartfelt devotion,

Dear Sir,
Your most humble servant,
Alexander Pushkin.

June 28, 1830.
Moscow.

[298]

To Mikhail Petrovich Pogodin
The second half of June, 1830. In Moscow.

I give you my hearty thanks, dear Mikhaylo Petrovich; you will receive my note of hand in a few days.[1] What do you think of Chaadaev's "Letter"?[2] And when shall I see you?

A.P.

[299]

To Vasily Semenovich Ogon-Doganovsky
May or June, 1830. In Moscow.
(Rough draft)

I would willingly undertake to buy up your debts, but the term for these promissory notes, according to your words, is two years, and I am obligated to pay the 24,800 rubles which I owe you, within four years.[1] I am in no position, because of poor returns, to pay 25 thousands all at once. All I can give for your promissory note of 25,000 is 20,000, with a discount of 10 percent per year—i.e., 18 thousand rubles. In case you wish it this way, be so good as to write me back, and I shall not fail to deliver it to you or to whomever you please.

[300]
To Mikhail Nikolaevich Zagoskin
July 14, 1830. In Moscow.

Dear Sir, Mikhayla Nikolaevich,

Shchepin, the brother of yesterday's Austrian Emperor, has conceived a powerful desire to be admitted to the theatrical school. I commend His Highness to your protection.[1]

Today or tomorrow I am going to Petersburg for several days. I hope to find you and all your family in good health when I return.

All yours,

July 14.   A. Pushkin.
Moscow.

[301]
To Natalia Nikolaevna Goncharova
July 20, 1830. From Petersburg to Moscow.
(In French)

I have the honor to present to you my brother (who finds you so pretty in his own judgment and whom I beg you to receive well in spite of that). My trip was deadly dull.[1] Nikita Andreevich[2] bought me a *bri̇̌cka*[3] which broke down at the first station—I repaired it with what came to hand. At the second station it was all to do over again —and so on. Finally, several miles from Novgorod I came upon your Vsevolozhsky, who had a broken wheel. We finished the trip together, talking a lot about Prince [D. V.] Golitsyn's tableaux.[4] Petersburg already seems very dull to me, and I expect to cut my stay as short as I can. Tomorrow my visits to your relatives will begin. Natalia Kirillovna[5] is in the country. Katerina Ivanovna[6] is in Pargolovo (a Finnish village, where Countess Polier lives).[7] Of very pretty women I have seen only Mme. and Mlle. Malinovskaya,[8] with whom to my complete astonishment I dined yesterday.

I am in a hurry. I kiss the hands of Natalia Ivanovna [Goncharova], whom I still do not dare call Mama, and your hands, too, my angel, since you do not permit me to embrace you.[9] My compliments to your sisters.[10]

July 20.   A.P.

[302]

To NATALIA NIKOLAEVNA GONCHAROVA
About (not later than) July 29, 1830.
From Petersburg to Moscow.
(In French)

Has my brother delivered my letter to you, and why do you not send me an acknowledgment, as you promised me? I am awaiting it with impatience, and the moment I get it I shall be compensated for the boredom of my stay here. I must tell you of my visit to Natalia Kirillovna [Zagryazhskaya]. I arrived, I had myself announced, she received me at her toilet, like a very pretty woman of the last century. "You are the one who is marrying my little niece?"—"Yes, Madame." —"Well, what do you think of that! I am very much astonished; I have not been informed of it. Natasha has written me nothing about it." (She was not speaking of you, but of Mama.)[1] Thereupon I told her that our marriage had been decided upon only a very short time ago, of Afanasy Nikolaevich's [Goncharov] disarranged business affairs, of Natalia Ivanovna's [Goncharova], etc., etc. She paid no heed: "Natasha knows how much I love her; Natasha has always written me upon all important occasions of life; Natasha will write me—and now, Sir, that we are relatives, I hope that you will come to see me often."

Then she asked for a lot of news of Mama, of Nikolay Afanasievich,[2] of you; she repeated to me the Emperor's compliments[3] about you—and we parted very good friends. Natalia Ivanovna will write her, won't she?

I have not seen Ivan Nikolaevich [Goncharov] yet. He was on maneuvers, and he returned to Strelna only yesterday. I shall go with him to Pargolovo, because I have neither the inclination nor the fortitude to do it by myself.

A few days ago I had my father write to Afanasy Nikolaevich, but perhaps he himself will come to Petersburg. What is the Grandmama of the Zavod doing, the bronze one, of course?[4] Won't this question put you under obligation to answer me? What are you doing?

Whom are you seeing? Where do you go walking? Will you go to Rostov? Will you write me? Incidentally, don't be frightened at all these questions; it is quite all right if you do not answer them—since you always think of me as a *sočinitel'*.[5] Recently I have been to see my Egyptian woman.[6] She has become very much interested in you. She made me draw your profile, she expressed to me the desire to make your acquaintance, and so I am taking the liberty of commending her to you. *Prošu ljubit' i žalovat'*.[7] And now I give you my best regards. My respects, my regards to Mama, to your sisters. Good-by.

[303]
To Natalia Nikolaevna Goncharova
July 30, 1830. From Petersburg to Moscow.
(In French)

Here is a letter from Afanasy Nikolaevich [Goncharov], which Ivan Nikolaevich [Goncharov] has just sent me. You cannot imagine how much inconvenience it is giving me. He will get the permission he is so eager for. But as regards the Zavod, I have neither the influence which he believes me to have nor the wish to act against the desires of Natalia Ivanovna [Goncharova], and without the knowledge of your oldest brother.[1] What is worse, I foresee new delays—truly, it is provoking. I have not yet seen Katerina Ivanovna [Zagryazhskaya]; she is at Pargolovo, at the Countess Polier's, who is almost insane, who sleeps until 6 o'clock in the evening, and who receives no one. Yesterday Mme. Bagreeva,[2] Speransky's daughter, sent for me, to haul me over the coals for not having yet complied with the formalities—but in truth I scarcely feel up to it. I go out little into society. You are being awaited here with impatience. The beautiful ladies ask to see your portrait, and they do not pardon my not having it. I console myself in not having it by spending hours on end in front of a blonde madonna who is as much like you as two drops of water, and which I would buy, if it did not cost 40,000 rubles.[3] Afanasy Nikolaevich [Goncharov] should have swapped the ugly Grandmama[4] for it, since up to the present he has not succeeded in melting her down. Seriously, I am afraid that all this may delay our marriage, unless Natalia Ivanovna [Goncharova] consents to entrust the matter of your trousseau to me. My angel, try, for goodness sake.

I am a scatterbrain, my angel: in rereading Afanasy Nikolaevich's [Goncharov] letter, I see that he is no longer thinking of mortgaging his Zavod estate, and that he wishes, in accordance with my advice, to ask for temporary assistance. That is another matter. In that case I shall go to my cousin Kankrin's[5] at once, and request an audience with him. I have not yet seen Benkendorf, and so much the better; I shall try to arrange everything in one single audience.

Farewell, *moj angel*.[6] My regards to all your family, whom I make bold to regard as mine.

July 30.

Will you send me an acknowledgment?

[304]

To Vera Fedorovna Vyazemskaya
August 4, 1830. From Petersburg to Moscow.

Greetings, Princess. How vexing that you did not catch me in Moscow; *j'avais tant de choses à vous dire. J'avoue à ma honte que je m'amuse à Pétersbourg et je ne sais trop comment et quand je serai de retour.*[1] Perhaps with the Prince; *en tout cas au revoir.*

A.P.

[305]

To Afanasy Nikolaevich Goncharov
August 14, 1830. From Moscow to Polotnyany Zavod.

Dear Sir, Afanasy Nikolaevich,

In accordance with your command I called upon Count Kankrin and talked about your piece of business, i.e., about monetary assistance;[1] I found the Minister rather ill-disposed. He said that this matter depends solely upon the Sovereign; I asked him for at least his promise not to express any objection to the Sovereign, if it should please His Majesty to render you this assistance from himself. The Minister gave me his word.

As regards the permission to melt down and recast the monument, you will receive without delay a paper from General Benkendorf to you. My fate depends on you; I again make bold to beseech you to resolve it.[2] All my life will be dedicated to gratitude.

With the most profound respect and heartfelt devotion, I have the happiness to be,

Dear Sir,

Your most humble servant,

August 14, 1830.   Alexander Pushkin.
Moscow.

[306]

To ELIZAVETA MIKHAYLOVNA KHITROVO
August 21, 1830. From Moscow to Petersburg.
(In French)

How much gratitude I owe you, Madame, for your kindness in giving me some acquaintance with what is going on in Europe! Nobody here receives periodicals from France, and as for political opinion regarding all that has just happened, the English Club has decided that Prince Dmitry Golitsyn was wrong in forbidding écarté by an ordinance.[1] I am condemned to live among these orangutans at the most interesting moment of our century. To top off my pain and distress, my poor Uncle Vasily Lvovich[2] has just died. It must be admitted that never did an uncle die more inopportunely. Here my marriage is delayed six more weeks, and God knows when I shall be able to return to Petersburg.

La Parisienne is not so good as *La Marseillaise.* The former song is vaudeville verses. I am dying of desire to read Chateaubriand's speech[3] in favor of the Duke of Bordeaux.[4] That was another fine moment for him. In any case here he is in the opposition again. In what does the opposition of *Le Temps*[5] consist? Does it wish a republic? Those who wished for one lately hastened the crowning of Louis Philippe; he owes them positions as chamberlains, and pensions. The marriage of Madame de Genlis and Lafayette would be completely fitting. And Bishop Talleyrand ought to unite them.[6] Thus the revolution would be consummated.

I beseech you, Madame, to tell your daughters the Countesses[7] that I am at their feet, and to be so kind as to accept the expression of my devotion and of my high esteem.

August 21.   A. Pushkin.
Moscow.

[307]
To Afanasy Nikolaevich Goncharov
August 24, 1830. From Moscow to Polotnyany Zavod.

Dear Sir, Afanasy Nikolaevich,

I am truly sorry that my efforts were in vain and that I have so little influence with our ministers;[1] I would count it happiness to be able to do something that would please you.

The death of my uncle Vasily Lvovich Pushkin and the bothers in connection with this sad event have again thrown my circumstances into disorder. I had hardly succeeded in getting out of debt when I was forced to go into debt again. I am setting out for my Nizhny Novgorod village in a few days, in order to assume possession of it.[2] My hope is in you alone. On you alone depends the resolving of my fate.[3]

With the most profound respect and with complete devotion, I have the honor to be,

Dear Sir,
Your most humble servant,
August 26.   Alexander Pushkin.
Moscow.

[308]
To Natalia Nikolaevna Goncharova
The last days of August, 1830. In Moscow.
(In French)

I am departing for Nizhny, uncertain of my fate. If your mother has decided to break off our marriage,[1] and you, to obey her, I shall subscribe to all the motives which she chooses to give for so doing, even though they may be as reasonable as the scene which she made yesterday and the insults which she pleases to lavish on me.

Perhaps she is right and I have been wrong in believing for a moment that happiness was made for me. In any case you are perfectly free; as for me, I give you my word of honor that I shall belong only to you or else I shall never marry.

A.P.

[309]

To Vera Fedorovna Vyazemskaya
The last part of August, 1830. In Moscow.
(In French)

I am departing, having had a falling-out with Mme. Goncharova.[1] The day after the ball she made the most ridiculous scene you could imagine. She said things to me which in all conscience I could not endure. I do not know yet whether my marriage is broken off, but the occasion is there, and I have left the door wide open. I did not wish to speak of it to the Prince, but tell him, and the two of you keep the secret for me. Oh, what an accursed thing happiness is! *Addio*, dear Princess. Write me a word to Lukoyanov,[2] to the Village Boldino.

[310]

To Peter Alexandrovich Pletnev
August 31, 1830. From Moscow to Petersburg.

A fine fellow you are! . . . You didn't take the trouble to say good-by to me,[1] and you don't write me a single line. Now I am going to Nizhny, i.e., to Lukoyanov, to the village Boldino—write me there, if you take the notion.

My dear one, I shall tell you everything I have on my soul: it's sad and there's anguish, anguish. The life of a thirty-year-old fiancé is worse than 30 years of the life of a gambler.[2] The affairs of my mother-in-law-to-be are in disorder. My wedding is being postponed further day after day. Meanwhile I am growing cold; I think of the cares of a married man, of the charms of bachelor life. Besides, Moscow gossip is reaching the ears of my fiancée and her mother— hence tiffs, caustic insinuations, shaky reconciliations. In a word, if I am not unhappy, to say the least I am not happy. Autumn is approaching. That is my favorite season. My health usually becomes more robust—the time of my literary labors is at hand. And I must bustle about with regard to a dowry and a wedding which God knows when we shall celebrate. None of this is very consoling. I am going to the village: God knows whether I shall have the time to work there, or the spiritual calm without which I won't produce anything except epigrams on Kachenovsky.

That's the way it is, my dear fellow. Let well enough alone. The devil prompted me to dream of happiness, as if I were created for it. I should have been satisfied with independence, for which I am obligated to God and to you.[3] I am sad, my dear fellow; I embrace you and kiss our fellows.

August 31.

[311]

To Natalia Nikolaevna Goncharova
September 9, 1830. From Boldino to Moscow.
(In French)

My very dear, my very lovable Natalia Nikolaevna—I am at your knees to thank you and to ask your forgiveness for the uneasiness[1] which I have caused you.

Your letter is charming and it has completely reassured me. My stay here could be prolonged by a completely unforeseen circumstance: I believed that the land which my father has given me was a separate estate, but it turns out to be a part of a village of 500 male peasants,[2] and it will be necessary to proceed to partition it. I shall try to arrange all this as quickly as possible. I am still more afraid of the quarantines which are beginning to be set up here. In our neighborhood we have the *cholera morbus*[3] (a very pleasant thing). And it could detain me an extra score of days. How many reasons there are for me to make haste! My respectful regards to Natalia Ivanovna [Goncharova]. I kiss her hands very humbly and very tenderly. I shall write to Afanasy Nikolaevich [Goncharov] at once. If you will pardon my saying so, he is very provoking. Thank Mlles. Katerina and Alexandra [Goncharova] very much for me for their having remembered me kindly, and, once more, pardon me and believe that I am happy only where you are.

September 9. Boldino.

[312]

To Afanasy Nikolaevich Goncharov
September 9, 1830. From Boldino to Polotnyany Zavod.

Dear Sir, Afanasy Nikolaevich,

From the letter I have been honored with receiving, I have observed with extreme regret that you surmise an insufficiency of zeal in me. Please be so kind as to accept my justification. I did not make bold to take it upon myself to be your intercessor in your matter of business,[1] solely because I was afraid of receiving a refusal if I should approach the Sovereign or his ministers with your petition at the wrong moment. My relations with the government are like spring weather: now, momentarily, there is rain, now there is sun. And now a cloud has come over. . . . It has pleased you to ask advice of me with regard to the channel through which you might forward to the Sovereign your petition for temporary assistance: I think that the best and shortest is via A. Kh. Benkendorf. He is an indulgent, well-intentioned person, and he may very well be the only great lord through whom the private benefactions of the Sovereign reach us.

Commending myself to your good will, I have the happiness to be, with the most profound respect and heartfelt devotion,

Dear Sir,

Your most humble servant,

September 9, 1830. Alexander Pushkin.

Village Boldino.

[313]

To Peter Alexandrovich Pletnev

September 9, 1830. From Boldino to Petersburg.

I wrote you a most melancholy letter,[1] my dear Peter Alexandrovich, but after all melancholy won't astonish you; you yourself know your stuff about that. Now my gloomy thoughts have been dispelled. I have arrived in the village, and I am resting up. The Cholera Morbus is about me. Do you know what kind of a wild beast it is? The first thing you know it will swoop down on Boldino, too, and it will bite us all—the first thing you know I shall set off to Uncle Vasily's,[2] and then you will be writing my biography. Poor Uncle Vasily! Do you know what his last words were? I came to see him, I found him unconscious; he came to, recognized me, was mournful and silent a little while, and then: "How boring Katenin's articles are!" And not another word. What do you think of that? That's what it means to die an honorable warrior on one's shield, *le cri de guerre à la bouche!*[3] You can't imagine how much fun it is to go dashing off from one's fiancée and then to settle down to writing verses. A wife is a different thing from a fiancée. Quite! Your wife is your buddy. With her present you can write as much as you please. But a fiancée is worse than the censor Shcheglov; she binds one's tongue and hands. . . . From mine I received today an extremely sweet little letter; she promises to marry me even without a dowry. The dowry can come later. She is calling me to Moscow—I shall arrive there not sooner than in a month, and from there to you, my joy. What is Delvig doing? Do you see him? Tell him, please, to lay up some money for me;[4] money is no joking matter; money is an important thing—ask Kankrin and Bulgarin.

Ah, my dear fellow! How charming this village is! Just imagine: steppe beyond steppe; of neighbors not a soul; you ride horseback to your heart's content; at home you write as much as you take a notion to, and nobody hinders you. Why, I'll cook you up a lot of all kinds of things, both prose and verse. Forgive me, my dear girl.[5]

September 9, 1830. Boldino.

What about my tragedy?[6] I have written a little elegiac preface; shouldn't I send it to you? Remember, however, that you promised me one of your own, a sensible, long one. And the price of the tragedy? Ten or twelve?

[314]
To Peter Alexandrovich Pletnev
September 29, 1830. From Boldino to Petersburg.
Boldino, September 29.

I have now just received your letter, and I am answering it immediately. Aren't you ashamed that you understood my spleen as you did? And Delvig is a fine fellow, and Zhukovsky is a fine fellow! Probably I expressed myself badly, but that does not justify the three of you. Here is what happened: it was my *mother-in-law* who was postponing the wedding on account of the dowry, and of course not I at all. I was furious. My mother-in-law began to give me scant welcome and to start up stupid quarrels with me, and that infuriated me. The spleen seized me and black thoughts took possession of me. Was *I* the one who wanted to back out or even thought of such a thing? But I saw a rejection coming, and I consoled myself as best I could. All you say about society is just; all the more just are my fears that aunts and grandmothers and little sisters may start turning my young wife's head with folderol. She loves me, but look, Aleko Pletnev, how the *free moon goes her way*, etc.[1] Baratynsky says that only a fool is happy when he is a fiancé, but a thinking person is disturbed and agitated about the future. Up to now it has been I—but now it will be we. A joke! This is the reason I have been trying to hurry my mother-in-law along; but she, like a peasant woman of whom only the hair is long,[2] did not understand me, and was fussing around about a dowry; to hell with it! Now do you understand me? You do? Well, thank God! Greetings, my dear fellow, how are you getting along? But I, having finished my business, am going to Moscow through a whole chain of quarantines. I shall be on the road a month at least. I have spent a month here without seeing a soul, without reading any journals, so that I don't know what [Louis] Philippe is doing and whether Polignac is in good health;[3] I should like to send you my sermon for the local peasants on the cholera;[4] you would die laughing, but you do not deserve this gift. Farewell, my dear fellow; give my greetings to your wife and daughter.

[315]

To NATALIA NIKOLAEVNA GONCHAROVA
September 30, 1830. From Boldino to Moscow.
(In French)

Here I am on the point of getting into the carriage, although my affairs are not settled, and I am indeed completely discouraged. You are very kind to promise a delay of only six days at Bogorodsk. I have just been told that five quarantines have been set up between here and Moscow, and that it will be necessary for me to spend fourteen days in each; do a little counting and then imagine what a bitch of a humor I must be in. As a crowning piece of good fortune, the rain has commenced and of course it will not stop before the beginning of sleighing. If anything can console me, it is the wisdom with which the roadways have been laid out between here and Moscow: imagine a parapet on each side, no ditch at all, no outlet for the water; which makes the entire road a mud hole. On the other hand, the pedestrians walk quite conveniently on completely dry footpaths and make fun of the bogged-down carriages. May the hour be accursed when I decided to part from you in order to come to this beautiful land of mud, pestilence, and conflagration—for we see nothing else.

What are you doing in the meantime? How are affairs going, and what does Grandpapa[1] say? Do you know what he has written me? The Grandmama[2] is worth, he says, only 7,000 rubles, and it is not worth while disturbing her in her retreat for that. It was indeed worth the trouble of making so much fuss over! Do not laugh at me, for I am furious. Our marriage always seems to flee before me, and isn't this pestilence with its quarantines the worst joke that fate could devise? *Moj angel*, your affection is the only thing in this world which keeps me from hanging myself in the main entrance of my sad manor house (where, parenthetically, my grandfather had a Frenchman hanged, an *outchitel*,[3] one abbé Nicole, with whom he was displeased).[4] Preserve your affection for me, and believe that all my happiness is in it. Do you permit me to embrace you? That is of no consequence at a distance of 350 miles and across five quarantines. I can't get these quarantines off my mind. So farewell, my angel. My tender regards to Natalia Ivanovna [Goncharova]; I greet with all my heart your sisters and Mr. Sergey.[5] Have you any news of the others?

September 30.

[316]
To NATALIA NIKOLAEVNA GONCHAROVA
October 11, 1830. From Boldino to Moscow.
(In French)

Entry into Moscow is forbidden,[1] and here I am, confined in Boldino. In the name of heaven, dear Natalia Nikolaevna, write me, even though you may not feel like it. Tell me, where are you? Have you left Moscow? Is there a roundabout route which might lead me to your feet? I am completely discouraged, and I really do not know what to do. It is clear that our marriage will not take place this year (accursed year). But you have left Moscow, haven't you? To expose oneself out of sheer wantonness right in the middle of the plague would be unpardonable. I well know that one always exaggerates the pictures of its ravages and the number of its victims; a young woman from Constantinople[2] told me once that only the rabble die of the plague—that is all very well, but genteel people nevertheless must take their precautions, because that is what saves them, and not their elegance and their good form. Then you are in the country, well sheltered from the cholera, aren't you? Then send me your address and a report on your health. As for us, we are encircled by quarantines, but the epidemic has not yet penetrated to here. Boldino has the air of a rock-bound island. No neighbors, no books. Frightful weather. I spend my time scribbling and fuming. I do not know what the wretched world is doing, and how my friend Polignac[3] is getting along. Write me some news of him, because I am not reading any periodicals at all here. I am becoming imbecilic with a vengeance. [In Russian:] How are grandfather and his bronze grandmother? Both are alive and well, aren't they? A map is now in front of me. I am looking to see how I might make a detour and come to you via Kyakhta, or Arkhangelsk. The point is that for a friend five miles is not really a detour. But to go straight to Moscow is to eat five miles of *kisel'*—and what kind, at that? Moscow![4] [In French:] But enough of bad jokes. I'm smiling yellow, as the fishwives say. Farewell. Tell your mother that I am at her feet; my very tender regards to all the family. Farewell, my beautiful angel. I kiss the tips of your wings, as Voltaire used to say to people who were no peers of yours.[5]

October 11.

[317]
To Peter Alexandrovich Pletnev
About (not later than) October 29, 1830.
From Boldino to Petersburg.

I tried to barge through to Moscow,[1] but when I discovered that nobody is being let through to there, I turned back to Boldino, and I am awaiting favorable weather. Well, what favorable weather we're having! I know the devil is not as dreadful as he is painted; I know that the cholera is no more dangerous than Turkish cross-fire. But remoteness, but lack of news—that's what is tormenting. When I set off on the trip, I wrote my folks[2] to expect me in 25 days. Then my fiancée stopped writing to me, and where she is and how she is, until now I don't know. What do you think of that? That is, my dear Pletnev, though I'm not the type, so to speak,[3] things are reaching the point that I might as well climb into the noose. Verses won't even come into my head, though it's a marvelous autumn, and there is rain and snow, and mud is knee-deep. I don't know where my girl is; I hope she has left plague-infected Moscow, but for where? For Kaluga? For Tver? For Bulgarin's at Karlovo?[4] I don't know a thing. I am not reading your journals; who is giving it to whom? Tell Delvig to stand firm,[5] that I shall come without fail to lend him a hand this winter, if I don't croak here. Meanwhile he can go ahead and order a vignette on wood, depicting me nude, as Atlas supporting on my shoulders *The Literary Gazette*. What about my tragedy?[6] Stand up for it, brave friends! Don't let the journalistic curs devour it. I was wanting to dedicate it to Zhukovsky with the following words: "I should have liked to dedicate my tragedy to Karamzin, but since he is no more, I dedicate it to Zhukovsky." Karamzin's daughters[7] have told me that I may dedicate my favorite work to the memory of their father. And so, if it is still possible, print on the title page:

To the Memory
Precious to all Russians
Of Nikolay Mikhaylovich
Karamzin,
This work, inspired by his Genius,
Is dedicated with veneration and gratitude.

A. Pushkin.

[318]

To NATALIA NIKOLAEVNA GONCHAROVA
About (not later than) October 29, 1830.
From Boldino to Moscow.

Dear Miss Natalia Nikolaevna, I do not know how to scold in French, so permit me to speak to you in Russian,[1] and you, my angel, answer me, even in Finnish, so long as you answer. I received your letter of October 1 on the 26th. It pained me for many reasons: in the first place, because it was exactly twenty-five days on the way; (2) because on October 1 you were still in Moscow, which had already been plague-infected for a long time; (3) because you had not received my letters; (4) because your letter was shorter than a calling card; (5) because apparently you are angry with me, whereas I am a most unhappy critter, even without that. Where are you? How are you? I have been writing to Moscow, but I get no answer. My brother does not write me,[2] assuming that his letters as usual are of no interest to me. In the time of the plague it is a different matter; I am glad of a pierced letter;[3] you know that he is at least alive—even that is good. If you are in Kaluga,[4] I shall come to you via Penza; if you are in Moscow, i.e., in the Moscow village, then I shall come to you via Vyatka, Arkhangelsk, and Petersburg.[5] I swear I am not joking—but write and tell me where you are, and address your letter to the Lukoyanov District, the village Abramovo, for forwarding to Boldino. It will reach me quicker. Farewell. I kiss your mother's little hands; I send a deep bow to your sisters.

[319]
To NATALIA NIKOLAEVNA GONCHAROVA
November 4, 1830. From Boldino to Moscow.
(In French)

On the 9th you were still in Moscow! My father writes me this; he also writes that my marriage is broken off. Isn't that enough to make me hang myself? I shall tell you once more that there are fourteen quarantines between Lukoyanov and Moscow. Enough said? Now I am going to tell you an anecdote. One of my friends was paying court to a pretty woman. One day when he comes to her house, he finds on her table an album which is unfamiliar to him. He wishes to look at it. Madame throws herself onto it and snatches it away from him; sometimes we men are as full of curiosity as you fair ladies are. My friend employs all his eloquence, all the resources of his wit, in order to get the album returned to him. Madame stands firm; he is obliged to forgo it. Some time afterward the poor little woman dies. My friend is present at her funeral, and he comes to console the poor husband. Together they rummage in the late departed's desk. My friend catches sight of the mysterious album. He seizes it, he opens it. It was all blank, with the exception of a single sheet on which were written these four bad verses of *The Prisoner of the Caucasus*:

> *Ne dolgo ženskuju ljubov'*
> *Pečalit xladnaja razluka,*
> *Projdet ljubov', nastanet skuka,*[1]

etc. . . . Now let us talk of something else. When I say let us talk of other things, I mean let's get back to the point. Aren't you ashamed to have remained on the Nikitskaya during the plague? It's all right for your neighbor Adrian,[2] who has profitable deals to make. But Natalia Ivanovna, but for you! Really, I do not understand you. I do not know how to get to you. I believe Vyatka is still free. In that case I shall go that way. Write me, however, to *Abramovo dlja dostavlenija v Boldino*.[3] Your letters will always reach me.

Farewell; God protect you. Tell your mother that I am at her feet.

November 4.

My respects to all the family.

[320]

To ANTON ANTONOVICH DELVIG

November 4, 1830. From Boldino to Petersburg.

I am sending you, Baron, my vassal's tribute, the floral by name,[1] for the reason that it is being paid in November, the very time for flowers. I report to you, my master, that the present autumn has been procreative, and that if your humble vassal does not croak of the Saracen's epizootic, the cholera by name, brought back by the Crusaders, i.e., the Volga boatmen, then in your castle *The Literary Gazette* the songs of the troubadours will not become silent the whole year round. My dear fellow, I have written a world of polemical articles, but not receiving journals I have fallen behind the age, and I do not know what is going on—or which one should be throttled, Polevoy or Bulgarin. My father does not write me anything about you. And that disturbs me, for all the same I am his son, i.e., mistrustful and spleeny (what do you think of the word?). Tell Pletnev that he would cover me with kisses if he saw my autumnal industriousness.[2] Farewell, my dear fellow; by the next post I shall perhaps send you something more.

November 4.

I am living in the village, as on an island, surrounded by quarantines. I am waiting for favorable weather to get married and finally get to Petersburg—but I still don't even dare think of that.

[321]
To Mikhail Petrovich Pogodin
The beginning of November, 1830. From Boldino to Moscow.

By *The Moscow Record*, the only periodical which is reaching me, I see, dear and honored Mikhaylo Petrovich, that you have not abandoned the Mother of us all.[1] Twice I tried to break through to you, but quarantines have again thrown me back onto my unendurable little island, from which I stretch forth my hands to you and cry out in a great voice.[2] Send me a living word, for God's sake. Nobody is writing me a thing. They think the cholera has grabbed me or that I have pined to death in quarantine. I do not know where or how my fiancée is. Do you know; can you find out? For God's sake find out and write and tell me: to the Lukoyanov District, the village Abramovo, for forwarding to the village Boldino. If you would send me, enclosed with this, your *Veche* tragedy,[3] you would be my benefactor, my true benefactor. I would give you a detailed critique at my leisure. But as it is I am not doing anything; there is not even anybody to scold with. God grant health to Polevoy! His second volume[4] is with me, and it is my solace. I am sending from my Patmos an Apocalyptical song.[5] Publish it wherever you please, even in *The Record*—but I ask and demand of you in the name of our friendship not to reveal my name to *anybody*. If the Moscow censorship won't pass it, send it to Delvig, but likewise without my name, and copied out in a hand other than mine. . . . But I haven't said the most important thing: the term of my debt[6] is next month, but I do not dare hope to pay you. It is not I that am telling the lie, and not my purse that is lying—the cholera is lying, and the five quarantines separating us are adding their own lie. Farewell; stay alive.

How is my brother?

[322]
To Peter Andreevich Vyazemsky
November 5, 1830. From Boldino to Moscow.

I am setting off, my dear fellow, for plague-infected Moscow—having received the news that my fiancée has not left there. What kind of a heart is hers? Her breast is girt with hard oak bark, with triple damask steel, like Horace's navigator.[1] She has written me a very

sweet, though unimpassioned letter. Brother Lev let me know about
you, about Baratynsky, and about the cholera. . . . Finally I have
received news from you, too. You say that a bad turn has come for
us. Right! Don't you see that the cards being dealt us are all stacked?
But we keep on playing! Not a single card to the left, but all the same
we keep coming for more. It would serve us right if we end up
naked as the suit of diamonds.[2] I have written a thing or two here.[3]
But it is vexing that I have not been receiving any journals. I have
been in the mood to scold, and I would have laid onto them in their
own manner. In polemics, shall we say, you and I, there is a drop of
our honey.[4] I am glad that you have taken up the Fonvizin.[5] Whatever you will say about him or apropos of him will all be good,
because it will get said. There is no reason for you to be worried
about the truth (i.e., about preciseness in applying the truth); the
bullet will seek out the guilty. All your literary surveys are full of
these random bullets. Just you collect your critical articles and see
what a cross-fire will arise. Shall we see each other someday? Did I
go so far into the Nizhny wilds that I myself don't know how to get
out? It's just like a fir cone up your a——; it went in fine, but it's
rough coming out. By the way, I don't have any news of naked Liza.[6]
Or of Polignac, either. Who's paying for the champagne, you or I?[7]
A pity, if I am. If I had known that I would stay here so long, I
would have started up a correspondence with her, with deep kisses
and stimulants,[8] i.e., by every post a sheet filled on both sides—and
in the Novgorod wilds I would have been reading *Le Temps* and
Le Globe. What do you think of the Sovereign? Fine fellow! The
first thing you know he will forgive our convicts.[9] God grant him
health. God grant all of you health, friends. Meanwhile there is no
use wishing for anything better. Here the peasants call their masters
by the title Your Health; the title is an enviable one, without which
all others mean nothing.

November 5.

[323]
To Praskovia Alexandrovna Osipova
November 5(?), 1830. From Boldino to Opochka.
(In French)
In the solitude of Boldino, Madame, I have received your two

letters together. In order to know the worth of a friendly voice and of a few lines penned by someone we cherish, one must have been completely alone, as I am now. I am very glad that my father, thanks to you, has borne up well under the news of the death of Vasily Lvovich.[1] I was very much afraid, I confess to you, for his health and nerves, which are so weakened. He has written me several letters in which fear of the Cholera appears to have taken the place of sorrow. This accursed Cholera! Shouldn't one call it a bad joke on the part of Fate? Try as I may, it is impossible for me to reach Moscow; I have been surrounded by a whole chain of quarantines, and on all sides at that, for the province of Nizhny is the very center of the plague. However, I am departing day after tomorrow,[2] and God knows how many months it will take me to make the 350 miles, which I usually cover in 48 hours.

You ask me, Madame, what I mean by the word *always*, in one phrase of my letter. I do not remember, Madame. But in any case the word can be only the expression and the motto of my feelings for you and all your family. I am sorry if my phrase appeared to have an unfriendly sense—and I beseech you to correct it. What you tell me about sympathy is very true and very nicely put. We sympathize with the unfortunate through a kind of egoism; we see that, after all, we are not the only unfortunate ones. To sympathize with happiness presupposes a very noble and a very disinterested soul. But happiness . . . is a great *perhaps*, as Rabelais said of paradise or eternity.[3] I am an Atheist as regards happiness; I do not believe in it, and only when I am near my good friends am I a little skeptical.

As soon as I am in Petersburg, you will receive, Madame, all that I have published. But here I have no way to send you anything. I greet you, Madame, with all my heart, you and all your family. Farewell; good-by. Please believe in my complete devotion.

A. Pushkin.

[324]

To NATALIA NIKOLAEVNA GONCHAROVA
November 18, 1830. From Boldino to Moscow.
(In French)
Boldino, November 18.

Again in Boldino, still in Boldino. When I learned that you had not left Moscow, I took post horses and set out. When I arrived at the main road, I saw that you were right, that the fourteen quarantines are only outposts—that there are only three real quarantines. I ride up boldly to the first (at Sivasleyka, the province of Vladimir), the inspector demands my travel warrant, informing me that I shall have only six days of delay to put up with. Then he casts his eyes on the sheet.

[In Russian:]

"You are not traveling on government business?"

—"No, on my own most essential business."

"Then be so good as to go back onto the other road. Here nobody is permitted through."

—"Has it been long?"

"Why, about three weeks already."

—"And these governors, the swine, don't let it be known?"

"That's not our fault, sir."

—"Not your fault! And does that make it any easier for me?"

There is nothing I can do—I go back to Lukoyanov; I demand a certificate that I am going from a place that is not plague infected. The local marshal of the nobility does not know whether, after my trip, he can give me this certificate. I have written the governor, and while awaiting his answer, the certificate, and a new travel warrant, I myself am staying in Boldino and moping. [In French:] This is how I have made three hundred miles but have not budged from my lair.

That is not all: I have been hoping, on my return to here, to have at least some letters from you. But blessed if the drunkard of a postmaster at Murom didn't take it upon himself to mix up the mail, in such a way that Arzamas receives the mail for Kazan, Nizhny that for Lukoyanov, and so that your letter (if there is one from you) is now wandering about I don't know where, and God knows when it will reach me. I am completely discouraged, and since now we are in the fast (tell your Mama that I shall not forget this fast for a long time), no longer do I wish to hurry; I shall let things go, and I shall stay here with folded arms. My father keeps on writing that my marriage is broken off. One of these days he will perhaps inform me that you are married. . . . That's enough to make one lose his head. May Prince Shalikov[1] be blessed, who finally informs me that the cholera has abated. This is the only good news which has reached me in three months. Farewell, *moj angel*, stay well, don't marry Mr. Davydov,[2] and pardon my bad humor. Tell your Mama that I am at her feet; my best wishes to everybody. Farewell.

[325]

To Natalia Nikolaevna Goncharova
November 26, 1830. From Boldino to Moscow.
(In French)

From your letter of November 19 I see clearly that I must explain myself. I was going to leave Boldino on the 1st of October. On the preceding day I went twenty miles from my house to Princess Golitsyna's,[1] to find out the precise number of quarantines, the shortest route, etc. Since her estate is located on the highway, the Princess has taken it upon herself to keep correctly informed on these matters.

The next day, the 1st of October, on returning home, I received the news that the cholera has penetrated to Moscow, that the Emperor is there, and *that all the inhabitants have deserted it.* This last piece of news reassured me a little. Having been informed, however, that certificates were being issued for free passage, or, at least, for the shortest period of quarantine, I wrote to that effect to Nizhny. I was answered that the certificate would be delivered to me at Lukoyanov (inasmuch as Boldino is not infected). At the same time I was informed that *entry into and departure from Moscow are forbidden.* This last piece of news and especially the uncertainty of your location (I have not received a letter from anyone, from my brother, who doesn't care a fig about me, on down) are keeping me in Boldino. I feared or rather hoped that upon arriving in Moscow *I would not find you there,* and *I was sure* that even if I were permitted to get there, *I would not be allowed to leave.* Meanwhile the rumor was confirmed that Moscow was deserted, and that reassured me.

Suddenly I received a little letter from you, in which you inform me that you have not dreamed of leaving. . . . I take post horses; I arrive at Lukoyanov, where I am refused a travel permit under the pretext that I have been selected to inspect the quarantines of my district.[2] I decided to send a complaint to Nizhny and to continue my trip. When I arrived in the province of Vladimir, I found the highway closed, and that nobody knew anything, things are in such fine order here. I returned to Boldino, where I shall remain until I receive the travel permit and the certificate; that is to say, till God knows when.

So you see (if you still deign to believe me) that my stay here is involuntary, that I am not living at the Princess Golitsyna's, although I have paid her one visit, that my brother is trying to shift the blame when he says that he wrote me at the beginning of the cholera, and that you are in the wrong to make fun of me.

And now, I extend my greetings.

November 26.

Abramovo is not Princess Golitsyna's estate, as you suppose, but a station nine miles from Boldino. Lukoyanov is thirty-five miles away from it.

Since you apparently are indisposed to take me at my word, I am sending you two documents about my enforced detention.[3]

I have not told you half of all the vexations I have had to endure. But it was not for naught that I have come and hidden myself here. If I had not been in a bad humor when I came to the country, I would have returned to Moscow from the second station, where I learned that the cholera was ravaging Nizhny [Novgorod]. But at that time I didn't care to retrace my steps, and I wanted nothing better than the plague.

[326]

To ALEXEY NIKOLAEVICH VERSTOVSKY

The second half of November, 1830. From Boldino to Moscow.

Today I was supposed to leave Boldino.—The news that Arzamas is surrounded again with quarantines halted me for another day. It was necessary for thorough inquiries to be made, and to take steps to get a certificate. Where did you get polish for your nails? Tell Nashchokin to be sure to stay alive; first, because he is in debt to me; (2) because I hope to be in debt to him; (3) because if he should die there would be nobody in Moscow for me to speak a living word to, i.e., an intelligent and friendly one. And so let him bathe in chlorinated water, let him drink mint—and in accordance with Count Zakrevsky's command,[1] let him not fall into despondency (to accomplish this, it would not be a bad idea to get into a quarrel with Pavlov,[2] as the person inducing despondency).

You cannot imagine how unpleasant it is to receive pierced letters: they are so rough that you can't wipe yourself with them—you would scratch up your *anus*.

[327]

To MIKHAIL PETROVICH POGODIN
The end of November, 1830. From Boldino to Moscow.

I again made an attempt to get to you; I rode up to Sevasleyka (the first quarantine). But at the barrier the station master, when he saw that I was traveling on my own most essential needs, would not let me through, and he chased me back to my Boldino. What is to be done? As consolation I found your letters and *Marfa*. I read it twice without putting it down. Hurrah! I was afraid, I confess, that the first impression might weaken afterwards; but no—I am still of the same opinion: *Marfa* has a European, a high merit. I shall analyze it as extensively as I can. For me this will be real study and pleasure. There is one rub: the style and language. You are endlessly incorrect. And you treat the language the way Ioann did Novgorod.[1] There is a multitude of errors in grammar—of truncations, shortened forms—contrary to the spirit of the language. But do you know what? Even this rub is no rub. More freedom must be given our language (of course, in keeping with its spirit). And your freedom is more to my liking than our prim correctness. Will your *Marfa* appear soon? I am not sending you any observations (specific ones), because you would not have time to change what needs changing. Leave that till the next edition. Meanwhile I shall tell you that only one place seemed anti-dramatic to me: Boretsky's conversation with Ioann: Ioann does not preserve his majesty (I don't mean in the manner of the speech, but in his relationship toward the traitor). Boretsky (though a Novgorodian) is on too familiar terms with him; he might have bargained thus perhaps with a boyar of Ioann's, but not with Ioann himself. Your heart is not well disposed toward Ioann. Though you developed his policy dramatically (that is, intelligently, in lively manner, profoundly), you were not able to add to it the captivating quality of your feeling—you were impelled even to make him express himself in a somewhat high-flown style. This is my chief criticism. The remainder . . . it will be necessary to praise the remainder to the accompaniment of the pealing of Ivan the Great,[2] which your most humble sexton will carry out with all zeal.

A.P.

How charming the scene of the ambassadors is! How well you have understood Russian diplomacy! And the Veche? and the Novgorod governor? and Prince Shuysky? and the independent princes? I tell you that all these merits are SHAKESPEAREAN! . . .

About the style I shall make only brief mention, leaving it up to the journals, which will probably raise a hullabaloo (and with reason), and you heed them. But I shall send a detailed interlinear critique for you. Farewell, good-by. My greetings to Yazykov.

[328]

To NATALIA NIKOLAEVNA GONCHAROVA

About (not later than) December 1, 1830.

From Platava to Moscow.

(In French)

Here is another document[1]—please turn the sheet over.

[On the second page]

I have been stopped at the quarantine of Platava.[2] They are not letting me through, because I am going by *perekladnaja*,[3] my own carriage having broken down. I beseech you to make my sad situation known to Prince Dmitry Golitsyn—and to beg him to exert his influence for me to be allowed to enter Moscow. With all my heart I greet you, as well as Mama and all the family. A few days ago I wrote you a letter[4] which was a little harsh—but that was because I was not in my right mind. Forgive my having done it, for I repent. Here I am 75 versts from you, and God knows whether I shall see you in 75 days.

P.S. Or else send me a carriage or a calash, in my name, to the quarantine at Platava.

[329]

To NATALIA NIKOLAEVNA GONCHAROVA

December 2, 1830. From Platava to Moscow.

(In French)

You need not trouble to send me a calash;[1] I had been incorrectly informed. Here I am in quarantine, with the prospect of remaining prisoner for 14 days—after which I hope to be at your feet.

Write me, I beseech you, to the quarantine at Platava. I fear that I may have angered you. You would pardon me if you knew all the unpleasantnesses which I have had on account of this plague. At the moment when I was about to depart, at the beginning of October, I was named inspector of the district—a responsibility which I definitely would have accepted, if I had not been informed at the same time that there was cholera in Moscow. I had the utmost difficulty in getting the task off my hands. Then the news came that Moscow was surrounded, that entry to it was prohibited. Then came my unsuccessful attempts at escape, then came the news that you had not left Moscow—finally came your last letter, which has cast me into despair. How could you have the heart to write it? How could you believe that I was remaining confined at Nizhny on account of that damned Princess Golitsyna?[2] Do you know this Princess Golitsyna? She is as big, by herself, as all your family put together, including me. In truth, I am ready to be harsh again. But here I am in quarantine, and for the moment I desire nothing more. *Vot do čego my dožili—čto rady, kodga nas na dve nedeli posodjat pod arest v grjaznoj izbe k tkaču, na xleb da na vodu!*[3]

Nizhny is no longer surrounded—the quarantines were abolished in Vladimir on the eve of my departure. This did not prevent me from being detained in Sivasleyka, since the governor had neglected to send word to the inspector that the quarantine no longer existed. If you could imagine only a quarter of the confusion which these quarantines have entailed, you would not understand how one can get clear of them. Farewell. My respectful regards to Mama. I greet with all my heart your sisters and Mr. Sergey [Goncharov].

Platava. December 2.

[330]
To PETER ALEXANDROVICH PLETNEV
December 9, 1830. From Moscow to Petersburg.

Dear fellow! I have been in Moscow since December 5. I found my mother-in-law full of animosity toward me, and I had difficulty in coping with her, but thank God I managed it. I also had difficulty in getting through the quarantines—twice I left Boldino and returned. But thank God I coped with that, too. Send me as much money as you can. Here the loan office is closed, and I am in the shallows. What about *Godunov*?¹ I shall tell you (as a secret) that in Boldino I wrote as I have not written for a long time. Here is what I have brought along: the two *last* chapters of *Onegin*, the eighth and ninth,² completely ready for the press. A tale,³ written in ottava rima (of about 400 verses), which let's bring out *Anonyme*. Several dramatic scenes or little tragedies, to wit: *The Avaricious Knight*, *Mozart and Salieri*, *Feast in the Time of the Plague*, and *Don Juan*. In addition to that I have written about 30 small poems. Good? That is still not all. (Completely secret)⁴ I have written five prose tales⁵ which are making Baratynsky hee-haw and kick about—and which we shall also publish *Anonyme*. It will be impossible under my name, for Bulgarin would rail. And so Russian literature has been delivered up, head, neck, and ears, to Bulgarin and Grech! A pity—but what was Delvig thinking of? Why should he have wanted to print the sticky-sweet piece of that unendurable Delavigne?⁶ But all the same Delvig must justify himself to the Sovereign. He can prove that in his *Gazette* there has never been even a shadow, not only of rebelliousness, but even of ill will toward the government. Talk this over with him. Otherwise the writer-spies will gnaw him to death as a *baran* instead of as a *Baron*.⁷ Farewell, dear fellow, stay healthy— that's the most important thing.

December 9.

[331]

To ELIZAVETA MIKHAYLOVNA KHITROVO
December 9, 1830. From Moscow to Petersburg.
(In French)

Upon returning to Moscow, Madame, I found at Princess Dolgorukova's¹ a packet from you. It was newspapers from France and Dumas' tragedy²—all were new to me, unfortunate plague-stricken man of Nizhny. What a year! What events! The news of the Polish insurrection³ has bowled me over. So our old enemies, then, will be exterminated, and thus nothing Alexander [I] did will remain, because nothing is based on the real interests of Russia, and all rests only on considerations of personal vanity, of theatrical effect, etc. . . . Do you know the scathing words of the Marshal [Kutuzov] your

father? Upon his entry into Vilna, the Poles came to throw themselves at his feet. *Vstan'te*, he told them, *pomnite čto vy russkie.*⁴ We
can only pity the Poles. We are too powerful to hate them; the war
which is about to begin will be a war of extermination—or at least
so it ought to be. The love of one's native land, such as it can be in a
Polish soul, has always been a gloomy feeling. Look at their poet
Mickiewicz.⁵ All this saddens me very much. Russia has need of
repose. I have just journeyed over her. The sublime visit of the
Emperor has cheered Moscow up again,⁶ but he could not be
in all the sixteen plague-infected provinces at the same time. The
common people are downcast and irritated. The year 1830 is a sad
year for us. Let us hope—it is always a good thing to hope.

December 9.

[332]

To Elizaveta Mikhaylovna Khitrovo
December 11, 1830. From Moscow to Petersburg.
(In French)

My father has just sent me a letter which you addressed to me in
the country. You ought to be as assured of my gratitude as I am of
the interest which you are so kind as to take in my fate. Therefore,
Madame, I shall not speak of it to you. As for the news of the
engagement being broken off, it is false, and it is founded only on
my lengthy seclusion and my customary silence with my friends.
The thing that interests me at the moment is what is taking place
in Europe. The French elections,¹ you say, are in a good spirit.
What do you call a good spirit? I tremble that they may inject the
irrepressibility of victory in all that, and that Louis Philippe may
be only too much a blockhead-king. The new election law will place
on the deputies' benches a young, violent generation, little afraid of
the excesses of the republican revolution, of which it has learned only
from memoirs, and which it did not go through. I still am not
reading the periodicals, because I have not yet had the time to get my
bearings. As for the Russian periodicals, I confess that the suppression of *The Literary Gazette* has greatly astonished me.² Without
doubt the editor was in the wrong, in inserting the sticky-sweet piece
by Casimir Delavigne—but the periodical is so inoffensive, so dull
in its solemnity that it is read only by men of letters, and allusions to

politics are completely foreign to it. I am sorry for Delvig, a calm man, the head of a family, a completely estimable man, and nevertheless a man whom momentary folly or inadvertence could injure in the eyes of the government, and at a moment when he was soliciting a pension from His Majesty for his mother, the widow of General Delvig.[3]

Please, Madame, tell your daughters for me that I am at their feet, that their good will is more than precious to me, and allow me to remain at your feet.

December 11.

[333]
To Nikolay Stepanovich Alexeev
December 26, 1830. From Moscow to Bucharest.

My dear fellow, how unjust[1] are your reproaches of me for forgetfulness and laziness! From your letters I see, my dear fellow, that mine are not reaching you. I do not know whom to blame; I dare not blame anybody. But I have written you several times, or (not to tell a lie), twice—in verse and in prose, as it used to be in days of old.[2] You write that you have grown old, my eternally young one; I should like to have a look at your bald spot and wrinkles; probably you would not recognize me, either: I have grown sideburns, I have had my hair cut short—I have grown sedate and fat and flabby. But that is still nothing—I am engaged, my dear fellow, I am engaged and getting married! And I shall certainly let you know what married life is like. Write me, my dear fellow, about those places where you are now being bored but which have already become sweet to my imagination: About the banks of the Byk, about Kishinev, about the beautiful women, who have probably grown old, about the Jewish girl,[3] your dark-complexioned friend, whom you so long and so persistently concealed from me; about Pulkheria,[4] about Stamo,[5] about Khudobashev,[6] about Inzov, about Liprandi—in a word, about all who are dear to my memory, men and women, alive and dead. My stay in Bessarabia has not left, up to now, any kind of trace, either in poetry or prose. Give me time—I hope you will see sometime that I have not forgotten anything. Farewell, my joy. Do write to me.

December 26.

[334]
To Pavel Voinovich Nashchokin
December (after the 5th), 1830. In Moscow.
Right now I am going to pray to God,[1] and I have taken with me
my last hundred. Find out, please, where my Tatar[2] lives, and, if
you can, obtain a couple of thousand on your part.[3]

[335]
To Nikolay Alexeevich Polevoy
January 1, 1831. In Moscow.
Dear Sir, Nikolay Alexeevich,
I sincerely thank you for sending *The Telegraph*, a pleasant piece of
proof for me that our literary variance[1] has not completely shattered
our former relationships. I regret that I still cannot deliver to you
Boris Godunov, which has already come out but which I have not
received.
With genuine respect, I have the honor to be,
Dear Sir,
Your most humble servant,
January 1, 1831.   Alexander Pushkin.

[336]
To Peter Yakovlevich Chaadaev
January 2, 1831. In Moscow.
(In French)
Here, my friend, is the one of my works which I love the most.[1]
You will read it, since it is by me—and you will tell me your opinion
of it. Meanwhile, I embrace you, and I wish you a happy New Year.
January 2.

[337]
To Peter Andreevich Vyazemsky
January 2, 1831. From Moscow to Ostafievo.
January 2, 1831.
Your verses are charming[1]—I don't feel like giving them for an
almanac; rather, let's send them off to Delvig. The wagon train, the
pigs, and the brigadier are marvellously amusing. Yakovlev[2] is

publishing before Carnival the almanac *Pancake*. It will be a pity if his first pancake comes out a lump.[3] Won't you give "Wagon Train" to him, and "The Maiden's Dream" to Maximovich? Yakovlev is also a fine fellow in that he is exceptionally valorous and is ready to smear his pancake with Bulgarin's grease and Polevoy's caviar—send him your satirical articles, if you have any. Do you know what New Year presents I have received? A subscription for *The Telegraph* and a subscription for *The Telescope* "from the publishers as a mark of their sincere respect." What do you think of that? And in *The Bee* they are proposing peace to me, reproaching us (you and me) with indomitable enmity and eternal service to Nemesis.[4] All this is excellent; one thing is a pity—in my *Boris* the scenes with the common people have been left out, and also the French obscenity and that of the language of our fatherland, but it is strange, though, to read a lot that is printed. *The Northern Flowers* [*for* 1831] are somehow pale. What do you think of the jester Delvig, who himself wrote nothing the whole year round and who then published his almanac in the sweat of our faces?[5] In a few days I shall be at your place, and I shall bring the champagne with pleasure—I am glad that I am to furnish the bottle. I have become reconciled with Polignac.[6] His second imprisonment in Vincennes, the meridian inscribed on the floor of his prison, the reading of Walter Scott, all this is romantically touching—but all the same the hall of justice is right. I am dissatisfied with the speeches of the advocates—all of them are timid. Only Lamennais[7] could *aborder bravement la question*.[8] About Poland[9] there's not a peep to be heard. I have seen Chicherin's[10] letter to his father, where he stated that *il y a lieu d'espérer qui tout finira sans guerre*.[11] Here a certain person bet a bottle of Veuve Cliquot Ponsardin[12] against a thousand rubles that Warsaw will be taken without a shot. Denis [Davydov] is here. He has written an eloquent *Eloge* on Raevsky.[13] We are advising him to write his Life. Our Kireevsky is here.[14] I saw him last evening. Naked Liza has written me a desperate, political letter. The recent occurrences seem to have produced a powerful effect on Petersburg society. If I were a bachelor, I would make a trip there and back. I met the New Year with the gypsies and with Tanyusha,[15] the genuine drunken Tatiana. She sang a song, made up in the gypsy camp, to the air *The Sleigh Came*:[16]

Davydov[17] and his nostrils,	D—Mityusha
Vyazemsky and his spectacles,	V—Petrusha
Gagarin[18] and his moustaches,	G—Fedyusha.

They frightened the wenches
And chased them all away, etc.

Do you know this song? *Addio*; my greetings to all your folks. Good-by.

[338]

To Mikhail Petrovich Pogodin
January 3, 1831. In Moscow.

Here is *Boris* for you. Do me the favor of delivering a copy to Nikodim Nadoumko,[1] who has sent me a subscription for *The Telescope*. We live in days of overturns—or turnabouts[2] (which is better?). They write me from Petersburg that *Godunov* has been having success. That's another wonder to me. Bring out your *Marfa*.

The copy for Nadezhdin was taken from me just now; tomorrow I shall send another.

[339]

To Peter Alexandrovich Pletnev
January 7, 1831. From Moscow to Petersburg.

What is the matter with you, my friend? Since you gave me a scolding in September for my spleen,[1] I haven't heard a peep out of you. I received the money (2000).[2] I have seen the charming edition of *Boris*. I have read your epistle to Gnedko [Gnedich], but I have not read his answer[3]—I know that you are alive, but still there are no letters from you. The Governor-General[4] hasn't forbidden you to have correspondence with me, has he? I wouldn't be surprised! You aren't angry, are you? I see no reason for you to be. You answer me, or else I shall be uneasy.

Now let's talk about business. My dear fellow, I have seen *The Flowers*. A strange thing, an incomprehensible thing![5] Delvig did not put a single line of his own in it. He has treated us the way a squire does his peasants. We toil—but he sits in the boat and berates us. That is not good and not reasonable. He opens our eyes for us, and we see that we are being made fools of. A strange thing, an incomprehensible thing! Poor Glinka works like a hired hand, but nothing worth-while comes of it. It seems to me that he has gone off his head with grief. Whom did he take the notion to ask to be god-parent of his child![6] Just imagine into what kind of a position he will put the priest and the deacon, the godmother, the midwife, and the godfather himself, whom they will make to renounce the devil, to spit, blow, to unite to Christ, and do other such stuff. Nashchokin assures us that everybody was spoiled by the late Tsar,[7] who stood godfather to everybody's children. Even now I can't get over Glinka's audacity. A strange thing, an incomprehensible thing!

They write me that my *Boris* is having a great success: a strange thing, an incomprehensible thing! At least I certainly did not expect it. What is the reason for it? The reading of Walter Scott? The voice of connoisseurs, of which elect there are so few? The clamor of my friends? The opinion of the Court?—However that may be, I do not understand the success of my tragedy where you are. In Moscow, is it different! Here they are regretting that I have completely, completely collapsed, that my tragedy is an imitation of Victor Hugo's *Cromwell*,[8] that unrhymed poetry is not poetry,[9] that the Pretender should not have revealed his secret to Marina so imprudently, that on his part this is very heedless and irrational—and similar profound critical observations. I am awaiting the translations and the judgment of the Germans,[10] but I am not disturbed about the French. In *Boris* they will seek political applications to the Warsaw uprising, and they will say to me, like our people, "For goodness sake, sir! . . ." It will be interesting to see the response of our Schlegels,[11] of whom only Katenin knows his business. The others are Inzov parrots or mag-pies which lisp only the often-repeated-to-them m——- f—— s.o.b.[12] Farewell, my angel. My greetings to you; my greetings also to all of you. By the way, Baratynsky's long poem is marvellous.[13] *Addio.*

January 7.

[340]

To PETER ANDREEVICH VYAZEMSKY
Between January 10 and 13, 1831. From Moscow to Ostafievo.
I shall try to take a leave of absence[1] and come for your name day. But I do not promise. My brother will probably come. [F. I.]

Tolstoy is intending to go to see you. Yesterday I saw Prince Yusupov[2] and carried out your commission. I questioned him about Fonvizin, and this is what I obtained: He knew Fonvizin very well and for some time lived in the same house with him. *C'était un autre Beaumarchais pour la conversation. . . .*[3] He knows of a world of bon mots of his, but he can't recall them. Meanwhile he told me the following: Maykov the tragedian,[4] meeting Fonvizin, asked him, stammering, as he usually did: "Have you seen my *Agriopa?*"— "I've seen it."—"What would you say about this tragedy?"—"I would say that *Agriopa* is a s——a——." Witty and unexpected! Isn't it? Put this in the biography, and I shall say thank you. As for *The Telescope* (another *Agriopa*), I don't have it at the moment—so write Salaev[5] to send you all this rubbish. I shall send your article about Pushkin to Delvig—why should you feed others' children?[6] Your own are hungry. However, I have grudgingly given Maximovich "The Wagon Trains."[7] I send my greetings to the Princess [Vera Vyazemskaya] and thank her for her kind invitation. About Poland nothing is to be heard. In England, they say, there is a revolt. The rabble have burned down Wellington's house.[8] In Paris it is quiet. In Moscow, too.[9]

[341]
To PETER ALEXANDROVICH PLETNEV
January 13, 1831. From Moscow to Petersburg.

Send me, my dear fellow, some twenty copies of *Boris* for the Moscow crafty rogues; otherwise I shall go broke buying it at Shiryaev's.

My dear fellow, here is my life's plan for you: I am getting married this month; I shall live half a year in Moscow; in the summer I shall come to you. I dislike Moscow life. Here you live, not as you wish, but as aunties wish. My mother-in-law is just such an aunty. It's quite a different thing in Petersburg! I'll start living in clover, as a petty bourgeois,[1] independently, and taking no thought of what Maria Alexevna will say.[2] What about our *Gazette*? We must take thought of it. Recently it has been very torpid; it cannot be otherwise: Russian literature is mirrored in it. In it recently there was talk of nobody but Bulgarin; thus it must be: in Russia only Bulgarin is writing. Here is the text for a fine philippic. If I were not lazy, and were not betrothed, and were not very kind, and could read and write, I would write a literary survey every week. But nothing doing—I don't have the patience, nor the fury, nor the time, nor the inclination. We shall see, though.

Money, money, that's the most important thing. Send me some money. And I shall tell you thanks. And just why don't you write me, you shameless fellow?

January 13.

[342]

To ALEXANDER KHRISTOFOROVICH BENKENDORF
January 18, 1831. From Moscow to Petersburg.

Dear Sir, Alexander Khristoforovich,

With the feeling of most profound gratitude I was honored to receive the well-disposed comment of the Sovereign Emperor, with regard to my historical drama. Written in the past reign, *Boris Godunov* is obligated for its appearance not only to the private protection which the Sovereign has honored me with, but also to the freedom which the Monarch boldly granted to Russian writers at such a time and in such circumstances when any other government would have tried to repress and fetter the publishing of books.[1]

Permit me to thank Your High Excellency also with all my heart, as the voice of the Highest's good will and as a man who has always taken such indulgent interest in me.

With the most profound respect and complete devotion, I am,

Dear Sir,

Your High Excellency's
Most humble servant,
January 18, 1831.   Alexander Pushkin.
Moscow.

[343]

To PETER ANDREEVICH VYAZEMSKY
January 19, 1831. From Moscow to Ostafievo.

Yesterday we received grievous news from Petersburg—Delvig has died of the putrid fever.[1] Today I am going to [M. A.] Saltykov's; he probably already knows everything. Leave *Adolphe*[2] with me—in a few days I shall send you the necessary observations.

[344]

To Peter Alexandrovich Pletnev
January 21, 1831. From Moscow to Petersburg.

What shall I say to you, my dear fellow? I received the terrible news on Sunday.[1] The next day it was confirmed. Yesterday I went to [M. A.] Saltykov's to announce everything to him—and I could not bring myself to do it. In the evening I received your letter. It's sad, agonizing. This is the first death I have ever wept over. Karamzin near the end was foreign to me; as a Russian, I was deeply sorry about his death. But nobody in the world was closer to me than Delvig. Of all the ties of childhood he alone remained in view—our poor little band was collected around him. Without him we are as though orphaned. Count on your fingers how many there are of us: you, I, Baratynsky, and that is all.

Yesterday I spent the day with Nashchokin, who has been hard hit by his death—we spoke of him, calling him the deceased Delvig, and this epithet was just as strange as it was terrible. Nothing can be done about it! Let us consent to it. The deceased Delvig. So be it.

Baratynsky is ill with grief. It is not all that easy to knock me off my feet. Stay well—and let's try to stay alive.

[345]

To Elizaveta Mikhaylovna Khitrovo
January 21, 1831. From Moscow to Petersburg.
(In French)

You are quite right, Madame, in reproaching me with my stay in Moscow. It is impossible to avoid becoming stupefied here. You know the epigram against companionship with a boring man:

On n'est pas seul, on n'est pas deux.[1]

This is the epigraph of my existence. Your letters are the only ray which can reach me from Europe.

You remember the good old days when the periodicals were dull? We used to complain about it. Most certainly, if we are dissatisfied today, we are hard to please.

The question of Poland is easy to decide. Nothing can save her except a miracle, and there are no miracles. Her safety is in despair, *una salus nullam sperare salutem*,[2] which is nonsense. Only a convulsive and general exaltation could offer the Poles any chance whatever. Hence the young people are right, but the moderates will triumph, and we shall have a province of Warsaw, which ought to have been done thirty-three years ago. Of all the Poles, only Mickiewicz interests me. He was in Rome at the beginning of the revolt; I fear that he may have come to Warsaw, to be present at the last crises of his fatherland.

I am dissatisfied with our official articles. In them predominates a tone of irony which ill becomes power. What good there is in them, that is to say the candor, comes from the Emperor; what bad, that is to say the bragging and the pugilistic posture, comes from his secretary.[3] There is no need to inflame the Russians against Poland. Our opinion has been completely decided for the last eighteen years.

The French have almost ceased to interest me. The revolution ought to be over with, but every day new seeds of it are sown. Their king,[4] with his umbrella under his arm, is far too bourgeois. They wish a republic, and they will have it—but what will Europe say, and where will they find a Napoleon?

Delvig's death gives me the spleen. Independently of his fine talent, he had an excellently organized mind and a soul of an uncommon stamp. He was the best among us. Our ranks are commencing to thin out.

I greet you very sadly, Madame.

January 21.

[346]

To Peter Alexandrovich Pletnev
January 31, 1831. From Moscow to Petersburg.

I have just now received the 2000 rubles, my benefactor.[1] *Satis est, domine, satis est.*[2] For this year I shall not need any more money. Give Sofia Mikhaylovna [Delvig] the remaining 4000—and I shall not disturb you any more.

Poor Delvig! Let us honor his memory with *The Northern Flowers*[3] —but I would be sorry if this would be a loss for Somov. He was sincerely attached to him—and the death of our friend can scarcely be other than hardest on him: the feelings of the soul weaken and change; the necessities of life never doze off.

Baratynsky is planning to write Delvig's life.[4] We shall all help him with our recollections, shan't we? I knew him in the Lyceum—was the witness of the first, unperceived development of his poetic soul—and of his talent, to which we have not yet done proper justice. With him I read Derzhavin and Zhukovsky—with him I discussed everything *that agitates the soul, that oppresses the heart.*[5] In a word, I know his first youth well, but you and Baratynsky know his early maturity better. You were the witnesses of his soul's full development. Let us write, as a threesome, the life of our friend, a life which was rich, not in romantic adventures, but in beautiful feelings, in clear pure reason, and in hopes. Give me your answer to this.

I see by your letter that Tumansky is in Petersburg—embrace him for me. Love him, if you don't love him already. In him there is much that is excellent, notwithstanding certain minor traits of a Little Russian character.[6]

What kind of an idea was it that came to Gnedich to send verses of his to *The Northern Bee*? I am glad Grech refused—how could one inscribe an anthological epitaph in a privy? And what is there in common between the poet Delvig and Faddey [Bulgarin], cleaner-out of police s——houses?[7]

My dear fellow, another request: make a trip to St. Florent's (i.e., to his successor's)[8] and pay him off for me. I owe him, as I remember, 1000 rubles. Excuse me to him—I was about to forget him completely.

How is the [Delvig's] widow?

January 31.

[347]

To Elizaveta Mikhaylovna Khitrovo
About (not later than) February 9, 1831.
From Moscow to Petersburg.
(In French)

You are very fortunate, Madame, to have a soul capable of understanding everything and of interesting itself in everything. The emotion you reveal in speaking of the death of a poet, in the midst of

Europe's convulsions, is a great proof of this universality of feeling. If the widow of my friend were in a state of distress, believe me, Madame, I would have had recourse only to you. But Delvig has left two brothers,[1] of whom he was the only support: couldn't it be arranged for them to enter the corps of pages? . . .

We are waiting to see what fate will decide. The Emperor's most recent proclamation[2] is admirable. It seems that Europe will merely keep its eyes on us. A great principle has just arisen from the womb of the revolutions of 1830: the principle of non-intervention;[3] it will replace that of legitimacy, which has been violated from one end of Europe to the other. Canning's system was not of this latter type.[4]

So M. de Mortemart[5] is in Petersburg, and one more agreeable and historical man is in your society. How I long to be back there again, and how sick and tired I am of Moscow and its Tatar nonentity!

You tell me of the success of *Boris Godunov*: really, I cannot believe it. Success did not enter into my calculations at all—when I wrote it. That was in 1825. And Alexander's [I] death, the unhoped-for favor of the present Emperor, his magnanimity and his so generous and so liberal way of looking at things were necessary—before my tragedy could be published. Besides, what good there is in it is so little designed to impress the respectable public (that is to say, the rabble that judges us), and it is so easy to criticize me rationally, that I thought to give pleasure only to fools, who might be witty at my expense. But in this lowly world we must take the bitter with the sweet, and *delenda est Varsovia*.[6]

[348]

To Nikolay Ivanovich Krivtsov
February 10, 1831. In Moscow.

I am sending you, my dear friend, my favorite work.[1] Once upon a time you pampered my first attempts—be well disposed to my more mature works, too. What are you doing in your solitude? This autumn I was not far from you.[2] My whole being craved to see you and chatter about old times—quarantines prevented me. As things are, God knows when and where fate will bring us together again. It is not so easy for us to get around. You are minus a leg,[3] and I am married.

Married—or almost. Everything you could say to me in favor of bachelor life and against marriage—all this I have already thought over. I have calmly weighed the advantages and disadvantages of the state I am choosing. My youth has passed tumultuously and fruitlessly. Up to now I have lived other than the way people usually live. There has been no happiness for me. *Il n'est de bonheur que dans les voies communes.*⁴ I am past thirty. At thirty, people usually get married —I am acting as people usually do, and I shall probably not regret it. Besides, I am marrying without rapture, without childish enchantment. The future presents itself to me not as all rosy, but in its austere nakedness. Trials and tribulations will not astonish me: they are included in my family budget. Any joy will be something I did not expect.

Today I have the *spleen*⁵—I am breaking off my letter so as not to pass my anguish on to you; you have enough of your own. Write me on the Arbat, to the house of Khitrovo.⁶ A few days ago I received via Vyazemsky a letter of yours written in 1824. I thank you, but I am not answering it.

February 10.

[349]

To Peter Alexandrovich Pletnev
About (not later than) February 16, 1831.
From Moscow to Petersburg.

In a few days I am getting married,¹ and I am presenting to you my financial report. I have mortgaged my 200 souls. I got 38,000²— and here is the way it has been distributed: 11,000 to my mother-in-law,³ who wanted her daughter to have a dowry without fail—write it as lost; 10,000 to Nashchokin, to rescue him from a bad situation: sure money. There remains 17,000 for settling down and a year's living. In June I shall be with you, and I shall start living *en bourgeois*, but here it is impossible to cope with the aunties.⁴ Their demands are stupid and ridiculous—but nothing can be done about it. Now do you understand what the dowry means and why I was angry? I can afford to take a wife who has nothing, but I cannot afford to go into debt for her rags. However, I am stubborn, and I had to insist on having the wedding at least. There's nothing else to do: I shall have to print my tales.[5] I'll send them to you next week, and let's print them by Easter.

How is the Baroness [Delvig]? I have written Khitrovo about Delvig's brothers.[6] Ask her how her affairs are, and whether my father has paid the debt to Delvig.[7] Won't she sell me the portrait of me?[8] They write me that her health is bad, but she writes Mikhail Alexandrovich [Saltykov][9] that she is well. Who is right? Why haven't you answered me about the life of Delvig? Baratynsky is seriously thinking about it. Your article about him is excellent.[10] The more I read it, the more I like it. But details are needed—an account of his opinions—anecdotes, a full-scale critique of his poems, etc.—— ——

Letter 271

1. Vyazemsky had asked an acquaintance to speak of Pushkin in the presence of Mme. Goncharova and her daughter Natalia; both spoke favorably of Pushkin and asked that he be given their regards.

Letter 272

1. Pushkin had formally proposed for the hand of Mlle. Goncharova on April 6 and had been tentatively accepted, with reservations because of his having no estate of his own, and because of his doubtful position vis-à-vis the police. As the result of the present letter, Pushkin was able to remove the first of these reservations, when his father, along with his parental blessing, gave him two hundred souls in the village of Kistenevo (not far from Boldino), in the Alatyrsky District, Nizhny Novgorod Province. Pushkin's next letter (Letter 273) was to Benkendorf, requesting that the Goncharovs' second objection be removed. When this petition was likewise successful, the official betrothal took place, on May 6. But in spite of Pushkin's eagerness for immediate marriage, the wedding was postponed several times and occurred nine months later, on February 18, 1831.

The end of the letter has not been preserved.

Letter 273

1. Nicholas I and Benkendorf had seen Natalia N. Goncharova while in Moscow in 1830.

2. Pushkin received in answer a letter from Benkendorf, along with permission to show it to whomever he wished, to the effect that Benkendorf's observing and advising Pushkin was from the Tsar's "paternal solicitude," that he was not then and never had been under police surveillance, and giving him permission to publish *Boris Godunov* under his "own responsibility."

3. The Decembrist Uprising of December 14, 1825.

4. Pushkin's proposal and the "consent" of the Goncharovs were kept secret until the official betrothal on May 6. See Letter 272, and note.

Letter 274

1. Countess Daria Fedorovna Ficquelmont (1804-1863), daughter of Elizaveta Mikhaylovna Khitrovo. Both she and her mother had famous literary salons in Petersburg. Her husband was the Austrian ambassador to Russia.

Letter 275

1. The novel *The Dead Ass and the Guillotined Woman* (1829) by Jules Gabriel Janin.

2. Victor Hugo's *The Last Day of a Condemned Man* (1829).

3. Pushkin, at the end of 1829, wrote his so-called "Don Juan" list in the album of Elizaveta N. Ushakova; this list includes thirty-seven names. Pushkinists have used much ingenuity in attempting to identify all of them. Natalia N. Goncharova's name appears last in the first column, consisting apparently of the more serious loves of Pushkin.

4. Pushkin mortgaged his Kistenovo serfs for 11,428.58 silver rubles in 1831.

5. "Female sponsor at a wedding."

Letter 276

1. Pushkin's letter was one of fifteen postscripts by friends of Shevyrev to a letter of Pogodin's.

Letter 277

1. That is, praises of Natalia N. Goncharova.

2. Vyazemsky was an admirer of Countess Ficquelmont at this time; he was serving in the Department of Finance, of which the Minister was Count Egor Frantsevich Kankrin (1774-1845).

3. Pushkin had just published a devastating, transparently veiled attack of Bulgarin in *The Literary Gazette* in an article about the *Memoirs* (1829) of Vidocq, notorious French detective and police spy.

4. That is, their journals, *Galatea* and *The Ladies' Journal*, respectively, both of which published news about ladies' fashions.

5. Third edition, 1830.

6. Nicholas I.

Letter 278

1. See letter 280.

2. Afanasy Nikolaevich Goncharov; the estate was Polotnyany Zavod ("Linen Factory"), in the province of Kaluga, which his own grandfather had established and which had made him wealthy.

3. Though Pushkin was impatient for the marriage to take place before the fast of St. Peter, which in 1830 began on June 1, it did not occur until the following February.

Letter 280

1. Pushkin had already cited Benkendorf's letter giving him permission to publish *Boris Godunov* under his "own responsibility," in Letter 278.

2. Maxim Yakovlevich Fon-Fok (1777-1831), chief subordinate of Benkendorf in the Third Division, the secret police.

3. Pushkin made several beginnings of a preface defending his "free, romantic, Shakespearean" approach to drama in *Boris Godunov*, but he never completed it. We have seen these principal ideas in Letters 139 and 248. Apparently Pushkin was thinking of making some general comments about critics and criticism in this preface, and this led him to speak of his desire to "crush" Bulgarin, whose most recent attacks on Pushkin had been an extremely unfavorable review (1830) of the seventh chapter of *Evgeny Onegin*, and an announcement containing a scarcely veiled attack on the price of the separately appearing chapters of Pushkin's novel in verse.

4. The review of *Evgeny Onegin*, chapter VII (see note 3).

5. They were published in the form of the "program" of a novel "The Real Vyzhigin," in which Pushkin used information about Bulgarin's previous life so as to make devastating references to Bulgarin and his novel *Ivan Vyzhigin*. Pushkin published these materials under the pseudonym Feofilakt Kosichkin in *The Telescope*.

6. See Letter 277.

7. Pletnev had proposed that Pushkin sell Smirdin the publication rights to his works for four years; Pletnev did not manage to persuade Smirdin to subtract a single month from the four years.

8. To kiss her hand.

9. Stepanida Alexandrovna Pletneva (ca. 1795-1839).

Letter 281
  1. Pushkin's future mother-in-law Natalia Ivanovna Goncharova. The new favor was permission to publish *Godunov*.

Letter 282
  1. Elizaveta M. Khitrovo's two daughters, Countesses Fiquelmont and Tizengauzen.

Letter 283
  1. Pushkin had lost at cards and was trying to borrow the money to pay the debt thus contracted. An entire series of letters, 283, 285, 288, 290, 291, 292, 293, 295, 296, 298, is concerned with this attempt to borrow money. It is published here as indicating the kind of joking Pushkin was capable of under these embarrassing circumstances.
  2. Pogodin's play *Marfa, the Novgorod Burgomaster's Wife* (1830).

Letter 284
  1. Victor Hugo's *Hernani* (1830); Sainte-Beuve's *La Vie, les poésies et les pensées de J. Delorme* (1829), and *Consolations* (1830).
  2. Nicholas I.
  3. "Papers, documents"—French transliteration of the Russian word.
  4. Neither Pushkin's means nor his pursuits had changed when he nevertheless, against his will, had conferred upon him the distinction of being a Kammerjunker, a court rank between Chamber-Page and Chamberlain, on January 1, 1834. Here Pushkin equates "Gentleman of the Chamber" with Kammerjunker.

Letter 285
  1. See Letter 283, and note 1.

Letter 286
  1 Pushkin paid a formal visit of several days' duration, to Natalia Nikolaevna Goncharova's relatives at Polotnyany Zavod in the second half of May, 1830.
  2. These two Kaluga members of the bourgeoisie walked the eleven miles to Polotnyany Zavod, in order to congratulate Pushkin upon his birthday and express their high regard for his poetry. An interesting insight into the difficulties and problems with regard to delivery of letters in Pushkin's day is connected with Antipin. In 1833, in Petersburg, Pushkin gave Antipin Letter 475 to deliver to Nashchokin in Moscow. When Antipin arrived in Moscow, Nashchokin was not to be found, and Antipin did not feel that he had the right to send the letter through the mail or give it to anyone else to deliver to Nashchokin; it was never delivered. Antipin was later a bookseller.

Letter 287
  1. Afanasy Nikolaevich Goncharov had inherited from his father a colossal statue of Catherine II; it had been ordered by her favorite, Prince Grigory Alexandrovich Potemkin (1739-1791), who, however, died before it was paid for. The statue was purchased by A. N. Goncharov's father and was to have been erected at Polotnyany Zavod in honor of Catherine II's visit there in 1775. However, it was never erected, and A. N. Goncharov conceived the idea of getting out of the statue the money that had been put in it, through Pushkin's connections, which he greatly overrated. The statue was not "deformed," but A. N. Goncharov thought it necessary to call the statue unsuccessful and promise to erect another before he could obtain permission to sell it. Pushkin obtained for A. N. Goncharov the permission to sell the statue; however, it was not

sold in Pushkin's time, for Goncharov was unable to realize the amount of money from it that he had hoped. Later it was sold and erected in Ekaterinoslav (now Dnepropetrovsk).

Letter 288
1. See Letter 283, and note 1.
2. Pogodin's *Marfa, the Novgorod Burgomaster's Wife.*

Letter 289
1. The street on which the Goncharovs' Moscow house was located. They normally spent winters there, and summers at their country estate of Polotnyany Zavod.
2. Apparently a servant of the Goncharovs'.
3. Pushkin's fears were that, though his engagement with Mlle. Goncharova had been publicly announced, it might nevertheless be broken off by her mother, who continued to raise objections of various kinds up to the wedding itself—and after. After Pushkin's visit to Polotnyany Zavod as the accepted fiancé of Mlle. Goncharova (see Letter 286, note 1), she remained there for a few days of additional visit.

Letter 290
1. Pushkin is still trying to borrow money (see Letter 283). Pogodin was trying to get it for him from Nikolay Ivanovich Nadezhdin (1804-1856), who wrote for *The Messenger of Europe* under the pen name of Nikodim Nadoumko, and who at this time was violently attacking Pushkin, who himself was answering in epigrams. Pushkin here has untranslatable multiple puns. The name Nadezhdin is related to the Russian word meaning "hope"; Nadezhdin's pen name Nadoumko is a Ukrainian form meaning an "adviser."

Letter 291
1. See Letter 283, and note 1.
2. Count Peter Alexandrovich Rumyantsev-Zadunaysky (1725-1796), field marshal, especially famed for his victory over the Turks at Kaluga in 1770, when he deployed his army in five *carrés* and withstood the Turks' offensive. The postscript apparently has to do with an article submitted for *The Moscow Messenger.*

Letter 292
1. See Letter 283, and note 1.

Letter 293
1. An untranslatable triple pun in the Russian (*tešit* "rough-hew," *češet* "scratch," *potešil* "gave comfort"). Nadezhdin had "rough-hewn" and "scratched" Pushkin in his articles in *The Messenger of Europe.* See Letters 283, 290, and notes.

Letter 294,
1. Pushkin was awaiting an answer to A. N. Goncharov's request for a loan from the government; the letter had been addressed to the Minister of Finance, E. F. Kankrin.
2. Of Catherine II. See Letter 287.
3. A. N. Goncharov promised to give his granddaughter Natalia Nikolaevna part of the village Katunka with 280 "souls," i.e., male peasants.

Letter 295
1. As so often in Pushkin, the biblical reference, from Luke 2:14, is humorous.
2. See Letter 283, and note 1.

Letter 296
   1. See Letters 283, 295, and notes.

Letter 297
   1. Grigory Kuzmich Zolotov, probably A. N. Goncharov's agent.
   2. The Minister of Finance.
   3. Natalia Nikolaevna Goncharova's brothers.

Letter 298
   1. See Letter 283, and note 1.
   2. P. Y. Chaadaev's "Philosophical Letter," written in 1829 and published in 1836, was widely read in manuscript form before its publication. When it appeared, Nadezhdin, then publisher of *The Telescope*, was exiled and the journal was forbidden; the censor who passed it was fired, and Chaadaev himself was declared mad. Pushkin's Letter 637 is a detailed answer to Chaadaev's letter.

Letter 299
   1. Pushkin had lost heavily at cards to Vasily Semenovich Ogon-Doganovsky (1776-1838), Smolensk nobleman and gambler. Apparently it was in connection with this debt that Pushkin was trying so desperately to borrow money, with the aid of Pogodin, as indicated by the series of letters beginning with Letter 283.

Letter 300
   1. Pushkin is here exerting influence on behalf of the violinist Artemy Mardarievich Shchepin, brother of the opera singer and producer Pavel Mardarievich Shchepin (d. ca. 1853), "yesterday's Austrian emperor." Zagoskin was the Director of the Office of Moscow Theaters.

Letter 301
   1. From Moscow to Petersburg. Pushkin made the trip in order to put his affairs into order and to have a conversation with his father about financial matters.
   2. Nikita Timofeevich Kozlov, Pushkin's serf.
   3. A britska, a long carriage with a calash top.
   4. *Tableaux vivantes* in the home of the Governor of Moscow; Natalia N. Goncharova had taken part in them.
   5. Natalia Kirillovna Zagryazhskaya (1747-1837), great-aunt of Natalia N. Goncharova; she had entrée at court. See Letter 302.
   6. Ekaterina Ivanovna Zagryazhskaya (1779-1842), a sister of Natalia N. Goncharova's mother, with entrée at court. She became very close to Pushkin and his family and was godmother of his children.
   7. Countess Varvara Petrovna Polier (1796-1870) had recently been widowed and was then living an isolated life on her luxurious estate, Pargolovo.
   8. Anna Petrovna Malinovskaya (1770-1847), who became a close friend of Pushkin and his wife, and her daughter Ekaterina Alexeevna Malinovskaya (1811-1872).
   9. According to the customs of the time, she might have allowed him to embrace her after their betrothal.
   10. Ekaterina Nikolaevna and Alexandra Nikolaevna Goncharova.

Letter 302
   1. Natalia Ivanovna Goncharova, Pushkin's future mother-in-law.

2. Nikolay Afanasievich Goncharov, the father of Pushkin's fiancée.
3. Nicholas I had met Natalia Goncharova at a ball in Moscow.
4. The statue of Catherine II.
5. "Writer."
6. Probably Alexandra Osipovna Rosset (1809-1882), a Lady in Waiting and a pupil of Pletnev's, an intelligent and beautiful woman with whom many of Pushkin's friends fell in love.
7. "Please love and be gracious." This is obviously a direct quotation.

Letter 303
1. The references are to Pushkin's attempt on behalf of A. N. Goncharov to secure permission to sell the statue of Catherine II and to obtain a loan on the estate Polotnyany Zavod. The "oldest brother" was Dmitry Nikolaevich Goncharov, who had the rights of primogeniture.
2. Elizaveta Mikhaylovna Frolova-Bagreeva (1799-1857), daughter of the famous Russian statesman Mikhail Mikhaylovich Speransky (1772-1839); she was a friend and admirer of Pushkin's and herself a writer.
3. The painting was Perugino's "Madonna and Child," which is now in the A. S. Pushkin State Art Museum in Moscow. Pushkin's famous sonnet "Madonna" (1830) is to and about Natalia N. Goncharova.
4. The statue of Catherine II.
5. Count E. F. Kankrin, Minister of Finance. Pushkin is jokingly using the form of address of one potentate to another, so as to underline the exaggerated view which A. N. Goncharov had of Pushkin's connections.
6. "My angel."

Letter 304
1. ". . . I have so many things to say to you. I acknowledge to my shame that I am having a good time in Petersburg and that I hardly know how or when I shall return." This short note is a postscript to a letter of Vyazemsky's to his wife. What Pushkin found to amuse him in Petersburg at this time is not definitely known. It is conjectured that the reference is to high-society conversations on the political news of the moment, the July (1830) Revolution in France. Nothing about the revolution was allowed to be published in Russian newspapers, though it was a common topic of conversation, especially in circles close to the court and the foreign embassies.

Letter 305
1. This monetary assistance was refused.
2. Pushkin is requesting that his wedding not be postponed because of the delay with his fiancée's dowry.

Letter 306
1. This letter is about the July, 1830, Revolution in France. Pushkin's low opinion of it comes out in various ways in this letter. By inference he compares (1) the objections of members of the Moscow English Club (some of whom were interested in politics) to the "ordinance" of Prince Dmitry Vladimirovich Golitsyn, Governor General of Moscow, forbidding the card game écarté, with (2) the French Parliament's objections to Charles X's ordinances leading to the Revolution. *La Parisienne* (1830), a song by Casimir Delavigne, became the anthem of the July Revolution, just as Rouget de Lisle's *La Marseillaise* (1792) had been the anthem of the French Revolution of 1789. Pushkin's

comment about the respective merits of the two songs is a comment upon the revolutions.

2. On August 20, 1830.

3. Chateaubriand, an extreme royalist from 1814 to 1824, was in the opposition from 1824 to 1830, but in 1830 he again joined the royalists. He subsequently supported King Louis Philippe. The speech referred to here was delivered on August 7, 1830.

4. The deposed Charles X vainly chose the Duke of Bordeaux to succeed him.

5. *Le Temps*, French newspaper founded in 1829, was in opposition to Charles X.

6. The supposition of this marriage is humorous. Countess de Genlis was a French writer and tutor of Louis Philippe. The Marquis de Lafayette, hero of the American Revolution and French statesman, was a leader of the opposition from 1825 to 1830, and again in the opposition when the conservative tendencies of Louis Philippe became clear. Talleyrand had been Bishop of Autun (1789) but was excommunicated (1791) for proposing that the French Revolutionaries take over church property; he was instrumental in securing restoration of the Bourbons in 1814, and he was involved in the July Revolution in 1830.

7. Countesses Tizengauzen and Ficquelmont.

Letter 307

1. The reference is to Pushkin's failure to get financial assistance from the government for A. N. Goncharov.

2. To Boldino, in order to take over management of Kistenevo.

3. The final permission for Natalia N. Goncharova to marry Pushkin.

Letter 308

1. Difficulties with Natalia I. Goncharova, Pushkin's future mother-in-law, come out in several other letters, before and after the marriage. By Nizhny, Pushkin means the estate Boldino in the Nizhny Novgorod Province. Pushkin went to Boldino in order to take care of legal formalities necessary for him to be able to mortgage the serfs on the nearby estate of Kistenevo.

Letter 309

1. See Letter 308.

2. Lukoyanov was capital of the district in which Boldino, the estate of Pushkin's father, was located.

Letter 310

1. Before Pushkin left Petersburg on August 10, 1830.

2. An allusion to Victor Ducange's melodrama, *Thirty Years, or the Life of a Gambler* (1827).

3. As Pushkin's agent.

Letter 311

1. See Letter 308.

2. The village of Kistenevo. Pushkin completed the legal steps necessary, on September 16.

3. The disease turned out to be, not the comparatively mild cholera morbus, but the most virulent form of cholera, called Asiatic cholera or Indian cholera. This was the first European invasion of the disease. As in the several other invasions of this disease during the nineteenth century, the Asiatic cholera made its way from India to Russia,

and from there to the rest of Europe and to the United States, dying out after several years, only to be followed a few years later by another, similar invasion from India.

The epidemic of Asiatic cholera reached Astrakhan in 1830, and from there it spread rapidly to cities on the Volga and then to Moscow; in 1831 it reached Petersburg and as far north as Arkhangelsk, and continued its spread over all European Russia. It next attacked Poland, where the Russian army was engaged in putting down the Polish Revolution of 1830-1831. In Poland, Grand Duke Constantine, brother of the Russian Tsar, and also General Dibich, Commander-in-Chief of Russian forces fighting against the Poles, both died of the disease. From Russia and Poland the disease spread to the rest of Europe and then, in 1832, to the United States. The height of the epidemic in Russia was reached in 1831; seven thousand people died of it in Petersburg alone. It did not die out in Europe until 1837.

As Pushkin notes in his letters, the symptoms of the disease were like those of poisoning. These symptoms of a hitherto unknown disease led the common people and the army to rise in riot in the so-called "Cholera Revolts" in 1831 in Petersburg, Novgorod, and Staraya Rus. As Pushkin observes, the use of quarantines to keep down the spread of the disease was ineffective. It is interesting that in his letters appears the idea which much later became central in the suppression of the disease—that the most effective preventive is proper sanitation. Pushkin himself thought personal courage the best protection against infection by the disease; he never showed any fear of it. It will be noted in his letters that he associated this epidemic of cholera with the plagues of antiquity and with the epidemics of the black plague and the bubonic plague in medieval and modern times. Pushkin's letters of the remainder of 1830 and of 1831 reflect the effects of the epidemic upon Pushkin's personal life, activities, and thinking, and also the effects upon Russia and Poland. The first important effect of the epidemic upon Pushkin was to keep him in Boldino longer than he had intended to stay. He had wished to leave Boldino about September 16, immediately after completing his Kistenevo business, but the quarantines held him back until the end of November. While he was constantly fretting at being prevented from returning to his betrothed, he was having an extremely productive literary period.

Letter 312

1. Of trying to obtain financial assistance for A. N. Goncharov.

Letter 313

1. Letter 310.
2. That is, to the other world; his uncle Vasily Lvovich Pushkin had just died.
3. "The war cry on his lips."
4. For articles in *The Literary Gazette*.
5. The reference here is obviously to his fiancée, Natalia N. Goncharova.
6. *Boris Godunov*; it was published without any preface.

Letter 314

1. Aleko is the hero of Pushkin's *Gypsies*, from which comes the quotation, an allusion to the inconstancy of women.
2. That is, her wit is short.
3. Pushkin's idea is that after Louis Philippe became King of France in the July, 1830, Revolution, Polignac, Charles X's minister who promulgated the ordinances of 1830 which brought on the revolution, would be executed.
4. It has not survived. Pushkin delivered the "sermon" in church. In it he made dire prediction of cholera infection for peasants who did not pay their quitrent.

Letter 315

1. A. N. Goncharov.
2. The statue of Catherine II.
3. "Teacher"—French transliteration of the Russian word.
4. Pushkin's grandfather Lev Alexandrovich Pushkin (1723-1790) was reputed to have hanged a French tutor on the suspicion of a liaison with his first wife.
5. Her brother Sergey Nikolaevich Goncharov.

Letter 316

1. Moscow was put under quarantine when cholera appeared there between September 10 and 20, 1830.
2. She has not been identified.
3. Pushkin's question is whether Polignac had been hanged (see Letter 314, and note 3).
4. Pushkin shifts to Russian, in order to make application of Russian folk expressions. The last, about the *kisel'*, means "the game is not worth the candle." "Grandfather and his bronze grandmother" are A. N. Goncharov and the statue of Catherine II. Either "detour" Pushkin wryly suggests would be tremendous: Kyakhta was a trading city north of Mongolia and south of Lake Baikal in Eastern Siberia, and thousands of miles in the opposite direction from Moscow; in Letter 318 Pushkin speaks similarly of a detour via *Vyatka* and Arkhangelsk, that is, from near the center of Russia to almost the northernmost point and then back to near the center.
5. In letters to the Count and Countess Argental.

Letter 317

1. Pushkin made an unsuccessful attempt to break through the quarantine about the first of October (see Letter 325 for a detailed account of it), and also another about the first of November.
2. The letter has not survived.
3. A slight paraphrase of a line from Pushkin's jocular, coarse, and harsh "Refutation of Beranger" (1828).
4. This preposterous notion was suggested by a then recent attack on Pushkin by Bulgarin, "A Second Letter from Karlovo to Kamenny Ostrov," in *The Northern Bee.* Bulgarin's village of Karlovo was located near Dorpat.
5. In his polemics with literary opponents.
6. *Boris Godunov.*
7. Sofia Nikolaevna Karamzina (1802-1856) and Princess Ekaterina Nikolaevna Meshcherskaya, nee Karamzina; there was a third daughter, Elizaveta Nikolaevna Karamzina (1821-1891).

Letter 318

1. This is the only letter which Pushkin wrote his fiancée in Russian—all the others are in French; after their marriage, all his letters to her were in Russian.
2. L. S. Pushkin was in Moscow at this time.
3. As a measure against the spread of cholera, letters were pierced many times, until, Pushkin complains in Letter 326 (q.v.), they were "rough."
4. That is, at Polotnyany Zavod, which is near Kaluga.
5. See Letter 316, and note 4.

Letter 319

1. "Not long does cold separation sadden woman's love; love will pass, boredom will come." The fourth line, which Pushkin does not quote, reads: "The beautiful one will fall in love again."

2. On September 9, 1830, Pushkin finished his "Undertaker," one of *The Tales of Belkin*; the hero Adrian Prokhorov, who invited his "clients" to celebrate his house-warming upon his moving from Basmannaya Street to Nikitskaya Street (where the Goncharovs' Moscow house was located) was obviously modeled on an undertaker whose house could be seen from the Goncharovs'.

3. "For delivery to Boldino."

Letter 320

1. That is, Pushkin's contributions for Delvig's *Northern Flowers for* 1831.

2. In Boldino during autumn, 1830, Pushkin had one of the literarily most productive periods of his life. In Letter 330 he lists most of the things he wrote at this time.

Letter 321

1. That is, Moscow. Pogodin published a daily bulletin, *The Record of the Condition of the City of Moscow*, in order to give a true report of the cholera in Moscow and thus keep down false rumors; it appeared from September 23, 1830, to March 6, 1831, as a supplement to Prince Shalikov's *Moscow Record*, and separately.

2. That is, he is surrounded by quarantines as an island is with water. This suggests to Pushkin St. John on the Island of Patmos, who often, in Revelation, "cries out in a great voice"; the image of stretching forth his hands is conventionally biblical—it is perhaps an echo of Psalms 143:6. Pushkin had used the image of a "rock-bound island" to describe his quarantine in Letter 316.

3. *Marfa*; the Veche was the parliament of old Novgorod.

4. Of his *History of the Russian People*.

5. Pushkin had similarly referred to his *Gavriiliada* in Letter 17 as a "composition in the manner of the Apocalypse." Here the "Apocalyptic song" is "Hero," a poem expressing the poet's disillusion at learning that the story of Napoleon's having touched the hand of a plague-infected man was false, and giving indirect praise of the act of Nicholas I in braving the dangers of going to cholera-infected Moscow, on September 29, 1830, in order to give courage to the populace there. Pogodin kept the secret of Pushkin's authorship for him, and the poem appeared without signature in Nadezhdin's *Telescope* in 1831. Pushkin's desire was realized, that his personal feelings on this event not be attributed to him, and that there be no opportunity of accusing him of being a flatterer of the Tsar; during Pushkin's lifetime his authorship of the poem was not suspected nor revealed.

6. See Letter 283, and note 1.

Letter 322

1. Pushkin is quoting from I. I. Dmitriev's translation of Horace's *Odes*, I, 3; in Horace it is "oak and triple bronze" that "must have girt the breast" of the navigator.

2. Some commentators think the allusion is to Nicholas I's policies and the unlikelihood of reforms, but the end of the letter seems to refute this idea. Perhaps the reference is to fate. See Letter 323.

3. See Letters 320 and 330.

4. Quotation from Krylov's fable "The Eagle and the Bee" (1813).

5. Vyazemsky's biography of Fonvizin.

6. Elizaveta M. Khitrovo. She had beautiful shoulders, which she bared even in excess of the fashion. The appellative is a quotation from an epigram on her, attributed to Pushkin.

7. Pushkin had bet Vyazemsky a bottle of champagne that Polignac would be executed. See Letter 314.

8. That is, Khitrovo would have written love letters, but she would also have sent news of the French July, 1830, Revolution, either in her own words or in the form of the French newspapers cited here.

9. Pushkin's reference is to Nicholas I's visit to cholera-infected Moscow (see Letter 321); the prediction of liberation of the Decembrist "convicts" did not come to pass.

Letter 323
1. Pushkin's parents were at Mikhaylovskoe, and thus in Osipova's neighborhood, when they received news of the death of V. L. Pushkin.

2. Pushkin did not succeed in getting through the quarantines this time, either.

3. Rabelais is reputed to have said, when dying, that he was going "into the great perhaps."

Letter 324
1. P. I. Shalikov was editor of *The Moscow Record*, which published news of the cholera epidemic in Moscow.

2. An unidentified suitor of Natalia N. Goncharova.

Letter 325
1. What Princess Golitsyna is unknown.

2. Pushkin tried to refuse to take this responsibility, but he was forced to, under the order making it compulsory for all to do whatever service was required of them in connection with the cholera.

3. They have not survived.

Letter 326
1. Count A. A. Zakrevsky at this time was Minister of Internal Affairs, and as such, in charge of measures to prevent the spread of the cholera.

2. Nikolay Filippovich Pavlov (1805-1864), actor and then dramatist. The allusion is to an anecdote about Paul I, that he released a certain general from the service because of his "face, which induced despondency."

Letter 327
1. Ivan III (the Great) conquered and annexed Novgorod in 1478. Ioann (Ivan III) and Boretsky are characters in Pogodin's play.

2. The famous bell tower in the Moscow Kremlin.

Letter 328
1. Pushkin's letter is on the back of a note by one Dmitry Yazykov, apparently a nobleman and landowner of the Nizhny Novgorod District, responsible for measures with regard to the cholera.

2. A village about seventy-five versts, or fifty miles, from Moscow, on the Nizhny Novgorod road.

3. "Stage horses."

4. Letter 325.

Letter 329

1. See Letter 328.
2. See Letter 325.
3. "Here's what we have lived to see—that we are glad when we are placed under arrest for two weeks in a weaver's dirty wooden house, on bread and water."

Letter 330

1. It was then in the press.
2. Renumbered the seventh and eighth chapters, when the projected seventh chapter, "Onegin's Journey," was abandoned.
3. *The Little House in Kolomna.*
4. "For you alone"—Pushkin's note.
5. *The Tales of Belkin.* In the preceding list, Pushkin calls his *Stone Guest* by the name of its hero, Don Juan.
6. Delvig's *Literary Gazette* was closed down in 1830 because of the publication of four verses of Delavigne's referring to the French July, 1830, Revolution, which it was forbidden to mention in the press. Bulgarin, referred to below as "writer-spy," had previously denounced Delvig and his journal to Benkendorf, and Delvig had already been given a stern warning before the above-mentioned verses were published.
7. Untranslatable pun on *baran* "ram" and *baron* "baron."

Letter 331

1. Princess Ekaterina Alexeevna Dolgorukova (1781-1870).
2. *Stockholm, Fontainebleau, et Rome*, by Alexandre Dumas, *père*, was presented in 1830 (written as *Christine*, 1828).
3. The Polish Revolution of 1830. Alexander I had given the Poles a constitution in 1815.
4. "Get up, . . . remember that you are Russians."
5. Adam Mickiewicz (1798-1855), greatest Polish poet. He was exiled to Russia from 1824 to 1829, where he made many friends among the *literati*, including Pushkin, from 1826. After he was allowed to leave Russia, in 1829, he spent the remainder of his life in Western Europe, actively engaged in attempts to liberate his native land. Pushkin always valued true poetic ability; he had a high opinion of Mickiewicz as poet and poetic improvisor. Pushkin's poetic masterpiece, *The Bronze Horseman* (1833), was written in answer to a poem by Mickiewicz. However, Pushkin's admiration for Mickiewicz as poet was mixed with his dislike for the Polish patriot in him, which Pushkin, as a Russian nationalist, contemned. It may be noted that in 1828 Pushkin had written a fruitless petition for Mickiewicz to be allowed to return from Russia to his native Poland.
6. See Letter 321 and note 5, and also Letter 325.

Letter 332

1. The election for seats in the French House of Deputies under the law introduced after the July, 1830, Revolution; Pushkin was afraid that the government of Louis Philippe would prove too weak, like that of the "blockhead king" in La Fontaine's fable "Frogs Seeking a King," which had been translated into Russian (1809) by Krylov.
2. See Letter 330, and note 6.
3. General Baron Anton Antonovich Delvig (ca. 1772-1828); his widow was Baroness Lyubov Matveevna Delvig (d. 1859).

Letter 333
1. The first verse of Pushkin's verse epistle "To Alexeev" (1821).
2. These letters have not survived.
3. Maria Egorovna Eikhfeldt. As he writes, Pushkin forgets that Alexeev is no longer in Kishinev.
4. Pulkheria Egorovna Varfolomey.
5. Ekaterina Zakharovna or Zemfirovna Stamo, the young wife of a middle-aged official in Kishinev when Pushkin was there. Pushkin paid court to her.
6. Artemy Makarievich Khudobashev, an Armenian, an official in Kishinev when Pushkin was there. Pushkin often joked good-naturedly at his expense.

Letter 334
1. Natalia Ivanovna Goncharova was taking her son-in-law-to-be to visit various churches and cathedrals in Moscow; she was an extremely religious person.
2. Pushkin had bought a shawl for his fiancée from him.
3. Pushkin's old friend Nashchokin took active part in the preparations for Pushkin's wedding, including, obviously, the financial arrangements.

Letter 335
1. The polemics in *The Literary Gazette* and *The Moscow Telegraph* with regard to Polevoy's *History*.

Letter 336
1. This letter is an inscription on a printed copy of *Boris Godunov*. It is a mark of Pushkin's estimation of Chaadaev that Pushkin, who had not yet received any copies of his play on January 1, sent a copy, obviously as soon as he obtained them, to Chaadaev on January 2.

Letter 337
1. Vyazemsky's "Winter Caricatures," which consist of four separate poems, the last of which is "Bumpy Roads, Wagon Train" and includes mention of pigs and a brigadier. Pushkin wished the poems to be sent to Delvig for his *Northern Flowers* or his *Literary Gazette*, but they appeared in Mikhail Alexandrovich Maximovich's (1804-1873) almanac *Dawn for* 1831. "The Maiden's Dream" (1831) was another poem by Vyazemsky.
2. Probably Pavel Lukianovich Yakovlev (1796-1835); the almanac did not appear.
3. That is, fail. A common Russian saying.
4. Pushkin's journalist-enemies calmed down a little in their attacks on him about this time. The reference is to an article "About Russian Journalistics," in *The Northern Bee* of December 27, 1830.
5. See Genesis 3:19.
6. Pushkin lost his wager when Polignac was sentenced to life imprisonment instead of being executed. The details of Polignac's imprisonment were drawn from newspapers of the time.
7. Félicité de Lamennais, French publicist and theologian.
8. "Grapple boldly with the question."
9. That is, the Polish Revolution of 1830.
10. Probably Alexander Petrovich Chicherin (b. ca. 1809), an officer, and son of Adjutant General Peter Alexandrovich Chicherin (1778-1848).
11. "There is room for hope that all will end without war."

12. A brand of champagne.

13. On N. N. Raevsky the Older; it was published in 1832.

14. Ivan Vasilievich Kireevsky (1806-1856).

15. Tatiana Demianovna (b. 1810), a beautiful gypsy singer. Pushkin alludes to an ancient Moscow song, the heroine of which is "drunken Tatiana" (*Tat'jana p'jana*).

16. A folk song.

17. Dmitry Alexandrovich Davydov (1786-1851), a friend of Vyazemsky's and a civil servant.

18. Prince Fedor Fedorovich Gagarin (1786-1863), Vyazemsky's brother-in-law.

Letter 338

1. Pseudonym of Nikolay Ivanovich Nadezhdin.

2. An allusion to the French and Polish revolutions of 1830, and also to his personal relationships with Nadezhdin and other journalists.

Letter 339

1. For Letter 310.

2. From Smirdin for *Boris Godunov*; Pletnev took all the responsibilities for publishing the work.

3. Pletnev's poem "To Gnedich" (1822) was published, along with Gnedich's answer "To P. A. Pletnev: Answer to His Epistle" in Delvig's *Northern Flowers for* 1831.

4. General Peter Kirillovich Essen (1772-1844), in 1831 Governor General of Petersburg; Pushkin is alluding to the inquiry instituted in 1826 as to the connections of Pletnev and Pushkin.

5. The burden of F. N. Glinka's poem "An Incomprehensible Thing," published in Delvig's *Northern Flowers for* 1831.

6. In the poem "Poverty and Consolation" (*Northern Flowers for* 1831) Glinka wrote: "God will give children? Well, what then? Let him be the godfather." Pushkin cites parts of the ceremony of Russian Orthodox baptism.

7. Alexander I.

8. Hugo's *Cromwell* (1827) was presented three years after Pushkin's *Boris Godunov* was written. Pushkin thought *Cromwell* devoid of both "action and interest."

9. In 1818 Pushkin had been of the same opinion, with regard to verses by Zhukovsky.

10. A German translation with a historico-critical introduction by Karl von Knorring appeared in 1831.

11. That is, Russian critics of the drama. Pushkin's guess as to the negative reaction of Russian drama critics, including Katenin, was accurate.

12. General I. I. Inzov's magpie(s) or parrot(s) repeated obscenities taught it (or them) by Pushkin himself.

13. *The Concubine* (1831).

Letter 340

1. That is, from his fiancée. Pushkin visited Vyazemsky at Ostafievo on December 17, 1830, and January 4, 1831. Pushkin was mistaken in thinking Vyazemsky celebrated January 16 as name day; he celebrated June 29.

2. Prince Nikolay Borisovich Yusupov (1750-1831), famous statesman.

3. "He [i.e., Fonzivin] was another Beaumarchais at conversation."

4. Vasily Ivanovich Maykov's drama *Agriopa* was staged in 1769 and published in 1775. Vyazemsky did not publish the anecdote, the wit of which seems to lie in the rhyme, untranslatable into English, and in the succinct judgment.

5. Ivan Grigorievich Salaev (d. 1858), Moscow bookseller and publisher.

6. That is, provide material for Maximovich's almanac instead of to Delvig. The article was one on the death of V. L. Pushkin.

7. See Letter 337.

8. The opposition of the Duke of Wellington, then leader of the Tories, to the Whig-sponsored Reform bill of 1831, which was adopted the following year, resulted for a time in making him extremely unpopular with the masses. He was jeered by the crowd on the anniversary of Waterloo, and he felt it necessary even to put up iron shutters over the windows of his house. The story that the house had been burned down was, however, false.

9. Pushkin refers to the July, 1830, Revolution in Paris and the cholera in Moscow.

Letter 341

1. An allusion to Pushkin's sardonic poem "My Genealogy," written in 1830.

2. That is, Mrs. Grundy. Pushkin slightly paraphrases the concluding words of Griboedov's *Woe from Wit*.

Letter 342

1. The allusion is to the French July, 1830, Revolution, the Polish Revolution of 1830, and the disorders in England and Belgium. One of the chief events bringing on the French Revolution of 1830 was Charles X's ordinance taking away the freedom of the press.

Letter 343

1. The disease then called "putrid fever" is now thought to have been typhus. Delvig's illness ran a rapid course; he became ill on January 6 and was dead eight days later.

2. That is, Vyazemsky's translation (1828-1829, pub. 1831) of Constant's novel.

Letter 344

1. Of Delvig's death (see Letter 343).

Letter 345

1. "One is not alone, and there are not [really] two." The epigram is by the French poet Ponce Denis Le Brun.

2. "The only deliverance [for the vanquished] is in hoping for no deliverance"— Vergil's *Aeneid*, II, 354.

3. That is, from Nicholas I's State Secretary, D. N. Bludov.

4. Louis Philippe.

Letter 346

1. As part of the purchase price of *Boris Godunov*, which Pletnev sold for Pushkin for 10,000 rubles, which were distributed as follows: 4000 to Pushkin, 5000 in repayment of a debt to Delvig, and 1000 rubles to Delvig's widow to buy a portrait of Pushkin done for Delvig by Orest Adamovich Kiprensky (1783-1836); see Frontispiece, Vol. I.

2. "It is enough, master, it is enough."

3. That is, by publishing *The Northern Flowers for* 1832, with the proceeds to go to Delvig's family. Delvig's widow was in financial straits, partly because sixty thousand rubles were stolen from Delvig's room the day after his death. Pushkin and Pletnev carried out the plan with regard to *The Northern Flowers*, and Somov received the usual salary for taking care of the technical side of the publishing.

4. Not accomplished.

5. Pushkin changes "attracts" to "oppresses" in borrowing a line from Zhukovsky's translation (1818) of Schiller's "Count von Habsburg" (1803).

6. It is not clear what traits Pushkin considered typical of the Little Russian, or Ukrainian, character.

7. Gnedich's elegy on the death of Delvig was published by *The Literary Gazette* in 1831, after the publication was turned down in Bulgarin's and Grech's *Northern Bee*, because of unfriendly relations between that journal and Delvig's.

8. Ferdinand Bellizard (d. 1863), bookseller.

Letter 347

1. Delvig had been bringing up two brothers, who were then twelve and fifteen years old. They did not enter the Corps of Pages.

2. Of January 25, 1831; it was composed in response to the resolution of the Warsaw Seim (parliament) that the Romanov rule in Poland was at an end and the Polish throne vacant. Thereupon the Poles sent diplomatic representatives to England, France, and other countries.

3. This principle in foreign affairs was upheld by Louis Philippe of France.

4. Canning's "system" from 1820 to 1827 was not that of legitimacy, but of non-intervention and of the encouragement of national and revolutionary governments in such countries as Mexico, Columbia, Argentina, and Greece.

5. The Duke de Mortemart, French general and diplomat, was then ambassador to Russia.

6. Pushkin, in applying to Warsaw Cato's dictum that "Carthage must be destroyed," is closer to the original usage than in Letter 43, where he applies it to the censorship. Pushkin follows Cato's style by adding the final tag, irrespective of its relevance to what has gone before it.

Letter 348

1. *Boris Godunov.*

2. When Pushkin was at Boldino, he was not far from Krivtsov's estate of Lyubichi.

3. Krivtsov had lost a leg in the battle of Kulm (1813) in view of Alexander I.

4. "There is no happiness except in the usual paths," the concluding words of Chateaubriand's *René* (1802).

5. Pushkin's English.

6. Anastasia Nikolaevna Khitrovo (1764-1840).

Letter 349

1. Pushkin's wedding was on February 18, 1831.

2. Paper rubles; i.e., 11,428.58 silver rubles.

3. Natalia Ivanovna Goncharova.

4. That is, his fiancée's female relatives.

5. *The Tales of Belkin*, published in the end of October, 1831.

6. Letter 347.

7. Nothing is known of this debt except that S. L. Pushkin sent the Baroness Delvig five hundred rubles in June, 1831.

8. By O. A. Kiprensky (1827); she let Pushkin have it for one thousand rubles.

9. Her father.

10. Pletnev's "Necrology" of Delvig, published in *The Literary Gazette* in 1831.

PART VIII

SETTLING DOWN—MOSCOW, TSARSKOE SELO

February, 1831—July, 1831

Natalia Nikolaevna Pushkina, 1831. *Water color by A. Bryullov.*

To Afanasy Nikolaevich Goncharov

February 24, 1831. From Moscow to Polotnyany Zavod.

Dear Sir, Grandfather, Afanasy Nikolaevich,

I hasten to inform you of my happiness[1] and to commend myself to your paternal good will, as the husband of your precious granddaughter Natalia Nikolaevna. Our duty and desire would be to go to your village to see you, but we are afraid we might disturb you, and we do not know whether our visit would be timely. Dmitry Nikolaevich [Goncharov] has been telling me that you are still worried about the dowry; my urgent plea is that you not further disorder your already disordered estate on our account; we can afford to wait. As regards the monument,[2] there is no way I can undertake the sale of it, being in Moscow, and I leave this whole matter to your disposing.

With the most profound respect and sincerely filial devotion, I have the happiness to be, Dear Sir, Grandfather,

Your most obedient servant and grandson,

Alexander Pushkin.

February 24, 1831.
Moscow.

[351]

To Peter Alexandrovich Pletnev

February 24, 1831. From Moscow to Petersburg.

My dear fellow, I am very much disturbed about you. There is said to be grippe in Petersburg; I am afraid for your daughter.[1] In any event, I am awaiting a letter from you.

I am married—and happy. My one desire is that nothing in my life change—I shall never see anything better. This state is so new for me that I seem to have been born again. I am sending you our calling card—my wife is not at home, and for that reason she is not in person commending herself to the good graces of Stepanida Alexandrovna.[2]

Farewell, my friend. How is the Baroness [Delvig]? The memory of Delvig is the only shadow on my sunny life. I embrace you and

Zhukovsky. From the newspapers I have learned of Gnedich's new appointment.[3] It does honor to the Sovereign, whom I sincerely love, and for whom I rejoice when he acts intelligently and like a tsar. *Addio.*

February 24.

Be well, everybody.

[352]
To Nikolay Ivanovich Khmelnitsky
March 6, 1831. From Moscow to Smolensk.
Dear Sir, Nikolay Ivanovich,

I hasten to respond to Your Excellency's proposal, which is so flattering to my self-esteem: I would consider it an honor to transmit my compositions to the Smolensky Library, but in consequence of the terms which I have contracted with the Petersburg booksellers, not a single copy remains in my possession, and the expensiveness of books does not permit me even to think of purchasing them.

With the most profound respect and with complete devotion, I have the honor to be, Dear Sir,

Your Excellency's
Most humble servant,
Alexander Pushkin.

March 6, 1831.
Moscow.

[On the other side]

After giving an official answer to your official letter, may I be permitted to thank you for remembering me, and to ask your forgiveness, not for myself, but for my booksellers, who have not sent you, notwithstanding my instructions, my annual tribute. It will be delivered to you without fail, to you, my favorite poet. But do not embroil me with the Smolensk governor, whom I nevertheless esteem as much as I love you.[1]

All yours.

[353]

To Elizaveta Mikhaylovna Khitrovo
March 26, 1831. From Moscow to Petersburg.
(In French)

The bustle and bothers of this month, which could hardly be called a honeymoon with us, have prevented me from writing you until now. My letters to you would have had to be full of nothing but excuses and thanks, but you are too much above both of them for me to permit them to myself. So my brother is going to owe all his future career to you;[1] he has departed, full of gratitude. I am expecting Benkendorf's decision any moment, so that I may forward it to him.

I hope to be at your feet, Madame, in one or two months at most.[2] I am eagerly looking forward to it. Moscow is the town of Nothingness. On its gates is written: "Abandon all intelligence, O ye who enter here."[3] Political news arrives to us late or distorted. For almost the last two weeks we have known nothing with regard to Poland—and there is not the slightest pang of impatience! If only we were quite dissolute, quite foolish, quite frivolous—but nothing of the kind. We are destitute, we are woebegone, and we are stupidly calculating the decline of our revenues.

You speak of M. Lamennais. I am well aware that he is a Bossuet Journalist. But his newspaper does not reach us. Let him prophesy; I do not know whether Paris is his Nineveh, but we are the pumpkins.[4]

Skaryatin[5] has just told me that he saw you before he left, that you were kind enough to remember me, that you even wished to send me some books. So I absolutely must thank you, even though thus I put you out of patience.

Please accept my respectful regards and extend them to your daughters, the Countesses.

March 26.

My address: *Khitrovo's house on the Arbat.*

[354]

To PETER ALEXANDROVICH PLETNEV
March 26, 1831. From Moscow to Petersburg.

My dear fellow, what do you mean by becoming completely silent? Here it has already been a month that I haven't seen a single line from you. A gracious prohibition against corresponding with me hasn't supervened from the Governor-General, has it?[1] I wouldn't be surprised! You aren't sick, are you? Is everything all right with you? Or are you simply being lazy and frightening your friends for nothing? Meanwhile here is a detailed report for you about me, about my domestic circumstances, and about my intentions. I have no intention whatever of remaining in Moscow; the reasons for this are known to you—and every day new ones arise. After Easter Week I am setting off for Petersburg. Do you know what? I want—so badly I don't know what to do—to go, not all the way to Petersburg, but to stop in Tsarskoe Selo. A blessed thought! In this way I would spend the summer and the *autumn* in inspirational solitude, near the capital amid sweet memories and other such comforts. And houses there are probably not expensive now: no hussars are there; the court is not there; but many empty apartments are there. I would see you every week, my dear fellow, and Zhukovsky, too. Petersburg is at hand—living is cheap, and there is no need to keep a carriage. What, I should like to know, could be better? Think this over at your leisure and send me your decision. I have received the books from Bellizard's, and I am grateful. Order him also to send me *Crabbe*, *Wodsworth*, *Southey*, and *Schakspear*,[2] to the house of Khitrovo on the Arbat. (I have rented this house in memory of my Eliza [Khitrovo]; tell this to the Southern Swallow, to our dark rosy-cheeked beauty.)[3] Tell Somov to send me, if he can, *The Literary Gazette* for last year (I don't need this one's; I am coming for it myself) and also *The Northern Flowers*, the last memorial to our Delvig. Let's talk about the almanac: I am not against publishing with you the last *Northern Flowers*.[4] But I am cooking up something else as well;[5] we'll talk about that, too. They have been telling me that Zhukovsky is very much pleased with *Marfa, the Novgorod Burgomaster's Wife*; if so, let him use his influence with Benkendorf or with whomever else he pleases, and obtain permission to publish the whole drama, an extremely remarkable work, notwithstanding the unevenness of its over-all merit and the weakness of its versification. Pogodin is a very, very sensible and honorable young man, a true German in his pure love for science, his industriousness, and his moderation. He must be given support, and also Shevyrev, whom it would not be at all bad to seat in the chair vacated by Merzlyakov, a kind sot, but a terrible ignoramus. This would be a victory over the University,[6] i.e., over prejudices and barbarity.

About my financial circumstances I shall tell you that, thanks to my father, who gave me the means of obtaining 38,000 rubles,[7] I have gotten married and have set up housekeeping after a fashion, without contracting any private debts. But it's no use to rely on my mother-in-law and my wife's grandfather, partly because their affairs are in disorder, and partly because one must not depend on words alone. At least on my part, I have acted honorably, and more than disinterestedly. I am not bragging, and I am not complaining—for my little wife is charming, and not only in outward appearance, and I do not consider what I had to do to be a sacrifice. And so, good-by, my dear one.

March 26.

[355]

To Lev Sergeevich Pushkin
April 6, 1831. From Moscow to Chuguev.

Everything had been decided.[1] They were awaiting only the answer from Count Paskevich when Benkendorf received *un rapport défavorable* about you from Moscow. I have no intention of making moralizing remarks, but if you had not been a chatterbox and had not been over-imbibing with French actors at the Yar,[2] probably you could have been already on the Vistula. You must not linger in Chuguev.[3] Go to your regiment immediately, and await there the determination of your fate. God grant that this prank may not cost you being stationed in Georgia forever.

April 6.

[356]

To Peter Alexandrovich Pletnev

April 11, 1831. From Moscow to Petersburg.

No matter what you say, you are unbearable: there's no use waiting for a line from you. Died, have you? If you are no longer in this world, then beloved shade,[1] greet Derzhavin for me and embrace my Delvig. If you are still alive, for God's sake answer my letters. Shall I come to you, shall I stop in Tsarskoe Selo or gallop past to Petersburg or Reval?[2] I am more than fed up with Moscow. You will say that Petersburg is very little better, but I am like Artur Potocki, to whom the proposal was made to go fishing: *J'aime mieux m'ennuyer autrement.*[3] I should think that if we get together in a band, then literature can't help getting warmed up and producing something: an almanac, a journal, or I wouldn't be surprised if even a newspaper![4] Vyazemsky is bringing you *The Life of Fonvizin*, a book that may very well be the most noteworthy one ever written in Russia (nevertheless excluding Karamzin's).[5] Peter Ivanych[6] has swum to Moscow, where he seems to have been received dryly enough. What kind of deviltry is this? We haven't succeeded in teaching sense to the public, have we? Or has she, the dove, figured him out, herself? But Bulgarin would seem to have been so created for her, and she for him, that they should not only live together but also die together. I have not yet made an attempt on *Vyzhigin II*, and since, they say, there is not a single word in it about me, I shall not make any. I mean, I am not going to read it, but all the same I shall berate. Somov has written me a long letter which I have not yet answered. Tell him that I shall bring him Delorme[7] myself, and therefore I am not sending it. How is the Baroness [Delvig]? Zhikhareva[8] has been telling me about you; how charming the anecdote about the notes is![9]

April 11.

Christ is risen!

[357]

To Peter Alexandrovich Pletnev

About (not later than) April 14, 1831. From Moscow to Petersburg.

You are right, favorite of the Muses[1]—one must be punctilious, even though that is a German virtue, and it is not bad to be moderate, though Chatsky laughs at both these talents.[2] And so here are point-by-point answers to your inquiries. Delaryu[3] writes too smoothly, too correctly, too primly for a young Lyceum pupil. I do not see a drop of the creative in him, but a lot of art. This is the second volume of Podolinsky's. But perhaps he will develop into something. Of the Gogol[4] I shall not say anything to you, because so far I have not had the leisure to read it. I am postponing reading until I get to Tsarskoe Selo, at which place, for God's sake, rent me an apartment. Of us there will be: we two, three or four menservants, and three womenservants. The cheaper the apartment the better, of course—but just the same two hundred rubles extra won't bankrupt us. We shall not need a little formal garden, for we shall have a big one at hand; we need a kitchen and a shed, and that is all. For God's sake, hurry it up! And let us know at once that, as they say, all is ready and we are welcome to come. Then we'll tumble in on you, like snow on your head.

Embrace Zhukovsky for his sympathetic interest, which I never doubted. I am not writing him, because I am not in the habit of corresponding with him. I am impatiently awaiting his new ballads.[5] And so the past is coming to pass with him again.[6] Thank God! But you do not write what his ballads are—translations, or original compositions. [I. I.] Dmitriev, thinking to criticize Zhukovksy, gave him extremely sound advice. Zhukovsky, he said, in his village has old women rub his feet for him and tell him fairy tales, which then he recasts into verses. Russian legends do not yield in the slightest in the poetry of the fantastic, to either the Irish or the German legends. If he still has the flux of inspiration, then advise him to read the *Menologion*,[7] especially the legends of the wonder-workers of Kiev, a charm of simplicity and fancy!

I am rereading my letter, and I see that I did not answer you precisely to your questions: (1) *where*, (2) *for how much time, and* (3) *of how many rooms* the apartment should be. The *answers*:

(1) On absolutely any street whatever of Tsarskoe Selo.

(2) Until January,[8] and therefore the apartment must be a warm one.

(3) There should be a special study—and the rest is all the same to me.

Upon this I embrace you, thanking you beforehand.

[358]

To AFANASY NIKOLAEVICH GONCHAROV
April 25, 1831. From Moscow to Polotnyany Zavod.

Dear Sir, Grandfather, Afanasy Nikolaevich,

I want to express to you my sincere gratitude for your receiving my agent and for the letter, a precious sign that you are well disposed toward me. Be assured of my unquestioning assent to everything that will be most convenient for you. It was impossible for me to accept a mere power of attorney,[1] for under it debts and arrears could increase, and the estate could, at last, be completely lost. If it please you to give Natalia Nikolaevna, instead of the three hundred promised serfs, for the time being, a power of attorney for the receipt of the income from them and a promissory note *with the stipulation that during your life the same promissory note remain not in effect* (God grant that it remain thus a very long time!), in that case the note must be given *as of serf affairs, for as many hundred thousand rubles as you wish to give of peasant souls*, in order that when the creditors assemble, three hundred serfs will actually fall to her share, and not one-tenth so many. You could give such notes, with just such stipulations, to your other grandchildren without any fear, and give a power of attorney for managing the estate only in case of their marriage.

I hope you will not be angry with me for my frankness. In any case, I await your decision, and I have the happiness, with the feeling of most profound respect and devotion, to remain,

Dear Sir, Grandfather,

Your most obedient servant and grandson,
Alexander Pushkin.

April 25.

[359]

To ELIZAVETA MIKHAYLOVNA KHITROVO
May 8, 1831. From Moscow to Petersburg.
(In French)

Enclosed here, Madame, is *The Pilgrim*,[1] which you asked me for. There is some genuine talent in this somewhat mannered chit-chat. The most curious thing about it is that the author is already thirty-five years old, and this is his first work. Zagoskin's novel[2] has not yet appeared. He has been obliged to recast several chapters which had to do with the Poles in 1812. The Poles in 1831 are much more troublesome, and their tale is not at an end. The news is being spread here of a battle which is said to have taken place on the twentieth of April. It must be false, at least as regards the date.

My trip has been postponed for several days because of business which is none of my affair.[3] I hope to be free of it by the end of the month.

My brother is a scatterbrain and a lazybones. You are indeed good, indeed kind, to take an interest in him. I have already written him an uncle's letter,[4] in which I give him a dressing-down, though I hardly know what for. By this time he ought to be in Georgia. I do not know whether I ought to send him your letter; I would prefer to keep it.

Without a farewell, Madame, as without a formal ending.

May 8.

[360]
To PAVEL VOINOVICH NASHCHOKIN
The second half (about the 20th) of May, 1831.
From Petersburg to Moscow.

We have arrived safely, my dear Pavel Voinovich, at the Demut Inn,[1] and in a few days we are setting off for Tsarskoe Selo, where my little house is not yet furnished (my future address: to Kitaeva's house). Polivanov[2] has just now been with me; he seems to be very much in love. Tomorrow he is setting off to Moscow. My affairs are in better order than I thought. In a few days I am sending you two thousand rubles for [V. P.] Gorchakov. I don't know whether you have received the thousand from Vyazemsky. I shall correspond with him. What are you doing, my dear fellow? How is your woman of the house?[3] How is Maria Ivanovna?[4] Have you gotten rid of her? And what about your efforts regarding my house and your debt? So far I have not yet received the rough draft of the power of attorney, and I wouldn't know how to draw one up myself. Hurry up and send it on.

My wife sends you her best regards.

[361]

To ELIZAVETA MIKHAYLOVNA KHITROVO
Between May 18 and 25, 1831. In Petersburg.
(In French)

Here are your books, Madame. I beseech you to send me the second volume of *The Red and the Black*. I am enchanted with it. *Plock and Plick* is a wretched thing. It is a pile of misconstructions, of absurdities, which do not even have the merit of originality. May one read *Notre Dame* already?[1] Good-by, Madame.

A. Pushkin.

[362]

To PAVEL VOINOVICH NASHCHOKIN
June 1, 1831. From Tsarskoe Selo to Moscow.

Here I have already been in Tsarskoe Selo a week, but I received your letter only day before yesterday. It was registered, and I had bothers with the police and the post. I shall send you the power of attorney without delay. I thank you very much for your friendly efforts with Maria Ivanovna,[1] and I congratulate you upon the cessation of your domestic war.[2] From one day to the next I have been expecting my baggage train and your letter. I would have sent Gorchakov at once what I owe him, with gratitude, but I have been forced during these two weeks to spend two thousand rubles, and therefore I have put it off a little. Now I seem to have settled everything, and I'm going to live quietly, without my mother-in-law, without a carriage, and consequently without great expenses and without gossip. How are you getting on with Polivanov-in-love? Is he following his loved one to Kaluga? At my house he met my wife's aunt, Katerina Ivanovna Zagryazhskaya, and I introduced him as a nephew-to-be. Only I'm afraid that grandfather[3] may bamboozle him—look after him. What is your domestic situation like? Hasn't a fiancé been found for a certain party? I'd make the trip from Tsarskoe Selo for that wedding, to celebrate your liberation, the lawful marriage of Olga Andreevna, and I would take you off to Petersburg. Then we'd really start living! Again there would be Negroes, dwarfs, Sauterne, etc. Farewell; write, and don't miss me too much. A certain person used to say, "If I lose a friend, I go to the club and choose myself another." My wife and I remember you every day. She sends her greetings to you. For the time being we are not acquainted with anybody else, and she misses you very much. June 1.

I have just now seen the very ill-disposed and unjust critique of Veltman[4] in *The Literary Gazette*. Let him not think that I have been somehow mixed up in it. In point of fact, I am at fault: I have been lazy about fulfilling my promise. I have not written a critique, but then I haven't had the time. I embrace Gorchakov. What about Vyazemsky's thousand?

[363]
To Peter Andreevich Vyazemsky
June 1, 1831. From Tsarskoe Selo to Moscow.

I am living in Tsarskoe Selo in Kitaeva's house on the highway. It will be a sin if you don't drop in to see me. All our Petersburg women acquaintances[1] send you greetings, and they are awaiting you. The local halls are very remarkable. The freedom of discussion has astonished me. Dibich[2] is being criticized openly and very severely. A week ago [Paskevich-] Erivansky was still in Petergof. You have read the news of the most recent battle, of May 14.[3] I do not know why there is no mention in it of certain details which I know of from private letters, and apparently from people who are reliable: Skrzynecki was in that battle. Our officers saw how he galloped up on his white horse, changed his mount to another, a chestnut-colored one, and began to command—they saw how, wounded in the shoulder, he dropped his broadsword and tumbled off his horse, how his suite hastened to him and seated him again on his horse. Then he began singing "Poland Has Not Perished Yet,"[4] and his suite began to chime in, but at that very moment another bullet killed a Polish major in the crowd, and the songs were broken off. All this is fine in a poetic sense. But all the same they must be throttled, and our slowness is tormenting. For us Poland's rebellion is a family affair, an ancient, hereditary dissension;[5] we cannot judge it by the impressions of Europeans, no matter what our own mode of thinking may be. But Europe must have general objects of attention and partiality; both the peoples and the governments must have them. Of course it is to the advantage of almost all governments to hold in such cases to the principle of *non-intervention*, i.e., to avoid getting involved in others' woes. But their people just bellow and bay. The first thing you know we'll have Europe on our neck. How fortunate that we didn't get mixed up last year in the most recent French mess![6] Otherwise, one good turn would deserve another. I shall now turn from politics to literature, i.e., to Bulgarin. Do you know why he was banished from Petersburg?[7] They say that upon the appearance of the epigram, "Figlyarin—Here Is an Exemplary Pole," he was so mortified that he addressed himself directly to the Sovereign with a tearful complaint against me, saying, "Your Majesty, do me the divine favor to make Pushkin stop it; he keeps on eenzolting me with his rhymes." The Sovereign couldn't be bothered with rhymes; this was not the first time he was fed up with the complaints and denunciations of this Bulgarin. So he commanded that he be banished as a bothersome person. But what do you think of Bulgarin's shamelessness and impertinence? As though it were not enough for him to have wheedled, by his roguery, the Sovereign's commendation of *Peter Ivanovich Vyzhigin*, and that he sells his own filthy lampoons from under the Emperor's purple mantle. Charles X[8] sits meekly in Edinburgh, but Faddey Bulgarin asks the Russian Emperor for auxiliary forces! The Lord my God, what we have lived to see! However, here is a piece of good news for you: Zhukovsky has actually written twelve charming ballads and many other charming things.[9] Farewell; I send my greetings to the Princess [Vyazemskaya].

June 1.

I send my hearty greetings to I. I. Dmitriev. How is his health?[10]

[364]

To Elizaveta Mikhaylovna Khitrovo

June 9(?), 1831. In Petersburg.

(In French)

I am very much vexed at being unable to spend the evening at your home. Something very dreary, that is to say, a duty, obliges me to go and yawn, I know not where. Here, Madame, are the books which you were so kind as to lend me. It is easy to understand your admiration for *Notre Dame*. There is much charm in all that invention. But, but . . . I dare not say everything I think about it. In any case, the priest's downfall is beautiful in all respects; it makes one feel dizzy. *The Red and the Black* is a good novel, in spite of several harangues out of key and several comments in bad taste.[1]

Tuesday.

[365]
To Pavel Voinovich Nashchokin
June 11, 1831. From Tsarskoe Selo to Moscow.

I have sent you, dear Pavel Voinovich, both the power of attorney and the money; I have received my entire Moscow baggage train,[1] but I haven't had a single word from you, and nobody from Moscow has written to me—neither to me nor my wife. My letters haven't been getting lost, have they? Please don't be lazy. Don't play cards with [N. F.] Pavlov, hurry up and get finished with Rokhmanov,[2] marry off Olga Andreevna, and come to us, leaving your cares behind you. We're living here quietly and cheerfully, as if in a remote village; even news has difficulty in reaching us, and what does, is not joyful. There would seem to be no use grieving about the death of Dibich.[3] He has injured Russia in the opinion of Europe, both with the slowness of his successes in Turkey and with his failures against the Polish rebels. Here they are saying that Vilna had been taken and burned and that Khrapovitsky has been hanged.[4] It is horrible, but I hope it is not true. They say the cholera still hasn't stopped raging. Is it true that there are quarantines in Tver? What a year! Farewell, dear fellow. My wife loves you very much and sends you her warmest greetings.

June 11. Tsarskoe Selo.

A.P.

[366]
To Peter Andreevich Vyazemsky
June 11, 1831. From Tsarskoe Selo to Moscow.

What kind of deviltry is this? I write and write—but nobody answers me. Have you received my letter?[1] Whether you have or not, here is another one for you; I have your thousand. Shall I send it to Moscow, or do you wish it to await you here? There is cholera and quarantine in Tver, they say. Just how are you going to get here? Surely not on a steamship, the way Count Paskevich went to the army.[2] We know nothing of what is going on there. The Poles must feel the loss of Dibich;[3] the estimate is that Tol[4] will be commander-in-chief for twenty days; maybe he will use this time for his and our benefit. Here they are saying that Vilna has been taken and Khrapovitsky has been hanged.[5] It is terrible in all respects! God grant that this news be false.

I have seen [A. I.] Turgenev, and I found little change in him: some gray hair here and there; the same liveliness, though, at least at our first meeting. I am expecting him to come to Tsarskoe Selo. He is going to Moscow, if a quarantine does not keep him from it. Try to ransack his *porte-feuille*,[6] which is full of European treasures. It will come in handy. Zhukovsky is still writing. He has translated several ballads by Southey,[7] Schiller,[8] and Uhland.[9] Among others, "The Deep-Sea Diver," "The Glove," "Polycrates' Ring," etc. He has also translated Walter Scott's unfinished ballad "The Pilgrim"[10] and has added a conclusion: it is charming. Now he is writing a fairy tale in hexameters,[11] something like his "Red Carbuncle,"[12] and the same personages are on the stage, the Grandfather, Luiza, the pipe, etc. All this will appear in a new edition of all his ballads, which Smirdin is publishing in two little volumes.[13] This is all we can console ourselves with in the present bitter circumstances. Here I am not receiving any journals, and I don't know what is going on in our slough,[14] or who is giving it to whom.

Farewell: I send my greetings to the Princess [Vyazemskaya] and to Katerina Andreevna [Karamzina], if she has already reached Ostafievo. If all of you are together, it would be difficult to lure you to come here; however it must be done. How is Sofia Nikolaevna [Karamzina]?[15] Is she reigning in the saddle? *A horse, a horse! My kingdom for a horse!*[16] Farewell until we meet again.

June 11.

A.P.

[367]

To Elizaveta Mikhaylovna Khitrovo

The middle of June, 1831. From Tsarskoe Selo to Petersburg.
(In French)

Svistunov[1] has told me that he would see you this evening; I take this opportunity, Madame, to ask a favor of you: I have undertaken a

study of the French Revolution;[2] I beseech you to send me Thiers
and Mignet, if you can. These two works are prohibited.[3] I have here
only *Memoirs Regarding the Revolution.* I am counting on coming to
Petersburg[4] for several hours within a few days. I shall take advantage of this opportunity to present myself at Chernaya Rechka.[5]

[368]

To ELIZAVETA MIKHAYLOVNA KHITROVO
About (not later than) June 20, 1831.
From Tsarskoe Selo to Petersburg.
(In French)

Thank you, Madame, for Mignet's *Revolution*;[1] I have received it
through Novosiltsev.[2] Is it true that [A. I.] Turgenev is leaving us,
and so abruptly, at that?

So the cholera is where you are;[3] have no fear, though. It's the old,
old story of the plague: "Ze genteel people, zey nevair die of it,"
as the little Greek girl says.[4] It is to be hoped that the epidemic will
not be violent, even among the common people. Petersburg is well
aired, and then there is the sea. . . .

I have carried out your commission. That is, I have not carried it
out—because what kind of an idea was it of yours to have me translate Russian verse into French prose,[5] when I do not even know
orthography? Besides, the verses are mediocre. I have written others[6]
which are no better, on the same theme, and which I shall send you
as soon as I find the opportunity to do so.

Keep well, Madame; at the moment that is the most urgent thing
I have to say to you.

[369]

To PAVEL VOINOVICH NASHCHOKIN
About (not later than) June 20, 1831.
From Tsarskoe Selo to Moscow.

Thank you very, very much for your letter of June 9. I don't know
whether I have answered it; in case I haven't, I have reread it and am
writing an answer. I have settled with the contractor;[1] he kept on
telling me that you promised I would pay him some more; on this
matter I await your instructions, but if it's left up to me, I shall not
add a cent. I don't understand very well what kind of contract you

were able to enter into with Rokhmanov; in Russia it has not yet become customary to insure one's life, but it will come sometime; as for now, we are not insured, but scared.[2] There is cholera here, i.e., in Petersburg, and Tsarskoe Selo has been surrounded with cordons[3] —just as at kings' courts they used to whip a page for the mischievousness of the prince. I am expecting high prices, and the inherited and acquired stinginess in me is uneasy. I have no information at all about my wife's business;[4] both her grandfather and my mother-in-law are keeping mum and are glad that God has sent their Tashenka such a meek little husband. What will happen with Alexander Yurievich [Polivanov]? Your news about him nearly tickled us to death. I can imagine him at the Zavod *en tête-à-tête* with the deaf old man, and Natalia Ivanovna [Goncharova] all a-flutter about her daughters, whom she has locked up quite securely.[5] How is Alexander Yurievich? Has his ardor cooled or not? How are you yourself? And will there soon be money? When there is, I shall come, regardless of any choleras and such like. But I am already despairing of seeing you. Farewell; answer me.

[370]
To Pavel Voinovich Nashchokin
June 26, 1831. From Tsarskoe Selo to Moscow.

I am very grateful for your letter, my friend. But what disease was it that you recuperated from so quickly? I have already written you that there is cholera in Petersburg, and since she is a new guest here, she is held in much more honor than with you indifferent Muscovites. A few days ago on the Hay Market there was a riot in her honor;[1] some six thousand Orthodox folk gathered together, broke into the hospitals, and (they say) killed a person or two; the Tsar himself appeared at the site of the riot and put it down. The thing was managed without cannons; God grant that it be also without the knout. These are difficult times, Pavel Voinovich! The body of the Tsarevich[2] is being brought back, and Dibich's, too. Paskevich arrived at the army on the thirteenth. We still do not have any news about military operations. This is general news of a social nature for you; now let's talk about our own woes. Write me by what time I am to appear in Moscow for the money and whether Doganovsky[3] is there. If he is there, then try to have a chat with him, i.e., to do some bargaining, and go ahead and finish the business without waiting for me—but, regardless of the cholera, I shall come to Moscow to see you without fail,[4] my joy. I have received a letter from Vyazemsky; he is leaving his thousand with me until further notice. I shall send you [V. P.] Gorchakov's thousand in a few days. The cholera has put the squeeze on us, and high prices have turned up in Tsarskoe Selo. I am doing without a carriage and without dessert, but all the same the money gets away. Just imagine, since the day of our departure I have drunk only one bottle of champagne, and that not all at once. Has your woe driven you to drink? I send my regards to Olga Andreevna. I am not sending foulards to her, for as I have already said all communications with Petersburg have been cut off. For the same reason you won't receive my picture any time soon. Bryullov[5] is in Petersburg and is married; consequently he won't set off for Italy so soon. Greet Shneyder for me;[6] I'm not seeing anybody here, and there is nobody to ask about his being presented. I also send my greeting to Andrey Petrovich.[7] Send me his song in the second, corrected, edition. I again send my regards to Olga Andreevna, Tatiana Demianovna, Matrena Sergeevna, and all the band.[8] Farewell, my charming fellow. My wife greets you cordially. Her sewing for you has come to a halt for lack of black silk. The cholera is all to blame.

June 26.

[371]

To Natalia Ivanovna Goncharova
June 26, 1831. From Tsarskoe Selo to Moscow.
(In French)

Madame,

I see by the letter which you wrote Natalia that you are very much dissatisfied with me because I have informed Afanasy Nikolaevich [Goncharov] of the intentions of M. Polivanov. As I remember, I spoke of it to you first. It is not my affair to marry off the young ladies, and whether M. Polivanov be accepted or not is quite the same to me; but you add that the step I took does me little honor. This expression is insulting, and I make bold to say that I have never deserved it.

I was obliged to leave Moscow in order to avoid mischief-making

interference which could in the long run have jeopardized more than
my peace of mind; I was being depicted to my wife as an odious man,
greedy, a vile usurer; she was told, "You are a fool to permit your
husband, etc." You will admit to me that this was preaching divorce.
A wife cannot with decency allow it to be said that her husband is a
scoundrel, and the duty of mine is to submit to what I choose. It is
not for a woman of eighteen years to govern a man of thirty-two.
I have displayed patience and tact, but it appears that both of them
allow one to be imposed upon. I love my peace of mind, and I shall
know how to assure myself of it.

At my departure from Moscow you did not see fit to speak to me
of business; you preferred to make a joke on the possibility of a
divorce, or something of the kind. It is nevertheless essential for me
to know definitely what you have decided with regard to me. I do
not speak of what has been intended to be done for Natalia; that
does not concern me, and I have never thought about it, in spite of
my avidity. I mean the eleven thousand rubles which I lent you.
I am not asking the payment of them, and I do not press you in any
manner. I only wish to know precisely what arrangements you will
see fit to make, so that I may make mine accordingly.[1]

I am, with the most profound respect,
>Madame,
>>Your most humble and most obedient servant,
>>>Alexander Pushkin.

June 26, 1831.
Tsarskoe Selo.

[372]
>To Praskovia Alexandrovna Osipova
>June 29, 1831. From Tsarskoe Selo to Opochka.
>(In French)

I have postponed writing you, expecting any moment to see you
arrive here; but the circumstances[1] do not permit me to hope it
any more. Therefore, Madame, I congratulate you by letter, and I
hope for Mlle. Evpraxia[2] all the happiness of which we are capable
here below and of which a being so noble and so sweet is worthy.

The times are very sad. The epidemic is making great ravages in
Petersburg. The common people have rioted several times. Absurd

rumors have been spread. The assertion has been made that the doctors were poisoning the populace. The raging rabble has massacred two of them. The Emperor has appeared in the midst of the mutineers. One person wrote me: *Gosudar' govoril s narodom. Čern' slušala na kolenax—tišina—odin carskij golos* **kak zvon svjatoj razdavalsja na ploščadi.**[3] He lacks neither courage nor oratorical powers; for this time the disturbance was quelled; but the disorders have been renewed since. Perhaps they will be obliged to resort to grapeshot. We are expecting the court at Tsarskoe Selo,[4] which so far has not been attacked by the contagion; but I believe that it will not be long in coming. May God preserve Trigorskoe from the seven plagues of Egypt;[5] may you live happy and tranquil, and may I again find myself some day in your neighborhood! And apropos of that, if I were not afraid of being indiscreet, I would beg you, as a good neighbor and a very dear friend, to let me know whether I might not be able to acquire Savkino,[6] and on what terms. I would build a thatched cottage there, I would place my books in it, and I would come there to spend several months of the year near my good and old friends. What do you say, Madame, of my castles in Spain, or, rather, of my thatched hut in Savkino? As for me, this scheme intrigues me, and I keep on coming back to it every moment. Receive, Madame, the assurance of my high esteem and of my complete devotion. My regards to all your family; accept also those of my wife, until I have the opportunity to present her to you.

Tsarskoe Selo.

June 29, 1830.[7]

[373]
To Mikhail Petrovich Pogodin
Between June 27 and 30, 1831. From Tsarskoe Selo to Moscow.

I thank you heartily both for your letter and for the *Old Statistics*.[1] I received all the copies yesterday from Petersburg. But I don't know how to deliver the copies intended for the Grand Dukes and Zhukovsky. You know that the cholera is here; Tsarskoe Selo has been surrounded by cordons, and it will probably be the refuge for the Tsar's family. In that case, Zhukovsky will come, and I shall wait till he arrives to hand him your packet. Your anger at him for his silence is unjust. He is a most unpunctual correspondent, and is in correspondence with nobody. I can assure you that he sincerely esteems you. You astonish me, that your tragedy[2] has not yet gone on sale. Venevitinov[3] told me that it had already appeared, and for that reason I have not done anything about it. It must appear without fail, and I shall write without fail to Benkendorf about it at the first opportunity.[4] The cholera and the death of the Tsarevich[5] have discomposed us completely; let me regain my senses.

Write Peter [the Great];[6] don't be afraid of his oak cudgel. In his time you would have been one of his assistants; in our time be at least his portrait painter. I am sorry that you have not yet dissociated yourself from Moscow University, which must sooner or later cast you from its midst, for no alien substance can remain in any body. And learning, activity, and intelligence are alien to Moscow University.

We have a little account to settle. I owed you 225 rubles of interest; of it I gave you, you remember, 75—a balance of 150 remains, which you will receive as soon as I receive my quitrent from Smirdin.

Write me directly to Tsarskoe, or Sarskoe, Selo. I am separated from Smirdin by the quarantine. For the time being I cannot fulfill your errands of buying the books for many reasons. Farewell; goodby.

A.P.

[374]
To Peter Alexandrovich Pletnev
July 3, 1831. From Tsarskoe Selo to Petersburg.

Do me the favor of telling me: Are you alive? What do you intend to do? How are our fellows? What horrors! Lord Jesus Christ!

For God's sake order Smirdin to send me some money, or I shall come to him myself, in spite of the quarantine.

Do you know what? I am alive and well.

Farewell.

July 3.

I have copied my five tales and the preface, i.e., the compositions of the late Belkin, a fine fellow. What do you want me to do with them? Shall we print them ourselves, or shall we make a bargain with Smirdin?[1] R.S.V.P.

My wife greets yours warmly and wishes health to both of you.

[375]

To Peter Andreevich Vyazemsky
July 3, 1831. From Tsarskoe Selo to Moscow.

I have received your letter (probably from Fedosey Sidorovich;[1] at least a cross and an anchor were engraved on the seal, together with the inscription, "God is my hope"). You want your furniture back. Oh, dear fellow! It will be difficult for me to find new furniture in Tsarskoe Selo. But nothing can be done about it; take it back. Only I shall be sorry to let you have it for the same price. By golly, Your Highness, it's worth more. I got it on the basis of a favorable opportunity and of acquaintanceship; truly, it wouldn't be a sin for you to add a hundred rubles or so. By the newspapers I have seen that [A. I.] Turgenev has set out for Moscow, where you are; won't you come back with him? That would be fine. We would start up something like an almanac, and we would ransack Turgenev[2] a little. I don't have any news about your *Adolphe*;[3] Pletnev is separated from me by the cholera; he writes nothing. I have been expecting Zhukovsky here, but the court no longer is coming to Tsarskoe Selo because the cholera has showed up in Pulkovo. In Petersburg the populace is wrought up; rumors of poisoning have become so widespread that even decent people repeat these absurdities with a clear conscience. The populace has killed two doctors. The Tsar has quelled the rebellion, but all is not quiet yet. We have no news from the army. There for you is all I know. Don't even ask about literature: I am not receiving a single journal except the *St. Petersburg Record*, and I don't read it. I have read *Roslavlev*,[4] and I'd very much like to know how you are berating it. I have not heard or seen any conversations about *Boris*;[5] I don't meddle in others' conversations. For the time being I am not writing anything: I am waiting for autumn. Eliza [Khitrovo] is preparing for a martyr's death and has already written me a touching farewell. How are you? Has your *Fonvizin* come out of the censorship and gone to press?[6] Apropos of the censorship, Shcheglov[7] has died; not the one from our regiment but from another. My father is moping in my neighborhood, in Pavlovsk;[8] on the whole it's boring enough.

July 3.

I greet all of you fellows, including Turgenev, too, if he is already there.

[376]

To Peter Yakovlevich Chaadaev
July 6, 1831. From Tsarskoe Selo to Moscow.
(In French)

My friend, I shall speak to you in the language of Europe;[1] I am more at home in it than in ours. And we shall continue our conversations, begun long ago at Tsarskoe Selo[2] and so often interrupted.

You know what is happening with us; in Petersburg the common people imagined they were being poisoned. The gazettes are wearing themselves out at scoldings and protestations, but unfortunately the common people cannot read, and bloody scenes are about to be repeated. We are encordoned at Tsarskoe Selo and at Pavlovsk, and we have no communication with Petersburg. That is why I have seen neither Bludov nor Bellizard. Your manuscript[3] is still with me; do you wish me to return it? But what will you do with it in Necropolis?[4] Leave it with me a little longer. I have just reread it. It seems to me that the beginning is too much linked up with previous conversations, to previously developed ideas which are very clear and definite to you but of which the reader is not informed. The first pages are, consequently, obscure, and I believe that you would do well to substitute for them a simple note, or else make an extract from them. I was prepared to call to your attention also the lack of order and of method of the whole piece, but I reflected that it is a letter and that the genre excuses and authorizes this negligence and unconstraint. Everything you say about Moses, Rome, Aristotle, the idea of the true God, about ancient Art, about Protestantism, is admirable in its force, truth, or eloquence. All that which is a portrait and a tableau is sweeping, dazzling, grandiose. Your mode of conceiving history is completely new to me, but I cannot always be of your opinion; for example, I do not understand your aversion for Marcus Aurelius or your predilection for David (whose Psalms I admire—if, however, they are by him). I do not see why the robust and naive painting of polytheism by Homer should rouse your indignation. Aside from its poetic merit, it is still, according to your own admission, a great historical monument. What bloodiness does *The Iliad* offer which is not to be found in the Bible? You see Christian unity in Catholicism; that is, in the Pope. Is it not in the idea of

Christ, which is also found in Protestantism? The first idea was monarchical; it became republican. I express myself poorly, but you will understand me. Write me, my friend, even if you must chide me. It is better, says the Preacher, to hear the rebuke of the wise than the song of fools.[5]

July 6. Tsarskoe Selo.

[377]

To PETER ALEXANDROVICH PLETNEV
About (not later than) July 11, 1831.
From Tsarskoe Selo to Petersburg.

The Court has arrived, and Tsarskoe Selo is full of excitement and has turned into the capital. I was sad to hear from Zhukovsky that you will not be here. But so be it: stay in your summer house and keep well. Rosset the dark-eyed[1] was disturbed about you, and wanted to write you, but Zhukovsky dissuaded her, saying, "He's alive, what more would you have." However she has commissioned me to send you 500 rubles of some sort of belated pension.[2] If you have some money of mine, pay it out of that—and let me know here; then I shall take the 500 rubles from her.

A few days ago I sent off to you via Gesling[3] the tales of my friend, the late Belkin.[4] Have you received them? I shall furnish the preface later. Give them to the censorship—the civil one, not that of the crown[5]—and let's sniff out an understanding with Smirdin; I am of the opinion that these tales can bring us in 10,000—and here is how:

2,000 copies at 6 rubles = 12,000
—1,000 for printing
—1,000 commission

Net   10,000

What about your plan for *The Northern Flowers* [*for* 1832] for the benefit of Delvig's brothers? I am giving *Mozart* [*and Salieri*] for it, and several short things. Zhukovsky is giving his fairy tale in hexameters.[6] Write Baratynsky; he will send us some treasures; he is in his village.—There's no use waiting for verses from you. If only you would get down to it and write something about Delvig, how good that would be! In any case we need prose; if you don't give anything, the prose will run aground.[7] There's no need of a survey of literature; what the devil kind of literature do we have? You'd have to berate Polevoy and Bulgarin. Would such a hallelujah be fitting on the tomb of Delvig? Think all this over well, and then take charge—but it's already time to publish, i.e., to prepare for publishing. Stay well, everybody; Christ be with you.

[378]

To PETER ALEXANDROVICH PLETNEV
About (not later than) July 16, 1831.
From Tsarskoe Selo to Petersburg.

I have been importuning you with letters,[1] and I did not know of your grief. Only yesterday I was told of the death of our good and intelligent blind man.[2] Knowing your attachment to the deceased Molchanov, I can vividly imagine your feelings. By the hour the world is becoming emptier, the road before us is becoming emptier. A difficult time, a difficult year. At least I console myself knowing that you in your Patmos[3] are unharmed and inaccessible. But the epidemic seems to be losing its force even in Petersburg. We who have already been under fire in Moscow and Nizhny have listened indifferently to the approaching cross-fire; but how many victims there are whom we know! However, except for Molchanov, we do not seem to have lost anybody close to our hearts. With us in Tsarskoe Selo everything is hurry-scurrying, exulting; the lying-in of the Tsaritsa is being awaited;[4] they are awaiting good news from Paskevich; they are awaiting the cessation of the cholera. As for me, I am awaiting a letter of yours; I am convinced that you and yours are well, just as I have always felt assured of the life and health of me and mine.

[379]

To MIKHAIL LUKIANOVICH YAKOVLEV
July 19, 1831. From Tsarskoe Selo to Petersburg.

My money, dear Mikhaylo Lukianovich,[1] is at Pletnev's. Do me the favor to take the trouble to make a trip to see him, and since he is a punctilious person, take my promissory note with you and write on it that the interest has been received.[2] Ask him for me to write me a couple of lines and send some money, which I have need of.[3] If he is staying in his summer house, afraid of the cholera, and is not having anything to do with anybody, then write me about him, whether he and his are well.

I cordially greet Sofia Mikhaylovna,[4] and I am very, very sorry that I shall not be able to say farewell to her. God grant her health and fortitude of soul. If she should come to need the money, ask her not to stand on ceremony with me, not only as regards my debt, but also in any event. How about *The Northern Flowers*? As for me, I am ready. A few days ago I looked through the letters of Delvig which I have; perhaps in due course we shall publish them. She has my letters to him, doesn't she? We might combine them.[5] Another request: two tragedies by our Kyukhlya[6] and his *Izhorsky*, as well as my "About a Knight in Love with a Maid,"[7] were at Delvig's, ready for the press. Can't Sofia Mikhaylovna let you have all this? Pletnev and I would try to make something of it.

What are you doing, friends, and who of our friends have set off for the place from which there is no returning?[8] Farewell, good-by.

July 19.
Tsarskoe Selo.

A.P.

Letter 350

1. Pushkin was married on February 18, 1831. This letter is typical in style of what was expected of a young member of a family to an older one at the time. For Pushkin's real opinion, see, for example, Letter 405.
2. The statue of Catherine II.

Letter 351

1. Olga Petrovna Pletneva (1830-1851), then less than a year old.
2. Stepanida Alexandrovna Pletneva, Pletnev's wife.
3. As a member of the Chief Directorate of Educational Institutions.

Letter 352

1. The "official answer" was written to Khmelnitsky in his capacity as Governor of Smolensk, a position he had occupied since 1829; the friendly part of the letter was to Khmelnitsky as dramatist and man of letters. Khmelnitsky had asked Pushkin to donate a copy of each of his books to the Smolensk Library.

Letter 353

1. Elizaveta M. Khitrovo and Pushkin (through Benkendorf) were trying to help L. S. Pushkin transfer into the Russian army engaged in putting down the 1830-1831 revolution in Poland. Their efforts were ultimately successful (see Letters 355, 380, and notes).
2. Pushkin left Moscow for Petersburg in the middle of May, 1831; after a week in Petersburg, he moved to Tsarskoe Selo.
3. Pushkin substitutes "intelligence" for "hope" in his reminiscence of Dante's *Inferno*, III, 9.
4. Pushkin's reference is to the oratorical and prophetical tone in Lamennais' newspaper *L'Avenir*. The prelate Bossuet's reputation for pulpit oratory had survived, by Pushkin's time, for a century and a half. The allusion to prophesying about Nineveh is to the Book of Jonah. According to the Slavic Bible, the plant which shaded Jonah was the pumpkin.
5. Fedor Yakovlevich Skaryatin (b. 1806).

Letter 354

1. Pushkin had already spoken of this possibility in Letter 339.
2. Pushkin's italics and spelling. Pushkin's earlier interest in English literature had to a considerable degree centered upon Byron and then Shakespeare. By this time, his interest had widened to Sir Walter Scott and other English authors including the ones mentioned here. In 1830, Pushkin wrote a poem, "Sonnet," based on Wordsworth's "Scorn Not the Sonnet, Critic" (1827).
3. Alexandra Osipovna Rosset.
4. Pushkin and Pletnev did publish *The Northern Flowers for* 1832.
5. The allusion is to Pushkin's hopes of publishing his own periodical, a desire which was not fulfilled until 1836.
6. Here, as elsewhere in the letters, Pushkin is paying his disrespects to Moscow University.
7. In bank notes; only some 11,000 in silver.

Letter 355
  1. For L. S. Pushkin's transfer from the Russian army in the Caucasus, then under the command of Count Paskevich, to the Russian army in Poland (see Letter 353).
  2. A famous restaurant in Moscow.
  3. Chuguev is a town in the Kharkhov province, on the road from Moscow to the Caucasus. The "unfavorable report" did not prevent L. S. Pushkin's being transferred to the Polish front, on May 20, 1831.

Letter 356
  1. A self-quotation from "The Incantation" (1830).
  2. Reval was a favorite summer resort for Russians at the time.
  3. "I prefer to be bored otherwise." Artur Potocki (1787-1832), Polish officer and author, and an acquaintance of Pushkin's during his Odessa years.
  4. See Letter 354.
  5. Karamzin's *History of the Russian State*. By "book" here Pushkin apparently means prose work.
  6. Bulgarin's novel *Peter Ivanovich Vyzhigin* (1831), which Pushkin calls *Vyzhigin II* below, to distinguish it from Bulgarin's *Ivan Vyzhigin* (1829).
  7. That is, Pushkin's own article (pub. 1831) on Sainte-Beuve's *La Vie, les poésies et les pensées de J. Delorme*.
  8. Probably Feodosia Dmitrievna Zhikhareva (1795-1850).
  9. An ironical allusion to the theft of fifty-four thousand rubles in bank notes after the death of Delvig, from the room in which his corpse was laid out.

Letter 357
  1. Quotation from Batyushkov's poetic epistle to I. M. Muraviev-Apostol.
  2. In Griboedov's *Woe from Wit*.
  3. Mikhail Danilovich Delaryu (1811-1868), minor writer.
  4. This is Pushkin's first mention of the great Russian novelist Nikolay Vasilievich Gogol (1809-1852), who had published several things, but whose fame began later in the same year, with the appearance of his *Evenings on a Farm Near Dikanka* (1831-1832).
  5. Ballads translated from Schiller, Southey, Uhland, and Bürger. See Letter 366.
  6. Line from Zhukovsky's poem "I Used to Meet the Young Muse . . . ," already quoted in Letter 127.
  7. See Letter 148, note 8.
  8. Pushkin actually moved from Tsarskoe Selo to Petersburg in the middle of October.

Letter 358
  1. A. N. Goncharov had proposed that he make over his Nizhny Novgorod estate to his three granddaughters—Pushkin's wife and her two sisters. The point of discussion is the dowry for Pushkin's wife.

Letter 359
  1. By the novelist Alexander Fomich Veltman (1800-1870). The first part appeared in 1831.
  2. Zagoskin's novel *Roslavlev* appeared during the following month.
  3. Pushkin's moving to Tsarskoe Selo was delayed by negotiations about his wife's dowry (see Letter 358).
  4. Letter 355.

Letter 360
1. A hotel where Pushkin had usually stayed while in Petersburg during his bachelor years.
2. Alexander Yurievich Polivanov (b. 1795) was then paying court to Alexandra Nikolaevna Goncharova, sister of Pushkin's wife. The courtship fell through because of the opposition of Pushkin's mother-in-law, who became angry with Pushkin for favoring Polivanov's suit.
3. Nashchokin's gypsy mistress, Olga Andreevna.
4. Pushkin's housekeeper, whom he left behind in Moscow to see to winding up his affairs with regard to his apartment there. Nashchokin took care of the financial matters for Pushkin in this connection, and therefore needed the power of attorney mentioned in the letter.

Letter 361
1. This letter shows Pushkin's dependency upon Mme. Khitrovo for contemporary French materials, and it also shows the immediacy of the reception of French literature into Russia at the time. Stendhal's *Le Rouge et le Noir* had appeared in 1830, and Eugène Sue's *Plock et Plick* and Victor Hugo's *Notre Dame de Paris*, in 1831.

Letter 362
1. The reference is to the assistance given Pushkin by Nashchokin in connection with Pushkin's moving from Moscow to Tsarskoe Selo. See Letter 360. Maria Ivanovna was Pushkin's Moscow housekeeper.
2. Nashchokin's "domestic war" was with his gypsy mistress, Olga Andreevna, who is called a "certain party" below. Nashchokin ended his liaison with her only in 1834.
3. A. N. Goncharov.
4. Of Veltman's novel, *The Pilgrim.*

Letter 363
1. Probably Elizaveta Khitrovo and her daughters, Countesses Tizengauzen and Ficquelmont. Both the latter had salons, to which Pushkin is probably referring in the expression "local halls."
2. Field Marshal Count Ivan Ivanovich Dibich had been Commander-in-Chief of Russian forces trying to put down the Polish revolution of 1830-1831. His campaign started off successfully, but then he retreated. When he died of cholera, on May 29, 1831, the accusation was made that he had poisoned himself. General Paskevich-Erivansky was his successor.
3. The battle of Ostrołęka, at which Dibich routed the Poles, led by their Commander-in-Chief, General Jan Skrzynecki (1787-1860). Skrzynecki was relieved of his command in August, 1831.
4. The Polish national anthem.
5. Pushkin voices the same opinion in his anti-Polish poem, "To the Calumniators of Russia" (1831).
6. The Revolution in France of July, 1830.
7. The rumor that Bulgarin had been banished from Petersburg was false. The epigram on Bulgarin, which Bulgarin attributed to Pushkin, was by P. A. Vyazemsky; Pushkin often refers to it, calling Bulgarin "Figlyarin." The name "Figlyarin" was made from the Russian *figljar*, which came from the Polish *figlarz*, and means "buffoon, mountebank." Thus the nickname refers to Bulgarin's being a Pole and to his despicable character.

8. Charles X of France fled to England after his abdication, on August 2, 1830.
9. See Letter 366.
10. He had recently been dangerously ill.

Letter 364
1. See Letter 361.

Letter 365
1. With the things from Pushkin's Moscow apartment.
2. Alexey Fedorovich Rokhmanov (1799-1862), a rich Muscovite to whom Pushkin was in debt, and who acted as Pushkin's agent for settling various financial affairs.
3. Dibich's death was greeted in Russia almost with joy, as presaging a change of command of the army, and accordingly, it was hoped, of military fortunes, in the war against the Poles.
4. The rumors proved to be false that Vilna had been taken, and that Lieutenant General Matvey Evgrafovich Khrapovitsky (1784-1847), the military governor there, had been hanged.

Letter 366
1. Letter 363.
2. Count Paskevich left Petersburg by steamship on June 6 en route to Memel. He arrived at the chief headquarters of the army on June 13, and hence there were only fourteen days between the death of Dibich and Paskevich's assuming command.
3. Pushkin's sarcastic comment shows his negative attitude towards Dibich.
4. Adjutant General Count Karl Fedorovich Tol (1777-1842), Chief of Staff under Dibich, served as Acting Commander-in-Chief between the time of Dibich's death and the arrival of his successor, Count Paskevich.
5. The rumors were false. See Letter 365, and note.
6. Pushkin here has a play on words on *porte-feuille*: "wallet" and "portfolio." The serious reference is to Turgenev's notes on his European impressions.
7. From Southey, Zhukovsky translated "God's Judgment on a Wicked Bishop," "Donica," and "Queen Orraca and the Five Martyrs of Morocco."
8. From Schiller, Zhukovsky translated "The Goblet," "The Glove," "The Ring of Policrates," and "The Lament of Ceres."
9. From Uhland, Zhukovsky translated "The Coming of Spring," "The Castle by the Sea," and "Alonzo."
10. Zhukovsky gave Scott's ballad "The Grey Brother" the title "Remorse." The hero is called a "Pilgrim." Perhaps Pushkin's use of this word was suggested by Scott's ballad "The Palmer." Scott published his "Grey Brother" as a "fragment," and hence it obviously lacked an ending.
11. "There Were Two Women and Another."
12. Zhukovsky had translated Hebel's tale in 1816.
13. Zhukovsky's *Ballads and Tales* were published by Smirdin in 1830.
14. In literature.
15. Sofia Nikolaevna Karamzina, daughter of the historiographer.
16. Pushkin quotes in English from Shakespeare's *Richard III*, V, iv. He is alluding to Vyazemsky's poem, "A Ride in the Steppe," dedicated to Sofia N. Karamzina, and using the quotation from Shakespeare as epigraph.

Letter 367
1. Alexey Nikolaevich Svistunov (1808-1872), a cavalry officer.

2. Only fragments survive.

3. This letter shows how Pushkin depended upon Mme. Khitrovo for receiving forbidden books, which she as mother-in-law of the Austrian Ambassador, Ficquelmont, could obtain. The books referred to here are all works in French: M. A. Thiers, *History of the French Revolution*, 10 volumes, 1823-1827; F. A. Mignet, *History of the French Revolution from* 1789 *to* 1814, 2 volumes, 1824; and *Collections of Memoirs Regarding the Revolution*, 23 volumes, 1821-1825.

4. Nothing is known of such a trip.

5. That is, at Mme. Khitrovo's house in this fashionable suburb of Petersburg.

Letter 368

1. See Letter 367.

2. Peter Petrovich Novosiltsev (1797-1869), an adjutant of the Moscow Governor-General Prince D. V. Golitsyn.

3. The cholera appeared in Petersburg in the middle of June, 1831, causing the court to move to Tsarskoe Selo.

4. Apparently the unidentified "woman from Constantinople" quoted in Letter 316.

5. The reference probably is to the poem "Kutuzov's Tomb," by Dmitry Yurievich Struysky (1806-1856), published under the pseudonym "Trilunny" in *The Literary Gazette* in 1831.

6. Pushkin's poem, "Before the Sacred Tomb," also written about Kutuzov, leader of Russian armies in the War Against Napoleon in 1812, and father of Mme. Khitrovo. See Letter 399.

Letter 369

1. The man who delivered Pushkin's "wagon train" of household goods from Moscow to Tsarskoe Selo.

2. An untranslatable pun: *my ne zastraxavany, a zastrašćeny*. The Russian word for "insured" is formed on a root similar to the one for "scared."

3. When cholera appeared in Petersburg, quarantines were placed around Tsarskoe Selo, in order that the court might have safe refuge there.

4. With her grandfather, A. N. Goncharov, who is called "the deaf old man" below.

5. Natalia Ivanovna Goncharova was violently opposed to Polivanov as suitor for the hand of her daughter Alexandra. See Letters 360 and 362.

Letter 370

1. In the Hay Market riot of June 23, 1831, the populace, convinced that deaths from the cholera were really from poisoning and that German physicians were to blame, destroyed one hospital and killed several physicians. See also Letter 372, and note 3.

2. Grand Duke Constantine, who died of the cholera on June 15, 1831.

3. V. S. Ogon-Doganovsky, to whom Pushkin owed gambling debts.

4. Pushkin went to Moscow at the beginning of December, 1831. See Letter 411.

5. Alexander Pavlovich Bryullov (1798-1877), architect and portrait artist.

6. Fedor Danilovich Shneyder, Moscow physician. Nashchokin had asked Pushkin to inquire whether Shneyder would receive an award for participation in two expeditions.

7. Andrey Petrovich Esaulov (ca. 1800-1850's), a composer under the protection of Nashchokin. His song was perhaps his musical setting of Pushkin's "Farewell."

8. That is, to the gypsy band which included the others in addition to Nashchokin's mistress, Olga Andreevna.

Letter 371
   1. Pushkin's wife probably succeeded in preventing this letter from reaching her mother.

Letter 372
   1. That cholera had appeared in the Opochka district.
   2. Expraxia Nikolaevna Vulf was married to Baron Boris Alexandrovich Vrevsky (1805-1888) nine days later, on July 8, 1831.
   3. "The Sovereign spoke with the common people. The mob listened on their knees —silence—only the Tsar's voice, *like a holy bell,* resounded on the square." Pushkin quotes from a letter from the writer, Baron Egor Fedorovich Rozen (1800-1860). The italicized expression is a quotation from Pushkin's *Boris Godunov*: the dying Tsar, in his advice to his son, tells him that the Tsar's voice should resound only on the occasion of a great grief or a great holiday, "like a holy bell."
   4. The court arrived on July 10.
   5. The cholera appeared in Trigorskoe in August, 1831.—According to the biblical account, "plagues" of Egypt numbered not seven, but ten (Exodus 7—12).
   6. An estate between Mikhaylovskoe and Trigorskoe, on the bank of the river Sorot. Pushkin did not acquire it.
   7. Slip of the pen for 1831.

Letter 373
   1. Pogodin sent Pushkin four copies of his publication, *The All-Russian State's Flourishing Condition, Into Which Peter the Great . . . Initiated, Led, and Left It. . . .* The work was compiled by the historian Ivan Kirillovich Kirillov (1689-1737). One of the four copies was for Pushkin himself; Pogodin asked Pushkin to arrange for the delivery of one copy each to Grand Dukes Alexander (1818-1881, as Alexander II, emperor, 1855-1881) and Constantine, and the fourth copy to Zhukovsky. Pogodin had complained of Zhukovsky's not answering his letters, and therefore he had asked Pushkin, instead of him, to present these books to the royal family.
   2. *Marfa, the Novgorod Burgomaster's Wife.*
   3. Alexey Vladimirovich Venevitinov (1806-1872), brother of the poet.
   4. Instead of writing, Pushkin went to see Benkendorf, but did not find him in (see Letter 385).
   5. Grand Duke Constantine.
   6. Pogodin's tragedy *Peter I* was not published until 1873, with a dedication to Pushkin modeled on Pushkin's dedication of *Boris Godunov* to Karamzin (see Letter 317).

Letter 374
   1. Pushkin's *Tales of Belkin,* which he sent along with this letter, to Pletnev, were published in 1831 by the publisher and bookseller Adolf Alexandrovich Plyushar (1806-1865).

Letter 375
   1. Feodosy Sidorovich Tolmachev, tutor in the Vyazemsky family.
   2. That is, his *porte-feuille,* as in Letter 366.
   3. Pletnev was then seeing through the press Vyazemsky's translation of Constant's novel *Adolphe.*
   4. Novel by Zagoskin.

5. Vyazemsky had referred to an anonymous pamphlet, *Conversation* (Moscow, 1831) on Pushkin's *Boris Godunov*.

6. It was not published until 1848.

7. Nikolay Prokofievich Shcheglov.

8. Pavlovsk was less than a mile away from Tsarskoe Selo.

Letter 376

1. Chaadaev had asked Pushkin to write him in Russian. Pushkin had developed an adequate literary language for poetry, but not yet a satisfactory language for expository, "metaphysical" prose. Pushkin still did abstract thinking in French, and hence the letter is in that language.

2. In 1816-1817, while Pushkin was still a student of the Tsarskoe Selo Lyceum and Chaadaev was a hussar officer stationed at Tsarskoe Selo. Perhaps no influence on Pushkin's intellectual development was more significant than that of Chaadaev. Though Chaadaev later greatly changed his views, Pushkin continued to have great friendship for him and great respect for him and his opinions.

3. The manuscript of two of Chaadaev's *Philosophical Letters*, written in French, first published as numbers two and three, but now numbered six and seven. Pushkin was trying to get Chaadaev's manuscript through the censorship with the aid of his old friend D. N. Bludov and published by Bellizard. Chaadaev's manuscript was, however, not passed by the censorship at this time. When the first of the *Philosophical Letters* was published in 1836, there was a tremendous uproar, and the central ideological battle of the nineteenth century in Russia, that of the Westerners versus the Slavophiles, was on. Chaadaev interprets history in his *Philosophical Letters* from the point of view of Roman Catholicism. He denies merit to pagan antiquity, including its literary and artistic monuments. He condemns Russian history and civilization as meaningless, because of Russia's having obtained its form of Christianity, Orthodoxy, from the Eastern side of the Great Schism of 1054, and hence missing the great period of the flowering of Roman Catholic thought, and also the Renaissance. Chaadaev similarly opposed Protestantism.

For Pushkin's reasoned views on the subject of Chaadaev's letters, and for further comment upon them, see Letter 637 and notes.

4. Chaadaev's *Philosophical Letters* were addressed from Necropolis ("City of the Dead")—that is, Moscow.

5. Ecclesiastes 7:5.

Letter 377

1. Alexandra Osipovna Rosset.

2. What sort of a "pension" is unknown.

3. Nikolay Nikolaevich Gesling (1806-1853), graduate of the Tsarskoe Selo Lyceum in 1826 and then civil servant.

4. Pushkin's *Tales of Belkin*.

5. Since Pushkin's *Tales of Belkin* were pseudonymous, allegedly by the Pushkin's "late friend," Pushkin was able to evade the censorship of Benkendorf and Nicholas I.

6. "A Battle with a Serpent."

7. Pletnev contributed nothing to this almanac.

Letter 378

1. The reference is to two letters which have not survived.

2. Peter Stepanovich Molchanov (b. 1770), in whose house Pletnev was living at this time, had died of the cholera on July 9, 1831.

3. Pushkin had already used the image of the Isle of Patmos in connection with exile n Letter 17, and with quarantine in Letter 321.

4. Empress Alexandra Fedorovna gave birth to Grand Duke Nicholas (1831-1891), on July 27, 1831.

Letter 379

1. Mikhail Lukianovich Yakovlev (1798-1868), a Lyceum comrade and friend of Pushkin's.

2. Yakovlev did as requested with the promissory note, which apparently was for the thousand rubles Pushkin agreed to pay Countess Delvig for the portrait of Pushkin.

3. The money Pushkin might expect from Pletnev was part of the ten thousand rubles for *Boris Godunov*.

4. Delvig's widow. Less than six months after Delvig's death, she remarried, in June, 1831. Pushkin could not go to Petersburg to see her off to Moscow, because Tsarskoe Selo was surrounded by quarantines. Yakovlev himself had proposed to her less than two months after Delvig's death.

5. Pushkin did not carry out the idea of combining and publishing their letters. It is noteworthy that Pushkin himself considered his letters of sufficient literary merit and general interest for publication.

6. Kyukhelbeker's tragedies here alluded to were probably *Archilochus* and *The Argives*. Thanks to the efforts of Pushkin, among others, the first and second parts of *Izborsky* appeared in 1835.

7. The first version of Pushkin's little poem, "There Was on Earth a Poor Knight." Later this poem plays a part in the action of Dostoevsky's novel, *The Idiot*.

8. Pushkin is thinking of deaths from the cholera.

PART IX

HISTORIAN—TSARSKOE SELO, PETERSBURG

July, 1831—July, 1833

To Pavel Voinovich Nashchokin
July 21, 1831. From Tsarskoe Selo to Moscow.

My poor goddaughter![1] Henceforth I shall not stand godfather for your children, dear Pavel Voinovich; I don't bring luck. Your wishes will be fulfilled precisely, if you take the notion to set out after Yusupov;[2] but that couldn't be; at least I absolutely cannot imagine you deceased. I keep on intending to come to you, but I fear there are quarantines. Now it is entirely impossible, when one sets out on the road, to be assured of how long it will take to make the trip. Instead of a three-day trip, if you don't watch out you will sit out three weeks in quarantine. A fine joke!—I am sending you a packet addressed to Chaadaev;[3] he is living on the Dmitrovka opposite the church. Do me the favor to deliver it to him. Where you are, everything seems quiet, one hears nothing of the cholera, there are no riots, no physicians or colonels are being murdered. Not without reason, the Tsar cited Moscow as an example for Petersburg! In Tsarskoe Selo, too, everything is quiet, but, God preserve us, what a mess there is around about.[4] You write me of some critical conversation[5] which I have not yet read. If you would read our journals, you would see that everything that is called criticism among us is equally stupid and ridiculous. As for me, I have given up. To object seriously is impossible, and I have no intention of playing the buffoon before the public. And, besides, neither the critics nor the public is worthy of sensible objections. This fall I shall get busy on literature, and this winter I shall hole up in the archives,[6] access to which has been permitted me by the Tsar. The Tsar is very gracious and amiable with me. The first thing you know I shall turn into a Tsar's favorite, and Zubkov and Pavlov will be coming to me with open arms.[7] My brother has been transferred to the Polish army.[8] There has been dissatisfaction with him because of his drunkenness and roistering, but there will be no consequences to all that. You know that we have crossed the Vistula without seeing the enemy. From hour to hour we are expecting important news both from Poland and from Paris. It seems that the business will blow over without a European war. God grant it may. Farewell, my dear fellow; don't be lazy, and stay well. July 21.

P.S. I have been chattering away with you, and I forgot about business. Here is the point; my money is in Petersburg at Pletnev's or at Smirdin's; my relationships with both have been broken off on account of the cholera. I do not know whether I shall receive by August 1 what is due me; in case I do, I shall send you Gorchakov's thousand. Otherwise, for the Lord God's sake, borrow it in my name if you wish and pay it at the due date. I am not to blame; the cholera is to blame, for it has cut me off from Petersburg, which is at hand, but they won't let me go there. It wouldn't be a bad idea, my lad, for us to get going on conversations or negotiations with Doganovsky —for the term of my first promissory note is approaching.

[381]

To Peter Alexandrovich Pletnev
July 22, 1831. From Tsarskoe Selo to Petersburg.

Your letter of the nineteenth has greatly saddened me. Again you are spleenful. Hey, look out: the spleen is worse than the cholera. One kills only the body; the other kills the soul. Delvig is dead, Molchanov is dead; just you wait, Zhukovsky will die, and we'll die, too. But life is still rich. We shall yet make new acquaintances. New friendships will ripen for us. Your daughter[1] will grow and then reach marriageable age. We shall be old grumblers, our wives, old grumblers, too, and the children will be fine, high-spirited young-sters. And the boys will start playing the rake, and the wenches, at being sentimental. And we shall love it that way.—Rub-bish, dear fellow. Don't be spleenful—the cholera will pass in a few days. If we be alive, sometime we shall be in high spirits as well.

I am sorry that you have not been receiving my letters.[2] Among them were some sensible ones. But there's no harm done. This Gesling, whom you do not know, is my Lyceum grandson, and he seems a fine fellow—I gave him the errand of delivering my tales[3] to you. Read them for your cholera-induced boredom, but there's no hurry about publishing them. Except for the two thousands for *Boris*, I have not yet received anything from Smirdin; I should think that about two thousands of money due me have accumulated; I'll write him to send it to me by the post after he delivers the five hundred Rosset rubles to you.[4] Incidentally, I shall tell you a piece of news (but let it remain between us for many reasons): the Tsar has taken me into service—not into the government office or the court or the military. No, he has given me a salary, has opened the archives to me, so that I may hole up there and do nothing.[5] That is very kind of him, isn't it? He said: *Puisqu'il est marié et qu'il n'est pas riche, il faut faire aller sa marmite.*[6] I swear he is very kind to me. When shall we see each other, my lad? Oh, this cholera! My [N. B.] Yusupov has died;[7] our Khvostov has died.[8] Maybe death will be content with these two victims. Farewell. I greet you and all yours. Stay well, all of you. Christ be with all of you.

[382]
To Pavel Voinovich Nashchokin
July 29, 1831. From Tsarskoe Selo to Moscow.

I asked you in my last letter to deliver a packet to Chaadaev:[1] they would not accept the packet at the post. I asked you to pay [V. P.] Gorchakov his remaining thousand. Here is this thousand. Deliver it, with my hearty thanks, to my good-natured creditor.

What are you doing? Are you awaiting your money, and will you rescue me from the toils of Doganovsky? Will it be necessary for me to come, as, I confess, I should like to, or shall I remain in Tsarskoe Selo, which is both cheaper and more tranquil?

Here with us everything, thank God, is quiet. The Petersburg riots have ceased; the cholera, too. The Sovereign made a trip to Novgorod,[2] where the colonies had revolted and where horrors had taken place. His presence quelled everything. The Tsaritsa gave birth to the Grand Duke Nikolay Nikolaevich day before yesterday.[3] Nothing is to be heard about Poland.

Farewell; good-by.

[383]
To Praskovia Alexandrovna Osipova
July 29, 1831. From Tsarskoe Selo to Trigorskoe.
(In French)
Your silence was beginning to disturb me, dear and kind Praskovia Alexandrovna; your letter has come to reassure me at exactly the

right time. I congratulate you once more,[1] and from the bottom of my heart I hope, for you all, prosperity, tranquillity, and health. I took your letters to Pavlovsk myself,[2] dying with the desire to know the contents, but my mother had gone out. You know the adventure that happened to them, Olga's escapade,[3] the quarantine, etc. Thank God, all is over now. My parents are no longer under arrest. The cholera is but little to be feared. It is almost over with in Petersburg. Do you know that there have been some disturbances in Novgorod[4] in the military colonies? The soldiers rioted, under the same absurd pretext, that they are being poisoned. The generals, officers, and physicians have all been massacred, with refined atrocity. The Emperor went there, and he quelled the riot with admirable courage and coolness. But the common people must not become accustomed to rioting, nor to his presence at riots. Everything has apparently finished. You judge of the disease better than the physicians and the government have done. *Bolezn' poval'naja, a ne zaraza, sledstvenno karantiny lišnee; nužny odni predostorožnosti v pišče i v odežde.*[5] If this truth had been known before, we could have avoided many evils. Now the cholera is being treated like any poisoning—*with oil and hot milk*, not overlooking steam baths. God grant that you have no need of making use of this prescription at Trigorskoe.

I put my interests and my plans in your hands. It matters little to me whether it be *Savkino*[6] or some other place; I desire to be your neighbor, and the proprietor of a pretty spot. Please let me know the price of this property or of another such. Circumstances, it appears, are going to keep me in Petersburg longer than I had wished, but that changes nothing in my plan or my hopes.

Accept the assurance of my devotion and of my complete esteem. I greet all your family.

July 29. Tsarskoe Selo.

[384]
To NIKOLAY MIKHAYLOVICH KONSHIN
June or July, 1831. In Tsarskoe Selo.

The dog has been found, thanks to your commands.[1] My wife thanks you kindly, but the dog catcher has put me in an embarrassing position. I offered him ten rubles for his labors, but he did not take it, saying "too little"; in my opinion he and the dog together are not worth that much, but my wife is of a different opinion. Are you well, and shall we see each other soon?

A.P.

[385]
To Mikhail Petrovich Pogodin
The end of July, 1831. From Tsarskoe Selo to Moscow.

Dear and honored one, I do not have time to answer your letter. I only inform you that your errand regarding the *Statistics of Peter I*[1] has been fulfilled; Zhukovsky has received the copies for the Grand Duke and for himself. He has made a different arrangement for the copy which was directed to Grand Duke Constantine. Zhukovsky will present it to the Empress. Be so kind as to write me an official note to *His Excellency Ivan Pavlovich Shambo*[2] (Her Majesty's secretary): "I make bold to place at Her Majesty's feet such-and-such a noteworthy book, etc."[3] I have been at General Benkendorf's on your business,[4] but I did not find him at home. He is remaining at Tsarskoe Selo; consequently I shall have a talk with him in a few days. Meanwhile I embrace you.

A.P.

[386]
To Pavel Voinovich Nashchokin
August 3, 1831. From Tsarskoe Selo to Moscow.

Father and benefactor! A few days ago I sent you Gorchakov's thousand; write me back, father, Pavel Voinovich, whether you have received everything all right, and another most humble request: Find out from Korotky[1] how much interest I owe the Loan Office on my loan of forty thousand and when is the deadline for repayment. Has Dorokhov's promissory note[2] been negotiated, and is Karniolin-Pinsky well? Are you well, my dear fellow? How are you getting along, and how are your folks? Why don't you send me the Esaulov song,[3] in the second, corrected edition? We would make it fashionable among the Ladies in Waiting. Everything here is getting along fine. My wife greets you.[4] She does not send a portrait,[5] for want of an artist. Whereupon, we beg forgiveness.

August 3.

P.S. And do me the favor of explaining how to make payments to the Loan Office. Should I come myself? Should I send a power of attorney to somebody? Or should I send the money by mail?

[387]

To Peter Andreevich Vyazemsky
August 3, 1831. From Tsarskoe Selo to Moscow.

August 3.

The Literary Gazette has for some reason become silent; of course Somov is sick or dissatisfied with the circulation.[1] Your observation about Bulgarin's little finger will not perish; I promise to set you laughing.[2] But for the present we don't feel like laughing: you probably have heard about the rebellions at Novgorod and Staraya Rus.[3] Horrible things. More than a hundred generals, colonels, and other officers were butchered in the Novgorod colonies with all the refinements of malignity. The rioters flogged them, beat them in their faces, jeered at them, plundered their houses, raped their wives. Fifteen doctors have been killed. One saved himself with the aid of the patients in the infirmary. After killing all their superiors, the rioters chose themselves others, from the engineers and communications men. The Sovereign arrived there after [A. F.] Orlov. He acted boldly, even audaciously: after giving them a sharp scolding, he bluntly declared that he could not forgive them, and he demanded that the instigators be surrendered. They promised and quieted down. But the Staraya Rus riot has not yet ceased. The military officials still do not dare show themselves on the street. One general there has been drawn and quartered, people have been buried alive, etc. The peasants participated; the regiments surrendered their commanders to them. It's bad, Your Highness. When such tragedies are before your eyes, there is no time to think about the dog show of our literature. The Polish business[4] seems to be ending; I am still afraid: a decisive battle, as Peter I said, is a very dangerous business. And even if we besiege Warsaw (which requires a great number of troops), Europe will have time to meddle in what's none of her affair. France will not butt in by herself; England has nothing to quarrel with us about; so maybe we shall muddle through.

In Tsarskoe Selo so far there have been no riots nor cholera. Russian journals are not reaching us; we are receiving the foreign ones, and life here is very endurable. Zhukovsky has the toothache;

he quarrels with [Alexandra Osipovna] Rosset; she turns him out of her room, and he writes her Arzamasian excuses in hexameters.

—by what shall I beseech you, O my heavenly Tsar— — — —
if you command it, I shall give my skin to be torn from my noble body for galoshes for you— —if you command it, I shall give my ears to be cut off for flyswatters, etc.

I shall send you this pure-Arzamasian work.

I thank Alexander Ivanovich [Turgenev] for his religio-philosophical postscript.[5] I don't understand why Chaadaev and the brotherhood are attacking the Reformation, *c'est à dire un fait de l'esprit Chrétien. Ce que le Christianisme y perdit en unité il le regagna en popularité.*[6] The Greek Church is a different matter: it came to a halt and separated itself from the general aspirations of the Christian spirit. I am glad that Chaadaev has appeared in society again. Tell him that I have been trying to send his manuscript[7] to him, but they still won't accept packets in the post. Make my excuses to him. I send my regards to all your folks, and I wish all of you health and tranquillity.

Tsarskoe Selo.

[388]
To Peter Alexandrovich Pletnev
August 3, 1831. From Tsarskoe Selo to Petersburg.

I have received, dear Pletnev, both the letter and the fifteen hundred. You are acting intelligently in sitting tight in your burrow and not showing your nose in Petersburg, which I cursed once upon a time. What is dangerous is not the cholera; what is dangerous is the fear, the moral state, the despondency, which must take possession of every thinking creature in the present terrible circumstances. The cholera will probably cease within a week, but Tsarskoe Selo will still be surrounded by quarantines for a long time. And so our meeting is still a long way off. How about *The Flowers*? I swear I don't know what I should do. Yakovlev writes that for the time being it is impossible to get started at them. Why so? The printing houses haven't stopped, have they? There is paper, isn't there? Somov isn't sick or refusing to publish, is he? By the way, what has happened to

The Literary Gazette? It is coming out more irregularly than *The Mercury.*[1] Apropos of that, Bestuzhev-Ryumin hasn't died, has he? They say the cholera carries off the drunkards. With deep sorrow I learned that Khvostov is alive. Among so many tombs, so many early or precious victims, Khvostov sticks out like some obscene fig. I was recently rereading Delvig's letters: in one of them he writes me of the death of D. Venevitinov. "I met Khvostov the very same day," he says, "and I could scarcely keep from berating him and asking why he is alive." Our poor Delvig! Khvostov outlived him, too. Mark my prophetic word: Khvostov will outlive me, too.[2] But in case he does, in the name of our friendship I adjure you to cut his throat—with an epigram, at least. Good-by, and stay well, all of you. My tales[3] returned to me, without reaching you.

August 3.

I often see Rosset; she loves you very much, and we often talk about you. Her engagement[4] has been publicly announced. The Sovereign has already congratulated her.

[389]

To Peter Andreevich Vyazemsky
August 14, 1831. From Tsarskoe Selo to Moscow.

Amiable Vyazemsky, poet and Chamberlain. . . .[1] (Have you recognized the manner of Vasily Lvovich?[2] Thus once he began a letter to a chamberlain decorated with the key to Loyalty and the Faith). So the sun has peeped out from behind the clouds at us, too! The same key is shining on your rear.[3] Hurrah! Praise and honor to the poet-chamberlain—please congratulate Princess Vera[4] for me.

When we heard of this event, so joyful for the Arzamas, we, the Arzamasians of Tsarskoe Selo, resolved to convoke a solemn assembly. All the members present here assembled together without delay, in the number of two. Mr. Zhukovsky was selected by lot as chairman; I, Cricket,[5] as secretary. The protocol of the session will be delivered without delay to Your Arzamasian and Chamberlainian Excellency (likewise Highness). The members asked why Asmodeus does not appear in a single periodical publication. The secretary responded in the same voice that he is sending off his articles, without his name, to *The Commercial Gazette*. The members inquired whether Asmodeus has long been occupying himself with the *Commercial*, whether he is winning at commercial play. The chairman responded, in the same voice, that he has won a key at the commercial, and now Asmodeus will transfer to the Bank.[6]

Leaving Arzamasian politics, I shall tell you that our Polish affairs are progressing, thank God: Warsaw has been surrounded, Skrzynecki has been relieved of his command by the impatient patriots. Dembiński,[7] who suddenly appeared in Warsaw from Lithuania, has been chosen commander-in-chief. The rebels were accusing Skrzynecki of inactivity. Hence they want battles; hence they will be crushed; hence the intervention of France will come too late;[8] hence Count Paskevich is astonishingly lucky. The King of Holland has flown into a passion,[9] but it looks as though he will be forced to give up the idea of Belgium; Prussia does not feel like fooling with him. If a general European war should break out, then I shall truly regret my marriage, unless I strap my wife to my saddle and take her along. Although Zhukovsky's poetic diarrhea has ceased, he is still squirting hexameters.[10] We are awaiting you. We really should start up a journal, but what kind? A *Quarteley*.[11] In three months we shall issue a little book—no, a big one, with the help of God and naked Liza.[12] By the way, Liza has written me a letter, a sort of last will and testament: *Croyez à la tendresse de celle qui vous aimera même au delà du tombeau*,[13] etc., but she became silent. I was calmly thinking to myself that she had died. But what do I learn? Eliza has fallen in love with the traveler Mornay,[14] and she is coquetting with him! What do you think of that? *O femme, femme! créature faible et décevante. . . .*[15] Farewell, Chamberlain, I greet you and yours with all my heart.

August 14.

[390]
To PAVEL IVANOVICH MILLER
The first half of August, 1831. In Tsarskoe Selo.

I cordially thank you for the books and for your kind letter. When will you fulfill your other promise—to pay me a visit? By so doing the grandson[1] would very much oblige his grandfather, who is devoted to him in heart.

A.P.

[391]
To Peter Alexandrovich Pletnev
About (not later than) August 15, 1831.
From Tsarskoe Selo to Petersburg.

I am sending you by Gogol the tales of my friend Ivan Petrovich Belkin;[1] give them to the plain censorship,[2] and let's proceed with their publication. I shall send the preface later. The rules by which we shall be guided in publishing are the following:

(1) Leave as much white space as possible, and spread the lines out as widely as possible.

(2) Put no more than eighteen lines on a page.

(3) Print the names *in full*, e.g., Ivan Ivanovich Ivanov, and not I. Iv. Iv—. Do the same with cities and villages.

(4) Spell out the numbers (except years).

(5) In the tale "The Station Master" call the hussar Minsky and replace the *** with this name everywhere.

(6) Whisper my name to Smirdin, for him to whisper it on to purchasers.

(7) From the most honored public take seven rubles apiece instead of ten[3]—for now there are hard times, a levy of recruits, and quarantines.

I think the public will pay this moderate quitrent without demurring, and will not force me to use stern measures.

The main thing: let's stay alive and well. . . . Farewell, my angel.

P.S. Print the epigraphs before the very beginning of the story, and the titles of the tales on a separate page (for the sake of the breadth). [. . .][4] Apropos of epigraphs: another must be chosen for "The Shot" —to wit, in A. Bestuzhev's "Novel in Seven Letters" in *The Polar Star*: "I had one shot left; I had sworn, etc."[5] Check it, my dear fellow.

[392]
To Nikolay Vasilievich Gogol
August 25, 1831. From Tsarskoe Selo to Petersburg.

Dear Nikolay Vasilievich,

I thank you very much for your letter and for delivering my packet[1] to Pletnev; especially for the letter. The project of your learned critique is extremely good.[2] But you are too lazy to put it into effect. F. Kosichkin's article[3] has not yet appeared. I don't know what that signifies. Nadezhdin hasn't become afraid of the anger of Faddey Venediktovich [Bulgarin], has he? I congratulate you upon your first triumph, upon the typesetters' snorting with laughter and their foreman's explications.[4] I am impatiently waiting for something else: what the journalists will say and the response of the sharp-witted shop clerk.[5] Here everything is all right: there are no riots, inundations, or cholera.[6] Zhukovsky has got into a writing vein: I feel autumn coming, and I am planning to set to work. Your Nadezhda Nikolavna, i.e., my Natalia Nikolavna,[7] thanks you for remembering her, and she cordially greets you. Embrace Pletnev for me, and stay alive in Petersburg, which seems to be hard enough to do.

[393]
To Peter Andreevich Vyazemsky
The end of August, 1831. From Tsarskoe Selo to Moscow.

(Between ourselves.) Delvig's two brothers have been left penniless and on the hands of his widow, who has lost a large part of her small estate. This present year we shall publish *The Northern Flowers* for the benefit of the two orphans. Send me some verses and some prose; we shall get our journal started afterwards.

On August 20, the anniversary of the death of Vasily Lvovich [Pushkin], the local Arzamasians had a funeral banquet in memory of our club elder, of cheesecakes,[1] into each of which was thrust a laurel leaf. Svetlana[2] pronounced the funeral oration, in which with especial feeling she recalled the ceremony of his initiation into the Arzamas.

[394]
To Pavel Voinovich Nashchokin
September 3, 1831. From Tsarskoe Selo to Moscow.

My dear Pavel Voinovich, I have not answered your last letter, which filled me with joy and gratitude, in the expectancy of the promised following one. But so far it has not come. God grant that success crown your diplomacy![1] I am awaiting Doganovsky's decision with trembling heart. Is everything all right with you? How are your cramps, headaches, trips to Elena Timofeevna,[2] and other tempests? With me, thank God, everything is quiet. My wife is well; the Tsar (between ourselves) has taken me into service[3]—i.e., has given me a salary and permitted me to burrow in the archives, to compile a history of Peter I. God grant the Tsar health! At my house a change of ministry has taken place. Alexander Grigoriev's accounts turned out to be erroneous; I demanded the accounts; the session was just as tempestuous as the one in which Ivan Grigoriev was annihilated; in consequence of this, Alexander Grigoriev gave his ministry over to Vasily (who has fleas of another kind).[4] On the same day my cook came to me asking to be retired; they want to make a soldier out of this minister, and he is going to Moscow to petition with regard to this matter; probably he will come to you, too.[5] I shall feel his absence, but perhaps all is for the best. I forgot to tell you that Alexander Grigoriev, upon going into retirement, received, as a testimonial from me, a slap in the face, on account of which he took the notion of carrying out an uprising, and he put in an appearance at my place with military force, i.e., with the section policeman. But this turned out to be to his own injury, for the shopkeepers, when they learned about everything, had him thrown into the dungeon, from which in my magnanimity I delivered him. There's no quieting my mother-in-law; nothing changes her, *ni le temps, ni l'absence, ni des lieux la longueur*;[6] she does nothing but scold me—and all on account of our friend Alexander Yurievich [Polivanov].[7] Not a peep from grandfather. Until now nothing has been done for Natalia Nikolaevna.[8] My affairs are progressing but slowly. I am publishing my tales[9] *incognito*; I shall send the first copy to you. Farewell, my dear fellow. And don't forget to do the inquiring about the Loan Office.[10]

September 3.

A.P.

My wife greets you very warmly. Good-by.

[395]
TO PETER ANDREEVICH VYAZEMSKY
September 3, 1831. From Tsarskoe Selo to Moscow.

First, about business: Nashchokin has no money of mine, and he probably hasn't got hold of any of his own.[1] I am having difficulty in receiving my revenues on account of the cholera. You will receive your five hundred rubles from Petersburg as soon as I can exchange letters with my correspondents. You write of starting a journal: Yes, the devil we shall! Who would authorize us to have a journal? Fon-Fok has died; the first thing you know N. I. Grech will step into his place. We'll be in fine shape! There's no use even thinking of a political newspaper, but we might try a monthly or a four-monthly, neutral journal. There is one rub: *without fashions* it won't sell, and *with fashions* for us to take a position alongside Shalikov, Polevoy, etc., would be shameful. What do you think—with or without?[2] We might put the correspondence of Avraam and Ignaty in the department of Classical Literature.[3] Zhukovsky is still writing away; he got six notebooks and began six poems at once; he simply has the flux. It's a rare day that he does not read me something new; this year he has probably written a whole volume. That would be fine for a journal. I have got the squirts, too. A few days ago I defecated a fairy tale of a thousand verses;[4] another is rumbling in my guts.[5] But still, the cholera. . . . What you say about *Roslavlev*[6] is the gospel truth; it makes me laugh to read the critiques in our journals; one begins with Homer, another with Moses, another with Walter Scott; they write books about a novel which you gave a complete evaluation of in three lines: "that the situations though far-fetched, are entertaining; that the conversations though they ring false, are lively, and that it all can be read with pleasure" (total $3\frac{1}{2}$ lines).

I was at Donna Sol's[7] yesterday; she doesn't have your letters here; she has no intention of burning them *et vous accuse de fatuité*. The fact is that she is extremely sweet, intelligent, and she mimics General Lambert's wife and the German Chamber-Lackey at Court[8] to perfection. Your judgment about the Russian proverb will not perish.[9] To the number of the most noble ones this one belongs, too: "You can't catch up with a shove," i.e., don't raise a fuss about a shove you have already received. Apropos of a shove, have you read the article in *The Telescope* by Feofilakt Kosichkin?[10] Farewell; I greet you and yours. Yesterday Donna Sol received, in the presence of me and Zhukovsky, a letter from her brother.[11] He asks Zhukovsky's opinion, for Katerina Andreevna [Karamzina], as to whether she should come to Petersburg or remain in Moscow.[12] Zhukovsky said that if he had a hundred tongues, they would all start saying,[13] "Come to us, to us, to us." Selfishness aside, I am of the same opinion; the cholera has ceased in Petersburg, and it is starting up again where you are. What times! Warsaw should have been taken on the twenth-fifth or twenty-sixth,[14] but there is no news yet.

September 3.

[396]

To Pavel Ivanovich Miller
About (not earlier than) September 4, 1831.
In Tsarskoe Selo.

I am very grateful to you, dear Miller, for the article by Feofilakt Kosichkin; I had already seen it.[1] I thank you kindly also for the news of the taking of Warsaw.[2] I congratulate you and all my Lyceum. Your devoted great-great-grandfather.[3]

[397]

To Praskovia Alexandrovna Osipova
September 11, 1831. From Tsarskoe Selo to Trigorskoe.
(In French)

Thank you very much, Madame, for the trouble which you are taking upon yourself, to negotiate with the owners of Savkino.[1] If one of them is too obstinate, may it not be possible to by-pass him and come to an agreement with the two others? There is no hurry, though. New pursuits are going to keep me in Petersburg at least two or three years.[2] I am vexed at this: I was hoping to spend them near Trigorskoe.

My wife is very grateful to you for the lines which you have been so kind as to address to her. She is a very good girl, and she is ready to love you with all her heart.

I do not speak to you of the taking of Warsaw.[3] You can judge with what enthusiasm we learned of it, after nine months of disasters. What will Europe say? That is the question which is on our minds.

The cholera has ended its ravages in Petersburg, but it is going to make its circuit of the provinces. Take great care, Madame. Your stomach ailments make me tremble. Do not forget that treatments for cholera are the same as for simple poisoning: some milk and oil—and take care not to catch a chill.

Farewell, Madame—please believe in my respect and my sincere affection. My regards to all your family.

September 11. Tsarskoe Selo.

[398]
TO ALEXANDRA OSIPOVNA ROSSET
The middle (after the 10th) of September, 1831.
In Tsarskoe Selo.
(In French)

You[1] are already familiar with these verses,[2] but since I have just sent a copy to the Comtesse de Lambert,[3] it is fitting that you should have a like copy.

From you I learned of the captivity of Warsaw.
....
You were the herald of glory and inspiration for me.

You will receive the second line as soon as I find it for you.

[399]
TO ELIZAVETA MIKHAYLOVNA KHITROVO
The middle (after the 10th) of September, 1831.
From Tsarskoe Selo to Petersburg.
(In French)

[. . . .][1]
These verses were written at a moment when it was permissible to be discouraged. Thank God, the moment has passed. We have regained the position which we ought not to have lost. It is no longer the one which was given to us by the hand of the Prince, your father, but it is still fairly good. We do not have a word to express *resignation*, although this state of soul, or, if you prefer, this virtue, is completely Russian. The word *stolbnjak* [stupor] is the most exact equivalent.

Although I have not importuned you with my letters during this time of calamities, I have had no lack of news of you; I knew that you were in good health and that you were enjoying yourself,[2] which is certainly worthy of *The Decameron*. You have been reading in time of plague, instead of listening to tales; that, too, is very philosophical.

I suppose that my brother was present at the assault of Warsaw;[3] I have no news of him. But wasn't it time Warsaw was captured! You have read, I suppose, Zhukovsky's verses and mine:[4] for God's sake, correct this one:

Svjatynju vsex tvoix gradov [The shrine of all your cities].

Put: *grobov* [tombs]. The reference is to the tombs of Yaroslav and the Saints of the Caves; this way it is instructive and has some meaning; *gradov* [cities] does not mean anything.

I hope to present myself at your house toward the end of this month.[5] There is an awful din in Tsarskoe Selo; Petersburg is much more of a retreat.

[400]
To Elizaveta Mikhaylovna Khitrovo
The end of September or the beginning of October, 1831.
From Tsarskoe Selo to Petersburg.
(In French)

Thank you, Madame, for the elegant translation of the ode[1]— I have noted in it two inexactitudes and one copyist's error. *Issjaknut'* means *to dry up*; *skrižali*—tables, chronicles. *Izmajl'skij štyk* is the bayonet of Izmail[2]—not Izmaylov's.

There is a letter for you[3] in Petersburg; it is an answer to the first one I received from you. Have it delivered to you—I enclosed in it the ode to your late father, the Prince.

M. Opochinin[4] has done me the honor of calling on me—he is a very distinguished young man—I thank you for his acquaintance.

In a few days I shall be at your feet.

[401]
To Pavel Voinovich Nashchokin
October 7, 1831. From Tsarskoe Selo to Moscow.

I regret, dear Pavel Voinovich, that the deal fell through over the five thousand.[1] I am grateful to you just the same for your trouble, and to Doganovsky and Zhemchuzhnikov for their indulgence. Don't you be angry. They wouldn't trust you because they don't know you; that's in the nature of things. But the person who, knowing you, would not entrust you at your word with his estate is not worthy of any trust whatever himself. I ask you to get in contact with them for the last time and offer them your fifteen thousand on hand, and *the remaining five thousand will be paid by me in three months.* I am ashamed at not being punctual, but my affairs have become completely upset. I thought that, getting married, I would spend three times as much as before; ten times as much has gone out. In Moscow they are saying that I receive a salary of ten thousand, but as for now I don't see even a penny; if I shall receive four thousand, then thank God for that.² Answer me as soon as you can, to Petersburg, to Kazachy Pereulok, the house of Dmitriev, in care of O[lga] S. Pavlishcheva, for delivery to A.S.P. Farewell, and stay well. I greet Olga Andreevna and your heir.³

October 7, 1831.   All yours,
Tsarskoe Selo.   A. Pushkin.

[402]
TO PETER ANDREEVICH VYAZEMSKY
The middle (about the 15th) of October, 1831.
From Tsarskoe Selo to Moscow.

Right now I am going from Tsarskoe Selo to Petersburg. I have left your furniture intact here to be delivered for you directly to the place where you will stay.¹ I have not sent off the money to you, for I have been expecting you here. But just when will you get here? We can hardly wait. See what you can get done for *The Northern Flowers*; send us some of your poetry and prose. And doesn't Yazykov have something? I hear he and Kireevsky are undertaking a journal.² Godspeed! But will there be fashions in it? That is the important question. At least it will be possible for us to appear somewhere, and Kosichkin³ is glad of that. Otherwise where would he be forced to take refuge! It's easy to say—in *The Telescope*! The Court is in Moscow. Zhukovsky and [Alexandra] Rosset are in Petersburg. Zhukovsky has written a world of good stuff, and he's still continuing up to now. He is translating a canto from *Marmion*.⁴ Wonderful. What do you think of the Gogol!⁵ My *Tales* are being published. *The Northern Flowers* will be interesting to see. Farewell, good-by. My address: At the Izmaylovsky Bridge on Voskresenskaya Street, in Bernikov's house.

[403]

To ALEXANDER KHRISTOFOROVICH BENKENDORF

The middle of October, 1831. From Tsarskoe Selo to Petersburg.

Dear Sir, Alexander Khristoforovich,

I make bold to disturb Your High Excellency with a most humble request for permission to publish in a separate book the poems of mine which have already been published during the last three years.[1]

In 1829, Your High Excellency was so kind as to inform me that it pleased the Sovereign Emperor henceforth to rely on me in the publication of my compositions.[2] The Sovereign's trust places on me the obligation to be a most strict censor toward myself, and after that it would be an indiscretion for me again to submit my composi- tions to His Imperial Majesty's examination. But permit me to hope that Your High Excellency, in accordance with the favor which you have always shown toward me, will vouchsafe me the preliminary permission.

With the most profound respect, gratitude, and complete devotion, I have the honor to be, Dear Sir,

Your High Excellency's

Most humble servant,

Alexander Pushkin.

Enclosed I am forwarding to Your High Excellency a letter de- livered to me by Mr. Pogodin.[3]

[404]

To SERGEY SEMENOVICH UVAROV

October 21, 1831. From Petersburg to Moscow.

Dear Sir, Sergey Semenovich,[1]

Prince Dondukov[2] has delivered to me the excellent, truly in- spired poem which in your modesty you chose to call an imitation. My poem served you as a simple theme for your brilliant fantasy to develop. It remains for me to thank you from my heart for the attention shown me and for the force and fullness of thoughts which you have magnanimously attributed to me.

With the most profound respect and complete devotion, I have the honor to be, Dear Sir,

Your Excellency's

Most humble servant,

October 21, 1831.   Alexander Pushkin.

SPb.

[405]

To Pavel Voinovich Nashchokin

October 22, 1831. From Petersburg to Moscow.

My dear Pavel Voinovich, here I am in Petersburg, where I have been forced to rent another house. Address me: *On the Galernaya, the house of Briskorn*. I have seen Zhemchuzhnikov. They have consented to accept my promissory note for five thousand and to accept the fifteen thousand immediately.[1] How shall we accomplish this? Shouldn't I come to Moscow myself? And somehow I should like to chatter with you a while, and I would take care in person of a couple of pieces of business; for example my wife's diamonds,[2] which I am trying to save from the bankruptcy of my mother-in-law and from the paws of Semen Fedorovich.[3] Grandfather is a swine; he is giving his third concubine in marriage, with a dowry of ten thousand, but he can't pay me my twelve thousand,[4] and he doesn't give anything to his granddaughter. Natalia Nikolaevna is with child[5]—the baby will come in May. All this will greatly change my way of living, and one must think of everything.

What about Moscow: how did you Muscovites receive the Sovereign,[6] and who will take it upon himself to justify the ancient Muscovite reputation for hospitality? The boyars have become extinct. There's no money; we don't feel up to celebrations. Moscow is a provincial city which receives the journals of fashions. It's bad. I am awaiting Vyazemsky; I don't know that I won't take up something literary—a journal, an almanac, or something of the kind. I'm lazy. By the way, I am publishing *The Northern Flowers* for the brothers of our deceased Delvig; make people buy them up—we shall do a good deed. My *Tales [of Belkin]* have been published; you will receive them in a few days. My greetings to your folks. I embrace you with all my heart.

October 22.

[406]

To Egor Fedorovich Rozen
October or the first half of November, 1831.
From Tsarskoe Selo to Petersburg, or in Petersburg.

Here for you, dear Baron, is *The Feast in the Time of the Plague* from Wilson's tragedy *à effet*.[1] Having undertaken the publication of the third volume of my shorter poems, I am not sending you certain of them, for they will probably appear before your *Alcyone*. I am burning with impatience to read your preface to *Boris*;[2] I am thinking of writing a letter to you for the second edition,[3] if you are willing, and of setting forth in it my ideas and rules by which I was guided in composing my tragedy.

[407]

To Nikolay Mikhaylovich Yazykov
November 18, 1831. From Petersburg to Moscow.

I cordially thank you, dear Nikolay Mikhaylovich, both you and Kireevsky, for the friendly letters and for the excellent verses;[1] if you had added your addresses as well, I would have been completely content. I congratulate all the brotherhood upon the birth of *The European*.[2] As for me, I am ready to serve you with whatever you please, with prose and poetry, in conscience, and against conscience. Feofilakt Kosichkin is touched to tears by the attention which you vouchsafe him.[3] A few days ago he received a letter of thanks from A. Orlov, and he is planning to answer him.[4] Take the trouble to locate him (Orlov) and deliver to him the answer of his friend (or from his friend, as Pogodin writes). Zhukovsky has arrived. The news he has brought is very consoling; the thousand you have raised[5] will greatly improve the domestic circumstances of our poor literature. I have hopes for Khomyakov;[6] his *Pretender* will be no longer a student, but his verses will continue to be as excellent as before. Hurry Vyazemsky up, have him send me some of his prose and verses; shame on him, and shame on Baratynsky, too. We are putting on a memorial feast for Delvig.[7] And this is the way they celebrate the memory of our fellows! And who? His friends! By golly, it's shameful. Khvostov had written an epistle to me, in which he has become rejuvenated and has shaken off old age. He says:

I became the ally of the Zodiac when I approached the sign of
the campaign; having no love for cholera pills, in old age I sang
of July,[8]

etc., in the same manner. I intend to answer befittingly the ally of
Aquarius, Cancer, and Capricorn. Generally speaking, with us
everything is all right.

[408]
To Fedor Nikolaevich Glinka
November 21, 1831. From Petersburg to Tver.
Dear Sir, Fedor Nikolaevich, we here have undertaken in memory
of our Delvig the publishing of the last *Northern Flowers*. Of all his
friends we have noted that only you and Baratynsky were lacking at
the poetic memorial feast: the two very poets with whom, after his
Lyceum friends, he was most closely connected. I have been told
that you are angry with me.[1] That is no argument: anger is one thing,
but friendship is another. And fine fellows they are who embroil us
against each other, with God knows what gossip. As for me, with
my sincere, profound esteem for you and your fine talent, I am
completely guiltless toward you.

I still rely on your good will and on your verses. Perhaps I shall
see you soon; at least it is pleasant to end my letter with this wish.
All yours, without ceremony, A. Pushkin.

November 21.

[409]
To Alexander Khristoforovich Benkendorf
November 24, 1831. In Petersburg.
(In French)
My General,
Not being yet definitely attached to the service, and some urgent
affairs necessitating my presence in Moscow,[1] I am obliged to absent
myself for two or three weeks without any other authorization than
that of the district police officer. I believe it my duty to give Your
Excellency notice of this.

I avail myself of this opportunity to speak to you of a completely
personal matter. The interest which you have always deigned to

show toward me encourages me to tell you of it in detail and in complete confidence.

About a year ago in one of our journals was printed a satirical article[2] in which a certain man of letters was spoken of, who manifested pretensions of having a noble origin, whereas he was only a bourgeois-gentleman. It was added that his mother was a mulatto whose father, a poor pickaninny, had been bought by a sailor for a bottle of rum. Although Peter the Great little resembled a drunken sailor, I was the one referred to clearly enough, since no Russian man of letters besides me may number a Negro among his ancestors. Since the article in question was printed in an official gazette, since indecency has been pushed to the point of speaking of my mother in a *feuilleton* which ought to be only literary, and since our gazeteers do not fight in duels, I believed it my duty to answer the *anonymous* satirist, which I did in verse, and very sharply. I sent my answer to the late Delvig, asking him to insert it in his journal. Delvig advised me to suppress it, calling to my attention that it would be ridiculous to defend oneself, with pen in hand, against attacks of this nature and to flaunt aristocratic feelings, when everything considered, one is only a gentleman-bourgeois, if not a bourgeois-gentleman.[3] I yielded to his opinion, and the affair rested there; however, several copies of this response circulated, at which I am not displeased, considering that nothing is in it which I wished to disavow. I confess that I pride myself on what are called prejudices: I pride myself on being as good a gentleman as anybody whatever, though it profits me little; lastly, I greatly pride myself on my ancestors' name, since it is the only heritage which they have left me.

But inasmuch as my verses could be taken as an indirect satire on the origin of certain prominent families, if one did not know that they are a very moderate response to a very reprehensible provocation, I have considered it my duty to give you this frank explanation, and to enclose the piece in question.[4]

Accept, General, the assurance of my high esteem.

Your Excellency's

Most humble and most obedient servant,

November 24.   Alexander Pushkin.
SPb.

[410]
To ELIZAVETA MIKHAYLOVNA KHITROVO
The second half of October, or November, 1831. In Petersburg.
(In French)
Thank you very much for *The Butcher Boy*.[1] There is true talent in all of it. But *Barnave* . . . *Barnave*; here is the Manzoni belonging to Count Litta.[2] Please have it returned to him, and pay no attention to my prophecies.

[411]
To NATALIA NIKOLAEVNA PUSHKINA
December 6, 1831. From Moscow to Petersburg.
I have just arrived at Nashchokin's on the Prechistensky Val, the house of Mme. Iliinskaya. I shall write you tomorrow. Today I'm all worn out. I kiss you, little wife, my angel.[1]
December 6.

[412]
To NATALIA NIKOLAEVNA PUSHKINA
December 8, 1831. From Moscow to Petersburg.
Hello, little wife, my angel. Don't be angry that I wrote you only three lines day before yesterday;[1] I was all worn out. Here is my *itinéraire* for you. I was intending to leave in a winter diligence, but they declared to me that because of the thaw I must leave in a summer one; they charged me thirty rubles extra and put me in a four-seated carriage together with two companions. And I had not even taken a manservant with me, in the hope of traveling alone. One of my travel companions was a Riga merchant, a good German who was choked up every morning with phlegm, and who at the station hawked a solid hour in a corner. The other was a Jew from Memel, traveling at the expense of the first. Just imagine what a jolly company. The German was drunk three times per day and twice per night punctiliously. The Jew amused him all along the way with pleasant conversation. For example, in German he recounted *Iwan Wijiguin*; (*ganz charmant!*).[2] I tried not to listen to them, and I pretended to be asleep. Behind us were riding in diligences three merchants, Princess Golitsyna (Lanskaya),[3] my friend [L. I.] Zhemchuzhnikov,

Lady in Waiting Kochetova,[4] etc. All these would stop together; there wasn't a minute's peace. In Valday we were compelled to change to winter carriages, and with difficulty we dragged ourselves to Moscow. I didn't find Nashchokin in his old apartment; with difficulty I tracked him down *at the Prechistenskie Vorota, the house of Iliinskaya* (don't forget the address). He's still the same: very sweet and intelligent. He had been winning at cards, but now he has lost it all, and is in debt and in the midst of bothers. I have fulfilled your commission: I kissed him for you and then declared that Nashchokin is a fool, a fool is Nashchokin.[5] The finishing touches are being put on his house[6] (remember it?). What candlesticks, what a silver service! He has ordered a piano a spider can play on, and a vessel which perhaps a Spanish fly might defecate in. I have seen the Vyazemskys, the Meshcherskys,[7] Dmitriev, [A. I.] Turgenev, Chaadaev, Gorchakov, Denis Davydov. All send their greetings to you. They ask a lot of questions about you, about your successes. I clarify the gossip, and there's a lot of gossip. I haven't seen any Moscow ladies yet; I probably shall not go to balls or to the Assembly.[8] I shall finish the business with Nashchokin and Doganovsky, probably soon;[9] I am waiting for information from you about your diamonds.[10] Here they are saying that I am a horrible usurer; they're mixing me up with my purse. Apropos of that, I have turned my purse into a money bag, and I shall celebrate births and christenings, besides the fixed name days. Moscow is still full of the presence of the Court,[11] in rapture over the Tsar, and it has not yet rested up from the balls. Sichler[12] in one month made eighty thousand net profit. A. Korsakova is marrying Prince Vyazemsky.[13] Here is all our news for you. I hope to see you in a couple of weeks. I miss you. In addition, since I left you, I am somehow afraid for you. You won't stay at home, you'll go to the palace, and the first thing you know you'll have a miscarriage on the hundred and fifth step of the grand staircase.[14] My darling, my little wife, my angel! Do me this favor; walk about your room two hours of the twenty-four, and take care of yourself. Ask your brother[15] to watch over you and not to let you have your way. Is Bryullov painting your portrait? Has Khitrovo or Ficquelmont been to see you? If you go to a ball, for God's sake don't dance anything except quadrilles; write me whether the servants are giving you trouble, and whether you can cope with them. Whereupon I kiss you affectionately. I have guests.[16]

December 8.

[413]
To NATALIA NIKOLAEVNA PUSHKINA
December 10, 1831. From Moscow to Petersburg.

I am still afraid that you may have sent the [pawn] tickets to Nashchokin's old apartment, and thereby prolonged my bothers. It's already been a week since I parted from you, and the end of my leave is near; I am undertaking another piece of business,[1] but it will not detain me. What shall I tell you of Moscow? Moscow is still dancing, but I have not been to any balls yet. Yesterday I dined at the English Club;[2] early this morning I was at Vlasov's[3] auction; I spent the evening at home, where I found a fool student, an adorer of yours.[4] He presented me with his novel *Teodor and Rozalia,* in which he describes our story. Killingly funny. But all this is none too amusing, and I feel drawn to Petersburg. I dislike your Moscow. I have not yet been to your place, i.e., to your Nikitskaya house.[5] I don't want your house serfs to know of my coming; and I don't want to learn from them of the arrival of Natalia Ivanovna [Goncharova], otherwise I shall have to go see her and have an unavoidable scene with her; she keeps on complaining all over Moscow of my covetousness; but enough of that, I have no intention of paying any heed to her. I kiss you, and I ask you to walk back and forth in the living room, not to go to the palace, and not to dance at balls.[6] Christ be with you.

December 10.

[414]
To NATALIA NIKOLAEVNA PUSHKINA
Before December 16, 1831. From Moscow to Petersburg.

I received both your letters at once,[1] and both of them pained and enraged me. Vasily [Kalashnikov] is lying that he spent two hundred rubles on me. I ordered that no money be given Aleshka,[2] on account of his bad conduct. I shall pay the board bill upon my arrival; nobody asked you to pay my debts. Tell these servants that I asked you to say that I am very much displeased with them. I ordered them not to disturb you, but I see they have rejoiced at my absence. How did they dare admit Fomin[3] to see you, when you did not want to receive him? And you are a fine one, too. You dance to their piping; you pay money to anybody who only asks for it; our finances won't succeed that way. Henceforth when they approach you, tell them that my business is no concern of yours, and that your orders are sacred. I'll square accounts with Aleshka upon my arrival. I shall probably be compelled to send Vasily packing, together with his sweetheart[4]—*enfin de faire maison nette.*[5] All that is very vexing. Don't be angry that I am angry.

My affairs[6] are in a difficult condition; Nashchokin has made a bigger muddle of his affairs than we suspected. He has two or three schemes, but he has not yet decided upon a single one of them. I have no intention of going to your grandfather's. But I shall try to hinder his piece of business.[7] I love you, my angel, so much that I cannot express it; since I have been here, I have been thinking only of how I might be able to make a bolt for Petersburg to you, my little wife.

I am unsealing my letter, my darling, to answer yours. Please don't lace yourself tightly, don't sit on your feet, and don't be friendly with countesses[8] to whom one can't bow in public. I am not joking, but speaking to you seriously and with concern. You did well in sending on Benkendorf's letter.[9] The point wasn't the rank, but it was necessary all the same. I am awaiting it. In a few days I shall describe my life with Nashchokin,[10] the ball at Soldaen's,[11] the evening at Vyazemsky's—and that's all. I am not reading your verses. What the devil good are verses of yours; I am fed up even with my own. Better, write me about yourself—about your health. Don't go up onto balconies—that is no place for you.

[415]
To Natalia Nikolaevna Pushkina
December 16, 1831. From Moscow to Petersburg.

My darling, you are very sweet, you write me so often, but there's one rub: your letters do not gladden me. What is this *vertige*? Fainting spells or nausea? Have you seen the midwife? Have they let blood for you? All this disturbs me horribly. The more I think about it, the more clearly I see that I acted stupidly in leaving you. In my absence you may pull some stunt on yourself. The first thing you know you'll have a miscarriage. Why don't you do some walking? And you gave me your word of honor that you would walk two hours out of the twenty-four. Is this good? God knows whether I'll get my business here finished, but I shall come to you by the holiday.[1] I have no intention to wait for any Golconda diamonds,[2] and I'll take you out in beads on New Year's. It is boring here for me; Nashchokin is busy with his affairs, and his house is such a muddle and jumble that one's head goes round. From morning till evening all kinds of people are with him: gamblers, retired hussars, students, lawyers, gypsies, spies, and, especially, moneylenders. There is free entry for everybody. Everybody has need to see him; everybody shouts, smokes a pipe, dines, sings, dances. There's not a vacant corner. What's to be done? Meanwhile he has no money, no credit— the time is passing, and my business is not getting disentangled.[3] All this enrages me in spite of myself. Besides, I have chilled my hand again, and my letter will probably smell of bay ointment,[4] like your calling cards. My life is monotonous; I seldom go out. I have been invited everywhere, but I have been only to Soldaen's and to Vyazemskaya's, where I saw your Davydov[5]—he's not married (be consoled). Yesterday Nashchokin fixed up a gypsy evening for us; I am so unaccustomed to that sort of thing that my head is still aching from the shouting of the guests and the singing of the gypsy girls. I miss you, my angel—good-by.

December 16.

[416]

To Praskovia Alexandrovna Osipova

About January 8 or 9, 1832. From Petersburg to Trigorskoe.

(In French)

Accept, Madame, my very sincere thanks for the troubles which you have been so kind as to take upon yourself with my books. I take advantage of your kindnesses and of your time, but I beseech you, as a final favor, to be so kind as to have our Mikhaylovskoe servants asked whether another box is not there, sent to the country with the cases containing my books. I suspect that Arkhip or others are holding it back at the request of Nikita, my domestic (at present,

Lev's). It ought to contain (I mean the box, and not Nikita) old clothes of his, his effects, and also mine, as well as several books which I cannot find.[1] Once more I beseech you to pardon my bothering you, but your friendship and your indulgence have completely spoiled me.

I am sending you, Madame, *The Northern Flowers* [*for* 1832], of which I am the unworthy editor. This is the last year of this almanac, and a tribute in remembrance of our friend,[2] whose memory will long be green. I am enclosing also some cock-and-bull stories;[3] I hope they will give you a moment's amusement.

We have learned here of your daughter's[4] pregnancy. God grant that it all end successfully and that her health be completely restored. They say that having the first baby makes a young woman more beautiful; God grant that it may be as favorable to her health.

Please accept, Madame, the assurance of my high esteem and of my unalterable affection.

A.P.

[417]

To Alexander Anfimovich Orlov
November 24, 1831, and January 9, 1832.
From Petersburg to Moscow.

Dear Sir, Alexander Anfimovich!

I sincerely thank you for the pleasure which your letter provided me. I rejoice that my defense, such as my powers allowed me to make it, of a talent which of course had no need of any defense, has earned your good will. You have appraised my zeal, and not my success.[1] *Mal" bex"*[2] in my brotherhood, but if my little stone banged Goliath Figlyarin in his brazen forehead, thanks be to the Creator! The first chapter of your new Vyzhigin[3] is a new proof of the inexhaustibility of your talent. But honored Alexander Anfimovich, restrain this noble, just indignation; curb the ferocity of your creative spirit! Do not reduce to despair with the fury of your pen the now tame publishers of *The Northern Bee*.[4] Leave me in the van, as a spy and sentinel. I give you my word that if they budge a whit, F. Kosichkin will cook up such a mess, or rather hodgepodge, that they will choke on it. I have read in the *Town Talk* an announcement of your desire to write a *History of the Russian People*.[5] Can this pleasant news be believed?

With true respect and unalterable zeal I remain always ready to be at your service.

November 24, 1831.   A. Pushkin.

P.S. This is a letter which you should have received, Dear Sir, Alexander Anfimovich.

However, when I was setting out for Moscow, I did not send it off to you, but hoped to see you in person. Fate did not bring us together, which I sincerely regret. I repeat here my request: leave in peace people who are not worthy of and who do not merit your anger. It seems that Mr. Polevoy is attacking you and me now.[6] I am about to get angry with him. Now Voeykov and Somov are messing about with him under the name of N. Lugovoy[7]—that is no business of mine.

January 9, 1832.   A.P.
SPb.

[418]
To Pavel Voinovich Nashchokin
January 8 and 10, 1832. From Petersburg to Moscow.

Hello, dear Pavel Voinovich; I had been expecting news from you all the time. I impatiently want to know how the mission came out,[1] what is your brother's *ultimatum*, and whether there is hope for you to put your affairs in order. Please don't be too lazy to describe all this to me in detail. And do me the favor to send me my *Loan Office certificate*, which I left in your secret chest of drawers; I dropped and lost a silver kopeck there. If you find it, send it, too. You don't believe in good luck from them, but I do. How is Rokhmanov, and how about my diamonds?[2] Do I need to enter into correspondence with him or not? What do you think? By the way, don't forget the *Revue de Paris*. Write me in detail about the mission of your German. It's an interesting business. When do you expect to receive your money, and won't you take it to court (which God forbid, but which there's no reason to be afraid of, though)? I found my wife well, in spite of her girlish imprudence—she dances at balls, coquettes with the Sovereign,[3] jumps off the porch. I must take the hussy in hand. She greets you and is preparing the sewing. She is awaiting the promised bribes.⁴ *Sur ce* I embrace you. I am sending the foulards to Olga Andreevna.⁵

January 8, 1832.

SPb.

January 10. My dear Pavel Voinovich, my business can be finished in a few days; if the diamonds have been redeemed, tell me Rokhmanov's address—I shall send him meanwhile 5500 rubles; for this money let him send me the diamonds (the ones pawned for 5500). I shall repawn them and redeem the remainder of them. Do me the favor not to be lazy about answering me. *All yours*.

[419]

To MIKHAIL OSIPOVICH SUDIENKO

January 15, 1832. From Petersburg to Moscow.

I am afraid, dear Mikhaylo Osipovich, that our long separation may have made us complete strangers to each other; however, I shall try to remind you of my existence and to talk about a matter which is important for me.

I must tell you that I have been married about a year and that in consequence my mode of life has changed completely, to the indescribable grief of Sofia Ostafievna¹ and the Cavalry Guard dead beats. I have left cards and dice alone for more than two years; to my misfortune I cashed in my chips when I was losing, and the expenses incidental to the wedding and setting up housekeeping, combined with the payment of my debts at cards, have disarranged my affairs. Now I turn to you: twenty-five thousand granted to me by you in the form of a loan for three, or at least two years, could consolidate my financial status. In the event of my death, I have an estate² which would guarantee your money.

The question is: can you do for me this, may I so call it, benefaction? *En fait de grands propriétaires* only three on this earth stand in more or less friendly relationships with me: you, [I. A.] Yakovlev, and still a third.³ This last one recently enrolled me in a certain government department and has already granted me (they say) an annual income of six thousand;⁴ I do not have the right to ask any more of him. In earlier days I would have gone to Yakovlev with some little drinking glasses and would have proposed to him *un petit déjeuner*; but he is stingy, and I certainly shall not make up my mind to ask money from him as a loan.[5] You remain. You are the only one I can speak to frankly, knowing that if you should refuse me, it will be the result not of stinginess or mistrustfulness, but simply of impossibility.

Another word: if my hope should not be a vain one, then I ask you to set for me a rate of interest, not because you need it, but because otherwise your money would be painful for me. I await your answer[6] and give you a friend's embrace. All yours,

January 15. A. Pushkin.

My address is—on the Galernaya, the house of Briskorn.

[420]

To ELIZAVETA MIKHAYLOVNA KHITROVO

The end of January (31?), 1832. In Petersburg.

(In French)

Most assuredly I shall not forget the ball of the Ambassador's wife,[1] and I request your permission to present my brother-in-law, Goncharov,[2] there. I am delighted that *Onegin*[3] has pleased you. I value your approbation.

Sunday.

[421]

To IVAN VASILIEVICH KIREEVSKY

February 4, 1832. From Petersburg to Moscow.

Dear Sir, Ivan Vasilievich,

Forgive me magnanimously for not having thanked you until now for *The European* and for not having sent you my humble tribute-payment. The blame for this lies in the distractions of Petersburg life, and also on the almanacs,[1] which have completely exhausted my treasury, so that I do not have even a couplet left for a rainy day, except for a tale which I have saved, a fragment of which I am forwarding for your journal.[2] God grant many years to your journal! If one may conjecture by the first two issues, *The European* will be long-lived. Until now our journals have been dry and insignificant, or intelligent and dry; it would seem that *The European* will be the first to combine intelligence and the ability to interest. Now a few words about journal economy: in your first two issues you published two capital pieces by Zhukovsky and a world of verses by Yazykov;[3]

such extravagance is out of place. There should have been at least three issues between "The Sleeping Tsarevna" and "Stepanida the Mouse." Two pieces by Yazykov would have been plenty. Save him for a rainy day. Otherwise what you'll do is squander what you have, and you will be compelled to live on Raich and Pavlov. Your article about *Godunov* and *The Concubine*⁴ gladdened all hearts; at long last we have lived to see true criticism. N.B.: Avoid learned terms, instead, try translating, that is, paraphrasing them. That will be both pleasant for the ignoramuses and useful for our language, which is still in the stage of infancy. Baratynsky's article is good, but it is too thin and watery (I am speaking of his answer to criticism).⁵ Your comparison of Baratynsky with Mieris⁶ is extremely striking and exact. His elegies and poems are precisely a series of charming miniatures, but this charm of finish, the distinctness in details, and the subtlety and accuracy of nuances—can all this be a guarantee for future success in comedy,⁷ which demands—just as the painting of stage scenery does—sharp and broad strokes? I hope *The European* will awaken him from his inactivity. I cordially greet you and Yazykov.

January⁸ 4, 1832.

[422]
To Alexander Khristoforovich Benkendorf
February 7, 1832. In Petersburg.

Dear Sir, Alexander Khristoforovich,

Your High Excellency has deigned to ask for explanations from me,¹ as to how it happened that my poem, "The Tree of Poison," was published in an almanac without preliminary examination by the Sovereign Emperor: I hasten to respond to Your High Excellency's inquiry.

I had always been firmly convinced that the Sovereign's *favor*,² with which I was unexpectedly honored, does not deprive me also of the *right* which the Sovereign has given to all his subjects: that of publishing with the authorization of the censorship. During the last six years, with my consent and without my consent, my poems have been published, without any obstacles, in all the journals and almanacs, and never has there been even the slightest reproof for this, either to me or to the censorship. I even, feeling ashamed to disturb His Majesty every moment, appealed a couple of times to your protection, when the censorship was in perplexity, and I have had the good fortune to find more indulgence in you than in it.

Since I need to explain personally certain difficulties to Your High Excellency, I make bold to ask you to fix an hour when I may come.

With the deepest respect and complete devotion, I have the honor to be, Dear Sir,

Your Excellency's

January[3] 7, 1832.   Most humble servant,
SPb.   Alexander Pushkin.

[423]
To Ivan Ivanovich Dmitriev
February 14, 1832. From Petersburg to Moscow.
Dear Sir, Ivan Ivanovich,

I want to express to Your High Excellency my most profound gratitude for the letter which you have been so kind as to honor me with[1]—a precious memento of your good will toward me. Your attention consoles me for the indifference of the uninitiated. I am glad that I have succeeded in pleasing you with my verses, even though they were blank ones. You must love rhyme, as your faithful servant that has never quarreled with you, and that has always been obedient to your slightest whim. It is consoling to every Russian to see the liveliness of your activity and of your attentiveness; judging by physiological signs, this is a pledge of longevity and health. Live long, Dear Sir! Outlive our generation, just as your powerful and harmonious verses will outlive the puny present-day productions.

Probably you already know that the journal *The European*[2] has been suppressed in consequence of a denunciation. Kireevsky, kind and shy Kireevsky, has been represented to the government as a madcap and a Jacobin! Everybody here hopes that he will succeed in justifying himself and that the slanderers—or at least the slander—will be abashed and unmasked.

With the deepest respect and complete devotion, I have the honor to be, Dear Sir,

Your Excellency's
Most humble servant,

February 14.   Alexander Pushkin.
SPb.

[424]

To ALEXANDER KHRISTOFOROVICH BENKENDORF
Between February 18 and 24, 1832. In Petersburg.
(Rough draft)

At Your High Excellency's command, I am forwarding to you a poem[1] of mine which has been accepted for an almanac and already passed by the censorship.

I have halted its publication until your authorization is given.

On this occasion I make bold to ask of Your High Excellency permission to explain my position frankly. In 1827[2] the Sovereign Emperor saw fit to announce to me that for me *except for His Majesty there would be no censor*. This unheard-of favor imposed on me the obligation to present for His Majesty's examination the compositions worthy of his attention, if not by their merit, then at least by their aim and contents. I have always felt pained and ashamed to trouble the Tsar with poetic trifles important only to me, for they have furnished me with an income of twenty thousand, and only this necessity has forced me to make use of the right granted me by the Sovereign.

Now Your High Excellency, having taken into consideration these my [. . .][3] has deigned to order me to submit to Your Excellency those poems of mine which I or journals wish to publish. Permit me to point out to Your High Excellency that to do so presents various inconveniences. (1) Your High Excellency does not always deign to reside in Petersburg, but the book *trade*, like every other trade, has its own *deadlines*, its market times; so that from a book's being published in March, and not in January, the writer can lose several thousand rubles, and publisher of a journal several hundred subscribers.

(2) If I am the only person who is subjected to an especial censorship depending solely on you, then, contrary to the right granted by the Sovereign, I alone of all writers would be subjected to a most cramping censorship, for, to put it quite simply, this censorship would look on me with prejudice and would find everywhere hidden meanings, *allusions*, and difficulties—and accusations of hidden meanings and implications have neither bounds nor justifications, if by the

word *tree* a constitution will be understood, or by the word *arrow*, the autocracy.[4]

I make bold to request one favor: henceforth to have the right to refer my shorter compositions to the usual censorship.[5]

[425]
To Alexander Khristoforovich Benkendorf
February 24, 1832. In Petersburg.

Dear Sir, Alexander Khristoforovich,

With the feeling of most profound veneration I have received the work[1] which has been most graciously bestowed upon me by His Imperial Majesty. This precious mark of the Tsar's benevolence toward me will awaken in me the strength for the completion of the work I have undertaken,[2] and which will be marked, if not with talent, then at least with zeal and conscientiousness.

Encouraged by Your High Excellency's indulgence, I make bold again to trouble you with a most humble request: for permission for me to examine in the Hermitage the library of Voltaire,[3] who made use of various rare books and manuscripts furnished him by Shuvalov[4] for the compilation of his *History of Peter the Great.*

At Your High Excellency's command I am forwarding to you a poem which I had given to an almanac and which had already been passed by the censorship. I have halted the printing of it until Your High Excellency's authorization is given.[5]

With the most profound respect and complete devotion, I have the honor to be, Dear Sir,

Your Excellency's
Most humble servant,

February 24, 1832.   Alexander Pushkin.
SPb.

[426]
To Vasily Ivanovich Kister
The second half (after the 18th) of February, 1832.
In Petersburg.
(Rough draft)

Titulary Counsellor Pushkin requests Mr. Kister[1] to appear to him in the Galernaya at the home of Mme. Briskorn, in order to receive the sum due to him according to a promissory note which was given in 1820.

[427]
To Alexander Khristoforovich Benkendorf
May 3, 1832. In Petersburg.
(In French)

My General,

His Majesty, having deigned to take an interest in my fate, has set a salary for me. But since I do not know *from where* I am to receive it and *counting from what day*,[1] I take the liberty of addressing myself to Your Excellency, asking you to remove me from the uncertainty. Please pardon my importunity and receive it with your customary indulgence.

I am, respectfully,
My General,
Your Excellency's
Most humble and most obedient servant,

May 3, 1832.   Alexander Pushkin.

[428]
To Praskovia Alexandrovna Osipova
May 16(?), 1832. From Petersburg to Trigorskoe.
(In French)

M. Alymov[1] is leaving tonight for Pskov and Trigorskoe, and he has kindly undertaken to deliver a letter to you, dear, good, and esteemed Praskovia Alexandrovna. I have not congratulated you upon the birth of a grandson.[2] God grant that he and his mother are getting along well and that we all may be present at his wedding, even though we have not been able to be present at his christening. Apropos of a christening, I may have one soon *on the Furshtatskaya in Alymova's house*.[3] Do not forget the address, if you should wish to write me a word. I do not give you any news, either political or literary. I suppose you are weary of it, like all of us. Nothing is wiser than to remain in one's village and to water one's cabbages.[4] An old truth which I apply every day in the midst of a completely worldly and completely topsy-turvy mode of life. I do not know whether we shall see each other this summer—which is one of my dreams—may it come to pass.[5]

Farewell, Madame; I greet you very tenderly, you and all your family.

[429]
To Alexander Khristoforovich Benkendorf
May 27, 1832. In Petersburg.
(In French)

General,

Mlle. Kyukhelbeker[1] has asked whether I would not take it upon myself to be the editor of several manuscript poems which her brother has left her. I thought that for me to do so, Your Excellency's authorization would be necessary, and that the censorship's would not suffice. I make bold to hope that the permission which I solicit cannot harm me: I was a schoolmate of M. Kyukhelbeker's, and it is natural that his sister, on this occasion, should address herself to me rather than to anybody else.

Now permit me to trouble you about something personal. Up to the present I have largely neglected my financial means. Now that I cannot be carefree without being remiss in my duty, I must think of making money, and I ask His Majesty for permission that I may do so. The service, to which he has deigned to attach me, and my literary pursuits oblige me to live in Petersburg, and I have no income except that which my labor provides me. The literary enterprise, the authorization of which I solicit and which would assure my fate, would be to be the head of the journal, about which M. Zhukovsky has told me that he has spoken with you.[2]

I am respectfully, General,
Your Excellency's

May 27. Most humble and most obedient servant,
Alexander Pushkin.

[430]
To Vera Fedorovna Vyazemskaya
June 4, 1832. From Petersburg to Moscow.
(In French)

Sejčas ot Xitrovoj.[1] No one could be more touched than she is at the condition of Batyushkov—with truly remarkable self-abnegation she offers to come herself to attempt the last remedy.[2] Apropos of self-abnegation: just imagine, my wife has had the maladroitness to give birth to a little lithograph of me.[3] I am in despair, in spite of all my self-conceit.

[431]

To ALEXANDER KHRISTOFOROVICH BENKENDORF
June 8, 1832. In Petersburg.
(In French)

General,

Two or three years ago M. [A. N.] Goncharov, my wife's grand-father, finding himself pressed for money, was on the point of melt-ing down a colossal statue of Catherine II, and I addressed myself to Your Excellency, in order to obtain permission for him to do so. Since I supposed that it was only a question of a misshapen mass of bronze, I was quite willing. But the statue turned out to be a fine work of art, and I felt shame and regret at destroying it in order to derive a few thousand rubles from it. Your Excellency, with your accustomed goodness, gave me the hope that the government might buy it from me; I therefore have had it brought here. If the fortune of a private individual does not permit him either to buy or to keep it, this fine statue could with propriety be placed in one of the establish-ments founded by the Empress, or at Tsarskoe Selo, where a statue of her is lacking among the monuments which she had erected to the great men who served her. I should like twenty-five thousand rubles for it, which is a fourth of what it cost[1] (the monument was cast in Prussia by a sculptor from Berlin).

The statue is at present at my house (Furshtatskaya Street, the house of Alymova).

I am respectfully, General,
Your Excellency's
Most humble and most obedient servant,

June 8, 1832.   Alexander Pushkin.
SPb.

[432]

To Ivan Vasilievich Kireevsky
July 11, 1832. From Petersburg to Moscow.

Dear Sir, Ivan Vasilievich,

I ceased corresponding with you, fearing to bring down on you additional dissatisfaction or unjust suspicion, in spite of my conviction that coal cannot be besmirched by soot.[1] Today I am writing you on an *occasion*, and I shall speak frankly to you. The suppression of your journal has produced a great impression here; everybody has been on your side; that is, on the side of complete innocence; the denunciation, so far as I have been able to find out, struck not from Bulgarin's dung heap, but out of the cloud.[2] Zhukovsky has stood up for you with his ardent straightforwardness; Vyazemsky has written Benkendorf a courageous, intelligent, and convincing letter. You are the only one who has not acted, and in this instance you are completely wrong. As a citizen you have been deprived by the government of one of the rights of all subjects; you should have justified yourself out of self-esteem, and, I even dare to say, out of esteem for the Sovereign; for attacks by him are not attacks by Polevoy or Nadezhdin. I do not know whether it is too late, but if I were you, even now I would not hesitate to make this justification. Begin your letter by saying that "having been long awaiting an inquiry from the government, you have been silent up to now, but," etc.[3] I swear that wouldn't be too much for you to do.

Meanwhile I address a cordial request to you, your brother,[4] and Yazykov. Recently I have received permission for a political and literary gazette.[5] Do not abandon me, brothers! If you will take upon yourself the trouble, after reading some book or other, to toss off several words about it for my beggar's wallet, the Lord God will not abandon you. Nikolay Mikhaylovich [Yazykov] is lazy, but since I shall have as few verses as I can get by with, my request will not trouble even him. Write me several words (having no fear of injuring my political reputation thereby) regarding the proposed gazette. I ask you for advice and aid.

July 11.

All joking aside: your supposition that you can harm anyone whatever with your letters is unjust. Correspondence with you would be as pleasant to me as your friendship is flattering to me. I am impatiently awaiting your answer—perhaps I shall be in Moscow in a few days.[6]

[433]
To Mikhail Petrovich Pogodin
July 11, 1832. From Petersburg to Moscow.

Dear Sir, Mikhaylo Petrovich,

I fulfilled your commission regarding Smirdin,[1] but, though I did not receive a satisfactory answer from him, I nevertheless could not make up my mind to write you about it. The barbarity of our literary trade makes me furious. Smirdin has got entangled in various obligations, has bought a lot of novels, etc., and is not entering into any contracts; tragedies are not "moving" now, he says in his technical language. And so let's wait it out. They tell me that you have been given a sharp scolding somewhere[2] for [*Marfa, the*] *Novgorod Burgomaster's Wife*; I hope this will have no influence whatever on your labors. Remember that for ten years in a row they praised me for God knows what, but they gave me a dressing down for *Godunov* and *Poltava*. With us criticism is of course beneath not only our literature itself, but even the public. One may become angry with it, but to put any credence whatever in it is unforgivable weakness. Your *Marfa*, your *Peter* are full of true dramatic power, and if they can ever be authorized by the theatrical censorship,[3] I predict for you such popular success as we cold Northern observers of the vaudevilles of Scribe[4] and the ballets of Didelot cannot even imagine.

Do you know that the Tsar has permitted me a political gazette?[5] The matter is important, for the monopoly of Grech and Bulgarin has fallen. You feel that you are indispensible for this business. But since a journal is a business undertaking, I do not have the audacity to proceed to anything, either offers or contracts, until I have looked things over thoroughly; I do not want to sell you the skin of a bear that is still alive, or to collect subscriptions for a *History of the Russian People* which exists only in my absurd pate. . . .[6] By the way, tell Nadezhdin that the recklessness of his judgments is unforgivable. Not long ago I read in his journal[7] a comparison between me and Polevoy: "Both hoax the public, one inveigles money from it by publishing his *Onegin* a chapter at a time, and the other, his *History* a volume at a time." The difference is between *collecting subscriptions, with the promise* of publishing twelve volumes in a year, and then in three years to publish three volumes on the interest from the swindled money— and of publishing, a chapter at a time, a composition regarding which it is said in the preface: "Here is the beginning of a composition which probably will never be finished." Nadezhdin is at liberty to find my verses bad, but to compare me with a swindler is swinishness on his part. How after that can a decent person have anything to do with these people? And what if we had to esteem, in addition, the opinions of Bulgarin, Polevoy, Nadezhdin? One would have to fight a duel after every issue of their journals. Thank God that public opinion (whatever it may be like among us) saves us the trouble.

I have not answered [A. A.] Shishkov and have not thanked him.[8] Embrace him for me. God grant him health, because of *Fortunat!*[9] Won't you come here? Hey, come.

July 11.

[434]

To DMITRY IVANOVICH KHVOSTOV
August 2, 1832. In Petersburg.

Dear Sir, Count Dmitry Ivanovich,

My wife sincerely thanks you for the charming and unexpected present.[1] Permit me also to present to Your Excellency my hearty thanks. I am in your debt: twice you have honored me by addressing me flatteringly and with the songs of a lyre meritorious and eternally young. In a few days I shall have the honor to appear, together with my wife, to pay our respects to the glorious and amiable patriarch.

With the most profound respect and devotion, I have the honor to be,

Dear Sir,
Your Excellency's
Most obedient servant,
Alexander Pushkin.

[435]

To MIKHAIL PETROVICH POGODIN
The first half of September, 1832.
From Petersburg to Moscow.

What kind of program do you want to see? The political part is officially insignificant, the literary part, essentially insignificant; news about the rate of exchange, about arrivals and departures: here is the whole program for you.[1] I wanted to destroy the monopoly, and I succeeded. The remainder interests me little. My gazette will be a little worse than *The Northern Bee*. I do not intend to play up to the public; to rail at the journals is all right once in five years, and then for Kosichkin,[2] but not for me. I have no intention of publishing poems, for even Christ has forbidden pearls to be cast before the public; prose-chaff is the thing for it.[3] One thing is egging me on: I'd like to destroy, to show all the repulsive meanness of present-day French literature, to say aloud once that Lamartine is more boring than Young[4] and does not have his depth, that Béranger is no poet, that V. Hugo has no life, i.e., no truth; that the novels of A. Vigny[5] are worse than the novels of Zagoskin; that their journalists are ignoramuses; that their critiques are scarcely better than our *Telescope's* and *-graph's*.[6] I am convinced in heart that the nineteenth century in comparison with the eighteenth, is in the dirt (I mean in France). The prose only barely makes up for the disgusting stuff they call poetry.

Let's have a talk about your client *Godunov* later.[7] I am going to Moscow in a few days, and I hope to see you.

[436]

To NATALIA NIKOLAEVNA PUSHKINA
September 22, 1832. From Moscow to Petersburg.

Thursday. Don't be angry, little wife;[1] let me say a word. I arrived in Moscow yesterday, Wednesday. The *vélocifère*[2]—in Russian, *Hasty Diligence*, notwithstanding the pleonasm—hastened like a tortoise, and sometimes even like a crawfish. In twenty-four hours I managed to make three stations. The horses threw their shoes, and—an unheard-of-thing!—they were reshod on the road. For ten years I've been riding on the highways, and I've never seen anything like it in my life. With difficulty I managed to drag to Moscow, which was

bepissed with rain and all excited about the arrival of the Court.[3]
Now hear whom I traveled with, whom I spent five days and five
nights with. Now I'll catch it! With five German actresses, in yellow
kacavejki[4] and black veils. What do you think of that? My dear, I
swear it wasn't I who coquetted with them, but they who flirted with
me in hope of a stray bill. But I pleaded ignorance of the German
language, and like little Joseph I came forth pure from temptation.
When I arrived in Moscow, I galloped to look for Nashchokin. I
found him, as before, distraught over his domestic circumstances,
but already more composed in his relationships with his Sarah.[5] He's
a cuckold, and he sees that this condition is a pleasant and independent
one. He went to the baths with me,[6] dined with me. He took me to
see Princess Vyazemskaya; the Princess took me to the French Theater,
where I almost dozed off from boredom and fatigue. I arrived at
Ober's,[7] and I went to sleep at ten o'clock in the evening. That's my
whole day for you; there was neither the time nor the physical
possibility for me to write. The Sovereign has been here since the
twentieth, and today he's setting off for Petersburg. So that I shall not
succeed in seeing Benkendorf, no matter now much I may need to.
The Grand Duchess[8] has been very ill; yesterday she was better, but
the Court is still upset, and the Sovereign has not attended a single
celebration. I saw Chaadaev in the theater; he invited me to go everywhere with him, but I was drowsy. My business, I should think, can
soon be completed,[9] and I, my angel, without delaying even a
minute, will gallop off to Petersburg. You can't imagine how I long
for you. I keep on worrying about whose hands I have left you in!
In Peter's,[10] the sleepy-headed drunkard, who is asleep all the time
and will never wake up, for he's a drunkard and a fool; in Irina
Kuzminichna's, who wars with you; in Nenila Onufrievna's,[11] who
plunders you. And how is Masha?[12] What about her scrofula, and
what about Spassky?[13] Oh, little wife, darling! What will become of
you? Farewell; write.

[437]

To Natalia Nikolaevna Pushkina
September 25, 1832. From Moscow to Petersburg.
What a clever little thing, what a sweet little thing you are! What
a long letter! How sensible it is! Thank you, little wife. Keep on as

you have begun, and I'll pray for you forever. Conclude whatever terms you wish with the cook,[1] providing only that I not be forced after dining at home, to have supper at my club.[2] My carriagemaker is a cheat. He charged me five hundred rubles for repairs, and within the month my carriage might as well be abandoned. Let this be a lesson to me not to deal with the semi-skilled. Frebelius or Iokhim[3] would have charged me a hundred rubles extra, but on the other hand they wouldn't have bamboozled me. For goodness sake don't smear Mashka either with plain cream or ointment. I don't much trust your Utkina.[4] Incidentally, see whether you aren't with child,[5] and in case you are, take care of yourself from the first. Don't go horseback riding, but do your coquetting some other way. Here everybody speaks of you very favorably. Your Davydov[6] is getting married, they say, to a plain little thing. Yesterday I was told an anecdote which I pass on to you. In 1831, on February 18, there was a wedding on the Nikitskaya, in the parish of Voznesenie.[7] During the ceremony two young men were talking with each other. One of them was tenderly consoling the other, an unlucky suitor of the maiden being wed. And the unlucky suitor, with sighing and tears, hoped, with time, to forget his mad passion, etc., etc., etc. The Princesses Vyazemskaya[8] heard the whole conversation and thinks the unlucky suitor was Davydov. But I think it was Petushkov or Buyanov or, more likely, Sorokhtin.[9] What do you think? An interesting anecdote, isn't it? Your intention to make a trip to Pletnev's is praiseworthy, but will you get it done? Make the trip, little wife, and I'll say thank you. What about our servants? How are you getting along with them? Yesterday I was at [Vera F.] Vyazemskaya's; she had a baggage train setting off,[10] and I meant to send off a letter to you along with it, but they forgot the letter, and I am dispatching it to you, so that not a single line of my pen may be lost, either for you or for posterity. Nashchokin is extremely nice. Two new personages have appeared at his house among his domestics: an actor who used to play the role of the secondary suitor, but now paralyzed and grown completely stupid; and a monk, a convert from the Jews, weighted down with fetters, who mimics the Jewish synagogue and tells us suggestive stories about the Moscow nuns. Nashchokin tells him, "Come here every day to dine and sup, pay court to my maids' room, but see that you don't play the pimp for

Okulova."[11] What do you think of the hermit? I split my sides laughing at him, but I don't understand how anybody can live surrounded with such riff-raff. I have sent the curls to the Malinovskys;[12] they have commanded that I be invited for an evening, but I probably shall not go. My business is assuming a good aspect.[13] Tomorrow I shall begin seeing what I can do about it, and if I don't finish in a week, I'll leave everything in the charge of Nashchokin, and I myself will set off to you—my angel, my sweet little wife. Farewell for now: Christ be with you and Masha. Do you see Katerina Ivanovna [Zagryazhskaya]? I greet her cordially, and I kiss her little hand, and yours, my angel.

Sunday.

An important discovery: Ippolit[14] speaks French.

[438]

To Natalia Nikolaevna Pushkina
September 27, 1832. From Moscow to Petersburg.

Yesterday I had just succeeded in sending off a letter[1] to the post when I received three whole letters from you. Thank you, wife. Thank you also that you are going to bed early. Only, it's not good that you are engaging in various coquetries. You really shouldn't have received Pushkin,[2] first, because he hasn't been at our house a single time when I was there, and second, because, though I have confidence in you, one mustn't give society grounds for gossip. In consequence of this I tweak your ear and kiss you tenderly as though nothing had happened. Here I am living quietly and respectably. I am hustling and bustling about my business,[3] listening to Nashchokin, and reading the *Mémoires de Diderot*.[4] Last evening I was at [Vera F.] Vyazemskaya's, and I saw there *le beau* Bezobrazov,[5] who treated me just as tenderly as Alexandrov did at Bobrinskaya's.[6] Remember? That touched my heart exceedingly. Farewell. Somebody is coming to see me.

A false alarm: Ippolit brought me some coffee. Today I'm going to listen to Davydov, not your *soupirant* but the professor;[7] but there's no love lost between me and any Davydovs except Denis—and so far as Moscow University is concerned, I'm a heathen. My appearance will cause a sensation and temptation, and that will pleasantly titillate my vanity.

Another disturbance: Mukhanov[8] sent me a huckster with a *pastila.*[9] Farewell. Christ be with you and Masha.

Tuesday.

Kiss Katerina Ivanovna's little hand for me. Now don't forget.

[439]

To NATALIA NIKOLAEVNA PUSHKINA
About (not later than) September 30, 1832.
From Moscow to Petersburg.

So you see that I am right: you shouldn't have received Pushkin.[1] You should have stayed at Idalia's[2] and not have got angry with me. Now thanks for your sweet, sweet letter. I expected thunder and lightning from you, for you didn't receive a letter from me before Sunday, as I figured it. But you're so calm, so indulgent, so amusing that it's marvelous. What does this mean? I'm not a cuckold, am I? Look to it! Who's telling you that I don't go to Baratynsky's? I shall spend this evening at his place, and I was there yesterday. We see each other every day. But we don't concern ourselves with wives. It's wrong for you to suspect me of infidelity to you and of predilection for the wives of my friends. I only envy those of them whose wives are not beauties, not charming angels, not madonnas,[3] etc., etc. You know the Russian song—

God, don't grant me a pretty wife; a pretty wife is often invited to a feast.

And as for the poor husband, he has a hangover at another's feast,[4] and he becomes nauseated at his own.—An almanacster[5] just left me. I had difficulty in talking myself free of him. He began to ask for verses for his almanac, and I for articles for my gazette.[6] Thus we parted. A few days ago I was invited to the University by Uvarov. There I encountered Kachenovsky (he and I used to rail at each other, you must be told, like women hawkers at a flea market).[7] But here he and I had such a friendly, such a sweet conversation, that all persons present began shedding tears of tender emotion. Pass this on to Vyazemsky. Thank you, my darling, for learning to play chess. That is absolutely necessary in every well-arranged family: I shall prove it later. A few days ago I was at a ball (at Princess Vyazemskaya's—consequently I am in the right). Countess Sollogub,[8] Countess Pushkina (Vladimir),[9] her sister Avrora,[10] and Natalia Urusova[11] were there. I behaved excellently: I exchanged compliments with Countess Sollogub (with the aunt,[12] *entendons-nous*), and I left to have supper at the Yar, as soon as the ball was in full swing. My business[13] is taking its normal course. I see Nashchokin every day. He had a feast in his *playhouse*:[14] a little mouse was served on the table in sour cream with horse-radish, like a pig. A pity there were no guests. By the terms of his will, he bequeaths you the playhouse. A novel has come into my head, and I shall probably get busy on it;[15] but meanwhile my head is going round at the thought of a gazette. Just how shall I cope with it? God grant health to Otryzhkov;[16] maybe he will save it. I kiss Masha and bless her, and you, too, my darling, my angel. Christ be with you both.

[440]

To Natalia Nikolaevna Pushkina
About (not later than) October 3, 1832.
From Moscow to Petersburg.

I shall answer your accusations point by point.[1] (1) A Russian does not change clothes on the road, but when he arrives at his destination, dirty as a pig, he goes to the baths, which are our second mother. Aren't you christened, that you don't know all this? (2) Letters are accepted in Moscow until 12 o'clock—and I entered the Tverskaya gates at exactly 11. Consequently I postponed writing you until the next day. Do you see that I'm in the right and that you're completely at fault? You are at fault, (1) because you get all kinds of rubbish into your head, (2) because out of vexation at me you sent off Benkendorf's packet[2] (probably an important one) to God knows where, (3) you coquette with all the diplomatic corps and still complain about your situation, as if it were like Nashchokin's! Little wife, little wife! . . . But let's drop it. I can just see you warring with the servants in my absence, changing servants, breaking down the carriages, checking the accounts, milking the wet nurse. 'At a girl! What's good is good.—Here I'm not all that active. I've succeeded with difficulty in getting two powers of attorney[3] written, but I shall not wait for the money. I'll leave the unfinished business in Nashchokin's charge. Your brother Dmitry Nikolaevich [Goncharov] is here. He did not find in Kaluga any document substantiating your father's state of illness, and he has come here to take steps to get one.[4] He and Natalia Ivanovna [Goncharova] have come to an understanding and have become reconciled. She does not want to take over the management of the estate, and in everything she is relying on Dmitry Nikolaevich. Your father keeps on talking about a will; in a few days he will be examined by the civil governor.[5] The power of attorney will be sent to you for your signature. Katerina Ivanovna [Zagryazhskaya] will inform you how to take care of all this. The Vyazemskys[6] are leaving after the fourteenth. And I in a few days.[7] Consequently there's no need for you to write. I miss you so much that I don't know where to incline my head. Want some gossip? Gorstkina married Prince Shcherbatov,[8] the youngster, yesterday. The handsome Bezobrazov is turning the little heads here, which are coiffured *à la Ninon*[9] by homebred hairdressers. Prince Urusov[10] is in love with Masha Vyazemskaya[11] (don't tell her father; he might get worried). Another Urusov[12] is getting married, they say, to Borozdina the Nightingale. Moscow is expecting the Tsar by winter, but, it seems in vain.[13] Farewell, my angel; I kiss you and Masha. Farewell, my darling. Christ be with you.

[441]

To Pavel Voinovich Nashchokin

December 2, 1832. From Petersburg to Moscow.

Let this be my justification for my unpunctuality. When I arrived here I found great disorders in my house; I have been compelled to discharge some servants, to change cooks, and finally to rent a new apartment, and consequently to use sums which would otherwise have remained untouched. I hope that by now you have received, dear Pavel Voinovich, the necessary papers for the remortgaging,[1] and that you will receive the mortgage money without any difficulty. If you do, after excusing me (as well as you can) to Fedor Danilovich [Shneyder] give him a thousand and take another for yourself, for you'll probably need it. As for the remainder of the debt, you will receive it in January—for I have already made arrangements, by selling to Smirdin the second edition of *Onegin*.[2] *Sur ce* let's talk about business. I have the honor to announce to you that the first volume of *Ostrovsky*[3] is finished and will be sent to Moscow in a few days for

your inspection and for the criticism of Mr. Korotky.[4] I wrote it in
two weeks, but I came to a halt because of severe rheumatism, with
which I suffered the next two weeks; so that I haven't taken up my
pen and I haven't been able to combine two ideas in my head. What
about your memoirs? I hope you won't give them up. Write them
in the form of letters to me. That would be both more pleasant for
me and easier for you. Imperceptibly a volume would grow, and
then, before you know it, a second one, too. My periodical[5] has
come to a halt, because authorization was for too long not forthcoming. It will not be published this year. And I am glad. I'll have
time to look around and prepare for the future; meanwhile I shall
skimp a little. I have not sold my statue yet,[6] but I'll sell it, come what
may. By summer I shall have fuss and bother on my hands. Natalia
Nikolaevna [Pushkina] is with child again, and she is having a pretty
hard time. Won't you come to christen Gavriil Alexandrovich?[7] I
am of the opinion that Petersburg would be a refuge and an ark of
salvation for you. Tell Baratynsky that Smirdin is in Moscow and
that I have spoken with him about publishing *The Complete Poems of
Evgeny Baratynsky.*[8] I spoke of eight or ten thousand rubles, but
Smirdin was afraid that Baratynsky would not consent; consequently, Baratynsky can make a deal with him. Let him try. How is
Veltman? How are his circumstances and how about his opera?[9]
Farewell; my greeting to your folks—I kiss Pavel.[10]
    October 2. SPb.
    On the Morskaya in the house of Zhadimirovsky.[11]

[442]
                   To ELIZAVETA MIKHAYLOVNA KHITROVO
    August or the first half of September, or between the end of October
                   and of December, 1832. In Petersburg.
                             (In French)
    Yes indeed—my brother-in-law[1] is very ill; yesterday I brought
him to my house. He is between madness and death; in an hour we
shall have the crisis—and you will have news of it.
    Aren't you ashamed to have spoken so lightly of *Karr*?[2] His novel
shows genius, and it is quite as good as your Balzac's[3] *marivaudage.*
Farewell, beautiful and good one.

[443]

To Pavel Stepanovich Sankovsky
January 3, 1833. From Petersburg to Tiflis.
(In French)

I have behaved so badly toward you,[1] I appear so ungrateful, that I am completely ashamed to write you. M. Kasassi[2] has brought me a very kind letter from you; in it you asked for some verses for an almanac which you had the intention of bringing out for this year. I have delayed in answering you for a good reason: I had nothing to send you, and I kept on waiting for a moment of inspiration, as the expression goes—that is, for a moment of scribble-mania. Well, inspiration has not come—I have not written a verse for two years[3]—and so the good intention I had of paying you the homage of my poor rhymes has gone to pave hell. For God's sake, do not be vexed with me, but pity me, for never doing what I ought or would like.

I have instructed [A. S.] Shiryaev to see that you get everything I have published since I returned from Tiflis—I do not know whether he has done so. As for me, I have many thanks to pay you for sending the Tiflis newspaper—the only one among those of Russia which has an original coloring and in which articles are to be found with a true and European interest. If you see A. Bestuzhev[4] sometimes, give him my compliments. We met on Mount Gut without recognizing each other, and since then I have had news of him only by the journals in which he has been publishing his charming tales. A story that he had died was spread about here; we bewept him quite sincerely, and we rejoiced greatly at his resurrection *v tretij den' po pisaniju*.[5]

This letter will be delivered to you by M. [K. O.] Rosset, a young man full of merit who is going to leave a brilliant world and a frivolous and dissipated existence, for the harsh occupation of being a soldier in Georgia. We recommend him to you, and we are sure you will thank us for this acquaintance.

Accept, Sir, the assurance of my high esteem.

January 3, 1833.

SPb.   Alexander Pushkin.

[444]
To ALEXANDER IVANOVICH CHERNYSHEV
February 9, 1833. In Petersburg.

Dear Sir, Count Alexander Ivanovich,

I want to express[1] to Your Excellency[2] my most sincere gratitude for the regard which has been shown to my request.

The following documents, regarding the history of Count Suvorov, should be located in the archives of the general staff:

(1) The dossier of the investigation regarding Pugachev.

(2) The official reports of Count Suvorov during the campaign of 1794.

(3) His official reports of 1799.

(4) His orders to his troops.[3]

I shall await from Your Excellency the permission to make use of these precious materials.

With the most profound respect, I have the honor to be, Dear Sir,
Your Excellency's
Most humble servant,
February 7,[4] 1833.   Alexander Pushkin.
SPb.

[445]
To PAVEL VOINOVICH NASHCHOKIN
About (not later than) February 25, 1833.
From Petersburg to Moscow.

What about it, dear Pavel Voinovich? Have you received the necessary papers,[1] have you taken a little something for yourself, have you paid Fedor Danilovich [Shneyder], have you managed to get the remaining thousand from the loan office, will you send me anything? If nothing has been done yet, then do this: *be so kind as to deliver 2,525 rubles to Senator Mikhail Alexandrovich Saltykov,[2] who is living on the Maroseyka, in the house of Bubuky, and get a receipt from him.* This is necessary, and it is very unpleasant for me.

How are your affairs? When we're not together I'm always afraid for you. I keep on imagining that you are perishing, that Weyer will do you in, and Rokhmanov is on your shoulders. God grant that I make some money; then, maybe, I'll get you rescued. Then, maybe, we'll get you separated from your mistress, we'll acquire the mill at Tyufly,[3] and you'll start living in clover, writing your memoirs. My life in Petersburg is neither fish nor flesh. The cares of living prevent me from being bored. But I don't have the leisure—the free bachelor life—a writer needs. I whirl in the great world; my wife is in great fashion. All that demands money. Money is obtained through my labors, and labors demand solitude.

Here is how I am planning my future. In the summer, after my wife's lying-in, I'll send her off to the Kaluga village to her sisters, and I shall make a trip to Nizhny and perhaps to Astrakhan.[4] On my way, we shall see each other and talk our fill. I need the trip both morally and physically.

[446]

To MIKHAIL PETROVICH POGODIN
March 5, 1833. From Petersburg to Moscow.
Keep this a secret.

Here is what is up: As we agreed, for a long time I had been intending to find a favorable time to request of the Tsar that you be my collaborator.[1] But somehow, I just couldn't find it. Finally, during Carnival the Tsar happened to begin talking with me about Peter I, and right then I presented it to him that it is impossible for me to labor alone in the archives, and that I need an enlightened, intelligent, and energetic scholar. The Tsar asked whom I want, and, at your name, he was about to frown (he mixes you up with Polevoy; forgive him magnanimously: he's not quite solid as a man of letters, though he's a fine fellow and glorious Tsar). I somehow managed to recommend you properly, and D. N. Bludov set everything to rights and explained that the only thing in common between you and Polevoy is the first syllable of your surnames. To this was added a favorable comment from Benkendorf. Thus the business was managed, and the archives are open to you (except the secret one). Now it remains to be decided on what basis you intend to approach the business: I think you should insist on your adjunct's[2] salary during all the time of your labors—and only that. But in no sense will your labors go for nothing. For *you* will publish all that can be published *and for yourself*; that will be both pleasing and profitable for you. How many different books can be compiled here! How many creative ideas can acquire their full development here! With your inspired activeness, with your pure conscientiousness, you will produce such marvelous things that we and our posterity will pray God for you, as we do for Schlözer[3] and for Lomonosov.

Write me an *official* letter, which I can show to Bludov, and I shall hasten to finish everything here. I await you with open arms.[4]

March 5.

[447]

To Alexey Petrovich Ermolov
The beginning of April, 1833. From Petersburg to Osorgino.
(Rough draft)

While collecting the monuments of the history of our fatherland, I have been expecting in vain that the description of your Trans-caucasion exploits would finally appear. Until now the campaign of Napoleon overshadows and chokes out everything—and only certain military people know what was going on in the East at the same time.

I have a request to make to Your High Excellency with regard to a matter which is important for me. I know that you will be unwilling to consent to fulfill it. But your glory belongs to Russia, and you do not have the right to keep it hidden. If in leisure hours you have turned your attention to your glorious memories and have composed memoirs about your wars, I ask you to vouchsafe me the honor to be your publisher. If your indifference has not permitted you to fulfill this, then I request you to allow me to be your historian, to present to me in brief the most essential bits of information, etc.[1]

[448]

To Ivan Timofeevich Kalashnikov
The beginning of April, 1833. In Petersburg.
(Rough draft)

I sincerely thank you[1] for the letter with which you have honored me. The pleasure of the readers whom we esteem is the best of all rewards.

You ask my opinion of *The Kamchatka Girl*. Frankness from my pen may seem to you to be only politeness. I wish rather to repeat to you the opinion of [I. A.] Krylov, a great connoisseur, and an impartial judge, of true talent. After reading *The Daughter of Zholobov*, he told me, "There's not a single Russian novel which I have read with more pleasure." *The Kamchatka Girl* is probably not inferior to your first work. As far as I have been able to observe, the part of the public which judges of books, not by the announcements in periodicals, but by their own impressions, has come to love you and has accepted both your pieces with complete cordiality. After this do not be concerned about the opinion of Polevoy;[2] he is a clever, obliging, and intelligent person, but of course certainly no man of letters. As a writer he has no talent at all; as a critic he repeats other's ideas. [. . .][3]

I have not read his novel, but judging by his *History*, how much below *The Kamchatka Girl* and *The Daughter of Zholobov* it must be!

The public loves him solely for his impudence and because the stupid listen with veneration to a person who boldly rails at everything, and they think: there's an intelligent man for you!

[449]
To Praskovia Alexandrovna Osipova
About (not later than) May 15, 1833. From Petersburg to Pskov.
(In French)

Excuse me, please excuse me, dear Paraskovia [sic] Alexandrovna, for having delayed in thanking you for your kind letter and for its interesting vignette. Difficulties of all kinds have kept me from doing so. I do not know when I shall have the happiness to present myself at Trigorskoe,[1] but I am dying of desire to do so. Petersburg does not suit me at all; neither my tastes nor my finances can adapt themselves to it. But for two or three years I shall have to be patient. My wife asks me to express a thousand kind regards to you, and also to Anna Nikolaevna [Vulf]. My daughter[2] has given us some uneasiness for the last five or six days. I suppose she is cutting some teeth. She does not have a single one so far. It is all very well to say that everybody has passed through this, but these creatures are so frail that it is impossible to keep from trembling when one sees them suffer. My parents have just arrived from Moscow. They are intending to go to Mikhaylovskoe about the month of July. I should very much like to go along.

[450]
To Peter Ivanovich Sokolov
The end (after the 27th) of May or the beginning of June, 1833.
In Petersburg.
(Rough draft)
Having received from Your Excellency the official notification regarding balloting for Senator Baranov as a member of the Russian Academy,[1] I hasten to provide you with my electoral vote.

With the most profound respect [. . . .]

[451]
To Modest Alexandrovich Korf
July 14(?), 1833. In Petersburg.
I have just now been at Smirdin's, and I think the matter is settled. Nikolay Modestovich[1] can go see him for the final conditions; I would advise him to check first how much is usually given for translations *à tant la feuille*, and demand the same price; in this way he probably will receive more than if he agrees to take an annual salary. In case of any difficulty, let him count on me; I am ready to serve him with all my heart.

I rejoice that I could answer your friendly letter satisfactorily, and could carry out your command. I cordially thank you for the congratulations.[2]

All yours,
Alexander Pushkin.

Friday.

Letter 380

  1. The dead daughter of Nashchokin and his gypsy mistress, Olga Andreevna.
  2. Nashchokin's "wishes" were that if he should die of the cholera, like Prince N. B. Yusupov, Pushkin would look after his financial affairs.
  3. The manuscript of two of his *Philosophical Letters*. See Letter 376.
  4. Pushkin is probably thinking of the quarantine, which still surrounded Tsarskoe Selo, though it had been removed from around Petersburg.
  5. About *Boris Godunov*. See Letter 375.
  6. Pushkin had just obtained permission from the Tsar to work in the state archives on a history of Peter the Great and his successors, up to Peter III. Pushkin never completed this historical work, though he left interesting notes and materials. Pushkin's receiving this permission resulted in his being officially returned to the civil service on November 14, 1831, with a salary of five thousand rubles.
  7. Vasily Petrovich Zubkov and Nikolay Filippovich Pavlov.
  8. See Letters 353 and 355. By the middle of August, 1831, L. S. Pushkin was engaging in actions with the Russian army against the Poles.

Letter 381

  1. Olga Petrovna Pletneva. Pletnev's wife was Stepanida Alexandrovna Pletneva.
  2. The two undelivered letters, which have not survived, referred to in Letter 378, and note 1.
  3. Pushkin's *Tales of Belkin*.
  4. The "pension." See Letter 377.
  5. See Letter 380, and note 6.
  6. "Since he is married and is not rich, his pot must be kept boiling." The small talk of the Tsar of All the Russias was in French. Pushkin, in his diary under the date of February 28, 1834, noted that the Tsar "speaks very well, not mixing the two languages, not making the usual errors, and using present-day expressions."
  7. See Letter 380.
  8. The rumor that Count D. I. Khvostov had died of the cholera proved to be false. See Letter 388 below for Pushkin's comment when he found out that Khvostov was still alive.

Letter 382

  1. See Letter 376.
  2. Nicholas I himself went to the Novgorod and Staraya Rus military colonies and put down the riots which had taken place because of the widespread notion that the deaths from the cholera were really from poisoning. Nicholas I took firm measures, with the result that 129 men died from corporal punishment.
  3. See Letter 378, and note 4.

Letter 383

  1. Upon the marriage of her daughter, Evpraxia Nikolaevna Vulf, to Baron B. A. Vrevsky (see Letter 372).
  2. The letters were addressed to Pushkin's parents, who were then living in near-by Pavlovsk.
  3. Pushkin's sister Olga, wishing to see her parents, slipped through the quarantine

to Pavlovsk, but she made a mistake in the house her parents were living in, and she was caught and sent back.

4. See Letter 382.

5. "It is an epidemic disease, but not a contagion; consequently quarantines are superfluous; only precautionary measures in food and clothing are necessary." The first clause is a quotation from her most recent letter.

6. Mme. Osipova had eagerly seconded Pushkin's suggestion of buying the estate Savkino, adjacent to her estate of Trigorskoe and to Pushkin's mother's estate of Mikhaylovskoe. Mme. Osipova promised to help arrange the purchase, and she wished details of how much he was prepared to pay.

Letter 384

1. The writer N. M. Konshin was the Director of the Chancellery of the Chief Directorate of Tsarskoe Selo at the time.

Letter 385

1. See Letter 373.

2. Ivan Pavlovich Shambo (1783-1848) was private secretary to the Empress Alexandra Fedorovna.

3. "And deliver the letter to me"—Pushkin's note.

4. Obviously with the idea of getting permission to publish Pogodin's *Marfa, the Novgorod Burgomaster's Wife.*

Letter 386

1. Dmitry Vasilievich Korotky was an official in the Loan Office where Pushkin borrowed forty thousand rubles on his peasants before his marriage.

2. Probably the promissory note given Pushkin by his Caucasian acquaintance Rufin Ivanovich Dorokhov (d. 1852) after losses to Pushkin at cards. Pushkin wanted to negotiate this note, in order to pay the interest on the forty thousand rubles.

3. See Letter 370 and note 7.

4. "And kisses you"—note by Mme. Pushkina.

5. Nashchokin had requested a portrait of Mme. Pushkina.

Letter 387

1. A paraphrase of the opening words of I. I. Dmitriev's fable, "The Sparrow and the Finch": "The nightingale has become silent. The poor fellow is sick or dissatisfied with his sweetheart." After Delvig's death, Somov continued the publication of *The Literary Gazette*, but it gradually died, the last issue being dated June 20, 1831.

2. Grech had asserted, in an article in defense of Bulgarin, that Bulgarin had "in his little finger alone more intellect than there is in the heads of his many reviewers." Vyazemsky's comment was that "one reader remarked, 'Too bad that Bulgarin does not write with his little finger alone.'" Grech's critique followed an attack on Bulgarin in *The Telescope*; it provoked one by Pushkin under the pseudonym of Feofilakt Kosichkin. Pushkin carried out his promise with another "Kosichkin" article in *The Telescope*, "A Few Words About Mr. Bulgarin's Little Finger, and Other Things."

3. See Letters 382 and 383.

4. The Polish revolution of 1830-1831.

5. Turgenev's "postscript," like Pushkin's Letter 376, to which it refers, contains objections to Chaadaev's historical ideas.

6. "That is, a manifestation of the Christian spirit. What Christianity lost of unity in it, it regained in popularity." Again, when Pushkin starts thinking of abstract matters

he shifts to the "language of Europe," in which, indeed, Chaadaev himself wrote. Pushkin's phraseology here is close to that of his then recent letter to Chaadaev (Letter 376).

7. The manuscript of two of Chaadaev's *Philosophical Letters*. See Letters 376 and 380.

Letter 388

1. The triweekly newspaper *The Northern Mercury* (1830-1832) came out more and more irregularly before it ceased. Its editor was Mikhail Alexeevich Bestuzhev-Ryumin (1800-1832), journalist and writer, who had earned Pushkin's dislike by publishing in almanacs a number of Pushkin's poems without permission.

2. Pushkin's prophecy was not fulfilled. Khvostov died two years before Pushkin.

3. *The Tales of Belkin*.

4. To Nikolay Mikhaylovich Smirnov (1807-1870), then a young diplomat, and later civil governor of Petersburg and a Senator. The marriage took place on January 11, 1832.

Letter 389

1. Prince Vyazemsky was made a Chamberlain on August 5, 1831.

2. Pushkin's little poem is "in the manner" of V. L. Pushkin's "To P. N. Priklonsky," where the lines occur, "Dear relative, poet, and Chamberlain. . . . You know my manner . . . ."

3. The Chamberlain's symbolical key was embroidered on the back part of the court costume.

4. Princess Vyazemskaya. Pushkin's poem centers on a pun on her name, which in Russian means "faith."

5. "Cricket" was Pushkin's Arzamas nickname, and "Asmodeus," Vyazemsky's.

6. The play on words here is not translatable. "Commercial play" (*kommerčeskaja igra*) has to do with games of skill, in contradistinction to games of chance (*azartnaja igra*); the banker was the dealer. As a civil servant in the Department of Foreign Trade, Vyazemsky had been writing articles published in *The Commercial Gazette*. As a result of his successful service, he attained the rank of Chamberlain. A decade or so later Vyazemsky did "transfer to the Bank"—he was Director of the Loan Bank from 1846 to 1853.

7. General Henryk Dembiński (1791-1864) succeeded Skrzynecki briefly to the command of the Polish forces. He gave up this position to Count Jan Krukowiecki (1770-1850), who surrendered Warsaw to General Paskevich on September 7, 1831.

8. Possible intervention by the French in the Polish Revolution was being discussed in the French House of Deputies.

9. William I became first king of the Kingdom of the Netherlands, made up of Holland and Belgium, in 1815. In 1830, Belgium declared its independence, and he was unable to prevent the separate establishment of Belgium as kingdom. The other powers, including Prussia, were too much occupied with the Polish question to come to his assistance.

10. Among the classical hexameters Zhukovsky was writing at the time was the humorous specimen quoted in Letter 387.

11. In speaking of his hopes for a journal, Pushkin usually uses the English words "Quarterly" (which he misspells, as in this letter) or, more frequently, "Review"—allusions to the great English-language quarterlies, such as *The Edinburgh Review* and *The Quarterly Review*.

12. Elizaveta M. Khitrovo. She had connection with the highest society and with

the court circle. Her participation, if it is meant seriously, would probably have been restricted to financial assistance and to the obtaining of information about foreign affairs.

13. "Believe in the affection of one who will love you even beyond the grave." Pushkin's letters to Mme. Khitrovo and her letters to him are all in French.

14. Unidentified.

15. "O woman, woman! Creature frail and deceiving"—Beaumarchais, *The Marriage of Figaro*, Act V, scene 3.

Letter 390

1. The letters to Pavel Ivanovich Miller (1813-1885) show Pushkin's continued interest in the Lyceum, of which Miller was then a student. The date of Miller's graduation was fifteen years after Pushkin's, hence the term "grandson," which Miller himself suggested. Miller struck up an acquaintance with Pushkin, and at Pushkin's request he had books and journals from the Lyceum library delivered to Pushkin.

Letter 391

1. Pushkin's *Tales of Belkin* were written under the pseudonym of Ivan Petrovich Belkin.

2. That is, Pushkin wished the tales to be sent to the usual censorship, instead of to Nicholas I and Benkendorf.

3. The actual sales price was 5.45 rubles in paper cover, and 6.45 in cloth.

4. A large part of the sheet is torn off here and lost—about nine lines of text.

5. The epigraph which Pushkin chose and quotes here is from Bestuzhev's "Evening at a Bivouac," not his "Novel in Seven Letters." Pushkin loved epigraphs and chose them with considerable care.

Letter 392

1. The manuscript of Pushkin's *Tale of Belkin*.

2. Gogol had suggested an article on A. A. Orlov and Bulgarin, including a comparison of the latter with Byron. Neither Pushkin nor Gogol wrote such an article.

3. Pushkin's critical attack on Bulgarin, written under the humorous pseudonym of "Feofilakt Kosichkin," was entitled "The Triumph of Friendship, or A. A. Orlov Justified." It appeared in Nadezhdin's journal, *The Telescope*, at the end of August, 1831.

4. Gogol's letter of August 21 describes the amusement of the typesetters as they were setting into type his *Evenings on a Farm Near Dikanka*, Gogol's first major literary work and the one that first gave him literary fame and popularity.

5. The "shop clerk" Pushkin had in mind was N. A. Polevoy.

6. Gogol had complained of the cholera and heavy rain in Petersburg. Mention of the cholera reminded Pushkin of the then recent riots in Petersburg in connection with the plague.

7. Gogol had erred in the given name of Pushkin's wife.

Letter 393

1. V. L. Pushkin, as the oldest member of the Arzamas literary society, was called its "elder." His Arzamas nickname, *Vot*, was often used in a corrupted diminutive form, *Votrushka* "cheesecake," instead of the theoretically possible *Votushka* "Little Vot." Hence the commemorative dish.

2. Zhukovsky's Arzamas nickname was "Svetlana," the name of the heroine of his poem of the same name, hence the "she."

Letter 394

1. The reference is to Nashchokin's efforts to settle Pushkin's affairs with Ogon-Doganovsky (see Letter 370) and others, and also the arranging of Nashchokin's domestic affairs.

2. Unidentified.

3. See Letters 380 and 381.

4. Alexander Grigoriev, Ivan Grigoriev, and Vasily Mikhaylovich Kalashnikov were servants of Pushkin's. Pushkin means that he discharged Alexander Grigoriev as his butler and gave the duties to Vasily Kalashnikov.

5. Pushkin's male cook actually went to Moscow and there saw Nashchokin, who wrote Pushkin that the cook had lied about being recruited.

6. "Neither time, nor absence, nor distance."

7. Because of Pushkin's favoring Polivanov's suit with Alexandra N. Goncharova. See Letter 360.

8. A. N. Goncharov had become completely silent about the promised dowry for his granddaughter.

9. *The Tales of Belkin.*

10. See Letter 386.

Letter 395

1. Pushkin owed Vyazemsky five hundred rubles. Vyazemsky asked Nashchokin to let him have five hundred rubles of Pushkin's money in his care, if he had them. This informal way of handling finances was quite common with Pushkin and his friends.

2. Neither Pushkin nor Vyazemsky wanted a fashion section in their projected journal, but Pushkin, feeling that a political or a fashion section was necessary for obtaining subscribers, and being refused permission for a political section, was suggesting the section on fashions. Vyazemsky hooted at the idea of a magazine with fashions coming out only quarterly. Pushkin's idea with regard to political and fashion sections being necessary for popularity of a journal was proved only too true in 1836, when his own literary journal did not prove lucrative.

3. Vyazemsky had spoken of the "classical dignity" of correspondence between Pushkin's father, here called for some reason Avraam (Abraham), and Ignaty Petrov, a serf who had formerly belonged to Vasily Lvovich Pushkin, brother of Pushkin's father.

4. Pushkin's masterpiece in the folklore genre and style, *The Tale of the Tsar Saltan.*

5. Probably *The Tale of the Priest and His Workman Balda.*

6. Novel by Zagoskin.

7. Alexandra O. Rosset. Vyazemsky had asked Pushkin to request her to burn all his poems and letters addressed to her before her marriage; she refused, accusing him of conceit.

8. General Count Karl Osipovich Lambert (1772-1843), a Senator, and his wife Uliana Mikhaylovna Lambert (b. 1791), were living across the street from Pushkin.

9. Vyazemsky had given interpretations of some Russian proverbs which he considered misunderstood.

10. See Letter 387.

11. Klementy Osipovich Rosset (1811-1866).

12. That is, Mme. Karamzina wished Zhukovsky's opinion as to whether Alexandra O. Rosset and her husband should live in Moscow or in Petersburg after their marriage. The couple settled down in Moscow after the wedding.

13. Zhukovsky is slightly paraphrasing Pushkin's poem "Losing Tongue and

Mind Simultaneously," which ends, "If I had a hundred eyes, all hundred would be looking at you" (see Letter 253).

14. Warsaw was taken on August 26.

Letter 396

1. There is salt in Pushkin's matter-of-fact comment: Pushkin wrote the article himself. See Letter 387.

2. See Letter 395.

3. See Letter 390.

Letter 397

1. See Letter 383. Mme. Osipova had told Pushkin that of the three owners of Savkino, one did not want to sell, and hence had set a price too high. Pushkin did not obtain the estate.

2. Pushkin's reference is to his going into the civil service to work on the history of Peter the Great. See Letters 380 and 381.

3. On August 26, 1831.

Letter 398

1. Although Alexandra O. Rosset was a good friend of Pushkin's, and although she is often mentioned in his letters, this is Pushkin's only surviving letter to her. She was an intelligent woman, and Pushkin liked to discuss his poems and literary ideas with her, though by doing so he aroused the jealousy of Mme. Pushkina, who had no literary interests.

2. The "verses" here are Pushkin's two poems on the Polish Revolution, "To the Calumniators of Russia" and "The Anniversary of Borodino," which were published, together with Zhukovsky's "An Old Song to a New Tune," in 1831, as *Three Poems on the Taking of Warsaw.* All three poems were intensely nationalistic, or even chauvinistic. The government's interest in them is shown by the great rapidity with which they passed through the censorship, were printed, and put on sale. This note is Pushkin's inscription on the copy which he gave Mlle. Rosset. The hiatus in the second line of the little inscription verse is Pushkin's own. No other copy of the little poem is known.

3. Countess Uliana Mikhaylovna Lambert.

Letter 399

1. Pushkin quotes the entire poem, "Before the Sacred Tomb," addressed to Mme. Khitrovo's father, General Kutuzov. The verses were written in the middle of 1831, when the Russians were still having difficulty in putting down the Polish Revolution. These verses became generally known only in 1836, when Pushkins's defense of another general of the War of 1812 against Napoleon, Barklay de Tolly, caused Pushkin to be accused of not properly revering Kutuzov, whereupon he published the poem.

2. This is probably another allusion to her "little affair" with the traveler Mornay. See Letter 389.

3. L. S. Pushkin did not participate in the taking of Warsaw.

4. See Letter 398. Pushkin's correction here cited is for his "Anniversary of Borodino," one of his two poems published together with Zhukovsky's in the little booklet.

5. Pushkin left Tsarskoe Selo for Petersburg in the middle of October.

Letter 400

1. A translation into French of Pushkin's "To the Calumniators of Russia." It has not survived, nor is it known who made this particular translation.

2. The allusion is to Suvorov's capture of Izmail (Ismail) in 1790 (it is described in Byron's *Don Juan*, cantos VI and VII).

3. Letter 399.

4. Konstantin Fedorovich Opochinin (1808-1848), Mme. Khitrovo's nephew.

Letter 401

1. Pushkin wished to clear up his gambling debts to Ogon-Doganovsky and Luka Iliich Zhemchuzhnikov (1783-1856) by paying fifteen thousand rubles and giving a note of hand for five thousand. Pushkin's proposal was not accepted.

2. Pushkin was officially given a position with the Collegium of Foreign Affairs, with a salary of five thousand rubles per year. Though he began his "duties" in November, 1831, he received his first salary only the following July.

3. Pavel Pavlovich, Nashchokin's son by his gypsy mistress, Olga Andreevna.

Letter 402

1. Pushkin had been using Vyazemsky's furniture. See Letters 362 and 366.

2. *The European*, edited by Kireevsky, Yazykov, and Baratynsky. Two issues of it appeared in 1832, and then it was suppressed.

3. That is, Pushkin himself, as a polemical journalist.

4. Zhukovsky translated a fragment of Sir Walter Scott's *Marmion*, under the title, "The Subterranean Trial."

5. Gogol's *Evenings on a Farm Near Dikanka*.

Letter 403

1. On October 19, Benkendorf answered, giving permission for republication of what Pushkin had already published.

2. Benkendorf answered that Nicholas I's permission concerned only *Boris Godunov* (see Letters 278 and 280), and that all other poems must be submitted for the Tsar's inspection.

3. About passing *Marfa, the Novgorod Burgomaster's Wife* through the censorship.

Letter 404

1. Sergey Semenovich Uvarov (1786-1855), from 1818 on, President of the Academy of Sciences, and from 1834, Minister of Public Education, and, as such, head of the censorship. In this latter capacity he is famous in Russian history for his motto of "autocracy, Orthodoxy, and nationality," which he used for furthering reactionary ideas. Pushkin later had many clashes with him.

2. Prince Mikhail Alexandrovich Dondukov-Korsakov (1794-1869), at this time in the Ministry of Internal Affairs. Later Pushkin had continuing difficulties with him, as an associate of Uvarov, when Dondukov and Uvarov were at the head of the censorship.

Letter 405

1. Pushkin owed twenty thousand rubles to Ogon-Doganovsky and Zhemchuzhnikov, and Nashchokin owed Pushkin fifteen thousand rubles. The affair ended by Nashchokin agreeing to undertake to pay the fifteen thousand to Pushkin's creditors.

2. Pushkin's mother-in-law gave her diamonds to her daughter Natalia before her marriage. They were pawned in 1831 to Nicette Weyer (1786-1841), merchant and pawnbroker in Moscow, and former French consul.

3. Semen Fedorovich Dushin (1792-1842), bailiff on Natalia I. Goncharova's estate, Yaropolets.

4. A. N. Goncharov had borrowed the money from Pushkin, before Pushkin's marriage, to purchase his granddaughter's trousseau.

5. Pushkin never uses the word *beremannaja* "pregnant," but always the coarser, more direct word *brjukhataja*, built on the word meaning "belly."

6. A series of balls and festivities were held for the royal family.

Letter 406

1. Pushkin enclosed his *Feast in the Time of the Plague* for Rozen's almanac, *Alcyone for 1832.* Pushkin's little play is based on *The City of the Plague* (1816) by the Scottish writer John Wilson (1785-1854), known also by his pseudonym of Christopher North. This little play was one of several which Pushkin wrote while he was held in quarantine by the plague in 1830.

2. Rozen proposed to translate Pushkin's *Boris Godunov* into German, but the translation did not appear. The "preface," a "rather stiff critique" appeared in Germany in 1833. Rozen himself was a poet and dramatist; in this capacity he is perhaps best known as the librettist for Glinka's opera, *Ivan Susanin* (*A Life for the Tsar*, 1836), first "national" Russian opera.

3. No second edition of *Boris Godunov* appeared during Pushkin's lifetime, nor did he ever write for publication his critical ideas behind the composition of the play.

Letter 407

1. Poetry by Yazykov for *The Northern Flowers for* 1832.

2. See Letter 402.

3. Yazykov had said that *The European,* though it would be devoted to things European, would always have room for anything by Kosichkin (that is, Pushkin).

4. The answer to Orlov is Letter 417. Pushkin's attack on Bulgarin in his "Triumph of Friendship . . . ," was in the form of a mock "justification" of Orlov, which the latter took seriously.

5. What news is not known unless it has to do with the "thousand," which apparently is money from advance subscriptions for *The European.*

6. Alexey Stepanovich Khomyakov (1804-1860), poet, historian, and later famous Slavophile and religious thinker, perhaps the most important theoretician of Russian Orthodoxy. His *Dimitry the Pretender* was finished in 1831 and published early in 1833. Pushkin's comment about "student" has to do with Khomyakov's earlier *Ermak*, the deficiences of which Pushkin hoped Khomyakov had outgrown.

7. The "memorial feast" for Delvig was *The Northern Flowers for* 1832. Pushkin wished all their friends to contribute literary works.

8. The quotation is from Khvostov's poem, "To A. S. Pushkin, Member of the Russian Academy, 1831, on the Occasion of Reading His Poem on the Caluminators of Russia." (Actually, Pushkin was elected a member of the Russian Academy about a year later.) In Khvostov's *Works,* the passage cited reads a little differently:

> I, bent, am like to the grasses of the field, but I have become an ally of the Zodiac. Fearing the arrows and bullets of the Cholera, I have sung, in Petropolis, *of July.*

No "answer" by Pushkin to Khvostov's verses is known.

Letter 408

1. F. N. Glinka had reason for anger at Pushkin in that in Pushkin's "Assembly of the Insects," in which various men of letters were characterized by various insects,

Glinka is called "ladybug" (*božja korovka*, that is, a meek, pious creature). Glinka answered Pushkin with a friendly letter and contributed several poems to *The Northern Flowers for* 1832.

Letter 409

1. Though Nicholas I's ukase naming Pushkin to a position in the civil service was dated November 14, 1831, Pushkin had not yet been informed of it.

2. The article was by Bulgarin, "The Second Letter from Karlovo to Kammeny Ostrov," and printed in *The Northern Bee* in August, 1830. It was transparently a personal attack on Pushkin, though Pushkin's name is not mentioned. Pushkin's great-grandfather, Abram Petrovich Gannibal, an abducted Ethiopian princeling, after being bought by Peter the Great, became a favorite of his and was made a nobleman. Pushkin's "answer" was an ironical poem on ancestors, "My Genealogy," in which he "admits" Bulgarin's charge that he, Pushkin, is a "bourgeois" at the court, retorting that Bulgarin is a courtier on Meshchanskaya (literally, Bourgeois) Street, the red light district, for Bulgarin had married a former prostitute. Pushkin wrote the poem on October 16, 1830. He enclosed a copy of it with this letter.

3. The allusion is to Molière's play *The Bourgeois Gentleman.*

4. In answer to this letter, Benkendorf sent to Pushkin Nicholas I's comments that he agreed with Delvig's reasoning, and that he desired that the poem not be circulated in manuscript.

Letter 410

1. This letter again shows how Mme. Khitrovo helped Pushkin keep abreast with contemporary European literature, as well as events, and how she provided connection with the society of the Court, to which Pushkin did not belong. The works spoken of in this brief note include three novels, *The Prima Donna and the Butcher Boy*, by Edmond Burat de Gurgy; *Barnave*, by Jules Janin; and a novel, probably *The Betrothed*, by the Italian poet and novelist Allessandro Manzoni.

2. Count Yuly Pompeevich Litta (1763-1839) was Head Chamberlain at the Court of Nicholas I.

Letter 411

1. This is Pushkin's first letter to his wife after his marriage to her. Like all subsequent letters to her, it is in Russian. Pushkin had left Petersburg on December 3, on a leave of twenty-eight days, for straightening out his affairs. He left Moscow for the return trip to Petersburg on December 24, probably arriving on December 27.

Letter 412

1. Letter 411.

2. Pushkin's ironical comment shows his contempt for Bulgarin's novel, *Ivan Vyzhigin*, and the "entirely charming" conversation about it.

3. Princess Anna Vasilievna Golitsyna, nee Lanskaya (1793-1868).

4. Ekaterina Nikolaevna Kochetova (d. 1867).

5. Mme. Pushkina had so called Nashchokin because of his expensive presents to her.

6. Nashchokin's expensive hobby was the outfitting of a mahogany play house, with expensive miniature piano, candelabra, table silver, oil paintings, and other furnishings, to the cost, it is said, of ten thousand silver rubles. It has been restored and is now located in the Historical Museum.

7. When Pushkin speaks of the Meshcherskys here and in later letters, he is referring

to Prince Peter Ivanovich Meshcherksy (1802-1876) and his wife, Ekaterina Nikolaevna Meshcherskaya, nee Karamzina (daughter of the historiographer).

8. The "Noble Assembly" of the Moscow nobility, where balls were given on Tuesdays in winter.

9. See Letter 405.

10. Mme. Pushkina's diamonds were pawned, and Pushkin was trying to arrange to redeem them. See Letter 405.

11. The Emperor and Empress had been in Moscow from October 11 to November 25, 1831.

12. Mme. Sichler was proprietress of a fashionable shop in Moscow.

13. Alexandra Alexandrovna Rimskaya-Korsakova was married to Prince Alexander Nikolaevich Vyazemsky (b. 1804) on February 12, 1832.

14. In the Winter Palace. Pushkin's prediction did not come true this time, but Mme. Pushkina had a miscarriage after dancing late at a court ball in 1834. See Letter 481.

15. Apparently Dmitry N. Goncharov.

16. This first long letter of Pushkin's to his wife after their marriage sets the tone of the further letters to her. The familiarity, simplicity, and directness of style provide perhaps the best sample in Russian of colloquial prose. Pushkin's love for his wife is clear, and also his solicitude about her and his conviction that she is not wise enough to take care of herself. Like succeeding letters to her, this one has a considerable amount of society gossip, but little discussion of literary, political, or social problems. One can learn much of the mind and character of Mme. Pushkina from Pushkin's letters to her, for his letters always have style, tone, and subject matter showing the relationship of Pushkin and his correspondents.

Letter 413

1. What business is not known.

2. Pushkin had been a member of the Moscow English Club (founded 1813), the most aristocratic of Moscow clubs, since 1829.

3. Alexander Sergeevich Vlasov (1777-1825) had a first-class collection of paintings, engravings, books, manuscripts, and jewels. His paintings included originals by such artists as Raphael, Leonardo da Vinci, Michelangelo, and Rubens. He died over a million rubles in debt, and his collections were sold at auction.

4. The minor writer Fedor Fominsky. His novel was published in 1832.

5. The Goncharovs' house on Nikitskaya Street.

6. Mme. Pushkina did not follow her husband's wishes, but, instead, became, that winter, the belle of the Petersburg balls.

Letter 414

1. Mme. Pushkina's letters, including these, have not survived.

2. One Alexey, a servant of Pushkin's. Pushkin uses the approbrious diminutive.

3. Probably Nikolay Iliich Fomin (died before 1848), a third-rate poet.

4. Vasily Kalashnikov married his "sweetheart," the servant Malania Semenova, then some nineteen or twenty years old, in 1832. Kalashnikov remained with Pushkin until Pushkin's death.

5. "To have a complete house cleaning."

6. The reference is to the business with Ogon-Doganovsky and Zhemchuzhnikov.

7. A. N. Goncharov's "piece of business" was probably "giving his third concubine in marriage," together with a large dowry, whereas he had given no dowry to his own

granddaughter nor repaid the money borrowed from him for her trousseau (see Letter 405).

8. The reference was no doubt made with specific people in mind. It has been pointed out that one of them must have been Countess Ekaterina Markovna Ivelich, noted for her coarse behavior.

9. Benkendorf's letter of December 10, 1831. It is discussed in Letter 409.

10. Pushkin describes life at Nashchokin's in Letter 415.

11. Vera Yakovlevna Soldaen (1790-1856), wife of the former secretary of the Dutch Embassy at the Russian Court.

Letter 415

1. Pushkin left Moscow on December 24, and hence he could not have arrived home for Christmas Day, for the travel time was three days.

2. Pushkin did not succeed in redeeming Mme. Pushkina's diamonds on this trip. For their pawning, see Letter 405.

3. The business with Ogon-Doganovsky and Zhemchuzhnikov.

4. Used for rheumatism.

5. No doubt the student V. Davydov, one of Mme. Pushkina's former admirers. He is mentioned banteringly several times in the Letters.

Letter 416

1. Mme. Osipova had sent Pushkin's books to him at the very beginning of the year. Pushkin hoped to find several of his books which had not been sent. "Arkhip" was probably the gardener at Mikhaylovskoe. "Lev" is Lev Sergeevich Pushkin. "Nikita" is no doubt Nikita Timofeevich Kozlov, Pushkin's peasant "uncle" and faithful servant. Mme. Osipova wrote back that the books were not to be found.

2. Delvig.

3. Perhaps the little book (1831) containing several fairy tales by Zhukovsky and Pushkin's *Tale of the Tsar Saltan.*

4. Baroness Evpraxia Nikolaevna Vrevskaya, nee Vulf.

Letter 417

1. Pushkin's tongue is in his cheek in this letter, which is in answer to Orlov's letter of thanks for Pushkin's taking his part in his articles, "The Triumph of Friendship, or Alexander Anfimovich Orlov Justified" and later, "A Few Words About Mr. Bulgarin's Little Finger, and Other Things." Orlov had taken Pushkin's defense of him vis-à-vis Bulgarin as being genuine: whereas it was simply ironical.

2. "I was small." Pushkin uses the Church Slavonic expression to point up the biblical allusion. Bulgarin is here called by the nickname used in epigrams on him, "Figlyarin." Pushkin's speaking of Bulgarin as Goliath and himself as David is ironical, but even the possibility of the joke indicates the power Bulgarin had in Russian letters at the time.

3. Orlov wrote a series of novels parodying Bulgarin's novel, *Ivan Vyzhigin.*

4. Bulgarin and Grech.

5. The story was that Orlov was to assist Polevoy with the latter's *History of the Russian People.* This rumor was intended as a jibe at Polevoy, who had taken subscriptions for a twelve-volume history which he said was ready for publication, but of which only three volumes had appeared.

6. In *The Moscow Telegraph,* 1831.

7. An article by Somov, under the pseudonym of Nikita Lugovoy, appeared in the literary supplement of Voeykov's *Russian Invalide.* The article defended Pushkin's works

and Gogol's *Evenings on a Farm Near Dikanka* and attacked Polevoy for unfavorable criticism of the latter. Pushkin is dissociating himself from Somov's article.

Letter 418
1. Nashchokin sent his agent, Heinrich Adam (Russian: Andrey Khristianovich) Knörzer (1789-1853), called "the German" below, to see whether he could obtain money from his brother, Vasily Voinovich Nashchokin (b. 1796). Apparently the "mission" was unsuccessful.
2. Rokhmanov had the task of redeeming Mme. Pushkina's diamonds.
3. Nashchokin is reported to have quoted Pushkin as saying that "Nicholas I courted [Pushkin's] wife as though she were an officer's wife, would ride past her windows on purpose mornings, and in the evenings at balls would ask her why her curtains were drawn."
4. Another allusion to Nashchokin's extravagant presents to Mme. Pushkina.
5. They were sent early in February.

Letter 419
1. "Madam" of a house of prostitution in Petersburg. See Letter 240.
2. Kistenevo.
3. The third "great owner of property" was Nicholas I.
4. The salary was finally set at five thousand rubles.
5. Pushkin must have arranged such "a light breakfast" with him in 1836; at least, he borrowed money from him then.
6. It is not known whether Pushkin received the loan here requested.

Letter 420
1. Daria F. Ficquelmont, the wife of the Austrian Ambassador and the daughter of Mme. Khitrovo.
2. Ivan Nikolaevich Goncharov.
3. That is, Chapter VIII of *Evgeny Onegin*, which appeared in January, 1832.

Letter 421
1. *The Northern Flowers for* 1832 and Baron Rozen's *Alcyone*.
2. Pushkin's humorous verse tale, *Little House in Kolomna*.
3. In the first two issues were published two poems by Zhukovsky, "The Sleeping Tsarevna" and "The War of the Mice and the Frogs" (which Pushkin calls "Stepanida the Mouse," after one of the characters), and six poems by Yazykov.
4. In his critique, "Survey of Russian Literature for 1831," Kireevsky included favorable criticism of Pushkin's *Boris Godunov* and Baratynsky's narrative poem, *The Concubine*.
5. Baratynsky's defense of his poem, *The Concubine*.
6. Franz van Mieris, seventeenth-century Dutch painter of small genre pictures and portraits.
7. Baratynsky wrote no comedies.
8. Slip of the pen, for February.

Letter 422
1. Pushkin's letter was in answer to an official letter from Benkendorf, inquiring how it happened that Pushkin's poem, "Anchar," which he here calls "The Tree of Poison," and other poems were published in *The Northern Flowers for* 1832, without having been censored by Nicholas I. See also Letter 424.

2. Nicholas I's becoming Pushkin's personal censor.

3. Slip of the pen, for February.

Letter 423

1. Dmitriev, in his letter, had expressed admiration for several of Pushkin's works, including the last chapter of *Evgeny Onegin*, and two plays in blank verse, *Boris Godunov* and *Mozart and Salieri*.

2. It was the Tsar himself who "discovered" political allusions unpleasant to himself in two articles by Kireevsky. When Kireevsky did not conceal, under interrogation, that he thought the serfs should be liberated, he was put under police surveillance and considered "dangerous."

Letter 424

1. Probably "Anchar."

2. Pushkin is referring to the scene of his forgiveness by Nicholas I, which occurred, not in 1827, but in September, 1826 (see Letters 189 and 190 and notes).

3. There is a hiatus in the manuscript at this point.

4. The allusions are to Pushkin's "Anchar," written in 1828 and published in *The Northern Flowers for* 1832. This perfect little poem is of the slave who dies after bringing poison from the Anchar, or Upas tree, to his "prince," who thereupon tips arrows with the poison and attacks his neighbors. On this first publication, the word "tsar" was printed instead of "prince."

5. Pushkin did not make a smooth copy of this letter nor send it to Benkendorf.

Letter 425

1. *The Complete Collected Laws of the Russian Empire from* 1649 [*to* 1825], in fifty-five volumes, 1830.

2. Pushkin's work on the history of Peter the Great.

3. Catherine the Great obtained Voltaire's library in 1779, and placed it in the Hermitage Museum in Petersburg.

4. Ivan Ivanovich Shuvalov (1727-1797), Russian Maecenas and great lord of the time of Catherine the Great. He bought many books and manuscripts for Voltaire to use in compiling his *History of the Russian Empire Under Peter the Great* (1759-1763).

5. Probably "Anchar."

Letter 426

1. This letter shows the financial practices of the time. Vasily Ivanovich Kister, a speculator in promissory notes, had obtained a promissory note of Pushkin's made out to Baron Sergey Romanovich Shilling, for five hundred rubles, and dated 1820; the note was probably the result of losses at cards. In 1830, Kister obtained a writ against Pushkin's personal property in security for the repayment of this loan. Whether Pushkin paid it is not known.

Letter 427

1. See Letter 401.

Letter 428

1. Probably Pavel Matveevich Alymov (1810-1891), Opochka Marshal of the Nobility, and son of the owner of the apartment where Pushkin was then living.

2. Alexander Borisovich Vrevsky (1832-1833), son of Mme. Osipova's daughter, Evpraxia Nikolaevna Vrevskaya, nee Vulf.

3. The address Pushkin gives here, in Russian, is his own. Pushkin's first child,

Maria Alexandrovna Pushkina (1832-1919), was born on May 19, 1832. Lev Nikolaevich Tolstoy (1828-1910) is said to have depicted some of her physical traits in the heroine of *Anna Karenina* (1875-1877).

4. Pushkin cites Horace in this connection in *Evgeny Onegin*, Chap. VI, stanza 7.

5. Pushkin did not visit Mikhaylovskoe until 1835.

Letter 429

1. Yulia Karlovna Kyukhelbeker, the younger sister of Pushkin's Lyceum friend, the Decembrist Vilgelm Karlovich Kyukhelbeker. Apparently Pushkin was not granted permission to publish whatever poems of Kyukhelbeker these may have been.

2. As a consequence of this letter, Pushkin received preliminary permission to publish a periodical called *Diary*, which would have been allowed to include news and articles about political events. The negotiations were long drawn out, and by the end of 1832 Pushkin had cooled toward the idea, for he discovered that he would have to follow closely the instructions of the government in writing the articles including political news.

Letter 430

1. "I have just left Khitrovo's."

2. The poet Batyushkov was mad. His physician had suggested that sexual intercourse might be used in treating his madness: Pushkin is jokingly saying that Mme. Khitrovo suggested herself for the purpose.

3. Pushkin's daughter Maria Alexandrovna Pushkina, born two weeks previously.

Letter 431

1. Pushkin did not succeed in his attempt to sell the statue to the government.

Letter 432

1. Pushkin's bitter irony is at Kireevsky's having fallen under the surveillance of the police after the suppression of his journal, *The European* (see Letter 423), and at his own position vis-à-vis the government. The then most recent indication of Pushkin's being considered "undependable" is reflected in Letter 422.

2. That is, Nicholas I himself was directly responsible, and not a denunciation by Bulgarin. Pushkin is paraphrasing a folk saying, "The lightning struck, not out of a cloud, but from a dung heap."

3. Kireevsky did not write such a letter as Pushkin suggested, but instead, when given the opportunity, expressed openly and directly his desire to establish a close connection "not with political Europe, but with thinking Europe," and pointing out the "necessity" for liberating the serfs in Russia.

4. Peter Vasilievich Kireevsky (1808-1856), a collector of folk songs.

5. To have been called *Diary* (see Letter 429).

6. Pushkin arrived in Moscow on September 21.

Letter 433

1. The "commission" was for Pushkin to ask Smirdin to buy up the entire edition of Pogodin's *Marfa, the Novgorod Burgomaster's Wife,* which was selling poorly, and also the entire edition of *The Selected German Theater,* translated by Alexander A. Shishkov (Moscow, 1830). Smirdin declined.

2. In *The Son of the Fatherland.*

3. Tsar Nicholas I refused to allow tsars to be presented on the stage, and hence the plays could not be performed.

4. The great contemporary popularity of the "well-made plays" of Scribe extended to Russia.

5. *Diary* (see Letter 429).

6. The allusion is to Polevoy's *History of the Russian People*. Pushkin proceeds to explain his point.

7. In *The Telescope*, 1832.

8. For a copy of his translated *Selected German Theater*, mentioned in note 1 above.

9. Tieck's play *Fortunat* was included in Shishkov's translated *Selected German Theater*.

Letter 434

1. The "present" was Khvostov's poem about Pushkin, "A Nightingale in the Tavrida Garden." Khvostov's other poem in praise of Pushkin was entitled "To A. S. Pushkin, Member of the Russian Academy, 1831, on the Occasion of the Reading of His Poem About the Calumniators of Russia." Pushkin quotes from the latter poem in Letter 407 (q.v., and note 8). It is interesting to compare Pushkin's polite and respectful tone in this letter (and in Letter 407) with his comments about Khvostov in his other correspondence with his literary friends.

Letter 435

1. Pushkin's comments about the "program" of his projected journal, *Diary*, show how much he had already cooled toward the idea of the conditions under which it would have had to be published. See Letter 429, and note 2.

2. That is, Pushkin might "rail at the journals," writing under a pseudonym, but not as himself writing under his own name.

3. In Matthew 7:6 the allusion is to swine.

4. This is the only mention in Pushkin's works of the English poet Edward Young. The popularity of his *Night Thoughts* (1742-1745) extended to Russia and lasted there even longer, perhaps, than in Europe in general.

5. Pushkin has in mind Vigny's *Cinq-Mars* (1826) and perhaps his *Stello* (1832).

6. Published by Nadezhdin and Polevoy, respectively. Pushkin may have intended puns by the way he divides the words: "castrate," for the former, and the title of "Count" for the latter. Pushkin may have been thinking of Nadezhdin as some sort of a castrate in criticism or journalism, and Pushkin may have been ironically applying the title of "Count" to the bourgeois Polevoy. Pushkin so loved puns and irony that one can hardly go wrong in assuming any possible double-meaning as intentional.

7. Pogodin was then at work on a play, *A History in Personages Relating to Tsar Boris Fedorovich Godunov*, which was finished in 1833 but published only in 1868.

Letter 436

1. At Pushkin's not having written the moment he reached Moscow. That she was angry, as he suspected, is clear from Letter 440.

2. Pushkin gives the word in Russian transliteration, *velosifer*.

3. Nicholas I was in Moscow from September 20 to September 22.

4. Open, short, fur-trimmed jackets.

5. Pushkin had already alluded in his letters to the story of Joseph and Potiphar's wife in Letter 270, in connection with Mme. Khitrovo. This biblical allusion immediately suggests to Pushkin another: The unpleasant scenes raised by Nashchokin's gypsy mistress, Olga Andreevna, because of Nashchokin's intentions of abandoning her and marrying, are here compared with the jealousy of Abraham's aged and still childless wife, Sarah, when the Egyptian handmaiden, Hagar, conceives by him (Genesis 16).

6. For the sake of privacy, Pushkin and Nashchokin would go to public steam baths for their long, friendly conversations.

7. Lavrenty Nikolaevich Ober (1802-1884), son of a French immigrant, proprietor of a fashionable shop in Moscow.

8. Elena Pavlovna, the wife of Grand Duke Mikhail Pavlovich, had had a miscarriage and was still seriously ill. Because of her illness, balls and other amusements which had been planned were cancelled.

9. Pushkin's "business," to which there are continued allusions during the letters written on this trip, was the attempt to remortgage his Kistenovo serfs for fifty additional rubles each. Pushkin's efforts during this trip and Nashchokin's later attempts on Pushkin's behalf were alike unsuccessful.

10. The Pushkins' cook.

11. Irina Kuzminichna and Nenila Onufrievna Arbenieva were both servants of the Pushkins'.

12. Pushkin usually speaks of his daughter, Maria Alexandrovna Pushkina, in the affectionate "Masha," or in the rough-affectionate "Mashka."

13. Ivan Timofeevich Spassky (1795-1861), the Pushkins' physician.

Letter 437

1. Peter (see Letter 436).

2. Pushkin refers to the Petersburg English Club, to which he had been elected in 1832.

3. Ivan Frebelius and Iokhim were well-known Petersburg carriagemakers of the time. Frebelius was "His Imperial Majesty's own carriagemaker"; he is mentioned in Gogol's *Inspector General*.

4. Probably a midwife.

5. She was not.

6. Probably the student V. Davydov, a suitor of Mme. Pushkina before her marriage.

7. Pushkin describes his own wedding.

8. Princesses Maria Petrovna Vyazemskaya (1813-1849) and Praskovia Petrovna Vyazemskaya (1817-1835), daughters of Pushkin's good friends, Prince Peter A. Vyazemsky and Princess Vera F. Vyazemskaya.

9. Pushkin is bantering. Sorokhtin, the third of these, had been, as a student, very much interested in Mme. Pushkina before her marriage. The names Petushkov and Buyanov are used jokingly; both occur in Pushkin's *Evgeny Onegin*, Chap. VI, stanza 17. Buyanov was the "hero" of V. L. Pushkin's risqué *Dangerous Neighbor*.

10. The Vyazemskys were moving to Petersburg.

11. One of five sisters of a brother-in-law of Nashchokin's. Two of them are mentioned in Letter 611, Varvara Alexeevna Okulova (1802-1879) and Elizaveta Alexeevna Okulova (1806-1886).

12. Alexey Fedorovich Malinovsky (1762-1840), Director of the Moscow Archives of the Ministry of Foreign Affairs, his wife Anna Petrovna Malinovskaya, and their daughter Ekaterina Alexeevna Malinovskaya. Mme. Malinovskaya helped Pushkin during his courtship of Natalia Goncharova, and she was her sponsor at his wedding. The "curls" were no doubt false and sent to Mme. Malinovskaya by Mme. Pushkina at her request.

13. The attempted remortgaging of Pushkin's Kistenevo peasants. See Letter 436.

14. A servant of Pushkin's who accompanied him on this trip.

Letter 438

1. Letter 437.

2. Probably Count Fedor Matveevich Musin-Pushkin, a second cousin of Mme. Pushkina.

3. The attempted remortgaging of Pushkin's Kistenevo serfs. See Letter 436.

4. Pushkin's library contained the *Memoirs* of the eighteenth-century French Encyclopedist, Denis Diderot, in the four-volume Paris edition of 1830-1831.

5. Sergey Dmitrievich Bezobrazov (1801-1879), an officer noted for his handsomeness. Pushkin's use of the adjective in French points up his play on words on the surname "Bezobrazov," which means "ugly."

6. Nothing is known about the incident Pushkin mentions. The people involved are Pavel Konstantinovich Alexandrov (1808-1857), natural son of Grand Duke Constantine; and probably Countess Anna Vladimirovna Bobrinskaya (1769-1846), widow of Count Alexey Grigorievich Bobrinsky (1762-1813), son of Catherine the Great by Count Grigory Grigorievich Orlov (1734-1783).

7. Not her former "admirer," the student V. Davydov, but Ivan Ivanovich Davydov (1794-1863), professor at Moscow University. For Pushkin's visit to Moscow University, see Letter 439 and note 7.

8. Probably Vladimir Alexeevich Mukhanov (1805-1876), an old acquaintance of Pushkin's.

9. In Russian, a kind of confection made with fruits.

Letter 439

1. Probably F. M. Musin-Pushkin. See Letter 438.

2. Idalia Grigorievna Poletika (d. 1889), who became a close friend of Pushkin's wife but an enemy of Pushkin. She played an important role later in the events leading up to Pushkin's fatal duel.

3. An allusion to Pushkin's poem to his wife, "Madonna" (1830).

4. Pushkin is playing on a Russian idiomatic expression meaning "to become involved in others' misfortunes, to bear another's burdens upon one's back," by using it in its literal meaning, "to have a hangover at another's feast."

5. Unidentified.

6. Pushkin's projected periodical, *Diary*.

7. At Moscow University, Pushkin and the journalist-professor Kachenovsky got into a rather warm discussion in which Pushkin defended and Kachenovsky disputed the genuineness of *The Lay of the Host of Igor*, the finest monument of ancient Russian literature. The genuineness of this work, attributed to the thirteenth century, has been questioned since its discovery in a manuscript identified as having been copied in the sixteenth century. Pushkin defended its authenticity on the same grounds most modern scholars take, of the language of the poem and its literary merits and qualities.

8. Countess Nadezhda Lvovna Solugub (d. 1903). Pushkin wrote a poem to her in 1832, and he is reported as having "openly courted her" at this time.

9. Countess Emilia Karlovna Musina-Pushkina, nee Shernval (1810-1846), wife of Count Vladimir Alexeevich Musin-Pushkin (1798-1854).

10. Avrora Karlovna Shernval (1813-1902), noted for her beauty.

11. Princess Natalia Alexandrovna Urusova (1812-1882), also a well-known beauty of the time.

12. Probably Countess Sofia Ivanovna Sollogub (1791-1854), mother of the writer Vladimir Alexandrovich Sollogub (1814-1882).

13. Regarding the Kistenevo peasants.

14. For Nashchokin's mahogany play house, see Letter 412.

15. Pushkin's *Dubrovsky*, which he at first named *Ostrovsky*. It remained unfinished.

16. Pushkin here follows his proclivity of punning on names, by jokingly changing

the name of Narkiz Ivanovich Tarasenko-Otreshkov (1805-1873) to Otryzbkov "belcher." Pushkin had given Tarasenko-Otreshkov a power of attorney to take steps necessary with regard to the projected periodical, *Diary*.

Letter 440

1. Pushkin is answering his wife's objections that he did not write her on the day of his arrival in Moscow, September 21. He had attempted to allay her expected anger in Letter 436.

2. Possibly Benkendorf's official acceptance of Tarasenko-Otreshkov as editor of Pushkin's proposed periodical, *Diary*.

3. Both had to do with Pushkin's attempts to remortgage his Kistenovo serfs.

4. A. N. Goncharov had possession of the family estates until his death on September 8, 1832. His son, N. A. Goncharov, Pushkin's father-in-law, who would normally have inherited them, was mad. Before N. A. Goncharov's oldest son, Dmitry N. Goncharov, could take over the management of the estate, he needed documentary proof of the disability of his father and the consent of the other heirs. D. N. Goncharov was named his father's guardian and took over the estates on November 1, 1832.

5. Nikolay Andreevich Nebolsin (1785-1846).

6. They were moving to Petersburg.

7. Pushkin left for Petersburg on October 10.

8. Sofia Nikolaevna Gorstkina (d. 1858); Prince Peter Alexandrovich Shcherbatov (b. 1811).

9. The coiffure, patterned on that of the famous seventeenth-century Paris courtesan, Ninon de Lenclos, was as follows: the hair is parted straight in the middle and long curly locks fall onto the shoulders. See illustration opposite Letter 528 for a portrait of Mme. Pushkina with this coiffure.

10. One of four brothers of Nikolay Alexandrovich Urusov (1808-1843).

11. Princess Maria Petrovna Vyazemskaya, daughter of Prince Peter A. Vyazemsky.

12. Nikolay Alexandrovich Urusov (see note 10 above). He married Anastasia Nikolaevna Borozdina (1809-1877), who was said to sing like a nightingale.

13. Pushkin was correct.

Letter 441

1. Of Pushkin's Kistenevo serfs.

2. The individual chapters had appeared separately; hence the "second edition" (1833) was the first edition of the work published as a whole. Smirdin paid Pushkin twelve thousand rubles for publication rights.

3. Renamed *Dubrovsky*.

4. Pushkin wished Korotky's criticism with regard to the use in *Dubrovsky* of court procedure, which Korotky knew well.

5. His projected *Diary*.

6. The statue of Catherine the Great.

7. Pushkin, assuming the baby would be a boy, is thinking of naming it in honor of his ancestor Gavriil Pushkin, who appears in *Boris Godunov*. When the baby, a son, was born, on July 6, 1833, he was named Alexander Alexandrovich Pushkin.

8. Smirdin bought the publication rights of Baratynsky's poems, but they were not published until 1835.

9. Veltman wrote the libretto, and A. P. Esaulov the music, of the opera *Summer Night*.

10. Nashchokin's son by the gypsy Olga Andreevna.

11. Pushkin moved to this address on December 1 or 2. He paid 3300 rubles per annum rent there. (His fixed income was still five thousand rubles.)

Letter 442

1. Pushkin uses the term *joli frère*, a pun on *joli frère* and *beau frère*, "nice brother" and "brother-in-law." The tone of the whole letter is joking, and the allusions are apparently of a private nature.

2. Pushkin is apparently referring to Alphonse Karr's novel *Under the Lindens* (1832).

3. Apparently the reference is to Balzac's novels which came out in 1831 and 1832, *The Fatal Skin* and *The Woman of Thirty*.

Letter 443

1. Pavel Stepanovich Sankovsky (1798-1832), editor of the Tiflis daily newspaper, *The Tiflis Record*, had died before Pushkin wrote this letter. Pushkin made his acquaintance while on the trip to Erzurum in 1829. Nothing is known of the almanac projected by Sankovsky.

2. Ivan Antonovich Kasassi (d. 1837), an army officer.

3. Pushkin exaggerates, though his poetic output had indeed decreased considerably at this time.

4. The Decembrist writer, A. A. Bestuzhev, under a pseudonym, was one of the contributors to Sankovsky's *Tiflis Record*. He became famous for his romantic tales with Caucasian setting, published under the pseudonym of Marlinsky.

5. "On the third day, according to the Scriptures." Pushkin shifts to Russian as he quotes from the Nicene Creed.

Letter 444

1. This is the first letter in which Pushkin displays interest in the Pugachev uprising. As a result of this interest, Pushkin turned his historical researches from the time of Peter the Great to that of Catherine the Great. The researches resulted in a historical work, *The History of Pugachev*, and a historical novel, *The Captain's Daughter*. It is interesting that Pushkin, who had been in hot water because of the liberal ideas and poems of his youth and who had so many friends among the Decembrists, would have turned his interests to the preceding abortive revolt, and that he would have dared to make use of his official position to investigate this uprising. Emelian Ivanovich Pugachev (ca. 1742-1775) was a Cossack soldier who proclaimed himself Peter III and led a revolt against Catherine the Great. The revolt was crushed, and he was executed.

2. Adjutant General Alexander Ivanovich Chernyshev (1786-1857), Minister of War from 1827 to 1852. Pushkin had obviously been carrying on negotiations for permission to work in the archives of the Ministry of War.

3. Pushkin was apparently interested only in the Pugachev documents, and his request for the others was merely a subterfuge, to give the impression that he wished to work on a biography of Suvorov, the greatest of all Russian military men. Chernyshev sent Pushkin three of the books he requested, but informed him that the documents about the Pugachev affair were in Moscow.

4. A slip of the pen for 9.

Letter 445

1. Concerning the attempted remortgaging of Pushkin's Kistenevo peasants.

2. Nothing is known of this debt.

3. Nashchokin hoped to acquire this estate and set up a mill on the Moscow River, in order to straighten out his finances.

4. Mme. Pushkina remained in Petersburg during the summer of 1833, instead of going to her mother's Kaluga estate, Polotnyany Zavod. Pushkin himself at this time made an extended trip to the Ural region, to gather information about Pugachev. He visited Nizhny Novgorod and other Volga towns. But he did not go to Astrakhan.

Letter 446

1. On Pushkin's historical researches on Peter the Great. Apparently the conversation between Pushkin and the Tsar took place at a ball, between February 5 and February 12, 1833.

2. The rank of "adjunct" in a university was below that of a professor. Unknown to Pushkin, Pogodin had just been appointed to the rank of professor.

3. August Ludwig von Schlözer (1735-1809), German historian, worked in Petersburg and specialized in Russian history. He published a number of Russian historical monuments, including *The Primary Chronicle* (Göttingen, 1802-1809).

4. Pogodin declined to go to Petersburg for this work, though he expressed considerable interest in Pushkin's request.

Letter 447

1. It is not known whether Pushkin sent this letter to Ermolov, who had been Commander-in-Chief of Russian forces engaged in subduing the Caucasus before the accession to the throne of Nicholas I in 1825. Ermolov's *Memoirs* were not published until 1863. At the time of this letter Pushkin was trying to persuade several important people of his time to write their memoirs. Pushkin visited Ermolov on his trip to the Caucasus in 1829, and his personal impressions of Ermolov were printed in his *Journey to Erzurum*.

Letter 448

1. Ivan Timofeevich Kalashnikov (1797-1863), third-rate author, quite popular at the time. His works included *The Daughter of the Merchant Zholobov* (1831) and *The Kamchatka Girl* (1833). Kalashnikov's letter accompanied copies of his works. This rough draft of Pushkin's answer is written in pencil and erased in many places.

2. Polevoy had published a sharp critique of *The Kamchatka Girl* in *The Moscow Telegraph*, 1833. Pushkin refers further along to Polevoy's *History of the Russian People* and his novel, *Oath at the Lord's Tomb* (1832).

3. The text of the whole letter is almost obliterated, and in places is illegible or readings are hypothetical. Some four lines are illegible at this point.

Letter 449

1. It was two years later before Pushkin made the trip. Pushkin's expression of this desire is prompted immediately here by Mme. Osipova's having visited the Pushkins in Petersburg, together with her daughter, Anna Nikolaevna Vulf, in February, 1833.

2. Maria Alexandrovna Pushkina.

Letter 450

1. Pushkin was elected a member of the Russian Academy on January 7, 1833. At first he took his membership seriously and attended meetings of the Academy on Saturdays for the remainder of the winter (seven times in 1833 and once in 1834). His active participation was confined to his voting in the election of new members—in this case, of Dmitry Osipovich Baranov (1773-1834), minor poet, who on August 5 was declared officially elected to the Academy. Pushkin's letter is addressed to Peter Ivanovich Sokolov (1764-1835), Permanent Secretary of the Russian Academy.

Letter 451

1. Korf had asked Pushkin to arrange for a position for Nikolay Modestovich Bakunin (1801-1838), as translator for Smirdin's new journal, *Library for Reading*, which began to appear in 1834. Pushkin was never on particularly friendly terms with his old Lyceum classmate Korf, but he was always ready, as in the present instance, to exert his influence on behalf of others. Pushkin's advice that a translator be paid by the "sheet" gives a side glance at journalistic practices of the time.

2. Upon the birth of Pushkin's second child, Alexander Alexandrovich Pushkin, on July 6, 1833. He died in 1914.

CONTENTS OF VOLUME III

ILLUSTRATIONS

PART X

INSPECTOR GENERAL IN THE
PUGACHEV COUNTRY

July, 1833 — December, 1833

Pushkin, 1836 or 1837.   *Portrait by A. Linev.*

[452]

To Alexander Khristoforovich Benkendorf
July 22, 1833. In Petersburg.
(Rough draft; in French)

My General,

Circumstances oblige me to go and spend two or three months in the near future on my lands in Nizhny Novgorod—I should like to take advantage of this opportunity, and make a trip to Orenburg and Kazan,[1] which I am not yet familiar with. I beseech His Majesty to permit me to see the archives of these two provinces.

[453]

To Alexander Nikolaevich Mordvinov
July 30, 1833. In Petersburg.
(Second rough draft)

Dear Sir, Alexander Nikolaevich,

I hasten to respond with all sincerity to Your Excellency's questions.[1]

In the course of the past two years I have occupied myself with historical researches alone, and I have not written a single line that is purely literary.[2] I need to spend some two months in complete solitude, so as to rest from these most important labors and to finish a book[3] which I began long ago and which will provide me with money, which I am in need of. I myself am ashamed to spend time on vain occupations, but what is to be done? It is they alone that provide me with independence and with the means to live with my family in Petersburg, where my labors, thanks to the Sovereign, have a more important and useful purpose.

Except for my salary, which has been appointed for me by the generosity of His Majesty, I have no fixed income; whereas, life in the capital is expensive, and with the increase in my family, expenses increase, too.

Perhaps the Sovereign will wish to know precisely what kind of book I want to finish writing in the village; it is a novel, the greater part of the action of which takes place in Orenburg and Kazan, and that is why I should like to visit both these provinces.

With the most profound respect and complete devotion, I have the honor to be, Dear Sir,

Your Excellency's
Most humble servant,
Alexander Pushkin.

July 30.
Chernaya Rechka.

[454]

To PAVEL VOINOVICH NASHCHOKIN (?)
July, 1833(?). Petersburg.

I am sending you my ugly phiz.[1] Say, how much do you want for your carriage? There are buyers.

A.P.

[455]

To NATALIA NIKOLAEVNA PUSHKINA
August 20, 1833. From Torzhok to Petersburg.

Torzhok. Sunday.

Dear little wife, here is my detailed Odyssey for you. You remember that when I left you I set off into the very storm. My adventures began at the Troitsky Bridge. The Neva was so high that the bridge was reared up. A rope was stretched across, and the police were not letting carriages through. I very nearly turned back to Chernaya Rechka.[1] However, I crossed the Neva higher up, and I left Petersburg. The weather was terrible. The trees along the Tsarskoselsky Prospekt were just strewn all around; I counted some fifty of them. The wind was blowing the puddles violently. The swamps were stirred up into whitecaps. Fortunately the wind and the rain were beating at my back, and I most calmly kept my seat all this time. Did anything bad happen to you Petersburg inhabitants? You didn't have a new inundation,[2] did you? What if, in riding about, I missed this one, too? That would be vexing. The next day the weather cleared up. Sobolevsky and I went ten miles on foot, killing, along the roadside, snakes which had foolishly surrendered to rejoicing at the sunshine and had crawled out onto the sand. Yesterday we arrived safely at Torzhok, where Sobolevsky raged because the linen was dirty. Today we woke up at 8 o'clock, breakfasted well, and now I'm turning off to Yaropolets,[3] and I'm leaving Sobolevsky alone with the Swiss cheese. There, my angel, is a detailed account of my journey. The coachmen are harnessing up six horses to the carriage, frightening me with the muddy side roads. If I don't drown in a puddle, like Anrep,[4] I'll write you from Yaropolets. I shall hope for letters from you in Simbirsk. Write me about your mastitis and the rest. Don't spoil Masha, and take care of your own health; don't coquet on the 26th.[5] But you'll say, there's nobody to do it with![6] But just the same, don't coquet. I greet Katerina Ivanovna [Zagryazhskaya] and kiss her hand with the tenderness of Ermolov. I give all of you a big kiss, and I bless you, Mashka, and Sashka.[7]

Greet Vyazemsky when you see him. Tell him that the storm prevented me from saying good-by to him and having a chat about the almanac.[8] I'll see what I can get done about it on the road.

[456]
To Natalia Nikolaevna Pushkina
August 21, 1833. From Pavlovskoe to Petersburg.

You couldn't guess, my angel, where I'm writing you from: from Pavlovskoe, between Bernovo and Malinniki,[1] about the last of which I have probably told you a lot. Yesterday when I turned off onto the country road to Yaropolets, I discovered with pleasure that I would go past the estates of the Vulfs, and I decided to visit them. At 8 o'clock last evening I arrived at my good Pavel Ivanovich's, who was as glad to see me as if I were a member of the family. Here I found a great change. Five years ago Pavlovskoe, Malinniki, and Bernovo were full of uhlans and young ladies, but the uhlans have been transferred and the young ladies have become dispersed. Of my old girl friends I found only the white mare, on which I made a trip to Malinniki. But she no longer prances under me, no longer is spirited, either. And in Malinniki, instead of all the Annettes, Evpraxias, Sashas, Mashas, etc.,[2] there lives only Praskovia Alexandrovna's manager Reichman,[3] who treated me to some schnapps. Veliasheva, whom I once lauded in verse, lives here in the neighborhood. But I'll not go to see her, for I know you wouldn't want me to. Here I am stuffing myself on jam, and I have lost three rubles in twenty-four rubbers of whist. You see that in all respects I am innocuous here. I am being asked about you a lot: whether you are just as pretty as they say and whether you are a *brunette* or a *blonde*, a *slender* or *plump* little thing. Tomorrow before dawn I'm setting off for Yaropolets, where I shall spend several hours and then set off for Moscow, where I suspect I shall have to stay three days or so. I forgot to tell you that in Yaropolets (my mistake, in Torzhok), the fat Mlle. Pozharskaya[4]—the same one who brews excellent kvas and fries excellent cutlets—as she was accompanying me to the doors of her inn, answered me in response to my compliments, "You ought to be ashamed to notice the beauties of others when you yourself have such a beauty that I, when I met her (?), gasped." And you should know that Mlle. Pozharskaya is the spit and image of Mme. George,[5] only a little older. You see, my little wife, that your fame has spread over all the provinces. Are you satisfied? Be healthy, all of you. Does Masha remember me? And she hasn't pulled some new pranks, has she?[6] Farewell, my plump little brunette (is that right?). I am behaving well, and there's nothing for you to pout at me about. This letter will reach you after your name day.[7] Have you looked in your mirror and assured yourself that nothing in the world can be compared with your face?[8] But I love your soul even more than your face. Farewell, my angel. I send you a big kiss.

[457]

To Natalia Nikolaevna Pushkina
August 26, 1833. From Moscow to Petersburg.

August 26. Moscow.

I wish you happiness on your angel's day,[1] my angel: I kiss you in the eyes, sight unseen. And I'm writing you the continuation of my adventures—from the attic of your Nikitskaya home,[2] where I arrived safely yesterday from Yaropolets. I arrived in Yaropolets late Wednesday. Natalia Ivanovna [Goncharova] couldn't have received me better. I found her well, though beside her was lying her walking cane, without which she can't get far. I spent Thursday at her house. We talked a lot about you, about Mashka, and about Katerina Ivanovna [Zagryazhskaya]. Your mother seems to be a little jealous of her on your account. However, although she complained about the past as usual, it was nevertheless with less bitterness. She very much wants you to spend next summer with her.[3] She lives very isolated and quiet in her ruined palace and is cultivating vegetable gardens over your great-grandfather Doroshenko's[4] ashes, to which I went to pay my respects. Semen Fedorovich,[5] a great friend of mine, took me to the tomb and showed me the other sights of Yaropolets. I found an old library in the house, and Natalia Ivanovna permitted me to take out some books I need. I picked out a score and a half or so of them, and they will arrive together with jam and liqueurs. Thus my foray on Yaropolets has been by no means fruitless.

Now, little wife, listen to what's happening to Dmitry Nikolaevich [Goncharov]. Like a reigning prince, he fell in love with Countess Nadezhda Chernysheva[6] *from her portrait*, after hearing that she is a plump, black-browed, and rosy-cheeked wench. Twice he made trips to Yaropolets in the hope of catching sight of her, and he actually did succeed in finding her in church. Then he up and went into a frenzy. He writes from the Zavod that he is head over heels in love with *la charmante et divine comtesse*, that he can't sleep at night, and that *son charmant image*, etc., and he asks that Natalia Ivanovna [Goncharova] without fail arrange a match for him with *la charmante et divine comtesse*; Natalia Ivanovna went to Kruglikova's[7] and carried out the commission. They invited *la divine et charmante*, who flatly refused. Natalia Ivanovna is worried about what effect this news will produce. I'll bet he won't shoot himself. What do you think? And you should know that he started up this affair away back last winter and very much suspected *la divine et charmante comtesse* of a propensity for Muraviev (the saintly).[8] For this reason he went once to ask him with all possible diplomatic subtlety, like Skotinin of his nephew: "Mitrofan, do you want to get married?"[9] You see what a rogue he is! And he didn't tell us a thing. Muraviev answered him that he is more likely to become a monk, and your brother rejoiced and went and asked of the countess *son coeur et sa main*, assuring her by letter *qu'il n'est plus dans son assiette ordinaire*.[10] I almost died laughing as I read his letter, and I regret that I didn't persuade him to let me have it for you.

I left Yaropolets at night and arrived in Moscow yesterday at noon. Your father[11] did not receive me. They say that he's quiet enough. Nashchokin told me that Yuriev's[12] money has been sent to you. Now I feel relieved. Sobolevsky is here *incognito* hiding from the moneylenders, like a real English *gentlemen* [sic],[13] and he is redeeming his promissory notes. On the road he behaved decently and fulfilled faithfully the conditions which I proposed, to wit: (1) to go halves in paying for the post horses, and not to shortchange his comrade. (2) Not to f——t, either openly or furtively, unless in sleep and at night, at that, and not after dinner. I shall stay in Moscow for some time; that is, two or three days. The calash needs some repairs. The country roads were nasty: six horses had difficulty in dragging me along. I shall be in Kazan about the third. From there I'm going to Simbirsk. Farewell; take care of yourself. I kiss all of you. Greet Katerina Ivanovna [Zagryazhskaya].

[458]

To NATALIA NIKOLAEVNA PUSHKINA
August 27, 1833. From Moscow to Petersburg.

Yesterday was your name day; today is your birthday. Many happy returns for you and for me, my angel. Yesterday I drank your health at [I. V.] Kireevsky's, together with Shevyrev and Sobolevsky; today I'll drink it at Sudienko's. I'm leaving day after tomorrow —my calash will not be ready before that. Yesterday when I arrived at home late I found on my table the calling card of Bulgakov,[1] the father of the beauties, and an invitation for an evening. It was his wife's name day, too. I didn't go, because I don't have ball dress, and so as not to have to shave off my mustache, which I'm letting grow out for the road. You see that it's hard to get to Moscow and not do a little dancing. However, Moscow is boring; Moscow is empty; Moscow is poor. There are even few cabs on its boring streets. On the Tverskoy Boulevard one comes across two or three beggar women in tatters, and some student in spectacles and a uniform cap, and Prince Shalikov. I was at Pogodin's, who they say is married to a beauty.[2] I didn't see her, and I cannot most humbly report to you with regard to her. I haven't seen Nashchokin the whole day. Chaadaev has become fleshier, handsomer, and healthier. Nikolay [N.] Raevsky is here. Neither he nor his brother[3] died—it was some Brigadier Raevsky[4] who died. Tell Vyazemsky that his namesake, Prince Peter Dolgorukov,[5] has died—after receiving a certain inheritance and not having time to squander it in the English Club, which local society laments. I haven't been in the club—very likely I have been expelled, for I have forgotten to renew my membership. I would have to pay a fine of three hundred rubles, and I'd be willing to sell the whole English Club for two hundred. [M. F.] Orlov, Bobrinsky,[6] and others of my old acquaintances are here. But I'm fed up with my old acquaintances—I'll not see anybody. An important piece of news: signs in French, which were destroyed by Rostopchin in the year you were born, have appeared again on the Kuznetsky Most.[7] I wandered along the bookshops as I usually do, but I found nothing worthwhile. The books which I took for the road have gotten beaten and rubbed to pieces in my trunk. I'm so angry today because of this that I wouldn't advise Mashka to get capricious or war with her nursemaid; I'd give her a thrashing. I kiss you. I greet Aunty.[8] I bless Mashka and Sashka.

[459]
To Natalia Nikolaevna Pushkina
September 2, 1833. From Nizhny Novgorod to Petersburg.

September 2. Nizhny Novgorod.

I didn't have time to write you before my departure from Moscow. Nashchokin saw me off with champagne, hot punch, and prayers. I had difficulty in getting the coachmaker to give me my carriage; I don't have much luck with coachmakers. The road is in good shape. But in the environs of Moscow no horses are to be had. Everywhere I had to wait several hours, and with difficulty I managed to drag to Nizhny today—that is, after five days and nights. I've had time only to go to the baths, and of the city I shall say only that *les rues sont larges et bien pavées, les maisons sont bien baties.*[1] I'm going to the Fair[2] which is displaying its last things, and tomorrow I'm setting out for Kazan.

My angel, I feel I have acted stupidly, in leaving you and beginning a nomadic life again. I can vividly imagine the 1st: Parasha, the cook, the cabby, the druggist, Mme. Sichler, etc., pester you for what is owed them. You don't have enough money. Smirdin makes excuses to you. You're worried, you're angry with me—and it serves me right. And this is still the good side of the picture—what if you have abscesses again, what if Mashka is sick? And other, unforeseen things that could happen . . . Pugachev isn't worth it. The first thing you

know I'll spit on him—and come to you. However, I shall go on
to Simbirsk, and there I expect to find some letters from you.
My angel, if you will be sensible—that is, well and calm—I'll bring
you from the village some goods worth a hundred rubles, as the
expression goes.[3] What weather we are having! Hot days, light frosts
in the morning—luxury! Is this the way it is where you are? Are you
taking walks along Chernaya Rechka, or are you still shut in?[4] In
any case, take care of yourself. Tell Aunty that though I'm jealous of
her over you, I ask in the name of Christ and God that she not
abandon you and that she look after you. Farewell, children, until
Kazan. I give all three of you an equally big kiss—you especially.

[460]

To NATALIA NIKOLAEVNA PUSHKINA
September 2, 1833. From Nizhny Novgorod to Petersburg.

September 2.

My angel, I wrote you today upon jumping out of the calash, and
still stupid from the road. I didn't tell you anything, and I didn't
report most humbly to you with regard to anything. Here's an
accounting for you from Saint Natalia's day[1] itself. In the morning I
went to [A. Y.] Bulgakov's to make my excuses and to thank him, and
while doing that to persuade him to give me a certificate[2] for the
station masters, who have very little esteem for me, notwithstanding
that I write excellent rhymes. At his house I found his daughters and
[N. V.] Vsevolozhsky le cocu,[3] who is galloping from Kazan to all
you people in Petersburg. They invited me to an evening at the
Pashkovs'[4] summer house; I didn't go, thus sparing my mustaches,
which have only scarcely bristled out. I dined at the home of
Sudienko, my friend, the comrade of my bachelor life. Now he's
married, too, and he has two youngsters,[5] and he has stopped playing
cards. But he has an income of 125,000, and with us, my angel, that's
yet to come. His wife is a quiet, shy un-beauty. We dined as a threesome, and without standing on ceremony I proposed the health of
my name-day celebrator,[6] and we all downed, without making a face,
a goblet of champagne apiece. The evening, at Nashchokin's—and
what an evening! Champagne, Lafite, hot pineapple punch—and all
to your health, my beauty. The next day I ran across Nikolay [N.]
Raevsky in a bookshop. Sacré chien, he said to me with tenderness,

pourquoi n'êtes-vous pas venu me voir?—Animal, I answered him with feeling, *qu'avez-vous fait de mon manuscrit petit-Russien?*[7] After this we set off together as though nothing had happened, with him holding me by the collar in plain sight of everybody, to keep me from jumping out of the calash. We dined together, the two of us (my error: in a threesome with a bottle of Madeira). Then to vary my life, I spent another evening at Nashchokin's. The next day he gave me a farewell dinner with sterlets and hot punch, they put me in my calash, and I went forth onto the highway.

Oh, little wife, I'm afraid! Now I must make an important confession. Shall I say the little word to you? Will your little heart survive it? I have purposely stretched out my letter with telling about my Moscow dinners, so as to reach this fateful spot as late as possible. Well, so be it. Be informed that at the second station, where they wouldn't give me horses, I ran across a certain town governor's wife who was going with her aunt from Moscow to her husband and was being slighted at all the stations. She received me quite badly and, in a drawling sing-song, began to try to shame and persuade me: "Aren't you ashamed? Who ever heard of such a thing? Two teams of three horses have been standing in the stable since yesterday, and you won't give me either one of them." "Really?" I said, and went to take these teams for myself. The town governor's wife, seeing that I am not the station master, became very much embarrassed, began to beg my pardon, and she so touched me that I yielded to her one team, to which she had every right, and hired myself another—i.e., a third, and left. You will think that there's no harm done yet. Wait, little wife. That's not all yet. The town governor's wife and her aunt were so enraptured by my knightly deed that they decided not to leave me, but to travel under my protection, to which I magnanimously consented. In this way we almost reached Nizhny itself—they have lagged three or four stations behind—and now I'm free and alone. You will ask whether the governor's wife is pretty. That's the trouble, she was not pretty, my angel Tasha. That's just what I'm grieving about. Ugh! I'm through. Let me go, and have mercy on me.

Today I was at the governor's, General Buturlin's.[8] He and his wife received me very kindly and affably; he persuaded me to dine with him tomorrow. The Fair has closed down—I walked about the emptied shops. They made the impression on me of the departure after a ball, when the Goncharovs' carriage has already left.[9] You see that notwithstanding the city governor's wife and her aunt I still love Natasha Goncharova, whom, sight unseen, I kiss just anywhere. *Addio mia bella, idol mio, mio bel tesoro, quando mai ti rivedro?* . . .[10]

[461]

To NATALIA NIKOLAEVNA PUSHKINA
September 8, 1833. From Kazan to Petersburg.

September 8. Kazan.

Hello, my angel. I've been in Kazan since the fifth, but till now I have not had the time to write you a word. Now I'm on the way to Simbirsk, where I hope to find a letter from you. Here I've been spending my time with old men, contemporaries of my hero;[1] I've gone all over the environs of the city, I've looked over the sites of the battles, I've been making inquiries, I have noted things down, and I'm very content that I have not visited this locale in vain. The weather is fine—but keep your fingers crossed. Before the rains, I hope to have toured every place I proposed to see and to be in the village[2] at the end of September. Are you well? Are all of you well? On the road I saw a little one-year-old girl who runs about on all fours like a kitten and already has two little teeth. Tell this to Mashka. Baratynsky is here. He's coming in to see me right now. Until Simbirsk. I'll tell you about Kazan in detail—now there's no time. I kiss you.

[462]

To ALEXANDRA ANDREEVNA FUCHS
September 8, 1833. In Kazan.

September 8, 1833.

Dear Madame, Alexandra Andreevna![1] I am sending you my address, together with my cordial thanks, and I hope that your promise to come to Petersburg is not merely a civility. Receive, dear Madame, the expression of my deep gratitude for your affably receiving a traveler to whom his momentary stay in Kazan will long be memorable. With the most profound respect, I have the honor to be [. . . .][2]

[463]
To Natalia Nikolaevna Pushkina
September 12, 1833. From Yazykovo to Petersburg.
The Village Yazykovo, forty miles from
Simbirsk. September 12.

I'm writing you from the village of the poet Yazykov, whom I've dropped in on, but have not found at home. Day before yesterday I arrived in Simbirsk, and from Zagryazhsky[1] I received the letter from you. It delighted me, my angel, but all the same I shall scold you a little. You have abscesses,[2] but you write me four whole pages. Aren't you ashamed of yourself! Why couldn't you have told me about yourself and the children in four lines? Well, so be it. God grant that you are well now. I'm glad that Sergey Nikolaevich [Goncharov] will be with you; he's very nice and won't bore you. There's nothing to tell you about Ivan Nikolaevich [Goncharov]. I hope that his wedding will be broken off. From everything it appears that all the family has taken advantage of his upset condition, in order to lure him into their toils. The authorities, if the matter ever gets to the authorities, will probable take this into consideration, too. It will be necessary to settle the business with money. If the girl is not with child, then there's no great harm done. I should think that there'll be no duel with the father or with the cobbler-uncle. If the house is suitable,[3] then there's nothing to do but take it —but stay there a while, at least. Your finances are worrying me a great deal; you have too little money. The first thing you know, you'll be making new debts without paying off the old. I'm traveling—with profit I think. But I'm not yet at my destination, and I haven't got anything written. I go to sleep and dream of arriving in Boldino and locking myself in there.

From Kazan I wrote you several lines[4]—I had no time. I was being dragged around the environs, the fields, the taverns, and I landed at an evening at the home of a *blue stockings*,[5] a forty-year-old, unendurable woman, with waxed teeth and dirty nails. She opened up her notebook and read me some two hundred verses,[6] as if there were nothing unusual in that. Baratynsky has written verses to her, and with astonishing shamelessness he praised her beauty and genius to the skies. I just expected that I would be compelled to write in her album—but God was merciful. However, she took my address and is threatening me with a correspondence and with coming to Petersburg, upon which I congratulate you. Her husband[7] is an intelligent and learned German, in love with her, and in amazement at her genius. However, he was very obliging to me, and I am glad that I made his acquaintance. Today I'm going to Simbirsk. I shall dine at the governor's, and by evening I'll set out for Orenburg, the final goal of my journey.

I found here Yazykov's older brother,[8] an exceptionally noteworthy person, and whom I'm ready to love as I love Pletnev or Nashchokin. I spent the evening with him, and I left him for you. But now I'm leaving you for him. Farewell, little angel wife. I kiss you and all the others—I bless the children with all my heart. Take care of yourself. I'm glad that you're not with child. I greet Katerina Ivanovna [Zagryazhskaya] and your brother Sergey [N. Goncharov].

Write me in Boldino.

[464]
To Natalia Nikolaevna Pushkina
September 14, 1833. From Simbirsk to Petersburg.

[September] 14. Simbirsk.

I'm in Simbirsk again. Night before last I left, setting out for Orenburg. I had barely gotten out onto the highway when a hare ran across in front of me.[1] The devil take it. I would have given a great deal to have hunted it down. At the third station when they began to harness up my horses for me I noticed that I had no coachmen—one was blind; the other was drunk and had hidden himself. After raising as much of a row as I could, I decided to return and to travel another road. On this road there are six horses at each station, and the post goes four times per week. They started back with me— I dropped off to sleep—I woke up in the morning—what did I see? I hadn't returned even three miles. A hill—the horses wouldn't pull up it—about twenty peasants around me. The devil knows how God helped—finally we climbed it, and I returned to Simbirsk. I would give a great deal to be a borzoi; I certainly would have hunted down that hare. Now I'm going by a different road.[2] Maybe it will be without adventures. I've kept on hoping that I would receive here, as consolation, at least some news of you. But no. How are you, my little wife? How are you and the children? I kiss and bless all of you. Write me often, and write all kinds of nonsense that has to do with you. I greet Aunty.

[465]

To NATALIA NIKOLAEVNA PUSHKINA
September 19, 1833. From Orenburg to Petersburg.
September 19. Orenburg.

I've been here since yesterday.[1] I reached here with difficulty. The road is most boring. The weather is cold. Tomorrow I'm going to see the Yaik Cossacks.[2] I'll spend some three days with them—and I'll set out for my village, by way of Saratov and Penza.

What is it, little wife? Do you miss me? I'm lonely for you. If I weren't ashamed to, I'd return straight to you, without having written a single line. But that's impossible, my angel. In for a penny, in for a pound—that is, I left to write: so write, then, novel after novel, long poem after long poem. And I just feel that the spell is coming over me—I'm composing, as it is, in the calash; what will it be like in bed?[3] One thing is greatly annoying me: my manservant.[4] Imagine the tone of a Moscow government office worker, stupid, talkative, drunk every other day, who eats my cold grouse for the road, drinks my Madeira, ruins my books, and at the stations calls me now a count and now a general. He simply infuriates me. What a fine fellow my Ippolit was![5] Apropos of the tribe of Ham,[6] how are you getting along with your household? I'm afraid you don't have enough servants. Shouldn't you hire somebody? I rely on the women, but how are you coping with the menservants? All this disturbs me—I'm as mistrustful as my father. I haven't said anything yet about the children. God grant health to them— and to you, little wife. Farewell, little wife. Don't you expect any letters from me until I get to the village. I kiss you and bless all of you.

How well I am behaving myself! How satisfied you would be with me! I'm not paying court to the young ladies, I'm not pinching the station masters' wives, I'm not coquetting with Kalmuck girls[7]— and a few days ago I refused a Bashkir girl, notwithstanding my curiosity, very forgivable in a traveler. Do you know, there is a proverb: in a foreign land, even an old woman is a gift of God. Look to it, little wife. Take example from me.

[466]
To Natalia Nikolaevna Pushkina
October 2, 1833. From Boldino to Petersburg.
October 2.

My darling, I've been in Boldino since yesterday—I thought I would find letters from you here, but I didn't find a single one. What's the matter with you? Are you well? Are the children well? My heart sinks when I think about what may be. As I was approaching Boldino, I had the gloomiest premonitions. So that when I found no news from you whatever, I almost rejoiced—I was so afraid of bad news. No, my darling, it's bad for a married man to travel. It's a different matter for a bachelor! He doesn't think of anything, no death saddens him. You should have received my last letter from Orenburg. From there I went to Uralsk. The local ataman[1] and the Cossacks received me famously, gave me two dinners, drank bottoms-up to my health, vied with each other in giving me all the information I wanted—and stuffed me on fresh caviar, prepared in my presence. As I was departing (on September 23) in the evening a rain came up, the first since I left. You should be told that this year there has been a general drought and that God obliged me alone by readying for me everywhere the finest kind of road. But on the return trip He sent me this rain, and in a half hour made the road impassable. And that's not all: there was a snowfall, and I broke in the winter road by going some thirty-five miles on a sleigh. As I was passing Yazykovo, I dropped in there. I found all three brothers.[2] I dined with them very merrily, spent the night, and set off for here. After entering the boundaries of Boldino, I met some priests, and I became as infuriated with them as at the Simbirsk hare.[3] All these encounters are not for nothing. Look out, little wife! The first thing you know, you'll get all spoiled in my absence, you'll forget me— you'll start really playing the coquette. My only hope is in God and Aunty. Maybe they will preserve you from the temptations of the social whirl. I have the honor to report to you that, as for me, I am as pure before you as a newborn babe. On the road I paid court only to old women of seventy and eighty—and I didn't even look at the very young, bepissed sixty-year-old ones. In the village of Berdy,[4] where Pugachev was encamped for six months, I had *une bonne fortune*—I found a seventy-five-year-old Cossack woman[5] who remembers that time as well as you and I remember 1830. I was in no hurry to get away from her, and I beg your pardon for not even thinking of you. Now I hope to bring a lot of things into order, get a lot written, and then come to you with the booty. The post arrives at Abramovo[6] on Sunday; I'm hoping for a letter—today is Monday, I'll be waiting for it a week. Farewell—I am leaving you for Pugachev.[7] Christ be with you, my children. I kiss you, little wife—be sensible and well.

[467]

To Natalia Nikolaevna Pushkina
October 8, 1833. From Boldino to Petersburg.

My angel, I have just now received two letters from you at once, the first ones since the Simbirsk ones. How they reached me, I don't understand: you write "to the Novgorod Province, to the village Abramovo, from there," etc. And not a single word about the district. Don't forget to add *in the Arzamas District*. If you don't, I wouldn't be surprised if there may be more than one village Abramovo in the Nizhny Novgorod Province, just as there may be more than one village Boldino. Two things are disturbing me; that I left you without money and perhaps with child, too. I can imagine your cares and vexation. Thank God you're well, that Mashka and Sashka are alive, and that you've rented a house, even though at a high price.[1] Don't scare me, little wife. Don't say that you have started really playing the coquette. I'll come to you without having succeeded in getting anything written—and without money our ship will go aground. You'd better leave me in peace, and I'll work and hurry. Here I've already been in Boldino a whole week. I'm bringing into order my notes about Pugachev, but for the time being verses are still dormant. If the Tsar will authorize the Notes[2] for me, we'll net some thirty thousands. We'll pay half our debts and start living in clover. Thank you very much for the news and for the gossip. If you see Zhukovsky, kiss him for me and congratulate him upon his return and upon his star; write me how his health is.[3] My cordial greeting to the Karamzins and Meshcherskys. Explain to Sofia

Nikolaevna [Karamzina] that if I didn't go to see them in Dorpat, it was solely because of not having the money for post horses for the 350 extra miles.[4] I didn't write them, because I kept on thinking I would get there. It's a pity that you haven't seen [Alexandra O.] Smirnova; she must be killingly funny after her trip to Germany;[5] [S. D.] Bezobrazov is acting sensibly in marrying Princess Khilkova.[6] He should have done it long ago. It's better to set up housekeeping for oneself than to dangle after others' wives all one's life and to claim others' verses as one's own. Don't coquette with Sobolevsky and don't be angry with Nashchokin; thank God he sent the 1500 rubles.[7] And have no regrets about the 180—just spit on it. Just what are those 50 rubles sent to you by my father? Aren't they the interest on the 550 he owes me?[8] I wouldn't be surprised! Here they're very strongly advising me to take over for myself the legacy of Vasily Lvovich [Pushkin];[9] and I'd like to, but for that, first, money, and, second, free time are necessary; and I don't have either. What do you think of Kraevskaya?[10] No wonder Otreshkov[11] has been dangling after her. I had no idea I would land in her memoirs and in that way attain immortality. Greet her for me, if you see her. And greet all my charmers: Khitrovo, first. How has she withstood my absence? I hope with the firmness worthy of the daughter of Prince Kutuzov. So the Ficquelmonts[12] have come? I rejoice for you; how successful will the balls turn out for you? Really, aren't you with child?[13] Why are you so touchy? Farewell, darling. I'm somehow not very well today. My little stomach aches, like [P. K.] Alexandrov's. I kiss and bless all of you. I greet and thank with all my heart Aunt Katerina Ivanovna [Zagryazhskaya] for her kind solicitude. Farewell.

October 8.

[468]
To Natalia Nikolaevna Pushkina
October 11, 1833. From Boldino to Petersburg.

My angel, one word: go see Pletnev and ask him to have all the ukases relating to Pugachev copied from *The Collected Laws*[1] (for the years 1774 and 1775 and 1773) *before my arrival*. Don't forget.

How are your finances? Are you with child? Don't expect me this month; expect me at the end of November. Don't hinder me, don't scare me, stay well, look after the children, don't coquette with the Tsar or with Princess Lyuba's fiancé.[2] I'm writing, I'm in the midst of bothers, I see nobody—and I shall bring you a world of all sorts of stuff.[3] I hope that Smirdin is punctual. In a few days I'll send him some verses.[4] Do you know what they're saying about me in the neighboring provinces? This is the way they describe my activities: when Pushkin writes verses—before him stands a quart of the *finest* liqueur—he gulps down a glass, a second, a third—and then he starts writing! That's fame. As for you, the fame of your beauty has reached our priest's wife, who assures me that you've got everything, not only face but figure. What more would you wish? Farewell. I kiss and bless all of you. I kiss Aunty's hand. Can Masha talk? Can she walk? What about some little teeth? I whistle along with Sasha. Farewell.

October 11.

[469]

To NATALIA NIKOLAEVNA PUSHKINA
October 21, 1833. From Boldino to Petersburg.

Today I received your letter of October 4, and I thank you heartily. Last Sunday I did not receive a letter from you, and I had the stupidity to pout at you. But yesterday such misery seized me that I can't remember such spleen coming over me before. I'm glad you're not with child and that nothing will prevent you from distinguishing yourself at the balls now going on. Apparently Ogarev[1] is very fond of the Pushkins; to hell with him. I don't prevent you from coquetting, but I demand of you coldness, propriety, dignity—still not to speak of the irreproachability of conduct which has to do, not with *tone*, but with what is really the most important of all. Why should you want, little wife, to vie with the Countess [Nadezhda Lvovna] Sollogub? You're a beauty, you're a real female woman—but she's a bag of bones. Why should you beat her out of her admirers? It's just as though Count Sheremetev[2] were to set about doing me out of my Kistenevo peasants. Who else besides Ogarev is paying court to you? Send me a list in alphabetical order. And write me, too, what places you go, and how the Karamzins, Meshcherskaya, and the Vyazemskys are. Tell Princess Vyazemskaya that she is wrong in being concerned about the portrait of Vigel, and that *on that side* my conduct is above any suspicion, but that out of esteem for her request I shall put his portrait *behind* all the others.³ Incidentally, she promised me her portrait, but up to now she has not kept her word. Reproach her for me. You probably have already seen Zhukovsky and Vielgorsky. How is Zhukovsky? They write me that he has become healthy and young again. Is it true? Just why did you want to marry him to Katerina Nikolaevna [Goncharova]? And what about Katerina Nikolaevna—will she come to see us or not? Just imagine, last Sunday instead of a letter from you I received a letter from Sobolevsky, who needs money for *pâtés de foie gras*, and who is undertaking an almanac⁴ to that end. You understand how his letter and requests for verses (what do I mean *requests*—commands, contracts for verses made to order) have angered me. And it's all your fault. Just how is my toothless *Puskina*? Oh, those teeth! And how is red-haired Sasha? And who'd he get red hair from?⁵ I hadn't expected that of him. Of myself I'll tell you that I am working in lazy, slip-shod manner. All these days my head has been aching, spleen has been gnawing on me. Now it's better. I've begun a lot, but I don't feel up to anything; God knows what's happening to me. I've become old and weak in mind.⁶ I'll come to rejuvenate myself with your youth, my angel. But don't expect me before the end of November; I don't want to come to you with empty hands—in for a penny, in for a pound. And don't you scold me. Thank for me my precious Katerina Ivanovna [Zagryazhskaya], who doesn't let you have your way in the loge. I kiss her little hands and ask her for God's sake not to leave you to the mercies of your adorers. I kiss and make the sign of the cross over Mashka, red-haired Sashka, and you. The Lord be with you. Farewell; I'm sleepy. October 21. Boldino.

[470]

To Natalia Nikolaevna Pushkina
October 30, 1833. From Boldino to Petersburg.

Yesterday I received, my darling, two letters from you. Thanks. But I want to upbraid you a little. You seem to have overdone your coquetting. Look here: it's not for nothing that coquetting is out of fashion and is considered a sign of bad tone. There's little sense in it. You rejoice that male dogs are running after you like a little bitch, with their tails like a poker, and sniffing you in the a——; that's something to rejoice over! It's easy, not only for you, but even for Paraskovia Petrovna[1] to train the bachelor ne'er-do-wells to run after you. All you need is to trumpet it about, "I," quote, "am quite willing." Here is all the secret of coquetry. *Where there's a trough, there'll be swine.* Why should you receive men who are paying court to you? You don't know whom you may run into. Read A. Izmaylov's fable about Foma and Kuzma.[2] Foma stuffed Kuzma on caviar and herring. Kuzma began to ask for something to drink, but Foma wouldn't give him anything. So Kuzma gave Foma a thrashing, for being a rascal. From all this the poet adduces the following moral: "Beauties! Don't feed men on herring if you don't want to give them something to drink; otherwise you may bump up against a Kuzma." Do you see? I ask that none of these academic luncheons[3] be at my house. Now, my angel, I kiss you as if nothing were amiss, and I thank you for describing to me your dissipated life frankly and in detail. Have your fun, little wife, only don't overdo it, and don't forget me. I want to see you coiffured *à la Ninon*[4] so much that I don't know what to do; you must look marvellously sweet that way. Why hadn't you thought before of that old whore and borrowed her coiffure from her? Describe for me your appearing at balls, which, as you write, have probably already begun—and, my angel, please don't coquette. I'm not being jealous, and I know, too, that you won't cast prudence to the winds. But you know how I dislike everything that smacks of the Moscow young lady, all that is not *comme il faut*, all that is *vulgar*. . . .[5] If upon my return I find that your sweet, simple, aristocratic tone has changed, I'll divorce you, Christ be my witness, and out of misery I'll become a soldier. You ask how I am getting along and whether I have not gotten better looking. In the first place, I have grown a beard: *a mustache and beard are a fine fellow's boast—when I go out on the street they call me uncle.* (2) I wake up at 7 o'clock; I drink coffee, and I lie around until 3 o'clock. Not long ago I got into a writing vein and I have already written a world of stuff.[6] At 3 o'clock I mount my horse, at 5, I take a bath, and then I dine on potatoes and buckwheat porridge. I read until 9 o'clock. There's my day for you. And they are all just alike.

Ask Katerina Andreevna [Karamzina] not to be angry with me. You were bearing a child, I didn't have any extra money, I was hurrying off in a different direction—and I just couldn't make it to

Dorpat.[7] I greet her, [Ekaterina N.] Meshcherskaya, Sofia Niko-laevna [Karamzina], the Princess [Vera] and Princesses [Maria P. and Praskovia P.] Vyazemskaya. Tell [Idalia G.] Poletika that I'll come in person for her kiss, for, tell her, they won't accept them in the mail. And how is it that Katerina Ivanovna [Zagryazhskaya] let you have your own sweet way? Oh, Lord Jesus Christ! I kiss Masha and ask her to remember me. What kind of rash does Sasha have? Christ be with you. I bless and kiss all of you.

October 30.

[471]

To Vladimir Fedorovich Odoevsky
October 30, 1833. From Boldino to Petersburg.

I am at fault, Your Highness! Completely at fault. I arrived at the village and thought I would get into a writing vein. Nothing of the kind happened. Headaches, financial cares, laziness—the laziness of the rural nobility, of the landowner—have so overcome me that God forbid. Don't expect Belkin; all joking aside, apparently he is deceased; he will not be at the housewarming, either in Gomozeyko's living room or in Panko's garret.[1] He is apparently not worthy to be in their company. . . . And it would not be a bit bad to get into that cellar! Now I shall report to Your Highness that when I was in Simbirsk I saw the unassuming woman-recluse[2] about whom you and I talked before my departure. She's not bad looking. The governor seems to be protecting her much more zealously than his wife does.[3] That is all that I was able to observe. Her lawsuit seems to be over with.

You gladdened me with the news of Zhukovsky.[4] God grant that his present store of health will suffice him for five years or so; and then somehow may he get well.

I greet Gogol. How about his comedy?[5] It's got something.

All yours,
A. Pushkin.

October 30.
Boldino.

[472]

To Natalia Nikolaevna Pushkina
November 6, 1833. From Boldino to Petersburg.
November 6, 1833. Boldino.

My darling little wife, I don't remember very well what I wrote you by the last post. As I remember I was a little angry—and my letter may have been a little harsh. I shall repeat to you a little more gently that coquetry leads to nothing good, and although it has its delights, nothing so quickly deprives a young woman of that without which there is neither domestic well-being nor tranquillity in her relationships toward society: *respect*. There's nothing for you to rejoice over in your victories. Ninon [de Lenclos], the whore from whom you've borrowed your coiffure (N.B.: you must be very pretty in that coiffure; I was thinking about that tonight), used to say: *Il est écrit sur le coeur de tout homme*: "*A la plus facile.*"[1] After that, take pride, if you will, in stealing men's hearts. Think this over well, and don't cause me needless worry. I'm leaving soon, but I shall stay in Moscow for some time on business.[2] Little wife, little wife! I'm traveling the highways, living three months in the remote steppe, stopping in nasty Moscow, which I hate—for what? For you, little wife. So that you may be tranquil and may sparkle with health, as is fitting at your years and with your beauty. But see that you take care of me, too. To the cares, inseparable from the life of a man, don't add family worries, jealousy, etc., etc.—not to speak of *cocuage*, about which I read a whole dissertation in Brantôme a few days ago.[3]

What is my brother doing? I don't advise him to go into the civil service, for which he's just as unfit as for the military. But at least he has a healthy a——, and he would nevertheless go farther in the saddle than in a chair in a government office.[4] It seems to me that we shan't get by without a European war. This Louis Philippe is like a cataract in my eye. The time will come for us to show him what's what—then Lev Sergeich will again go reap, as our assessor says, some laurels and myrtles. Meanwhile I advise him to twiddle his thumbs, a pleasant and healthful occupation. Here I was about to take the notion to take over Vasily Lvovich's legacy.[5] But the trusteeship has so plundered him that it's not even to be thought of, unless Benkendorf might intercede. I'll try it, when I arrive in Petersburg. A letter to my father is enclosed. He is probably already there. I shall bring you a lot of verses, but don't noise it about: if you do, the almanacsters will pester me to death. I kiss Mashka, Sashka, and you. I bless you, Sashka, and Mashka. I kiss Mashka—and so forth, up to seven times. I should like to be with you by Aunty's name day.[6] But God knows.

[473]

To Pavel Voinovich Nashchokin
November 24, 1833. From Petersburg to Moscow.

What about it, Pavel Voinovich, how are your domestic circumstances? Has it been decided?[1] I'm so eager to find out the dénouement that I don't know what to do; I left your novel at the most intriguing point. I don't dare hope—but one may hope. *Vous êtes éminemment un homme de passion*[2]—and in an impassioned state you are able to do what you would not even dare to think of in a state of sobriety; just as once when drunk you swam across a river, though you didn't know how to swim. The present affair is like that—take off your shirt, cross yourself, and splash off from the bank. We— Prince Fedor [F. Gagarin] and I—shall follow you in a boat, and somehow or other you'll scramble out onto the opposite side. Now I'll tell you about my journey.[3] I accomplished it successfully. Lelenka[4] did not bother me; he's very nice, i.e., silent. All our relationships were bounded by my pushing him away with my elbow when he would lean against my shoulder at night. I arrived with him well and unharmed. And since the river has not yet frozen hard and there are no bridges yet, I sent him off to Lev Sergeevich [Pushkin], by doing which I have probably done him a favor. When I was leaving Moscow my Gavrila was so drunk and he so enraged me that I ordered him to climb down from the coach box, and I left him on the highway, in tears and hysterics, but all that had no effect on me— I thought of you. . . . Just you order your Gavrila in a skirt and *kacavejka*[5] to climb down from the coach box—enough of this brawling. At home I found everything in order. My wife was at a ball; I went to get her—and I took her away to my place, like a uhlan taking off a young provincial lady from the name-day celebration of a town governor's wife.[6] My financial affairs have got all tangled up in my absence, but I am thinking of untangling them.[7]

I have seen my father. He is very glad of my proposal to take over Boldino.[8] He has no money. My brother's in evening dress and is very decorous. Sobelevsky has won his lawsuit,[9] and he's going to where you are. Write me, if you have time. Give the note to my manager.[10] My respects to Olga Andreevna.   November 24.

[474]
To Alexander Khristoforovich Benkendorf
December 6, 1833. In Petersburg.

Dear Sir, Count Alexander Khristoforovich,

I make bold to forward to Your Highness a poem which I should like to publish,[1] and on the occasion of this to request from you an authorization which is important to me. The bookseller Smirdin is publishing a journal,[2] in which he has asked me to participate. I can consent only in case he may undertake to present my compositions to the censorship and take the necessary steps with them, on a basis of equality with the other writers who are participating in his enterprise. But I did not wish to tell him anything definite without your knowledge.

Though I have attempted to utilize as infrequently as possible the permission, so precious to me, of burdening the attention of the Sovereign Emperor, I now nevertheless make bold to request the Highest's gracious permission for me to do so: I once thought of writing a historical novel relating to the times of Pugachev,[3] but after finding a multitude of materials, I abandoned that notion and wrote *The History of the Pugachev Affair*.[4] I make bold to request through Your Highness the permission to present it for His Highest's examination. I do not know whether it will be permissible for me to publish it, but I dare to hope that this historical fragment will be of interest to His Majesty, especially in connection with the military actions of that time, which are until now little known.[5]

With the most profound respect and complete devotion, I have the honor to be,

                    Dear Sir,
                    Your Highness's
                    Most humble servant,
December 6, 1833.   Alexander Pushkin.
SPb.

[475]
To PAVEL VOINOVICH NASHCHOKIN
Between December 13 and 20, 1833.
From Petersburg to Moscow.

I have received two sad letters from you, dear Pavel Voinovich,[1] and I've been waiting for a third, while impatiently wanting to know what's happening to you, and what direction your affairs of house and heart are taking.[2] But you are probably too distraught, and I don't know what to hope for: has your fate changed, has it quieted down? Do write me about that, and in detail.

On your name day[3] my family (including Grigory Fedorovich)[4] drank your health and wished you all good luck. About Lelenka[5] I have no news. He is living at Eristov's, and I'm receiving letters addressed to him from Moscow. His insane father wrote me an insane letter, which I am already tardy in answering. He is worried about the calligraphic labors of his son, and about whether the boy isn't weeping and whether he isn't homesick for his family. Reassure the old man as best you can.

I don't know whether I'll be in Moscow in January. Uncle's heirs are making me foolish proposals—I have rejected the legacy.[6] I don't know whether they will enter into new negotiations. Here I've been having financial unpleasantnesses. I came to an agreement with Smirdin, but I was compelled to break the contract because the censorship did not pass *The Bronze Horseman*.[7] That's a real loss for me. If they won't pass *The History of Pugachev*, then I'll have to go to the village. All this is very unpleasant. I'm relying on getting your money for you, however; I'm thinking of proceeding in the spring to my complete works.[8]

All my folks are well—your godson [Alexander A. Pushkin] kisses you; he's a fine boy. I haven't talked yet with Pletnev about Pavel,[9] because there's no hurry. Farewell; I greet Prince [F. F.] Gagarin— and I wish happiness to you both.

A.P.

Letter 452

1. Pushkin wished to make the trip to Orenburg and Kazan in order to visit the scene of the Pugachev uprising, for historical researches on Pugachev and for his novel, *The Captain's Daughter*. The Pushkins' lands in the province of Nizhny Novgorod were the paternal estates of Boldino and Kistenevo. This letter also includes, in its final form, which has not survived, Pushkin's request for permission to go to Dorpat to visit Ekaterina Andreevna Karamzina, who was in deep mourning because of the death in 1833 of her fifteen-year-old son, Nikolay Nikolaevich Karamzin. Pushkin was at once given permission to go to Dorpat, but he was asked for more information regarding his reasons for wishing to make the trip to the Ural region. Pushkin's further explanations are given in Letter 453.

Letter 453

1. In the absence of Count Benkendorf, his assistant, Alexander Nikolaevich Mordvinov (1792-1869), handled Pushkin's request (Letter 452) for permission to visit the Ural region. Pushkin's letter is in response to Mordvinov's letter transmitting Nicholas I's inquiry as to why Pushkin wished "to interrupt his activities" and make a trip to Orenburg and Kazan. Pushkin received the desired permission to make the trip, and a four-month leave of absence.

2. Pushkin exaggerates. He had written his unfinished *Dubrovsky* and several shorter things, though, to be sure, his literary output had decreased greatly.

3. Pushkin's novel of the Pugachev uprising, *The Captain's Daughter*, the preface of which is dated August 5, 1833. However, upon his return from the Ural region, Pushkin did not complete the novel at once, but wrote his *History of Pugachev*, a work of historical research. He did not complete his *Captain's Daughter* until 1836.

Letter 454

1. Pushkin's self-deprecatory remark is in agreement with the recorded opinion of many of his contemporaries, who often alluded to his "African" features and appearance. When Pushkin married Mlle. Goncharova, there were comments about the wedding of "beauty and the beast."

Letter 455

1. Pushkin departed from Petersburg, together with his friend S. A. Sobolevsky, during a storm on August 17. He left his wife and children behind in a summer house in the suburb of Chernaya Rechka.

2. The allusion is to the Petersburg flood of November 7, 1824, which occurred while Pushkin was in exile in Mikhaylovskoe and which is mentioned in several letters. Pushkin described this flood in *The Bronze Horseman*, perhaps his poetic masterpiece, which he wrote while on this trip.

3. Yaropolets was the estate of Pushkin's mother-in-law, in the Volokolamsk District, in Moscow Province.

4. Roman Romanovich Anrep (d. 1830), an officer Pushkin met in the Caucasus in 1829. He died of exposure after wandering into a swamp in an attack of madness.

5 Mme. Pushkina's name day and the date of the annual ball commemorating the Battle of Borodino.

6. The allusion is undoubtedly to Nicholas I, who was abroad—for which reason the ball was postponed.

7. Sasha is the affectionate diminutive, and Sashka the rough-affectionate diminutive of the first name of Pushkin's son, Alexander Alexandrovich Pushkin.

8. Vyazemsky had proposed to Pushkin that together they publish another *Northern Flowers*. Nothing came of the idea.

Letter 456

1. Pavlovskoe was the estate of Pavel Ivanovich Vulf. It was near Ivan Ivanovich Vulf's estate of Bernovo and Praskovia Osipova's estate of Malinniki.

2. The "Annettes" included Anna Nikolaevna Vulf, Anna Ivanovna Vulf, and Anna Petrovna Kern. There was only one person present with each of the other names or diminutives mentioned: Evpraxia Nikolaevna Vrevskaya (nee Vulf), Alexandra Ivanovna Osipova, and Maria Ivanovna Osipova.

3. Karl Reichman (d. 1835), a German, manager of Osipova's estate, Malinniki. In 1834 Pushkin invited him to manage his paternal estate of Boldino, but Reichman declined.

4. Daria Evdokimovna Pozharskaya, proprietress of an inn in Torzhok.

5. She has been variously identified as the tragic actress Marguerite Joséphine Wemmer (1787-1867) and as the Pushkins' midwife.

6. Apparently Pushkin is asking whether his daughter has been ill again.

7. August 26.

8. Pushkin set to rhyme the story of Snow White, in his *Tale of the Dead Tsarevna and of the Seven Heroes*, before he returned home from this trip. It was written on November 4, 1833, at Boldino.

Letter 457

1. On her name day, Saturday, August 26.

2. The Goncharovs' Moscow house.

3. The invitation was accepted. Pushkin's wife and children spent the summer with her mother at Yaropolets in 1834.

4. Peter Dorofeevich Doroshenko (1627-1698), hetman of the Ukraine, Mme. Pushkina's great-great-great-grandfather, the ancestor to whom the estate Yaropolets was given.

5. Semen Fedorovich Dushin, manager of the estate Yaropolets.

6. Countess Nadezhda Grigorievna Chernysheva (1813-1853).

7. Countess Sofia Grigorievna Kruglikova, nee Chernysheva (1799-1847), sister of Nadezhda Grigorievna Chernysheva.

8. Andrey Nikolaevich Muraviev (1806-1874), writer on religious themes.

9. Pushkin's quotation is from Fonvizin's famous comedy *The Adolescent*, Act II, scene 4. Pushkin, in an epigram on Muraviev in 1827 had called him, instead of Apollo Belvedere, "Mitrofan Belvedere."

10. Pushkin is obviously giving direct quotations in all the French in this letter, including Dmitry Goncharov's offering of "his heart and hand," and his statement that "he is not his usual self."

11. Nikolay Afanasievich Goncharov, who was mad.

12. Vasily Gavrilovich Yuriev, an officer who lent money at interest.

13. Pushkin's English.

Letter 458

1. Alexander Yakovlevich Bulgakov (1781-1863), the Moscow Post Director, and

as such in charge both of the mail and of post horses. Pushkin had met him in 1826; their relationships were good, though not close, until Bulgakov intercepted one of Pushkin's letters to Pushkin's wife (Letter 488, q.v.). His wife was Natalia Vasilievna Bulgakova (1785-1841), and his daughters were Ekaterina Alexandrovna Bulgakova (b. 1811) and Olga Alexandrovna Dolgorukova, nee Bulgakova (1814-1865).

2. Pogodin married Elizaveta Vasilievna Vagner (1809-1844) on July 8, 1833.

3. Alexander Nikolaevich Raevsky.

4. Unknown. "Brigadier" was a rank between colonel and general.

5. Prince Peter Mikhaylovich Dolgorukov (1784-1833), had just died of the cholera.

6. Count Alexey Alexeevich Bobrinsky (1800-1868), grandson of Catherine the Great.

7. Count Fedor Vasilievich Rostopchin (1763-1826), the Commander-in-Chief in Moscow in 1812, the year Mme. Pushkina was born. He is presented at considerable length in Tolstoy's *War and Peace*. Kuznetsky Most (literally, Smith's Bridge) is a street in Moscow.

8. "Aunty" here and in subsequent letters is Katerina Ivanovna Zagryazhskaya, Mme. Pushkina's aunt.

Letter 459

1. "The streets are broad and well paved; the houses are well constructed." Pushkin seems to be quoting some book of travels.

2. The famous Nizhny Novgorod Fair, which opened on July 15 and closed on September 8—the most famous of all Russian fairs.

3. Pushkin is quoting from a song.

4. After giving birth to their son Alexander Alexandrovich Pushkin, on July 6.

Letter 460

1. August 26.

2. The excuses were for not attending a ball given by Bulgakov. Bulgakov, as Post Director, could give Pushkin a "certificate" so that he could more easily receive horses for traveling by post chaise.

3. "The cuckold."

4. Sergey Ivanovich Pashkov (1801-1883) and his wife, Nadezhda Sergeevna Pashkova (1811-1880).

5. In 1829 Sudienko married Nadezhda Mikhaylovna Miklashevskaya (d. 1876). The sons mentioned are Iosif Mikhaylovich Sudienko (1830-1892) and Alexander Mikhaylovich Sudienko (1832-1882).

6. Mme. Pushkina.

7. "You dirty dog, . . . why haven't you come to see me?"—"You beast, . . . what have you done with my Little Russian manuscript?" The manuscript is unknown.

8. Mikhail Petrovich Buturlin (1786-1860), military and civil governor of Nizhny Novgorod. His wife was Anna Petrovna Buturlina (1793-1861). Pushkin dined with them on September 2 and probably September 3. Buturlin suspected Pushkin of being an inspector general sent by Nicholas I, and Buturlin sent on a letter to Orenburg, where Pushkin's old friend, Count Vasily Alexeevich Perovsky, was the governor, warning of Pushkin's being en route, and telling of his suspicions as to the reason for Pushkin's trip. Pushkin gave the theme to Gogol, who used it in his *Inspector General*. It is ironic that whereas Pushkin was being taken for an inspector general by one official, actually the secret police sent out instructions that surveillance be maintained over him and

his conduct while he was in the Pugachev country. However, the order for this surveillance did not catch up with him while he was there.

9. That is, in 1830, before Pushkin's marriage.

10. "Farewell, my beauty, my idol, my beautiful treasure. When shall I see you again.?"

Letter 461

1. That is, of Pugachev.
2. Boldino.

Letter 462

1. Alexandra Andreevna Fuchs (d. 1853) kept a literary salon for twenty-five years. She herself wrote verses and ethnographical articles. She was the wife of Karl Fuchs (1776-1846), a German who became Professor and then Rector of the University of Kazan, and who was also noted as an amateur local historian and ethnographer. It is perhaps worthy of note that Pushkin's letter to her is in Russian, though his letters to women (except his wife) are predominantly in French.

2. This letter, like Pushkin's other letters to Mme. Fuchs, was published later by her, and without the complimentary close and signature. The original manuscript copies of these letters have not survived.

Letter 463

1. Alexander Mikhaylovich Zagryazhsky (1796-1878), governor of Simbirsk, and a relative of Mme. Pushkina.

2. From mastitis.

3. Apparently Mme. Pushkina and the children moved into this house in September. The rent was 4800 rubles per year, 96 percent of Pushkin's official salary. Their landlord was Alexander Karlovich Olivio.

4. Letter 461.

5. Pushkin's English. The reference is to Alexandra Andreevna Fuchs. Pushkin's description of her is obviously completely unjust. Mme. Pushkina's inclinations to be jealous are clear from several comments Pushkin makes in the letters written during this trip.

6. Poems addressed to her were by Khomyakov, Yazykov, Baratynsky, and Ivan Kireevsky, among others.

7. Karl Fuchs.

8. Peter Mikhaylovich Yazykov (1798-1851).

Letter 464

1. Pushkin was very superstitious. A hare crossing his path was the equivalent, among us, of a black cat.

2. There were three different routes which Pushkin could take. Pushkin left Simbirsk on September 12, and, the second time, on September 15.

Letter 465

1. Pushkin spent three days in Orenburg, the house guest of the Simbirsk governor, his old friend Vasily Alexeevich Perovsky. On the day Pushkin wrote this letter, he visited the town of Berdy, some five miles from Orenburg (see Letter 466).

2. Cossacks who lived along the Yaik (now Ural) River. They were in the town of Uralsk, where Pushkin spent three days.

3. Pushkin usually wrote mornings in bed, with his notebook propped up on his knees. For Pushkin's literary works written during this trip, see Letter 468, and note 3.

4. Gavrila. Some of these traits are depicted by Gogol for the servant in his *Inspector General*.

5. Pushkin's former servant.

6. That is, hinds, boors.

7. The allusion is to an event which happened to Pushkin in the Caucasus in 1829, and which he describes in his *Journey to Erzurum*. His attempts at "coquetting" with the Kalmuck girl were unsuccessful, but the occurrence led to his poem, "To a Kalmuck Girl" (1829).

Letter 466

1. Vasily Osipovich Pokatilov (d. 1838).

2. Pushkin spent the night of September 29 at Yazykovo, and left for Boldino the next day. The three Yazykov brothers were Peter Mikhaylovich Yazykov, the poet Nikolay Mikhaylovich Yazykov, and Alexander Mikhaylovich Yazykov (1799-1874).

3. See Letter 464. Priests were also "bad luck."

4. A settlement about five miles from Orenburg. Pushkin visited it on September 19.

5. Buntova (d. after 1848). When she was fourteen or fifteen, Pugachev saw her on the street and ordered that she be taken to a public bath for him. She gave Pushkin considerable information which he made use of in his works on the Pugachev uprising. Tolstoy presents as typical a hussar of Pushkin's generation similarly using a public bath for relations with a woman, in his *Two Hussars* (1856).

6. A post station eight miles from Boldino.

7. That is, to work on the Pugachev materials.

Letter 467

1. See Letter 463, and note 3.

2. Pushkin is thinking of the separate publication of the historical materials which he compiled and published in his *History of Pugachev*.

3. Zhukovsky had returned to Tsarskoe Selo in September, after spending the summer abroad for his health. Zhukovsky received the "star" of the order of St. Stanislav, on August 30, 1833.

4. For Pushkin's earlier intention to visit Mme. Karamzina in Dorpat, see Letter 452, note.

5. The Smirnovs spent the first ten months of 1833 in Germany.

6. Princess Lyubov Alexandrovna Khilkova (1811-1859). The marriage took place in November, 1833.

7. What money Pushkin means is not known.

8. Nothing is known of Pushkin's financial affairs with his father at the time.

9. Boldino had been jointly owned by Pushkin's father, S. L. Pushkin, and his uncle, V. L. Pushkin. His uncle's heirs wished Pushkin to buy their inherited share (see Letter 472).

10. Neither she nor her memoirs have been identified.

11. Probably N. I. Tarasenko-Otreshkov.

12. Count Karl Ludwig Ficquelmont, the Austrian ambassador, and his wife, Countess Daria Fedorovna Ficquelmont, daughter of Elizaveta Khitrovo.

13. She was not.

Letter 468

1. Pushkin had been given a copy of the *Complete Collected Laws* in February, 1832 (see Letter 425). Pushkin wished these materials for his *History of Pugachev*.

2. S. D. Bezobrazov, fiancé of Lybov (Lyuba) Alexandrovna Khilkova (see Letter 467).

3. During his stay at Boldino in October and early November, 1833, Pushkin had his last really productive short literary period, which can be compared in this respect, only with the autumn of 1830. During early autumn, 1833, Pushkin wrote, in addition to *The History of Pugachev*, *The Bronze Horseman*, *The Tale of the Fisherman and the Fish*, *The Tale of the Dead Tsarevna and the Seven Heroes*, and *Angelo* (an adaptation of Shakespeare's *Measure for Measure* into the form of a narrative poem), in addition to a number of shorter things (for some of which, see note 4).

4. Pushkin no doubt is referring to the works of his which appeared in 1834 in Smirdin's *Library for Reading*: the poems, "The Hussar," "Budrys and His Sons," "The Voevoda," *The Tale of the Dead Tsarevna and the Seven Heroes*, and the tale, "The Queen of Spades."

Letter 469

1. Nikolay Alexandrovich Ogarev (1811-1867). Apparently his attempts at paying court to Mme. Pushkina were described in a letter of hers.

2. Count Dmitry Nikolaevich Sheremetev (1803-1871) was an extremely wealthy landowner.

2. Mentioning Vigel, Pushkin again refers to his homosexual proclivities.

4. It did not appear.

5. Pushkin forgets that his brother Lev had red hair.

6. *Staram stala, i umom ploxam.* Pushkin is quoting an expression used by a Kazan Tatar about Catherine the Great's vicegerent in Kazan, Prince Platon Stepanovich Meshchersky (1713-1799).

Letter 470

1. Probably Praskovia Petrovna Vyazemskaya.

2. "The Forbidden Beer" (1829). Pushkin spells out Izmaylov's meaning.

3. Pushkin was dissatisfied with the luncheons at meetings of the Russian Academy; vodka was served there instead of wine.

4. See Letter 440, note 9. The illustration opposite this letter shows a portrait of Mme. Pushkina, made much later, with this hairdress.

5. Pushkin uses the same expressions, in French and English, with regard to the heroine Tatiana, who lives up to these standards, in *Evgeny Onegin*, Chap. VIII, stanzas 14-15.

6. See Letter 468, and note 3.

7. For the projected trip to Dorpat, see Letter 452, note.

Letter 471

1. Pushkin's *Tales of Belkin* were attributed by him to his "deceased" friend Belkin. Pushkin further speaks of Gomozeyko, pseudonym of Odoevsky, and Panko, pseudonym of Gogol. Odoevsky had proposed that he, Gogol, and Pushkin publish an almanac in the "form of a three-story house," of which Odoevsky would take the living room, Gogol the attic, and Pushkin the basement. Pushkin declined, and the almanac did not materialize.

2. Unidentified.

3. The governor was Alexander Mikhaylovich Zagryazhsky. His wife was Karolina Osipovna Zagryazhskaya.

4. That his health was better. See Letter 467.

5. Gogol's *Vladimir, Third Class.*

Letter 472

1. "It is written on the heart of every man: '*to the easiest to get.*' "
2. Pushkin spent three days in Moscow, about the middle of November. He arrived in Petersburg before November 24.
3. Pushkin refers to *La Vie des dames galantes*, by Pierre de Bourdeille, Seigneur de Brantôme, sixteenth-century memoirist and historian. This book begins with a discussion of cuckoldry.
4. Lev Sergeevich Pushkin, who had served in the Russian army which put down the Polish Revolution, had retired from the military service, and was "twiddling his thumbs" in Petersburg.
5. See Letter 467, and note 9.
6. November 24. Pushkin was in Petersburg on that day and attended the name-day celebration of Ekaterina A. Karamzina.

Letter 473

1. Nashchokin was still in the midst of extreme domestic turmoil with his gypsy mistress, Olga Andreevna, because of his desire to leave her and marry Vera Alexandrovna Narskaya (d. 1900).
2. "You are to a high degree a man of passion."
3. From Moscow to Petersburg.
4. Unidentified. He is mentioned again in Letter 475. "Lelenka" is a diminutive of the name Alexey.
5. That is, Olga Andreevna.
6. Pushkin went to the place where the ball was being held, found and seated himself in his wife's carriage, and had a servant tell her to come home on very important business. When she climbed into the carriage, it was into his embraces. L. N. Tolstoy, twenty years later, presents a hussar and a provincial lady in such an adventure in his *Two Hussars*, as being typical of hussars in Pushkin's generation.
7. Pushkin had in mind selling the works he had written in the autumn of 1833 to Smirdin at a good price.
8. Pushkin took over the management of his father's estate Boldino in April, 1834.
9. Unknown.
10. M. I. Kalashnikov. The note undoubtedly had to do with the attempted remortgaging of Pushkin's Kistenevo serfs.

Letter 474

1. *The Bronze Horseman*. Nicholas I allowed the publication of only a fragment of it during Pushkin's lifetime.
2. *A Library for Reading*, which began to appear in 1834. Pushkin contributed to it until plans for his own journal, *The Contemporary*, began to crystallize, late in 1835. Smirdin offered Pushkin fifteen thousand rubles per annum to continue to collaborate with him, instead of publishing his own journal.
3. *The Captain's Daughter*.
4. *Istorija Pugačevščiny*. Pushkin actually entitled his work *The History of Pugachev*, but Nicholas I required him, before he would allow publication, to change the title to *The History of the Pugachev Revolt*.
5. Benkendorf transmitted to Pushkin the Tsar's permission for the poems Pushkin wished Smirdin to publish to be sent to the usual censorship, but the Tsar wished to see *The History of Pugachev*.

Letter 475

1. This letter was never delivered. See Letter 286, and note.

2. Nashchokin fled from his gypsy mistress Olga Andreevna in January or February, 1834, leaving her in possession of his Moscow house and considerable money. Shortly afterward, he married Vera Alexandrovna Narskaya.

3. Rather, his birthday, December 8. Nashchokin celebrated his name day on the Day of Peter and Paul, June 29.

4. A dwarf who was attached to the Goncharov family.

5. See Letter 473, and note 4.

6. V. L. Pushkin's heirs included his common-law wife, Anna Nikolaevna Vorozhey-kina, and his daughter by her, Margarita Vasilievna Bezobrazova, nee Vasilieva (1810-1889).

7. See Letter 474.

8. Pushkin's complete works were not published during his life.

9. Nashchokin's son by Olga Andreevna.

PART XI

GRAY-HAIRED KAMMERJUNKER — PETERSBURG

December, 1833—August, 1834

Pushkin, 1836 or 1837. *Gravure by T. Wright.*

To ALEXANDER KHRISTOFOROVICH BENKENDORF
Between February 7 and 10, 1834. In Petersburg.
(Second rough draft; in French)

In submitting to His Majesty the second volume of Pugachev, I take the liberty of speaking to Your Excellency about circumstances concerning me, and of having recourse to your customary kindness.

By permitting the publication of this work, His Majesty has assured my fortune. The sum which I shall be able to realize from it puts me in the position even to accept an inheritance which I have been forced to renounce for lack of some forty thousand rubles which I did not have. This work will procure them for me. If I can be the publisher of it myself—without having recourse to a bookseller—fifteen thousand would be enough for me.

I request two things: one, that I be permitted to publish my work at my own expense in the special printing house under M. [M. M.] Speransky's supervision, the only one where I am sure of not being tricked—the other request is to receive, as a two-year loan, fifteen thousand, a sum which will permit me to devote to the publishing all the time and care which I should.[1]

I have no right to the favor which I solicit, except the kindnesses which I have already received—and which give me the courage and the confidence to have recourse to you again.—I entrust my very humble request to Your Excellency's protection.

I am, Count,

Your Excellency's

Most humble [. . . .]

[477]

To STEPAN DMITRIEVICH NECHAEV
February 12, 1834. In Petersburg.

Dear Sir, Stepan Dmitrievich,[1]

I make bold to have recourse to Your High Excellency with a most humble request.

By the wish of the Sovereign Emperor, the archdeacon[2] of the

Court church at Tsarskoe Selo, on account of drunkenness, has been expelled from the Court department and has been transferred to that of the diocese. According to the order of the Synod, he must be sent back to his diocese. The archdeacon, a man no longer young, and with a family, requests, as a favor, that he be left in the local diocese. The sense of the Sovereign's command would be fulfilled just the same, for not a word was said in it to the effect that he be sent to his *own* diocese.

The archdeacon, I know not why, has addressed himself to me, supposing that my weak voice might be honored with your attention. In any case, I could not refuse to intercede for him, and I commend my client to your magnanimous protection.

With the most profound respect, I have the honor to be,
Dear Sir,
Your Excellency's
Most humble servant,
Alexander Pushkin.

February 12, 1834.

[478]
To ALEXANDER KHRISTOFOROVICH BENKENDORF
February 26, 1834. In Petersburg.

Dear Sir, Alexander Khristoforovich,

Not having now the means, independently of the booksellers, to proceed to the publication of the work which I have written, I make bold to have recourse to Your Excellency with my request for the disbursement from the Treasury, in the form of a loan at the established interest rates, of twenty thousand rubles, the same to be repaid in full in two years, with payments to be made at whatever dates the authorities may choose to set.[1]

With the most profound respect, I have the honor to be,
Dear Sir,
Your Excellency's
Most humble servant,
Alexander Pushkin.

February 26, 1834.

[478a]
To Countess Elizaveta Ksaverievna Vorontsova
March 5, 1834. From Petersburg to Odessa.
(In French)
Dear Countess,

Here are several scenes of a tragedy which I had intended to write.¹ I desired to place at your feet something less imperfect; unfortunately, I have already made disposition of all my manuscripts, and I have preferred to be at fault toward the public, rather than not obey your commands.

May I dare, Madame, to speak to you of the moment of happiness which I experienced upon receiving your letter, at the mere idea that you have not completely forgotten the most devoted of your slaves?

I am, with respect,
Countess,

March 5   Your most humble and most
1834   obedient servant,
Petersburg.   Alexander Pushkin.

[479]
To Vladimir Fedorovich Odoevsky
March 15 or 16, 1834. In Petersburg.

Are you going to the meeting at Grech's? If so, then let's go together. It is terrifying to go alone: they might beat us up.¹

[480]
To Vladimir Fedorovich Odoevsky
March 16, 1834. In Petersburg.

The point is the *Konversations-Lexikon*:¹ I sniffed it out. I agree with Your Highness that this evening has its loathsome and its interesting side. I shall go to Grech's, for I have received permission to do so from Pletnev, who is conscience incarnate. Let's go. What can we lose? After all, this will be a communal gathering of all the republic.² We'll watch and listen to everything—but we'll not join the gang of thieves.³

A.P.

[481]
To Pavel Voinovich Nashchokin
The middle of March, 1834. In Petersburg.

You can't imagine, dear friend, how I rejoiced at your letter. In the first place, I receive from you a whole notebook: proof that you have the time to spare, the paper to spare, the peace of mind, and the urge to chat with me. From your first lines I see that you are calm and happy. Every word destroys gossip, half of which I did not believe, but the other half of which disturbed me greatly. Sobolevsky and Lev Sergeevich were dining with me. When I read your letter first to myself and then in the hearing of your friends, we were all pleased; we all wished you happiness. Natalia Nikolaevna [Pushkina] is impatiently desirous of becoming acquainted with your Vera Alexandrovna,[1] and she asks you to make them friends sight unseen. She sincerely loves you and congratulates you. . . . But first let's talk business, i.e., about money. When you sent me off from Moscow, you remember that we thought that you could get along without money from me; for that reason I have not made my arrangements. I had in my hands, and quite recently, a good round sum, but it has melted away, and I shan't have any money before October. But I'll provide you with your three thousand in a short time, in instalments which I shall set, taking my circumstances into consideration. Here they have been saying that you lost *on credit* all that you were due to receive from your brother.[2] You can't imagine how that has disturbed me, but now I am relying on the change in your life. You no longer need the shocks of *quinze el va* and *plié*[3] in order to dispel your domestic woes. They say that unhappiness is a good school: perhaps. But happiness is the best university. It provides the finishing touches for the education of a soul capable of the good and the beautiful, such as yours is, my friend; such as mine is, as you know. Of course, we're even, if you are obligated to me for your marriage— and I hope that Vera Alexandrovna will love me, just as Natalia Nikolaevna loves you. Just imagine, my wife came very near to dying a few days ago. The present winter has been horribly abundant in balls. In Carnival there was dancing even twice a day. Finally came the last Sunday before Lent. I think: "The balls are over with, thank God!" My wife was in the palace. Suddenly I saw that she was becoming ill—I took her away, and after we got home she had a miscarriage.[4] Now she's (keep our fingers crossed) well, thank God, and in a few days she's going to the Kaluga village to her sisters', who are suffering terribly from the caprices of my mother-in-law.[5] I had already taken over your debt to Vyazemsky before I received your letter. Andrey Petrovich [Esaulov] is in a terrible state. He has been dying of hunger and going out of his mind. Sobolevsky and I have been helping him parsimoniously with money, but generously with counsels. Now I'm thinking of sending him off to the regiment as a bandmaster. He's an artist in soul and in habits, i.e., nonchalant, indecisive, lazy, proud, and flighty. He prefers independence to everything else. But a beggar is yet more independent than a day laborer. I'm holding up to him as examples the German geniuses who have overcome so much woe, to win fame and a crust of bread. How much do you owe him? Do you want me to pay him for you? My circumstances have become still more difficult, and here's the occasion for it: A few days ago my father sent for me. I arrived. I found him in tears, my mother in bed—all the house in horrible agitation. "What's going on?"—"They're levying a distress on the estate."—"You must hurry up and pay the debt."—"The debt is already paid. And here's the letter of the manager."[6]—"Then what's the trouble?"—"There's nothing to live on until October."—"Go to the village."—"There's nothing to do it on." What's to be done? I'll have to take the estate in hand and set support money for my father. New debts, new bothers. But I must do it: I should like to set at ease my father's old age and arrange the affairs of my brother Lev, who in his way is just such another artist as Andrey Petrovich [Esaulov], with the difference that he has no knowledge of any art. My sister Olga Sergeevna has had a miscarriage and is with child again. This is all simply marvellous.

Here are some other pieces of news for you: I've been a Kammer-junker[7] since the month of January. *The Bronze Horseman* was not passed. Losses and unpleasantnesses! On the other hand, *Pugachev* has been passed, and I am publishing it at the Sovereign's expense. This has quite solaced me; all the more that, of course, in making me a Kammerjunker the Sovereign was thinking of my rank rather than of my years—and he surely didn't intend to humilitate me. As soon as I get my affairs arranged, I'll get busy on yours. Farewell; expect some money.

[482]

To MIKHAIL PETROVICH POGODIN
About (not later than) April 7, 1834.
From Petersburg to Moscow.

I rejoice at the opportunity to have a frank talk with you. The Society of Lovers[1] has treated me in such a way that I absolutely cannot have anything to do with it. It elected me a member along with Bulgarin, at the very time when he was unanimously black-balled in the English Club (N.B.: in the Petersburg one) as a spy, a turncoat, and a slanderer, at the very time when I was compelled in answer to his vilifications to publish the article on Vidocq;[2] I had to prove to the public, which was rightly astonished at my long-suffering, that I have the full right to disdain Bulgarin's opinion and not to demand satisfaction from a notorious scoundrel prating of honor and morality. And then what happens? At the same time I read in Shalikov's gazette: "*Alexander Sergeevich and Faddey Venediktovich, these two coryphaei of our literature,* have been awarded, etc."[3] No matter what you say, it's a slap in the face. I believe that the Society, in this case, behaved like Famusov, without having any intention of insulting me:

I'm glad to have just anybody, you know.[4]

But it was my duty to return at once the certificate of membership which was sent to me. I did not do so, because at that time I did not feel like being bothered with membership certificates—but I simply cannot have anything to do with the Society of Lovers.

You ask me about *The Bronze Horseman*, about *Pugachev*, and about *Peter*. The first will not be published. *Pugachev* will come out by fall. I am approaching *Peter*[5] with fear and trembling, as you are the chair of history.[6] Altogether, I am writing a lot for myself, but I am publishing against my will and solely for money. Why should one want to appear before the public, which does not understand one, so that four fools may berate one just short of obscenity in their journals for the next six months? The time was when literature was a noble, aristocratic field of endeavor. Now it is a flea market. So be it.

[483]

To GRIGORY ALEXANDROVICH STROGANOV
About (not earlier than) April 11, 1834.
In Petersburg.
(In French)

I am very sorrowfully paying the penalty for the vain fancies of my youth. Lelewel's[1] accolade seems harsher than exile to Siberia; I thank you,[2] however, for having been so kind as to transmit to me the article in question:[3] it will serve me as the text for a sermon.

Please, Count, tell your wife[4] that I am at her feet, and accept the assurance of my high esteem.

Alexander Pushkin.

[484]

To IOSIF MATVEEVICH PENKOVSKY
April 13, 1834. From Petersburg to Boldino.

Father has seen fit to put at my complete disposal the management of his estate; accordingly, confirming the power of attorney which he has given you, I hereby notify you that you are to refer directly to me with regard to all business having to do with Boldino. Send me without delay an accounting of the money which has been delivered by you to my father from the time you took over the management, and also which you have received on loan and in payment of indebtedness, and next how much unsold grain remains, how much uncollected quitrent, and how much (if any) arrears. You are to proceed also with the chattel inventory of Boldino, so that the same will be ready by the month of September.[1]

April 13.   A. Pushkin.

[485]

To IVAN IVANOVICH LAZHECHNIKOV
The first half of April, 1834. From Petersburg to Tver.
(Rough draft)

With keenest gratitude I received your letter of March 30, and the manuscript about Pugachev.[1] The manuscript was already known to me; it was written by the academician Rychkov, who was in Orenburg at the time of the siege. In your copy I found several interesting additional points which I shall make use of without fail.

In passing several times through Tver, I have always wished for an opportunity to present myself to you and to thank you, in the first place, for that true pleasure which you provided me in your first novel,[2] and, in the second place, for the consideration with which you have honored me.

With impatience I await your new novel, an excellent fragment of which I have read in Maximovich's almanac.[3] Will it come out soon? And how are you thinking of publishing it? For God's sake, not in parts. These instalments are hard on the patience of the numerous people who read and esteem you.

With the most profound, etc.

[486]

To Natalia Nikolaevna Pushkina
April 17, 1834. From Petersburg to Moscow.

April 17.

How are you, little wife? How's your trip?[1] And how are Sashka and Mashka? Christ be with you! Be hale and hearty, and hurry up and get to Moscow. I am expecting a letter from you from Novgorod, but meanwhile here is an accounting of my bachelor mode of life. Day before yesterday I returned from Tsarskoe Selo at five o'clock in the afternoon and found on my table two cards, one to a ball on April 29, and an invitation to appear the following day at Litta's; I guessed that he was intending to give me a dressing down for not having been at mass. And indeed that same evening I found out from Zhukovsky, who dropped in on me, that the Sovereign has been displeased at the absence of many Chamberlains and Kammer-junkers, and that he commanded that we be informed of it. In the palace Litta harangued us with great heat, saying: *Il y a cependant pour les Messieurs de la Cour des règles fixes.* To which Naryshkin observed to him, *Vous vous trompez: c'est pour les demoiselles d'honneur.*[2] I made my excuses in writing. They say that we are going to march in pairs, like Institute girls. Just imagine that I, with my gray beard, would have to strut alongside Bezobrazov[3] or Remer[4]—nothing would induce me to do it! *J'aime mieux avoir le fouet devant tout le monde,* as M. Jourdain says.[5] This morning I was sitting in my study, reading Grimm[6] and waiting for you, my angel, to ring,[7] when Sobolevsky came to see me with the question of where we were going to dine. Then I remembered that I had wanted to fast and prepare for the mass, but I nevertheless had already broken the fast. Nothing could be done about it; we decided to dine at Dumé's, and meanwhile we began to bring the library into order. Your aunt came to ask about you, and learning that I was in my dressing gown and for that reason would not come out to her, she herself came in to me —I fulfilled your commission, we talked, grieved, and worried about you a little, and we decided to reiterate our requests and demands—that you take care of yourself and remember our exhortations. Then I went to Dumé's, where my appearing produced general merriment: "Bachelor, bachelor Pushkin!" They began to ply me with champagne and punch and to ask whether I wouldn't go to Sofia Ostafievna's.[8] All that embarrassed me so that I don't intend to go to Dumé's any more, and I'm dining at home today, having ordered Stepan[9] to bring cold fish-and-vegetable soup and *beaf-steaks*.[10] I spent yesterday evening at home; today I woke up at seven o'clock, and I began writing this detailed report to you. I'm sending you your mother's letter, which arrived day before yesterday. I'll write her. Meanwhile I send you a hug and a kiss, and I bless all three of you.

[487]

To NATALIA NIKOLAEVNA PUSHKINA
April 19, 1834. From Petersburg to Moscow.

My darling, I am sending you two letters which I unsealed out of curiosity and stinginess (so as to pay less postage for weight), and also a prescription for some drops. As a favor to me, don't forget to reread Spassky's[1] instructions and to follow them. By now, little wife, you ought to be near Moscow. The farther you go, the better you feel; but, as for me! . . . Your sisters are expecting you. I can imagine everybody's joy. See to it that you don't act like a little girl. Don't forget that you already have two children, and that you have lost a third by miscarriage. Take care of yourself. Be careful. Dance in moderation. Don't overdo your fun. And, most important, hurry up and get to the village. I kiss you affectionately and bless all of you. How is Mashka? I'll bet she's really glad that she can rampage to her heart's content! Now here's an accounting of my behavior for you. I stay at home, I dine at home, I don't see anybody, and I receive only Sobolevsky. Day before yesterday I played a fine trick on Lev Sergee-vich. Sobolevsky, as if with nothing special in mind, asked him to dine at my house. Lev Sergeevich showed up. I made my excuses to him, as to a gourmet, that, not expecting him, I had ordered myself only cold fish-and-vegetable soup and *beafsteaks*.[2] Lev Sergeevich is content with that. We sit down at the table. Fine fish-and-vegetable soup is served. Lev Sergeevich gulps down two plates. He sops up the sturgeon. And then he asks for wine. He is answered that there is no wine.—"What do you mean, there's not any?"—"Alexander Sergee-vich has ordered that it not be put on the table." And I state that I've been on a diet since Natalia Nikolaevna's departure—and drink water. You should have seen the despair and the sardonic laughter of Lev Sergeich, who probably won't come to dine with me again. During all this time Sobolevsky kept on adding water, now in a tumbler, now in a wineglass, now in a long goblet—and he plied Lev Sergeich with it, who kept standing on ceremony and refusing. Here's an example for you of my innocent doings. I am impatiently awaiting your letter from Novgorod, and I'll take it immediately to Katerina Ivanovna [Zagryazhskaya]. For the present—farewell, my angel. I kiss and bless all of you. Yesterday we had our first thunder—thank God, spring is over.

April 19.

[488]
To Natalia Nikolaevna Pushkina
April 20 and 22, 1834. From Petersburg to Moscow.

Friday.

My little angel wife! I have just now received your letter from Bronnitsy—and I thank you with all my heart. I shall impatiently await news from Torzhok. I hope you will get over your tiredness from the journey all right, and that in Moscow you will be healthy, merry, and beautiful. I sent your letter to Aunty, instead of taking it to her myself, because I am reporting myself as being ill, and I am afraid I might meet the Tsar. I am spending all these holidays at home. I have no intention of going to see the Heir, with congratulations and greetings; his reign is yet to come, and I probably shall not live to see it. I have seen three tsars: the first ordered my little cap to be taken off me, and gave my nurse a scolding on my account; the second was not gracious to me; although the third has saddled me with being a Kammerpage close upon my old age,[1] I have no desire for him to be replaced by a fourth.[2] Better let well enough alone. We shall see just how our Sashka will get along with his namesake born to the purple: I didn't get along with mine.[3] God grant that he not follow in my footsteps and write verses and quarrel with tsars! Then he wouldn't outshine his father in verses, but neither would he fight windmills. But now enough of nonsense; let's talk about business: Please take care of yourself, especially at first. I dislike Easter Week in Moscow. Don't heed your sisters and gad about having a good time from morning till night. Don't dance at a ball until matins. Be moderate in having your fun; go to bed early.—Don't let your father get at the children. He could frighten them and goodness knows what else.[4] Take better care of yourself during your periods. While in the village, don't read the nasty books in your grandfather's library; don't soil your imagination, little wife. I permit you to coquette to your heart's content. Don't ride horses that are too spirited (on which point I humbly beseech Dmitry Nikolaevich). In addition, I ask you not to spoil either Mashka or Sashka, and if you should not be satisfied with your German woman or wet nurse, I ask you to get rid of her immediately, without any scruples, and without standing on ceremony.

Sunday. Christ is risen, my dear little wife. I am lonesome, my angel. I am lonesome with you away. I can't get your letter out of my head. You seemed to me to have gotten too tired. You will arrive in Moscow. You will rejoice your sisters. Your nerves will be taut. You will think that you are completely well. You will stand up all night at the Easter service. And next you'll be lying all stretched out in hysterics and fever. That's what is alarming me, my angel. So much that my head is going round and round, and I can't get it off my mind. Will I be able to wait it out until you have dashed off to the village? The Grand Duke has recently taken the oath of fealty. I was not at the ceremony, because I am reporting myself ill, and I really am not very well. Kochubey[5] was made a chancellor. There is a multitude of gracious acts: six Ladies in Waiting, your friend Natalia Obolenskaya[6] among others, but still not our Mashenka Vyazemskaya.[7] It's a pity and a vexation. The Heir was very touched; the Sovereign, too. In general, they say, all this produced a powerful effect. On the one hand I very much regret that I did not see the historical scene and that when I get old I shall not be able to speak of it as a witness. Another piece of news: Merder[8] has died. It is still a secret from the Grand Duke, and it will poison his youthful joy. Arakcheev has died, too. I am the only one in all Russia who regrets it[9]—I had not succeeded in arranging to see and have a long talk with him. Aunty has given me a chocolate billiard table—it is charming. She sends you lots of kisses and has a fit of the spleen on your account. Farewell, all my folks. Christ has risen; Christ be with you.[10]

[489]
To NATALIA NIKOLAEVNA PUSHKINA
April 24, 1834. From Petersburg to Moscow.

Tuesday. I thank you, my angel, for your letter from near Torzhok. You are sensible, you are well—you are feeding the children porridge —you're near Moscow. All that made me very glad and calmed me; otherwise I wouldn't be myself. We are having a noisy, stormy Easter Week. Yesterday I was at [Ekaterina Andreevna] Karamzina's, and Timiryazeva[1] and I quarreled. Today I'm going to Aunty's with your letter. Tomorrow I'll write you a lot. For the present I kiss you and bless all of you.

[490]
To NATALIA NIKOLAEVNA PUSHKINA
April 28, 1834. From Petersburg to Moscow.

Well, little wife! At long last we have received a letter from you. As I count it, you were to have arrived in Moscow on Maundy Thursday (and thus it happened), and for nine whole days there was no news from you. Aunty got very scared. I was more calm, knowing that you had dragged up to Torzhok all right, and supposing that the bothers of the arrival and the joys of seeing everybody would keep you from thinking about letters during your first days there. However, I had begun to feel bad, too. Thank God that you have arrived, that you and Masha are well, that Sashka is better. Probably he has recovered completely. Isn't he sick on account of his wet nurse? Order her to be examined, and wean him. It's time. Give my regards to your sisters. Ask them from me not to spoil Mashka—i.e., not to heed her tears and cries. Otherwise I won't have any peace on account of her. Take care of yourself, and, as a favor to me, don't catch cold. What's to be done with your mother? If she herself does not want to come to see you, go see her for a week or two, though that means extra expenses and extra bothers. I'm horribly afraid of family scenes for you. May the Lord remind you of King David and all his meekness!—Please do not enter into close relationships with your father, and don't show the children to him. He can't be depended on in his condition. If you don't watch out, he might bite off Mashka's little nose.¹ Now here's my most humble report. I spent Easter Week decorously at home; the only thing I did was to go yesterday (Friday) to [Ekaterina Andreevna] Karamzina's and [Alexandra Osipovna] Smirnova's. I didn't put in an appearance at the park where the swings are; tomorrow there'll be a ball,² at which I won't appear either. This ball is turning everybody's head, and it has become the subject of all the talk of the town. There will be eighteen hundred guests. It has been calculated that, assuming a minute per carriage, it would take ten hours for everybody to drive up. But the carriages will arrive three at a time, and consequently the time will be cut to a third. Yesterday all the city, except me, went to see the hall. Sobolevsky is here, but he borrowed fifty rubles from me, and since then he hasn't been back. Lev Sergeevich is moving today from [V. V.] Engelgardt's to our parents'. I have the honor to observe to you that your cabman asked, not for Rhine wine, but Rhenish (i.e., every white, dry, grape wine is called Rhenish). Your observation about the education of the Russian people is very just, though, and it does you honor and gives me pleasure. *Dis-moi ce que tu bois, je te dirai qui tu es.*³ Do you drink camomile tea or *eau d'orange*? Aunty dropped in on me day before yesterday to find out about your health, and she coquetted with me from her carriage. Today I'll take your letter to her. Farewell, my angel. I kiss you, and I bless all of you. I send my regards to your sisters. . . . Oh, I'd like to let slip *une bonne plaisanterie*, but I'm afraid of you. *Addio.*

Saturday.

[491]

To Natalia Nikolaevna Pushkina
April 30, 1834. From Petersburg to Moscow.

St. Thomas' Monday.

Yesterday the nobility ball finally was held.[1] The carriages began to drive up at six o'clock. I went out strolling around the city, and I passed by [D. L.] Naryshkin's house. A multitude of people was thronging. The police were clamoring at them. An illumination was being prepared. Without waiting until twilight, I went to the English Club, where a fantastic thing happened to me. In the club I was robbed of 350 rubles,[2] robbed not as at *tintere*, not at whist, but as people are robbed on the city squares. What do you think of our club? We've outdone even the Moscow [English Club]! You think I've been angry; not in the slightest. I'm cross at Petersburg, and I rejoice at its every loathsomeness. Returning home, I received your letter, my dear angel. Thank God you're well, the children are well, you're a good little girl, you leave the ball before the mazurka, and you're not gadding about the parishes. One thing's bad; you couldn't refrain from going to Princess Golitsyna's ball.[3] And going there is just what I asked you not to do. I don't want my wife to go where the hostess permits herself discourtesy and disrespect. You're no Mlle. Sontag,[4] who is invited to a party and then not even looked at. Moscow ladies are not my idea of a good example. Let them gad about in the anterooms of people who don't even look at them. Good enough for them. Little wife, little wife! If you don't heed me in such a trifle, then how am I to keep from thinking. . . . But God save you. You say: "I didn't go to see her; she herself came up to me." That's just what's bad. You could and should have paid her a visit, because she has a position of high honor at court and you're the wife of a Chamber Page;[5] that's an obligation of service. But there was no need for you to go to a ball at her house. I swear it vexes me—I don't even want to continue my letter.

[492]

To Natalia Nikolaevna Pushkina
April 30, 1834. From Petersburg to Moscow.

My dear wife, my little angel wife—I've already written you today, but somehow my letter got off on the wrong foot. I began with *Te*

Deum, but I shifted over to *De Profundis*. I began with tendernesses, and I ended with a slap in the face. Pardon me, little wife. Forgive us our debts, as we forgive our debtors. I forgive you for the ball at Golitsyna's,[1] and I'll talk to you about yesterday's ball, which all the city is talking about, and which they say was very successful. Nothing more magnificent was ever seen. It was not too crowded and there were plenty of ices; so that it would have been very good for me. But I was among the common people, and the whole city passed in front of me in carriages (except the poet Kukolnik,[2] who passed in some old *fourgon* with some sort of tattered boy footman on the box—which was a true, poetic manifestation). I'll check about the gowns and let you know. I wrote you that some money was stolen from me in the club. Don't believe it. That's low slander. The money has been found and brought to me.[3] You are wrong in thinking that I'm in Sobolevsky's clutches and that he is soiling your furniture. I don't see him at all, and I've made friends again with Sofia Karamzina. She's at a wedding today, Bakunina's.[4] There's another fine wedding: Vorontsov is getting married—to K. A. Naryshkin's daughter,[5] who has not yet had her coming-out. Now, of wealthy eligibles, only Novomlensky[6] remains, for Sorokhtin, you say, has died. Whom will he choose? Alexandra Nikolaevna [Goncharova] or Katerina Nikolaevna [Goncharova]? What do you think? You'll probably get this letter only in Yaropolets. I've already written to Natalia Ivanovna [Goncharova]. Kiss her little hands for me, and tell her a lot of tender things. Farewell, wife. I kiss and bless you, and all of you.

A.P.

[493]

To DMITRY NIKOLAEVICH BANTYSH-KAMENSKY
May 1, 1834. From Petersburg to Moscow.
Dear Sir, Dmitry Nikolaevich,
Permit me to express to you my most profound gratitude for the letter, a precious token of your favor, and for the photograph of the seal of the Pretender, which I immediately sent off to be engraved.[1] I have his portrait, and it, too, is being engraved. With impatience I shall await the biography of Pugachev, which you are so kind as to promise me, with such indulgence.

I regret that time does not permit me to submit my work for your examination. The opinions and observations of such a person as you would serve as guidance for me and would encourage my first historical endeavor.

With the most profound respect and complete devotion, I have the honor to be, Dear Sir,

Your Excellency's

May 1, 1834.   Most humble servant,

SPb.   Alexander Pushkin.

[494]

To NIKOLAY IVANOVICH PAVLISHCHEV

May 4, 1834. From Petersburg to Warsaw.

Dear Sir, Nikolay Ivanovich,

I thank you for your letter.[1] It is sensible and business-like; consequently it is not hard to answer.

When I consented to take over the management of Father's estate, I demanded a clear accounting of the indebtedness to the government and to private individuals, and of the revenues.

Father answered me that, on the entire estate, there is about 100,000 of debt, that there is about 7000 of interest to be paid, that there is about 3000 of arrears, and that there is about 22,000 of revenues.

I asked that all this be determined with more exactness, and when Father did not succeed in doing it himself, I addressed the Loan Office and ascertained that there is

Of debt to the government	190,750
Of annual interest	11,826
Of arrears	11,045
(Of debts to private individuals I estimate about	10,000)

I am unable to ascertain how much the revenues amount to, but relying on Father's word and placing it at 22,000, it will result that after payment of interest to the government up to 10,000 will be left.

If Father will assign 1500 of this money to Olga Sergeevna, and the same amount to Lev Sergeevich, then 7000 will be left for him. This ought to be enough for him. But there are the arrears to the government, the debts to private individuals, Lev Sergeevich's debts.

And Father has already received and spent part of this year's revenues.

Until I have brought these confused affairs into order and clarified them, I cannot and do not promise anything to Olga Sergeevna. My financial condition permits me to get by without taking anything from the revenues of Father's estates, but I cannot afford to add money *of my own*.

In a few days [. . .]² the 74 serfs which have not been mortgaged [. . .]² *I hope* to receive some [. . .]² thousands, if there are no judgments against the estate. Out of this money, I'll send you what Lev Sergeevich owes you.

With true respect and devotion, I remain,

Your most humble servant,

A. Pushkin.

May 4, 1834.

SPb.

I have not yet received the power of attorney³ from Father, and I have already paid, in one month, 866 [rubles] for Father and 1330 for Lev Segreevich *out of my money*: more I cannot do.

[495]

TO NATALIA NIKOLAEVNA PUSHKINA

About May 5, 1834. From Petersburg to Yaropolets.

What's this, wife? Here it has already been five days that I haven't had any news of you. I hope that only the bothers of departure and arrival have prevented you from writing to me, and that you and the children are well. I'm writing to you at Yaropolets. I don't know where to send money for you, whether to Moscow or to Volokolamsk or to Kaluga.¹ In a few days I'll come to some decision. What shall I tell you about myself? My life is very monotonous. I dine at Dumé's about 2 o'clock, so that I won't encounter the bachelor gang. In the evening I'm usually at the club. Yesterday I was at Princess Vyazemskaya's and your Countess [Nadezhda Lvovna] Sollogub was there, too. From there I went to [V. F.] Odoevsky's, who is leaving for Reval. I often see Aunty, who's disturbed that there has been no news about you for a long time. We're having fine weather, but where you are it's probably still better. It's time for you to go to the village for medication, for baths, and for fresh air.

My angel, I have just now received your letter of the first of May. Thank you for deciding to wait until your monthly is over. This proves to me your good sense, and I love you three times as much for it. I rejoice that you're becoming prettier, although that's *du superflu*. Aunty was just now (at five o'clock) sitting with me. She sends you a kiss. The Summer Garden is full. Everybody's promenading. Countess Ficquelmont has invited me to a party. That will be my first appearance in society since your departure. I'm not paying court to Sollogub, Christ be my witness, nor to Smirnova, either. Smirnova has become horribly big-bellied and will bear within a month.[2] Everybody sends regards to you. I'll write some more tomorrow.

Don't you dare go swimming—have you gone out of your mind? Day after tomorrow I'm dining at Spassky's—and I'll complain about you. I didn't go to [Countess] Ficquelmont's, but remained at home; I have reread your letter, and now I'll go to bed. Your brother Ivan [N. Goncharov] is with me. Lev Sergeevich and my father make me very angry, and Olga Sergeevna is already beginning to make me angry. I'll turn the whole thing down[3]—and start living in clover.

[496]
To Natalia Nikolaevna Pushkina
May 12, 1834. From Petersburg to Yaropolets.
What a fool you are, my angel! Of course I'm not going to be disturbed because you let three days go by without writing me a letter, just exactly as I'm not going to be jealous if you waltz three times in a row with a cavalry guardsman. Yet it doesn't follow from this that I'm indifferent and incapable of jealousy. I sent you off from Petersburg with great anxiety; your letter from Bronnitsy has agitated me still more. But when I found out that you had reached Torzhok in good health, a mountain fell from my heart, and I haven't begun being melancholy again. Your letter is very sweet. And your fears with regard to the true reasons of my friendship for Sofia Karamzina are very pleasant for my self-esteem. I answer your questions thus: [Alexandra Osipovna] Smirnova does not go to the Karamzins'—she would not be able to climb that kind of a staircase with her big belly. I think she's already in her summer house.

Countess Sollogub does not go there, either; I saw her at Princess Vyazemskaya's. As for gallivanting, I'm not gallivanting after anybody. My head's going round and round. I rue the day I took over the estate,[1] but what could I do? I did it, not for myself, but for the children. Aunty spent yesterday with me; she sends you a kiss. Yesterday there was a big parade which, they say, didn't turn out well. The Tsar has placed the Heir under arrest.[2] They're expecting the Prussian Prince[3] here and many other guests. I hope to get by without being at a single festival. Your absence has the one advantage for me that I'm not obliged to doze at balls and glut myself on ices. I'm addressing you at Yaropolets, where you should have been since day before yesterday. I send my cordial respects to Natalia Ivanovna [Goncharova]; I kiss you and the children. Christ be with all of you.

Do you know that Princess [Ekaterina N.] Meshcherskaya and Sofia Karamzina are going abroad? Sofia has been weeping for about two weeks already. I'll probably take her as far as Kronshtadt.[4]

[497]
To NIKOLAY VASILIEVICH GOGOL
May 13, 1834. In Petersburg.

I agree with you completely.[1] I shall go this very day to exhort Uvarov, and apropos of the death of *The Telegraph*, I shall also talk about yours.[2] From this, I shall make an imperceptible and skillful transition to the immortality awaiting him. Maybe we shall bring it off.

[498]
To NATALIA NIKOLAEVNA PUSHKINA
May 16, 1834. From Petersburg to Yaropolets.

My angel! I have not received any letters from you for a long time. Apparently you haven't had the time. Now you are probably in Yaropolets and are already getting ready for the road again. I miss you so much that, first thing you know, I'll come to you. I've spoken with Spassky about the Pyrmont waters.[1] He wishes you to take them. And he went into details with me which I don't want to write to you about by mail, because I don't want a husband's letters to his wife to circulate among the police.[2] Write me about your health

and the health of the children, whom I send a kiss and my blessing. I send my respects to Natalia Ivanovna. I send you a kiss. In a few days you'll receive letters by an *occasion*. Farewell, my darling.
                              May 16.

[499]
                    To Natalia Nikolaevna Pushkina
              May 18, 1834. From Petersburg to Yaropolets.
   My angel! Best wishes upon Masha's birthday.[1] I kiss you and her. God grant that she have some little teeth, and good health. I wish the same to Sasha, though it's not his name day. You haven't written me for so long, so very long, that although I dislike getting disturbed to no purpose, I am nevertheless disturbed. I should have received at least two letters from Yaropolets. Are you and the children well? Are you calm? I haven't written you, because I've been cross—not with you, but with others. One of my letters has fallen into the hands of the police,[2] and so forth. Look, little wife. I hope that you won't give my letters to anybody to make copies of. If the post has unsealed a husband's letter to his wife, then that's its affair. But there is one unpleasant thing in that: the privacy of family relationships, intruded upon in a foul and dishonorable manner. But if you are to blame, then that would be painful for me. Nobody must know what may take place between us; nobody must be received into our bedroom. Without privacy there is no family life. I write to you, not for the press. And there's no reason for you to accept the public as confidant. But I know that couldn't be. And it has been a long time since swinishness in anybody has astonished me.
   Yesterday I was at a concert given for the poor in [D. L.] Naryshkin's magnificent, really magnificent, hall. What a pity that you didn't see it. They sang new music by Vielgorsky, to words by Zhukovsky. I don't see anybody. I don't go anywhere. I've set to work, and I write mornings. Without you, I'm so bored that every minute I think of setting off to see you, if only for a week. Here it's already a month I've lived without you. I'll stick it out until August. And you take care of yourself; I'm afraid of your horseback rides. I still don't know how you ride. Probably fearlessly. But do you sit firmly in the saddle? That's the question. God grant that I find you well and the children safe and sound! And spit on Petersburg, and turn in my

resignation, and scamper off to Boldino, and live as a country squire! Dependency is unpleasant, especially for a man who has been independent for some twenty years. This is not a reproach to you, but muttering at my own self. I bless all of you, children.

[500]

To Alexander Nikolaevich Mordvinov
May 26, 1834. In Petersburg.

Dear Sir, Alexander Nikolaevich,

I make bold to disturb Your Excellency with a most humble request for permission for me to reprint, in one volume, my compositions in prose[1] which have been published up to now, and also for permission to provide Vilgelm Kyukhelbeker with a copy of all my compositions.[2]

With the deepest respect, I have the honor to be, Dear Sir,

Your Excellency's
Most humble servant,
May 26, 1834.   Alexander Pushkin.
SPb.

[501]

To Natalia Nikolaevna Pushkina
About (not later than) May 29, 1834.
From Petersburg to Polotnyany Zavod.

I thank you, my angel, for the good news about Masha's little tooth. Now I hope she will cut the rest of them without any trouble. Now it's Sasha's turn. Why do you get things mixed up and say, "I'm not writing about myself, because that's not interesting?" It would have been better for you to have written about yourself than about [Countess] Sollogub, about whom you get all kinds of nonsense into your head—to the laughter of all honorable people, and of the police, who are reading our letters.[1] You ask what I'm doing. Nothing worth-while, my angel. However, I stay at home and work until four o'clock. I don't go out into society; I've become unaccustomed to my frock coat; I spend the evenings in the club. The books have come from Paris, and my library is growing and getting crowded. A *Ventriloque*[2] who has made me laugh until I cried, has come to us in Petersburg; I'm truly sorry that you won't get to hear him. The bothers with regard to the estate[3] infuriate me; with your leave, it will be necessary, I'm afraid, for me to go into retirement[4] and to lay aside with a sigh my Kammerjunker court-dress uniform, which has so pleasantly flattered my self-esteem, and in which I unfortunately haven't had time to play the dandy. You're young, but you're already the mother of a family, and I'm convinced that it won't be more difficult for you to fulfill the duty of a good mother than it is for you now to fulfill the duty of an honest and good wife. Lack of independence and of order in one's domestic affairs is terrible in a household. And no successes of vanity can take the place of tranquillity and content. Here's a moral for you.—You call on me to come to you before August. I'd be glad to go to paradise, but my sins won't let me. Do you really think that swinish Petersburg is not loathsome to me? That I'm having a gay time living in it among the lampoons and denunciations to the police? You ask me about the *Peter*? It's coming along so-so. I'm accumulating materials—bringing them into order—and all at once I'll cast a bronze monument[5] which can't be dragged from one end of the city to the other, from square to square, from alley to alley. Yesterday I saw Speransky, the Karamzins, Zhukovsky, Vielgorsky, Vyazemsky—all send greetings to you. Aunty keeps on spoiling me. For my birthday she sent me a basket of melons, wild strawberries, garden strawberries—so that I'm afraid that I may meet the thirty-sixth year of my stormy life with the flux. Today I'm going to take your letter to her. Meanwhile, farewell, my darling. I am bilious; so excuse my angry letters. I send my kiss and blessing to all of you.

I am sending money in care of Dmitry Nikolaevich [Goncharov].

[502]
To Natalia Nikolaevna Pushkina
June 3, 1834. From Petersburg to Polotnyany Zavod.

What, my darling, is happening to you? This is already the ninth day that I haven't had any news of you. This disturbs me in spite of myself. Let's suppose you have left Yaropolets. All the same you could have taken time to write me a couple of lines. I haven't written you because the swinishness of the post has so chilled me that I haven't had the strength to take a pen in hand. The thought that anybody is eavesdropping on you and me *à la lettre* is driving me mad.

It's quite possible to live without political liberty; without family inviolability (*inviolabilité de la famille*) it's impossible: penal servitude is a lot better. This was written, not for you.[1] But here's what I write for you. Have you begun the mineral baths? Does Masha have any new teeth? And how did she stand cutting her first ones? Guess who is staying with me: Sergey Nikolaevich [Goncharov], who went to his brother's[2] in Tsarskoe Selo, but they quarreled, and he was compelled to flee with all his baggage. I'm very glad to have him. Checkers have been resumed. Aunty left with Natalia Kirillovna [Zagryazhskaya]. I haven't been to see her yet. Dolgorukova-Malinovskaya[3] has had a miscarriage, but she seems to be well. Today I'm dining at Vyazemsky's, whose son is having a name day; Karamzina has left, too. Have I written you that the Meshcherskys have set off for Italy, and that Sofia [Karamzina] simply gushed tears for three days together, accusing herself of hardheartedness, and feeling remorseful that she's leaving Katerina Andreevna [Karamzina] alone? I accompanied them to the steamship. Last Sunday I was presented to the Grand Duchess.[4] I went to Her Highness's on Kamenny Ostrov, in that pleasant mood in which you are accustomed to see me when I put on my magnificent full-dress uniform. But she was so pleasant that I forgot both my unhappy role and my vexation. The censor [A. I.] Krasovsky was presented together with me. The Grand Duchess said to him: *Vous devez être bien fatigué d'être obligé de lire tout ce qui paraît.—Oui, Votre Altesse Impériale*, he answered her, *d'autant plus que ce que l'on écrit maintenant n'a pas le sens commun.*[5] And I was standing beside him. She, as an intelligent woman, somehow managed to smooth it over. Smirnova is about due to have her baby. Her belly is horrible; I don't know how her delivery will be, but she is walking a lot, and she's not like what she was last year. I met Countess Sollogub not long ago. She commanded me to send you a kiss, and her aunt did the same. I'm mostly at home and in the club. I am behaving myself decently; the only thing that's not good is that my stomach has got upset and biliousness is bothering me so. But here you can't safeguard yourself against biliousness. There's no news, and even if there were, I wouldn't tell it. I kiss all of you; Christ be with all of you. My father and mother are going to the village[6] in a few days, and I'm bustling about for them. Lev [Pushkin] goes to Tsarskoe Selo on foot, and Sobolevsky to Oranienbaum. Apparently they don't have anything to do. Farewell, my angel. Don't be angry at the coldness of my letters. I'm having to force myself to write.

June 3.

[503]
To Dmitry Nikolaevich Bantysh-Kamensky
June 3, 1834. From Petersburg to Moscow.

Dear Sir, Dmitry Nikolaevich,

I do not know how to thank you enough for furnishing me with the documents regarding Pugachev.[1] Although I already had a multitude of precious materials in my hands, I found here hitherto unknown details of curious interest, which I shall utilize without fail. I have given Smirdin your excellent article about [P. I.] Panin.[2] He accepted it with thanks. Won't you consent to participate in his journal, and on what conditions?

You have probably heard about Plyushar's commercial and literary undertaking, the Russian *Conversations Lexicon*:[3] a great multitude of biographical articles prepared by you might enter into the make-up of this lexicon. Won't you enter into relationships with Plyushar? In case you will, I request that you choose me as your agent;[4] we are glad to do our best.[5]

With the most profound respect and complete devotion, I have the honor to be, Dear Sir,

Your Excellency's
Most humble servant,
June 3, 1834.   Alexander Pushkin.
SPb.

[504]
To Natalia Nikolaevna Pushkina
June 8, 1834. From Petersburg to Polotnyany Zavod.

My dear angel! I have written you a four-page letter, but it turned out to be so bitter and gloomy that I did not send it to you, and I'm writing you another. I definitely have the spleen.[1] It is boring to live without you and not even to dare to write you everything that comes into my heart.[2] You speak of Boldino. It would be good to settle down there for good, but that is hard to do. We shall have time to talk more about it. Do not be angry, wife, and do not interpret my complaints the wrong way. I have never thought of reproaching you for my dependent state. I had to marry you because without you I would have been unhappy all my life. But I did not have to enter the service, and what is still worse, to entangle myself with financial obligations. The situation of dependency caused by family life makes a man more moral. The situation of dependency which we impose on ourselves from ambition or from need lowers us. Now they look on me as a flunky, whom they may treat as they please. Disgrace is easier to bear than disdain. Like Lomonosov, I do not want to be a clown, even before the Lord God.[3] But you are not to blame in any of this. I am to blame, because of the good nature with which I am filled to the point of stupidity, notwithstanding my experience in life.

I thank you for the scales, a luxurious token of my stinginess. Aunty sent them to me without a note. Probably she is now in the midst of cares and is preparing Natalia Kirillovna for the news of the death of Prince Kochubey, who did not reach you as he had intended, but died in Moscow. I am not sending you any money yet. I have been compelled to outfit my old folks[4] for the road. I am being pestered mercilessly. Probably I shall heed you and soon give up the management of the estate. Let them make a mess of things as they please. It will suffice for their lifetime. And we shall try to leave Sashka and Mashka a piece of bread, shan't we? There is no news. [Count] Fiquelmont is ill and horribly depressed. Vielgorsky is going to Italy to his sick wife.[5] Petersburg is deserted; everybody is in summer houses. I stay at home and write until four o'clock. I dine at Dumé's. In the evening I am at the club. And that is my whole day. I took the notion, for relaxation, to play cards in the club, but I have been compelled to stop. Card playing agitates me—and my biliousness does not abate. I send my kiss and blessing to all of you. Farewell. I am expecting a letter from you about Yaropolets. But be careful . . . your letters are probably being unsealed, too. National security requires it.

[505]

To Natalia Nikolaevna Pushkina

June 11, 1834. From Petersburg to Polotnyany Zavod.

You've found something to scold about! . . . The Summer Garden[1] and Sobolevsky. To be sure, the Summer Garden is my kitchen garden. When I get up after my nap, I go there in my dressing gown and house slippers. After dinner I take a nap in it, I read and write there. I'm at home in it. And Sobolevsky? Sobolevsky is one thing, and I'm another.[2] He makes his schemes, and I make mine. My scheme is to scamper off to the village to you. What is it you write me about Kaluga? Why should you care to see it? Kaluga is a little more loathsome than Moscow, which is much more loathsome than Petersburg. What is there for you to do there? It's your sisters who are prodding you on, and probably my favorite one, at that.[3] That's just like her. I ask you, my darling, not to go to Kaluga. Stay at home. It will be better that way. Aunty's at her summer house, but I haven't been to see her yet. I'm going today with your letters. Natalia Kirillovna [Zagryazhskaya] has learned of Kochubey's death. *Je ne croyais pas*, she said, *que la mort de Kochubey me fit tant de peine*.[4] She is consoling herself that he was the one that died, and not Masha.[5] Today my folks[6] are going to the village, and I'm going to accompany them—to the carriage, not to Tsarskoe Selo, to which place Lev Sergeevich [Pushkin] goes on foot. Oh, how they have pestered me; I was reminded of you, my angel. But there is nothing else to be done. If I don't take over the estate,[7] then it will be lost, with nothing to show for it. Olga Sergeevna and Lev Sergeevich will have to be turned out to graze, and then I'll have them on my hands, and then how much grief and expense I'll have— but a lot they'll care. They'll jeer at me. Oh, my family, my family!

Please, my darling, don't make a trip to Kaluga. Whom do you want to have anything to do with there? The governor's wife?[8] She's very pleasant and intelligent, but I don't see any reason for you to go pay your respects to her. With Dmitry Nikolaevich's fiancée?[9] Now, that's a different matter. You arrange this wedding, and I'll come and be his sponsor at the wedding. Write me, little wife, how you spent your time in Yaropolets, how you got along with your mother and the others. I hope you parted in friendly fashion and didn't manage to quarrel and get jealous of each other. Here the Prussian Prince[10] is expected. Yesterday Ozerov[11] arrived from Berlin with his wife who is three embraces in girth. A real woman. Looking at her, I thought of you and wanted you to return from the Zavod just such a fat slob. Enough of your being lean as a rake. Farewell, wife. My spirits have brightened up. I've received letters from you two days in a row, and with all my heart I've become reconciled with the mails and with the police.[12] The devil take them. What are the children doing? I bless them, and I kiss you.

June 11.
The same day.

Aunty has just now left me. She asks you to write her, and me to pull your ears. She's moving to Tsarskoe Selo, to Prince Kochubey's house, along with Natalia Kirillovna [Zagryazhskaya], who is astonishingly pleasant and kind. Tomorrow I'll go say farewell to her. Why don't you write Aunty? What a scatterbrain you are! She asks me to let you go to Kaluga, but, after all, you'll dash off, even without my permission. You're gifted at that. I have just said farewell to my father and mother. He is depressed, and his thoughts are melancholy. You know what I'm thinking? Shouldn't I come to you for the summer? No, wife, there are things to be done. Let's stick it out another month and a half. And then I'll come to you like a bolt from the blue. If only they will let me. Why should you want to install your sisters in the Palace?[13] In the first place, they'll probably be refused, and in the second, if they are accepted, then think what vile talk will spread over swinish Petersburg. You're too pretty, my angel, to go in for being a petitioner. Wait a little. You'll become a widow, you'll get a little older—then go ahead and be a beggar in rags and tatters, and a titular counsellor's[14] wife. My advice to you and your sisters is to stay as far away from the Court as you can; there's little good in it. You three aren't wealthy. All of you shouldn't tumble in on Aunty. My God! If the Zavod were mine, then you wouldn't lure me to Petersburg even with a Moscow *kalač*.[15] I'd live as a country squire! But you females don't understand the happiness of independence and are ready to bind yourself to eternal servitude, just in order that it might be said about you: *Hier Madame une telle était décidément la plus belle et la mieux mise du bal.*[16] Farewell, *Madame une telle*, Aunty has sent me your letter, for which I thank you very much.

Stay well, intelligent, sweet. Don't ride on spirited horses. Look after the children so that their nursemaids will look after them. Write me oftener. Kiss your sisters for me without ado—and Dmitry Nikolaevich, too. Bless the children for me. I send you a kiss. I'm going on the steamship to accompany Vielgorsky, who probably won't find his wife alive.[17] *Peter I* is coming along; the first thing you know I'll publish the first volume by winter. I've ceased to be angry with *him*,[18] because, *toute réflexion faite*, it's not he that's to blame for the swinishness surrounding him. But if you live in a privy, in spite of yourself you'll get used to s——, and its stench won't bother you, even though you are a *gentleman*.[19] Ugh, I'd like to scamper off to where the air is fresh.

[506]
To Natalia Nikolaevna Pushkina
About (not later than) June 19, 1834.
From Petersburg to Polotnyany Zavod.

I'm sad, little wife. You're sick; the children are sick. How all this will end, God knows. Here I am being pestered and infuriated without mercy. My debts and others' give me no peace. The estate is disorganized, and there is need to cut expenses and bring it into order, but they've taken cheer and begun badgering me. Now it's one thing, now it's another. Here's Spassky's letter for you.[1] If you're well, what do you need baths for? I saw Aunty a few days ago. She's going to Tsarskoe Selo. Farewell, little wife. Pletnev is coming into my room now.

A.P.

I send a kiss to all of you, and my blessing to the children.

[507]
To Alexander Khristoforovich Benkendorf
June 25, 1834. In Petersburg.
(In French)

Count,

Since family matters necessitate my presence, now in Moscow, now in the interior, I am forced to retire from the service, and I beseech Your Excellency to obtain this permission for me.

I would ask, as a last favor, that the permission which His Majesty has deigned to grant me, of visiting the archives, not be withdrawn from me.[1]

I am, respectfully,

Count,

Your Excellency's

Most humble and most obedient servant,

June 15.[2]   Alexander Pushkin.

St. Petersburg.

[508]

To NATALIA NIKOLAEVNA PUSHKINA
About (not later than) June 27, 1834.
From Petersburg to Polotnyany Zavod.

"Your Honor, you always deign to yowl about nothing" (*The Adolescent*).[1]

For pity's sake, what indeed are you scolding me about? Because I missed one post? But, after all, we have the post every day, so that you can write as much as you please and when you please. It's not the way it is from Kaluga, from which letters come every ten days. Your next to the last letter was so sweet that I would have given you a good kissing, and this one is so scatterbrained that I'd like to pull your ears. I'll answer you point by point. When I was presented to the Grand Duchess,[2] the Lady in Waiting on duty was not [Countess] Sollogub, but my cousin by marriage Chicherina,[3] whom I'm not very fond of, and even if Sollogub had been on duty, why then if one is to fall in love. . . . — — — Oh, little wife! The post prevents, otherwise I would really give you an earful. I wrote you that I've become unaccustomed to a frock coat, and you try to catch me in a lie as in a *petite misère ouverte*,[4] adducing as evidence that I saw this person and that person, and consequently I am going out in society. That doesn't prove anything. The main thing is that I've again become accustomed to Dumé's and to the English Club—and that's nothing to brag about. Smirnova has been delivered successfully, and just imagine: of twins. What do you think of the little woman, and what of the red-eyed rabbit, Smirnov? They so fashioned the first child that he couldn't get out, and this time they had to divide it into two.[5] Today is I think the ninth day—and the report is that the mother and children are well. You write me that you're thinking of marrying off Katerina Nikolaevna to Khlyustin,[6] and Alexandra Nikolaevna to Ubri.[7] Nothing of the sort will happen. Both men will fall in love with you. You are hindering your sisters—because one must be your husband, to court others in your presence, my beauty. Khlyustin is lying to you, and you even believe him. Where does he get the notion that I won't come to you in August? Can it be that he was drunk on cold-fish-and-vegetable-soup-with-onions? One thing is keeping me in Petersburg: mortgaging the Nizhny Novgorod estate.[8] I even intend to entrust my Pugachev to [M. L.] Yakovlev,[9] and tear off to Polotnyany Zavod to you, my angel.

That's where I'd like to scamper away from life, to slip away to! I send you and the children a kiss, and I send my blessing to all of you with all my heart. I'll bet you have grown so good-looking in the village that nobody ever heard of the like. Thank you for the anecdote about Dmitry Nikolaevich.[10] Hasn't he fallen in love? Aunty's in Tsarskoe Selo. I'm going to see her in a few days. *Addio, vita mia; ti amo.*[11]

[509]

To Natalia Nikolaevna Pushkina

About June 28, 1834. From Petersburg to Polotnyany Zavod.

My angel, I have just now sent Count Litta an excuse to the effect that I cannot be at the Petergof celebration,[1] on account of illness. I'm sorry that you won't see it; it's worth seeing. I don't even know whether you'll ever succeed in seeing it. I'm thinking strongly about resigning.[2] We must think about our children's fate. My father's estate, as I have ascertained, is in disorder to the point of impossibility, and only by strict economy can it be straightened out. I may have large sums, but we run through a lot, too. If I were to die today, what would happen to you? It's little consolation that they would bury me in a striped caftan and in the crowded Petersburg cemetery, at that, and not in a church in the open spaces as is fitting for a decent person.[3] You're an intelligent and good woman. You understand what necessity is. Let me become wealthy—and then perhaps we might go on a spending spree to our hearts' content. Petersburg is horribly boring. They say that the world is living on the Petergof road. On Chernaya Rechka are only Bobrinskaya[4] and [Countess]

Ficquelmont. They recieve—but nobody comes. There will be great celebrations after Petergof. But I certainly won't go anywhere. One thing is holding me here: the printing house.[5] My error, one more thing: the mortgaging of the estate.[6] But will it be possible to mortgage it? How right you were, that I ought not to have taken onto myself all these bothers, for which nobody will say thanks, and which have already spoiled so much of my blood that all the leeches in our house couldn't suck it out for me. Apropos of our house: I must tell you that I've quarreled with our landlord,[7] and here's why. A few days ago I was returning home at night. The doors were locked. I knocked and knocked; I rang and rang. With difficulty I at long last succeeded in awakening the yardman. And I had already told him several times not to lock up before I come in. In my anger with him I gave him a father's punishment. The next day I discovered that Olivio was declaiming against me in his yard and had ordered the yardman not to heed me but to lock up the doors about 10 o'clock, so that thieves won't steal the staircases. I immediately ordered that an announcement be nailed to the doors, written in Sergey Nikolaevich's hand, that the apartment is for rent—and I wrote Olivio a letter which the fool hasn't answered up to now. My war with the yardman hasn't ceased, and yesterday I had some trouble with him again. I'm sorry for him, but there's nothing to be done. I'm stubborn, and I want to out-argue the whole household—including thereby even the leeches. I'm entirely at fault toward you, with regard to money. There was money . . . and I lost it at cards. But what was I to do? I was so bilious that I had to amuse myself with something. He[8] is to blame for everything. But God forgive him. If he would only let me go to my estate. Your letter isn't before me. It seems that there's something that I'm obliged to object to—but until tomorrow. Meanwhile, farewell. I kiss you and the children, I bless all three. Farewell, my darling. Give my regards to your sisters and brothers. Sergey Nikolaevich was commissioned an officer a few days ago,[9] and he's fussing about, getting a full-dress uniform.

A.P.

[510]

To Natalia Nikolaevna Pushkina
June 30, 1834. From Petersburg to Polotnyany Zavod.

Your Shishkova[1] was mistaken: I have not been paying court to her daughter Polina, because I haven't seen her. But I made a trip to the Academy, to see Alexander Semenovich Shishkov, and I did that, not for a wedding, but for jettons,[2] *pas autrement*.[3] The story about the princesses[4] is entirely correct, but I don't see anything funny in it. Thank you for your sweet, very sweet letter. Of course, my dear, there's no consolation in my life except you—and to live separated from you is just as stupid as it is hard to bear. But what can be done? After tomorrow I'll begin printing my *Pugachev*, which has been lying at Speransky's[5] until now. It will delay me about a month. In August I'll be with you. Tomorrow is the Petergof celebration, but I'll spend it in Pletnev's summer house with him alone. We'll drink to your health. I have quarreled with our landlord, Olivio, once and for all, and we'll have to have another apartment, especially if your sisters come with you. Sergey [N. Goncharov] is still with me; yesterday he came to see me in his officer's full-dress uniform, and he's a fine-looking fellow. The story of how Ivan Nikolaevich quarreled with Yuriev[6] and how they became reconciled is killingly funny, but it would take too long to tell it to you. I have discomfiting news from the village. The new manager whom I sent found everything in such disorder that he refused the management and left.[7] I'm thinking of following his example. He's an intelligent man; Boldino could muss up five more years.

Farewell, little wife. I thank you for promising not to coquette. Even though I have permitted you to do that, all the same it's better not to make use of my permission. I am glad that Sashka has been weaned. It was long overdue. And that the wet nurse would get drunk as she would go off to sleep—that's no misfortune, either. The boy will get used to wine, and will be a fine fellow and favor Lev Sergeevich [Pushkin]. Tell Mashka not to be capricious, or else I'll come, and it'll be bad for her. I bless all of you—I kiss you especially.

June 30.

Please don't demand tender love letters of me. The thought that my letters are being unsealed and read in the post, among the police, and so on, numbs me, and I'm dry and boring in spite of myself. Just you wait. I'll go into retirement, and then corresponding won't be necessary.

[511]
To Mikhail Lukianovich Yakovlev
July 3, 1834. In Petersburg.

Dear Sir, Mikhaylo Lukianovich,[1]

In consequence of the commission which the authorities have entrusted to you with regard to the publishing of my manuscript, entitled *The History of the Pugachev Revolt*, and in accordance with my conversation in person with you on this matter, I hasten to inform you:

1st. I desire that the aforesaid manuscript be printed in 8-vo, with the same kind of format as *The Code of Laws*.

2nd. I fix the number of copies at 3000; I request that paper for 1200 of them be stocked at government expense, and I shall myself deliver to the printing house the necessary quantity of paper for 1800 copies.

3rd. As for the type font and the publishing of the book in general, I rely on your discretion for everything.

I have the honor to be, with the most profound respect,
Dear Sir,
Your most obedient servant,
Alexander Pushkin.

July 3, 1834.
SPb.

[512]
To Alexander Khristoforovich Benkendorf
July 3, 1834. In Petersburg.
(In French)

Count,

Several days ago I had the honor to make application to Your Excellency, in order to obtain permission to retire from the service. This step being improper, I beseech you, Count, not to act upon it. I prefer seeming inconsistent to seeming ungrateful.[1]

However, a leave of absence of several months would be absolutely necessary for me.

> I am, respectfully,
> Count,
> Your Excellency's
> Most humble and most obedient servant,

July 3.   Alexander Pushkin.

[513]

To Vasily Andreevich Zhukovsky
July 4, 1834. From Petersburg to Tsarskoe Selo.

When I received your letter, I immediately wrote to Count Benkendorf, asking him to stop my retirement, *ma démarche étant inconsidérée*, and I said *que j'aimais mieux avoir l'air inconséquent qu'ingrat*.[1] But after this I received official notification that I shall receive my retirement, but that access to the archives will be forbidden me.[2] This grieved me in all respects. I submitted my resignation in a moment of spleen and vexation at everybody and everything. My domestic circumstances are difficult. My position is not a cheering one. A change in my mode of living is almost a necessity. I lacked the courage to explain all this to Count Benkendorf—and for this reason my letter must have seemed dry; whereas, it was simply stupid.

But I certainly had no intention of bringing about what has resulted. I don't dare, I swear, to write a letter directly to the Sovereign[3]—especially now. My justifications would be like petitions, and he has already done so much for me. Lizaveta Mikhaylovna [Khitrovo] has just now gone from me. She brought me your two further letters. This, of course, touches me. But just what am I to do! I shall write again to Count Benkendorf.

[514]

To Alexander Khristoforovich Benkendorf
July 4, 1834. In Petersburg.

Dear Sir, Count Alexander Khristoforovich,

I was honored with receiving last evening Your Excellency's letter of June 30.[1] I am extremely grieved that my ill-considered petition, forced from me by unpleasant circumstances and vexing petty cares, could appear to be insane ingratitude and opposition to the will of him who has until now been rather my benefactor than Sovereign. I shall await the determination of my fate, but in any case nothing will change the feeling of my deep devotion to the Tsar or my filial gratitude for his previous favors.

With the most profound respect and complete devotion, I have the honor to be, Dear Sir,

Your Excellency's
Most humble servant,

July 4, 1834.   Alexander Pushkin.
SPb.

[515]

To Mikhail Lukianovich Yakovlev
July 5, 1834. In Petersburg.

Here, my benefactor, is the first chapter for you[1]—God speed it.

[516]

To Vasily Andreevich Zhukovsky
July 6, 1834. From Petersburg to Tsarskoe Selo.

I myself truly don't know what's happening to me. What crime—what ingratitude—is there in going into retirement when my circumstances, the future fate of my family, and my own peace of mind demand it? But the Sovereign is nevertheless able to see in this something resembling what I cannot understand. In that case I do not submit my resignation, but I ask to be left in the service. Now, why are my letters dry? And just why should they be running like snot? In the depths of my heart I feel myself in the right toward the Tsar. His wrath grieves me, but the worse my position is, the more tongue-tied and numb-tongued I become. What am I to do? Ask forgiveness? All right. But for what? I'll go see Benkendorf and explain to him what I have on my heart—but I don't know wherein my letters are improper. I'll try to write the third.[1]

[517]
To Alexander Khristoforovich Benkendorf
July 6, 1834. In Petersburg.
(In French)

Count,

Permit me to speak to you with open heart. In asking to retire,[1] I was thinking only of troublesome and distressing family affairs. I had in view only the inconvenience of being obliged to make a number of trips while attached to the service. I swear on my God and on my soul that that was my only thought; it gives me profound sorrow to see it interpreted so cruelly. The Emperor has showered me with favors since the first moment his royal thought directed itself upon me. Among these favors are some which I cannot think of without profound emotion, for he placed so much straightforwardness and generosity in them. He has always been my providence, and if in the course of these eight years I have happened to murmur, never, I swear it, has a feeling of bitterness been mixed with those feelings which I have pledged toward him. And at this moment, not the idea of losing an all-powerful protector fills me with sorrow, but that of leaving in his mind an impression which, fortunately, I have not deserved.

I repeat, Count, my most humble entreaty that the request which I so thoughtlessly made not be acted upon.

Commending myself to your powerful protection, I make bold to present to you the assurance of my high esteem.

I am, respectfully,
Count,
Your Excellency's
Most humble and most obedient servant,
July 6.   Alexander Pushkin.
SPb.

[518]
To Mikhail Nikolaevich Zagoskin
July 9, 1834. From Petersburg to Moscow.

Dear Sir, Mikhaylo Nikolaevich,

You were kind enough to remember me, and you sent me your

most recent, excellent work,[1] but you have not heard any thanks from me. You have the full right to consider me an ignoramus, a barbarian, and an ingrate, But my friend Sobolevsky is to blame, who every day says he is off for Moscow—but it is already more than six months since he took from me the letter which he promised to deliver to you without delay.[2]

I apply to you about an important matter. M. Alexandre, a very noteworthy person (or even persons)[3] is planning to go to Moscow, and he offers you the following conditions: the gross receipts for the performances to be halved with the management (the expenses of the performance at its expense) and a benefit performance. Honor me with your answer and console little Mother Moscow.

With the most profound esteem and complete devotion, I have the honor to be, Dear Sir,

Your Excellency's
Most humble servant,
July 9. Alexander Pushkin.

[519]
To Natalia Nikolaevna Pushkina
July 11, 1834. From Petersburg to Polotnyany Zavod.

You, my little wife, are most featherbrained (I had trouble in writing the word). Now you get angry with me over [Countess] Sollogub, now over the briefness of my letters, now over my cold style, now because I don't come to you. Think everything over, and you'll see that toward you I'm not only in the right, but you might even say a saint. I'm not coquetting with Sollogub, because I don't see her at all. I write briefly and coldly on account of circumstances which you are well aware of.[1] I don't come to you on account of business affairs, for I'm printing *Pugachev*, and I'm mortgaging the estates, and I'm in the midst of cares and bothers. And your letter grieved me, but at the same time it gladdened me, too. If you cried from not receiving a letter from me, it follows that you still love me, little wife. For that I kiss your little hands and feet.

If you could see how diligent I have become; how I am reading proofs—how I am hurrying Yakovlev along! Only that I may be with you in August. Now I'll tell you about yesterday's ball. I was at the Ficquelmonts'. You must bear in mind that since your departure I have not been going anywhere except to the club. Here yesterday, when I entered the illuminated hall, with the elegantly dressed ladies, I was as full of confusion as a German professor; with difficulty I found the hostess, with difficulty I muttered a few words. Then I looked things over and saw that not all that many people were there, and that the ball was one without ceremony and not a rout.[2] There were several Prussian ladies whom I didn't know (our ladies are better looking, to say nothing of you), and dressed like Ermolova[3] in desperate days. Then I ate my fill of ices, and I came home—at one. I don't think there's anything to chide me about. In society they inquire about you a lot, and are eagerly awaiting you. I tell them that you went off to Kaluga to dance. All praise you for that. And they say: " 'At a girl!" And my heart rejoices. Aunty dropped in to see me yesterday, and she chatted with me in her carriage. I complained to her about my mode of living, and she consoled me. A few days ago I came within a hair's breadth of committing a disastrous thing: I came within a hair's breadth of quarreling with *him*. And how I had to show the white feather! And I became depressed.[4] If I quarrel with this one—I won't live to see another. But I can't be angry with him long—even though he's not in the right. Today I was at Pletnev's summer house; it was his daughter's[5] name day. Only instead of him, I found his one-eyed girl cousin[6]—and nothing else. He had left for Oranienbaum—to teach the Grand Duchess.[7] It was vexing, but there was nothing to be done. Farewell, little wife—I'm sleepy. I send you and the children a kiss—and my blessing to all of you. Christ be with you.

July 11.

[520]

TO PRASKOVIA ALEXANDROVNA OSIPOVA
June 29 and July 13, 1834. From Petersburg to Trigorskoe.
(In French)

I thank you with all my heart, dear, good, and kind Praskovia Alexandrovna, for the letter which you were so kind as to write me. I see that you still keep the same friendship and the same interest in me. I am going to answer you frankly, as to what regards Reichman. I know him to be an honest man, and for the moment that is all I need. I cannot have confidence in either Mikhail[1] or Penkovsky, seeing that I know the first and do not know the second. Having no intention to to go Boldino and settle down, I cannot even consider restoring an estate, which, be it said between us, is bordering on complete ruin. I wish only not to be robbed, and to pay the interest to the Loan Office. The improvements will come later. But be calm: Reichman has just written me that the peasants are in such a state of misery and affairs are in such bad condition, that he could not undertake the administering of Boldino, and that at this moment he is at Malinniki.[2]

You cannot imagine how much administering this estate is weighing on me. There is no doubt that Boldino deserves to be saved, if only for Olga and Lev, who have for their prospect beggary or, at the very least, poverty. But I am not rich. I have a family of my own dependent on me, and which without me would fall into destitution. I have taken an estate which will produce only anxieties and unpleasantnesses. My parents do not know that they are on the verge of total ruin. If they could take it upon themselves to remain for several years at Mikhaylovskoe, affairs might be managed, but that will never be.

I am counting on seeing you this summer,[3] and as a matter of course, to stop at Trigorskoe. Please present my regards to all your family and accept once more my thanks and the expression of my respect and unalterable friendship.

June 29.   A.P.
SPb.

July 13. This letter should have been at your house two weeks ago. I do not know why it is not yet on its way. My affairs will keep me in Petersburg for some time yet. But I still plan to present myself at your door.

[521]

To Natalia Nikolaevna Pushkina
About (not later than) July 14, 1834.
From Petersburg to Polotnyany Zavod.

You want to know without fail whether I'll be at your feet soon? Gladly, my beauty. I'm mortgaging my father's estate; that will be finished within a week. I'm publishing *Pugachev*; that will take a whole month. Little wife, little wife, have patience until the middle of August, and then how I'll come to you and embrace you and what a kissing I'll give the children! Do you really think that I like bachelor life so terribly much? I sleep and dream of coming to you. And if only I might remain in one of your villages near Moscow, I would light a candle to God; I'd be glad to go to heaven, but my sins won't permit me.[1] Let me make some money, not for myself but for you. I have little love for money—but I esteem in it the sole means of decent independence. And about which neighbor are you writing me arch letters? With whom are you frightening me? From here I can see what sort of thing it is. A man of some thirty-six years. A retired military man or a civil servant in an elective post. With a paunch and in a military cap. He has three hundred souls and he's en route to remortgage them—on account of a poor harvest. And on the eve of departing he sentimentalizes in front of you. Isn't this correct? And you, my little wench, for lack of *him*[2] or another, choose even him as an adorer: good going. And how is it that balls have not palled on you, that you go even to Kaluga for them. Astonishing!—I must talk to you about my woe. A few days ago the spleen took possession of me; I submitted my resignation. But I received such a tongue-lashing from Zhukovsky and such a dry dismissal from Benkendorf that I had to show the white feather, and I am begging for Christ's and God's sake that they not retire me. And you're even glad of it, aren't you? All right, if I live twenty-five more years; but if I curl up my toes in less than ten, I don't know what you'll do, and what Mashka and especially what Sashka will say. There will be little consolation for them in little papa's having been buried as the court jester and in their little mama's having been terribly pretty at the Anichkov balls.[3] Well, there's nothing to be done. God is great; the most important thing is that I don't want them to be able to suspect me of ingratitude. That's worse than liberalism.[4] Stay well. Kiss the children and bless them for me. Farewell; I send you a kiss.

A.P.

[522]
To Natalia Nikolaevna Pushkina
July 14, 1834. From Petersburg to Polotnyany Zavod.
All you ladies are cut to the same pattern. How very interesting

are the little fool D.'s[1] adventures and his family quarrels! But how glad you are of them. How you've burst out coquetting, too, I'll bet. How about Kaluga? So you will reign there a while? Little wife, I'm not chiding you for that, though. All that's in the nature of things. Be young, because you are young—and reign, because you're beautiful. I kiss you with all my heart. Now let's talk about a serious matter. If you really have taken the notion of bringing your sisters here, then it's impossible for us to remain at Olivio's.[2] There's no room. But are you bringing both your sisters? Hey, little wife, look here. . . . My opinion is that a family must be *alone* under *one* roof: the husband, the wife, the children while they're small; the parents, when they have become very aged. Otherwise there will be no end of bothers, and there'll be no domestic tranquillity. We'll talk some more about this, though. Yakovlev promises to let me go to you in August. I'll leave *Pugachev* in his care. August is close. Thank God, we've waited it out. I hope you're pure and innocent toward me and that we'll meet as we parted. It seems to me that you are beginning to like Sashka. I am glad. He's a lot nicer than Mashka, who'll lead you a merry dance. Smirnova again came within a hair's breadth of dying. She became angry with the doctor, and her blood rushed to her head; thank God it wasn't her milk.[3] She's receiving now, but I haven't been to see her yet. Today there are fireworks—Sergey Nikolaevich [Goncharov] is going to see them, but I'll stay in the city. With us it's the third day of terrific heat—and we don't know what to do. I sleep and dream of getting away from Petersburg to you. But you don't believe me, and you scold me. Today I'll make a trip to Pletnev's. We'll talk about you. I'm having great bothers with regard to Boldino. In a year I'll spit on the whole thing—and I'll get busy on my own affairs. Lev Sergeevich is behaving very badly. Of money, he doesn't have a single kopek, but he loses fourteen bottles of champagne at a time at dominoes at Dumé's. I don't say anything to him, because, thank God, the fellow is thirty. But I'm sorry for him, and I'm vexed. Sobolevsky is directing him, and just what they do, God only knows. Both are empty-headed enough. Aunty is in Tsarskoe Selo. I keep on planning to go to see her, but I don't ever get there. Farewell. I hug you tight—I bless the children —you, too. Do you pray every day, standing in the corner?

July 14.

[523]

To Natalia Nikolaevna Pushkina
About (not later than) July 26, 1834.
From Petersburg to Polotnyany Zavod.

My angel Natasha, do you know what? I'm taking the story[1] now being occupied by the Vyazemskys. The Princess is going abroad; her daughter[2] is seriously ill; they're afraid it's consumption. God grant that the South help her. Today I dreamed she had died, and I awoke in horror. For God's sake, take care of yourself. Woman, says Galiani, *est un animal naturellement faible et malade.*[3] What kind of helpers or workers are the lot of you? You work only with your little feet at balls, and you help your husband squander. And thank you for that. Please don't be angry with me because I'm slow in coming to you. Truly, my soul is longing, but my purse forbids. I'm working my pants off.[4] I'm reading the proofs of the two volumes[5] at once, writing notes, mortgaging villages—sending Lev Sergeich packing to Georgia.[6] I'll take care of everything—and I'll come galloping headlong to you.—Just now proofs were brought to me, and I left you for *Pugachev.* I have read in the proofs that "Pugachev entrusted to Khlopusha the plundering of the factories."[7] I'm entrusting to you the plundering of the Factories—do you hear, my Khlo-Pushkina? Plunder the Factories and return with the booty.[8] I don't go out in society. Smirnova has commanded that I be told that she's writing me into the category of foreigners who are not to be received. She's well, but she came within a hair's breadth of dying (*animal naturellement faible et malade*). I kiss Masha, and I laugh at her pranks, sight unseen. She's an intelligent wench. But for the time being it's not intelligence I want of her, but health. Are you satisfied with your German woman and the wet nurse? You did badly in not getting rid of the wet nurse. How can you believe the promises and tears of a drunkard, and keep her with the children? Hush, I'll settle all that. Nine sheets remain between me and you. That is, when I have examined nine printed sheets and have written at the bottom *print*, then I'll dash off to you. And meanwhile I'll request a leave of absence. There is no news of any kind—except that poor Marshal Maison[9] came very near to getting crushed to death on maneuvers. See what fine fellows ours are! I kiss you and them. The Lord bless all of you.

[524]

To Natalia Nikolaevna Pushkina
About (not later than) July 30, 1834.
From Petersburg to Polotnyany Zavod.

What does this mean, wife? Here it's already more than a week since I've received any letters from you. Where are you? How are you? In Kaluga? In the village? Respond. What could so occupy and amuse you? What balls? What conquests? You aren't ill, are you? Christ be with you. Or do you simply want to make me hurry and come to you? Please, little wife, away with these military stratagems which, all joking aside, torment me, seven hundred miles away from you. I'll come to you as soon as Yakovlev lets me off. My affairs are progressing well. The two volumes[1] are being printed at once. For one week's difference, don't make me abandon everything and then moan a whole year, if not two or three. Be sensible. I'm very busy. I work all morning—until four o'clock—and I don't allow anybody in to see me. Then I dine at Dumé's. Next I play billiards in the club. I return home early, hoping to find a letter from you—and every day I'm disappointed. How lonesome I am.

I've already come to an agreement with Prince Vyazemsky. I'm taking his apartment.[2] By August 10 I'll have 2500 rubles laid up for him. I'll have our things moved, and I myself will gallop off to you. There's not long to wait.

Farewell. All of you, keep well. I kiss your portrait,[3] which somehow seems at fault. Look to it ——

[525]

To Natalia Nikolaevna Pushkina
August 3, 1834. From Petersburg to Polotnyany Zavod.

You ought to be ashamed, little wife. You get angry with me, without investigating which is at fault—I or the post—and you leave me for two weeks without any news about you and the children. I have been so disturbed that I haven't known what to think. Your letter calmed me, but it didn't console me. The description of your trip to Kaluga, however comic, is not at all amusing to me. Why should you want to gad about to a foul, provincial little town, in order to see vile actors vilely performing an old, vile opera? Why should you want to stop at an inn, go visiting merchants' daughters, observe with the mob the provincial fireworks, when in Petersburg you would never even think of paying any attention to the Karatygins[1] and you wouldn't be lured into a carriage by any fireworks. I asked you not to make trips to any Kalugas, but that's apparently just the kind of nature you have. There's nothing for me to say with regard to your coquettish relationships with your neighbor. I myself gave you permission to coquette—but I don't at all need to read a sheet covered on both sides with detailed description of it. After chiding you, I take you tenderly by the ears and kiss you—thanking you that you pray to God on your knees in the middle of the room. I pray to God too little, and I hope that your pure prayer is better than my prayers are, both for me and for us. You are expecting me at the beginning of August. Here it's already the third now, and I still am not getting under way; Yakovlev will let me off about the middle of the month. But even then I won't be completely free. I've taken the Vyazemskys' apartment.[2] I'll have to move myself and the furniture and books, and then I'll cross myself and set off on the trip. God grant that I arrive by your name day;[3] that would make me happy.

The Vyazemskys are here. Poor Polina[4] is very weak and pale. It's pitiful to look at her father. How crushed he looks. They're all going abroad. God grant that the climate may help her. Maria [Vyazemskaya] has grown prettier, and in poor and slighted Moscow she has produced a great effect. Talk is still clattering about you, after your momentary appearance. They found that you had become thin—I'll bring you back a fat slob, as you promised. Look to it! Don't make a liar of me. A few days ago I met Mme. George. She stopped me on the street and asked about your health; I said that in a few days I'm going to you *pour te faire un enfant.* She began to curtsey, and said over and over: *Ah, Monsi, vous me ferez une grande plaisir.*[5] However, I'm afraid of a lying-in for you, after you've had a miscarriage. I hope, however, that you've rested up. I've seen Smirnova; she's begun to recuperate, but she looks bad and yellow. Aunty has returned from Tsarskoe Selo, and she has been to see me. She's very sweet, but she has become completely fed up with Natalia Kirillovna [Zagryazhskaya]. Natalia Kirillovna is angry with everybody, especially with Prince Kochubey: how could he die and thereby grieve her Masha?[6] She pouts at the Princess, too, and says: *Mon Dieu, mais nous toutes nous avons perdu nos maris et cependant nous nous sommes consolées.*[7] Aunty says that you don't write her at all. That's not good. And she is always putting herself to trouble for you. Sergey [Goncharov] is in camp. I do not see your brother Ivan. Farewell; Christ be with you. I kiss all of you, you especially. They've brought some proof sheets.[8]

August 3.

[526]

To Mikhail Lukianovich Yakovlev

About (not later than) August 12, 1834. In Petersburg.

And just why? Voltaire was a very respectable man, and his relations with Catherine are a matter of history.[1]

[527]

To Mikhail Lukianovich Yakovlev

Between August 10 and 20, 1834. In Petersburg.

Here's the eighteenth sheet.[1] I've checked it against the other copies,[2] and I didn't find any sense there, either. Voltaire's name (you're right, favorite of the Muses!)[3] will have to be removed from the Preface,[4] though I love him very much.

Letter 476

1. As a result of this letter and a visit to Benkendorf, Pushkin received from the Tsar a loan of twenty thousand rubles, to pay for the publication of his *History of Pugachev*.

Letter 477

1. Stepan Dmitrievich Nechaev (1792-1860) was the Head Procurator of the Holy Synod, and also a poet and archaeologist.

2. Fedor Fedotovich Lebedev. This letter gives another instance of Pushkin's generous willingness to use his influence in favor of almost anyone who sought it.

Letter 478

1. This letter is Pushkin's official request for a loan for the publication of his *History of Pugachev*. It was written after Pushkin's personal conference with Benkendorf on February 26. See Letter 476.

Letter 478a

1. This letter was discovered and first published in 1956. It is the only letter which has been so far discovered, from Pushkin to Countess Vorontsova. Pushkin had been in love with her in 1824 ("Elise" is included in his "Don Juan List"), but their relationships are still not entirely clear. Pushkin is responding to Countess Vorontsova's letter of December 26, 1833, in which she requested something from his pen for an almanac sponsored by her for the benefit of the poor in Odessa. Countess Vorontsova's letter was signed, almost illegibly, "E. Wilbemans[?]," which has been interpreted as being an anagram of her name. Pushkin recognized her handwriting or deciphered the anagram, and he fulfilled her request, in the midst of his fuming over being made a Kammerjunker, and in his concern over the health of his pregnant wife—who had a miscarriage on the night of this letter (see Letter 481). Under the entirely "correct" words can be sensed a warm personal attachment.

What work Pushkin sent Countess Vorontsova is not known. Perhaps it was his *Rusalka*, which he was working on at this time, and which he never finished. Pushkin's manuscript arrived too late for inclusion in Countess Vorontsova's almanac, which was signed by the censorship on March 8, 1834.

Letter 479

1. Pushkin and Odoevsky attended, at Grech's invitation, a meeting at Grech's house to discuss participation in the compilation of *The Encyclopedic Lexicon*, to be published by the Petersburg bookseller Adolf Plyushar and edited by Grech. The encyclopedia was planned for twenty-four volumes, of which only seventeen ever appeared (1835-1841). See Letter 480.

Letter 480

1. *The Encyclopedic Lexicon* (see Letter 479). Pushkin calls it by the title of the famous *Konversations-Lexikon*, published by Brockhaus in Leipzig in 1809.

2. That is, of the literary proletariat, in contradistinction to the literary aristocracy, to which Pushkin and Odoevsky belonged.

3. Pushkin and Odoevsky attended the meeting at Grech's and both agreed to par-

ticipate in the compilation of the encyclopedia, but they made such reservations that their participation was rejected. Pushkin speaks of the meeting and enterprise in his diary (under March 17) as follows: "Yesterday at Grech's there was a literary conference concerning the publication of a Russian *Konversations Lexikon*. Of us there were about a hundred great Russian people, most of whom were unknown to me. Grech told me as a preliminary, 'Plyushar in this business is a charlatan, and I am his stooge: I drink his medicine and praise him.' Thus it turned out. I detected much charlatanry and very little sense. An enterprise of a million rubles, but I see nothing to be gained from it. I do not speak yet of honor. But why should one want to crawl into the slough where Bulgarin, Polevoy, and Sviniin are splashing about." In commenting about the "exclusion" of Odoevsky, Pushkin, and others who had made reservations about participating in the encyclopedia, Pushkin in his diary (under April 2), adds: "An honorable man, says Odoevsky, can be deceived once, but only a fool is deceived a second time. This lexicon will be nothing but *The Northern Bee* and *A Library for Reading*, with a new arrangement and scope."

Letter 481

1. Nashchokin had finally abandoned his gypsy mistress, Olga Andreevna, and had married Vera Alexandrovna Narskaya.

2. V. V. Nashchokin.

3. The terms have to do with card playing: fifteen times the stake and twice the stake, respectively.

4. On March 4, 1834. Pushkin's account of it in his diary, under the date of March 6, is as follows: "Thank God! Carnival has ended, and, with it, the balls. A description of the last day of Carnival (March 4) will give an understanding of the others. Selected ones were invited to the palace for a matinee ball, at 12:30. Others, to the evening ball, at 8:30. I arrived at 9. They were dancing the mazurka, with which the matinee ball was ending. The ladies were assembling, and those who had been in the palace since morning changed their finery. There was a world of displeased ones; the ones who were invited for the evening envied the matinee lucky ones. . . . All this ended with my wife having a miscarriage. That's what all the dancing led to."

5. Mme. Goncharova was living on the estate Polotnyany Zavod, together with her still unmarried daughters, Alexandra Nikolaevna Goncharova and Ekaterina N. Goncharova.

6. Iosif Matveevich Penkovsky (d. 1885 or 1886), manager of Boldino.

7. Pushkin was made Kammerjunker on December 31, 1833. At this time, this rank was given to young nobles in their early twenties. Pushkin felt insulted that this rank was conferred upon him instead of the superior rank of Chamberlain, a rank which his friend Vyazemsky and his Lyceum classmate Korf, for example, already had. Pushkin had not attained a rank in government service commensurate with his age; his official rank in the service was allowed by the Tsar to determine the court rank given him. Pushkin's humiliation and his fury at this "honor" are clear in subsequent letters.

Letter 482

1. The Moscow Society of Lovers of Russian Literature. Pushkin had been elected a member in 1829 (see Letter 269). Pogodin had been insisting that Pushkin send the Society one of his poems to be read there before it would appear in print.

2. Pushkin's attack on Bulgarin, in the guise of an article on Vidocq (see Letter 277, and note).

3. *The Moscow Record*, edited by Prince P. I. Shalikov, commented approvingly in

1830 of the election of the men of letters, Pushkin, Baratynsky, Bulgarin, and the composer Verstovsky, as members of the Society.

4. The heroine's father, Famusov, so greets the hero, Chatsky, in Griboedov's *Woe from Wit*.

5. That is, his historical researches on Peter the Great.

6. Pogodin had recently been promoted from adjunct to professor at Moscow University (see Letter 446).

Letter 483

1. Joachim Lelewel (1786-1861), Polish historian and politician, a leader in the Polish Revolution of 1830-1831, and President of the Polish National Committee. He continued his revolutionary activities after the revolution was crushed.

2. Count Grigory Alexandrovich Stroganov (1770-1857), a member of the State Council, Mme. Pushkina's great-uncle. Count Stroganov was noted as an extremely handsome man in his youth; in Byron's *Don Juan*, Julia held out even against his attractiveness. Count Stroganov to a considerable degree took the side of d'Anthès and Heeckeren against Pushkin in the events leading up to Pushkin's death, but after Pushkin's death, he became one of his children's guardians.

3. Count Stroganov had sent Pushkin the *Journal de Francfort*, No. 101, of April 24 (April 12, Old Style), 1834, which gave an account of Lelewel's reading aloud one of Pushkin's early, revolutionary poems and attributing revolutionary ideas to him. The article was a corrective to Lelewel's remarks: it pointed out Pushkin's recent anti-Polish poems and his being in good standing with the Tsar and the Court. How Pushkin was struck by the event is indicated by the fact that he copied part of the article in his diary. Scholars have noted the violence of Pushkin's remarking in this letter that to be accepted by a Pole as continuing to be a believer in the revolutionary ideas of his youth was worse than to be in exile in Siberia as a Decembrist revolutionary.

4. Countess Yulia Pavlovna Stroganova (d. 1864).

Letter 484

1. This letter marks Pushkin's officially taking over the financial management of his father's estate, Boldino. Pushkin gave Penkovsky another power of attorney on October 30, 1834. Managing his father's estate was a source of continuing harrassment to Pushkin from the time he took it over until he gave it up in June or July, 1835.

Letter 485

1. Ivan Ivanovich Lazhechnikov (1792-1869), author of historical novels, and at this time Director of Educational Institutions of the Province of Tver. The manuscript which Lazhechnikov sent Pushkin was the description of Pugachev's siege of Orenburg, by Peter Ivanovich Rychkov (1712-1777). Pushkin received copies of this manuscript from Spassky, Yazykov, and Lazhechnikov. He published Rychkov's account in one of the Appendices to his *History of Pugachev*.

2. Lazhechnikov's first novel was *The Last Novik* (1831-1833). His "new" novel was *The House of Ice* (1835). In Muscovite Russia, a *novik* was a young nobleman who had recently begun obligatory service at court.

3. *Dawn for* 1834.

Letter 486

1. Natalia Nikolaevna Pushkina and the Pushkin children left to visit their Goncharov relatives in Moscow, Yaropolets, and Polotnyany Zavod, on April 15. They spent the summer visiting.

2. Pushkin also wrote in his diary of how Count Litta, Head Chamberlain, "dressed down" the Kammerjunkers, insisting that there were " fixed rules" for the "Gentlemen of the Court," and how Kirill Alexandrovich Naryshkin (1786-1838), Head Marshal of the Court, answered that Litta was mistaken, that the rules were for the Ladies in Waiting. There is an untranslatable pun on *règles* "rules, periods."

3. Probably S. D. Bezobrazov.

4. Nikolay Fedorovich Remer (1806-1889), who was made a Kammerjunker, along with Pushkin, in 1833.

5. "I would rather be whipped in front of everybody."—In Molière's *Bourgeois gentilhomme*.

6. Probably the *Correspondence littéraire* (1753-1773) of Baron Friedrich Melchior von Grimm, French critic and *Philosophe*.

7. Pushkin probably means that he was expecting the postman to ring with a letter from Mme. Pushkina.

8. "Madam" of a "fashionable" house of prostitution.

9. A servant of the Pushkins'.

10. Pushkin's English and spelling.

Letter 487
1. That is, their family physician's instructions. Mme. Pushkina's trip was for convalescence from her miscarriage on March 4, 1834. See Letter 481.

2. Pushkin's English and spelling.

Letter 488
1. Pushkin shows his contempt for his court rank of Kammerjunker as being for younger men of his class, by using the term *Kammerpaž*, or Chamber Page, granted only to boys.

2. The three tsars were Paul I, Alexander I, and Nicholas I.

3. Pushkin's "namesake" was Alexander I. The "namesake" of Pushkin's son became Alexander II; at this time he was Grand Duke Alexander, the "Heir" to the throne. The celebrations were upon the "Heir's" attaining his sixteenth birthday (on April 17, 1834) and hence his legal majority, and upon his taking the oath of fealty.

4. Pushkin is thinking of his father-in-law's madness.

5. Prince Viktor Pavlovich Kochubey (1768-1834), statesman, Senator, and Chairman of the Committee of Ministers of the State Council. The rank of chancellor was the highest civil rank, and it corresponded with the military rank of field marshal.

6. Natalia Andreevna Ozerova, nee Obolenskaya (1812-1901), wife of Sergey Petrovich Ozerov (1809-1884).

7. Princess Maria Petrovna Vyazemskaya.

8. Karl Karlovich Merder (1788-1834), tutor of the Heir, died on March 24, 1834.

9. Count A. A. Arakcheev died on April 21, 1834. He was hated by all Russian liberals as the symbol, instigator, and administrator of the reactionary policies of the last ten years of the reign of Alexander I, and especially for the establishment of the military colonies in 1817. Though Nicholas I continued many of the policies of Arakcheev, he considered him a "monster" (*izverg*).

10. This letter, with its expression of clear displeasure at the court rank of Kammerjunker, with its admission of giving lying excuses for avoiding court functions, and with its critical approach to tsars in general, was opened by the Moscow postmaster, Bulgakov, and the contents reported to Nicholas I, who did not hesitate to speak of the letter to members of the court. Pushkin's rage at this action, clearly stated in subsequent letters,

led him to attempt, unsuccessfully, to resign from the service and retire to the country. These events are climactic in Pushkin's life.

Pushkin speaks thus of the event in his diary, under the date of May 10, 1834: "A few days ago I received from Zhukovsky a note from Tsarskoe Selo. He was informing me that a certain letter of mine was circulating about the city, and that the Sovereign had spoken to him about it. I imagined that the point was foul verses, full of repulsive obscenity, which the public was indulgently and graciously attributing to me. But it proved otherwise. The Moscow post unsealed a letter written by me to Natalia Nikolaevna, and, finding in it an account concerning the oath of the Grand Duke, written, apparently, not in the official style, made a report about it to the police. The police, without making out the meaning, presented the letter to the Sovereign, who flared up and did not understand it, either. Fortunately, the letter was shown to Zhukovsky, who then explained it. Everything quieted down. It did not please the Sovereign that I referred to my becoming a Kammerjunker, without tender emotion and without gratitude. However, I can be a subject, even a slave, but I shall not be a flunky and a clown even before the Tsar of Heaven. But what profound immorality there is in the customs of our government. The police unseal a husband's letters to his wife, and take them for reading to the Tsar (a well-bred and an honorable man), and the Tsar is not ashamed to admit it—and to set in motion an intrigue worthy of Vidocq and Bulgarin! No matter what you say, being an autocrat is hard."

Letter 489
1. Sofia Fedorovna Timiryazeva (b. 1799) and her husband, General Ivan Semenovich Timiryazev (1790-1867), were among Pushkin's good friends in the last years of his life.

Letter 490
1. Another reference to her father's madness.
2. The ball was in celebration of the attaining of his "majority" by the Heir to the throne, Grand Duke Alexander, who was born in 1818. It was given by the nobility of the Petersburg Province, at the home of Dmitry Lvovich Naryshkin (1764-1838). Pushkin did not attend. (See following letter.)
3. "Tell me what you drink, and I'll tell you what you are." Pushkin substitutes the word "drink" for "eat" in the aphorism of the French gastronome, Anthelme Brillat-Savarin, in his *Physiology of Taste* (1826).

Letter 491
1. See Letter 490, and note 2.
2. Pushkin was mistaken. See Letter 492.
3. That of Princess Tatiana Vasilievna Golitsyna (1782-1841), wife of the Governor General of Moscow, Prince D. V. Golitsyn.
4. Henriette Gertrude Walpurgis Sontag (1806-1854), wife of Count Rossi. She was a well-known singer of the time.
5. Pushkin again speaks of himself as a Chamber Page instead of a Kammerjunker. See Letter 488, note 1.

Letter 492
1. See Letter 490, and note 2.
2. Nestor Vasilievich Kukolnik (1809-1868), author of romantic and patriotic dramas in blank verse in a bombastic style.
3. See Letter 491.

4. Ekaterina Pavlovna Bakunina (d. 1869) married Alexander Alexandrovich Poltoratsky (1792-1855), a cousin of Anna Petrovna Kern, on April 30, 1834.

5. Count Ivan Illarionovich Vorontsov-Dashkov (1790-1854) married Countess Alexandra Kirillovna Naryshkina (1817-1856), daughter of Kirill Alexandrovich Naryshkin.

6. Novomlensky, probably a student and admirer of Mme. Pushkina before her marriage, as was also Sorokhtin.

Letter 493

1. In a letter of April 10, 1834, the historian Dmitry Nikolaevich Bantysh-Kamensky (1788-1850) sent Pushkin a sketch of Pugachev's seal and offered to send him a biography of Pugachev. In response to Pushkin's letter, Bantysh-Kamensky sent Pushkin a biography of Pugachev, twenty short biographies of followers of Pugachev, and a biography of Count Peter Ivanovich Panin.

Letter 494

1. Pushkin's brother-in-law, Pavlishchev, in his letter asked Pushkin, who had taken over the management of his father's estate Boldino, to send the money owed Pavlishchev by Lev Pushkin and also asked for information as to when he would receive the 1500 rubles annually which Pushkin's sister Olga had been promised after her marriage. Lev Pushkin owed Pavlishchev some 500 rubles. From the time Pushkin took over his father's estate, Pavlishchev continually peppered him with long, detailed, complaining letters, which provided one of the major irritations of Pushkin's management of the estate.

2. The sheet is torn at this point.

3. For managing Boldino and for disposing of the revenues from it. Pushkin managed his father's estate from April, 1834, until June or July, 1835.

Letter 495

1. That is, to the Goncharovs' Moscow house, to their estate Yaropolets in the Volokolamsk District, or to the estate Polotnyany Zavod in the Kaluga District.

2. Alexandra Osipovna Smirnova (nee Rosset) bore twin daughters on June 18, 1834.

3. The management of his father's estate Boldino.

Letter 496

1. His father's estate of Boldino.

2. Pushkin wrote in his diary that Nicholas I was dissatisfied because his son "galloped instead of trotted."

3. Frederick William (1795-1861), who as Frederick William IV was King of Prussia from 1840 to 1861, the brother of the Russian Empress Alexandra Fedorovna. He arrived in Russia on June 13 and left on August 1, 1834.

4. Pushkin notes in his diary that on May 26 he "was on the steamship, and accompanying the Meshcherskys, who were setting off for Italy."

Letter 497

1. Gogol was trying to obtain the post of professor in Kiev University, his request being motivated by bad health. He asked Pushkin to speak of Gogol's poor health to the Minister of Education, S. S. Uvarov.

2. Polevoy's *Moscow Telegraph* was closed down on April 3, 1834, as the result of a deposition by Uvarov. Pushkin's remark is mordantly ironic. Pushkin wrote thus in his diary of the closing down of this journal: "Zhukovsky says, 'I'm glad that *The Telegraph*

is forbidden, though I regret that they forbade it.' *The Telegraph* deserved its lot; it would be hard to preach Jacobinism with greater impudence under the nose of the government, but Polevoy was a pet of the police. He was able to assure them that his liberalism was only an empty mask."

Letter 498

1. Mineral waters and muds in the town of Pyrmont, Principality of Waldeck, Germany, on the Emmer River.
2. The last clause of this sentence was struck out but is still legible. Pushkin had discovered that Letter 488 (q.v., and note) has been intercepted.

Letter 499

1. May 19.
2. Letter 488.

Letter 500

1. *Tales Published by Alexander Pushkin* appeared in 1834. The edition included Pushkin's *Tales of Belkin*, *The Blackamoor of Peter the Great*, and "The Queen of Spades."
2. Special permission was required for sending his works to his friend Kyukhelbeker, the Decembrist.

Letter 501

1. See Letters 498 and 499.
2. Alexandre Vattemare, a French ventriloquist, actor, and mimic.
3. Boldino.
4. Pushkin made the official request a month later (Letter 507).
5. The allusion is to the monument of Peter the Great in Petersburg; this monument forms the center of Pushkin's *Bronze Horseman*. Pushkin was again working on the history of Peter the Great. Pushkin's comment here is reminiscent of his "Monument" ("I have erected myself a monument, not made by human hands"), which he wrote two years later.

Letter 502

1. Pushkin's strong language was for those who intercepted his private letters and for those who read them. Pushkin was well aware that in this number were included not only post officials, but also the secret police and the Tsar himself.
2. Ivan Nikolaevich Goncharov was then an officer and stationed in Tsarskoe Selo.
3. Princess Ekaterina Alexeevna Dolgorukova, nee Malinovskaya.
4. Elena Pavlovna, wife of Grand Duke Mikhail Pavlovich. Pushkin was presented to her on May 27, 1834. He quotes the conversation a little differently in his diary entry of June 2.
5. "You must be quite tired of being obliged to read all that appears." "Yes, Your Imperial Highness, . . . the more so that what is being written now has no common sense."
6. Pushkin's parents left on June 11 to spend the summer at Mikhaylovskoe (see Letter 505).

Letter 503

1. See Letter 493, and note.
2. In response to Pushkin's Letter 493, Bantysh-Kamensky sent Pushkin the article about Panin, for publication if found suitable.

3. See Letter 480, and note 1. Pushkin's spelling.

4. At this time Pushkin was interested in becoming literary agent for people such as Bantysh-Kamensky.

5. Pushkin jokingly concludes with the tsarist soldier's conventional response to a commendation.

Letter 504

1. Pushkin transliterates the English word into Russian orthography.

2. The allusion is to Pushkin's letters being intercepted and read (see Letter 488, and note 10).

3. On May 10, Pushkin had written almost exactly the same thing in his diary (see Letter 488, note 9). The quotation from Lomonosov is from a letter to Shuvalov, dated January 19, 1761.

4. His parents.

5. Countess Luiza Karlovna Vielgorskaya (1791-1853).

Letter 505

1. The Pushkins' Petersburg apartment was near the Summer Garden, near the Summer Palace of Peter the Great. It was a center for court life.

2. *Sobolevskij sam po sebe, a ja sam po sebe.* Pushkin jokingly adapts the proverbial soldier's distinction between a cannon and a mortar: *puška sama po sebe, a edinorog sam po sebe.* The remark is particularly apt, because Pushkin's own surname comes from *puška,* "cannon."

3. Pushkin's "favorite" of Mme. Pushkina's sisters was Alexandra Nikolaevna Goncharova.

4. "I would not have believed . . . that Kochubey's death would grieve me so."

5. Princess Maria Vasilievna Kochubey (1779-1844), Kochubey's widow, and Natalia K. Zagryazhskaya's niece.

6. Pushkin's parents.

7. Boldino.

8. The governor of Kaluga at the time was Illarion Mikhaylovich Bibikov (d. 1861), and his wife was Ekaterina Ivanovna Bibikova (1795-1849).

9. Pushkin is jokingly referring to Countess Nadezhda Grigorievna Chernysheva. See Letter 457.

10. Frederick William (see Letter 496).

11. Sergey Petrovich Ozerov and his wife, Natalia Andreevna Ozerova, nee Obolenskaya.

12. Another allusion to his letters being opened and read.

13. That is, to have them made Ladies in Waiting.

14. Pushkin's rank in the government service.

15. A *kalač* is a kind of roll. Pushkin is playing on the Russian saying, "You couldn't lure me, even with a *kalač*," meaning "nothing would induce me to come," by adding a particular place to which he could not be lured (Petersburg), and a special kind of *kalač* (Moscow).

16. "Yesterday Madame such-and-such was definitely the most beautiful and best dressed at the ball."

17. Mme. Vielgorskaya died in 1853.

18. Nicholas I.

19. Pushkin's English.

Letter 506

1. Spassky's letter no doubt contained medical advice for Mme. Pushkina, who was convalescing.

Letter 507

1. Pushkin's request to be allowed to retire was prompted by his indignation at the interception of his letters by the police, by the humiliation of his "promotion" to Kammerjunker, and by his ever-worsening financial situation in Petersburg. The letter itself was naturally considered by Nicholas I and Benkendorf to be "dry," for it lacked any explanation or justification for the request. On June 30, Pushkin received Benkendorf's answer, that "His Imperial Majesty [did not] wish to keep anyone against his will," and hence Pushkin might retire, but that permission to use archive materials could not then be granted, "for this right can belong solely to people enjoying the especial trust of the authorities." Zhukovsky and Mme. Khitrovo pleaded Pushkin's case with the authorities. He eventually felt compelled to take back his request (see Letters 512, 516, 517, and notes).

2. Slip of the pen for June 25.

Letter 508

1. This is a good example of the way Pushkin uses an epigraph for a letter. The quotation is from Fonvizin's *Adolescent*, Act IV, and it is addressed to the block-headed "hero" of the play.

2. Elena Pavlovna. See Letter 502.

3. Ekaterina Petrovna Chicherina (d. 1874), one of the Grand Duchess Elena Pavlovna's Ladies in Waiting. She was a third cousin of Pushkin's.

4. The second highest bid in the card game of Boston: the bidder contracts to discard one card and lose the twelve tricks. Eighty white counters would be won from or lost to each of the other players, depending upon the success of the play.

5. Alexandra O. Smirnova was unable, in 1832, to bear her first child, in seventy-two hours of labor; the child had to be destroyed before it could "get out."

6. Semen Semenovich Khlyustin (1810-1844), a nephew of Tolstoy the American.

7. Sergey Pavlovich Ubri, then in exile in Kaluga.

8. His father's estate of Boldino.

9. Yakolev saw Pushkin's book through the press. A number of the succeeding letters are to him in this connection.

10. The anecdote is unknown.

11. "Farewell, my life; I love you."

Letter 509

1. In the beginning of June, Nicholas I and his court went to Petergof, a suburb of Petersburg. Special celebrations and amusements occurred.

2. Pushkin had already sent in his letter of resignation three days earlier (Letter 507) and was awaiting its results. It will be seen that Pushkin is not candid with his wife on this matter.

3. Pushkin died less than three years later in Petersburg, but he was buried by "a church in the open spaces," at the monastery Svyatye Gory, near his mother's estate of Mikhaylovskoe.

4. Countess Anna Vladimirovna Bobrinskaya. Pushkin, on December 18, 1834, wrote in his diary that "she always lies for me and gets me out of scrapes."

5. The printing of his *History of Pugachev*.

6. Boldino, of which Pushkin was his father's financial manager at the time.
7. Alexander Karlovich Olivio.
8. Nicholas I.
9. On June 22, 1834.

Letter 510
1. Ekaterina Vasilievna Shishkova; her daughter "Polina" was Praskovia Dmitrievna Shishkova.
2. Metal tokens were given upon members' attendance at meetings of the Russian Academy, and they were redeemed later. Alexander Semenovich Shishkov was President of the Russian Academy. Pushkin had been a member since January 7, 1833. Though Pushkin attended several sessions of the organization in 1833, he attended only one in 1834, that on December 8.
3. "Not otherwise."
4. Unknown.
5. That is, at the printing plant.
6. Perhaps V. G. Yuriev.
7. Karl Reichman refused the management of Boldino, in his letter of June 22, 1834.

Letter 511
1. Pushkin's old friend M. L. Yakovlev was at this time the head of the printing house of the Second Section of His Majesty's Chancellery. Yakovlev saw Pushkin's *History of Pugachev* through the press for him. The letter is written in the form of an official note.

Letter 512
1. See Letter 507. Zhukovsky had undertaken to smooth things out between the Tsar and Pushkin, after Pushkin's attempted resignation. The present letter is the direct result of a letter by Zhukovsky to Pushkin (of July 2, 1834), in which Zhukovsky gives the Tsar's response to Zhukovsky's question "Can't all this be corrected somehow?" The Tsar answered as follows: "Why not? I never hold anybody back, and I shall give him his retirement. But in that case all is finished between us. He can, however, still ask for his letter to be returned." Pushkin realized what reason he had to fear the Tsar's words "in that case all is finished between us."

Letter 513
1. "My step being ill-considered . . . that I prefer seeming inconsistent to seeming ungrateful." See Letter 512, and note. Pushkin quotes himself a little imprecisely.
Zhukovsky, in addition to his letter of July 2, had written Pushkin a long letter on July 3, in which he roundly berated Pushkin for sending in his resignation without having consulted in advance either with him or Prince Vyazemsky, and advised him to "accuse" himself for his "stupid deed" in a letter to the Tsar, and to explain what moved him to send in the resignation. Zhukovsky says that if Pushkin does not so act, he will harm himself for his "whole life," and that he will earn his friends' "disapprobation"— at least Zhukovsky's. Zhukovsky also sent a second version of the letter, one that could be shown to Benkendorf.
2. See Letter 507, and note 1.
3. Pushkin did not write directly to Nicholas I, but, instead, again to Benkendorf.

Letter 514
1. See Letter 513, and notes.

Letter 515

1. This note was written on the manuscript of *The History of Pugachev*.

Letter 516

1. This letter was written hurriedly, like Letter 517, upon Pushkin's receiving still another letter from Zhukovsky, likewise dated July 6, complaining that neither of Pushkin's letters to Benkendorf (Letters 512, 514) is satisfactory, because the first does not say whether he wishes to continue in the service, and the second "is so dry that it might seem to the Sovereign to be a new impropriety." Zhukovsky emphasized that Nicholas I considered Pushkin's resignation as "ingratitude" and insisted that Pushkin write what his "heart will say." The "third" letter was Letter 517.

Letter 517

1. See Letter 507. Nicholas I's response to this letter, made to Benkendorf, was as follows: "I forgive him, but you summon him again to explain to him the senselessness of his behavior and what all this could end with; what might be forgiven a twenty-year-old madcap cannot be applied to a man of thirty-five years, a husband and father of a family." Pushkin understood this hint of another exile, and he tersely wrote in his diary on July 22: "The last month has been stormy. I came within a hair's breadth of quarreling with the Court—but everything came out all right. Just the same, I won't get away with it."

Pushkin did not get away with it. His last chance of living as he chose disappeared when he submitted to the Tsar's desire that he remain in Petersburg. After Pushkin's death, three years later, Zhukovsky changed his opinion considerably with regard to Pushkin's reasons for "gratitude" towards Nicholas and his "ingratitude" in wanting to get away, when Zhukovsky, given the task of reading and sorting all Pushkin's papers, became so aroused at the suspicious treatment of Pushkin during Nicholas' reign, that he wrote an indignant letter to Benkendorf.

Letter 518

1. Zagoskin's novel, *Askold's Tomb* (1833).

2. No such letter survives.

3. Alexandre Vattemare, the ventriloquist, and hence "persons." Vattemare had asked Pushkin to write to Zagoskin, in the latter's capacity as Director of the Moscow Imperial Theater. Zagoskin's answer is unknown.

Letter 519

1. Namely, that some of Pushkin's letters had been opened and read by post officials, the police, and the Tsar.

2. "Routs" were fashionable in Russia at the time. See Letter 243 and note 8.

3. Josephine Charlotte Ermolova, nee Comtesse de Lasalle. Pushkin comments about the filthiness of her clothing, in his diary, under the date of December 5, 1834: "N.N. said, 'Here is Mme. Yermolova *la sale* (Lassale).'"

4. Pushkin is referring to his submitting his resignation to Nicholas I, and the upshot. Pushkin's attitude toward his wife's judgment, and his opinion of what her attitude would be toward his wishing to retire is clear from the dates of his letters to her during the "stormy month." His letters to her, during her trip, had been dated, on the average, about four days apart, until the letter of June 11, in which he expressed clear displeasure with the Tsar and his desire to get away to "fresh air." His next letter, dated June 19. was only a brief note. Obviously the desire to resign was growing and growing

in him. Then he sent in his resignation on June 25. While he was waiting for the answer, he wrote his wife three letters in about four days. Then, on June 30, when he received the Tsar's curt acceptance of his resignation, the second act of the drama began— of his trying to take back the resignation. Pushkin did not write his wife again until July 11, almost two weeks later, when the drama was completed.

5. Olga Petrovna Pletneva.
6. Unidentified.
7. Grand Duchess Elena Pavlovna.

Letter 520
1. M. I. Kalashnikov.
2. Reichman was manager of Mme. Osipova's estate of Malinniki; she had suggested him as manager of Boldino. He refused this management in a letter of June 22, 1834.
3. Pushkin next visited Trigorskoe in 1835.

Letter 521
1. The equivalent English proverb is less colorful: If wishes were horses, beggars would ride.
2. Nicholas I.
3. Court balls in the Anichkov Palace. Pushkin wrote in his diary, under January 1, 1834, that he was made a Kammerjunker because "the court wanted Natalia Nikolaevna to dance in the Anichkov."
4. "Liberalism" was the charge leading to Pushkin's exile under the guise of an administrative transfer in 1820.

Letter 522
1. Unidentified.
2. Pushkin's landlord.
3. In Letter 508, of June 27, 1834, Pushkin had reported that Mme. Smirnova had recently borne twins.

Letter 523
1. Pushkin moved there in the middle of August, 1834. The house was on the Gagarinskaya Embankment, and it was owned by Sila Andreevich Batashev.
2. Princess Praskovia Petrovna Vyazemskaya; she died in Rome on March 11, 1835.
3. Woman "is a naturally feeble and sickly animal."
4. *Do nizlozenija riz.* It has proved impossible to preserve the biblical flavor of the expression, which has to do with Noah's taking off his clothes while drunk after the Flood (Genesis 9:21). The quotation has humorous connotations in Russian.
5. Of his *History of Pugachev.*
6. Lev S. Pushkin re-entered the military service and went to Caucasian Georgia to serve, but not until 1836.
7. Khlopusha was the nickname of Afansy Timofeevich Sokolov, one of Pugachev's military leaders. The incident is recounted in the first volume of Pushkin's *History of Pugachev.*
8. Pushkin makes a double pun, on Khlopusha's name and his own, and on the name of the Goncharov estate, Polotnyany Zavod, "Linen Factory."
9. Count Joseph Maison (1771-1840), French ambassador at the Russian court. Pushkin wrote of the event in his diary (under the date of July 22), as follows: "Marshal Maison fell from his horse on maneuvers and came very near to being crushed by the

Obraztsov Regiment. Arendt has announced that he is out of danger. At Austerlitz he smashed our cavalry guards. One good turn deserves another."

Letter 524

1. Of Pushkin's *History of Pugachev.*
2. See Letter 523.
3. Probably the portrait of Mme. Pushkina as a bride, by A. P. Bryullov, in water colors. See Illustration opposite Letter 350.

Letter 525

1. The actor Vasily Andreevich Karatygin and his wife, the dramatic actress Alexandra Mikhaylovna Karatygina, nee Kolosova. Pushkin knew both personally.
2. See Letters 523 and 524.
3. August 26.
4. Princess Praskovia Petrovna Vyazemskaya. See Letter 523, and note 2.
5. "To make a baby for you." "Oh, Sir, you will give me great pleasure."
6. Princess Maria Vasilievna Kochubey (see Letter 505).
7. "Good Lord, but we have all lost our husbands, and yet we have consoled ourselves."
8. Of Pushkin's *History of Pugachev.*

Letter 526

1. This note and the following one show the strictness of the censorship under which Pushkin operated. This note was written on the manuscript of the Preface of Pushkin's *History of Pugachev,* in response to Yakovlev's question, "Can't Voltaire be dispensed with?" Pushkin had included Voltaire's name in the list of historical figures "whose names are met" in Pushkin's work, a "historical page," which "must not be lost for posterity." Pushkin was forced to remove Voltaire's name from the Preface (see Letter 527).

Letter 527

1. Of the proofs of Pushkin's *History of Pugachev.*
2. The other copies of Rychkov's description of the siege of Orenburg by Pugachev (see Letter 485, note 1).
3. A quotation from Batyushkov's poetic epistle to I. M. Muraviev-Apostol (already quoted in Letter 184).
4. See Letter 526, note.

PART XII

CARES AND WOES—PETERSBURG

August, 1834—December, 1835

Natalia Nikolaevna Pushkina, 1844.

To Ivan Ivanovich Lazhechnikov
About August 20, 1834. From (?) to Tver.

I have kept on hoping, honored and amiable Ivan Ivanovich, to thank you in person for your favorable attitude toward me, for the two letters, for the novels, and for the Pugachev materials,[1] but unsuccess pursues me. I'm passing through Tver by post chaise, and in such an appearance that I simply dare not come to see you and renew our ancient, momentary acquaintance. I postpone it to September, that is, until my return trip. Meanwhile, I commend myself to your indulgence and good will.

One who heartily esteems you,
Pushkin.

To Natalia Ivanovna Goncharova
About (not later than) August 25, 1834.
From Polotnyany Zavod to Yaropolets.

Dear Madame, Mother, Natalia Ivanovna,

How I regret that I didn't drop in to Yaropolets on my way from Petersburg. I would have had the happiness of seeing you, and I would have shortened the trip by several miles. Besides, I would have missed Moscow, which I am not very fond of, and in which I spent several hours too many. Now I'm at the Zavod, where I found all my family well, except Sasha. I'm leaving them for several more weeks and going on business for my father to his Nizhny Novgorod village,[1] and I'm sending my wife off to you, where I myself will come as soon as possible. My wife is sad that she won't spend with you the name day[2] of you both. What's to be done! I'm sorry, too, but it can't be helped. Meanwhile I congratulate you upon the day of August 26—and I heartily thank you for the 27th.[3] My wife is charming, and the longer I live with her the more I love this sweet, pure, kind creature, whom, before God, I have in no way deserved. I have been seeing my brother-in-law Ivan Nikolaevich often in Petersburg, and Sergey Nikolaevich was even living with me almost up to my departure. He's now bustling around, outfitting himself.[4] Both of them, thank God, are well.

I kiss your little hands, and I commend myself and all my family to your favor.

A. Pushkin.

[530]

To ALEXANDER IVANOVICH TURGENEV
About (not later than) September 9, 1834. In Moscow.

My wife has selected the pins, and she cordially thanks you. It goes without saying that you'll be the first to receive my *Pugachev*,[1] as soon as it comes forth from the press. Simbirsk was besieged not by him but by one of his confederates, nicknamed Firska. I shall leave the book at my wife's, who will pass it on to you. All yours—good-by.

A.P.

In 1671 Simbirsk held out against Stenka Razin,[2] the Pugachev of that time.

[531]

To SERGEY ALEXANDROVICH SOBOLEVSKY
September 9, 1834. From Moscow to Petersburg.

Moscow, September 9.

Please, dear Sergey Alexandrovich, explain to my wife[1] where *notre ami l'usurier*[2] lives. I am relying on your sluggishness, and I consider it a certainty that you are still in Paris[3]—and that I shall even find you're there upon my arrival in Petersburg.

[532]

To ALEXANDER IVANOVICH TURGENEV
September 9 or 10, 1834. In Moscow.

I already have all this—and it will be printed in an appendix.[1] I am grateful to Polevoy[2] for his being kindly disposed toward the historiographer of Pugachev, the Kammerjunker,[3] etc. I am leaving right now. The horses are already harnessed up.

[533]

To Natalia Nikolaevna Pushkina
September 15 and 17, 1834. From Boldino to Petersburg.

September 15.

The post goes on Tuesday, but today is still only Saturday. And so this letter won't reach you very soon. I arrived day before yesterday, Thursday, in the morning—that's how one creeps along the provincial roads—and, at that, I have paid almost everywhere double the post-horse fee. True, horses had been taken from everywhere for the Sovereign, who must go from Moscow to Nizhny. The first snow met me in the village,[1] and now the yard in front of my little window is all white; *c'est une très aimable attention*.[2] However, I haven't got down to writing yet, and I'm taking my pen for the first time, in order to have a little chat with you. I'm glad that I have got to Boldino; it looks as though there will be less bother than I expected. I should very much like to write something or other. I don't know whether inspiration will come. Here I found Bezo-brazov[3] (just why are you so astonished? It wasn't your adorer,[4] but my cousin Margaritka's husband). He's bustling about and managing the estate and probably will buy half of Boldino. Oh! If I only had a hundred thousand! How I would get all that settled. But Pugachev, my little peasant on quitrent, won't bring me even half of that, and, besides, you and I will squander every kopeck he brings in, won't we? Well, nothing can be done about it. If I live, there'll be some money, too. . . . Here's Bezobrazov coming to see me—farewell.

Ugh! I had difficulty in getting rid of him. He stayed with me for two hours. We both tried to outsmart each other—God grant that I outsmarted him in deed; in words, I think, I outsmarted him. I can see from here your mistrustful smile. You think I'm a tomfool, and that they'll hoodwink me again. We'll see. When I get to Moscow, I'll finish the deal in two days, and I'll come to Petersburg with a "well done," the owner of the village Boldino. . . .[5]

Just now some peasants came to see me, with a petition. I was forced to try to outsmart them, but they probably will outsmart me. . . . Even though I've become an awfully clever politician since I've been reading *Conquêtes de l'Angleterre par les Normands*.[6] What's this, now? A peasant woman with a petition. Farewell; I'll go listen to her.

Well, little wife, some humor. A soldier's wife asks that her son be registered as one of my peasants. However, she says, he has been registered as a bastard, though she gave birth to him, she says, only thirteen months after husband was sent off as a recruit. So how, then, can he be a bastard? I shall do what I can for the honor of the insulted widow.[7]

17th.

Now you're probably in Yaropolets, and you're probably already thinking about departing. I'm impatiently awaiting a letter from you. Don't forget my address: *in the Arzamas District*, to the village Abramovo, thence to the village Boldino. I'm all right here, but I'm bored, and when I'm bored, I feel drawn to you, just as you cuddle up to me when you're frightened. I kiss you and the children, and I bless all of you. I haven't begun writing yet.

[534]

To NATALIA NIKOLAEVNA PUSHKINA

Between September 20 and 25, 1834. From Boldino to Petersburg.

Here it will soon be two whole weeks that I've been in the village, and I still haven't received a letter from you. I'm bored, my angel. Verses won't come into my head, and I'm not copying the novel.[1] I'm reading Walter Scott and the Bible, and I keep on thinking of you. Is Sashka well? Have you given his wet nurse the sack—have you gotten rid of the damned German woman? How were you when you reached there? There are many things that I'm disturbed about. Apparently I'm not to stay long in Boldino this autumn. I have settled my affairs some way or other. I'll hang around a little and see whether I won't get into a writing vein. If not—then Godspeed, and onto the road. I'll stay in Moscow three days, at Natalia Ivanovna's twenty-four hours—and then I'll come to you. And, indeed, can it really be that near you I won't get into a writing vein? Nonsense. I've been expecting [A. M.] Yazykov to come see me, but apparently he won't make it.

Tell me, please, whether you aren't with child. If you are with child, I ask you, my darling, to be careful, not to jump, not to fall, not to kneel in front of Masha (or even in prayer). Don't forget that you've had a miscarriage, that you must take care of yourself. Oh, if only you were already in Petersburg. But according to all my calculations, you won't reach there before October 3. And how are things going to be for you there? Without money, without Amelian,[2] with your two fool nurses and slatternly maidservants (let this not be said in anger to Pelagea Ivanovna,[3] whom I kiss, sight unseen). I'll bet your head's going round and round. There's one hope: Aunty. But you can't make two Aunties out of one—it's obvious that I must hurry. Farewell; Christ preserve all of you. A big kiss to you— all of you keep well.

[535]

To NIKOLAY MIKHAYLOVICH YAZYKOV
September 26, 1834. From Boldino to Yazykovo.

I was delighted, in my solitude, at the coming of Alexander Mikhaylovich [Yazykov], who, unfortunately, spent only a few hours with me. He tempts me with his proposal to go to the village Yazykovo[1] with him to be a witness of his wedding, promising to make good use of me. But it is impossible for me—my wife and children. . . .

In conversing about various subjects, we decided that it would not be at all bad for me to begin an almanac, or better yet, a journal.[2] I have nothing against it, but if I am to do so I must be assured of your collaboration. What do you think, sir? You see, yourself: the hack writers are getting the better of us. It's time, by golly it's time, to give them a sizable repulse. I am setting off for Petersburg in a few days. If you have the leisure to write me a couple of lines, address them to the Dvortsovaya Naberezhnaya, to the house of Batashev—at the Prachechny Bridge. Alexander Mikhaylovich is in a hurry—and I am ending my letter by commending myself to your good will.

One who prays for you,

September 26.   A. Pushkin.
V[illage] Boldino.

My sincere respects and my greetings to Peter Alexandrovich [Yazykov].

[536]

To Mikhail Lukianovich Yakovlev
October 19, 1834(?). In Petersburg.

It's at your house we're celebrating the Anniversary, isn't it?
October 19.   No. 14.[1]

[537]

To Alexandra Andreevna Fuchs
October 19, 1834. From Petersburg to Kazan.

October 19, 1834. SPb.

Yesterday, upon returning to Petersburg after three months of boring traveling over the provinces, I was delighted by an unexpected boon; a letter and a parcel[1] from Kazan. I avidly read your charming poems and, among them, your epistle to me, the unworthy admirer of your Muse. In exchange for the productions of your imagination, which are filled with charm, intelligence, and sensitiveness, I hope in a few days to deliver to you the repulsively horrible *History of Pugachev*. Do not scold me. Poetry seems to have dried up for me. I am doing nothing but prose, and what kind at that! . . . I am truly ashamed, especially before you.

You wrote that Baron Lützerode[2] should have delivered to me a letter as long ago as last year. To my extreme regret I have not received it, probably because Baron Lützerode was no longer in Petersburg when I returned from Orenburg. He had already been recalled to Dresden. E. P. Pertsov,[3] whom I had the pleasure of seeing for a moment in Petersburg, was telling me that he had at his house a letter from you to me, but it has not reached me, either. He has left Petersburg, without delivering to me this valuable token of your kind remembrance of me. I understand his distractedness under his circumstances of that time, but I cannot help complaining. I forgive him magnanimously, but only on condition that he send me the letter which he forgot to deliver to me here.

Please take the trouble, dear Madame, to present my most profound respects to Karl Fedorovich [Fuchs], whose amiability and favorable inclination will be eternally memorable to me.

With the most profound respect and cordial devotion, I have the honor to be [. . . .][4]

[538]

To Nikolay Vasilievich Gogol

The second half of October, 1834. In Petersburg.

I have reread it with great pleasure. It all, I should think, can be passed. It would be a pity to have to omit the flogging;[1] I think it necessary for the full effect of the evening's mazurka. Maybe God will bring it through. Godspeed!

A.P.

[539]

To Iosif Matveevich Penkovsky

November 10, 1834. From Petersburg to Boldino.

I have received your letter of October 30, and I hasten to answer you. I myself shall pay *my* debt to the Guardian Council, but not a single kopek must be spent from the Boldino revenues. As regards the 1270 which are demanded for an extension of Father's debt, if you can find such a sum, then pay it. I am sending you the power of attorney by the next post. You have done well in that up to now you have not started selling the grain. Prices are bound to rise. Fortunately, I can wait a while longer.[1]

A.P.　　　　　　November 10.

[540]

To Alexander Khristoforovich Benkendorf

November 23, 1834. In Petersburg.

Dear Sir, Count Alexander Khristoforovich,

The History of the Pugachev Revolt has been printed, and I have been awaiting Your Excellency's permission for its release. Meanwhile, permit me to trouble you with one more humble request. I should like to have the happiness to present to the Sovereign Emperor the first copy of the book, augmenting it with certain notes which I decided not to publish, but which may be of interest to His Majesty. I make bold to have recourse to Your Highness in order to receive this permission.

The bookseller Smirdin wants to publish in one book my poems which have already appeared in print;[2] I have made bold to send them to the chancellery of His Excellency A. N. Mordvinov, according to the prescribed form for so doing.

With the most profound respect, complete devotion, and gratitude, I have the honor to be,

Dear Sir,

Your Excellency's

November 23, 1834.   Most humble servant,
SPb.   Alexander Pushkin.

[541]

To ALEXANDER IVANOVICH TURGENEV
Between December 1 and 11, 1834. In Petersburg.

I don't have a *French* copyist, but as many Russian ones as you
like. Tomorrow I'll scare one up. For the time being, I don't need
anything from Paris,[1] unless maybe Maistre's *Pope*.[2]

[542]

To ALEXANDER KHRISTOFOROVICH BENKENDORF
December 17, 1834. In Petersburg.
(In French)

I am in despair at having to trouble Your Excellency again, but
M. Speransky has just had me informed that, since *The History of the
Pugachev Revolt* has been in his section by order of His Majesty the
Emperor, it is impossible for him to deliver the edition *bez vysočajšego
na to soizvolenija*.[1] I beseech Your Excellency to pardon me and to
extricate me from this difficulty.

I am, with the most profound respect,

Count,

Your Excellency's

Most humble and most obedient servant,

December 17, 1834.   Alexander Pushkin.

[543]

To ALEXEY ALEXEEVICH BOBRINSKY
January 6, 1835. In Petersburg.
(In French)

We have received an invitation from Countess Bobrinskaya:[1]
M. and Mme. Pushkin *and her sister*, etc. There is a great clamor
among the females over it (as W. Scott's Antiquary[2] says): *which*?[3]
Since I suppose it is simply an error, I take the liberty of addressing

you in order to remove us from the quandary and to restore peace in my household.

I am, respectfully, Count,

Your most humble and most obedient servant,

January 6, 1835. A. Pushkin.

[544]

To Pavel Voinovich Nashchokin

About (not later than) January 8, 1835.

From Petersburg to Moscow.

Dear Pavel Voinovich,

You can't imagine with what pleasure I have finally received a letter from you. But first of all, let's talk about business. Sobolevsky, with whom I have financial dealings, *without delay* will deliver to you the two thousand rubles. Consequently, don't be uneasy. I could find a lot to tell you in excuse for my insolvency, but to write that by the post would be a superfluous thing; God grant that my belated money may arrive at a good time for you. I congratulate you upon your daughter Katerina Pavlovna;[1] I wish good health to the recently confined mother. (You don't write me when her confinement was.) All summer I scoured Russia, but I couldn't find you anywhere. You had been driven out of Tula by the fires. A whole week in Moscow I couldn't find you. In Torzhok nobody could give me news of you. I'm glad, Pavel Voinovich, of your letter, by which I see that your astonishing good nature and your sensible, patient indulgence have undergone no change, neither from the bothers of a life new for you, nor from your friend's culpability toward you. If only we might see each other! I would tell you a lot of things; this year much has piled up that it wouldn't be bad to have a chat with you about, at your place on the divan, with a pipe between my teeth, far from gypsy tempests[2] and Rokhmanov's forays![3] Write me, if you can, a little oftener: *On the Dvortsovaya Naberezhnaya* to the house of Batashev at the Prachechny Bridge (where Vyazemsky used to live), and not to Smirdin's, who keeps your letters for whole months, and sometimes, probably, even mislays them. I would take a peep at your domestic and village life with curiosity. I have always known you tempest-tossed. What kind of effect is tranquillity having on you? Have you ever seen horses unloaded on the Petersburg

Exchange? They stagger and can't walk. Isn't it that way with you, too? I don't want to talk to you about myself, because I have no intention of taking as my confidant the Moscow post, which this present year has committed astonishing swinish acts with regard to me;[4] I'll write you by an *occasion*. Meanwhile I embrace you with all my heart, and I kiss the hands of the recently confined mother.

[545]

To PAVEL VOINOVICH NASHCHOKIN
January 20, 1835. From Petersburg to Moscow.

I'm sending you, dear Pavel Voinovich, fifteen hundred rubles; the remaining five hundred would have gotten to you, but yesterday a young man touched me for them as a loan, for a stake at cards. Commiserating with a state in which you and I, too, have chanced to get caught on occasion, you'll probably be magnanimous and forgive me. However, please send me a full reckoning of my debt.[1]

My wife sends her cordial greetings to your Vera Alexandrovna [Nashchokina]; at Mme. Sichler's she has ordered her a hat, which today is being sent off to Moscow. My wife says that *comme Mme. Nashchokin est brune et qu'elle a un beau teint*,[2] she has chosen for her a hat of such-and-such a color, and not of another. But that's a ladies' affair.

You probably have seen my *Pugachev*, but I hope you haven't bought it. I am keeping a special copy for you. What do you think of these times? Pugachev has become a good, punctual payer of his quitrent—Emelka Pugachev, my peasant on quitrent! He has brought me in money enough, but since I had been living on credit for a couple of years, I'm keeping nothing hidden in my bosom, but everything's going for paying off debts. Now I embrace you with all my heart, kiss Vera Alexandrovna's little hand, and I'm setting off for the post.

January 20, 1835.
SPb.

[546]

To Alexander Khristoforovich Benkendorf
January 26, 1835. In Petersburg.

Dear Sir, Count Alexander Khristoforovich,

I have the honor to forward to Your Highness certain observations which could not enter into *The History of the Pugachev Revolt* but which may be of interest. I asked for permission to present them to the Sovereign Emperor, and I have had the happiness to receive the Highest's assent to my so doing.[1]

Along with this I make bold to ask Your Excellency to solicit a favor which is important for me: the Sovereign's authorization for me to read the Pugachev dossier, which is in the archives.[2] In my free time I would be able to make a brief excerption from it, if not for publication, then at least in order to make complete my work, which without this is imperfect, and in order to set my historian's conscience at rest.

With the most profound respect and with complete devotion, I have the honor to be,

Dear Sir,
Your Highness's
Most humble servant,
Alexander Pushkin.

January 26, 1835.
SPb.

[547]

To Dmitry Nikolaevich Bantysh-Kamensky
January 26, 1835. From Petersburg to Moscow.

Dear Sir, Dmitry Nikolaevich,

With gratitude I am returning to you the articles which your good will toward me has allowed me to utilize in the compilation of my *History*.[1] Along with them I am also forwarding a copy of the *History* itself. Your opinion of it, whatever it may be, is precious to me. Praise from a genuine historian, and not from a superficial narrator or transcriber, would be flattering for me; whereas, from censure I would learn a great deal (which you know, yourself, I cannot expect to do from the observations of our inveterate critics).

I ask you to take upon yourself the labor of correcting two errors which have been justly noted in *The Son of the Fatherland*:[2] On page 128 *was already* 10 *miles* should read 35. And in a note to the fifth chapter (16), instead of *Tobolsk*, *Tabinsk*.

With the most profound respect and gratitude, I have the honor to be,

Dear Sir,

Your Excellency's

January 26.   Most obedient servant,
SPb.   Alexander Pushkin.

[548]

To Ivan Ivanovich Dmitriev

February 14, 1835. From Petersburg to Moscow.

Dear Ivan Ivanovich, young [Andrey Nikolaevich] Karamzin showed me Your High Excellency's letter, in which you reproach me with unforgivable impoliteness. I hasten to justify myself. I have not delivered you my tribute[1] until now, because I have been momentarily expecting the portrait of Emilian Ivanovich [Pugachev], which is being engraved in Paris; I have wanted to present my book to you in perfect condition. Not to fulfill that would be, on my part, not only stinginess, but also ingratitude: my chronicle is indebted to you for a striking and vivid passage,[2] for the sake of which much will be forgiven me by even the severest readers.

You scoff at our generation, and of course you have full right to do so. I am not going to take up for the historians[3] and versifiers of my time. In olden days the historians had less charlatanry and more erudition and diligence, the versifiers, more sincerity and spiritual warmth. As regards financial profits, permit me to observe that Karamzin was the first among us to show an example of large enterprise in the trade of literature.[4]

I do not know whether you feel interested in the fate of our academy, which not long ago lost its secretary,[5] who died on his shield—that is, on the last proof sheet of its dictionary.[6] It is not known who will be his successor. The holy place will not remain empty—but the place of the permanent secretary was empty enough, even before it was vacated.

Your contemporary,[7] whom you mention in your letter to Andrey

Nikolaevich Karamzin, is well, thank God, and continues to visit Smirdin's bookshop daily and the academy on Saturdays. In the bookshop he takes his own works which are still unsold, and he gives them out to his fellow members of the academy with touching financial disinterestedness.

With the most profound respect and devotion, I have the honor to be, Dear Sir, Your High Excellency's most humble servant.

February 14, 1835.   Alexander Pushkin.
        SPb.

[549]
To Pavel Alexandrovich Katenin
April 20, 1835. From Petersburg to Stavropol.
(Fragment)

I am at fault toward you, in not having answered your letter for so long. The point is that I had nothing good to tell you in answer. Your "Sonnet" is exceedingly good, but I was not able to publish it. Now the censorship has become just as arbitrary and muddle-headed as in the times of the blessed[1] Krasovsky and Birukov: it passes things for which it deservedly gets a dressing-down, and then, out of fright, it will no longer pass anything. Your next to the last verse was enough to arouse all the censorship committee against your[2] sonnet.[3]

[550]
To Lev Sergeevich Pushkin
April 23 or 24, 1835. From Petersburg to Tiflis.
(In French)

I have delayed answering you because I have not had much to tell you. Since I had the weakness to take my father's affairs in hand, I have not touched 500 rubles of the revenues; and as for the loan of 13,000, it has already been spent. Here is the accounting which concerns you.[1]

to Engelgardt[2]	1,330
to the restaurant	260
to Dumé	220 (for wine)
to Pavlishchev	837
to the tailor	390

to Pleshcheev[3]   1,500
Besides, you have received; in bills   280
(*In August*, 1834) in gold   950
                                              ———
                                              5,767

Your promissory note (10,000) has been redeemed.[4] Thus, in addition to rent, board, and the tailor, which have cost you nothing, you have received 1230 rubles.

In view of the fact that my mother has been very sick, I am still taking care of affairs, in spite of a thousand unpleasantnesses. I am counting on giving them up at the first opportunity. I shall try, at that time, to arrange for you to receive your share of the lands and the peasants. Probably then you will busy yourself with your affairs and you will lose your indolence and the ease with which you allow yourself to live from one day to the next. From this moment on, address yourself to your parents. I have not paid your petty gambling debts, because I have not gone to seek out your companions—they should have addressed themselves to me.

[551]

To Ivan Ivanovich Dmitriev
April 26, 1835. From Petersburg to Moscow.

Dear Sir, Ivan Ivanovich, I want to express my sincere gratitude to Your High Excellency for your friendly word and for your consoling encouragement to my historical fragment.[1] It is being berated,[2] and deservedly: I wrote it for myself, not thinking that I would be able to publish it, and I strove only for a clear exposition of occurrences which were involved enough. Readers love anecdotes, the pecularities of the locality, etc.—but I thrust all that back into the notes. As regards those thinkers who are indignant with me because Pugachev is presented in my book as Emelka Pugachev and not as Byron's Lara,[3] I willingly refer them to Mr. Polevoy, who probably for a suitable sum will undertake to idealize this personage according to the very latest fashion.

You ask who is the secretary in our academy. I do not think it has been decided yet. Ulysses Lobanov and Ajax Fedorov are quarreling over the arms of Achilles. But they may very well fall to Yazykov-

Nestor (at least to the publisher of Nestor).[4] You are a prophet in your own country.

A black year has come onto our academies; scarcely had Sokolov passed away in the Russian Academy when Dondukov-Korsakov[5] appeared in the Academy of Sciences as the Vice President. Uvarov is a clown, and Dondukov-Korsakov is his stooge. Somebody said that where one goes, there goes the other; one turns flips on the rope, and the other, under him on the floor.

With the most profound respect and with complete devotion, I have the honor to be, Dear Sir, Your High Excellency's most humble servant,

Alexander Pushkin.

April 26, 1835.
SPb.

[552]

To VASILY ALEXEEVICH PEROVSKY
March or April, 1835. From Petersburg to Orenburg.

I am sending you *The History of Pugachev*, in memory of our jaunt to Berdy;[1] and three more copies for Dal,[2] Pokatilov, and for the hunter[3] who compares woodcocks with Wallenstein or with Caesar. I regret that in Petersburg we succeeded in meeting only at a ball. Good-by until we meet again, in the steppes or high in the Urals.

A.P.

[552a]

To GUSTAV NORDIN
After the middle of April, 1835. In Petersburg.
(In French)

Sir, please accept my most sincere thanks for your kind contraband.[1] Will you pardon my importuning you once more? I very much need the work on Germany[2] by that scapegrace, Heine. May I dare to hope that you will have the kindness to obtain it, too?

Accept, Sir, the assurance of my high esteem.

A. Pushkin.

[553]

To Iosif Matveevich Penkovsky
May 1, 1835. From Petersburg to Boldino.

All your arrangements meet with the full measure of my approval. I am thinking of being there in July. My affairs in Petersburg have taken a bad turn, but I hope to set them straight. According to my agreement with Father, the revenues from Kistenevo from now on are assigned exclusively to my brother Lev Sergeevich and my sister Olga Sergeevna.[1] Consequently, send all the revenues from my share to wherever my sister or her husband Nikolay Ivanovich Pavlishchev requests; and send the revenues from the other half (except the interest which is due to the government Loan Office) to Lev Sergeevich, wherever he may direct. Boldino will remain for Father.

In a few days I shall write you in more detail.

May 1.   A. Pushkin.

[554]

To Lev Sergeevich Pushkin
May 2, 1835. From Petersburg to Tiflis.

Father has agreed to give you complete control of half of Kistenevo. I am yielding my own share to our sister (i.e., only the revenues). I have already written to this effect to the manager.[1] You will have a net income of about two thousand rubles. I advise you to leave up to the manager the payment of the interest—and that you yourself receive only this sum. Two thousand is not a great deal, but all the same one can live on it. Our Mother was dying; now she is better, but not completely well. I don't think she can live long.

[555]

To Nikolay Ivanovich Pavlishchev
May 2, 1835. From Petersburg to Warsaw.

Dear Sir, Nikolay Ivanovich,

I have not answered you for a long time, because I could write nothing definite. I am answering both your letters today. You are right about almost everything, and there's no use discussing what you're not right about. Let's talk about business. You demand a sister's lawful share. You know our family circumstances; you know how difficult it is for us to proceed to anything sensible or business-like. Let us postpone this until another time. Here are the arrangements which I proposed to Father a few days ago, and to which, thank God, he agreed. He is letting Lev Sergeevich have half of Kistenevo; I am yielding my half to my sister (i.e., the revenue), with the proviso that she receive the revenues and pay the interest to the government Loan Office: I have already written to this effect to the manager.[1] Boldino remains Father's. Of course, this is neither a sacrifice nor a favor on my part, but a consideration for the future. My own family and my affairs are not in good condition. I am thinking of leaving Petersburg and going to the village, if only I can avoid incurring displeasure in so doing.

For the clasp and the pin I am offered 850 rubles.[2] What do you want me to do? It would not be a bad idea for you to come to Petersburg, but we still have time to exchange letters about it.

I have been still managing the estate up to now, but I am thinking of giving it up by July. Mother is better, but she is by no means so well as she thinks; the doctors have no hope for a complete recovery.

I send cordial greetings to you and my sister.

May 2.   A. Pushkin.

[556]
To MIKHAIL PETROVICH POGODIN
The beginning of May, 1835. From Petersburg to Moscow.
(Rough draft)
Dear Sir, Mikhaylo Petrovich,

I have just now received the most recent issue of *A Library for Reading*, and in it I have noticed some tale with the signature *Belkin*[1]—and I ran across your name. Since I shall not read the story, I hasten to announce to you that this Belkin is not my Belkin, and that I am not answerable for any absurdities of his.

This letter will be delivered to you by Mr. Semen,[2] the editor of *The Pictorial Annual*. He is planning to describe Moscow, and I am sending him to one who loves her.

Tell the Observers[3] that they should be a little more punctual in delivering.

[557]

To Natalia Ivanovna Goncharova
May 16, 1835. From Petersburg to Yaropolets.

Dear Madame, Mother, Natalia Ivanovna,

I have the happiness to congratulate you upon your grandson Grigory[1] and to commend him to your favor. Natalia Nikolaevna gave birth to him successfully. But she was in pain longer than usual. And her condition now is not exactly good—though, thank God, there is no danger whatever. I was absent when the baby was born; I had been forced to make a trip to the Pskov village on personal business,[2] and I returned the day after her delivery. My arrival disturbed her, and she suffered all day yesterday; today she is better. She has commissioned me to solicit your blessing on her and the new-born child.

Yesterday the hatbox was received from you, together with the note, which I have not shown my wife, so as not to cause her pain, in her condition. She seems not to have carried out your errand satisfactorily, and she might conclude from the note that you have become angry with her.

I kiss your little hands, and I have the happiness to be, with the most profound respect and heartfelt devotion,

Your most humble
Servant and son-in-law,
A. Pushkin.

[558]

To Semen Semenovich Khlyustin
May 25, 1835(?). In Petersburg.
(In French)

I beseech you to excuse me. It will be impossible for me to come and dine at your house. My wife has suddenly become very ill. Please be so kind as to send me the address of M. de Circourt.[1]

All yours,
May 25.   Pushkin.

[559]

To Vladimir Fedorovich Odoevsky
April or May, 1835. In Petersburg.
What do you take me for? I heard the fool[1] once in Moscow, and I'm not going to any more. One must listen to him, however, in order to berate him properly in the Chronicler.[2] And so, subscribe, Prince! Be so kind as to pay up, Your Highness—you'll get used to it and come to love it. Don't be stingy. And shall we see each other some fine day?

A.P.

[560]

To Alexander Khristoforovich Benkendorf
April or May, 1835. In Petersburg.
(Rough draft; in French)
I make bold to submit for Your Excellency's decision the following:

In 1832 His Majesty deigned to grant me the permission to be the publisher of a political and literary journal.[1]

This profession is not mine, and it is distasteful to me in quite a few respects, but circumstances oblige me to have recourse to a measure which until now I believed I could avoid. I am living in Petersburg, where, thanks to His Majesty, I can devote myself to pursuits which are more important and more to my taste. But the life I am leading entails expenses, and my family affairs are so disorganized that I find myself in the necessity of either abandoning historical labors,[2] which have become dear to me, or of having recourse to the Emperor's kindnesses, to which I have no claim other than the benefactions which he has already showered upon me.

A journal offers me the means of living in Petersburg and of meeting my sacred obligations. I therefore should like to be the editor of a gazette similar in every way to The Northern Bee, and I should like permission to publish separately items of a purely literary nature (such as long and detailed critiques, tales, short novels, long poems, etc.), for which room could not be found in a feuilleton (a volume every three months in the manner of the English Reviews).[3]

I beg your pardon, but I am obliged to tell you everything. I have had the misfortune to incur the enmity of the Minister of Public Instruction,[4] and also that of Prince Dondukov, born Korsakov. Both of them have already made me feel this in a rather disagreeable manner. In entering upon a field of endeavor where I shall be dependent upon them, I would be lost without your immediate protection. I therefore make bold to beseech you to grant my journal a censor drawn from your chancellery. This is all the more indispensable to me in that, since my journal is to appear at the same time as *The Northern Bee*, I must have time to translate the same articles, under the penalty of otherwise being obliged to republish on the morrow the news already published the preceding evening—which would indeed suffice to ruin the whole undertaking.

[561]

To Alexander Khristoforovich Benkendorf
April or May, 1835. In Petersburg.
(Second rough draft; in French)

When I asked for permission to become the publisher of a literary and political gazette, I myself felt all the objections to this undertaking. I was compelled to do so by painful circumstances. Neither I nor my wife, so far, has an estate; that of my father is so disorganized that I have been obliged to take over the direction of it, in order to assure a future to the rest of my family. I wanted to become a journalist only so as not to reproach myself with having neglected a means which, by giving me an income of 40,000, would deliver me from my difficulties. I confess that, my plan not meeting with His Majesty's approval,[1] I was relieved of a great burden. But I am, as a consequence, obliged to have recourse to the kindnesses of the Emperor, who is now my only hope. I ask your permission, Count, to explain my situation to you and to entrust my request to your protection.

Finding a way to borrow 100,000 would suffice me to pay my debts and to be able to live, to arrange my family affairs and finally to be free to devote myself without any worries to my historical labors and to my pursuits. But in Russia it is impossible.

The Emperor, who up to the present has never wearied of showering me with favors, but what is painful to me [. . . .],[2] in deigning to take me into his service, he did me the favor of setting my salary at 5,000. This sum represents the interest on a capital of 125,000. If, instead of my salary, His Majesty would do me the favor of giving me the capital as a *loan* for ten years and without interest—I would be perfectly happy and tranquil.[3]

[562]

To Alexander Khristoforovich Benkendorf
June 1, 1835. In Petersburg.
(In French)

Count,

I am ashamed of always troubling Your Excellency, but the indulgence and the interest which you have always deigned to display toward me will be the excuse for my indiscretion.

I have no property; neither I nor my wife has yet the portion which is to come to us. Up to the present I have lived on only the fruits of my labor. My fixed income is the salary which the Emperor has deigned to grant me. Working in order to live has, most certainly, no humiliation for me. But it is completely impossible for me, accustomed to independence, to write for money; and that idea alone is enough to reduce me to inaction. Life in Petersburg is horribly expensive. Up to the present I have looked rather indifferently upon the expenditures which I have been obliged to make, because a political and literary journal—a purely commercial undertaking— would give me immediately the means of having an income of 30,000–40,000. However, this work was so repugnant to me that I have considered having recourse to it only as the last resort.

I see myself in the necessity of cutting short expenditures which only entail my making debts and which are preparing for me a future of anxiety and cares, if not of destitution and despair. Three or four years of retirement to the country would make it possible for me again to come and resume in Petersburg the pursuits for which I am still indebted to the favors of His Majesty.

I have been showered with benefactions by the Emperor; I would be in despair if His Majesty could suppose, in my desire to depart from Petersburg, any other motive than that of absolute necessity. The least sign of displeasure or of suspicion would suffice to keep me in the status where I now am, because, in short, I would rather be in financial difficulties than be ruined in the opinion of the one who has been my benefactor, not as Sovereign, not from duty or justice, but from a free feeling of noble and generous benevolence.[1]

Entrusting my fate into your hands, I have the honor to be, with the most profound respect,

Count,

Your Excellency's

Most humble and most obedient servant,

June 1.   Alexander Pushkin.

SPb.

[563]

To NIKOLAY IVANOVICH PAVLISHCHEV

June 3, 1835. From Petersburg to Warsaw.

Dear Sir, Nikolay Ivanovich,

You wish to know just what Father's estate consists of. I am sending you a listing of it:

In the village of Boldino, according to the seventh revision, 564 souls.

In the little village of Kistenevo (also called Timashevo), 476.

The late Vasily Lvovich [Pushkin] owned *the other half of Boldino,* in which there were also about 600 souls. This part was sold three years after the heir himself renounced the inheritance. I was not able to take upon myself the debts of the deceased, because I was already hard up, even without doing that.[1] And I should think that Lev Sergeevich [Pushkin] could not have even thought of it, for, the very first thing, one would have had to pay at least 60,000. It's a pity that you did not get in touch with me at that time. If I could have supposed that you would take over the management of this estate, I might not have renounced it.

You want to have a power of attorney[2] for managing that part of Kistenevo, the income of which I am yielding to my sister. Gladly. Only write me whether I am to send it to you or whether you yourself will come for it. It would not be a bad idea to talk everything over.

June 3, 1835.   All yours, A. Pushkin.

[564]

To Vasily Andreevich Durov
June 16, 1835. From Petersburg to Elabuga.

Dear Sir, Vasily Andreevich,[1]

I was sincerely gladdened by receiving your letter, which reminded me of our old, pleasant acquaintanceship, and I hasten to answer you. If the author of the Notes[2] will agree to entrust them to me, then I shall willingly undertake the cares of their publication. If he is thinking of selling them in manuscript, then let him set the price himself. If the booksellers do not agree to it, I shall probably buy them. I should think their success can be vouched for. The author's fate is so curious, so well known and so mysterious, that the solution of the riddle cannot help producing a powerful, a general impression. As for the style, the simpler it is, the better. The most important thing is truth, sincerity. The subject in itself is so interesting that it needs no adornments. They would even harm it.

I congratulate you upon your new mode of living; I am sorry that of your hundred thousand ways to obtain a hundred thousand rubles, not one seems to have been employed by you with success. But money will come with time. The main thing: may we stay alive.

Farewell—I am awaiting your answer with impatience.

With the most profound respect and complete devotion, I have the honor to be,

Dear Sir,

Your most humble servant,

June 16, 1835. A. Pushkin.

SPb.

On the Dvortsovaya Naberezhnaya, the house of Batashev.

[565]

To Andrey Alexandrovich Kraevsky
June 18, 1835. In Petersburg.

I have not written anything to the Moscow brotherhood. But do me the favor of correcting the next to the last verse in "The Cloud."[1]

And the wind, *caressing the little leaves* of the trees [. . . .]

[566]
To Alexander Khristoforovich Benkendorf
July 4, 1835. In Petersburg.

Dear Sir, Count Alexander Khristoforovich,

It was the Sovereign's pleasure to jot down on my letter to Your Highness[1] that I may not leave for several years in the village, unless I first resign. I commit my fate completely to the Tsar's will, and I wish only that His Majesty's decision[2] be not a sign of disfavor toward me, and that access to the archives not be forbidden me, when circumstances permit me to be in Petersburg.

With the most profound respect, devotion, and gratitude, I have the honor to be,

Dear Sir,

Your Highness's

July 4, 1835.	Most humble servant,
SPb.	Alexander Pushkin.

[567]
To Natalia Ivanovna Goncharova
July 14, 1835. From Petersburg to Yaropolets.

Dear Madame, Mother, Natalia Ivanovna,

I sincerely thank you for the present which you have been so kind as to bestow upon my new-born son,[1] and which arrived very opportunely. We expected Dmitry Nikolaevich [Goncharov] for the christening, but he didn't get here. He writes that his affairs detained him, and that his anticipations with regard to Countess N.[2] were not fulfilled. He does not seem to be in despair. As you instructed, I kissed my wife with all possible tenderness; she kisses your little hands and is intending to write you. We are now living in a summer house, on Chernaya Rechka, and we are thinking of moving from here to the village and even for several years.[3] Our financial circumstances require it. However, I am awaiting the decision of my fate by the Sovereign, who has been very gracious to me, and whose wish will be my law.

I have a request and domestic explanations to address to you: Until now our chief bothers have come from our not being able to cope with our male cooks, who in Petersburg, are spoiled and excessively expensive. If you have any male cook in Yaropolets whom you do not need (if only he be of good, honorable, and undebauched conduct), then you would do us a true benefaction by sending him to us—especially in case we leave for the village. Forgive me for speaking to you without ceremony and directly, relying on your indulgence and good will.

My wife, children, and sisters-in-law⁴—all, thank God, at my house are well, and they kiss your little hands. Masha is asking to go to a ball, and she says she has already learned to dance from the little doggies. You see how precocious they are among us; the first thing you know she will be marriageable.

With the most profound respect and devotion, I have the happiness to be,

Dear Madame, Mother,
Your most humble servant and son-in-law,
July 14.   A. Pushkin.

[568]
To Alexander Khristoforovich Benkendorf
July 22, 1835. In Petersburg.
(In French)

Count,

I have had the honor of waiting upon you at Your Excellency's door, but I did not have the good fortune to find you in.

Showered with favors by His Majesty, I, Count, am writing you now in order to thank you for the interest which you have been so kind as to display toward me, and to explain my situation frankly to you.

During my last five years' residence in Petersburg, I have incurred debts of close to sixty thousand rubles. Moreover, I have been obliged to take in hand my family's affairs, which have so encumbered me that I have been obliged to forego a legacy,¹ and so that the only means that I had of putting my affairs in order were either to retire to the country, or else borrow, once and for all, a large sum of money. But this latter course is almost impossible in Russia, where the law grants too weak a guarantee to the creditor, and where loans are almost always debts between friends and on one's word.

Gratitude is not for me a painful feeling, and most certainly my devotion to the person of the Emperor is not troubled by any mental reservations of shame or of remorse. But I cannot conceal from myself that I have absolutely no right to benefactions from His Majesty and that it is impossible for me to ask for anything.[2]

It is therefore to you, Count, that I entrust once more the deciding of my fate, and beseeching you to accept the assurance of my high esteem, I have the honor to be, with respect and gratitude,

Count,

Your Excellency's

July 22, 1835.　　　Most humble and most obedient servant,
St. Petersburg.　　　　　　　　　　Alexander Pushkin.

[569]

To Vladimir Dmitrievich Volkhovsky
July 22, 1835. From Petersburg to Tiflis.

I have a friendly and most humble request to make of you, my honored Vladimir Dmitrievich:[1] Count Zabela is en route to Georgia to serve under your command. His friends and relatives ask, on his behalf, your protection and good will, which of course he needs in his situation. I know that my intercession is completely superfluous in this instance, but I rejoice at the chance to remind you from afar of your Lyceum comrade, who is sincerely devoted to you.

I am sending you my most recent composition, *The History of the Pugachev Revolt*. In it I was trying to investigate the military actions of that time, and I was thinking only of the clear exposition of them, which cost me no little labor, for the commanders, who operated confusedly enough, wrote their reports still more confusedly, boasting or justifying themselves equally unintelligibly. It was necessary to check all this, to verify, etc. Your opinion regarding my book would be precious to me in every respect.

Be healthy and happy.

July 22, 1835.　　　　　　　　　　　A. Pushkin.
SPb.

[570]
To ALEXANDER KHRISTOFOROVICH BENKENDORF
July 26, 1835. In Petersburg.
(In French)

Count,

It pains me, at the moment when I am receiving an unexpected favor, to ask for two more, but I have resolved to have recourse in all frankness to the one who has deigned to be my Providence.

Of my sixty thousand in debts, half are debts of honor. In order to pay them, I see myself under the necessity of contracting usurious debts, which will redouble my difficulties, or even place me in the necessity of having recourse again to the generosity of the Emperor.

I therefore beseech His Majesty to do me a full and complete favor: first, to grant me the possibility of paying off these thirty thousand rubles; and, second, to deign to permit me to regard this sum as a loan and, accordingly, to have the payment of my salary suspended until my debt be paid off.[1]

Commending myself to your indulgence, I have the honor to be, with the most profound respect and with the most heartfelt gratitude,

Count,

Your Excellency's,

July 26, 1835.   Most humble and most obedient servant,
St. Petersburg.   Alexander Pushkin.

[571]
To ALEXANDRA ANDREEVNA FUCHS
August 15, 1835. From Petersburg to Kazan.

August 15, 1835. SPb.

I have long delayed delivering your tribute to you, while I was awaiting the portrait of Pugachev from Paris. Finally I have received it, and I hasten to forward my book to you.[1] Relying on your indulgence, I have made bold to send in care of you a copy for delivery to Mr. Rybushkin,[2] from whom I had the honor to receive his interesting history of Kazan.

I commend myself to your precious good will, and to the friend-ship of honored Karl Fedorovich [Fuchs] (to whom I apologize for the imperfections in the publishing of my book).

With the most profound respect and devotion, I have the honor to be [. . . .]³

[572]

To Efim Petrovich Lyutsenko
August 19, 1835. In Petersburg.

Dear Sir, Efim Petrovich!¹

I am truly ashamed for the bothers which I am letting Your Excellency in for. Smirdin has not kept his word; I suspect that actually his circumstances are in a muddle. The printing of your poem² cannot cost fifteen hundred rubles; he is mistaken. My departure for the village prevents me from undertaking the business myself. I have just now written to Baron Korf, asking him to intercede for you, as for one connected with the Lyceum. I hope that on his part he will do everything possible.

With genuine respect and complete devotion, I have the honor to be, Dear Sir, Your Excellency's most humble servant.

August 19, 1835.   A. Pushkin.

[573]

To Vasily Alexeevich Polenov
August 28, 1835. In Petersburg.

Dear Sir, Vasily Alexeevich,¹

I have the honor to make a most humble request of Your Excellency.

The Sovereign Emperor has been so kind as to empower me to unseal the Pugachev dossier, in order to compile a Historical Extract.² In the eight binders provided me from the St. Petersburg Senate, I have not found the most important document: the deposition taken from Pugachev himself, in the Committee of Inquiry established in Moscow. I make bold most humbly to request Your Excellency that you have this matter referred to A. F. Malinovsky,³ who probably knows where this essential document is located.⁴

With the most profound respect and with complete devotion, I have the honor to be,

Dear Sir,
Your Excellency's

August 28, 1835.   Most humble servant,
SPb.   Alexander Pushkin.

[574]

To EGOR FRANTSEVICH KANKRIN
September 6, 1835. In Petersburg.

Dear Sir, Count Egor Frantsevich,

Having a most humble request to make of Your Highness, I make bold to burden your attention with a preliminary explanation of my piece of business.

As a consequence of domestic circumstances, I was compelled to request retirement, in order to go to the village for several years. The Sovereign Emperor most graciously deigned to say that he does not want me to be torn away from my historical labors, and he commanded that I be given 10,000 rubles,[1] as a grant in aid. This sum was not sufficient to rectify my financial status. Remaining in Petersburg, I could not avoid either further muddling my affairs by the hour, or having recourse to grants in aid and to favors, an expedient to which I am not accustomed, for until now, thank God, I have been independent and have lived by my labors.

And so I have made bold to ask His Majesty for two favors: (1) that I be given, *instead of a grant in aid, a loan of 30,000 rubles, every ruble of which I need* for payment of debts which must be paid; (2) that my salary be withheld until this sum has been repaid. The sovereign has been kind enough to consent to both.[2]

But from the State Treasury I was given, instead of 30,000 rubles, only 18,000, for there was a deduction of various amounts of interest and of the 10,000 (ten thousand rubles) which had been given me as a loan for the publishing of a certain book.[3] Thus I am in a more constrained position than ever, for I am compelled to remain in Petersburg, with my debts not paid and deprived of my 5000 rubles of salary.

I make bold to request Your Highness for the authorization for me to receive in full the sum which I was forced to request of the Sovereign, and for permission to pay the interest on the sum which was given me in 1834, until my circumstances permit me to pay the sum itself in full.[4]

Commending myself to Your Highness's good will, with the

most profound respect and with complete devotion, I have the honor to be,

Dear Sir,

Your Highness's

Most humble servant,

September 6, 1835.   Alexander Pushkin.

[575]

To NATALIA NIKOLAEVNA PUSHKINA

September 14, 1835. From Mikhaylovskoe to Petersburg.

You and I are fine ones. I didn't give you my address, and you didn't ask me for it. Here it is: to the Pskov Province, to Ostrov, to the village Trigorskoe.[1] Today is September 14. Here it has already been a week since I left you, my darling, but I have seen no benefit in having done so. I haven't begun writing, and I don't know when I'll begin. Instead, I think of you constantly, and I won't think up anything worth while. I'm sorry I didn't bring you along with me. What weather we're having! Here I've just spent three whole days jaunting about—now on foot, now on horseback. Thus I'll jaunt away my whole autumn, and if God doesn't send some decent frosts, I'll return to you without having accomplished anything. Praskovia Alexandrovna [Osipova] isn't here yet. She's either in the village at Begicheva's,[2] or she's fussing around in Pskov. She's expected in a few days. Today I saw the moon over my left shoulder,[3] and I began to be very much disturbed about you. How's our expedition?[4] Have you seen Countess Kankrina, and what's the answer? As a last resort, if Count Kankrin turns us off, we have Count Yuriev[5] left; I direct you to him. Write me as often as you can; and write everything you're doing, so that I may know whom you're coquetting with, where you go, whether you're behaving yourself well, what your gossiping is like, and whether you're waging war successfully with your surnamesake.[6] Farewell, darling: I kiss Maria Alexandrovna's[7] little hand, and I ask her to be my intercessor with you. I kiss Sashka on his round forehead. I bless all of you. To Aunts Azya and Koko,[8] my cordial greeting. Tell Pletnev to write me about our mutual affairs.

[576]
To Peter Alexandrovich Pletnev
Between September 1 and 15, 1835.
From Mikhaylovskoe to Petersburg.
(Rough draft)
You advise me to continue *Onegin*, assuring me that I haven't
finished it [. . . .]¹

[577]
To Alexandra Ivanovna Bekleshova
Between September 11 and 18, 1835. From Trigorskoe to Pskov.
My angel,¹ how sorry I am that I found you were no longer here,
and how glad Evpraxia Nikolaevna [Vrevskaya, nee Vulf] made me,
by telling me that you intend to come to our parts again! Do come,
for God's sake; at least by the 23rd. I have heaps of confessions,
explanations, and all sorts of stuff for you. We might, at our leisure,
even fall in love. I am writing you, and cater-cornered from me you
yourself are sitting, in the form of Maria Ivanovna [Osipova].² You
wouldn't believe how she calls to mind a former time

And journeys to Opochka³

and so forth. Forgive me my friendly chatter. I kiss your little hands.
A.P.

[578]
To Natalia Nikolaevna Pushkina
September 21, 1835. From Mikhaylovskoe to Petersburg.
My wife, here it's already the 21st, and I haven't received a single
line from you yet. This disturbs me in spite of myself, though I
know that you probably didn't learn my address before the 17th, in
Pavlovsk. Did you? Besides, the mail from Petersburg comes only
once a week. However, I am constantly uneasy, anyhow, and I'm
not writing anything. And time is passing. You can't imagine how
vividly the imagination operates when we sit alone within four walls,
or when we walk in the woods, when nobody hinders us from thinking—from thinking until the head begins to whirl. And what do I

think about? Here's what: what are we going to live on? My father won't leave me the estate; he has already squandered half of it. Your estate is within a hair's breadth of ruin. The Tsar doesn't permit me to join the ranks of the landowners or the journalists. God sees that I can't write books for money. We don't have a penny of sure income, but a sure outgo of thirty thousand. Everything hangs on me and Aunty. But neither I nor Aunty is eternal. How all this will come out, God knows. Meanwhile, it's sad. Just give me a kiss; maybe the woe will pass. But it's no use—your little lips won't stretch two hundred fifty miles. I just sit and pine—what would you have! Now listen to my diary: I was at the Vrevskys[1] day before yesterday, and spent the night there. Praskovia Alexandrovna [Osipova] was expected, but she didn't come. Vrevskaya is a very kind and sweet little woman, but she's as fat as Mefody, our Pskov bishop. And you'd think, looking at her, she's with child; she's still just the same as when you saw her. I borrowed Walter Scott from them, and I'm reading him. I'm sorry that I didn't bring the English along with me. By the way: send me, if you can, *Essays de M. Montagne* [sic][2]—four dark blue books on my long shelves. Look them up. Today the weather is gloomy. Autumn is beginning. Maybe I'll set to work. I'm expecting Praskovia Alexandrovna, who probably will arrive in Trigorskoe today.—I walk a lot, I ride horseback a lot, on jades which are very glad of it, for in reward they're given oats, to which they're not accustomed. I eat baked potatoes, like a Finn, and soft-boiled eggs, like Louis XVIII. That's my dinner. I lie down at 9 o'clock; I get up at 7. Now I require of you a similar detailed accounting. I kiss you, my darling, and all the children. I bless all of you with all my heart. Stay well, all of you. To my sisters-in-law, my greeting. How must one say it: *bel' sery* or *bel' seri*?[3] Farewell.

[579]

To NATALIA NIKOLAEVNA PUSHKINA
September 25, 1835. From Trigorskoe to Petersburg.

I am writing you from Trigorskoe. What's this, little wife? Here it's already the 25th, and all this time I haven't had a single line from you. This angers and disturbs me. How are you addressing your letters to me? Write *To Pskov*, to Her Honor, Praskovia Alexandrovna Osipova, for delivery to A.S.P., the well-known writer—and that's all there is to it. That way it'll be surer that I'm reached by your letters, without which I will get completely stultified. Are you well, my darling? And how are my young ones? How's our home, and how well are you managing it? Just imagine, I haven't written a line up till now, and all because I'm not tranquil. In Mikhaylovskoe I found everything as of old, except that my nursemaid[1] is no longer here, and that near the old familiar pines there has grown up during my absence a young pine family which it's vexing for me to look at,[2] just as it's sometimes vexing for me to see young cavalry guardsmen at balls, at which I no longer dance. But there's nothing to be done. Everything around me says that I'm growing old, and sometimes even in plain Russian. For example, yesterday I was met by a peasant woman I know, whom I couldn't help telling that she had changed. Then she, to me: "And you, too, my provider, you've grown old and ugly." Though I can say of myself, as my deceased nursemaid used to, that I never was good-looking—but I once was young. All that is no great matter. There is one great matter: don't notice, my darling, what I am noticing all too well. What are you doing, my beauty, in my absence? Tell me what occupies you, where you go, what new gossip there is, etc. [Sofia Nikolaevna] Karamzina and the Meshcherskys, I've heard, have arrived.[3] Don't forget to give them my cordial greeting. It's roomier now at Trigorskoe: Evpraxia Nikolaevna [Vrevskaya, nee Vulf] and Alexandra Ivanovna [Bekleshova, nee Osipova] are married, but Praskovia Alexandrovna [Osipova] is still the same, and I love her very much. I am behaving myself with modesty and decency. I go on jaunts on foot and horseback. I'm reading Walter Scott's novels, which I'm in rapture over, and I am moaning for you. Farewell. I give you a big kiss; I bless you and the children. How are Koko and Azya?[4] Are they married, or not yet? Tell them not to get married without my blessing. Farewell, my angel.

[580]

To NATALIA NIKOLAEVNA PUSHKINA
September 29, 1835. From Mikhaylovskoe to Petersburg

My darling, yesterday I received two letters from you; they grieved me very much. What's Katerina Ivanovna [Zagryazhskaya] ill of? You write *terribly ill*. Consequently there's danger? With impatience

I am awaiting your *bulletin*. All that proceeds from her inhuman mode of living. Will we live to see the day when Countess Polier has finally married her prince?[1] Kankrin jokes—but I'm in no mood for jokes. The Sovereign promised me a *Gazette*,[2] but then he forbade it; he makes me live in Petersburg but does not give me the means of living by my own labors. I am wasting my time and spiritual powers, I'm throwing my hard-earned money out the windows, and I don't see anything in the future. My father is squandering his estate away, without pleasure and without prudence; your folks are losing theirs on account of the stupidity or the heedlessness of the deceased Afanasy Nikolaevich [Goncharov]. What will come of all this? The Lord knows. Your fire occurred probably from the negligence of your Ladies in Waiting; may they thrive in my absence! Thank God that the affair was limited to the curtains. You have sent me a note from Mme. Kern; the fool has taken it into her head to translate [George] Sand,[3] and she asks that I act the pander for her with Smirdin. The devil take them both! I have commissioned Anna Nikolaevna [Vulf] to answer her for me that if her translation is as faithful as she herself is a faithful copy of Mme. Sand, then her success is undoubtable, but that I have no business connections with Smirdin.—What about Pletnev? Is he thinking about our mutual piece of business?[4] Probably not. I am spending my time very monotonously. Mornings I am not getting anything done, but I am merely milling the wind. In the evening I ride to Trigorskoe, burrow in old books, and nibble on nuts. But I'm not even thinking of writing either poetry or prose. Tell Sashka that I have white plums here which there's no comparing with the ones he steals from you, and that I ask him to eat some with me. How's Mashka? What do you think of her friendship with the little *Peassant*?[5] And what do you think of her conquests? Write me the political news, too. I don't read newspapers here—I don't go to the English Club or see [Elizaveta M.] Khitrovo. I don't know what's happening in the great wide world. When will the Tsars be there? And isn't there something to be heard about a war, etc.? I bless all of you—stay well. I kiss you. How stupidly you addressed your letter to me; what a dainty dish! "To the Pskov Province, to the village Mikhaylovskoe." Oh you, you dove! But you didn't say what district. And I'll bet there is more than one village Mikhaylovskoe. And even if only one, then just who knows where it is? What a featherbrain! You see that I keep on grumbling, but what's to be done? There's nothing to be glad about. Write to me about Aunty—and about your mother. *Je remercie vos soeurs,*[6] as Natalia Ivanovna [Goncharova] writes, although, truly, there's nothing to thank them for.

[581]
To NATALIA NIKOLAEVNA PUSHKINA
October 2, 1835. From Mikhaylovskoe to Petersburg.

My dear little wife, we have a filly here which takes either harness or the saddle. She's good in every way, but just let something frighten her on the road, and she will take the bit in her teeth and she'll take you six or eight miles over mounds and ravines—and then there is no way you can curb her in until she herself is all fagged out.

I have received, angel of skittishness and beauty! your letter, where you see fit to take the bit in your teeth and kick out your dainty and shapely little hoofs shod by Mme. *Katherine*.[1] I hope that now you are all fagged out and have calmed down. I am awaiting from you some decent letters wherein I may hear you and your voice—and not abuse, which I have not deserved at all, for I am behaving myself like a fairy-tale maid. Since yesterday I have begun to write (but knock on wood). Our weather is becoming worse and worse, and fall seems to be approaching in earnest. Perhaps I shall get in a writing vein. From your angry letter I conclude that Katerina Ivanovna [Zagryazhskaya] is better;[2] you wouldn't have abused me so spiritedly if she were seriously ill. All the same, write me about everything, and in detail. Why don't you write anything about Masha? After all, though Sashka is my favorite, I still love her pranks. I look out the window and think: it wouldn't be bad if suddenly a carriage entered the yard—and Natalia Nikolaevna were sitting in the carriage! But no, my darling. Stay in Petersburg, and I'll try to hurry up and come to you sooner than the appointed time. How about Pletnev?[3] How are the Karamzins, the Meshcherskys, etc.?—Write me about everything. I kiss you, and I bless the children.

[582]

To Peter Alexandrovich Pletnev
About (not later than) October 11, 1835.
From Mikhaylovskoe to Petersburg.

I was made glad by receiving from you a letter (a sensible one, as yours usually are). I shall try to answer point by point and in detail: You have received the *Journey*[1] from the censorship, but what did the committee decide with regard to my most humble petition?[2] The little ass Nikitenko won't kick and the bull Dunduk[3] butt me to death, will they? They won't get rid of me so easily, though. My thanks, my great thanks to Gogol for his "Calash";[4] the almanac can travel a long way in it. However, my opinion is this: don't accept "The Calash" for nothing, but set a price for it; Gogol needs money. You ask a name for the almanac: let's call it Arion or Orion. I love names which don't make any sense; there's nothing for jokes to stick to. Have Langer[5] also sketch a vignette without any sense. There should be some little flowers, and lyres, and chalices, and ivy, as in Alexander Ivanovich's apartment in Gogol's comedy.[6] That will seem very natural. I would be glad to come to you in November; all the more that I've never had such a fruitless autumn in my life. I'm writing, but bungling the job. For inspiration one must have spiritual tranquillity, and I'm not tranquil at all. You're doing badly in becoming indecisive. I have always found that everything which you have devised has succeeded for me. Let's begin the almanac with the *Journey*. Send the proofs along to me, and I'll send you some poems. Who will be our censor? I rejoice that Senkovsky is trafficking on the name of Belkin. But can't we (of course stealthily and unobtrusively, for example, in *The Moscow Observer*) announce that the real Belkin is dead and refuses to accept responsibility for the sins of his homonym?[7] That truly wouldn't be a bad thing to do.

[583]

To Egor Frantsevich Kankrin
October 23, 1835. In Petersburg.

Dear Sir, Count Egor Frantsevich,

Upon returning from the village,[1] I discovered that Your High-

ness had been so kind as to inform me of the Sovereign's approving
my most humble request, which I conveyed to you. I want to express
to Your Highness my sincere, profound gratitude for the indulgent
attention with which you, in the midst of your labors, have honored
me, and for your well-disposed intercession, to which I am obligated
for the success of my piece of business.[2]

With the most profound respect and with complete devotion, I
have the honor to be,

Dear Sir,

Your Highness's

Most humble servant,

October 23.   Alexander Pushkin.
St. Petersburg.

[584]

To ALEXANDER KHRISTOFOROVICH BENKENDORF

About (not earlier than) October 23, 1835. In Petersburg.

(Rough draft)

I address myself to Your Excellency with a complaint and a most
humble request.

On the occasion of the censorship's finding difficulties in
authorizing the publication of one of my poems, I was compelled
during your absence to direct a petition to the Censorship Committee
that the misunderstanding which had arisen be resolved. But the
Committee has not honored my petition with an answer.[1] I do not
know how I could have deserved such neglect—but not a single
Russian writer has been more oppressed than I.

My compositions, approved by the Tsar, have been stopped at
their appearance—they are published with arbitrary emendations by
the censor; my complaints have been left without attention. I do not
dare to publish my compositions—for I do not dare [. . . .][2]

[585]

To PRASKOVIA ALEXANDROVNA OSIPOVA

About (not later than) October 26, 1835.

From Petersburg to Trigorskoe.

(In French)

Here I am, Madame, arrived in Petersburg. Just imagine, my

wife's silence proceeded from her having taken it into her head to address her letters to Opochka. God knows how she came to do that. In any case I beseech you to send one of our servants there, so that the post master will be informed that I am no longer in the country and that he should forward to Petersburg all the mail he has for me.

I have found my poor mother at death's door.[1] She had come from Pavlovsk to seek lodgings, and suddenly fell in a faint at Mme. Knyazhnina's,[2] where she had stopped. Raukh[3] and Spassky have no hope. In this sad situation I also have the affliction of seeing my poor Natalia the object of the hatred of society. Everywhere it is being said that it is dreadful that she should be such a woman of fashion when her father-in-law and her mother-in-law do not have the wherewithal to eat, and that her mother-in-law is dying at the home of outsiders. You know how things really stand. Strictly speaking, no one can say that a man who has twelve hundred peasants is poverty-stricken. It is my father who has something and I who have nothing. In any case, Natalia has nothing to do with all this; I am the one who should be answerable. If my mother had come to take up her abode at my house, Natalia, as a matter of course, would have taken her in. But a cold house, full of little ones, and crowded with company, is hardly suitable for an ill person. My mother is better off at her own house. I have found her already moved.[4] My father is in a very pitiable state. As for me, I am in a fret, and I am completely dumbfounded.

Believe me, dear Madame Osipova, all life, *süsse Gewohnheit*[5] that it is, has a bitterness which ends by rendering it disgusting, and society is a nasty pile of filth. I prefer Trigorskoe. I greet you with all my heart.

[586]

To Ivan Ivanovich Lazhechnikov
November 3, 1835. From Petersburg to Moscow.

Dear Sir, Ivan Ivanovich!

In the first place, I must ask your forgiveness for my laggardliness and unpunctuality. I received the portrait of Pugachev a month ago,[1] and upon returning from the village I discovered that until now your copy of the *History* of him has not been delivered to you. I am returning to you Rychkov's manuscript,[2] which, by your benevolence, I was able to utilize.

Permit me, Dear Sir, to thank you now for the excellent novels which we all have read with such avidity and with such enjoyment. Perhaps, as regards artistry, *The House of Ice* stands even higher than *The Last Novik*, but it does not abide by historical truth, and that, in time, when the Volynsky[3] affair is made available to the public, will of course harm your work. But poetry will always remain poetry, and many pages of your novel will live as long as the Russian language is not forgotten. On behalf of Vasily Trediakovsky,[4] I confess, I am ready to argue with you. You injure a person who is in many respects worthy of our esteem and gratitude. In the Volynsky affair he plays the role of a martyr. His report to the Academy is extremely touching. It is impossible to read it without indignation at his tormentor. One might also discuss Biron a little. He had the misfortune to be a German; on him has been dumped all the horror of Anna's reign, which was in accordance with the spirit of its time and the mores of the populace. Incidentally, he had great intelligence and great talents.

Permit me to pose for you a philological question, the resolving of which is important for me: in what sense did you use the word *xobot* in your last work, and according to what dialect?[5]

Commending myself to your favor, I have the honor to be, with the most profound respect,

Dear Sir,
Your most obedient servant,

November 3, 1835.   Alexander Pushkin.
St. Petersburg.

[587]

To PRASKOVIA ALEXANDROVNA OSIPOVA
December 26, 1835. From Petersburg to Pskov.
(In French)

Madame, I have finally had the consolation of receiving your letter of November 27. It was almost four weeks on the way. We did not know what to think of your silence. I do not know why I am assuming that you are at Pskov, and I am addressing this letter to you there. My mother's health has improved, but there is not yet a convalescence. She is weak; however, the malady has subsided.

My father is very much to be pitied. My wife thanks you for remembering her and commends herself to your friendship. *Rebjatuški takže.*[1] I wish you health and merry holidays, and I say nothing to you of my unalterable devotion.

The Emperor has just granted a pardon to the majority of the conspirators of 1825, to, among others, my poor Kyukhelbeker. *Po ukazu dolžen on byt' poselen v južnoj časti Sibiri.*[2] It is a beautiful region, but I should like to have him closer to us; and perhaps he will be permitted to withdraw to the lands of Mme. Glinka, his sister. The government has always treated him with gentleness and indulgence.

When I consider that ten years have elapsed since these unfortunate disturbances,[3] it all seems a dream. How many occurrences, how many changes in everything, beginning with my own ideas—my situation, etc., etc. Actually, only my friendship for you and your family do I rediscover in my soul still the same, still unaltered and undiminished.

December 26.

Your promissory note[4] is ready, and I shall send it to you next time.

Letter 528
1. Lazhechnikov's novels were *The Last Recruit* and *The House of Ice*. The "Pugachev materials" were in Rychkov's manuscript. See Letter 485, and note 1.

Letter 529
1. Boldino.
2. August 26.
3. Mme. Pushkina's birthday.
4. Sergey Nikolaevich Goncharov had been made an army officer on June 22, 1834.

Letter 530
1. It appeared at the end of December, 1834. There is information about the seige of Simbrisk by Firska in the eighth chapter.
2. Pushkin's various mentions of Stenka Razin show that Pushkin was very much interested in his uprising, in the seventeenth century, as well as that of Pugachev, in the eighteenth, and the Decembrist Uprising, in the nineteenth.

Letter 531
1. This letter was probably delivered by Pushkin's wife.
2. What pawnbroker Pushkin meant is not known.
3. Pushkin often joked at his friend Sobolevsky's "sluggishness" and laggardliness. Sobolevsky had been planning for years to make a trip to Paris. He did not make it until 1837.

Letter 532
1. The reference is obviously to Pugachev materials.
2. Probably K. A. Polevoy, who managed the book trade of the brothers Polevoy and who offered to co-operate with Pushkin in selling Pushkin's *History of Pugachev*.
3. Pushkin's allusions are to K. A. Polevoy's brother N. A. Polevoy, author of *The History of the Russian People*, and also to the fact that the Polevoys belonged to the literary proletariat or bourgeoisie, rather than the literary aristocracy, to which Pushkin belonged.

Letter 533
1. Pushkin left Petersburg on August 25. He spent a few hours in Moscow, and then went to Polotnyany Zavod, where his wife was visiting relatives. After spending about two weeks there, he returned with Mme. Pushkina to Moscow, where they spent a few days. Then she left for Petersburg, and he to visit his father's estate of Boldino. He arrived there on September 13. He returned to Petersburg on October 18.
2. "That is very nice of it."
3. Peter Romanovich Bezobrazov (1797-1856), husband of Vasily Lvovich Pushkin's natural daughter, Margarita Vasilievna Bezobrazova. The Bezobrazovs did not succeed in keeping Mme. Bezobrazova's inherited share of Boldino. Pushkin's father owned the other half share of it. Pushkin uses the contemptuous form, Margaritka, in referring to his cousin.
4. S. D. Bezobrazov.

5. Pushkin did not buy all or part of Boldino.

6. By Augustin Thierry. The third edition (Paris, 1830) was in Pushkin's library.

7. A recruited peasant's service as a soldier was so long (twenty-four years) that, if married, his wife was left, in effect, a widow and usually without resources. Such "widows" often resorted to prostitution.

Letter 534

1. Probably his *Captain's Daughter*.

2. That is, Emelian, apparently a servant.

3. Unknown.

Letter 535

1. The three brothers Yazykov were still living together on their estate of Yazykovo in the Province of Simbirsk.

2. Pushkin's idea of a journal finally materialized, in his *Contemporary*, in 1836. N. M. Yazykov contributed to it.

Letter 536

1. Members of the first class continued to celebrate faithfully October 19, the anniversary of the founding of the Tsarskoe Selo Lyceum. The celebration in 1834 was at Yakovlev's house. Pushkin's room at the Lyceum was number 14.

Letter 537

1. *The Poems of Alexandra Fuchs* (Kazan, 1834).

2. Baron Karl Theodore Lützerode, then Ambassador from Saxony to Russia. The letter in point has not survived, nor has the other letter mentioned.

3. One Erast Petrovich Pertsov.

4. The original of this letter has not survived—only the form in which Mme. Fuchs later published it, with the omission of the complimentary close and signature.

Letter 538

1. The reference is to Gogol's tale, "The Nevsky Prospect." The scene of Pirogov's being flogged by the German shopkeepers was taken out by the censor. The word Pushkin uses for "flogging," *sekutija*, is a humorous formation from the Russian verb "to flog" (which has the root of *sek*) and based on the analogy of the Russian transliteration, *èksekucija*, of the French word *exécution*.

Letter 539

1. The letter has to do with financial and legal arrangements for Penkovsky to manage Boldino and Kistenevo, under the direction of Pushkin, who was still his father's business manager. Pushkin is keeping his own finances, in connection with Kistenevo, carefully separate from his father's, in connection with Boldino. Penkovsky paid the 1270 rubles alluded to. Pushkin signed the power of attorney for Penkovsky to manage Boldino and Kistenevo, on November 20, 1834. The Guardian Council was the government office through which the serfs were mortgaged.

Letter 540

1. Pushkin received the desired permission.

2. *The Long Poems and Verse Tales of Alexander Pushkin* appeared in 1835.

Letter 541
1. Turgenev was about to set off for Paris.
2. Count Joseph de Maistre's *Du pape* appeared in 1817.

Letter 542
1. "Without the Sovereign's authorization to do so." The Russian passage was underlined, and it is apparently a direct quotation. Nicholas I gave permission for the book to be released, "if there is nothing besides what I have read." Benkendorf, on December 23, authorized the issuance of the book. Speransky was the head of Section II of His Imperial Majesty's Chancellery, which included the typography.

Letter 543
1. Countess Sofia Alexandrovna Bobrinskaya (1799-1866), wife of Count Alexey Alexeevich Bobrinsky.
2. Oldbook, a character in Sir Walter Scott's *Antiquary* (1816).
3. When Mme. Pushkina returned to Petersburg from her visit to her relatives in 1834, she brought both her sisters along. They continued to live in Petersburg with the Pushkins.

Letter 544
1. Nashchokin, in a letter written a month earlier, had informed Pushkin of Mme. Nashchokina's having given birth to their daughter Ekaterina Pavlovna Nashchokina (b. 1834), had asked Pushkin to pay at once the two thousand rubles Pushkin owed him, and had asked that Mme. Pushkina buy a hat and some dress materials (see Letter 545) in Petersburg for Mme. Nashchokina.
2. The allusion is to Nashchokin's earlier tempestuous life with his former mistress, the gypsy Olga Andreevna.
3. Rokhmanov had been an agent of Pushkin and of Nashchokin in 1831-1832, and 1833. For example, he was given the task of redeeming Mme. Pushkina's pawned diamonds.
4. Another allusion to the interception of Letter 488 by the post officials and the police.

Letter 545
1. See Letter 544 and note 1.
2. "Since Mme. Nashchokina is a brunette and has a beautiful complexion."

Letter 546
1. See Letter 540, and note 1.
2. Pushkin received the requested permission. On February 21, the Minister of Justice reported that the Pugachev dossier had been transferred to the State Archive for Pushkin's use.

Letter 547
1. Pushkin's *History of Pugachev*. See Letter 503, and note 2.
2. In January, 1835.

Letter 548
1. A copy of Pushkin's *History of Pugachev*.

2. Dmitriev's description, as a spectator, of the execution of Pugachev. Pushkin quotes this description in a note to Chapter VIII.

3. The allusion is to Polevoy's *History of the Russian People* and perhaps also to Kachenovsky and his skeptical attitude towards the genuineness of *The Lay of the Host of Igor*.

4. Russian editors have pointed out that Pushkin is mistaken. Nikolay Ivanovich Novikov (1744-1818), in the period between 1769 and 1791, had made excellent profits publishing satirical and other periodicals, a historical dictionary of Russian writers, a series of old Russian chronicles, and other things.

5. Peter Ivanovich Sokolov.

6. *The Dictionary of the Russian Language*. As an old Arzamasian, Pushkin here takes a sarcastic attitude toward the Russian Academy and its activities, though he was at this time a member.

7. Count D. I. Khvostov. Pushkin often laughs at the way he bought up copies of his own works at booksellers and donated them to his acquaintances.

Letter 549

1. The implication of the word here is "idiotic." The term "blessed" was a common appellative for the *jurodivye*, wandering holy fools.

2. Variant reading: "the whole."

3. Katenin had requested that Pushkin print his sonnet "Caucasus Mountains" in *A Library for Reading*. The next-to-the-last verse reads as follows: "The thicker the darkness around, the brighter the shining of the star."

Letter 550

1. When Pushkin took over the managing of his father's estate Boldino (see Letter 494), he agreed to pay the debts of his brother, L. S. Pushkin. Pushkin's brother-in-law, Pavlishchev, who watched the Pushkin family's finances like a hawk, pointed out that Pushkin by January, 1835, had already paid eighteen thousand rubles of his brother's debts.

2. L. S. Pushkin had rented an apartment from V. V. Engelgardt for the staggering sum of two hundred rubles per week.

3. L. S. Pushkin had gone into debt with Alexander Pavlovich Pleshcheev in Warsaw.

4. A promissory note given in November, 1833, to Ilia Alexandrovich Boltin, with a term of four years, for a gambling debt.

Letter 551

1. Pushkin's letter is a point-by-point answer to Dmitriev's letter of April 10, 1835.

2. In his diary, Pushkin further notes, "and what is worse, they are not buying it."

3. Hero of Byron's verse tale of the same name; Byron's romantic verse tales continued to be in vogue in Russia in the 1830's, and romantic tales in prose with Byronic heroes, but authors such as Bestuzhev-Marlinsky and Polevoy, were extremely popular.

4. The question was who would succeed P. I. Sokolov, "Achilles." The play on the names of Greek heroes from Homer's *Iliad* was suggested to Pushkin by the fact that Dmitry Ivanovich Yazykov (1773-1845), writer and translator, who, as Pushkin predicts, received the post, had published a translation of Schlözer's *Nestor: Russian Chronicles in the Ancient Slavic Language* . . . (Petersburg, 1809-1819). The other two contenders were Mikhail Estafievich Lobanov and Boris Mikhaylovich Fedorov.

5. He was appointed on March 7, 1835.

Letter 552

1. During Pushkin's visit to the Ural region, while doing research on Pugachev, in 1833. See Letter 466.

2. Vladimir Ivanovich Dal (1801-1872), write, lexicographer, and physician, most famous as the compiler of the four-volume *Dictionary of the Great-Russian Language* (1861-1868). Dal was present, as physician, at Pushkin's suffering and death, in January, 1837, after Pushkin received his mortal wound.

3. Konstantin Demianovich Artyukhov, an army captain of engineers. Dal recounts how Artyukhov gave Pushkin a lively account of hunting the woodcock, including how, after being shot, the bird would "pause stock-still in the air, dying, like Brutus." Pushkin puns on the name Wallenstein and the Russian word for woodcock, *val'dšnep* (German, *Waldschnepfe*). Pushkin wrote in his presentation copy, "To the officer who compares a woodcock with Wallenstein."

Letter 552a

1. This letter was first published in 1956. Gustav Nordin (1799-1867) was in 1835 secretary of the Swedish Embassy in Petersburg. It is not known what "contraband," i.e., foreign book prohibited in Russia, Nordin had given Pushkin.

2. The reference is to the fifth and sixth volumes of a French-language edition of Heine's *Works*, published in Paris in 1834-1835; the two volumes have the title "On Germany." The term "scapegrace," as has been noted, does not necessarily reflect Pushkin's own opinion of Heine, but the disfavor with which he was looked upon by official Russia. This is the only mention of Heine in Pushkin's letters. Apparently Pushkin's request to Nordin was fulfilled; the two volumes "on Germany" were in Pushkin's library, one of them with a presentation note from Count Ficquelmont, dated April 27, 1835, referring to the "two volumes of contraband."

Letter 553

1. This letter announces Pushkin's giving up the managing of his father's estate of Boldino. Pushkin directly informed his brother and his sister in Letters 554 and 555, respectively.

Letter 554

1. See Letters 553 and 555. Pushkin had received his "share" (half) of Kistenevo just before his marriage.

Letter 555

1. Letter 553. See also Letter 554 and note.

2. In addition to continually peppering Pushkin with letters querulously demanding Olga's "lawful share," Pavlishchev asked Pushkin to see about the sale of some of her valuables.

Letter 556

1. The tale was "A Tale Lost to the World," and it was really by Senkovsky. It contained ironical comment about a story by Pogodin. Pushkin is informing Pogodin that the author of *The Tales of Belkin* (Pushkin) did not write this tale.

2. Avgust Semen, bookseller and publisher of the Moscow publication, *Pictorial Review of Memorable Objects from the Sciences, Fine Arts, Trade, and Society.*

3. Publishers of the journal *The Moscow Observer* (1835-1837), edited by Pogodin and Shevyrev, and with contributors, the same group who had supported *The Moscow*

Messenger and *The European*. Pushkin contributed to the journal when it began to appear, but his relationships with it and its editors and contributors cooled in 1836.

Letter 557
1. Pushkin's son, Grigory Alexandrovich Pushkin, was born on May 14, 1835.
2. Pushkin left for the village of Mikhaylovskoe on May 5 and returned on May 15.

Letter 558
1. Count Adolphe de Circourt, French publicist, who was well acquainted with Russian men of letters of the day, including for example, A. I. Turgenev, Zhukovsky, and Chaadaev. Count Circourt was the husband of Khlyustin's sister, Anastasia Semenovna de Circourt.

Letter 559
1. Unidentified.
2. Pushkin wrote and then crossed out the word "Review" in English. In May, 1835, Pushkin was trying to establish a periodical; it was to have had a supplement called "The Contemporary Chronicler of Politics, the Sciences, and Literature." Pushkin obtained permission to establish a journal, which he called *The Contemporary*, in 1836 (see Letters 560, 561, and 568).

Letter 560
1. The projected periodical, *Diary*. See Letter 429, and note 2.
2. The work on Peter the Great.
3. The word "Review" is in English in the original. Pushkin was eventually given permission to publish a literary, but not a political journal (see Letter 588).
4. S. S. Uvarov, against whom Pushkin directed his satirical "On the Convalescence of Lucullus." About this time Pushkin wrote in his diary: "Uvarov is a great scoundrel. He screams about my book [*The History of Pugachev*] as being a subversive work. His stooge Dundukov (a fool and the dregs of society) persecutes me with his censorship committee. He does not consent for me to print my works with the consent of the Sovereign alone. The Tsar likes, but the whipper-in dislikes."

Letter 561
1. See Letter 560, and note 3.
2. The phrase was left unfinished.
3. Pushkin may not have sent this letter; it may have been replaced with Letter 568. Pushkin's debts were becoming more and more crushing, and he was forced to project and to take more and more radical actions to cope with them.

Letter 562
1. Pushkin's request for a lengthy leave of absence (or a temporary retirement) from the service was rejected by Nicholas I, with a threatening note recalling Pushkin's attempt to retire a year earlier. Pushkin had to give in. It may be noted that this request to retire, thus presented, strengthened Pushkin's position in his request to be allowed to publish a journal and also in his efforts to borrow money from the government, for its rejection deprived him of one of the alternatives.

Letter 563
1. For Pushkin's unrealized idea of taking over the inheritance of his uncle, Vasily Lvovich Pushkin, see Letters 475 and 533.
2. Pushkin did not give it to him.

Letter 564

1. Vasily Andreevich Durov (b. 1799). Pushkin had made Durov's acquaintance in the Caucasus in 1829. Pushkin wrote in his "Table Talk" a character-sketch of Durov, including examples of his "hundred thousand schemes to obtain a hundred thousand rubles."

2. Nadezhda Andreevna Durova, by marriage Chernova (1783-1866), sister of Durov. Disguised as a man, she fought as a Russian soldier and officer in the wars against Napoleon from 1807 to 1814. She wrote under the masculine penname of Alexander Andreevich Alexandrov and hence here and elsewhere Pushkin uses the masculine pronoun in speaking of or to her.

Letter 565

1. Andrey Alexandrovich Kraevsky (1810-1889), journalist and later well known as editor of the journal, *Memoirs of the Fatherland* (1839-1884). At this time he was an intermediary between Pushkin and Moscow journals, particularly *The Moscow Observer*, in which "The Cloud" appeared. As always, Pushkin takes great interest in his works being published accurately, including minor textual revisions.

Letter 566

1. Letter 562 (q.v., and note).

2. The original word, struck out in the rough draft, was "retiring [me]." Obviously Pushkin had not given up all hope of being allowed to retire for several years, but he nevertheless was careful to remove the word.

Letter 567

1. Grigory Alexandrovich Pushkin.

2. Countess Nadezhda Grigorievna Chernysheva.

3. See Letters 562 and 566. The request was denied.

4. Mme. Pushkina's two sisters were still living with the Pushkins.

Letter 568

1. That of his uncle, Vasily Lvovich Pushkin. See Letters 475, 533, and 563.

2. Nicholas I offered Pushkin a loan of ten thousand rubles and a six-month leave of absence, during which he would see "whether he needed to go into retirement or not."

Letter 569

1. Vladimir Dmitrievich Volkhovsky (1798-1841), a Lyceum comrade of Pushkin's, at this time a general in the Russian army in the Caucasus. This letter shows another instance of Pushkin's willingness to help others with what influence he had. Nothing is known of the Count Zabela for whom "protection and good will" are sought.

Letter 570

1. Pushkin's request was granted by Nicholas I.

Letter 571

1. The portrait of Pugachev, engraved in Paris, was received considerably later than the appearance of Pushkin's *History of Pugachev*.

2. Mikhail Samsonovich Rybushkin (1792-1849), an Adjunct Professor of Kazan University. His book was *A Brief History of the City of Kazan* (1834).

3. The original of the letter has not survived. In the published form, the complimentary close and signature were omitted.

Letter 572

1. Efim Petrovich Lyutsenko (1776-1854), an official and man of letters. From 1811 to 1813 he had been an official at the Tsarskoe Selo Lyceum.

2. Lyutsenko wished Smirdin to publish his translation of Wieland's verse tale, *Die Wünsche oder Pervonte*. The deal with Smirdin fell through. Then Pushkin himself published it, without the name of the translator, and with the title page reading as follows: "Vastola, or Desires: A Tale in Verse, Composed by A. Wieland, Published by A. Pushkin, Petersburg, 1836." Pushkin obviously hoped that his name as publisher would attract more purchases than Lyutsenko's name would have attracted as translator. Misunderstanding resulted, and Pushkin was attacked by his journalist enemies as being the uninspired translator of the poem (see Letter 592 and notes).

Letter 573

1. Vasily Alexeevich Polenov (1776-1851), Director of the State Archives.

2. Pushkin had requested this permission in Letter 546 (q.v.).

3. Alexey Fedorovich Malinovsky was Director of the Moscow Archives of the Ministry of Foreign Affairs.

4. It is noteworthy that Pushkin continued his researches in the Pugachev affair after his book had been published, compiling materials which he had no hope of publishing.

Letter 574

1. See Letter 568, note 2.

2. See Letter 570, and note.

3. Pushkin's *History of Pugachev*. The loan was twenty thousand rubles, instead of ten thousand. See Letter 476 and note.

4. Pushkin's request was granted. Pushkin wrote the letter to Kankrin as Minister of Finance.

Letter 575

1. Pushkin left Petersburg for Mikhaylovskoe on September 7. He remained there until October 20, when he departed for Petersburg, upon hearing of his mother's poor health. Pushkin is asking that his mail be sent to Mme. Osipova's address.

2. Mme. Osipova's niece, Anna Ivanovna Begicheva.

3. In Pushkin's poem, "Portents" (1829), he makes poetic utilization of the superstition that seeing the moon over the left shoulder is associated with sadness and despondency.

4. The "expedition" was to Countess Ekaterina Zakharovna Kankrina (1796-1879), the wife of the Minister of Finance, Count Kankrin. Pushkin was hoping through Mme. Kankrina to influence her husband with regard to the business of Letter 574, that none of the loan of thirty thousand rubles, which Nicholas I granted Pushkin, be withheld.

5. Count Vasily Gavrilovich Yuriev, an officer who lent money.

6. Probably Countess Emilia Karlovna Musina-Pushkina.

7. His three-year-old daughter. Pushkin gives a special effect by using the mode of address of a young lady for his daughter, and following it immediately with the rough-affectionate diminutive for his son.

8. Mme. Pushkina's sister, Alexander N. Goncharova, and Ekaterina N. Goncharova, respectively.

Letter 576

1. Only this small fragment of the letter exists, if indeed it is a letter. It was first published among Pushkin's letters in the Academy of Sciences of the Soviet Union editions of Pushkin's *Works*, both large (XVI [1949], 431), and small (X [1949], 546). In the Index volume to the large Academy *Works*, which became available while this edition was already in the press, it is stated (p. 76) that what was printed as a letter is really a sketch of the plan of the uncompleted poem "To Pletnev" ("You Advise Me, Dear Pletnev," 1835).

One of the interesting problems in Puskin criticism is whether his novel in verse, *Evgeny Onegin*, is a completed work. "Onegin's Journey," at first projected as Chapter VIII, was not completed and was omitted by Pushkin. Pushkin began a Chapter X, but it exists only in fragments. He is reported as having said in 1829 that Onegin was to have become a Decembrist and to have died in the Caucasus.

Letter 577

1. Alexandra Ivanovna Bekleshova, nee Osipova, had been, since 1833, the wife of the Pskov Chief of Police, Peter Nikolaevich Bekleshov.

2. Maria Ivanovna Osipova was the half-sister of Alexandra Ivanovna Bekleshova and of Evpraxia Nikolaevna Vrevskaya.

3. Pushkin quotes a verse from his love poem, "Confession," which he had written to the addressee of this letter nine years earlier. The time called to mind is that of Pushkin's exile in Mikhaylovskoe, when almost all of the Osipova-Vulf family were more or less in love with him and/or he with them.

Letter 578

1. Baron Boris Alexandrovich Vrevsky and his wife, Evpraxia Nikolaevna Vrevskaya, nee Vulf. Pushkin visited them on September 19.

2. Pushkin's library contained a copy of the Paris, 1828, edition of Montaigne's essays.

3. Pushkin's question has to do with the plural form, in Russian orthography, of the French expression, *belle-soeur*.

Letter 579

1. Arina Rodionova.

2. The next day, September 26, 1835, Pushkin wrote his lyric, "Again I Visited. . . ," in which is presented the experience of his revisiting Mikhaylovskoe after ten years. He speaks there of his nursemaid "who is no more," and of the "green family" of pines that has grown up, and which he will not live to see mature.

3. They had gone abroad in May, 1834 (see Letter 470).

4. Mme. Pushkina's two sisters.

Letter 580

1. Countess Varvara Petrovna Polier married the Neapolitan ambassador in Petersburg, Prince Giorgio Butera di Ridali, in 1836.

2. See Letter 429, note 2.

3. Anna Petrovna Kern had translated George Sand's novel, *André* (1835).

4. Probably a projected joint publication of an almanac (see Letter 582).

5. *Muzik* (instead of *mužik*).

6. "I thank your sisters."

Letter 581

1. Perhaps her sister, Ekaterina Nikolaevna Goncharova; perhaps the proprietress of a fashionable shop.
2. See Letter 580, regarding her illness.
3. Apparently the allusion is to a projected almanac. See Letter 580.

Letter 582

1. Pushkin's *Journey to Erzurum*, a travel-account of his trip to the Caucasus and Erzurum in 1829. It appeared in the first issue of Pushkin's journal, *The Contemporary*, in 1836.
2. Pushkin had made an official petition to the Chief Directorate of the Censorship, on August 28, 1835, for clarification of his position with regard to the double censorship: of the ordinary censorship, on the one hand, and that of Benkendorf and Nicholas I, on the other. See also Letter 584.
3. Pushkin usually calls Prince M. A. Dondukov-Korsakov *Dunduk*, "muddlehead." Pushkin used the term in an epigram on him. Alexander Vasilievich Nikitenko (1805-1877) was a censor and Dondukov-Korsakov an official in the censorship.
4. Gogol's tale, "The Calash," was published in the first issue of Pushkin's *Contemporary* in 1836.
5. Valerian Platonovich Langer, an artist.
6. Part of Gogol's play *Vladimir, Third Class* was also published in the first issue of *The Contemporary*.
7. Under Pushkin's pseudonym of Belkin, Senkovsky had published "A Tale Lost to the World." (See Letter 556). In *The Russian Invalide* there appeared a vitriolic critique in 1836, showing that Pushkin could not be the author of the tale, and hinting at Senkovsky as the author.

Letter 583

1. Pushkin left Mikhaylovskoe on Occtober 20, after a month and a half's absence from Petersburg, upon hearing of his mother's serious illness.
2. See Letter 574. Pushkin received, as a four-year loan, the entire thirty thousand rubles he had requested.

Letter 584

1. The censorship refused to pass the "second, corrected" edition of Pushkin's *Angelo*, an adaptation into a poem, of Shakespeare's *Measure for Measure*, though Nicholas I himself had approved the original manuscript. Pushkin's petition of August 28, 1835 (see Letter 582, note 2) was left unanswered. Thus Uvarov was avenging Pushkin's epigram on him.
2. No fair copy of this letter survives. Whether it was sent is not known.

Letter 585

1. See Letter 583, note 1.
2. Princess Varvara Alexandrovna Knyazhnina (1774-1842), a childhood friend of Pushkin's mother.
3. Egor Ivanovich Raukh (1789-1864), like Spassky, a physician.
4. Pushkin's parents had moved into a small and uncomfortable apartment in the home of his sister, Olga Sergeevna Pavlishcheva.
5. "Sweet habit."

Letter 586

1. See Letters 548 and 571. Apparently Pushkin received the portrait in February, 1835.

2. See Letter 485, where Pushkin also mentions Lazhechnikov's novels alluded to below. *The House of Ice* appeared in 1835.

3. Artemy Petrovich Volynsky (1689-1740), Russian statesman and diplomat, was executed as head of the "Russian" opposition to "German" influence of Count Ernst Johann Biron (1690-1772), favorite of the Russian Empress Anne (reigned 1730-1740).

4. Eighteenth-century neo-classical poet.

5. In a lengthy letter of November 22, 1835, Lazhechnikov defends his conception of Volynsky, Trediakovsky, and Biron against Pushkin's objections. He further states that the word *xobot*, in the expression *kakim-to xobotom*, was still used in the "Great Russian dialect" by narrators of folk tales to mean *kakim-to putem*, *kakim-to obrazom*, "in a certain way, manner."

Letter 587

1. "The youngsters, likewise."

2. "According to the ukase he must be settled in the southern part of Siberia." Pushkin cites the ukase of December 14, 1835, according to the provisions of which the punishment of several Decembrists was somewhat eased. Kyukhelbeker was allowed to settle in the Irkutsk Province of Eastern Siberia. He was not permitted to live in the village of his sister, Yustina Karlovna Glinka, nee Kyukhelbeker.

3. The Decembrist Uprising of 1825.

4. Apparently Pushkin must have borrowed some money from Mme. Osipova.

PART XIII

CONTEMPORARY JOURNALIST—PETERSBURG

December, 1835 — October, 1836

To Alexander Khristoforovich Benkendorf

December 31, 1835. In Petersburg.

Dear Sir, Count Alexander Khristoforovich,

I have the happiness to submit for His Majesty's inspection the memoirs of the Brigadier Moreau de Brasey[1] about the expedition of the year 1711, along with my notes and introduction. These memoirs are interesting and sensible. They are an important historical document, and they very well may be the sole one (except for the journal of Peter the Great himself).

I make bold to disturb Your Excellency with a most humble request. I should like during next year, 1836, to publish four volumes of items of a purely literary (e.g., of tales, poems, etc.), historical, scholarly nature, and also critical analyses of Russian and foreign literature; something on the order of the English quarterly *Reviews*.[2] In refusing to participate in all our journals, I have been deprived also of my own revenues. The publication of such a *Review* would again provide me with independence, and, along with that, the means of continuing the labors which I have begun. This would be a new benefaction for me on the part of the Sovereign.

Commending myself to the favor which you always show toward me, I have the honor to be, with the most profound respect and with complete devotion,

Dear Sir,

Your Excellency's

December 31, 1835.　　　　　　Most humble servant,

SPb.　　　　　　　　　　　　Alexander Pushkin.

To Nadezhda Andreevna Durova

January 19, 1836. From Petersburg to Elabuga.

Dear Sir, Alexander Andreevich,[1]

I have been exceedingly disturbed by your last letter, of January 6. I have not received your manuscript, and here is what I suspect to be the reason. Though I left for three months in the village, I spent only three weeks there, and then was compelled to return hastily to Petersburg. Your manuscript has probably been sent to Pskov. Do me the favor not to be angry with me. I am going now to take what steps I can with regard to it; I shall try to make up for the delays.

I was about to be in complete despair of ever receiving the Memoirs, which I have been awaiting so impatiently. Thank God that now I have managed to get on their trail.

With the most profound respect and with complete devotion, I have the honor to be,

> Your most zealous and most humble servant,
> January 19, 1836.   A. Pushkin.

[590]

To Pavel Voinovich Nashchokin

Between January 10 and 20, 1836. From Petersburg to Moscow.

My dear Pavel Voinovich,

I have not written you because I am at odds with the Moscow post.[1] I have heard that you were planning to come see me at my village. I rejoice that you didn't come, because you would not have found me there. The illness of my mother has forced me to return to the city. There have been various rumors about you with regard to your winnings; but what has truly consoled me is that all people have been unanimously justifying you, and you alone. I am thinking of spending some time in Moscow, if I don't croak on the road. Have you a corner for me? Then wouldn't we chatter to our heart's content! But here there's nobody to do it with. My financial circumstances are bad—I have been forced to undertake a journal.[2] I don't know yet how it will go. Smirdin is already offering me fifteen thousand to renounce my undertaking and become again a collaborator of his Library [for Reading]. But though that would be profitable, I nevertheless cannot agree to it. Senkovsky is such a knave and Smirdin such a fool that one cannot have anything to do with them. I should like to get a glimpse of your family life and rejoice at it. After all, I had something to do with it, for I had an influence on the decisive turning point of your life.[3] My family is increasing, growing, being noisy about me. Now, I should think, there's no reason to murmur at life or to fear old age. For a bachelor it's boring in society: he's vexed to see new, young generations. Only the father of a family looks without envy at the youth surrounding him. From this it follows that we did well in getting married. How are your affairs? How are Knörzer and your little Jewish doctor[4] whom Natalia Nikolaevna so dislikes? And she has a most perceptive heart. Look, get rid of him; your really must. But let's talk all this over later. Good-by, my friend.

[591]

To ALEXANDER NIKOLAEVICH MORDVINOV (?)
The second half of January or the beginning of February, 1836.
Petersburg.
(Rough draft; in French)

I beseech you to pardon my obtruding myself upon you, but, since yesterday I was not able to make my justification to the minister[1] [. . . .][2]

My ode was sent to Moscow without any explanation. My friends had no knowledge of it. Any sort of allusion in it has been carefully removed. The satirical part strikes at the vile avidity of an heir, who at the moment of his relative's illness, already has seals affixed to the effects which he covets. I confess that a similar story had been widely spread and that I have picked up a poetical expression which has slipped out on this theme.

It is impossible to write a satirical ode without the malign immediately finding innuendoes in it. Derzhavin in his "Noble Lord" portrayed a sybarite plunged in voluptuousness, deaf to the cries of the people, and who exclaims,

> To me a moment of my tranquillity is more pleasing than centuries in history.

These verses were applied to Potemkin and to others[3]—however, all these declamations were commonplaces, which had been repeated a thousand times. That is to say, in the satire of the basest and the most common vices, portrayed [. . . .][2]

Fundamentally they were the vices of the great lord, and I have no way of knowing to what degree Derzhavin was innocent of indulging in personalities.

In the portrait of a vile miser, of a foxy fellow who steals wood belonging to the Crown, who presents to his wife inaccurate accounts, of a toady who becomes children's nursemaid at great lords' houses, etc.—the public has recognized, it is said, a certain great lord, a rich man, a man honored with an important office.⁴

So much the worse for the public—it is enough for me that I not only have not named names, but have not even hinted to anyone whatever that my ode [. . . .]²

I ask only that anyone prove to me that I have named him, what feature of my ode could be applied to him, or even what I have insinuated.

All this is very vague; all these accusations are commonplaces.

It matters little to me whether the public is wrong or right. What matters much to me is to prove that never in any manner have I *insinuated* to anyone that my ode was leveled against anyone whatever.⁵

[592]
To SEMEN SEMENOVICH KHLYUSTIN
February 4, 1836. In Petersburg.
(In French)

Sir,

Permit me to correct several points where you appear to me to be in error.¹ I do not remember having heard you quote anything from the article in question. What prompted me to express myself, perhaps with too much heat, is the remark which you made to me, that I was wrong last evening to take Senkovsky's words to heart.

I answered you: *Ja ne seržus' na Senkovskogo; no mne nel'zja ne dosadovat', kogda porjadončye ljudi povtorjajut neleposti svinej i merzavcev.*² To put you on the same footing with *svin'i i merzavcy*³ is certainly an absurdity, which could neither have entered my head nor have escaped me, even in all the heat of an altercation.

To my great surprise, you replied to me that you take complete responsibility for Senkovsky's injurious article, and in particular for the expression *obmanyvat' publiku.*⁴

I was all the less prepared for such an assertion coming from you *in that neither last evening nor at our last interview did you say anything whatever to me which related to the article in the journal.* I believed that I did not understand you and I requested you to be so kind as to explain yourself, which you did in the same terms.

I then had the honor to make the observation to you that what you have just put forth turns the question into something quite different, and I held my tongue. Leaving you, I told you that I could not leave things thus. That can be regarded as a provocation, but not as a threat. Wherefore, to sum things up, I am obliged to repeat: I can pay no attention to the words of a Senkovsky, but I cannot disdain them when a man like you adopts them. In consequence, I have commissioned M. Sobolevsky to request of you in my name to be so kind as to retract the words purely and simply, or else to grant me the customary satisfaction. The proof of how repugnant this last course was to me is that I have specifically told Sobolevsky that I shall not insist upon an apology. I am sorry that M. Sobolevsky has displayed his usual negligence in all this.

As for the incivility which I showed in not bowing to you when you left me, I pray you to believe that it was a completely involuntary inadvertence, and I ask your pardon for it with all my heart.

I have the honor to be, Sir, your most humble and most obedient servant.

February 4.   A. Pushkin.

[593]

To Nikolay Grigorievich Repnin-Volkonsky
February 5, 1836. In Petersburg.
(In French)

Prince,

To my regret I am compelled to trouble Your Excellency.[1] But as a gentleman and the father of a family, I must watch over my honor and the name which I am to leave to my children.

I do not have the honor to be personally acquainted with Your Excellency. Not only have I never offended you, but for certain reasons known to me, up to the present I have had for you a true feeling of respect and of gratitude.

However, a M. Bogolyubov[2] has publicly repeated remarks which I consider insulting, and as coming from you. I pray Your Excellency to be so kind as to let me know what to believe.

No one knows better than I the distance which separates me from you: but I hope that you who are not only a great lord, but also a representative of our ancient and genuine nobility, to which I too belong—I hope that you will understand without difficulty the imperious necessity which has dictated this step to me.

I am, respectfully,
Your Excellency's
Most humble and most obedient servant,

February 5, 1836.   Alexander Pushkin.

[594]

To Vladimir Alexandrovich Sollogub
The first days of February, 1836. In Petersburg.
(Rough draft; in French)

You[1] have put yourself to useless trouble in giving me an explanation which I have not asked of you. You have permitted yourself to address improper remarks to my wife, and you have boasted that you have *uttered impertinences* to her.

Circumstances do not permit me to set out for Tver before the end of the month of March.[2] Please excuse me [. . . .][3]

[595]

To Nikolay Grigorievich Repnin-Volkonsky
February 11, 1836. In Petersburg.

Dear Sir, Prince Nikolay Grigorievich,

I want to express to Your Highness my sincere, most profound gratitude for the letter which you were so kind as to honor me with.

I cannot help acknowledging that Your Highness's opinion with regard to compositions which are insulting to the honor of a private person is completely just. It is difficult to excuse them even when they are written in a moment of chagrin and blind vexation. As an amusement for an idle or depraved mind, they would be unforgivable.[1]

With the most profound respect and with complete devotion, I am,
Dear Sir,
Your Highness's
Most humble servant,

February 11, 1836.   Alexander Pushkin.

[596]

To ALEXANDRA ANDREEVNA FUCHS
February 20, 1836. From Petersburg to Kazan.

Dear Madame, Alexandra Andreevna,

I am so much to blame toward you that I do not make bold even to try to justify myself. Not long ago I returned from the village[1] and I found at my house the letter which you were so kind as to honor me with. I do not understand how it can be that my tramp Emelian Pugachev[2] has not reached Kazan, a memorable place for him; apparently he has made side excursions and has gone on a spree, according to his wont. Now Count Apraxin[3] has indulgently undertaken to deliver my book to you. Along with this, permit me, Dear Madame, to forward to you also a subscription for *The Contemporary*, which I am publishing. Dare I hope that you will embellish it some time with the productions of your pen?[4]

I testify my most profound respect toward amiable, honored Karl Fedorovich [Fuchs], commending myself to your and his good will.

I have the honor to be, with the most profound respect and complete devotion,

Dear Madame,
Your

SPb.   Most humble servant,
February 20, 1836.   Alexander Pushkin.

[597]

To VASILY DMITRIEVICH SUKHORUKOV
March 14, 1836. From Petersburg to Pyatigorsk.

My very dear Vasily Dmitrievich,[1]

I am writing you in the room of a compatriot of yours, a pleasing young man[2] from whom I not infrequently receive news of you. He has just now told me that you are married.[3] I congratulate you with all my heart; I wish you happiness, which you deserve in all respects. I send my respects to Olga Vasilievna and my regrets that I cannot tell her all that I think, and everything good that I know, about you.

Have I written you since our separation in the Erzurum Palace? I don't think I have written; forgive my eternal lack of leisure, and don't attribute my procrastination to anything else. Now let us talk about business. You know that I have become a journalist (which reminds me that I have not sent you *The Contemporary*;[4] excuse me— I'll try to make up for my fault). And so, having become a confrere of Bulgarin and Polevoy, I address you with astonishing shamelessness and ask for *some articles* from you. Really, do send me something out of your sensible, conscientious, interesting works. In the vicinity of Beshtau and Elbrus both leisure and inspiration dwell. Meanwhile, it wouldn't be a bad idea to talk about value (monetary). I pay two hundred rubles per printed sheet. Shan't we enter into commercial relationships, too?

Farewell; all yours,

March 14, 1836.   A.P.
SPb.

[598]

To Vladimir Fedorovich Odoevsky
The end of February or the first half of March, 1836.
In Petersburg.

I am highly, very highly pleased and grateful.[1] If it will be possible to print five sheets per week, that's capital—and our business is in the bag. However, have the proofs of my *Journey*[2] sent to me. There are many mistakes in the manuscript. What about your tale "Zizi"?[3] It's a capital thing.

A.P.

[599]

To Peter Andreevich Vyazemsky
About (not later than) March 17, 1836. In Petersburg.

Hurrah! We have won![1] Kozlovsky's article[2] came through all right; I am beginning to print it now. But poor [A. I.] Turgenev! ... all his political gossip has been stopped. Even the names of Fieschi and of all the ministers have been blotted out; only the orthodox spelling of the names of our Russian Catholic women and diplomats' wives remains.[3] However, I shall address myself to Benkendorf— won't he intercede? You spoke to me about your verses to Pototskaya.[4] Have you obtained them? Can't you at least recall them?

A.P.

[600]

To MIKHAIL ALEXANDROVICH DONDUKOV-KORSAKOV
March 18, 1836. In Petersburg.

Dear Sir, Prince Mikhail Alexandrovich,

Utilizing the permission granted me by Your Highness, I make
bold to have recourse to you with a most humble request.

The Censorship Committee could not pass the "Letters from
Paris," as an item containing political news. Will you permit me,
Dear Sir, in order that I may receive this permission to address myself to Count Benkendorf? Or will you command that this be left to
the Committee?[1]

With the most profound respect and with complete devotion, I
have the honor to be,

Dear Sir,
Your Highness's
Most humble servant,

March 18, 1836.   Alexander Pushkin.
SPb.

[601]

To ALEXANDER LUKICH KRYLOV
Between March 20 and 22, 1836. In Petersburg.
(Rough draft)

Dear Sir, Alexander Lukich,

Prince M. A. Korsakov has written me that the "Letters from
Paris" will be examined in the Highest Committee. I am forwarding
them to you. One observation: Turgenev's "Letters from Paris" are
being published in *The Moscow Observer* not as political, but as
literary, articles.[1]

[602]

To ALPHONSE JOBARD
March 24, 1836. From Petersburg to Moscow.
(In French)

Sir, I have received with genuine pleasure your charming translation of the "Ode to Lucullus" and the very flattering letter
accompanying it.[1] Your verses are as pretty as they are barbed, which

is saying a great deal. If it is true, as you say in your letter, that the attempt was made to establish legally that you have lost your mind, one must acknowledge that since then you have devilishly found it again!

The good will which you apparently bear me, and which I am proud of, justifies my speaking to you in full trust. In your letter to the Minister of Public Instruction, you seem inclined to publish your translation in Belgium, supplementing it with some notes, which are necessary, you say, for comprehending the text: I make bold to beseech you, Sir, to do nothing of the kind. I am sorry for having published a piece which I wrote in a moment of bad humor. With its publication I have incurred the displeasure of a certain one[2] whose opinion is dear to me, and whom I cannot defy without ingratitude and without folly. Be so good as to sacrifice the pleasure of publicity to the idea of obliging a brother-writer. Do not revive, with the aid of your talent, a production which otherwise would fall into the oblivion which it deserves. I make bold to hope that you will not refuse me the favor which I am asking of you, and I pray you to be so kind as to receive the assurance of my complete esteem.

I have the honor to be, Sir, your most humble and most obedient servant.

March 24, 1836.   A. Pushkin.
St. Petersburg.

[603]
To Vasily Andreevich Durov
March 17 and 27, 1836. From Petersburg to Elabuga.

Dear Sir, Vasily Andreevich,

I thank you very much for sending the memoirs and for the trust which you have shown in me. Here are my proposals. (I) I publish a journal; in the second issue of it (i.e., in the month of July) I am publishing *The Memoirs of* [18]12 (all or a part of them), and I shall send you money at once, at the rate of two hundred rubles per printed sheet. (II) Now that I have finally received your brother's other memoirs, I am thinking of combining *The Memoirs of* [18]12 with them.[1] In this way the book will be thicker, and consequently more expensive.

The Complete Memoirs will probably sell well, after I trumpet them in my journal. I am ready either to buy or to print them on the author's behalf—whichever he likes and is most profitable for him. In any case, be assured that I shall exert every possible effort for the success of our mutual piece of business.

Your brother writes that he will be in Petersburg this summer. I await him with impatience. Farewell. Be happy, and God grant that you grow rich on the lucky little hand of brave Alexandrov, which little hand I ask you to kiss for me.

All yours,

March 17, 1836.   A. Pushkin.
 SPb.

I have just now read the *Memoirs* copied out: it's charming. It's lively, original, and the style is excellent. Its success is indubitable. March 27.[2]

[604]

To George Borrow
Between the end of October, 1835, and March, 1836.
In Petersburg.

Alexander Pushkin has received Mr. Borrow's book with the most profound gratitude, and he heartily regrets that he has not had the honor of becoming personally acquainted with him.[1]

[605]

To Vladimir Fedorovich Odoevsky
The beginning of April, 1836. In Petersburg.

In my first issue there won't be a single line from your pen. That grieves me. But we lacked the time—and my friends had made a vow to the public, in my name, that *The Contemporary* would be issued in St. Thomas' Week.[1]

I am thinking of beginning the second issue with your sensible, intelligent, and powerful article—which I should like to entitle "Of Enmity Toward Enlightenment,"[2] for I should like to put in the same issue, as well, a critique of *The Inn*, under the title "Of Certain Novels."[3] Do you permit it?

The censorship seems to have fallen into a quandary over "Segeliel."[4] But I am not very content with the work—besides, printing it as a fragment might harm the publication of your complete work.

I am leaving on Tuesday.[5] Shall I see you before then?

All yours,

A.P.

I did not include "The Conversation of the Discontented Ones,"[6] because I already had Gogol's "Scenes"[7] in type—and because you two might damage the effect of each other.

[606]

To Mikhail Alexandrovich Dondukov-Korsakov
April 6, 1836. In Petersburg.

Dear Sir, Prince Mikhail Alexandrovich,

I make bold to make a most humble request of Your Highness.

Of course I do not have the right to complain of strictness on the part of the censorship: all the articles which have gone into my journal were passed. But I am obliged for the authorizing of them solely to Your Highness's good-natured indulgence, for the censor, Mr. [A. L.] Krylov, in and of himself could not make up his mind to pass them. Though I feel in full measure the value of the protection which you have shown toward me, I nevertheless make bold to observe, in the first place, that it is shameful and unseemly for me to disturb Your Highness every moment with paltry requests, whereas I should like to utilize the right which you have granted me, only in cases which are truly difficult and which really require the authorization of the higher authorities; in the second place, that such a double censorship takes an excessive amount of time for me, so that my journal cannot come out on schedule. I do not complain of superfluous mistrustfulness on the part of my censor. I know that on him lies a responsibility which is perhaps not delimited by the Censorship Regulations. But I make bold to request Your Highness for the authorization to choose myself an additional censor, in order that thus the examining of my journal may be made twice as rapid. Without this, it will come to a halt and fail.[1]

With the most profound respect and with complete devotion, I have the honor to be,

Dear Sir,

Your Highness's

April 6, 1836.   Most humble servant,
SPb.   Alexander Pushkin.

[607]
To Mikhail Petrovich Pogodin
April 14, 1836. From Mikhaylovskoe to Moscow.
Dear Sir, Mikhaylo Petrovich,
I am writing to you from the village, where I have come in consequence of mournful circumstances.[1] My journal came out in my absence,[2] and you have probably already received it. The article about your aphorisms[3] was not written by me, and I had neither the time nor the strength to examine it decently. Do not be angry with me if you are dissatisfied with it. Won't you enter into literary and commercial relationships with me? In case you will, I ask you to state your demands, with no beating around the bush. If you should see Nadezhdin, thank him for me for his *Telescope*. I shall send him *The Contemporary*. Today I am going to Petersburg. But I shall be in Moscow in May—to do some burrowing in the archives and to see you.

April 14.   All yours, A.P.
Mikhaylovskoe.

[608]
To Nikolay Mikhaylovich Yazykov
April 14, 1836. From Golubovo[1] to Yazykovo.
Guess where I'm writing you from, my dear Nikolay Mikhaylovich. From the land

—where the free ones used to dwell, etc.[2]

where exactly ten years ago we three were feasting—you, [Alexey N.] Vulf, and I; where your verses chimed and also our capacious goblets, where now we are remembering you—and old times. A greeting to you from the hills of Mikhaylovskoe, from the portals of Trigorskoe, from the waves of the blue Sorot, from Evpraxia Nikolaevna, once upon a time a semi-ethereal maid, and now a plump wife, and already with child for the fifth time, and at whose house I'm a guest. A greeting to you from everything and everybody devoted to you in heart and memory!
Alexey Vulf is here, a retired student and hussar, a mustachioed

agriculturalist, the Lovelace of Tver[3]—pleasant as before, but he has already crossed the threshold of his thirtieth year. My visit in Pskov is not so boisterous and merry now as during my exile, in the days when Alexander reigned; but it has reminded me of you so keenly that I could not help writing you a few words in the expectation that you will respond, in turn. You will receive my *Contemporary*; I hope that it may merit your approbation. One of the critical articles is mine: about Konissky.[4] Do be my collaborator, without fail.[5] Your verses are living water, ours are dead water.[6] We have doused *The Contemporary* with ours; besprinkle it with your seething drops. Your "Epistle to Davydov" is charming! Our warrior with black curls had dyed his gray hair and had tinted his white forelock, too, but after your verses he washed it out again—and he did well.[7] This is a mark of veneration for poetry. Farewell—write me, and, by the way, do send to Vyazemsky, as well, an answer to his epistle which was printed in *The Housewarming*[8] (as I remember), and which you haven't said a word about to him. Stay well, and write. That is: *Live and let live*.[9] All yours, A.P.

April 14.

Send me, for God's sake, *The Verses About Alexey, Man of God*[10] and some other legend—*it's essential*.

[609]
To Alexander Nikolaevich Mordvinov
April 28, 1836. In Petersburg.

Dear Sir, Alexander Nikolaevich,

I hasten to forward to Your Excellency the letter which I received. It was delivered to me about a week ago. Upon my return from a walk, I discovered that it had been given to my servants without any verbal message, I do not know by whom. I supposed that the letter had been delivered to me with your knowledge.[1]

With the most profound respect and with complete devotion, I have the honor to be,

Dear Sir,
Your Excellency's

April 28, 1836.   Most humble servant,
SPb.   Alexander Pushkin.

[610]

To Mikhail Alexandrovich Dondukov-Korsakov
Between April 19 and 30, 1836. In Petersburg.
(Rough draft)

I have had the happiness to receive the letter with which Your Highness has honored me,[1] and the article about the Occupation of Dresden.[2]

Although the censorship could not pass for publication General Davydov's justification—nevertheless, Dear Sir, I am grateful to Your Highness for the attention with which you have been so kind as to honor my most humble request.

With the most profound respect
And complete devotion [. . . .]

[611]

To Natalia Nikolaevna Pushkina
May 4, 1836. From Moscow to Petersburg.
May 4. Moscow at Nashchokin's—opposite
Stary Pimen,[1] the house of Mme. Ivanova.

Here is a detailed report for you, my Tsaritsa: my trip[2] went all right. I spent the night of May 1 in Tver, and I arrived here on the night of the 2nd. I have stopped at Nashchokin's. *Il est logé en petite maîtresse.*[3] His wife is very sweet. He is happy, and he has plumpened up a little. We were, it goes without saying, very glad to see each other, and yesterday we chattered the whole day through, about God knows what. I have already succeeded in visiting Bryullov. I found him in the studio of some sculptor, at whose house he's living.[4] I was greatly taken with him. He has a fit of the spleen, he is afraid of the Russian cold, etc., he yearns for Italy, and he's very much discontented with Moscow. At his place I saw several sketches which he has begun, and I thought of you, my charming one. It can't be that I won't have a portrait of you, painted by him! It's impossible that, upon seeing you, he wouldn't want to paint you; please don't drive him off, the way you drove off the Prussian Kridner.[5] I very much want to bring Bryullov to Petersburg.[6] Why, he's a genuine artist, a fine fellow, and he's ready for everything. Here Perovsky[7] made a prisoner of him; he took him to his own house, shut him up under lock and key, and made him work. Bryullov had difficulty in getting away from him. Nashchokin's little house[8] has been brought to perfection—the only thing lacking is some living tiny people. What fun Masha would have with it! Here is some local news for you. Okulova, the long-nosed singer, yesterday was married to the widower Diakov.[9] Her sister Varvara has gone mad of love. She was in love and had hoped to get married. Her hope was not realized. She fell into melancholy, began to talk incoherently. Her sister's wedding completely addled her brains. She ran off to Troitsa.[10] They had difficulty in catching her and in taking her away. I am very sorry for her. They hope that what she has is only fever with delirium,[11] but that's hardly it. I have seen our match-maker, [F. I.] Tolstoy. His daughter[12] is almost mad, too. She lives in a dream world, surrounded by visions, translates from the Greek of Anacreon, and is being given homeopathic treatments. I have not yet succeeded in seeing Chaadaev, [M. F.] Orlov, [A. N.] Raevsky, and the Observers[13] (whom Nashchokin calls *les treize*). I intend to coquette with the Observers and the booksellers, and I'll try to take care of *The Contemporary* as best I can.—Here is Nashchokin coming, and I'm leaving you for him. I kiss and bless you and the children. I greet your ladies. Here they're already talking about Maria Vyazemskaya's wedding[14]—I'm being secretive for the time being. Farewell. My dear—I kiss you again.

[612]

To Natalia Nikolaevna Pushkina
May 6, 1836. From Moscow to Petersburg.

Here I have already been in Moscow three days, and I still have not done anything. I have not seen the archives,[1] have not struck a bargain with the booksellers, have not paid all my calls, have not been to the Solntsevs[2] to pay my respects. What would you have me do? Nashchokin gets up late, I start chattering with him—look, it's time to dine, and then to have supper, and then to sleep—and the day is gone. Yesterday I was at [I. I.] Dmitriev's and at [M. F.] Orlov's, [F. I.] Tolstoy's; today I'm planning to go see the others. The poet [A. S.] Khomyakov is getting married to Yazykova,[3] the sister of the poet. A wealthy groom, a wealthy bride. What Moscow gossip should I pass on to you? There seems to be a lot of it, but I can't remember. What Moscow says about Petersburg is killingly funny. For example: "In Petersburg there is a certain *Saveliev*, a cavalry guardsman, an excellent young man. He's in love with Idalia Poletika, and on account of her he has slapped Grinvald in the face. Saveliev, in a few days, will be shot. Imagine how pathetic Idalia is!"[4] And about you, my darling, some talk is going about which isn't reaching me in its entirety, because husbands are always the last in the city to discover about their wives. However, it seems that you have driven a certain person[5] to such despair with your coquetry and cruelty that he has acquired himself in solace a harem of theatrical trainees. That is not good, my angel. Modesty is the best adornment of your sex. In order to regale, with something or other, Moscow, which expects some fresh news from me, as a visitor, I tell them that Alexander [N.] Karamzin (the son of the historiographer) wanted to shoot himself, from love *pour une belle brune*, but that fortunately the bullet only knocked out a front tooth.[6] However, enough nonsense. Send for Gogol, and read him the following: I have seen the actor Shchepkin,[7] who asks him, for Christ's sake, to come to Moscow and read *The Inspector General*.[8] Without him the actors won't put it over. He says that the comedy will be a caricature and *filthy* (toward which Moscow has always had a sneaking inclination). For my part, my advice to him is the same; *The Inspector General* must not crash in Moscow, where they love Gogol more than in Petersburg. Enclosed is a *packet* for Pletnev, for *The Contemporary*. If the censor [A. L.] Krylov won't pass it, give it to the committee,[9] and for God's sake print it in the second issue. I await a letter from you with impatience. How about your belly,[10] and how about your money? I don't regret coming to Moscow, but I feel nostalgia for Petersburg. Are you at the summer house? How did you make out with the landlord? How are the children? Woe is me! I see that I absolutely must have an income of eighty thousand. And I shall have it. It's not for nothing that I have let myself in for speculating on a journal—after all, that's the same thing as *honey bucketing*, which [S. D.] Bezobrazov's mother wanted to get farmed out to her: to clean up Russian literature means to clean out privies and to depend on the police. The first thing you know. . . . The devil take them! My blood is turning to bile. I kiss you and the children. I bless them and you. I greet the ladies.[11]

[613]

To Peter Andreevich Vyazemsky
May 7, 1836. In Moscow.

Here is the point:

A recommendation (No. 11,483) has been made by the governor of Ryazan regarding the pension which is due to the widow of Stepan Savelievich Gubanov, provincial land surveyor. His wife is in dire need and requests that they hasten the day when she will receive the pension.

Please, my dear fellow, accomplish this through D. V. Dashkov, whom this matter depends on. You will also oblige Okulov, at whose house I am writing you this note, and who makes the same request of you.[1]

May 7.   A. Pushkin.

[614]

To Natalia Nikolaevna Pushkina
May 10, 1836. From Moscow to Petersburg.

I have just now received a letter from you, and it has so touched me that I hasten to send you nine hundred rubles. I'll write you an answer later on; now for the time being, farewell. Ivan Nikolaevich [Goncharov] is sitting with me.

[615]

To Natalia Nikolaevna Pushkina
May 11, 1836. From Moscow to Petersburg.

I thank you very, very much for your letter. I can imagine your bothers, and I ask your forgiveness for myself and the booksellers. They are horribly bad tone, as Gogol says,[1] i.e., worse than swindlers. But God will help us. I thank [V. F.] Odoevsky, too, for his typographical bothers.[2] Tell him to print however he takes the notion—the sequence is of no importance. How about the memoirs of [Nadezhda A.] Durova?[3] Have they been passed by the censorship? They are essential for me—without them I'm sunk. You write about the *Goltsov* article. What's that? One by Koltsov[4] or by Gogol? Print the Gogol,[5] but scrutinize the Koltsov. That's not important, though. Yesterday Ivan Nikolaevich [Goncharov] was at my place. He assures me that his affairs are going well. Dmitry Nikolaevich [Goncharov] knows that better than he does, though. My life is most dissipated. I am not staying at home—I am not burrowing in the Archives. Today I'm going to Malinovsky's[6] for the second time. A few days ago I dined at [M. F.] Orlov's, at whose house the Moscow Observers gathered together, and among others, [A. S.] Khomyakov, the engaged. Orlov is an intelligent man and a very fine fellow, but I'm somehow not overly fond of him, on account of our old relationships. Raevsky (Alexander), who last time seemed to me to have grown a bit stultified, seems to have livened up again and become more intelligent. His wife[7] is no beauty—they say she's very intelligent. Since being a journalist has now been added to my other merits, I have a new charm for Moscow. Not long ago, I was told that Chertkov[8] had come to see me. We had never visited each other in our lives. But on this reliable opportunity he remembered that his wife is kin to me, and therefore he brought me a copy of his *Journey to Sicily*. Oughtn't I give him a good scolding *en bon parent*? Yesterday I had supper at Prince Fedor Gagarin's and I returned at 4 o'clock in the morning—in just such a good mood as if it had been from a ball. Nashchokin is my only solace here. But he sleeps until noon, and in the evening he goes to the club, where he plays until dawn. I have seen Chaadaev only once in all. My letter is like one of Turgenev's[9]—and it can prove to you the difference between Moscow and Paris. I'm going out to see what I can do about the affairs of *The Contemporary*. I'm afraid the booksellers may take advantage of my softheartedness and wheedle some concessions in spite of your strict instructions. But I'll try to show a noble firmness. I have been at Solntseva's.[10] He is not here, he's in the village. She is inviting Father to their village for the summer. My little cousins are squealing like jackdaws. I have been at Perovsky's, who showed me some unfinished pictures of Bryullov's. Bryullov, who had been imprisoned at his house,[11] escaped from him and has quarreled with him. Perovsky, as he was showing me "The Taking of Rome by Genseric" (which is as good as his "Last Day of Pompeii")[12] kept saying: "Notice how excellently that scoundrel, such a swindler, has painted this horseman. How he managed, the swine, to express his rascally, brilliant idea, the rogue, the knave. How he has painted this group,

the drunkard, the cheat." Killingly funny. Well, farewell. I kiss you
and the youngsters. Stay well, all of you. Christ be with you.
    May 11.

[616]
To Ksenofont Alexeevich Polevoy
May 11, 1836. In Moscow.
Dear Sir, Ksenofont Alexeevich,
    I have not answered your last letter, for I have been hoping to see
you in person. The bookseller Farikov[1] has provided me with the
book[2] which you have done me the honor to send addressed to me.
As regards *The Contemporary*, Farikov did not want to take it from
me for you, for he had already sent it to you himself.[3] The money
(275 rubles)[4] about which you were so kind as to write was not
delivered to me by him, either. I most humbly request that if henceforth you should choose to have business with me, you not entrust
anything to Mr. Farikov—for he seems an undependable and un-
punctilious person.
    With true respect, I have the honor to be
                            Your most humble servant,
                                        A. Pushkin.
    May 11.

[617]
To Natalia Nikolaevna Pushkina
May 14 and 16, 1836. From Moscow to Petersburg.
What's this, little wife? You began so well, and have ended so
badly. Not a line from you. You haven't had the baby already,
have you? Today is Grishka's[1] birthday. Many happy returns of
the day to him and to you. I shall drink to his health. He doesn't
have a new little brother or little sister, does he? Wait until I arrive.
And I'm already preparing to come to you. I've been in the Archives,
and I shall be compelled to burrow into them for some six months.
What'll happen to you then? I'll bring you with me, if you like. My
life in Moscow is staid and respectable. I stay at home—I see only
the male sex. I don't go out walking, I don't cut capers—and I'm
getting fat. A few days ago [A. D.] Chertkov invited me for dinner.
I arrived there—and his wife had had a miscarriage. This didn't

prevent us from dining very boringly and very badly. I am playing the coquette with Moscow literature as well as I know how. But the Observers hold me in no high esteem. Nobody except Nashchokin loves me. But *tintere*[2] is my rival with him, and I'm being sacrificed to it. When I listen to the small talk of the local men of letters, I am astonished at how decent they can be in print and how stupid in conversation. Confess: Is that the way it is with me? Truly, I'm afraid it is. Baratynsky, however, is very pleasant. But somehow we're cold towards each other. I'm pressing Bryullov to come to Petersburg—but he's ill and is having a fit of the spleen. Here they want a bust of me to be sculptured.[3] But I don't want it. Then my Negro ugliness would be committed to immortality in all its dead immobility; I tell them that I have a beauty at home, whom we'll sculpture some time. I have seen Khomyakov's betrothed.[4] I couldn't get a good look at her in the twilight. As the late Gnedich used to say, she is *pas un bel femme*, but *une jolie figurlette*.[5] Good-by for a minute. Two buffoons are coming in to see me. One is a major and a mystic;[6] the other is a drunkard and a poet.[7] I am leaving you for them.

May 14.

I had difficulty in getting rid of the buffoons—including Norov. Everybody is inviting me to dinner, but I am refusing everybody. I'm beginning to think about departing. You are probably already in your suburban swamp.[8] Just how are my children and my books? Just how was the moving of the former and the hauling of the latter? And however did you manage to get your belly hauled? I bless you, my angel. God be with you and the children. Stay well, all of you. I greet your equestriennes.[9] I kiss Katerina Ivanovna's [Zagryazhskaya] little hands. Farewell.

A.P.

I have received an extremely sweet letter from you—I haven't the time to answer it. I thank you and kiss you, my angel.

May 16.

[618]
To Natalia Nikolaevna Pushkina
May 18, 1836. From Moscow to Petersburg.
Wife, my angel, though thanks for your nice letter, all the same

I'll scold you a little. Why did you write: "This is my last letter; you won't receive any more"? You want to compel me to come to you before the twenty-sixth. That's not the thing to do. God will help; *The Contemporary* will come out even with me away. But you won't give birth with me away. Can you give Odoevsky five hundred out of the money you have received? No? Well, let them wait until I get there—and that's all there is to it. Your new dispositions regarding your own revenues are your affair. Do as you like, though, I should think, it's better to have dealings with Dmitry Nikolaevich [Goncharov] than with Natalia Ivanovna [Goncharova]. This I say only *dans l'intérêt de M. Durier et Mme. Sichler;*[1] it's all the same to me. Your Petersburg news is horrible. What you write about Pavlov has reconciled me with him. I am glad he had challenged Aprelev.[2]— With us murder can be a vile way of settling scores: it saves one from a duel and exposes one to only a penal sentence—but not to capital punishment. Stolypin's drowning is horrible![3] Was it really impossible to help him? With us, here in Moscow, everything, thank God, is quiet: Kireev's fight with the Yar has produced great indignation in our prim local public. Nashchokin takes Kireev's[4] part very simply and very sensibly: what matter that a hussar lieutenant got drunk and beat up an innkeeper, who undertook to defend himself? In our day, when we used to beat the Germans in the Red Tavern,[5] didn't we, too, get what for, and did the Germans take being shoved around, with their arms folded? In my opinion Kireev's brawl is much more excusable than the fine dinner of your cavalry-guards, and the prudence of the young men, whose eyes get spit in, and they wipe them with a batiste handkerchief, opining that if an unpleasantness results, they won't be invited to the Anichkov Palace.[6] Bryullov has just now left me. He's going to Petersburg reluctantly; he fears the climate and lack of freedom. I try to console and encourage him. But at the same time my own heart drops into my boots when I recall that I'm a journalist. Though still a decent person, I have received police reprimands, and I have been told, *Vous avez trompé,*[7] and such like. What will happen to me now? Mordvinov will look on me as he does Faddey Bulgarin and Nikolay Polevoy—as a spy. The devil prompted my being born in Russia with a soul and with talent! It's great fun, I must say. Farewell; stay well, all of you. I kiss you.

[619]
TO PAVEL VOINOVICH NASHCHOKIN
May 27, 1836. From Petersburg to Moscow.

My dear Pavel Voinovich,

I arrived home at my summer cottage on the twenty-third at midnight, and on the threshold I learned that Natalia Nikolaevna had given birth successfully to a daughter, Natalia, a few hours before my arrival. She was asleep. The next day I congratulated her and gave her, instead of a ten-ruble gold piece, your necklace, which she is in raptures over. Knock on wood; all's going well. Now let's talk about business. I left you two extra copies of *The Contemporary*. Give one to Prince [F. F.] Gagarin, and send the other from me to Belinsky[1] (N.B.: but keep it secret from the Observers), and have him told that I regret very much that I didn't succeed in seeing him. *Secondly*, I forgot to bring along your Memoirs[2] with me; do me the favor to hurry and send them. *Thirdly*, money, money! I need it desperately.

My trip went all right, though I had to repair the calash three times, but thank God, I did it on the spot, i.e., at a station, and it didn't take over two hours *en tout*.

The second issue of *The Contemporary* is very good, and you will thank me because of it. I am beginning to love it myself, and I'll probably start working at it actively. Farewell, be lucky at *tintere* and all else. I send my cordial greetings to Vera Alexandrovna [Nashchokina]. I have not yet succeeded in carrying out her commissions. In a few days I'll see what I can do about them.

May 27.

Here's an anecdote about my Sashka for you. He is being forbidden (I don't know why) to ask for what he wants. A few days ago he says to his aunt: "Azya![3] Give me some tea! I shan't ask."

[620]
TO DENIS VASILIEVICH DAVYDOV
Between May 24 and 30, 1836. From Petersburg to Moscow.
(Rough draft)

I have just now arrived from Moscow—

I cannot send you your article about Dresden[1] until it has been

printed, for it is a censored document. You will have time to look at
its noble wounds to your heart's content.

Meanwhile, I thank you for the permission to publish it in its
present form. But it's a pity. Why didn't we print it in the second
issue of *The Contemporary*, which will be all full of Napoleon?[2]
How fitting it would have been, in the same place, to slaughter
General Wintzengerode[3] at the foot of the Vendôme Column,[4]
as a propitiatory sacrifice! I was about to roll up my sleeves to
do it! He got away, damn him. God be with him, the devil take
him.

Vyazemsky advises me to publish "Your Eyes"[5] without your
permission. I would be glad to, but I'm a little afraid. What do you
think? Mayn't I—without your name? . . .

I'm expecting some letters from Yazykov.

[621]
To Lev Sergeevich Pushkin
June 3, 1836. From Petersburg to Tiflis.

Here for you is a brief accounting of our proposed apportioning.[1]

The 80 souls and 1900 acres of land in the Pskov Province are
worth (at the rate of 500 rubles per soul, instead of the usual price
of 400 rubles)

	—40,000 rubles
From them is excluded a 7th share for our father	5,714
And a 14th share for our sister	2,857
Total	8,571—

Our father has declined his own share and granted it to our sister.

For our share, it remains to divide equally	31,429 rubles
For your share will come	15,715.

We shall not have time to get anything done before the month of
September.

Write what debts you have in Tiflis, and if you have time,
buy up your notes of hand before your creditors find out about your
inheritance.

I see from your letter to Nikolay Ivanovich [Pavlishchev] that
you don't know anything about your own affairs. Your note of hand,
given to Boltin, has been bought up by me. The debt to Pleshcheev[2]

has been paid (except 300 rubles which he wrote me about after I had already given up the management of the estate). The debt to Nikolay Ivanovich [Pavlishchev] has also been paid. Of the petty ones, your debt to Gut[3] has not been paid, *nor have certain others which you know of*, Nikolay Ivanovich tells me.

June 3.

My opinion: to spread out the payment of these 15,000 to you over three years, for you probably need money, and you couldn't consent to receive only the revenues from half of Mikhaylovskoe. About what has been assigned to you by Father I shall talk with him, although that will probably lead to nothing. When I gave the estate back to him,[4] I thought I had bespoken for you the net revenues from half of Kistenevo.[5] But apparently our father has changed his mind. As for me, under no circumstances do I want to meddle in the administration, or ruination, of our father's estate.

[622]
To ANDREY ALEXANDROVICH KRAEVSKY
June 6, 1836. In Petersburg.

In Vyazemsky's article about Julius Caesar and Napoleon there are errors against the nature of the language in the proper names. For example, *Tarkvin* instead of *Tarkvinij* [Tarquin], *Parfy* instead of *Parfjane* [Parthians], *Tiverij* instead of *Tiberij* [Tiberius]—and others. Do me the favor of correcting them, if you run across them.[1]

June 6.

[623]
To NADEZHDA ANDREEVNA DUROVA
About June 10, 1836. From Petersburg to Elabuga.

Here is the beginning of your notes. All the copies have already been printed and are now being bound. I do not know whether it would be possible to stop the edition.[1] My sincere and disinterested opinion is, leave it as it is. "The Memoirs of an Amazon" is a little too far-fetched, precious; it reminds one of German novels. "The Memoirs of N. A. Durova" is simple, sincere, and noble. Be brave—step onto the literary field of endeavor just as courageously as onto the one which has made you famous. Half measures are good for nothing.

All yours, A.P.

My house is at your service. On the Dvortsovaya Naberezhnaya, the house of Batashev at the Prachechny Bridge.

[624]
To Ivan Ivanovich Dmitriev
June 14, 1836. From Petersburg to Moscow.

Dear Sir, Ivan Ivanovich, upon returning to Petersburg I had the good fortune to find at my house a letter from Your High Excellency. Father has entrusted me with testifying of his most profound gratitude for the sympathetic interest which you take in the misfortune which has come upon us.[1]

Your favorable comment about *The Contemporary* encourages me in a field of endeavor which is new for me. I shall try also henceforth to justify your kind opinion.

The observation about your homonym[2] will adorn the second issue of *The Contemporary* and will be printed word for word. Your Sosie is no son of Jupiter,[3] and his encounter with you is unprofitable for him in all respects.

God grant you health and many years! Outlive our young literary men, just as your poetry will outlive our young literature.

With the most profound respect and with complete devotion, I have the honor to be, Dear Sir, Your High Excellency's most humble servant.

June 14.   Alexander Pushkin.
SPb.

[625]
To Iosif Matveevich Penkovsky
June 14, 1836. From Petersburg to Boldino.

Upon returning from Moscow, I found your letter at my house. I hope that you have already received the receipt from the Moscow Council.[1] There is no need to increase the quitrent. If it is possible and financially advantageous to put Kistenevo to the plow,[2] then go to it. But it will hardly be possible.

Father plans to spend this year there, but it is hardly likely that he will really do it. He probably will not consent to reside in Boldino. If he does not remain in Moscow, then I think he will settle down in Mikhaylovskoe.

I am very grateful to you for taking care of our estate. I know that last year you halted Father in his intention of selling this estate and thereby depriving, if not me, then my children, of their last dependable crust of bread. Be assured that I shall never forget it.

June 14, 1836.   A.P.
SPb.
I shall write you about Mikhaylo and his family.[3]

[626]
To Nikolay Ivanovich Ushakov
About June 14, 1836. In Petersburg.
(Rough draft)
Upon returning from Moscow, I had the honor to receive your book[1]—and I have read it avidly.

I shall not undertake to judge it as the work of a learned military man, but I am delighted with the clear, eloquent, picturesque account. From now on the name of the subjugator of Erivan, Erzurum, and Warsaw[2] will be coupled with the name of his brilliant historian. With astonishment I noticed that you have also granted me immortality—with one stroke of your pen. You have admitted me to the Temple of Glory, just as once upon a time Count Erivansky permitted me to enter conquered Erzurum after him.[3]

With the most profound, etc.

[627]
To Nadezhda Andreevna Durova
About (not earlier than) June 25, 1836.
From Petersburg to Elabuga.
I thank you very much for your frank and decisive letter.[1] It is very pleasing, because it bears the genuine stamp of your fiery and impatient character. I shall answer you *item by item*, as the court clerks say.

(1) Your notes are still being copied out. I felt obliged to give them only to someone I could depend on. Because of this, the business has been held up.

(2) The Sovereign has seen fit to be my censor. That's true. But I do not have the right to submit *others'* works for his examination. You of course will be an exception, but a pretext is necessary for doing so, and that is what I should like to talk with you about, in order that the business not be spoiled by our being hasty.

(3) You have passed through one field of endeavor with glory; you are entering upon a new one, still foreign to you. The bothers of the writer are still incomprehensible to you. It is impossible to publish a book in one week; at least some two months are required for that. The manuscript must be copied, presented to the censorship, one must apply to the printing house, etc., etc.

(4) You write me: "Take action or let me take action." As soon as I receive the copied-out manuscript, I shall begin immediately. This cannot and must not prevent you from taking action on your part. My aim is to provide you with as much profit as possible, and not to leave you a victim of the mercenary and careless booksellers.

(5) It is impossible for me to go see the Tsar on maneuvers for many reasons. I had even thought of applying to him *as a last resort*, if the censorship does not pass your notes. I shall explain all this to you when I have the pleasure of seeing you in person.

I shall have the honor of delivering the remaining five hundred rubles to you by July 1.[2] With me, payment usually (as with other journalists) occurs only when the article purchased is issued.

I know a man who would have willingly bought your memoirs; but his terms probably would have been more profitable for him than for you. In any case, whether you sell them or whether you have them printed yourself, please entrust me with all the troubles of the publication, of the proofs, etc. Be assured of my devotion, and for God's sake do not be hasty and blame me as lacking in zeal.

With the most profound respect and with devotion, I have the honor to be, Dear Sir,[3]

Your most humble servant,

Alexander Pushkin.

P.S. In a few days the second issue of *The Contemporary* will come out. Then I shall be more free and in funds.

[628]

To Ivan Alexeevich Yakovlev
July 9, 1836. In Petersburg.

Dear Ivan Alexeevich,

I am so much at fault toward you that I shall not even try to justify myself. Money has been coming to me and slipping through my fingers. I have been paying others' debts, trying to buy up others' estates[1]—and my own debts have remained on my neck. My extremely disordered affairs have made me insolvent . . . and I am compelled to ask of you another extension until autumn. Meanwhile I congratulate you upon your arrival. Where may we see you? I am in mourning[2] and do not go anywhere, but I would be glad to meet you, even though you are my creditor.[3] I am relying on your only too well tried magnanimity.

July 9, 1836.   All yours,
     Kamenny Ostrov.   A. Pushkin.

[629]

To Nikolay Ivanovich Pavlishchev
July 13, 1836. From Petersburg to Mikhaylovskoe.

I well knew that the steward[1] was a swindler, although, I confess, I had not suspected him of such impudence. You have done well in dismissing him and taking over the management of the estate yourself. One thing is bad. From your letter I see that, in defiance of my orders, the steward had already succeeded in selling off everything. What are you going to live on meanwhile? By golly, I don't know. Your Polonsky[2] has not come to see me. But since I do not yet have a power of attorney from Lev Sergeevich [Pushkin],[3] I have not tried to look him up. However, where am I to find him when I need him? Father left Petersburg on July 1—and I have not received any news of him. I shall forward Sister's letter to him as soon as I find out where to write him. How is her health? With all my heart I embrace her. I also send my greetings to dear and honored Praskovia Alexandrovna [Osipova], who has forgotten me completely. Here my head's going round and round. I am thinking of coming to Mikhaylovskoe, as soon as I have brought my affairs into a little order.

July 13.

[630]

To Nikolay Ivanovich Pavlishchev
About (not later than) August 13, 1836.
From Petersburg to Mikhaylovskoe.

Do me the favor to compose on the spot the *announcement of the sale* of Mikhaylovskoe,[1] and send it to me; and I shall print it that way. But try to talk it over with the *best* buyers there on the spot. One of our neighbors here, who knows both the region and our land, has offered me 20,000 rubles for Mikhaylovskoe. I confess that it is hardly likely that anyone will give twice that, and I don't dare even to think of 60,000. I cannot agree to the transaction you propose,[2] and here is why: Father will never consent to give Olga her share of his estate while he is alive, and I can't rely on Boldino. Father has already lived up and lost, through poor management, half of the estate, and has even wanted to sell the remainder already. You write that for me Mikhaylovskoe would be only a toy. So it would—for me. But my children are not a bit richer than your Lelya,[3] and I cannot play jokes with their future and their property. If you took Mikhaylovskoe and then it should become necessary for you to sell it, then it wouldn't be a toy for me, either. Your appraisal of 64,000 is a good price, but one must find out whether so much would be given. I might even give it, but I don't have the money, and if I had it, I could use the capital more advantageously. I send greetings to Olga. God grant her good health—and us good buyers. This fall I shall be in Mikhaylovskoe—probably for the last time. I should like to find you still there.

A.P.

[631]

To Andrey Andreevich Zhandr
July or August, 1836. In Petersburg.
(Rough draft)

I make bold to trouble you with a request for a young man whom I am not acquainted with, but who finds himself in circumstances which require immediate aid. Mr. Khmelnitsky[1] arrived from Little Russia a few days ago. He is here without money and without protectors. He is twenty-three years old. Judging from his conversation and a letter which I received from him, he is intelligent and has noble feelings. Here is the point: he wishes to get a place in the Navy, but up to now he has not had admission to see Prince Menshikov.[2] I have promised to introduce him to you, vouching for your readiness to do him a good turn, if only it be possible.

[632]

To Denis Vasilievich Davydov
August, 1836. From Petersburg to Maza.
(Rough draft)

You thought your article "Of Partisan Warfare"[1] would pass through the censorship whole and unharmed. You were mistaken: it did not get by without some red ink. Really, the military censors seem to blot out, to prove that they read.

It's hard, one must say. With one censorship you have to dance a merry tune; but what is it like to depend on all four?[2] I do not know what offense has been committed by Russian writers, who not only are mild but are even, in and of themselves, in accord with the spirit of the government. But I know that never have they been so oppressed as now, not even in the last five years of the reign of the late Emperor,[3] when all literature remained in manuscript, thanks to Krasovsky and Birukov.

The censorship is a civilian matter; the *opričina* has been separated from it—but the members of the *opričina* are guided, not by the code, but by their extreme notions.[4]

[633]

To Peter Alexandrovich Korsakov
About (not later than) September 27, 1836.
In Petersburg.

Dear Sir, Peter Alexandrovich,

Once upon a time, when I was taking my first steps in the literary field of endeavor, you gave me a friendly hand.[1] Now I make bold to have recourse again to your indulgent protection.

You alone among us have been able to combine the ticklish duty of the censor with the feeling of a man of letters (the best ones—not those of the present times). I know how burdened you are with your duties. I am ashamed to trouble you. But you are the only one to whom we can have recourse with full confidence and with sincere esteem for your ultimate decision. You have only yourself to blame.

I make bold to forward to you the first half of my novel for authorization; I ask you to preserve the secret of my name.

With the most profound respect and with complete devotion, I have the honor to be,

Dear Sir,
Your most humble servant,
A. Pushkin.

[634]

To NIKOLAY IVANOVICH GRECH
October 13, 1836. In Petersburg.

Dear Sir, Nikolay Ivanovich,

I sincerely thank you for your kind word about my "Great Leader."[1] The stoic figure of Barklay is one of the most remarkable in our history. I do not know whether he can be fully justified with respect to military art, but his character will remain eternally worthy of astonishment and admiration.

With sincere respect and with devotion, I have the honor to be,

Dear Sir,
Your most humble servant,

October 13, 1836.   Alexander Pushkin.

[635]

To MODEST ALEXANDROVICH KORF
October 14, 1836. In Petersburg.

What you sent me yesterday[1] is valuable to me in all respects and will remain with me as a memorial. I am truly sorry that the governmental service has deprived us of a historian. I have no hope of replacing you. Upon reading this list of names, I became frightened and ashamed: a great part of the books cited are unknown to me. I shall exert all possible efforts to obtain them. What a field modern Russian history is! And when you reflect that it is as yet completely untilled, and that except for us Russians nobody can even undertake it! But history is long, life is short, and worst of all, human nature is lazy (Russian nature especially). Good-by. Tomorrow we shall probably see each other at Myasoedov's.[2]

Devoted to you in heart,

October 14. A.P.

[636]

To Mikhail Lukianovich Yakovlev
Between October 9 and 15, 1836. In Petersburg.

I agree with the opinion of No. 39.[1] There is no point in changing the ancient customs of the Lyceum for the twenty-fifth anniversary. That would be a bad omen. It has been said that even the last Lyceum student will celebrate October 19 *alone*.[2] It is not a bad idea to call that to mind.

No. 14.

[637]

To Peter Yakovlevich Chaadaev
October 19, 1836.
(In French)

October 19.

I thank you for the booklet which you sent me. I was delighted to read it again, although very much astonished at seeing it translated and published. I am pleased with the translation; it has preserved the energy and the unconstraint of the original. As for the ideas, you know that I am far from being entirely of your opinion.[1] There is no doubt that the Schism separated us from the rest of Europe and that we have not participated in any of the great occurrences which have agitated it. But we have had our own special mission. Russia, in its immense expanse, was what absorbed the Mongol conquest. The Tatars did not dare to cross our western frontiers and leave us to their rear. They withdrew to their deserts, and Christian civilization was saved.[2] For this purpose we were obliged to have a life completely apart, one which though leaving us Christians left us such complete strangers to the Christian world that our martyrdom did not provide any distraction to the energetic development of Catholic Europe. You say that the well to which we went to draw Christianity was contaminated, that Byzantium was contemptible and contemned, etc. Well, now, my friend! Was not Jesus Christ himself born a Jew, and was not Jerusalem the laughing-stock of nations? Are the Gospels the less wonderful for that? We have taken the Gospels and traditions from the Greeks, but not the spirit of puerility and controversy. The customs of Byzantium were never those of Kiev. The Russian clergy, up to Feofan,[3] was worthy of respect; it was never besmirched by the infamies of papism, and most certainly it would never have provoked the Reformation at the moment when humanity had the most need of unity.[4] I acknowledge that our present-day clergy is behind the times. Do you want to know the reason why? Because it wears the beard; that is all. It does not belong to good society.[5] As for our history being nil, I absolutely cannot be of your opinion. The Wars of Oleg and of Svyatoslav, and even the wars of appanage —are these not that life of adventurous effervescence and of ruthless, pointless activity which characterizes the youth of all peoples? The invasion by the Tatars is a sad and a grand picture. What? Are the awakening of Russia, the development of its power, its march toward unity (Russian unity, of course), the two Ivans,[6] the sublime drama begun at Uglich and concluded at the Ipatiev Monastery[7]—is all this to be not history, but a pallid and half-forgotten dream? And Peter the Great, who in himself alone is a universal history! And Catherine II, who placed Russia on the threshold of Europe? And Alexander, who led us to Paris? And (cross your heart) do you find nothing impressive in the present-day situation of Russia, nothing which will strike the future historian? Do you believe that he will place us outside Europe? Although I personally am sincerely attached to the Emperor, I am far from admiring all that I see around me; as a man of letters, I am embittered; as a man of prejudices,[8] I am offended. But I swear to you on my honor that not for anything in the world would I be willing to change my fatherland, nor to have any other history than that of our ancestors, such as God gave it to us.

This is a very long letter. After having taken issue with you, I must tell you that many things in your letter are profoundly true. One must admit that our social life is a sad thing. The absence of public opinion, the indifference toward all duty, justice, and truth, the cynical disdain for human thought and dignity are truly distressing. You have done well to say it out loud. But I fear that your historical opinions may do you harm ... in a word, I am vexed that I was not near you when you delivered your manuscript to the journalists. I do not go anywhere, and I cannot tell you whether your article is attracting attention. I hope that it will not be puffed. Have you read the third issue of *The Contemporary*? The article "Voltaire" and the "John Tanner"[9] are mine. Kozlovsky would be my providence if he were to consent once and for all to become a man of letters. Farewell, my friend. If you see [M. F.] Orlov and [A. N.] Raevsky, remember me kindly to them.—What are the lukewarm Christians saying of your letter?[10]

[638]

To Sergey Lvovich Pushkin
October 20, 1836. From Petersburg to Moscow.
(In French)

My dear Father, here, first of all, is my address: *On the Moyka at the Konyushenny Bridge, in the house of Princess Volkonskaya.*[1] I have been obliged to leave Batashev's house, the caretaker of which is a rascal.

You ask me for news of Natalia and the youngsters. Thank God, all are healthy. I have no news of my sister, who left the country, ill. Her husband, after having put me out of patience with his perfectly useless letters,[2] is giving no further signs of life, when the thing to be done is to straighten up his affairs. Do send him a *power of attorney* for the share which you have given Olga. It is needed. Lev has entered the service,[3] and is asking me for money, but I am not in position to support everybody. I myself am in very disordered circumstances, burdened with a numerous family, supporting them by dint of hard work, and not daring to look to the future. Pavlish-chev reproaches me with the expenditures I make, though I am not a burden upon anyone, and though I do not have to give an accounting to anyone but my children. He asserts that all the same they will be richer than his son. I know nothing of the sort. But I neither can nor will be generous at their expense.

I had counted on going to Mikhaylovskoe; I have not been able to. This will upset my affairs for another year, at least. In the country I would have worked a great deal. Here I do nothing but fret.

Farewell, my dear Father. I kiss your hands and embrace you with all my heart.

October 20, 1836.

[639]
To Peter Alexandrovich Korsakov
October 25, 1836. In Petersburg.

Dear Sir, Peter Alexandrovich,

I hasten to answer your questions.[1] The name of the maiden Mironova is fictitious. My novel is based on a tradition I once heard, that one of the officers, who was unfaithful to his duty and went over to Pugachev's gangs, was pardoned by the Empress at the request of his aged father, who threw himself at her feet. The novel, as you see, departed far from the truth. I would ask you not to mention the real name of the author, but to state that the manuscript was delivered via P. A. Pletnev, whom I have already informed in advance.

Permit me, Dear Sir, to testify again of my most profound respect and my cordial gratitude.

I have the honor to be,
Dear Sir,
Your most humble servant,

October 25.   Alexander Pushkin.

[640]
To Vladimir Fedorovich Odoevsky
1835 or 1836. In Petersburg.

I am at home, ill, with a cold in the head. I am ready to receive a dear guest in my cubicle—but I myself shall not come out of my cubicle.[1]

A.P.

[641]
To Anna Petrovna Kern
1835 or 1836 (?). In Petersburg.
(In French)

My pen is so poor that Mme. Khitrovo cannot use it, and so I have the privilege of being her secretary.[1]

[642]
To Anna Petrovna Kern
1835 or 1836 (?). In Petersburg.
(In French)

Here is Sheremetev's[1] answer. My wish is that it be agreeable to you. Mme. Khitrovo has done what she could. Farewell, beautiful lady. Be calm and happy, and believe in my devotion.

[643]
To Anna Petrovna Kern
1835 or 1836 (?). In Petersburg.
(Fragments; in French)

When you could not obtain anything, you, a pretty woman, what, then, will I be able to do, I who am not even a handsome lad? [. . .] All that I can advise is to turn again to the expedient [. . . .][1]

[644]
To Peter Andreevich Vyazemsky
In the second half of 1835 or in 1836.
In Petersburg.

Arab (does not have a feminine), a dweller or native of Arabia, an Arabian. *Karavan byl razgrablen stepnymi arabami* [The caravan was plundered by the Arabs of the steppes].

Arap, feminine *arapka*; this is what negroes and mulattoes are usually called. *Dvorcovye arapy*, negroes serving in the palace. *On vyezžaet s tremja narjadnymi arapami* [He is leaving with three finely dressed negroes].

Arapnik, from the Polish *Herapnik* (*de* **harap**), *cri de chasseur pour enlever aux chiens la proie. Reiff*).[1] N.B.: **harap** *vient de* **Herab** [down].

Really, it wouldn't be a bad idea to get busy on a Lexicon or at least a critique of lexicons.[2]

[645]
To Mikhail Lukianovich Yakolev
1836(?). In Petersburg.

Smirdin has plunged me into misfortune; this tradesman is

always going back on his word, and a promised day, with him, means God knows when.[1]

Tomorrow I shall receive the money at 2 o'clock in the afternoon. And in the evening I shall deliver it to you.

All yours, A.P.

[646]

To ACHILLE TARDIF DE MELLO
1836(?). In Petersburg.
(In French)

You have made me find my verses very beautiful,[1] Sir. You have reclothed them in that noble garment in which poetry is truly a goddess, *vera incessu patuit dea*.[2] I thank you for your precious packet.

You are a poet and you are teaching youth; I invoke two benedictions upon you.

A. Pushkin.

·

Letter 588

1. Pushkin's edition of "The Memoirs of Brigadier Moreau de Brasey" was published in *The Contemporary* in 1837, after Pushkin's death.

2. Pushkin uses the English word "Review" here and below. This official request resulted in Pushkin's obtaining permission to publish a literary journal, *The Contemporary*, which began to appear in April, 1836.

Letter 589

1. Pushkin addresses Mme. Durova, the "Amazon" who fought, disguised as a man, in Russia's wars against Napoleon, by her masculine pseudonym, Alexander Andreevich Alexandrov (see Letter 564, and note). Pushkin printed a fragment from her memoirs in his *Contemporary* in 1836, but he did not publish the edition in book form.

Letter 590

1. Pushkin's wrath had not cooled in the almost two years since the Moscow postmaster had intercepted one of his letters and given it to the police, who gave it to the Tsar (see Letter 488, and note).

2. *The Contemporary.*

3. The allusion is to Nashchokin's abandoning his mistress, Olga Andreevna, and marrying.

4. A certain V—— who called himself doctor, and who practiced alchemy. Nashchokin spent considerable money on his experiments to produce gold.

Letter 591

1. Probably Benkendorf. This letter concerns Pushkin's clash with Uvarov, Minister of Public Education, over Pushkin's "Ode on the Convalescence of Lucullus," in which Uvarov is satirized and the charges are leveled against him as indicated in this letter. Benkendorf asked Pushkin in person at whom the satire was directed. Pushkin replied, "At you." Benkendorf laughed at the absurdity. Then Pushkin inquired why people thought it might be about Uvarov.

2. Pushkin did not complete the sentence.

3. That is, to favorites of Catherine the Great. Derzhavin's poem was written in 1794, two years before Catherine's death.

4. In his diary in February, 1836, Pushkin makes these specific charges—and worse— against Uvarov.

5. It may be noted that Pushkin does not deny that the poem is a personal satire on Uvarov. He only says that the charges are commonplace and that he has never told anyone that the poem was a satire on anyone.

Letter 592

1. Pushkin's letter is in answer to a letter of the same day from Khlyustin, challenging Pushkin to a duel. The challenge resulted from hot words of Pushkin's upon hearing Khlyustin repeat Senkovsky's charge that Lyutsenko's translation of *Vastola* was Pushkin's own (see Letter 572). Khlyustin demanded satisfaction on three points: (1) that Pushkin included him among the "swine and scoundrels" he accuses, (2) that Pushkin made threats equal in significance to a challenge and then did not send a

challenge, and (3) that Pushkin was impolite in not bowing when he left Khlyustin. In this letter Pushkin answers all three points, but Khlyustin was satisfied with the answer to only the third. Further negotiations and conversations, with Sobolevsky as intermediator, were necessary to prevent a duel. The last twelve months of Pushkin's life begin with him in an irritated mood and making intemperate charges. This is the first of several almost-duels which were averted in 1836, before the fatal duel occurred in January, 1837.

2. "I am not angry with Senkovsky, but I cannot help being vexed when decent people repeat the absurdities of swine and scoundrels." Pushkin's self-quotation in Russian shows that the conversation in point had been in Russian, though Khlyustin's challenge and Pushkin's reply are both in French. Pushkin could consider Senkovsky a "swine and a scoundrel," but he was not "angry" with him, that is, he would not challenge him to a duel, as a member of a lower social class.

3. "Swine and scoundrels."

4. "To deceive the public." Pushkin left himself open for this charge by publishing Lyutsenko's translation of *Vastola*, without the name of the translator, but with his own name as publisher on the title page—with the result that it could be assumed that Pushkin was the translator.

Letter 593

1. Prince Nikolay Grigorievich Repnin-Volkonsky (1778-1845), a member of the State Council and brother of the Decembrist S. G. Volkonsky.

2. Varfolomey Filippovich Bogolyubov (ca. 1785-1842), an official serving in the Collegium of Foreign Affairs, and a man close to Uvarov. He informed Pushkin that Repnin-Volkonsky considered Pushkin's satire on Uvarov, "On the Convalescence of Lucullus" (see Letter 591, and note), as directed at him, Repnin-Volkonsky. Repnin-Volkonsky had been removed from the post of Governor-General of Little Russia in 1834, because of irregularities in his accounts, and hence he might very well feel that he had reason to think that Pushkin's poem was about him. (See Letter 595.)

Letter 594

1. Count Vladimir Alexandrovich Sollogub, later a well-known writer of short stories. At a ball in December, 1835, or January, 1836, Sollogub answered some bantering comments of Mme. Pushkina's with a remark which she considered offensive. Pushkin, sensitive about his wife's honor, immediately sent off a challenge to Sollogub, but it remained undelivered, because Sollogub had left to serve under the Governor of Tver. When Sollogub learned of the challenge, which has not survived, he wrote a letter of explanations, which Pushkin is here answering. The affair ended without a duel. Pushkin was "satisfied" when Sollogub, after extended personal negotiations, wrote a letter asking Mme. Pushkina's pardon. Though Pushkin was willing to fight, his attitude toward dueling at this time is clear from one thing he said to Sollogub: "Surely you don't think it's fun for me to duel? But what can I do? I have the misfortune to be a public man, and, you know, that's worse than being a public woman." Sollogub, after this event, was in very friendly relations with Pushkin. Pushkin chose him as his second for negotiations with Georges Charles d'Anthès-Heeckeren (1812-1895) with regard to a duel in November, 1836. This duel did not take place, and Sollogub had no part in the arrangements for Pushkin's fatal duel two months later.

2. Pushkin traveled through Tver on May 1, 1836, and tried to have a meeting with Sollogub, but Sollogub was then out of town. Three days later Sollogub went to Nashchokin's house in Moscow, where Pushkin was then on a visit, and the satisfactory explanations took place.

3. The sentence was left uncompleted. The fair copy of this letter is unknown. In the version published from memory by Sollogub in 1865, the following sentence occurs, which is not in this rough draft: "The name which you bear and the society which you frequent oblige me to demand of you the reason for the impropriety of your conduct." Like Pushkin, Sollogub was an aristocrat and a Kammerjunker.

Letter 595
1. Repnin-Volkonsky, in his letter (in Russian) of February 10, 1836, in answer to Letter 593, stated that he had never spoken of Pushkin at all in the presence of Bogolyubov. He added that "to you I shall sincerely say that your genius and talent will bring benefit to the fatherland and glory to you, in lauding the Russian faith and loyalty, rather than in insulting honorable men." Repnin-Volkonsky was "grieved" that Pushkin had not "contemned tales so repugnant to [his] principles."

Letter 596
1. Pushkin's letter is a tardy answer to Mme. Fuch's letter of November 15, 1835. Pushkins last previous trip to the "village" had been in September and October, 1835.
2. Pushkin's *History of Pugachev*.
3. Unidentified.
4. Mme. Fuchs sent various works to Pushkin, as a result of this invitation, but he did not print any of them in *The Contemporary*.

Letter 597
1. Vasily Dmitrievich Sukhorukov (1795-1841), army officer and writer, implicated in, but not a participant of the Decembrist Uprising of 1825. Materials which he collected for a history of Don troops and, later, of the Russian expedition to Erzurum in 1829, were confiscated by the authorities and never returned to him. Pushkin met him in the Caucasus, "in the vicinity" of the mountains of Beshtau and Elbrus, when Pushkin also took part in the expedition to Erzurum. In his *Journey to Erzurum*, Pushkin mentions meeting Sukhorukov (Chapter V).
2. Possibly one F. I. Shumkov.
3. To Olga Vasilievna Shvetsova.
4. Pushkin no doubt means a notification that Sukhorukov would receive it. Pushkin was sending such announcements to his friends and prospective contributors at the time. No articles by Sukhorukov appeared in the journal during Pushkin's lifetime.

Letter 598
1. Odoevsky was Pushkin's closest collaborator in *The Contemporary*. The discussion here is about the first issue.
2. Pushkin's *Journey to Erzurum*.
3. Odoevsky's tale "Princess Zizi" did not appear in Pushkin's *Contemporary*, but in *Memoirs of the Fatherland* (1839).

Letter 599
1. The letter has to do mainly with difficulties with the censorship in connection with articles for Pushkin's *Contemporary*. All the items mentioned in this letter appeared in the first issue of *The Contemporary*.
2. Prince Peter Borisovich Kozlovsky (1783-1840), writer and diplomat. His article was "Review of the Paris Mathematical Annual for 1836."
3. The reference is to A. I. Turgenev's "Letters from Paris," which contained comment about social and political events of the time, including the unsuccessful

attempt on the life of King Louis Philippe of France, made by Giuseppi Fieschi, Corsican conspirator, on July 28, 1835. Brief mentions of Fieschi and several French ministers, including among others Guizot and Thiers, were nevertheless permitted to occur in the printed "Letters."

4. Vyazemsky's poem, "The Rose and the Cypress," addressed to Princess Maria Alexandrovna Pototskaya (d. 1845).

Letter 600

1. Pushkin's point is that, after the Censorship Committee made substantial cuts in A. I. Turgenev's "Letters from Paris," Pushkin wished to present them at once to Benkendorf for approval, thus by-passing the Chief Directorate of the Censorship. Prince Dondukov-Korsakov answered, however, that the article would be presented to the Chief Directorate of the Censorship. Pushkin noted on the back of Dondukov-Korsakov's letter, "With the censorship you can quarrel, he says, but not with His Grace."

Letter 601

1. See Letters 599 and 600. Alexander Lukich Krylov (1798-1853), professor of history at Petersburg University, as the censor of A. I. Turgenev's "Letters from Paris," had made cuts which Pushkin wished restored. This letter calls attention again to the close scrutiny which the censorship under Nicholas I kept over all foreign news of any political interest.

Letter 602

1. Alphonse Jean Jobard (1793—after 1845) had been professor of Latin and Greek at Kazan University in the 1820's. He was expelled from Russia in 1836, as the result of clashes with Uvarov, Minister of Public Education. On March 16, 1836, Jobard sent his own translation of Pushkin's satire on Uvarov, "On the Convalescence of Lucullus," to Pushkin, along with a copy of a letter addressed to Uvarov, in which Jobard proposed that Uvarov accept the translation and publish it as his own, as he was in the habit of doing with others' work. Upon receiving Pushkin's letter, Jobard agreed not to publish the translation and letter to Uvarov "for a time," but he stated that he had sent copies to relatives in France and Belgium, and that they might be published there if Jobard did not receive "justice" in Russia.

2. Nicholas I.

Letter 603

1. Pushkin published only a part of Nadezhda Andreevna Durova's memoirs in his journal, *The Contemporary*. Durova was Durov's sister; Pushkin calls her Durov's "brother" and "him" because she wrote under a masculine pseudonym, Alexander Andreevich Alexandrov, in recounting her experiences of serving in the army disguised as a man.

2. The letter was sent off only on April 18.

Letter 604

1. This is the only known letter of Pushkin's to an English man of letters. The book in question is Borrow's *Targum, or a Metrical Translation from Thirty Languages*, which he published in English in Petersburg in 1835. It contains some translations from Pushkin.

Letter 605

1. The first issue of Pushkin's *Contemporary* appeared on April 11, 1836. St. Thomas' Week is the second week after Easter.

2. Odoevsky's article, "Of Enmity Toward Enlightenment, as Observed in Most Recent Literature," was published in the second issue of *The Contemporary*, but not at the beginning of it.

3. Odoevsky's critique of the novel, *The Inn* (1835), by Alexander Petrovich Stepanov (1781-1837), was published in the third issue of *The Contemporary*, under the title "How Novels Are Written Among Us."

4. Odoevsky's "fragment" remained unfinished; it did not appear in *The Contemporary*.

5. Pushkin left for Mikhaylovskoe on April 7 or 8, 1836, for the burial of his mother, who died on March 29.

6. A dramatic fragment by Odoevsky. It did not appear in *The Contemporary*.

7. Gogol's "Morning of a Man of Business: Petersburg Scenes," which appeared in the first issue of *The Contemporary*.

Letter 606

1. As a result of this request, an additional censor was named for Pushkin's *Contemporary*, Pavel Ivanovich Gaevsky. Gaevsky proved so severe a censor that Pushkin soon had reason to regret having made the request.

Letter 607

1. The death of his mother on March 29.

2. The first issue of *The Contemporary* appeared on April 11, during the first week of Pushkin's absence from Petersburg.

3. The review of Pogodin's *Historical Aphorisms* (Moscow, 1836) was written by Gogol. During Pushkin's lifetime one article by Pogodin appeared in *The Contemporary*.

Letter 608

1. The estate of the Vrevskys. Pushkin was visiting the family of Evpraxia Nikolaevna Vrevskaya, nee Vulf.

2. The quotation is from Yazykov's poem "Trigorskoe."

3. In 1829, Pushkin had called Vulf "Lovelace Nikolaevich" (Letter 254), and in another letter he called himself "the Lovelace of Tver" and Vulf "Valmont" (Letter 238).

4. An unsigned article about *The Collected Works* of Georgy Konissky (1717-1795), Belorussian Archbishop.

5. Yazykov, in response to this request, contributed "A Dramatic Tale About Ivan Tsarevich . . . " to *The Contemporary* in 1836.

6. In Russian fairy tales, "dead water" causes the parts of a dismembered body to grow back together, and "living water" then brings it back to life. Puskin utilized this folklore motif in *Ruslan and Lyudmila*.

7. In Yazykov's poetic "Epistle to Davydov," which had been published in *The Moscow Observer* during the previous year, he alludes to a well-known physical trait of D. V. Davydov, as he says, "You are a warrior with curly black hair, with a white lock on your forehead."

8. Yazykov's answer to Vyazemsky's poem, "To Yazykov" (1834), was published in 1844.

9. The quotation is from Derzhavin, "On the Birth of Tsaritsa Gremislava: To Lev Alexandrovich Naryshkin."

10. Yazykov answered that he had sent the work to his brother to be given to

Pushkin, but that Pushkin should obtain a copy of the work from Peter Vasilievich Kireevsky, whose copy had been collated with many copies.

Letter 609

1. The letter in question was from Kyukhelbeker, whose prison sentence in connection with the Decembrist Uprising had been commuted to permission to settle in Eastern Siberia (see Letter 587). Pushkin is answering Mordvinov's letter stating that Benkendorf wanted the letter from Kyukhelbeker and wanted to know via whom Pushkin received it.

Letter 610

1. Dondukov-Korsakov's letter of April 10, 1836, in which he named Gaevsky as second censor of Pushkin's *Contemporary*, in response to Pushkin's request (Letter 606).

2. Denis V. Davydov's essay, "The Occupation of Dresden . . .," which contained criticism of certain military leaders and self-justification by Davydov. Because of the military matters involved, it had to be sent to the military censorship. See Letter 620.

Letter 611

1. A church in Moscow.

2. Pushkin left on April 28 for what turned out to be his last trip to Moscow. He went there to work in the archives and to accomplish certain business with regard to his *Contemporary*.

3. Pushkin is playing on the idiom "he is lodged foppishly," so as to include the idea that "he is lodged with a little mistress."

4. The painter Karl Pavlovich Bryullov (1799-1852). The sculptor he was living with was probably Ivan Petrovich Vitali (1794-1855).

5. Probably an error, for Alexander Julius Klinder, a portraitist.

6. Bryullov visited Petersburg at the end of May or the beginning of June, 1836, after Pushkin returned from Moscow.

7. The writer, Alexey Alexeevich Perovsky. Bryullov was painting his portrait at the time, but did not finish it.

8. Nashchokin's play house (see Letter 412 and notes). Some "tiny people" were added later, including a figurine of Pushkin.

9. Elizaveta Alexeevna Okulova and Varvara Alexeevna Okulova were sisters of Nashchokin's brother-in-law. The former married Alexey Nikolaevich Diakov (1790-1837) on May 3, 1836.

10. The Troitse-Sergieva Lavra (Monastery).

11. *Belaja gorjačka.*

12. Sarra Fedorovna Tolstaya (1820-1838). She died of tuberculosis.

13. The publishers of the journal, *The Moscow Observer.*

14. Princess Maria Petrovna Vyazemskaya married Peter Alexandrovich Valuev (1815-1880) on May 22, 1836.

Letter 612

1. To work on materials regarding Peter the Great.

2. Pushkin's aunt and uncle and their family.

3. Ekaterina Mikhaylovna Yazykova (1817-1852). The wedding took place a month later.

4. Judging from Pushkin's tone, Moscow gossip must have had the story all wrong. According to other information, Peter Yakovlevich Saveliev (1801—after 1838), a Cavalry Guard Officer, was made a private in the Nizhny Novgorod Dragoon Regiment

three days after this letter was written, as the upshot of a quarrel with one Staff-Captain Gorgoli. There is no evidence that he slapped the face of Rodion Grigorievich Grinvald (1797-1877), the commander of the regiment in which he had been serving as an officer. What interest Idalia Poletika took in Saveliev is not known.

5. Nicholas I.

6. No other record of the love of Alexander Nikolaevich Karamzin (1815-1888) for a beautiful brunette or attempt at suicide is known.

7. Mikhail Semenovich Shchepkin (1788-1863), who became perhaps the most famous Russian realistic actor. He became famous in the role of the Town Mayor in Gogol's *Inspector General*. That the first Moscow performance of the play was by no means a complete success is attributed to the fact that Shchepkin, denied a free hand in directing the play, refused to continue as its director.

8. Gogol's *The Inspector General*, one of the greatest of all Russian dramas, had been presented for the first time less than a month earlier, on April 19, 1836, in the presence of Nicholas I himself, who joined in the praise of the satire. There were also attacks on it by the journalists Senkovsky, Bulgarin, and Polevoy, and they contributed to Gogol's going abroad on June 9, 1836.

9. The Censorship Committee.

10. Pushkin is, as usual, unceremonious in his query concerning his wife's pregnancy. The expected child was born on May 23.

11. Mme. Pushkina's aunt, Mme. Zagryazhskaya, and her two sisters.

Letter 613

1. This letter shows Pushkin's continued willingness to exert his influence on behalf of anyone who requested him to. Nothing more is known about Stepan Savelievich Gubanov and his widow. The Governor of Ryazan at the time was Stepan Vasilievich Perfiliev (1796-1878). The surveying office, in which Gubanov had served, was administratively subordinate to the Ministry of Justice, of which the head was Pushkin's old friend Dashkov. What interest Matvey Alexeevich Okulov (1793-1853) may have had in the affair is not known.

Letter 615

1. Gogol's *The Inspector General*, Act V.

2. For his work in seeing the second issue of *The Contemporary* through the press.

3. See Letter 589.

4. Alexey Vasilievich Koltsov (1809-1842), self-taught poet, particularly effective in folk-type lyrics on peasant subjects. His poem, "The Harvest," appeared in the second issue of *The Contemporary*.

5. Gogol's tale "The Nose" was also published in the second issue of *The Contemporary*.

6. Alexey Fedorovich Malinovsky, Director of the Archives in Moscow.

7. Ekaterina Petrovna Raevskaya, nee Kindyakova (1812-1839). The marriage had taken place on November 11, 1834.

8. Alexander Dmitrievich Chertkov (1789-1858), historian and archaeologist. His *Recollections of Sicily* had been published in Moscow during the preceding year.

9. That is, like A. I. Turgenev's "Letters from Paris," which were being published in *The Contemporary*. See Letters 599, 600, and 601, and notes.

10. Pushkin's aunt, Elizaveta Lvovna Solntseva, his father's sister. "He" in the next sentence is her husband, M. M. Solntsev, and the "little cousins" referred to further along are their children.

11. See Letter 611.

12. Paintings by Bryullov. "The Taking of Rome by Genseric" (1836), remained an unfinished sketch. His "Last Day of Pompeii" (1833) was a sensational success when it was shown in 1834, the same year that Edward Bulwer-Lytton's novel *The Last Days of Pompeii* appeared.

Letter 616

1. One of the minor Petersburg booksellers.

2. Ksenofont Polevoy's *Mikhail Vasilievich Lomonosov* (Moscow, 1836).

3. Apparently Pushkin wished to give K. A. Polevoy a free subscription to *The Contemporary*, but Farikov wished K. A. Polevoy to subscribe to it through him.

4. K. A. Polevoy had offered to be Pushkin's agent in obtaining subscriptions for *The Contemporary*. The reference here is apparently to payment for subscriptions to Pushkin's journal.

Letter 617

1. Rough-affectionate diminutive for Grigory (Alexandrovich Pushkin), Pushkin's second son.

2. A card game.

3. Apparently the sculptor I. P. Vitali proposed that he sculpture Pushkin. This was accomplished only after Pushkin's death, and at the behest of Nashchokin.

4. Ekaterina Mikhaylovna Yazykova.

5. Pushkin is laughing at the commoner Gnedich's self-acquired French.

6. Avraam Sergeevich Norov (1795-1869), minor poet whose left leg had been torn off in the Battle of Borodino in 1812. He later (1853-1854) published accounts of his travels in Europe, Egypt, Nubia, and Palestine.

7. Unidentified.

8. In their summer home on Kamenny Ostrov.

9. Mme. Pushkina's two sisters.

Letter 618

1. M. Durier and Mme. Sichler were proprietors of fashionable shops. The point of reference is Mme. Pushkina's own income from family estates. Pushkin thinks she would do better to deal with her oldest brother, Dmitry, than with her mother.

2. Alexander Fedorovich Aprelev (1798-1836) seduced the sister of one Pavlov. After Aprelev refused either to marry the girl or to give "satisfaction" in a duel, Pavlov, on May 8, 1836, stabbed Aprelev to death on the church porch on the day of Aprelev's wedding with another woman.

3. Pavel Grigorievich Stolypin (1806-1836), retired cavalry officer, drowned on May 9, 1836.

4. Nothing is known of Kireev in addition to what Pushkin says here.

5. A restaurant in Petersburg.

6. The Court balls were presented in the Anichkov Palace in Petersburg.

7. "You have deceived."

Letter 619

1. Vissarion Grigorievich Belinsky (1811-1848), who was to become the greatest of all Russian critics and the greatest literary power in his own day. During the 1840's his perceptive criticism of Pushkin, Lermontov, and Gogol resulted in their being generally accepted in the esteem they have held ever since; he lived to hail and champion many of the later great Russian realistic writers, including Turgenev, Goncharov, and

Dostoevsky, among others. Belinsky had sharply attacked *The Moscow Observer*. Pushkin wished to attract Belinsky to work on his *Contemporary*, but he did not wish to arouse the "Observers" prematurely. Pushkin did not live to accomplish the hope of adding Belinsky to his collaborators.

2. Nashchokin began writing his memoirs at this time, after long insistence on the part of Pushkin (see Letter 441). The manuscript survives, with Pushkin's extensive corrections, a good sample of the kind of editorial work Pushkin did for his journal.

3. The child's aunt, Alexandra Nikolaevna Goncharova.

Letter 620

1. Davydov's article, "The Occupation of Dresden . . .," which was published in the fourth issue of *The Contemporary*, suffered considerably from the censorship. See Letter 610 and note.

2. Napoleon figures in two articles by Vyazemsky, "Napoleon and Julius Caesar" and an article on Edgar Quinet's poem "Napoleon" (1836), both in the second issue of Pushkin's *Contemporary*.

3. Baron Ferdinand von Wintzengerode (1770-1818), German-born field marshal and diplomat in Russian service, had been the military superior of the famed guerilla leader, D. V. Davydov, in the War Against Napoleon of 1812-1813. Davydov had clashed with Wintzengerode when Davydov took Dresden without orders from his superior. Davydov's defense of this action was excised by the censorship from the published article.

4. Napoleon had the Vendôme Column constructed (1806-1810) to celebrate the defeat of the Russians and Austrians at Austerlitz in 1805. The statue of Napoleon which was placed on it in 1812 was replaced with another of him in 1833.

5. Davydov's poem here referred to, "I Remember—Deeply . . .," was first published four years later.

Letter 621

1. The point of discussion of this letter is the apportionment of the estate of Mikhaylovskoe after the death of Pushkin's mother. Pushkin's father inherited a seventh share of the estate and his sister a fourteenth; Pushkin and his brother Lev shared equally the remainder. Pushkin here discusses buying his brother's share. Lev S. Pushkin answered with a power of attorney for Pushkin to manage the estate, and he gave Pushkin his blessing to buy or mortgage the estate, for all he was interested in was the money. Pushkin did not, however, manage to buy the estate, because of disagreement with his brother-in-law Pavlishchev about the value of it.

2. For Lev S. Pushkin's debts to Boltin, Pleshcheev, and Pavlishchev, see Letter 550.

3. Unidentified person.

4. That is, when Pushkin gave up the financial management of his father's estate of Boldino and half of Kistenevo. See Letter 553 and notes.

5. See Letter 554, and also Letters 553 and 555.

Letter 622

1. This is another instance of Pushkin's insistence upon accuracy and purity in the use of language, and also of his editorial conscience and care. Kraevsky made the corrections which Pushkin here enumerates, in Vyazemsky's article, "Napoleon and Julius Caesar," in the second issue of *The Contemporary*.

Letter 623

1. Nadezhda Andreevna Durova was vexed that Pushkin had entitled her recollections

of serving in the Russian army while disguised as a man as "The Memoirs of N. A. Durova," instead of "Notes by the Own Hand of the Russian Amazon Known Under the Name of Alexandrov." See Letter 589.

Letter 624

1. In a letter of May 5, 1836, Dmitriev had expressed sympathy to Pushkin and his father upon the death of Pushkin's mother. In the same letter, Dmitriev gave an extremely favorable estimate of the first issue of Pushkin's *Contemporary*.

2. Dmitriev's "observation" was that "your journal moved and refreshed me for a whole week and made me forget my step-brothers." By "step-brothers" Dmitriev alludes to an article signed "I.D." and a poem signed "Ivan Dmitriev" which had recently appeared in *The Moscow Record* and in *The Russian Invalide*, respectively. Pushkin did as he said and published the comment in the second issue of his *Contemporary*.

3. The allusion here is to Molière's play *Amphitryon*, in which the servant confuses his master with Jupiter, in the form of his master. Pushkin uses the term conventionally for a double being mistaken for the original.

Letter 625

1. The Loan Office where Kistenevo was mortgaged.

2. Pushkin means, if it is more profitable to cultivate the entire estate on the basis of *barščina* (with the serfs working part-time, usually half, on the owner's part and the remainder of the time on their own), instead of quitrent (money payment in lieu of part-time work for the owner).

3. M. I. Kalashnikov, his son Vasily, and his daughter Olga.

Letter 626

1. *The History of the Military Activities in Asiatic Turkey in* 1828 *and* 1829 (Moscow, 1836), by General Nikolay Ivanovich Ushakov (1802-1861), a military writer and historian.

2. General Paskevich-Erivansky.

3. In a footnote, Ushakov remarks that "our glorious poet" Pushkin participated in the cross fire of June 14, 1829. Pushkin recounts the campaign in detail, including his entering Erzurum, in his *Journey to Erzurum*.

Letter 627

1. In a letter of June 25, 1836, the self-styled Amazon, Durova, expressed impatience with Pushkin for the delays in the appearance of her memoirs. When difficulties with the censorship arose, she insisted that Pushkin show her memoirs to the Tsar himself, and even take them to him on maneuvers, threatening otherwise to take other action. After this polite but firm refusal, she made other arrangements for their publication; they appeared in 1838.

2. The money was in payment for a fragment from her notes, published in the second issue of *The Contemporary*, which had not yet appeared.

3. As in other letters to Durova, Pushkin addresses her in accordance with her masculine pseudonym, Alexander Andreevich Alexandrov. She used the masculine pronoun to refer to herself in her letter to him.

Letter 628

1. Pushkin is alluding to his projected purchase of his brother's share of his late mother's estate of Mikhaylovskoe. See Letter 621.

2. Because of his mother's death, some three and a half months earlier.

3. Pushkin had owed Yakovlev six thousand rubles since 1828-1829.

Letter 629
  1. The steward at Mikhaylovskoe, a German named Ringel. Pavlishchev dismissed him, after discovering many irregularities in the accounts.
  2. One Vasily Ivanovich Polonsky.
  3. Early in July, 1836, Lev Pushkin sent a power of attorney for Pushkin to manage or dispose of the estate of Mikhaylovskoe; however, Pushkin had not yet received it. See Letter 621.

Letter 630
  1. In his letter of July 11, 1836, Pavlishchev proposed that Pushkin buy the estate of Mikhaylovskoe at the price of 64,000 rubles, and pay Olga and Lev their shares in that case, or else advertise and sell the estate. Pushkin himself had evaluated the estate at 40,000 rubles in Letter 621.
  2. The "transaction" proposed by Pavlishchev was that he, Pavlishchev, buy the estate of Mikhaylovskoe for 64,000 rubles, and that Pushkin assume his sister Olga's share of the inheritance of their father's estate, Boldino, for Pushkin's share in Mikhaylovskoe, which would thus be counted at 25,000 rubles. Pushkin was well aware that his sister Olga was hardly likely to inherit 25,000 rubles from their father.
  3. Pavlishchev's son, Lev Nikolaevich Pavlishchev.

Letter 631
  1. Alexander Ivanovich Khmelnitsky, later a journalist. Whether Pushkin's request was of avail is not known. Pushkin's old friend Zhandr was at this time Director of the Chancellery of the Ministry of the Navy.
  2. Vice Admiral Alexander Sergeevich Menshikov (1787-1849). Khmelnitsky's appointment in the Navy depended upon him.

Letter 632
  1. Davydov's article was published in the third issue of *The Contemporary* in 1836. Being on a military subject, it had to be passed by the military censorship, as well as the usual one.
  2. The various censorships included the usual one, the religious censorship, the censorship of the Ministry of Foreign Affairs, and the military censorship; for Pushkin there was a fifth, that of the Court.
  3. Alexander I.
  4. Ivan the Terrible divided Russia into the *zemščina* and the *opričina*. The latter were his special bodyguard and troops and were greatly favored; they were used by Ivan to subjugate the nobles to his will and were allowed liberty to pillage and persecute the *zemščina*, the remainder of the populace. Pushkin is comparing the depredations of the military censors on Davydov's article to the arbitrary lawlessness of the *opričina* under Ivan the Terrible.

Letter 633
  1. Peter Alexandrovich Korsakov (1790-1844), a writer, translator, and censor, and brother of Prince M. A. Dondukov-Korsakov. In 1817, Korsakov had published some of Pushkin's poems in *The Northern Observer*. His reputation of being a mild and reasonable censor was immediately justified, as he passed Pushkin's novel, *The Captain's Daughter*, and kept the secret of its authorship.

Letter 634

1. Grech, in a letter of October 12, 1836, had given a rapturous appreciation of Pushkin's poem on Barklay de Tolly, which had appeared in the third issue of Pushkin's *Contemporary*. Pushkin's poem aroused considerable controversy. The praise of Barklay, who was replaced in the war against Napoleon of 1812 as Commander-in-Chief of the Russian Army of the West by Kutuzov, as a result of dissatisfaction with his refusal to come to decisive battle with Napoleon's forces, seemed directly contradictory to the traditional Russian patriotic view of praise of Kutuzov and blame of the "foreigner" Barklay de Tolly. Pushkin was forced, in self-defense, to prove his own admiration for Kutuzov by publishing part of his poem written earlier to Kutuzov, "Before the Sacred Tomb" (1831).

Letter 635

1. A bibliography, which Korf had compiled, of foreign books relating to Peter the Great and his time, and which he sent Pushkin in connection with the latter's historical labors.

2. Pavel Nikolaevich Myasoedov (1799-1868), like Korf, a Lyceum schoolmate of Pushkin's. He gave a dinner for his old Lyceum comrades on October 15, 1836, and attended the anniversary celebration of the opening of the Lyceum, on October 19.

Letter 636

1. That is, with the opinion of Yakovlev, that the celebration on October 19, 1836, the twenty-fifth anniversary of the opening of the Tsarskoe Selo Lyceum, should be limited to members of the first graduating class. The numbers were those of the rooms at the Lyceum. Yakovlev's room was number 39, and Pushkin's number 14.

2. A self-quotation from Pushkin's own poem, "October 19" (1825).

Letter 637

1. The " booklet " was a copy of the issue of *The Telescope* (1836) containing a Russian translation of the first of Chaadaev's *Philosophical Letters* (the original was in French). In the "Philosophical Letter," Chaadaev, postulating religion as the prime historical moving force and Roman Catholicism as the proper form of Christianity, argued that Russia, having received Christianity from Byzantium and having fallen on the side of Greek Orthodoxy in the Great Schism of 1054, had no real history, culture, or tradition; he includes a devastating attack on contemporary Russian society, based on serfdom. The result of the publication of this letter was that the editor of the journal, Nadezhdin —who had published the letter in order to publish later refutations of it—was exiled to Siberia. The censor, Alexey Vasilievich Boldyrev (1780-1842), who had passed it, was discharged. Chaadaev was declared mad, and put under the daily observation of a physician.

Chaadaev's letter may be considered the opening gun in the Westerner-Slavophile controversy, which became the central ideological controversy in Russia in the nineteenth century. Later Westerners, like Alexander Herzen (1812-1870), rejected Chaadaev's arguments regarding religion, but agreed with his interpretation of the status of Russia at the time. The Slavophiles rejected his arguments *in toto*, arguing that Orthodoxy is the only true form of Christianity and that Russia's culture before its Westernization under and after Peter the Great had been in essence far superior to the culture of Western Europe. To the government party, under Uvarov's motto of "Orthodoxy, autocracy, and nationality," all of Chaadaev's opinions were anathema.

Chaddaev's first "Philosophical Letter" was dated December 1, 1829. Pushkin read it probably soon after it was written; in the summer of 1831, he read the second and third of these letters (see Letter 376). Pushkin respected Chaadaev's ideas, though he by no means agreed with all of them. Pushkin's letter in answer to Chaadaev is the most important of all his letters, from the point of view of social and political ideas. It shows how, as a historian, he was interested in a broad view of history, how as a patriot he defended Russian history as it was, and how as a man of his own day, he was in substantial agreement with Chaadaev in his criticism of Russian society of the time.

Pushkin did not send the letter to Chaadaev. On October 22, 1835, Pushkin received a letter from K. O. Rosset, informing him of the action being taken against Chaadaev, Nadezhdin, and Boldyrev, and advising him to "reread" his own letter, or "still better," that he "defer" sending it by the post. Pushkin kept the letter, noting on it, " 'A falcon does not peck out another falcon's eye,' a saying quoted by Walter Scott in *Woodstock*."

Vyazemsky, like Pushkin, basically disagreed with Chaadaev, but it is interesting that in a letter he made an attempt to minimize Chaadaev's "guilt" (see Letter 662). Vigel presented the denunciation which led immediately to the action against Chaadaev, Boldyrev, and Nadezhdin.

2. Pushkin had already developed this idea in his unfinished article "Of the Nullity of Russian Literature" (1834), where he indignantly rejects the idea that it was Poland that thus saved Europe during the time of the Tatar yoke in Russia (1240-1480).

3. Feofan Prokopovich (1681-1736) drew up the "Spiritual Regulation" (1721) which abolished the patriarchate and established the Holy Synod, making the Russian Church subordinate to the Russian state. The Over-Procurator of the Holy Synod, a government appointee, obtained almost complete authority in Church administration.

4. That is, at the time of the invasion of Europe by the Turks, who besieged Vienna in 1529 and 1683.

5. Peter the Great had forced noblemen, but not the clergy, to shave, and thereby separated the clergy from "good society."

6. Pushkin is thinking of Ivan III (the Great), ruler of Russia from 1462 to 1505, under whose rule the Tatar yoke was thrown off, who annexed Novgorod, who married Sophia Paleologue, niece of the last Byzantine emperor, and who adopted the Byzantine double-headed eagle, and gave a basis to the claim of Moscow as the "Third Rome"; and Ivan IV (the Terrible), who ruled from 1533 to 1584, who first took the title of "Tsar" (Caesar), who conquered Kazan, and in whose reign western Siberia was annexed to Russia. It may be noted that under each of the rulers mentioned here by Pushkin there were added sizable conquests.

7. The greatest drama in the history of the Russian government before 1917 had to do with the ending of the house of Ryurik and the accession of the house of Romanov. The drama began with the murder of Dimitry, son of Ivan the Terrible, at Uglich in 1591, leaving no descendant of Ryurik to ascend the throne upon the death of Tsar Fedor in 1598. Boris Godunov, son-in-law of Ivan the Terrible, ruled as elective Tsar until 1605. Then the Time of Troubles began, with two False Dimitrys and invasions by Poland and Sweden before the house of Romanov (reigned 1613-1917) was established with the election of Michael Romanov, which was announced to him in the Ipatiev Monastery in 1613.

8. Pushkin's "prejudices" are those of a member of the old aristocracy against the aristocracy of service, established by Peter the Great in his Table of Ranks in 1722. See rough-draft variant of this letter, note 10 below.

9. The latter article is a review of the memoirs of John Tanner, a white American who was captured as a boy and brought up by the American Indians. The book was published in New York in 1830, and a French edition was published in Paris in 1835.

Pushkin begins his article with the expression of distaste for democracy in the United States, as depicted in Alexis de Tocqueville's *De la Démocratie en Amérique* (1835).

10. The rough-draft variants to this letter are interesting and important enough to justify quoting at length:

> [Peter the Great] tamed the nobility by promulgating the *Table of Ranks*, and the clergy, by abolishing the patriarchate (N.B.: Napoleon said to Alexander: "You are *Pope* at home; that is not so stupid"). But it is one thing to make a revolution, and another to enshrine the results. Up to Catherine II, Peter's revolution was continued among us, instead of being consolidated. Catherine II was still afraid of the aristocracy; Alexander was a Jacobin himself.[a] The *Table of Ranks* has already been doing away with the nobility for 140 years, and the present emperor was the first to place a dike (very feeble, so far) against inundation by a democracy worse than that of America. (Have you read Tocqueville? I am still all hot and bothered and quite frightened by his book.)
>
> As for the clergy, it is outside society, it is still bearded. One does not see it anywhere, not in our salons, not in literature; it does not belong to good society. It is not above the people, it does not wish to be of the people. Our sovereigns have found it convenient to leave it where they found it. Like eunuchs, it has no passion but for power. Consequently it is dreaded. And, I know, a certain one, in spite of all his energy, yielded to it on one grave occasion. I was enraged by this at the time.[b]
>
> Religion is, fortunately, foreign to our thoughts and to our habits, but there is no need to say so.
>
> Your booklet appears to have produced a great sensation. I do not speak of it the society I frequent.
>
> What needed saying and what you have said is that our present society is as contemptible as stupid. That this absence of public opinion, this indifference toward all duty, justice, right, and truth, this cynical disdain for all that is not necessity. This cynical disdain for thought and the dignity of man.[c] It was necessary to add (not as a concession, but as the truth) that the government is still the only European in Russia, and that as brutal and cynical as it is, it could have been a hundred times worse. Nobody was paying the slightest attention to it.
>
> The conquest of Ryurik[d] is as important as that of the Norman Bastard.[e] The youth of Russia passed joyfully in the invasions of Oleg and of Svyatoslav, and even in the wars of appanage, which were nothing but continual duels—the result of this effervescence and of this activity springing from the youth of peoples, of which you speak in your letter. The invasion is a sad and a grand picture. Oh, isn't the invasion of the Tatars a memory.

Notes to rough-draft variants (Note 10).

a. In a conversation with Grand Duke Michael in 1834, Pushkin went so far as to tell him that "all the Romanovs have been revolutionaries and levellers," and he expressed his objections to the nobility of service (see his Diary, under December 22).

b. Pushkin is apparently speaking of the removal of Gerasim Petrovich Pavsky (1787-1863) as teacher of divine law to Grand Duke Alexander (later Alexander II), on the complaint of the Moscow Metropolitan Filaret. (See Pushkin's Diary, under February, 1835.) The "certain one" was Nicholas I.

c. The sentence fragments are Pushkin's.

d. Original reading: "of Igor, of Ryurik, and of Oleg." All three were heroes of Kievan Rus. Ryurik (d. 879) was the reputed Varangian, or Scandinavian, founder of the empire of Russia and the ruling house, which lasted until 1598. Igor (d. 945, ruled 912-945) and Oleg (see Letter 101, note) were princes of Kiev.

e. The reference is to the conquest of England by William the Conqueror in 1066.

Letter 638

1. Pushkin gives the address, as usual, in Russian spelling. The house was owned by Princess Sofia Grigorievna Volkonskaya.

2. See Pushkin's answers to Pavlishchev's letters: Letters 494, 555, 563, 629, 630.

3. Lev S. Pushkin had re-entered the military service and left for Caucasian Georgia for active duty, in July, 1836.

Letter 639

1. In a letter of the same date, Korsakov agreed to be the censor of Pushkin's novel, *The Captain's Daughter* (see Letter 633). He also raised two questions regarding the novel: (1) whether the heroine Mironova was a historical person and whether she actually went to see Catherine the Great, and (2) whether Pushkin, who wanted authorship of the novel to remain unknown, wished Korsakov to tell the Censorship Committee that Pushkin had delivered the manuscript to him. In the case of an anomymous manuscript, someone had to take responsibility for it. In order the better to preserve his anonymity, Pushkin asked Pletnev to do this for him.

Letter 640

1. Russian editions place Letters 640 through 646 at the end of the letters of 1836. It has seemed best for this edition to place these letters, all of which were apparently written before Letter 647, in this position, in order to make a separate chapter of the letters of the final stage of Pushkin's life.

Letter 641

1. This short note is a postscript to a brief note by Elizaveta M. Khitrovo to Anna Petrovna Kern, sent in Pushkin's hand. Like the following two letters, it shows Pushkin's continuing friendly relationship with Mme. Kern, with whom he had been so much in love a decade earlier. This letter and the following two have to do with Mme. Kern's unsuccessful attempt to buy up the estate given her as dowry and then sold by her father to a Count Sheremetev—probably Dmitry Nikolaevich Sheremetev.

Letter 642

1. See Letter 641, note. Sheremetev's answer was a refusal.

Letter 643

1. *Revenir à la charge*, "to renew an attempt, to become again a dependant." Mme. Kern quoted this note in her *Memoirs*, adding, "etc., etc., and playing on the last word." This letter also has to do with Mme. Kern's attempts to buy back her family estate from Sheremetev (see Letter 641 and note).

Letter 644

1. "Hunter's cry, to call dogs off their prey." Pushkin is quoting from Philipp Reiff's *Russo-French Dictionary . . . or Etymological Dictionary of the Russian Language*, the first volume of which (A-O) appeared in Petersburg in 1835. Pushkin used the word *arap* in the title of his own uncompleted novel about his Abyssinian ancestor: *Arap Petra Velikogo* (*The Blackamoor of Peter the Great*).

2. Pushkin has in mind a critique of the Russian Academy *Dictionary* and Plyushar's *Encyclopedic Lexicon*.

Letter 645

1. Pushkin's little poem includes play on words on two idioms relating to the days of the week. It reads, literally, as follows:

Smirdin has plunged me into misfortune. With this tradesman there are seven Fridays in a week, and his Thursday is really Thursday after a little rain.

Letter 646

1. Achille Tardif de Mello, French man of letters, very much interested in Russian literature, especially in the works of Pushkin. In a letter to Pushkin, he had enclosed his own translation of Pushkin's *Prisoner of the Caucasus*.

2. "A true goddess appears in her gait."

PART XIV

SOLE DEFENDER OF HONOR — PETERSBURG

November, 1836 — January, 1837

Pushkin in His Coffin.   Painting by A. Kozlov.

To Egor Frantsevich Kankrin
November 6, 1836. In Petersburg.

Dear Sir, Count Egor Frantsevich,

Encouraged by the indulgent attention which Your Highness has already been so kind as to honor me with, I make bold to disturb you again with a most humble request.

According to arrangements of which Your Highness's ministry is aware, I stand indebted to the Treasury (without security) for 45,000 rubles, of which 25,000 must be repaid by me in the course of five years.

Now, wishing to repay my debt in full and immediately, I discover that to my so doing there is one obstacle, which can be easily removed, but only by you.

I have 220 souls in the Nizhny Novgorod Province, of which 200 are mortgaged for 40,000. According to the arrangements of my father, who has bestowed this estate upon me, I do not have the right to sell them during his lifetime, although I may mortgage them either to the Treasury or to private individuals.[1]

But the Treasury has the right to recover what is due it, regardless of any private individual's agreements, unless they are confirmed by the Sovereign.

As payment of the aforesaid 45,000, I make bold to give over this estate, which surely is worth that much, and probably even more.

I make bold to burden Your Highness with still another request, which is important for me. Since this matter is quite unimportant and may fall within the scope of a customary procedure, I most earnestly request Your Highness not to bring it to the notice of the Sovereign Emperor, who in his magnanimity probably would not wish such a repayment (although it is not at all burdensome to me), and he might even order that my debt be forgiven me, which would place me in an extremely painful and embarrassing situation: for in such a case I would be compelled to refuse the Tsar's favor, and that might seem an impropriety, vaingloriousness, and even ingratitude.[2]

With the most profound respect and complete devotion, I

have the honor to be, Dear Sir, Your Highness's most humble servant.

November 6, 1836.   Alexander Pushkin.

[648]

To Nikolay Borisovich Golitsyn
November 10, 1836. From Petersburg to Artek.
(In French)

St. Petersburg, November 10, 1836.

Thank you very much, dear Prince,[1] for your incomparable translation of my piece of verse leveled against the enemies of our country. I have already seen three translations,[2] one of which is by a powerful personage *from among my friends*, but none is so good as yours. Why didn't you translate the piece at the opportune time;[3] I would have sent it off to France, to throw it in the teeth of all the noisy clamorers of the Chamber of Deputies.

How I envy you your excellent Crimean climate:[4] your letter has awakened in me many memories of all kinds. It is the cradle of my *Onegin*, and you are sure to have recognized certain personages.[5]

You give me notice of a verse translation of my *Fountain of Bakhchisaray*. I am sure that you will succeed in it, as in all that comes from your pen, although the genre of literature which you are taking up is the most difficult and the most thankless I know of. In my opinion nothing is more difficult than to translate Russian verses into French verses, because, owing to the conciseness of our language, one can never be so brief. Honor, then, to the one who performs it as well as you do.

Farewell. I do not despair of seeing you soon in our capital, considering your aptitude for travel. Truly yours,

A. Pushkin.

[649]

To Vladimir Alexandrovich Sollogub
November 17, 1836. In Petersburg.
(In French)

I do not hesitate to write what I can declare verbally. I have challenged M. G. Heeckeren to a duel, and he has accepted, without entering into any explanations. I am the one who now prays the witnesses of this affair to be so kind as to consider this challenge as not having taken place, for I have learned from popular report that M. Georges Heeckeren has decided to declare his intentions of marriage with Mlle. Goncharova, after the duel. I have no reason to attribute his resolve to considerations unworthy of a man of gallant soul.[1]

I request, Count, that you make whatever use of this letter you judge appropriate.

Accept the assurance of my complete esteem.

November 17, 1836.   A. Pushkin.

[650]
To Mikhail Lukianovich Yakovlev
November 19, 1836. In Petersburg.
My dear and honored Mikhaylo Lukianovich! Excuse me! I invited you to dine at my house today, but I shall not be at home. Until another time, forgive me magnanimously. Do not forget to deliver the note about the saints,[1] to me, a sinner.

[651]
To Louis van Heeckeren
Between November 17 and 21, 1836. In Petersburg.
(Reconstructed text of unsent letter; in French)
Baron,

First of all, permit me to summarize everything that has just taken place.[1] The behavior of your son had been fully known to me for a long time and could not be a matter of indifference to me, but since it was kept within the bounds of the proprieties and since, moreover, I knew how much on that score my wife deserved my trust and my respect, I contented myself with the role of an observer free to intervene when I might think proper. I well knew that a handsome face, an unlucky passion, two years' perseverance always may end by producing some effect on a young woman's heart, and that then the husband, at least if he is not a fool, becomes quite naturally the confidant of his wife and the master of her conduct.[2] I shall admit to you that I was not without misgivings. An incident, which at any other moment would have been very disagreeable, came quite fortunately to rescue me from the difficulty: I received anonymous letters. I saw that the moment had come, and I availed myself of it. You know the rest: I made your son play a role so ludicrous and pitiful that my wife, astonished at so much truckling,[3] could not refrain from laughing, and that the emotion which she had perhaps come to feel in response to this great and sublime passion, faded into the coolest and most deserved disgust.

But you, Baron, will permit me to observe that your role in all this affair is not of the most seemly. You, the representative of a crowned head, have paternally acted as the pander of your bastard, or the one so called; all the behavior of this young man has been directed by you. You dictated the sorry jokes which he has just been reciting and the vacuous things which he has taken a hand in writing. Like an obscene old woman you would go and lie in wait for my wife in every corner, in order to speak to her of your son, and when, ill with the syphilis, he was kept at home for treatments, you would say, vile man that you are, that he was dying of love for her. You would murmur to her, "Give me back my son." That is not all.

You see that I know all about it. But wait, that is not all: I have told you that the affair was getting complicated. Let us return to anonymous letters. You well surmise that they may be of interest to you.

On November 2 you received a piece of news from your son which gave you much pleasure. He told you that I was angry, that my wife was afraid . . . that she was losing her head. You decided to strike a blow which you thought would be decisive. An anonymous letter was composed by you.

I received three copies of the half a score which were delivered. This letter had been fabricated with so little caution that at the first glance I was on the trail of the author. I did not trouble myself about it further; I was sure of finding my knave. Sure enough, in less than three days of searching, I knew positively what to believe.

If diplomacy is only the art of knowing what is done at others' houses and of making game of their plans, you will do me the justice to admit that you have been vanquished on all points.

Now I am arriving at the object of my letter. Perhaps you desire to know what has prevented me up to the present from dishonoring you in the eyes of our court and of yours. I shall tell you.

I am, you see, a good, unsophisticated person, but my heart is sensitive. A duel is no longer enough for me, and whatever may be its outcome, I shall not consider myself sufficiently avenged, either by the death of your son, or by his marriage, which would seem to be a good joke (which, it must be added, troubles me very little), or finally by the letter which I have the honor to be writing you, and a copy of which I am keeping for my personal use. I want you yourself to take the trouble to find the reasons which would suffice to make me pledge not to spit in your face, and to annihilate even the last traces of this miserable affair, from which it will be easy for me to make an excellent chapter in my history of cuckoldry.[4]

I have the honor to be, Baron,

Your most humble and most obedient servant,

A. Pushkin.[5]

[652]

To Alexander Khristoforovich Benkendorf
November 21, 1836. In Petersburg.
(In French)

Count!

I have just cause and I believe myself obliged to inform Your Excellency of what has just taken place in my family. On the morning of November 4 I received three copies of an anonymous letter, injurious to my honor and that of my wife. From the appearance of the paper, from the style of the letter, from the manner in which it was worded, I recognized from the first moment that it was written by a foreigner, by a man of high society, by a diplomat.[1] I started making inquiries. I learned that seven or eight persons had received, on the same day, a copy of the same letter, in a double envelope, the inner of which was sealed and addressed to me. The majority of the persons who received them, suspecting a vile deed, did not send them on to me.

People in general were indignant at such a despicable, such an unprovoked insult. But while repeating that the conduct of my wife has been irreproachable, they said that the pretext of this infamy was the assiduous court which M. d'Anthès has been paying her.

It did not suit me to see the name of my wife linked on this occasion with the name of anyone whatever.[2] I had M. d'Anthès so informed.

The Baron de Heeckeren came to my house and accepted a duel for M. d'Anthès, asking for a delay of fifteen days.

It turns out that in the interval granted, M. d'Anthès fell in love with my sister-in-law, Mlle. Goncharova, and that he made her a marriage proposal. Public report having informed me of this, I had the request made to M. d'Archiac (M. d'Anthès' second) that my challenge should be regarded as not having taken place.[3] Meanwhile I made sure that the anonymous letter was from M. Heeckeren, which I believe it my duty to call to the attention of the government and of society.

Being the sole judge and defender of my honor and that of my wife, and consequently asking for neither justice nor vengeance, I neither can nor will provide anyone whatever with the proofs for what I assert.

In any case, I hope, Count, that this letter is a proof of the respect and of the trust which I bear toward you.[4]

With these feelings, I have the honor to be,
                    Count,
                        Your most humble and most obedient servant,
November 21, 1836.   A. Pushkin.

[653]
To Egor Frantsevich Kankrin
About (after) November 21, 1836. In Petersburg.
(Rough draft)

I have had the happiness to receive the letter with which Your Highness was so kind as to honor me. I regret extremely that the expedient which I have made bold to propose has proved to be unsuitable.[1] In any case, I shall count it a duty to rely absolutely in everything on Your Highness's good judgment.

Expressing to Your Highness my sincere gratitude for the consideration with which you were so kind as to honor me, with the most profound [. . . .]

[654]
To Vladimir Fedorovich Odoevsky
December 7, 1836(?). In Petersburg.

I am very grateful to you. I am always at home, and I am completely at fault toward you—but the devil knows how lazy I have become.

December 7.

[655]

To AMABLE GUILLAUME BARANTE
December 16, 1836. In Petersburg.
(In French)

Baron,

I hasten to send Your Excellency[1] the information which you wished to have, concerning the regulations which treat of literary property in Russia.

Literature has become with us an important branch of industry only during the last score of years or so. Up till then it was regarded as only an elegant and aristocratic pursuit. Madame de Staël said in 1811: "In Russia a few gentlemen have engaged in literature" (*Ten Years of Exile*).[2] Nobody dreamed of deriving any other fruit from his works than triumphs in society. Authors themselves encouraged reprinting without authorization and prided themselves upon it, and our academies, at the same time, were setting the example of this offense with a clear conscience and in freedom from apprehension. The first complaint for such reprinting was lodged in 1824.[3] It was discovered that the case had not been foreseen by the law-giver. Literary property has been recognized in Russia by the present sovereign. Here are the terms of the law:

"Every author or translator of a book has the right to publish and to sell it as acquired (non-hereditary) property.

"His legitimate heirs have the right to publish and to sell his works (provided that the property has not been alienated) during the period of twenty-five years.

"After twenty-five years from the date of his death have passed, his works and his translations become public property."
(*The law of April* 22, 1828.)

The amendment of April 28 of the same year explains and supplements these regulations. Here are its principal articles.

"A literary work, either in printed or in manuscript form, may not be sold either during the lifetime of the author or after his death, in order to satisfy creditors, unless he insists upon it himself.

"The author has the right, notwithstanding any previous agreement, to make a new edition of his work if two-thirds of it have been altered or else completely recast.

"He will be regarded as pirate (1) who in reprinting a book does not observe the formalities required by the law; (2) who sells a manuscript or the right to publish it to two or more persons at once, without having their consent for his so doing; (3) *who publishes a translation of a work printed in Russia (or else one which has been approved by the Russian censorship), while at the same time adding to it the original text itself;* (4) *who reprints in a foreign country a work published in Russia, or else one which has been approved by the Russian censorship, and sells copies of it in Russia.*"

These regulations are far from resolving all questions which might arise in the future. The law stipulates nothing with regard to posthumous works. The legitimate heirs ought to have sole property in them, with all the privileges of the author himself. Does the author of a pseudonymous work, or else one attributed to a known writer, lose his property rights, and what is the rule to be followed in this event? The law says nothing about it.

The reprinting of foreign books is not prohibited and ought not be. Russian booksellers will always have a great deal to gain, when they reprint foreign books, and the sale of them will always be assured for them, even without exporting; whereas, the foreigner would not be able to reprint Russian works, for lack of readers.

The statute of limitations for the offense of pirating is fixed at two years.

The question of literary property is very much simplified in Russia, where nobody can present his manuscript to the censorship without giving the name of its author, and without placing it, by this same token, under the immediate protection of the government.

       I am, respectfully,

          Baron,

              Your Excellency's,

                  Most humble and most obedient servant,

December 16, 1836.   Alexander Pushkin.

SPb.

[656]

To Nikolay Mikhaylovich Konshin
December 21 or 22, 1836. From Petersburg to Tsarskoe Selo.

Your letter made me very glad, dear and honored Nikolay Ivanovich,[1] as a sign that you still have not forgotten me. I shall set your memorandum going this very day.[2] I shall see Zhukovsky and I shall turn you over from my hands to his. Alas! I am not in such friendly relationships with Uvarov, but Zhukovsky will, I hope, fix everything up. Upon taking over the place of Lazhechnikov, won't you, too, on the example of your predecessor, take up writing novels? How good that would be! All the same, you had forgotten me, although finally you did remember me. And I permit myself to give you a little friendly reproach because of that.

Aren't you going to be in Petersburg? In the event you are, I hope I shall see you. I shall try to provide you with an answer as soon as possible.

A.P.

[657]

To Praskovia Alexandrovna Osipova
December 24, 1836. From Petersburg to Trigorskoe.
(In French)

You won't believe, my dear Praskovia Alexandrovna, how much pleasure your letter has given me. I had not had any news of you in more than four months; and only day before yesterday M. Lvov[1] gave me some. On the same day I received your letter. I had been hoping to see you in the autumn, but I was prevented from doing so partly by my affairs, partly by Pavlishchev, who has put me in such bad humor that I have not wished to seem to be coming to Mikhaylovskoe in order to arrange the partition of it.

With much regret I have been obliged to give up the idea of being your neighbor, but I still hope not to lose that place, which I prefer to many another. *Vot v čem delo:*[2] At first I proposed to take over the estate at once for myself alone, agreeing to pay my brother and my sister the shares which are due them, at the rate of five hundred rubles per soul. *Pavliščev ocenil Mixajlovskoe v* 800 *r. dušu—ja s nim i ne sporju, no v takom slučae prinužden byl otkazat' sja i predostavil imenie prodat'. Pered svoim ot''ezdom pisal on ko mne, čto on*

imenie ustupaet mne za 500 *r. dušu,* **potomu čto emu den'gi nužny.**[3]
I have sent him about his business, telling him that if the estate is
worth twice that much, I would not wish to profit at the expense of
my sister and my brother. There the matter dropped. Do you want
to know what my wish would be? I would have liked you to be the
proprietress of Mikhaylovskoe and to reserve for myself the *usad'ba,*[4]
together with the garden and a half score of *dvorovye.*[5] I have a great
longing to come to Trigorskoe for a little while this winter. We
would speak of all that. Meanwhile, I greet you with all my heart.
My wife thanks you for remembering her. *Ne privezti li mne vam ee?*[6]
My regards to all your family—to Evpraxia Nikolaevna[7] especially.

[658]
To Vladimir Fedorovich Odoevsky
About (not later than) December 29, 1836.
In Petersburg.

It is just as caustic as sensible.[1] I don't think, though, that the
censorship will destroy it all. In any event, there is no harm in asking.
Shan't we see each other at the Academy of Sciences, where sits
Prince Dunduk?[2]

[659]
To Adolf Alexandrovich Plyushar
December 29, 1836. In Petersburg.
(In French)

Sir,

I am completely in agreement on all the conditions which you are
so obliging as to propose to me concerning the publication of a
volume of my long poems[1] (in your letter of December 23, 1836). It
is, then, agreed that you will have 2500 copies printed on paper
which you will choose, that you alone will be encharged with the
sale of the edition, for the consideration of 15 percent discount,
and that proceeds of the first volumes sold will be used to reimburse
you for all the costs of publication, as well as the 1500 rubles in
bills which you have been so kind as to advance me.

Please accept, Sir, the assurance of my complete esteem.

December 29, 1836.   A. Pushkin.
St. Petersburg.

[660]
To Vladimir Fedorovich Odoevsky
The end of November or in December, 1836. In Petersburg.
Of course, "Princess Zizi" has more truth in it and is more entertaining than "The Sylphide."[1] But any gift of yours is a benefaction. The father-in-law's letter seems cold and too insignificant. On the other hand, in the others there is much that is charming. I have noted one place with the mark (?)—it seemed to me unintelligible. In any case, whether it is "The Sylphide" or whether it is the "Princess," finish it and send it off. Without you *The Contemporary* is done for.

A.P.

[661]
To Vladimir Fedorovich Odoevsky
The end of November or in December, 1836. In Petersburg.
Mr. Volkov's article[1] is indeed very noteworthy, sensibly and intelligently written, and interesting for everybody. However, I shall not put it in, because in my opinion there is no need at all for the government to get mixed up with the project of this Gerstner. Russia cannot afford to throw away 3,000,000 on the attempt. The business of the new railroad is one for private persons: let them be the ones to take the necessary steps. All that they can be promised is the franchise for twelve or fifteen years. A railroad from Moscow to Nizhny Novgorod may be needed still more than one from Moscow to Petersburg—and my opinion would be: start with it. . . .
I am of course not against railroads. But I am against the government undertaking this matter. Several objections to the project are irrefutable. For example: the snowdrifts. To take care of that a new machine must be *invented*, a *sine qua non*. There's no use thinking of sending out people or hiring laborers for clearing away the snow. That is an absurdity.
Volkov's article is written in a lively, pointed manner. Otreshkov is polished off very humorously. But one must not forget that many members of the State Council have been against railroads, and so the *tone* of the article in general must be softened greatly. I should like for the article to be published separately or in another journal; then

we might present an advantageous account of it, with an abundance of excerpts.

I agree with you that the epigraph chosen by Volkov is unfitting. The words of Peter I [the Great] would be the most fitting ones, but for this time send me the following: "But ask the German, doesn't he want to f—— us?"

[662]

To PETER ANDREEVICH VYAZEMSKY
December, 1836. In Petersburg.

Your letter is excellent: I should think that whether the form is *Dear Sergey Semenovich*, or *Of*, etc.,[1] is of no significance: the main thing is to give the article as wide circulation and as much vogue as possible. But in any event the censorship will not dare to pass it, and Uvarov will not provide the birches to be used on himself. It would be difficult, and awkward, to mix Benkendorf up in this matter. Just what is to be done? I think: leave the article as it is, and at some later time extract from it all that can be gotten by with, as you once used to do in *The Literary Gazette* with the articles which Shcheglov would not pass. It's a pity that you didn't criticize Ustryalov according to the formula devised by Voeykov for Polevoy.[2] How good it would have been! I am copying the verses for you.

[663]

To VLADIMIR FEDOROVICH ODOEVSKY
December, 1836. In Petersburg.

Saints alive, Your Highness! Have some fear of God: I'm neither kith nor kin to Lvov, Ochkin, or the children.[1] Why should I play the fool[2] for *The Children's Journal*? As it is, they're already saying that I am falling into my second childhood. Unless maybe for the money? Oh, that's not a childish—but a sensible matter. At any rate, let's talk it over.

[664]

To SERGEY LVOVICH PUSHKIN

The end of December, 1836. From Petersburg to Moscow.

(In French)

It has been a very long time since I have had any news of you. Venevitinov[1] has told me that he found you sad and agitated, and that you are planning to come to Petersburg. Is it true? I need to go to Moscow. In any case I hope to see you soon. Well, the new year is almost upon us. God grant that it may be happier for us than that which has just passed. I have no news of my sister or Lev. The latter must have been a member of the expedition, and all that is sure is that he has not been killed or wounded.[2] What he wrote about General Rozen[3] has turned out to be unfounded. Lev is touchy, and spoiled by the familiarity of his former superiors. General Rozen did not ever treat him like a dog, as he said, but like a staff captain, which is a completely different thing. We are having a wedding. My sister-in-law Katerina is getting married to Baron Heeckeren, the nephew and adopted son of the ambassador of the King of Holland.[4] He is a very handsome and fine fellow, very much in fashion, rich, and four years younger than his intended. Preparations for the trousseau are occupying and amusing my wife and her sisters much, but they are driving me wild. For the house has the air of a millinery and lingerie shop. Venevitinov has presented his report on the state of the province of Kursk. The Emperor was impressed by it, and has made a lot of inquiries about Venevitinov; he said to I don't remember whom: "Introduce him to me the first time we are together." There's a career made. I have received a letter from Peshchurov's cook,[5] who proposes that I take his apprentice back. I have answered him that I shall await your commands as to that. Do you wish to keep him? And what were the conditions of his apprenticeship? I am very busy. My journal and my Peter the Great are taking a lot of time. This year I have managed my affairs badly enough; next year will be better, I hope. Farewell, my very dear father. My wife and all my family embrace you and kiss your hands. My respects and my best wishes to my aunt and her family.[6]

[665]

To Nikolay Ivanovich Pavlishchev
January 5, 1837. From Petersburg to Warsaw.
(Fragment)

Let Mikhaylovskoe be sold. If a good price is given for it, then it will be better for you. I shall see whether I shall be able to keep it for myself.

[666]

To Fedor Afanasievich Skobeltsyn
January 8, 1837. In Petersburg.

Can't you, dear Fedor Afanasievich, lend me for three months, or obtain for me, three thousand rubles?[1] You would oblige me extremely, and you would save me from the hands of the booksellers, who are glad to give me the squeeze.

January 8, 1837.   A. Pushkin.

[667]

To Alexander Ivanovich Turgenev
January 16, 1837. In Petersburg.

Here are your letters for you. It will be necessary to blot out the stereotyped official phrases and also certain sincere, cordial words, for don't cast,[1] etc. Try to write as legibly as you can whatever you insert. Here is the sort of title I am thinking of giving to all this: "The Labors, Researches, of *Such-and-Such*, or of *A. I. T.*, in the Archives of Rome and Paris." The article is profoundly interesting.[2]
Here are my verses to Vyzemsky for you:

So the sea, the ancient killer of man, is inflaming your genius; with golden lyre you glorify the trident of awesome Neptune. . . . Do not glorify him: in our vile age Gray Neptune is the ally of Land. In all the elements, man is tyrant, traitor, or prisoner.[3]

January 16.

[668]

To ALEXANDRA OSIPOVNA ISHIMOVA
January 25, 1837. In Petersburg.

Dear Madame, Alexandra Osipovna,[1]

A few days ago I had the honor to call at your home, and I regret extremely that I did not find you there. I hoped to talk over a matter of business with you. Peter Alexandrovich [Pletnev] has given me hope that you will be kind enough to collaborate in the publication of *The Contemporary*. I agree in advance to all your terms, and I hasten to take advantage of your good will: I should like to acquaint the Russian public with the works of Barry Cornwall.[2] Won't you consent to translate several of his Dramatic Sketches? In that case I shall have the honor of forwarding his book to you.

With the most profound respect and with complete devotion, I have the honor to be,

Dear Madame,
Your most humble servant,
January 25, 1837.   A. Pushkin.

[669]

To LYUBOV MATVEEVNA ALYMOVA
Between March, 1833, and January 25, 1837.
In Petersburg.

Dear Madame, Lyubov Matveevna,

I most humbly request that Mr. Yuriev be permitted to take out of your yard the bronze statue which is there.[1]

With true respect and with devotion, I have the honor to be, Dear Madame,

Your most humble servant,
Alexander Pushkin.

[670]

To LOUIS VAN HEECKEREN
January 26, 1837. In Petersburg.
(In French)

Baron!

Permit me to summarize what has just taken place.[1] The behavior of your son had been known to me for a long time, and could not be a matter of indifference to me. I contented myself with the role of an observer free to intervene when I might think proper. An incident which at any other moment would have been very disagreeable came quite fortunately to rescue me from the difficulty: I received the anonymous letters.[2] I saw that the moment had come, and I availed myself of it. You know the rest: I made your son play a role so pitiful[3] that my wife, astonished at so much cowardice and truckling, could not refrain from laughing, and that the emotion which perhaps she had come to feel in response to this great and sublime passion faded into the coolest disdain and the most deserved disgust.

I am obliged to point out, Baron, that your role has not been altogether seemly. You, the representative of a crowned head, have paternally acted as your son's pander. It appears that all his behavior (clumsy enough, at that) has been directed by you. You probably dictated the sorry jokes he has just been reciting and the vacuous things which he has taken a hand in writing. Like an obscene old woman, you would go and lie in wait for my wife in every corner, in order to tell her of the love of your bastard, or the one so called, and when, ill with the syphilis, he was kept at home, you would say that he was dying of love for her. You would murmur to her, "Give me back my son."

You well realize, Baron, that after all this I cannot permit my family to have anything at all to do with yours. On this condition I consented not to follow up this filthy business and not to dishonor you in the eyes of our court and of yours, as I had the power and the intention of doing. I do not care for my wife to hear any more of your paternal exhortations. I cannot permit your son, after the despicable conduct which he has demonstrated, to dare to speak a word to my wife, nor still less to recite guardhouse puns[4] to her and play at devotion and unlucky passion, for he is only a coward and only a soundrel. I am therefore obliged to address myself to you, in order to pray you to put an end to all this little game, if you desire to avoid a new scandal, from which most certainly I shall not shrink.

I have the honor to be, Baron,

Your most humble and most obedient servant,

Alexander Pushkin.

January 26, 1837.

[671]

To ALEXANDER IVANOVICH TURGENEV
January 26, 1837. In Petersburg.

I can't get away. I expect you before 5 o'clock.[1]

[672]

To KARL FEDOROVICH TOL
January 26, 1837. In Petersburg.

Dear Sir, Count Karl Fedorovich,

The letter with which Your Highness[1] has been so kind as to honor me will remain for me a precious memorial of your good will, and the attention with which you have honored my first historical effort fully rewards me for the indifference of the public and the critics.

I was no less gladdened by Your Highness's opinion of Mikhelson,[2] who has been too much forgotten among us. His services have been obscured by slander; it is impossible to see without indignation what he was forced to endure on account of the jealousy or the incompetence of his peers and his superiors. I am sorry that I did not succeed in placing in my book a few strokes of your pen for the full justification of the meritorious warrior. No matter how strong may be the prejudice of ignorance, no matter how avidly slander may be accepted, one word spoken by such a person as you destroys them forever. Genius discloses the truth at the first glance, and "the truth is mightier than the Tsar," says the Holy Writ.[3]

With the most profound respect and with complete devotion, I have the honor to be,

Dear Sir,

Your Excellency's

Most humble servant,

January 26, 1837.   Alexander Pushkin.

[673]

To AUGUSTE D'ARCHIAC
Between 9:30 and 10:00 A.M. January 27, 1837. In Petersburg.
(In French)

Viscount,

I do not have the slightest desire to let Petersburg idlers into the secrets of my family affairs; therefore I reject all negotiations between seconds. I shall bring mine only to the place of meeting. Since it is M. Heeckeren who is challenging me and who is offended, he can choose one for me, if that is agreeable to him; I accept him in advance, even though he be his lackey. As for the time and the place, I am completely at his command. According to our Russian customs, that is enough. I pray you to believe, Viscount, that this is my last word, and that I have nothing more to say in reply to anything concerning this affair, and that I shall not budge again, except to go to the place.[1]

Please accept the assurance of my complete esteem.

January 27.   A. Pushkin.

[674]
To ALEXANDRA OSIPOVNA ISHIMOVA
January 27, 1837. In Petersburg.

Dear Madame, Alexandra Osipovna,

I regret extremely that it will be impossible for me to come at your invitation today.[1] Meanwhile I have the honor to forward the Barry Cornwall.[2] You will find at the end of the book some pieces marked with a pencil; translate them as you can—I assure you that your translating couldn't be better. Today I chanced to open your *History in Tales*,[3] and I couldn't help becoming engrossed in them. That is how writing should be done!

With the most profound respect and with complete devotion, I have the honor to be,

Dear Madame,
Your most obedient servant,
January 27, 1837.   A. Pushkin.

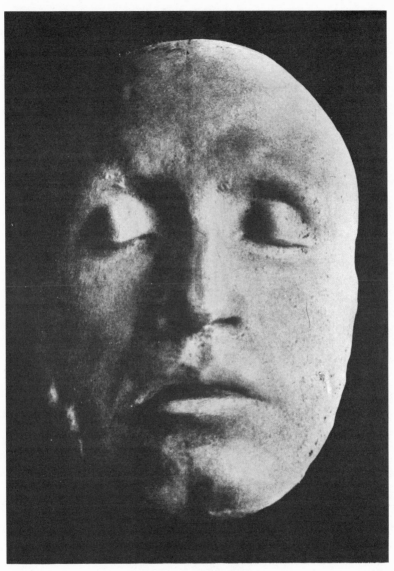

Pushkin. Death Mask.

Letter 647

1. On November 4, 1836, Pushkin received several copies of a fake "certificate" in French, which read as follows:

> The Grand-Cross Commanders and Chevaliers of the Most Serene Order of Cuckolds, convened in plenary assembly under the presidency of the venerable Grand Master of the Order, His Excellency D. L. Naryshkin, have unanimously elected M. Alexander Pushkin coadjutor of the Grand Master of the Order of Cuckolds and historiographer of the Order.
>
> Perpetual Secretary, I. Borkh.

Dmitry Lvovich Naryshkin was husband of the acknowledged mistress of Alexander I. The mention of Naryshkin in the "certificate" and the designation of Pushkin as "historiographer" could be interpreted as a scarcely concealed hint at his own position, receiving a salary from the government for doing historical research and holding the court rank of Kammerjunker, and attending court functions, where the popularity of Mme. Pushkina extended, as the Letters indicate, to the Tsar himself.

Pushkin attributed the writing of the letter to Louis van Heeckeren (1791-1884), Dutch ambassador to the Russian court, who had recently legally adopted Georges Charles d'Anthès, French legitimist exile then in Russian service. D'Anthès-Heeckeren had been paying court, ever more openly, to Mme. Pushkina for two years (see Letters 651, 652, and 670).

Pushkin immediately took two actions: he challenged d'Anthès-Heeckeren to a duel, and he made the attempt through this letter to settle his financial accounts with the government of Nicholas I. In this letter, Pushkin is proposing that the government buy the estate of Kistenevo, in settlement of Pushkin's debt. Pushkin's father had given him the right to manage Kistenevo and to receive the revenues and to mortgage the serfs there (see Letter 349), but Pushkin had no legal right to sell it before his father's death.

2. Kankrin answered on November 21 that he considered the government's acquiring private lands "unsuitable in general" and that in any case it could not be done without His Majesty's command.

Letter 648

1. Prince Nikolay Borisovich Golitsyn (1794-1866), a retired army officer and musician, who translated Russian poetry into French. His French translation of Pushkin's "To the Calumniators of Russia" was published in Moscow in 1839, and of Pushkin's *Fountain of Bakhchisaray*, in 1838.

2. The three translations include the one sent him by Elizaveta M. Khitrovo (see Letter 400), the translation done by Baron B. A. Vrevsky or Countess Alexandra Grigorievna Laval, and the translation done by Uvarov (see Letter 404).

3. That is, while the Polish Revolution of 1830-1831 was going on.

4. Prince Golitsyn was then living in his summer house in the Crimea, which recalled to Pushkin his own visit to the Crimea in 1820 (see Letters 11, 169).

5. Apparently members of the Raevsky family.

Letter 649

1. D'Anthès-Heeckeren was out of Petersburg when Pushkin sent him a challenge to a duel, on November 5, 1836, the day after Pushkin received anonymous letters. Heeckeren, d'Anthès-Heeckeren's adoptive father, persuaded Pushkin to postpone the duel for fifteen days. In the meantime, he made all possible efforts to get Pushkin to take back his challenge. Pushkin was willing to take back his challenge only when he learned that d'Anthès-Heeckeren wished to marry Mme. Pushkina's sister, Ekaterina Nikolaevna Goncharova. D'Anthès-Heeckeren insisted that Pushkin make no allusion to the forthcoming marriage in his letter taking back the challenge. Pushkin had no real faith that d'Anthès-Heeckeren would really marry Mme. Pushkina's sister, and he flatly refused to omit mention of the marriage in the letter necessary to prevent the duel. However, he consented to add phraseology to the effect that d'Anthès-Heeckeren was not acting dishonorably in deciding to marry Mme. Pushkina's sister. The enraged Pushkin intended to make d'Anthès-Heeckeren the laughing stock of Petersburg, by setting up a situation in which d'Anthès-Heeckeren would appear a coward. Pushkin was successful at this point.

Letter 650

1. Probably about Yakovlev's and Eristov's *Historical Dictionary of the Saints* (1836). A review of this book was published in the third issue of *The Contemporary*.

Letter 651

1. Though Pushkin had just taken back his challenge to d'Anthès-Heeckeren (Letter 649), his anger now turned toward d'Anthès-Heeckeren's adoptive father, Heeckeren, whom Pushkin considered the author of the "anonymous letter" which Pushkin received on November 4 and the abettor of d'Anthès-Heeckeren, as the latter paid open court to Mme. Pushkina.

2. This passage indicates that Mme. Pushkina was seriously attracted to d'Anthès-Heeckeren, that d'Anthès-Heeckeren had been paying marked court to her for a long time, and that Mme. Pushkina had admitted "everything" to her husband.

3. This is a plain hint at cowardice in that d'Anthès-Heeckeren was satisfied with Pushkin's taking back his challenge on the basis of rumors of the approaching marriage of d'Anthès-Heeckeren and Ekaterina Goncharova.

4. The allusion is to Pushkin's being called, in the "anonymous letter" of November 4, the "historiographer" of the order of cuckolds.

5. Pushkin showed this letter to Zhukovsky and to Sollogub, his second in the negotiations with d'Anthès-Heeckeren regarding the duel, but he did not send it, probably as the result of advice from Benkendorf (after sending Letter 652) and of . Nicholas I himself, with whom Pushkin had an audience on November 23. However, Pushkin kept the letter, and he used it as the basis for Letter 670, the provocation which resulted in the duel which was mortal for him. Pushkin tore the final version of this letter to shreds as he utilized phrases for the composition of Letter 670. The letter in the form here presented is a reconstruction from two existing versions, and the final form is to some degree conjectural. It should be compared with Letter 670.

Letter 652

1. Pushkin is hinting here that Heeckeren, the Dutch Ambassador, was the author of the "anonymous letter" of November 4.

2. Pushkin may possibly be alluding here, not only to d'Anthès-Heekeren, but to Nicholas I himself.

3. Letter 649. Vicomte Auguste d'Archiac, attaché at the French consulate and first cousin of d'Anthès-Heeckeren, was d'Anthès-Heeckeren's second, not only in connection with the duel in November, 1836, which did not take place, but also in the duel of January 27, 1837.

4. Two days after this letter, Pushkin had an audience with Nicholas I in the presence of Benkendorf on November 23. Apparently Nicholas I persuaded Pushkin not to send Letter 651 to Heeckeren nor to take any further action with regard to anonymous letters or his suspicions.

Letter 653

1. Pushkin's letter is in response to Kankrin's refusal of his petition for the government to buy Kistenevo (Letter 647).

Letter 655

1. Baron Amable Guillaume Barante, French writer, historian, and, at this time, Ambassador to Russia. Barante had written Pushkin on December 11, 1836, requesting information regarding copyright laws in Russia from Pushkin, as the person in Russia best qualified to speak on the subject, and informing Pushkin that the whole question of authors' rights, including those of translation, was then under consideration in France.

2. Her *Ten Years of Exile* was published in 1821.

3. Pushkin is referring to himself and the Oldekop "swindle," when with impunity Oldekop published Pushkin's *Prisoner of the Caucasus*, together with Oldekop's German translation of it. See Letter 77.

Letter 656

1. Pushkin errs in Konshin's patronymic.

2. In a letter of December 20, 1836, Konshin had asked Pushkin to obtain Zhukovsky's intercession with Uvarov, Minister of Public Education, for Konshin's receiving the post of Director of the Tver Gymnasium and the Educational Institutions of the Province of Tver, a position which had become vacant upon the retirement of the historical novelist Lazhechnikov. Though Pushkin often laughed at the minor poet Konshin in his letters, Pushkin immediately fulfilled Konshin's request. Konshin obtained the appointment early in 1837.

Letter 657

1. Possibly one Alexey Ivanovich Lvov.

2. "Here is the situation."

3. "Pavlishchev appraised Mikhaylovskoe at eight hundred rubles per soul. I have no intention of quarreling with him, but that being the case I was forced to refuse and I offered the estate for sale. Before his departure, he wrote me that he is letting me have the estate for five hundred rubles per soul, 'because he needs the money.' "

4. "Manor house and outbuildings."

5. "House serfs."

6. "Shouldn't I bring her along for you?"

7. Baroness Vrevskaya, nee Vulf.

Letter 658

1. "It" is probably an article by Vigel against Bulgarin, on the occasion of fierce attacks on Pushkin in an article in *The Northern Bee* in 1836.

2. The last sentence of the letter is a paraphrase of Pushkin's epigram on Prince M. A. Dondukov-Korsakov: "In the Academy of Sciences sits Prince Dunduk. They say such

an honor is not fitting for Dunduk. Why is he sitting there? Because he has an a———."
The conclusion of the epigram is double-edged—it includes allusion to the suspected
homosexual relationships between Prince Dondukov-Korsakov and his superior,
Uvarov. *Dunduk* means a muddle-headed person. Pushkin's reference to the meeting of
the Academy of Sciences is to that of December 29, 1836. Pushkin attended it, and
according to the testimony of Kraevsky, there he pointed at Dondukov-Korsakov and
alluded to the epigram.

Letter 659

1. Pushkin here is accepting the proposal made by the bookseller and publisher
Plyushar for the publication of a one-volume edition of Pushkin's long poems. The
edition did not materialize, because of Pushkin's death.

Letter 660

1. Stories by Odoevsky, which Pushkin wished for the fifth issue of *The Contemporary*.
Odoevsky rewrote the father-in-law's letter as a result of Pushkin's comment.

Letter 661

1. This letter shows Pushkin's interest in contemporary civic developments, and it
also shows the peculiar difficulties of publishing in Russia in Pushkin's day. The article in
question is one by Matvey Stepanovich Volkov (1802-1878), engineer and professor,
in objection to an article, by N. I. Tarasenko-Otreshkov, which favored the construction of a railroad from Petersburg to Moscow, as proposed by the German-Czech
engineer František Gerstner (1793-1840). Gerstner proposed in 1835 that the Russian
government finance the construction of three railroads, from Petersburg to Moscow,
from Moscow to Nizhny Novgorod, and from Petersburg to Tsarskoe Selo and
Pavlovsk. This third railroad was authorized, and completed in the summer of 1836.
Then sharp discussion arose about the desirability of the longer railroads. Gerstner
attempted to obtain a monopoly on railroad construction in Russia. He advanced, among
other proposals, that foreign capital be used for constructing railroads in Russia. He
did not receive permission for the construction of any railroad except the short line from
Petersburg to Pavlovsk. Pushkin later consented to publish Volkov's article, but he
died before it could appear. Then Tarasenko-Otreshkov became one of the guardians
of Pushkin's family, and the article could not be published in Pushkin's journal.

Letter 662

1. Vyazemsky's article was written in the form of a letter; Pushkin means that it
does not matter whether a letter-form or article-form is used. Vyazemsky's article-
letter was addressed to Uvarov, Minister of Education, and was directed against the
doctoral dissertation, "Of the System of Pragmatic Russian History," by Nikolay
Gerasimovich Ustryalov (1805-1870), in which Ustryalov attacked the historian
Karamzin. Vyazemsky, in the article, accuses Uvarov of retreating from his famous
formula of "Orthodoxy, autocracy, and nationality" by allowing such a dissertation,
and of "allowing and even encouraging historical skepticism." The letter is an indirect
defense of Chaadaev and his presentation of his historical views (see Letter 637), for
which Chaadaev had been declared mad. Vyazemsky, however, was far from sharing
Chaadaev's opinions. Vyazemsky's letter was not published until 1879.

2. Voeykov, in the journal, *The Slav* (1827-1830), in a section called "The Chame-
leonist," published a collection of stupid expressions from articles by Polevoy and sharp
criticisms on Polevoy, in the form of a "wreath, plaited by a brigadier's wife."

Letter 663

1. Odoevsky apparently suggested that Pushkin contribute to the journal, *A Child's Library*, published by Prince Vladimir Vladimirovich Lvov (1804-1856) and Amply Nikolaevich Ochkin (1791-1865). Odoevsky participated actively in the journal in 1836. Pushkin declined.

2. Pushkin's expression is an untranslatable bilingual pun: *sot-dejstvovat'*, "to cooperate" and "to play the fool."

Letter 664

1. Alexey Vladimirovich Venevitinov, brother of the poet, D. V. Venevitinov.

2. Pushkin means that if Lev Pushkin, who was serving in the army in the Caucasus, had been killed or wounded, they would have received the information from official reports.

3. General Baron Grigory Vladimirovich Rozen (1782-1841), Lev Pushkin's commanding officer in the Caucasus at the time.

4. The wedding of Ekaterina Nikolaevna Goncharova and d'Anthès-Heeckeren took place on January 10, 1837. Pushkin refused to attend, but sent Mme. Pushkina, instead. Pushkin refused to receive the couple after their marriage.

5. The cook of A. N. Peshchurov, the Opochka Marshal of the Nobility.

6. The Solntsevs, in Moscow.

Letter 666

1. Fedor Afanasievich Skobeltsyn (b. 1781), a rich landowner and gambler, was then staying at Vyazemsky's, in the same house where Pushkin was living. Skobeltsyn refused Pushkin's request.

Letter 667

1. Pushkin was fond of the biblical injunction against casting pearls before swine (see Letter 435).

2. At the command of Nicholas I, A. I. Turgenev had been doing research in materials relating to Russian history of the sixteenth to eighteenth centuries, in the state archives of France and the Papal States. His article was intended for publication in Pushkin's *Contemporary* in 1837, but it did not appear.

3. Pushkin had written the poem in 1826, upon hearing the rumor, which turned out to be false, that A. I. Turgenev's brother, N. I. Turgenev, had been arrested in London in connection with the Decembrist Uprising of 1825. A. I. Turgenev heard of the poem only in 1837. He was, naturally, interested in the poem because of its connection with his brother, to whom he sent it on January 21, 1837. Pushkin had quoted the poem in his letter to Vyazemsky of August 14, 1826 (Letter 188). This time Pushkin quotes the poem without division into stanzas, and he makes changes in the punctuation.

Letter 668

1. Alexandra Osipovna Ishimova (1806-1881) became well known as a writer for children.

2. Pushkin had been very much interested in the works of Barry Cornwall, pseudonym of the English poet and dramatist Bryan Waller Procter, since 1830. Pushkin borrowed from him the form of the dramatic scene for his "little tragedies" in blank verse, which include some of his best works. Pushkin had in his library a copy of *The Poetical Works of Milman, Bowles, Wilson, and Barry Cornwall* (Paris: Galignani, 1829).

Wilson's *City of the Plague*, in the same volume, was the source of Pushkin's *Feast in Time of Plague* (see Letter 406, and note 1). See Letter 674 and notes.

Letter 669
1. Lyubov Matveevna Alymova (b. 1808) was sister of the owners of the house on Furshtatskaya Street, where Pushkin lived from May to December, 1832. He apparently had the statue of Catherine II (see Letter 287) brought to Petersburg at that time. Pushkin hoped to sell it to Vasily Gavrilovich Yuriev, probably in settlement of a gambling debt.

Letter 670
1. D'Anthès-Heeckeren did not cease his attentions to Mme. Pushkina after his own marriage on January 10, 1837. He continued to attempt to monopolize her at balls, though he was refused admittance into the Pushkins' home. Mme. Pushkina recounted to her husband their conversation, but she was unwilling or unable to take such action that d'Anthès would cease his attentions to her. She even consented to a rendezvous with him, in the home and presence of her friend Idalia Poletika. Mme. Poletika slipped away, on some excuse, and d'Anthès-Heeckeren pressed his case, but one of Poletika's children interrupted them, and Mme. Pushkina slipped away. A curious point is that an officer, Peter Petrovich Lanskoy (1799-1877), who stood guard outside Poletika's house while this meeting was taking place, married Mme. Pushkina seven years later. Pushkin received an anonymous letter on the following day, telling of this "assignation." He then proceeded to write this letter, reworking Letter 651. As he rewrote the earlier letter, Pushkin tore it to shreds, piecing together many of the expressions he had written earlier into this final form. This method of composition, plus the surviving rough-draft variations, show that Pushkin wrote this letter in cold rage. He made his letter as insulting as possible, in order that a duel would be inevitable. It is possible that Pushkin really wrote and sent the letter on January 25 and inadvertently misdated it. The letter was sent to Heeckeren so as to implicate him in the whole business; Pushkin was aware that the duel would be with d'Anthès-Heeckeren.
2. Pushkin still considered Heeckeren the author of the anonymous letters of November 4, 1836, and he is here hinting at him as the author.
3. The assertion here is of cowardice, upon d'Anthès-Heeckeren's accepting Pushkin's letter taking back his challenge of November 5, 1836. See Letter 651, note 2.
4. Mme. Pushkina dutifully reported to her husband what d'Anthès-Heeckeren said to her. A sample of his "guardhouse puns" is the following: Mme. Pushkina and her sister, now Mme. d'Anthès-Heeckeren, had the same chiropodist, which gave him the occasion to tell Mme. Pushkina: *Je sais maintenant que votre cor est plus beau, que celui de ma femme* [I know now that your corn is more beautiful than my wife's], with a pun on *cor* "corn" and *corps* "body."

Letter 671
1. A. I. Turgenev noted on this letter, "Pushkin's last note to me, on the eve of the duel." This is Pushkin's last letter to an old friend. A. I. Turgenev, who had been to a considerable degree responsible for Pushkin's attending the Tsarskoe Selo Lyceum, and who had been Pushkin's friend all his life, was the person who was permitted to accompany Pushkin's corpse from Petersburg to the burial place at the Svyatye Gory Monastery, near Mikhaylovskoe.

Letter 672
1. Adjutant General Karl Fedorovich Tol had participated notably in the wars against

Napoleon and the Polish Revolution of 1830-1831. Pushkin is answering Tol's letter thanking him for a copy of Pushkin's *History of Pugachev*.

2. Ivan Ivanovich Mikhelson (1740-1807), who took an important part in putting down the Pugachev uprising. Tol's opinion was that history would finally give Mikhelson his due.

3. I have been unable to trace this quotation.

Letter 673

1. This letter was written in answer to insistent demands by d'Archiac, d'Anthès-Heeckeren's second, that Pushkin send a second for negotiations about the conditions of the duel between Pushkin and d'Anthès-Heeckeren. Pushkin asked Arthur Magenis, secretary of the English embassy, to be his second, but Magenis declined when Pushkin refused to tell him the reasons for the quarrel. Pushkin had been infuriated that his second in November, Sollogub, had attempted to enter into negotiations, and this time he meant to make it impossible. A few hours later, Pushkin met his old Lyceum comrade and friend, Konstantin Karlovich Danzas (1801-1871), and half-persuaded, half-commanded him to be his second, but he did not permit any further negotiations at all.

Letter 674

1. This letter, written a few hours before Pushkin's fatal duel with d'Anthès-Heeckeren, contains the last words he wrote. The calm tone of the letter, discussing in a matter-of-fact manner business regarding his *Contemporary*, and also the polite praise of the work that Ishimova had previously done, show Pushkin's control of himself. Perhaps it was most fitting that he died on his literary shield, like his uncle, Vasily Lvovich Pushkin (see Letter 313).

The duel took place in knee-deep snow at Chernaya Rechka, in the suburbs of Petersburg, about 4:30 p.m. on the same day. D'Anthès-Heeckeren fired first and Pushkin fell, wounded in the abdomen. Pushkin summoned enough strength to fire his shot, which wounded d'Anthès-Heeckeren only slightly, but was enough to knock him down. Pushkin's doctors, Spassky, Arendt, and Dal, never had hopes of his recovery, nor did he. During the two days he lay dying, he was surrounded by his old friends the Vyazemskys, Zhukovsky, Ekaterina Karamazina, and Danzas. Though he tried to hide his suffering from his wife, he wished it not to be concealed from her that his wound was mortal. He died at 2:45 p.m. on January 29.

2. Mme. Ishimova translated, from the book containing the works of Barry Cornwall (see Letter 668), five dramatic scenes marked by Pushkin, including *Ludovico Sforza, Love Cured by Kindness, The Way to Conquer, Amelia Wentworth*, and *The Falcon*. They were published in *The Contemporary* in 1837.

3. Ishimova's *History of Russia in Tales for Children*, the first volume of which appeared in December, 1836. The work went through several editions.

INDEX

INDEX

MAPS

A R C T I C   O C

SWEDEN

FINLAND

BALTIC SEA

PRUSSIA

POLAND

Riga

St. Petersburg

• Arkhangelsk

• Vyatka

URAL MOUNTAINS

Moscow •

Kiev •

Kishinev

Odessa

• Nizhny Novgorod

• Kazan

Simbirsk •

Volga River

• Samara

Uralsk •

• Ufa

Orenburg •

BLACK SEA

CAUCASUS

Astrakhan •

KIRGHIZ LANDS

OTTOMAN

Kars •

Erzurum •

• Tiflis

CASPIAN SEA

EMPIRE

TURKESTAN

PERSIA

AFGHANISTAN

INDIA

THE RUSSIAN EMPIRE IN PUSHKIN'S DAY (1830)

Miles

0   200   400   600

ESTATES

1 Mikhaylovskoe
  Trigorskoe
2 Malinniki
3 Yaropolets
4 Polotnyany Zavod
5 Boldino
  Kistenevo
6 Yazykovo

SWEDEN

FINLAND

WHITE SEA

• Arkhangelsk

BALTIC SEA

• Reval
Dorpat•
Riga• Ostrov•
  Opochka•

• St. Petersburg

Pskov• Novgorod
    • Staraya Russa

1

2• • Torzhok
  3• • Tver

PRUSSIA

Vistula R.

• Warsaw

POLAND

Smolensk •

Dneper R.

• Kiev

HUNGARY

Jassy •

Prut R.

• Kishinev
  Odessa •

Danube R.

OTTOMAN EMPIRE

BAKHCHISARAY
Bakhchisaray •

CRIMEA
• Kerch

BLACK   SEA

OTTOMAN EMPIRE

• Moscow

4• • Kaluga

Don River

• Ekaterinoslav

Kuban R.

Terek R.

CAUCASUS

• Vyatka

• Nizhny Novgorod

Arzamas
5•   • Kazan

6• • Simbirsk

• Samara
Orenburg •

Uralsk •

Ural River

• Ufa

KIRGHIZ LANDS

Volga River

Astrakhan •

Kars •

Tiflis •

GEORGIA

Erzurum •

CASPIAN

SEA

PERSIA

PERSIA

RK

EUROPEAN RUSSIA IN PUSHKIN'S DAY (1830)

Miles

0   100   200   300   400